Praise for
WASHINGTON'S SPIES

"Fascinating . . . tells how the work of the spies proved to be the tipping point in the summer of 1778, helping Washington begin breaking the stalemate with the British . . . [and] brings to light their crucial help in winning American independence." —*The Dallas Morning News*

"Gen. George Washington, who brushed 'counter liquor' across seemingly innocuous letters to reveal messages written in invisible ink, knew that intelligence is a mosaic formed from many small parts, some fitting more precisely than others. In *Washington's Spies*, Alexander Rose has done an admirable job of investigating and reporting on Washington's wartime intelligence service."
—*The Virginian-Pilot*

"After working on Washington, I knew there was a story to tell about his reliance on spies during the Revolutionary War. But I believed the story could never be told because the evidence did not exist. Well, I was wrong, and Alexander Rose tells this important story with style and wit."
—JOSEPH J. ELLIS, author of *His Excellency: George Washington*

"First in war, first in peace, first in covert ops—Alex Rose unfolds the story of a Long Island–based spy ring of idealists and misfits who kept George Washington informed of what was going on in enemy-occupied New York. Making brilliant use of documentary sources, Rose gives us intrigue, crossed signals, derring-do, and a priceless slice of eighteenth-century life. Think of Alan Furst with muskets."
—RICHARD BROOKHISER, author of *Founding Father: Rediscovering George Washington*

"This fascinating and carefully crafted book shows us a side of the Father of Our Country that hero-worshippers since Reverend Weems never imagined—and the almost forgotten covert side of the Revolutionary War. . . . [Rose] gives us a compelling portrait of [a] rogues' gallery of barkeeps, misfits, hypochondriacs, part-time smugglers, and full-time neurotics that will remind every reader of the cast of a John le Carré novel."
—ARTHUR HERMAN, *National Review*

"Offers fascinating new research on how Washington organized an intelligence-gathering network that helped turn the American Revolution in his side's favor."
—*Chicago Tribune*

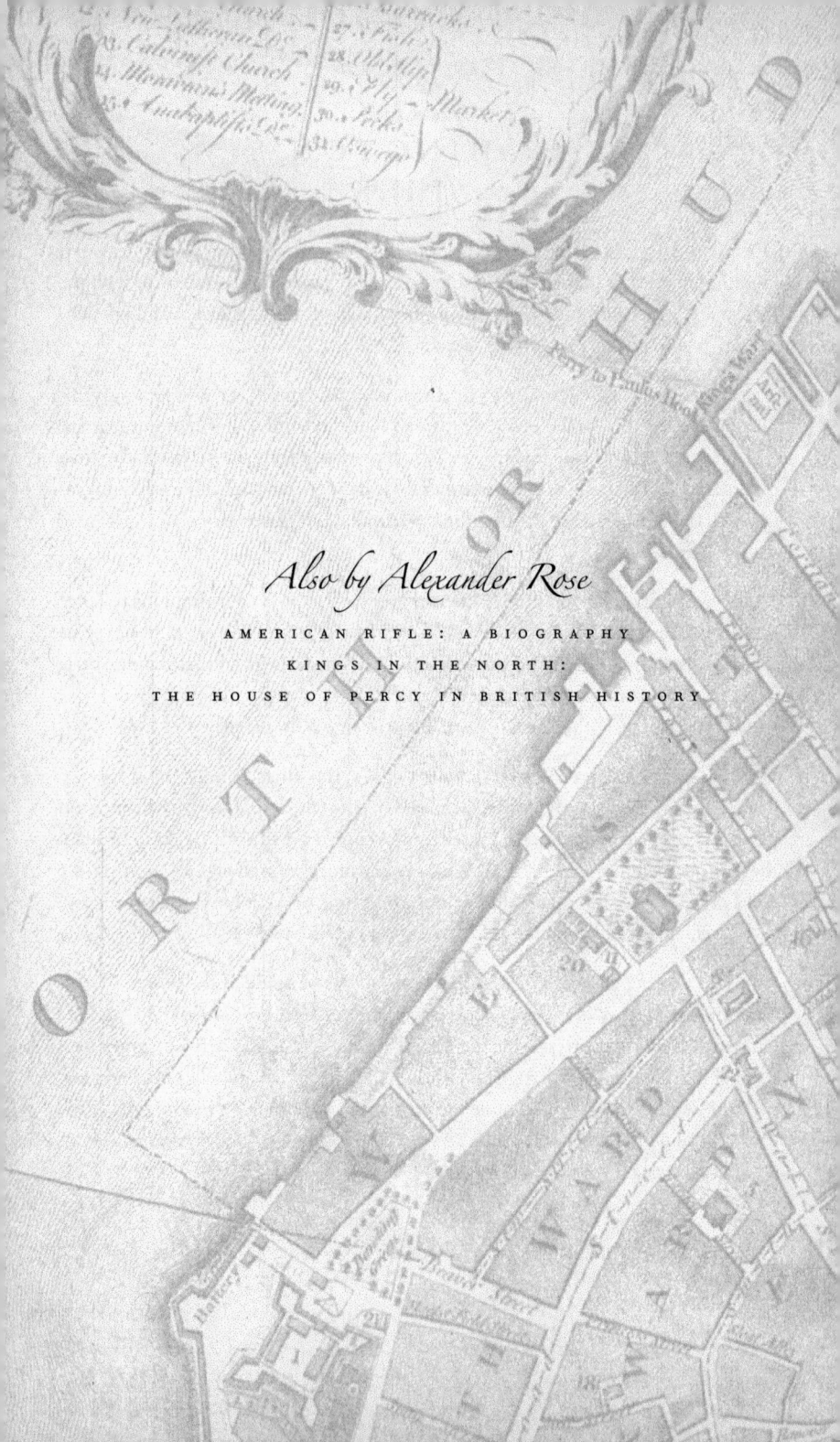

Also by Alexander Rose

AMERICAN RIFLE: A BIOGRAPHY

KINGS IN THE NORTH:
THE HOUSE OF PERCY IN BRITISH HISTORY

WASHINGTON'S SPIES

THE STORY OF AMERICA'S FIRST SPY RING

Alexander Rose

BANTAM BOOKS TRADE PAPERBACKS

NEW YORK

To My Family

I will keep my mouth with a bridle, while
the wicked is before me.
Psalm 39

In passing him they did not even see him, or hear him, rather they
saw through him as through a pane of glass at
their familiars beyond.
Thomas Hardy, JUDE THE OBSCURE

Worse than having no human sources is being seduced
by a human source who is telling lies.
*Report of the Commission on the
Intelligence Capabilities of the United States
Regarding Weapons of Mass Destruction, 2005*

Lord, now lettest thou thy servant depart in peace.
Luke 2:29

Intelligence is the life of every thing in war.
*Letter, General Nathanael Greene
to Major John Clark,
November 5, 1777*

CONTENTS

LONG ISLAND, CONNECTICUT,
AND THE HUDSON, 1776

---- THE CULPER ROUTE

NEW YORK CITY
1776

N
W E
S

King's College

Barclay

"Holy Ground"

The boundary of the 1776 fire

Trinity Church

Greenwich Road

Location of Templeton & Stewart

Morris Street

Broadway

Wall Street

Hercules Mullig Tailor Store

Queen Street

Water Street

Fort George

Broad Street

Hanover Square

Fly Marke Long Islar Ferry

The Exchange

The Battery

Whitehall Slip

CANVAS TOWN

Fresh Water Pond

Broadway

Barracks

The Poor House

City Jail

Bowry Lane

Location of Townsend's Store & House

Peck's Slip

Burling's Slip

| 0 | 500 | 1000 | 1500 | 2000 | 2500 |

SCALE OF FEET

CHAPTER ONE

"As Subtil & Deep as Hell Itself":
Nathan Hale and the Spying Game

The Yankee soldier, flinty once but now wizened and gnarled, flashed in and out of lucidity. Sometimes his memories of a war fought sixty years before gushed liberally from his lips, but more often, for half hours at a time, he would slouch in vacant-eyed silence. His visiting relative, R. N. Wright, recorded despondently that Asher Wright "is now in the eighty-second year of his life, and besides the infirmities of advanced age, has been affected in his mind, ever since the melancholy death of his young master, Captain Nathan Hale. What is gathered of him, can be learnt only at intervals and when he is in the humor of conversation."[1]

One evening in 1836, though, Asher was particularly loquacious, and spoke so excitedly his companion taxed himself hard to scribble down the old man's words. Wright the Younger used whatever came to hand—a blank leaf in the book he had been reading (Hume's *History of England*, as it happened)—for he knew that he was listening to one of a diminishing band of brothers of the Revolutionary War. Indeed, Asher was a particularly venerated member of that generation: Not only one of the few remaining men who had known the legendary Captain Hale, Asher Wright was also the last surviving Patriot to have seen Hale alive. He had shaved and dressed him on the very morning of his departure.[2]

"When he left us, he told me he had got to be absent a while, and wanted I should take care of his things & if the army moved before he returned, have them moved too.... He was too good-looking to go so. He could not deceive. Some scrubby fellows ought to have gone. He had marks [scars] on his forehead, so that anybody would know him who had ever seen him—having had [gun]powder flashed in his face. He had a large hair mole on his neck just where the knot come. In his boyhood, his playmates sometimes twitted him about it, telling him he would be hanged."

One of those playmates might well have been Asher Wright. A local boy, he had grown up with Hale, but they had parted ways after Nathan went off to Yale, a place far beyond the modest means of Wright's family. They met again during the war, when Hale's first "waiter," his servant, had fallen sick, and though the man eventually recovered (Wright ascribed it to Hale's practice of praying for him), he could not continue in the post. "Capt. Hale was [of] a mind I should take his place," recalled Wright. "And I did & remained with him till he went on to Long Island."

Tired of his exertions, Wright could add little more to his recollections—apart from one nugget. Nathan Hale, today immortalized as the "Martyr-Spy of the Revolution," wasn't even supposed to have become a spy in the first place. "James Sprague, my aunt's cousin... he was desired by Col[onel] Knowlton, to go on to Long Island. He refused, saying, I am willing to go & fight them, but as for going among them & being taken & hung up like a dog, I will not do it." No soldiers, let alone officers, in Knowlton's Rangers—Hale's regiment—wanted to take the ignoble job of secret agent, an occupation considered inappropriate for gentlemen, and one best suited for blackguards, cheats, and cowards. And it was then, remembered Asher, that "Hale stood by and said, I will undertake the business."[3]

Born on June 6, 1755, the sixth child in a large family, Nathan Hale was of good and middling, and most respectable, Connecticut stock. The first Hale—one Robert, reputedly descended from a knightly family in Kent—arrived in Massachusetts from England in the early 1630s, and turned his hand to blacksmithing. He was evidently an assiduous one, for he managed to acquire several fields along the Mystic River. His son John attended the newly founded Harvard College, graduating in 1657 and becoming a Calvinist pastor of robust persuasion near Salem, where he participated in the witch trials but later recanted his temporary insanity. One of John's sons, Richard—Nathan's father—left for Connecticut in about 1744 and settled in Coventry, twenty miles east of Hartford, where fertile farming land was still to be had. On his mother's side, Nathan was descended from Elder John Strong, an immigrant who sailed aboard the *Mary and John* in 1630 from Plymouth. It was his great-great-granddaughter, Elizabeth, who married Richard and begat Nathan.

As was only to be expected of strict New England Congregationalists, Nathan was taught to revere magistrates and ministers as God's chosen servants, and to observe each Sabbath as if it were his final one on this earth. He pronounced grace thrice daily, attended church twice on Sundays, and declaimed prayers once before bed.

When Nathan was twelve, his mother died, and the Strongs took his education in hand. As there were several men of the cloth on the Strong side, Nathan was marked down for a clerical career, for which a college education was essential. In preparation for his entry to Yale—where the Strongs had connections—Nathan had Cicero, Cato, and Horace beaten into him by the Reverend Dr. Huntingdon, a man of pronounced liberal tendency, who, in between his classes on Latin declensions and conjugations, subjected Nathan to a series of jeremiads on the iniquity of the Stamp Act.

By the summer of 1769, young Hale, all of fourteen, was at last ready to go up to Yale. Along with thirty-five other promising teenagers, he entered that September as a member of the Class of '73 (there were about one hundred students at the college). For freshmen, Yale could be a most forbidding and mystifying place, a Bedlam of confusing rituals and hierarchies where no rule could be bent, no corners cut, no blind eye turned. A fearsome regime of fines, ranging from a penny (for missing mandatory chapel services) to twelve shillings for graver misdemeanors (missing them twice), ruthlessly controlled the pupils' behavior. Every student doffed his hat when the president approached, and bowed as he passed, or faced his wrath. Freshmen, meanwhile, acted as flunkies for the upperclassmen, who exacted a very painful form of punishment on those unwise enough to tell them where to go.

The first priority, apart from striving to avoid attracting an upperclassman's attention, was work. Hale imbibed a curriculum of Hebrew, Latin, Greek, logic, rhetoric, disputes, geometry, classics, natural philosophy, divinity, astronomy, mathematics, metaphysics, and ethics. Roger Alden, a good friend of his, told Hale that he dreaded the curriculum as much as he did "the morning prayer bell or Saturday noon recitations." That prayer bell rang at 4.30 a.m. in the summer, and at 5 a.m. in the winter; as for the Saturday recitations, terrified pupils were interrogated by their tutors in the three classical languages.[4]

Still, college days were not all drudgery. Hale evidently managed to have a good time. His father, confronted with mounting bills for Nathan's living expenses, instructed him in December 1769—just three months after his once-studious boy arrived in New Haven—to "carefully mind your studies that your time be not lost." He also asked his errant son to remember to attend chapel to avoid more fines. A year later, Hale Senior heard that Hale minor was not minding his studies as carefully as he ought, and anxiously urged him to "shun all vice, especially card-playing." (Yale students, if caught three times gambling, were expelled from the college.)

One baleful influence on Hale was his classmate Benjamin Tallmadge, the son of a churchman who had diligently taught him his Virgil and Plato. He had more time for mischief making than his peers, for, as Tallmadge self-mockingly wrote in his memoirs, "being so well versed in the Latin and Greek languages, I had not much occasion to study during the first two years of my collegiate life."[5] In March 1771, Tallmadge, Nathan, and Nathan's older brother Enoch (also attending Yale) were fined heavily (a shilling and five pence) for breaking windows following a prolonged visit to a local tavern. Tallmadge, who had drunk deeper of the amber nectar than the Hales, was amerced another seven pence for additional damage to college property.[6]

Students entertained themselves. Debating societies were always popular: In 1773, for example, Hale and Tallmadge debated the motion "Whether the Education of Daughters be not, without any just reason, more neglected than that of sons." (They argued for the pro-daughter side, and won, an event that James Hillhouse, a Yale contemporary, said "received the plaudits of the ladies present.")[7]

He was a member of the Linonia, the most "social" of the debating clubs, and it was noted in the minutes that the meeting of December 23, 1771, "was opened with a very entertaining narration by Hale." Hale also took part, with relish, in amateur theatrical productions; contemporaries thought him excellent in Robert Dodsley's frothy farce *The Toy Shop* (a hit on the London stage in 1735). When they weren't arguing or acting, the students joined such literary societies as the Brothers in Unity, whose members adopted nicknames derived from classical myth (Hale chose Damon, while Tallmadge went with Pythias). Ostensibly, they intended to improve their rhetorical writing style, but all too often, being bored with the starchy formality of Latin, they fell into the kind of flowery purplishness popular at the time in artistic circles in England and America.[8]

A letter from Tallmadge to Hale gives an indication of the predominant style: "Friendly Sir, In my delightsome retirement from the fruitless bustle of the noisy, with my usual delight, &, perhaps, with more than common attention, I perused your epistle—replete as it was with sentiments worthy to be contemplated, let me assure you with the strongest confidence of an affectionate friend, that with nothing was my pleasure so greatly heightened, as with your curious remarks upon my preceding performance, which, so far from carrying the appearance of a censuring critick's empty amusement, seemed to me to be wholly the result of unspoted regard & (as I may say) fraternal esteem."[9]

Tiresome to read today, but the letter, and the several others like it between the two men, signals how immensely fond Tallmadge and Hale were of one another. Leafing through their correspondence, it's still touching to read the encomiums "I remain your constant friend" and "a heart ever devoted to your welfare."[10] If anything malign ever happened to one, the other would be merciless toward his assailants.

Thus, Yale of the 1770s, despite its addiction to protocol and pomposity, was a place where comradeship and camaraderie flourished. Paradoxically, too, the college inspired a rebellious, insubordinate ethos, not least when its inmates frequently (and loudly) complained about the dire food served in hall and the usurious cost of books for sale. On no other issue, however, were the students more agitated than that of relations with the Mother Country. In the years before the Revolution, Yale was notorious for its politics. Afterwards, one fierce Loyalist, Thomas Jones, recalled bitterly of his alma mater that it was nothing but "a nursery of sedition, of faction, and republicanism," while General Thomas Gage, commander of the British forces in North America, branded the place "a seminary of democracy" full of "pretended patriots."[11] For all Gage's disparagement, Yale students were the first American students to organize a boycott against British-made goods, and when Hale was entering, the graduating class voted almost unanimously to appear "wholly dressed in the manufactures of our own country" at their commencement ceremony.

Upon graduation, Hale was obliged to find a job, the clerical life having lost whatever attractions it may once have had. He became a schoolmaster in East Haddam (Tallmadge taught in Wethersfield), a town sixteen miles from the mouth of the Connecticut River, in the fall of 1773. The school was rather small, and worse, isolated, and still worse, paid poorly. Even had the wages been sufficient, there was nothing in East Haddam to spend it on. He boarded with James Green: His descendants were reported some time ago to possess the only chair that Hale is known to have sat upon. Unsurprisingly, considering that East Haddam's nightlife consisted of sitting on chairs, Hale was bored numb, mentally as well as physically. By March 1774, he couldn't bear it any longer and applied to New London, to the Union School, a wealthy private academy.[12]

In the meantime, he fell in love. Or rather, re-fell in love, with the same woman. In his last year at college, Hale had been introduced to Alice Adams, a pretty, vivacious thing, but one, alas, about to be married off to a wealthy man, Elijah Ripley, considerably older than herself. Fortunately for Hale, Mr. Ripley's talents did not include longevity, and he died on December 26, 1774. Hale waited, decently, until her period of mourning was over before launching his suit. In early 1775, Alice was overjoyed to receive a Hale-penned poem:

Alicia, born with every striking charm,
The eye to ravish or the heart to warm
Fair in thy form, still fairer in thy mind,
With beauty wisdom, sense with sweetness joined
Great without pride, and lovely without art. . . .

The two began to court, but Hale put duty before pleasure.[13] Just a few months into his wooing, the Revolution came to Connecticut. The battles of Lexington and Concord on April 19, 1775, galvanized young men into joining the colors—including two of Hale's brothers, who signed up for the Connecticut militia marching to Massachusetts. Of the thirty-five members of Yale's 1775 class, for instance, thirteen continued into the ministry, but no fewer than thirteen others joined the Continental army.[14]

Inescapably shaped by his background, his milieu, and his education, Hale was by temperament and inclination a pronounced Patriot. Tallmadge, who wrote to him on July 4, 1775, allows us a penetrating glimpse into what two young American idealists felt at the time: "I consider our country, a land flowing as it were with milk & honey, holding open her arms, & demanding assistance from all who can assist her in her sore distress. . . . [W]e all should be ready to step forth in the common cause."[15]

While Tallmadge would join the Continentals the following year, Hale went to the recruiting station just two days after that inspirational letter was written. It was the same day—July 6—that the governor of Connecticut commissioned officers in the newly raised Seventh Regiment. Hale's name is on the list as first lieutenant of the third company. The Seventh was commanded by Colonel Charles Webb, whose own first lieutenant was William Hull, one of Hale's friends from Yale. On September 8, Washington requested Governor Jonathan Trumbull to send his new Connecticut regiments, and within two weeks, Hale was on the march. From his diary—albeit abbreviated, and hurriedly jotted down—we know that the Seventh marched to Providence, then through Massachusetts to Cambridge, headquarters of the American forces surrounding Boston, where they had Gage and his forces bottled up. Once there, the regiment was assigned to General John Sullivan's brigade at Winter Hill; Hale was promoted to captain-lieutenant, and signed up for another contract of service for 1776 at a time when many refused to reenlist when their terms were up. His regiment was then renamed the "Nineteenth Foot in the service of the United Colonies," as part of Washington's effort to mold his gaggle of ragtag militias into a professional volunteer force.

Hale had missed a great battle on June 17, when the newly arrived General William Howe put to flight the American militia from their fortified positions atop Bunker and Breed's hills. Howe's multiple assaults, though eventually achieving their objective, proved abnormally costly in his own men's lives; of Howe's field staff, only he remained unshot. One Tory, Peter Oliver, who witnessed the battle, ascribed "the sacrifice of a greater disproportion of heroick officers than perhaps ever fell in one battle" to the Americans' "savage way of fighting, not in open field, but by aiming at their objects from houses & behind walls and hedges."[16] Two decades earlier, during the Seven Years' War, Howe had made his name with his dashing attacks; Bunker Hill turned him into an overly cautious commander reluctant to administer the coup de grace to his downed, albeit still dangerous, enemies for fear of having victory snatched from him at the last moment. Though he remained a master tactician—Washington would repeatedly find himself at a disadvantage on the battlefield whenever he was present—Howe's experience at Bunker Hill convinced him that the Americans, even when seemingly vanquished, were far more potent than his superiors in London realized. Howe's preferred strategy became one of attrition: Secure one's base, muster overwhelming numbers, outmaneuver the enemy, defeat him in open battle when necessary, and wait until his army collapsed. To this end, as it became evident to Howe over the subsequent months that Boston was ultimately untenable, he began planning an evacuation to Canada.

By the time Hale arrived, the excitement was over, and the two armies were in stalemate. Hale spent his time doing virtually nothing during his stay outside Boston. Apart from a few brief bursts of action around him ("Considerable firing upon Roxbury side in the forenoon, and some P.M. No damage done as we hear," he wrote in his army diary), life was pretty uneventful, even dull—with all the attendant ill effects on discipline that breeds. Indeed, in September the Virginian regiment of riflemen mutinied out of boredom, and when a British doctor visited the New England camp, he described the soldiers there as nothing but "a drunken, lying, praying, hypocritical rabble, without order, subjection, discipline, or cleanliness."[17] In his free time, which was plentiful, Hale played checkers, watched the men wrestle (even placing a few bets on the burlier ones), drank wine at Brown's Tavern, read whatever books came his way, and listened to chaplains give sermons. He also composed poetry for his Yale friends about army life, and provided an admiring portrait of Washington:

> *When coming here from Watertown,*
> *Soon after ent'ring Cambridge ground,*
> *You spy the grand & pleasant seat,*
> *Possess'd by Washin[g]ton the great.*

Though his sense of rhyme failed to scale the Himalayan heights he intended, Hale occupied his hours on duty drilling, sorting out pay disputes, organizing supplies, setting pickets, listing guard rosters—all the humdrum minutiae of army life. "Studied the method of forming a regiment for review, of arraying the companies, also of marching round the reviewing officer," he noted of one day's activities.

In mid-March 1776, short of supplies and awed by Washington's artillery newly emplaced atop Dorchester Heights, the British finally evacuated Boston and departed for Halifax, Nova Scotia, to recuperate under their new supreme commander, General Howe. Though Washington could not predict when and where Howe would return, he was confident that New York—wealthy, easily supplied, situated between the South and New England, and possessing a magnificent harbor—would be the target. In this, he was right. In their Canadian fastness, Howe and his generals planned to use New York as their base of operations. Ownership would permit him to march north up the Hudson River, thereby severing the fiery New Englanders from their less hostile brethren in the Middle States and the South, and British control over the region would gradually tighten until the rebellion asphyxiated.

In mid-March, Washington began transferring his forces south to New York. On the nineteenth of that month, accordingly, Hale's regiment was ordered to leave Roxbury. On the thirtieth, they sailed across Long Island Sound and disembarked at Turtle Bay in Manhattan, at the foot of what is now East Forty-fifth Street.[18] Then into the city itself, at the southern end of the island, where they fortified their positions against a possible, and increasingly probable, British onslaught. Throughout May, Hale and his men were stationed on the west side of the Bowery. Shortly after, his unit was rotated out to post guard at the western end of Long Island, a region rife with anti-Patriot sentiment and where the inhabitants eagerly awaited "liberation" from these rebels by His Majesty's troops, rumored to begin landing on Staten Island in late June.

Writing to his brother Enoch on May 30, Hale was dismissive of the Long Island Tories, observing that "it would grieve every good man to consider what unnatural monsters we have as it were in our bowels." He wanted robust measures taken against them. Until that happened, there was more cheerful news to consider: On July 9, when the regiments were summoned to their customary evening roll call, "the declaration of the Congress, declaring the United Colonies FREE, SOVEREIGN, AND INDEPENDENT STATES, was published at the head of the respective brigades, in camp, and received with loud huzzas."[19]

How long that independence would last depended on the resilience of the Continentals stockaded in New York City (i.e., what is now lower Manhattan), with a fortified bulwark in Brooklyn. These few were expected to dissipate the fury of an empire. On August 20, we have the last, hasty dispatch Hale wrote (to his brother): "For about six or eight days the enemy have been expected hourly whenever the wind and tide in the least favored. We keep a particular look out for them this morning. The place and manner of attack time must determine. The event we leave to Heaven."[20]

Two days later, General and Admiral Howe—"Black Dick," the latter, was the commander's brother—began ferrying their army to Long Island, their intention being to storm the Brooklyn fortifications, cross the East River, conquer Manhattan, and crush the rebellion before Christmas. Hale's Nineteenth Regiment was sent to Brooklyn, but did not assume front-line positions. His eighty-man company was kept in reserve behind the breastworks, and he witnessed from afar the disaster that befell Washington's soldiers at the hands of the best army in the world on August 27 and 28, when General Howe felt confident enough in numbers to assault the American positions. Washington's front collapsed, and on August 30, he evacuated Brooklyn and withdrew to Manhattan. He had lost one island only to be trapped on another. Across the East River, the thin blue ribbon separating Washington and oblivion, an observer could see the tens of thousands of scarlet-clad soldiers and hundreds of troop-transports awaiting a decent tide and a fair wind so they could invade Manhattan. There was nothing else for it but to leave, while they still had the chance. Sooner or later, the British would come and Washington could ill afford to have his army besieged in the city. The decision was quickly made: The Americans would retreat north to Manhattan's Harlem Heights, whose rocky slopes afforded useful cover for a last-ditch defense of the Revolution.

Washington and his commanders furiously debated what to do with the abandoned city. The New Englanders wanted to burn it, so as to leave the British with nothing but a blackened husk in which to spend the approaching winter; the New Yorkers, sensibly enough, were reluctant to raze their own property.[21]

General Nathanael Greene, a Rhode Islander, favored burning. In a lengthy letter to Washington, he laid out the purely military justifications for doing so: "The city and island of New York are no objects for us.... Part of the army already has met with a defeat; the country is struck with a panic; any capital loss at this time may ruin the cause.... Two-thirds of the property of the city of New York and the suburbs belongs to the Tories. We have no very great reason to run considerable risk for its defence.... I would burn the city and suburbs, and that for the following reasons. If the enemy gets possession of the city, we never can recover the possession without a superior naval force to theirs. It will deprive the enemy of an opportunity of barracking their whole army together.... It would deprive them of a general market; the price of things would prove a temptation to our people to supply them for the sake of gain, in direct violation of the laws of their country. All these advantages would result from the destruction of the city."[22] He would be proved right in every respect.

But New Yorkers pressured Washington not to listen to the likes of Greene, and the Convention of the State of New York asked him to ensure that if it came to "the fatal necessity" of destroying the city, then its "twenty thousand inhabitants may not be reduced to misery by the wanton act of an individual."[23] The Convention was referring to a rumor running round the army "that any man is authorized to set [New York] on fire" if the order to retreat was given. Not yet having made up his own mind about what to do, but wanting to soothe their fears of an overzealous arsonist, Washington hedged whether he would give an order to burn-and-retreat. "Nothing but the last necessity and that such as should justify me to the whole world," he wrote, "would induce me to give orders for that purpose."[24]

For political cover, Washington passed the buck to Congress; if there were to be fallout in later years, the general needed to be able to claim he was following the directions of the nation's elected representatives. On September 2, in his report to the body, Washington spoke frankly, and despondently: "Our situation is truly distressing.... Till of late I had no doubt in my own mind of defending this place, nor should I have yet, if the men would do their duty, but this I despair of.... If we should be obliged to abandon the town, ought it to stand as winter quarters for the enemy?" Congress replied from Philadelphia the very next day: "Resolved...that no damage be done to the said city by his troops, on their leaving it; the Congress have no doubt of being able to recover [New York] tho the enemy should for a time obtain possession of it."[25]

Washington was off the hook, and the Americans made their preparations to vacate. The issue that now vexed him was, having departed New York, how would he fend off the British once his troops were stretched across middle and upper Manhattan, and living off the land, especially as winter drew on? At least when they were tightly boxed into the city, apart from being billeted in warm quarters, the Americans could leverage their numbers and benefit from their short supply lines. Better still, the enemy's choice of possible attack strategies was severely limited. At some point, the Howes would have to undertake an amphibious landing, followed by an infantry assault on tenaciously held fortifications—maneuvers fraught with danger and almost certain to result in heavy losses. Still, eventually the Howes would do it, and Washington would be finished. Better, perhaps, to run now and live to fight another day. Accordingly, on September 11, Washington informed Congress that he was "ordering our stores away [so] that if an evacuation of the city becomes inevitable, and which certainly must be the case, there may be as little to remove as possible."[26]

Between September 7 and 15, apart from a few thousand who would depart a few days hence, American troops left the city of New

York and marched north. Washington now at least enjoyed a line of retreat into Connecticut or New Jersey should the fortunes of war continue to tell against him, but his first priority was to divine the probable British line of attack. They could come from almost any direction. Across the water, Washington could see with his own eyes the British busying themselves, but would they land in the city and advance up the island, or would they land to his north and drive south, or would they do both and entrap him within their pincers? Perhaps they would do neither and attempt an invasion midway up the island, then divide their forces and take New York at the same time as marching to Harlem. Washington knew Howe was ploddingly slow, but he was methodical, and it was a dead certainty he had something up his sleeve.

Washington needed accurate and timely intelligence of Howe's designs and motions. Previous efforts had proved a mixed bag. As early as July 14, General Hugh Mercer—Scotland born, he was a former apothecary from Virginia—regretfully informed Washington that he could find no one suitable to sneak into the British camp (though he did succeed two days later). Five weeks later, General William Livingston—soon to resign his commission to become the governor of New Jersey—said that "very providentially I sent a spy last night on Staten Island to obtain intelligence of the movements of the enemy.... He has this moment returned in safety."[27] The spy, whose name was almost certainly Lawrence Mascoll (Washington's warrant-book records a payment on August 23 for him "going into the enemy's line to obtain information"), had visited an "informant" employed by Howe to carry "baggage" who had "heard the orders read and heard the generals talk."[28]

Mascoll brought back some useful intelligence, such as the British army figures, the revelation that provisions were running very low, and the news that the "Tories on the Island are very illy treated lately, so that the inhabitants who at first were all pleased would now be willing to poison them all. They take from them every thing they choose, and no one has any thing they can call their own." But Mascoll's assertion that the next attack would fall on New Jersey (at Bergen Point,

Elizabeth Town Point, and Perth Amboy) didn't impress a skeptical Washington.[29] He believed that an imminent strike on Long Island was being prepared, and in that he was right. A few hours after Washington told Congress of his suspicions on August 22, Admiral Howe fired his guns as a signal and his brother launched his invasion with some four hundred vessels.

On September 1, Washington ordered Generals William Heath, a former Massachusetts farmer (he had urged Washington not to abandon New York), and George Clinton (then serving as a militia commander but soon to become governor of the state) to establish "a channel of information" on the Long Island side. "Perhaps some might be got who are really Tories for a reasonable reward to undertake it. Those who are friends would be preferable, if they could manage it as well." Then, four days later, Washington wrote again, a little anxiously, to Heath: "As everything in a manner depends on intelligence of the enemy's motions, I do most earnestly entreat you and General Clinton to exert yourselves to accomplish this most desirable end. Leave no stone unturned, nor do not stick at expense to bring this to pass, as I was never more uneasy than on account of my want of knowledge on this score.... Much will depend on early intelligence, and meeting the enemy before they can intrench. I should much approve of small harassing parties, stealing, as it were, over in the night, as they might keep the enemy alarmed, and more than probably bring off a prisoner, from whom some valuable intelligence may be obtained."[30] Following orders, Clinton managed to get over William Treadwell and Benjamin Ludlum, who had pledged "to run every risk to gain the necessary intelligence." For good measure, he had conceived a plan to kidnap two Tory neighbors of his, whom he thought might prove reluctant to talk. But never mind, Clinton jauntily assured Washington, "If I can catch them I'll make them willing."[31]

The Tories escaped falling into Clinton's clutches, but Treadwell and Ludlum managed to return from Long Island two days later. Clinton "examined them" and dispatched their intelligence to Washington. Despite Treadwell and Ludlum's bravery, their intel was of little use and of low quality: Troop figures were exaggerated and their revelations were either vague or pointless, or both (i.e., "a party of the Light Horse . . . seized upon some bread flour and salt which was in a store, but can't tell the exact place").[32] It was not a successful mission.

During these early days of the intelligence war, Washington focused nearly exclusively on obtaining *military intelligence*—that is, tactical information on the enemy's positions and movements—an activity he had himself performed as a young officer during the French and Indian War, and which was regarded in Europe as a respectable pursuit for a gentleman.[33] He made no attempt to infiltrate and implant an agent permanently behind enemy lines to report back periodically. Consequently, Washington's agents were required to operate at night and return before dawn, or at most, spend just a few days out in the cold. The Americans also commonly failed to provide any training or backup for their agents, which is partly why the success in getting Treadwell and Ludlum over was marred by their lack of expertise in knowing what to look for.

Even so, at least Treadwell and Ludlum were in the thick of things, unlike Hale. Soon after the defeat at Brooklyn, Hale—frustrated at having been present at a battle and at a siege and yet never firing his musket at a redcoat, let alone bayoneting one—transferred to another regiment, one guaranteed some action: Knowlton's Rangers, a new outfit trained for special scouting service. It was commanded by thirty-seven-year-old Lieutenant Colonel Thomas Knowlton, a former farmer who had been a ranger in the French and Indian War and who had fought at Bunker Hill. Courageous to a fault, remembered one of his men, he never cried, "Go on, boys!" but always, "Come on, boys!"[34]

As early as September 1, Captain Hale was leading a company of Knowlton's men reconnoitering potential American positions in the north, at Harlem and Hell Gate, though in the absence of the enemy he saw no fighting. It was clear, however, that Howe was planning to attack Manhattan in the very near future, thereby making imperative an accurate appraisal of his preparations on Long Island. To this end, a few days before September 15—when Howe launched an amphibious landing at Kip's Bay—Washington asked Knowlton to recruit a few spies from amongst his men. This was not Knowlton's first brush with intelligence: In July he had helped General Mercer dispatch an agent, Captain John Mersereau ("who undertook the service very cheerfully"), to Staten Island.[35]

Hale, hearing of Knowlton's inquiries, sought his friend William Hull to discuss whether he should volunteer. When they met, Hale "remarked that he thought he owed to his country the accomplishment of an object so important and so much desired by the commander of her armies," and asked Hull's candid opinion. Hull replied that he thought the business of spying a murky and unwholesome one, adding that he thought Hale too open and frank to carry it off in any case. He warned that he would die an ignominious death. "I am fully sensible of the consequences of discovery and capture in such a situation," mused Hale. "But for a year I have been attached to the army, and have not rendered any material service." Spying, he agreed, was not an honorable undertaking, but "if the exigencies of my country demand a peculiar service its claims to perform that service are imperious."[36]

Washington had his man. And now that man, according to the recollections of Hale's sergeant, twice visited Washington to discuss his route, precautions, and cover story.[37] (Washington vaguely knew Hale, having distributed General Orders on June 16 noting the court-martial of Hale's second-in-command, a Lieutenant Chapman, for "Disobedience of orders, and refusing to do his duty.")[38] Washington's previous attempts to gather intelligence by sending men through the "front door"—landing them directly in heavily fortified Brooklyn or on Staten Island—had all proved fruitless; Hale, this time, would sneak in through the back by making his way to Connecticut, crossing the Sound, and landing on Long Island behind (or to the east of) the British encampments in Brooklyn. From his intended destination of Huntington, Long Island, it was about two days' unrushed travel to Brooklyn, plenty of time for Hale to observe the massive baggage trains trundling west, count the regiments mustering for a final attack, and see when they embarked on the fleet of transports, tenders, and men-of-war congregating at Hell Gate. Importantly, Hale's orders never stipulated that he was to travel to Manhattan, since at the time Howe had not yet attacked the island. He was only to spy out Long Island and come home.[39]

Hale's brother Enoch later heard that Nathan left between the tenth and fourteenth of September. Accompanied by Sergeant Stephen Hempstead, Hale left the American camp and traveled first to Westchester and then, early on September 15, arrived in Norwalk, Connecticut—home ground for Hale and also a place where it was easy to pick up a ride across the Sound to Long Island. In his pocket Hale kept a letter from Washington directing captains of armed craft to take him anywhere he designated. Hale already knew whom he wanted for the task: Captain Charles Pond of Milford, Connecticut, a friend of his from their days in the Nineteenth Regiment.

Hempstead observed, several decades later, that at Norwalk, "Captain Hale had changed his uniform for a plain suit of citizen's brown clothes, with a round, broad brimmed hat; assuming the character of a Dutch [i.e., New York] schoolmaster, leaving all his other clothes, commission, public and private papers with me, and also his silver shoe buckles, saying they would not comport with his character of schoolmaster, and retaining nothing but his college diploma, as an introduction to his assumed calling."[40]

Traversing the Sound had turned dangerous. Ruthless smugglers and gunrunners, for both sides or just for themselves, now abounded, and British patrols scouted for rebel privateers. Pond, however, was an old hand at evading (and avoiding) trouble, having been given command of the fast four-gun sloop *Schuyler* in May, while he was temporarily seconded from the army. Its big sister was the fourteen-gun *Montgomery*, under Captain William Rogers, and together, throughout the summer of 1776, they had patrolled the coast between Sandy Hook and Montauk. Pond plundered a valuable English merchantman off Fire Island on June 19, but once the British controlled Long Island, the *Merlin, Cerberus,* and *Syren* began stalking these Congress-approved privateers in earnest.[41]

Particularly feared among these British commanders was Captain William Quarme, an adept hunter-killer commanding the sixteen-gun brig *Halifax*, which often carried a complement of Rangers for the dirty work.[42] Cruising off Huntington, on Long Island's north shore, at 4 a.m. on September 17, Quarme heard word that two Continental vessels—*Schuyler* and its escort, *Montgomery*—had been spotted the day before, lurking suspiciously. According to the ship's log, Quarme "sent the tenders and boats armd to serch the [Huntington] Bay for two rebel privateers haveing interlagence of them." Quarme tarried at Huntington until the next day, when, at 6 p.m., "the tenders and boats returnd not being able to find any rebel privateers."[43]

By dropping anchor at 4 a.m., Quarme had missed *Schuyler* and *Montgomery* by mere hours. Having left Norwalk on the sixteenth, the two privateers waited off Huntington until inky blackness fell, then Hale was rowed ashore, and they raced home before the dawn of the seventeenth revealed their presence. The vessels had only a few miles' head start over the *Halifax*, but that was more than enough to discourage any pursuit.

As the *Halifax* weighed anchor, one man aboard—his senses sharpened by decades as a frontiersman, warrior, and ranger—suspected something murky afoot. Why had two Continental vessels appeared so close to an enemy-held shoreline and vanished before sunup? Could they have dropped off something—or someone? He resolved to keep a beady eye peeled for anything untoward. The man's name was Robert Rogers, and he was a killing gentleman.

Rogers had once been described by a subordinate "as subtil & deep as Hell itself … a low cunning cheating back biting villain," and by a superior (General Thomas Gage) as a man who would "stick at nothing." He had been born of yeoman farmer stock on the New Hampshire frontier forty-five years before, and at the age of fourteen, saw his first action in 1744–45 after French-backed Indians raided settlements, stripping corpses, scalping them, and then jerking out the entrails before quartering the limbs and severing the genitals. Having imbibed some knowledge of the techniques of the local Pennacook Indians, Rogers volunteered to help track the killers. Over the next decade, Rogers associated with Indians, Indian fighters, and hunters, and learned to make his way through the immense, mostly unexplored wilderness of valleys and hills, gorges and forests, lakes and rivers.[44]

By the beginning of the French and Indian War, Rogers was a captain in a New Hampshire regiment, and honed his skills at reconnaissance by probing the French positions a hundred miles distant from his own lines. Already, Rogers was not averse to rough soldiering, recalling that during one of these missions he and a companion tried to capture a Frenchman for interrogation, "but he refused to take quarter so we kill'd him and took of his scalp in plain sight of the fort." He scouted and raided in all weather, from the mosquito-tortured summer to the freezing winters—when even the hardiest of eighteenth-century armies put aside their muskets. He was notorious for aggressively pursuing his enemies, as well as for his equal-opportunities policy of recruiting Indians into his unit, to serve alongside the ruffians, Irish, and Spaniards he also thought fit to employ.

In 1756, William Shirley, commander-in-chief of the British army in North America, commissioned Rogers to command the "Independent Company of Rangers," a newly formed unit whose mission was "to make discoveries of the proper routes for our own troops, procure intelligence of the enemy's strength and motions, destroy their... magazines and settlements, pick up small parties... upon the lakes, and keep them under continual alarm." There's little doubt that "Rogers's Rangers" were a tough bunch. Kitted in coarse, woolen green jackets and canvas trousers, they wore brown leggings up their thighs, buttoned, like spatterdashes, from the calf downwards, and were shod in moccasins (an idea borrowed from the Indians). Betokening the Scottish origins of many of the Rangers, they adopted the flat bonnets of their homeland, with caplike hats for the officers. Along with the usual musket, powder horns, bayonet, and canteen distributed to regulars, they wielded tomahawks and knives.

A day in the life of a Ranger could be a terrifying one. During one winter mission deep in the woods, Rogers and seventy-four of his men were ambushed by the French and their Indian allies. As they ran low on ammunition, the heavily outnumbered Rangers heard the French (in Rogers's words) "calling to us, and desiring us to accept of quarters, promising that we should be ... used kindly." If they didn't surrender soon, however, "they would cut us to pieces." Rogers defiantly shouted back that he and his Rangers would be the ones doing the cutting, only to be shot "thro my wrist which disabled me from loading my gun."

After a firefight lasting five and a half hours, it now being nighttime, Rogers and his officers decided to carry off their wounded and vanish into the hinterland. Unfortunately, they had overlooked some of the wounded, including Private Thomas Brown, who found two other casualties, Captain Speakman and a soldier, Baker, also left behind. Brown crawled into the underbrush to hide, whence he saw an Indian first scalp Speakman alive, and then kidnap Baker, who tried to commit suicide but was prevented.

Speakman, lying there with the back of his head peeled off, his brain exposed, and his blood soaking into the snow, saw Brown and "beg'd me for God's sake! to give him a tomahawk, that he might put an end to his Life! I refus'd him, and exhorted him as well as I could to pray for mercy, as he could not live many minutes in that deplorable condition, being on the frozen ground, cover'd with snow. He desir'd me to let his wife know if I lived to get home the dreadful death he died." Brown was soon captured anyway and later saw Speakman's head stuck on a pole, staring glassily out at the wilderness. Baker was never heard from again. Brown, however, did witness another Ranger stripped and tied to a stake by the Indians, who thrust pine skewers into his flesh and set them alight. As for Rogers, he got the rest of his broken men back to the fort—with heavy losses, but that was not unusual in the Rangers. His friend, Captain Abercrombie, was sportingly sanguine about the affair, telling Rogers that "I am heartily sorry for Spikeman [sic] ... as likewise for the men you have lost, but it is impossible to play at bowls without meeting with rubs."[45]

After the French and Indian War, Rogers married Elizabeth

Browne, a minister's daughter, and began an unillustrious career of being dunned constantly by creditors as a result of business ventures gone sour. No matter what Rogers did—land speculation, fur trading, trying to discover the Northwest Passage, or organizing a lottery to build a road in New Hampshire—it never quite panned out. In the mid-1760s, he moved to London, where his military exploits and rough frontiersman demeanor still made him a minor celebrity. By all accounts, he enjoyed the metropolitan lifestyle, perhaps a little too much, for he was committed in 1771 to the "Prince of Prisons," the Fleet—a debtors' jail—where he began drinking heavily.

He spent three miserable years there, and was released in August 1774. The next spring, he was given a belated break and allotted the retirement pay of a full major. Suddenly liquid again, Rogers sailed to America, not only to see his wife for the first time in half a decade, but also because he suspected that his very special talents, degraded through indolence and age though they were, might prove useful sooner than many thought.

When he arrived in September 1775, no one quite knew what to do with him, or what his intentions were. General Gage, the British commander, had loathed him—it was a personal thing—ever since the French and Indian War, so Rogers's pickings looked a little slim in Boston. The Americans weren't too hospitable, either. On September 22, the Philadelphia Committee of Safety, suspecting Rogers as a retired British army major (which indeed he was), locked him up for a day.[46] He was released only after he promised not to take up arms against Americans.[47]

Still, Rogers remained deeply in debt, so his strategy was to play both sides to see who would bid highest for his services. Fortunately for him, Gage resigned in October, and was replaced by General Howe, who was far more solicitous of Rogers's talents. In November 1775, Rogers offered him his services (and heightened his attractiveness by fibbing that the Americans had already "made considerable overtures to him"). Howe was enthusiastic, telling the prime minister that he had asked Rogers to name his terms.[48]

Rogers, having hooked Howe, went to the Americans in December and sought out Washington, a fellow French and Indian War veteran well acquainted with Rogers's fearsome reputation. Washington was surprised by Rogers's approach, for all he wanted, apparently, was to pass through the American lines so he could "go unmolested where my private business may call me." And then, a casual aside revealed the deeper harmony playing beneath the charming melody: "I have leave to retire on my half-pay, & never expect to be call'd into the [British] service again. I love North-America, it is my native country and that of my family's, and I intend to spend the evening of my days in it."[49]

Washington did not long mull Rogers's proposal. He was already suspicious. Two weeks before, the Reverend Eleazar Wheelock, the Congregational minister who founded Dartmouth College in 1769, had written him a lengthy note relating the details of a visit from Rogers, who "was in but ordinary habit for one of his character" and "treated me with great respect." Two of Wheelock's recollections drew Washington's attention. Rogers claimed he "had been offered and urged to take a commission in favor of the Colonies but as he was [still] in half pay from the Crown he thought proper not to accept it," a statement that proved him a liar. If anyone knew whether Rogers had been offered a position in his army, it was Washington. While Rogers's untruth could possibly be dismissed as bluster or a misunderstanding, the second nugget was more alarming. Wheelock said two soldiers, recently arrived from Montreal, had remarked that Rogers "had lately been seen in Indian habit" in Canada, which could imply that Rogers was planning to stir up the Indians and cause trouble for the Americans in the north.[50]

It was all very fishy. After checking out the Canadian rumor, Washington told General Philip Schuyler (head of the Northern Department and charged with the invasion of Quebec) that while he suspected Wheelock's information about the Indians to be inaccurate, Rogers was anyway "much suspected of unfriendly views to this country, [so] his conduct should be attended to with some degree of vigilance and circumspection."[51] He directed Generals Sullivan and

Schuyler to surveil and to "strictly examine" Rogers.[52] Unfortunately, like a good Ranger chieftain, the latter had disappeared since his visit to Wheelock.

Rogers reappeared in early February, in New York of all places, then under American control. His intent was blazingly obvious: General Henry Clinton was due to arrive any day to discuss "matters" with the royal governor, William Tryon, who had been obliged to rule New York (what parts weren't already in rebel hands, that is) from aboard the *Dutchess of Gordon*, anchored in the harbor. Clinton, born in 1738 and the aristocratic son of a former New York governor, had just recently emerged from a long depression caused by the death of his wife. Ever since his recovery, Clinton—in his youth something of a charmer—had turned into a cantankerous and egotistical, yet paradoxically shy and self-doubting, character who brooked no dissent from his subordinates and had nothing but criticism for superiors. For his part, Howe intensely disliked working with his second-in-command, foisted on him by London. Taken together, the two supreme commanders of the British forces in America—both adequate individually—were the worst possible combination with which to combat as audacious a general as Washington or to fight a new kind of people's war in a vast military theater far removed from the familiarities of Europe.[53]

Rogers, for Clinton, was a welcome guest, he being one of the few soldiers who knew the terrain. Clinton recorded their conversation on February 8 in his diary: "[I told] Major Rogers that if he chose to join me, I did believe that his services would be such as would induce me to recommend him to gov't & the commander in chief. [He] said that if he could get rid of the oath [of parole forbidding him to fight against Americans] he would[;] I told him he was the best judge how it was tender'd to him & if he was reconciled to coming I should be glad to receive him."[54]

Hoping to extract more cash from the other side, Rogers applied—unaware that Washington wanted him "strictly examined"—to Congress for a commission. Snatched by troopers at South Amboy, he was taken to Philadelphia, where Washington, now certain that Rogers was two-timing, interrogated him. He remained in jail until Congress declared independence, and two days later, on July 6, 1776, he was ordered to be transported under armed guard to New Hampshire—"to be disposed of as the government of that state shall judge best."[55]

Perhaps his guards wrote Rogers off as a drunken old soldier. Perhaps they were merely incompetent. In any event, Rogers escaped his captors on the night of July 8, and lay low, living off the land and covering his tracks, until the hue and cry died down. Ten days later, bearded and smelly, he stealthily clambered up the anchor chain of the British flagship in New York harbor, slipped past the guards, and magically appeared in the dining room. The surprised officers at the table welcomed the famous frontiersman gladly—a pleasant change from his treatment at the hands of Washington and the rebels. On August 6, General Howe reported to Lord Germain in London that "Major Rogers, having escaped to us from Philadelphia, is empowered to raise a battalion of Rangers, which, I hope, may be useful in the course of the campaign."[56]

Officially, they were called the Queen's American Rangers, but were instantly dubbed Rogers's Rangers. As part of his terms of service, Rogers—now luxuriating in the official rank of Lieutenant-Colonel-Commandant, but invariably known as "Major Rogers" (his rank during his French and Indian heyday)—insisted on appointing his own officers and choosing his own men. He'd always detested the British practice of buying and selling commissions (he could never afford to do it), and preferred the New Hampshire way of giving officerships to the men, no matter their background or circumstances, who recruited the most soldiers. Inevitably, his captains and lieutenants could sometimes be of a distinctly ungentlemanly hue and demeanor.[57]

As one disgusted British report noted of the Rangers: "Many of those officers were men of mean extraction without any degree of education sufficient to qualify them to bear His Majesty's commission.... [M]any...had been bred mechanecks others had kept publick houses, and one or two had even kept bawdy houses in the City of New York." One of them, "Mr. Brandon...kept a tavern and eating house in New

York" while "Captain Griffiths kept a dram Shop in the flea market [and] Captain Eagles was still more illeterate and low bred than Frazer [while] Welsh was the [least] exceptionable [since he was once] a petty constable in the City of New York."[58]

Rough they certainly were, as that horrified British officer noticed, but Rogers's subordinates were tough and seasoned (some had served under him in the French and Indian War), and bonded to their chieftain with clanlike loyalty. In the case of the ones just mentioned, Daniel Frazer had served twenty-three years in the British regulars and been wounded at Ticonderoga in 1758; John Brandon had fought in the French and Indian War, and in Boston under General Gage; Patrick Welsh was in the Thirty-fifth Foot for fifteen years, to which he added four years as an adjutant in a Connecticut unit, and another four at the same rank in a New York outfit. John Eagles and John Griffiths, though lacking hard military experience, had made their stripes recruiting Loyalist platoons in heavily, and sometimes violently, Patriot locales. They had seen their share of street fighting and pub brawls.[59]

The Americans had heard no word of Rogers from the moment he scarpered into the July night. It was only in late August that Washington discovered what he had been getting up to. In Westchester County, after his unit had ambushed a detachment of Rangers, a Continental officer named Flood searched the pockets of their commander, William Lounsbury, who had been killed in the melee. Aged about fifty, Lounsbury had retreated to a cave and heroically held off his assailants with a club before succumbing to seven bayonet wounds.[60] Flood discovered "a commission signed by Genl Howe to Major Rogers, empowering him to raise a battalion of Rangers." The officer passed the intelligence to the New York Committee of Safety, which, startled that the infamous Rogers was back in business, immediately alerted Washington.[61]

The return of Rogers, and the threat that once he'd finished recruiting his Ranger units Americans would be faced with a succession of Indian-style guerrilla attacks on their vulnerable supply lines, worried Washington enough to warn Congress that it needed to sweeten the pot for new recruits. Even then, he added, "Nothing less in my opinion, than a suit of cloaths annually...in addition to the pay and bounty, will avail, and I question whether that will do, as the enemy...are giving ten pounds bounty for Recruits; and have got a battalion under Majr. Rogers nearly compleated upon Long Island."[62] He was right. By the beginning of October 1776, the Rangers had formed into ten companies, making about five hundred men, all snappily uniformed in short, double-breasted green coats with blue facings and cuffs, white waistcoats and breeches, and dark brown leggings.[63] To help him, Admiral Howe donated a sloop that Rogers used for trawling the shoreline of Long Island Sound for volunteers and to launch lightning raids on the enemy from his headquarters in Huntington (he kept a sort of regional office at Flushing, as well).[64]

Rogers wanted information, and was willing to pay lavishly for it. He had dozens of informers on Long Island and along the Connecticut coast willing to provide tip-offs about troop movements and naval activities. Connecticut's governor, Jonathan Trumbull, informed Washington in mid-October that Rogers knew what was happening in "every inlet and avenue into the towns of Greenwich, Stamford and Norwalk." "The design of Rogers," he continued, "is from Huntington to make a sudden descent in the night more especially on the town of Norwalk, not only to take the stores there, but to burn, and destroy all before them."[65]

So, when Nathan Hale slipped across the Sound in the company of Captain Pond late on the night of September 16, he was entering Rogers's den. One of Rogers's numerous informers in Norwalk had noticed the presence of Pond's *Schuyler* in port, as well as the arrival of two men, both army types, only one of whom departed quietly in the night with the sloop while the other, Sergeant Hempstead, headed westwards back toward American lines. Having also been alerted by a lookout on the Long Island side that two rebel vessels—one named *Schuyler*, last seen berthed in Norwalk—were in the vicinity of Huntington, Rogers had shrewdly suspected that a man was being transported across the

Sound. But he received the intelligence a little too late, which explains why he and his Rangers were aboard the warship *Halifax* when it nosed around Huntington a few hours after the *Schuyler* and *Montgomery* had hightailed it. Rebuffed in his attempt to capture the spy *in flagrante delicto*, an annoyed Rogers was forced to cool his heels aboard the *Halifax* all day on Tuesday, September 17.

Hale, a Connecticut Yankee in the midst of King George's army, must soon have heard that Howe had begun the invasion of Manhattan and that Washington was abandoning New York. Instantly, the *raison d'être* of his mission had vaporized. Should Howe succeed in storming the island and taking the city, he would drain Brooklyn of men and materiel and funnel them into Manhattan, thereby leaving Hale to spy on only the newly deserted fortifications and emptied barracks of Long Island. There was nothing for it but for Hale to hasten westwards the fifty miles to Brooklyn, gather whatever information he could along the way, and then try to reach the American lines. In his hurry, Hale got careless. He spent too much time in the open and asked too many impertinent questions of the locals. Worse still, he was an easy mark for the thousands of Tory refugees who had flooded into Long Island from Connecticut after being purged from their houses by vengeful Patriots. Someone, perhaps someone sitting outside a tavern or riding to Hempstead, may have noticed Hale ambling by, and recalled, with a start, that young Nathan of the Connecticut Hales had, it was rumored, joined the rebels after leaving Yale. It would not have been too much trouble to tell a passing Ranger of what one had seen. And it would not have taken too long for Rogers to elicit from his Ranger that some excited Connecticut refugee had recently spotted a known or suspected rebel-traitor wearing a brown summer suit and impersonating a New York schoolmaster.

Though Hale had a head start on him, Rogers not only knew the ground but also did not have to worry about enemy patrols slowing him down. Then again, since Hale was alone, he could blend into the crowd if he suspected he was being tailed. Instead of disembarking at Huntington, then, Rogers, guessing that Hale would head west along the coastal road toward the city, planned to lie in wait to intercept him. At 10 p.m. on Wednesday the eighteenth, according to the *Halifax*'s log, "the party of Rangers" disembarked at Sands Point—a spot midway between Huntington and Flushing—and set off to hunt their prey.[66]

The next day, just as Rogers had supposed, Hale was scoped traveling along the coastal road. Rogers spent the next several hours watching the innocent from afar. Was he an agent or not? He almost certainly was, but spring the trap too early, and Hale could claim a case of mistaken identity, especially if no incriminating maps or notes were found on him. Rogers needed Hale to condemn himself. All the next day, Rogers watched his quarry, and saw Hale scribbling notes whenever he saw a British detachment or passed a barracks. He now probably had enough to hang him, but he wanted to make the kill certain.

That night, a Friday, Hale took a room at a roadside tavern and was sitting alone at a table eating supper when Rogers "happened" to sit across from him. Hale looked nervous, so Rogers made some small talk, remarking by the by on the recent battles. Soon, the two men began chatting about the war and Rogers—playing the part of an American militiaman caught behind enemy lines—complained of being "detained on an island where the inhabitants sided with the British against the American Colonies." Hale's interest, of course, was piqued, and Rogers took the opportunity of intimating "that he himself was upon the business of spying out the inclination of the people and motion of the British troops." Rogers's stratagem persuaded Hale that he had found a friend, and one who could be trusted with his secret. Amid the tavern's unsuspecting customers, they discreetly raised their glasses and toasted Congress, whereupon Hale confided everything about himself and his mission. Rogers had hooked Hale, but hadn't yet reeled him in; for that, he needed witnesses to his confession. As they bade each other good night, Rogers smiled and asked Hale to come dine with him the next day at his quarters. Hale enthusiastically accepted: Traveling with such an amiable companion as Rogers to New York would be pleasanter than wending his own way there.

On Saturday afternoon, Hale arrived at Rogers's tavern. Waiting with him were three or four men—Rangers disguised as civilians—whom Rogers introduced as friends to the cause. Rogers ordered ales for them all and together they talked of the revolution, Hale's undertaking, and his excitement at being reunited with his beloved Alice. In the meantime, the rest of Rogers's men had silently surrounded the inn. At last, Rogers gave the signal and Hale, openmouthed and panicked, was seized and manacled. Accused by Rogers of being a spy, Hale pointlessly denied it, but as Rogers dragged him out of the tavern, several passersby pointed him out and said they knew him as being a Hale of Connecticut and a known rebel.[67]

Hale was taken to Flushing—where the Rogers maintained a recruitment office—and bundled aboard Rogers's private sloop for the hour-long voyage to Howe's Manhattan headquarters. Rogers said little, if anything, to his captive. For a bloodied warhorse like him, bagging this Hale, straight out of Yale with a year's drill duty on his card, had been too easy.

Very late on Saturday night, Rogers unceremoniously deposited Hale at the Beekman Mansion at what is now First Avenue and Fifty-first Street, but was then being used by General Howe. Hale's execution for espionage was a formality. Howe was in the midst of orchestrating a major battle campaign and had no time to conduct a full court-martial for espionage, even if one had been required. The evidence was incontrovertible and entirely uncontroversial: Rogers had provided witnesses who attested to Hale's declaration that he had been sent by Washington; Hale had admitted that he was an officer in the Continental army; Hale was captured in civilian clothes behind enemy lines; Hale was carrying a sheaf of incriminating documents. There was neither reason nor need for Howe to agonize over this spy.

After Howe, roused from his bed, had sleepily signed Hale's death warrant, he was detained in the greenhouse under the guard of the provost marshal, sixty-year-old William Cunningham, a red-haired, red-faced drunk and notorious bully unlikely to look upon traitors like Hale with much regard for their welfare. (Some months later he showed a captured American officer, Captain John Palsgrave Wyllys, his souvenir: Hale's Yale diploma. Cunningham would be hanged in London in 1791 for forgery. On the scaffold he confessed to having caused two thousand prisoners to die by starvation and general cruelty, such as slipping poison into the food of the bolshier ones. He sold their rations for his own profit.)[68]

After breakfast, it was time. Hale's destination was the artillery park, about a mile away, next to the Dove Tavern, at what is now Third Avenue and Sixty-sixth Street.

Hale's hands were pinioned behind his back, and he was outfitted with a coarse white gown trimmed with black—which would be used as a winding-sheet for his corpse—over his rumpled brown suit, plus a rough, woolen white cap, also black-trimmed. A couple of guards led the way, and behind him a squad of redcoats marched with loaded muskets and fixed bayonets—in case the prisoner made a last-minute break for freedom (it occasionally happened, the spectacle of embarrassed guards chasing and tackling a condemned man being considered quite comical). Accompanying the party was a cart loaded with rough pine boards for his coffin. At the site, the noose was swung over a rigid horizontal branch about fifteen feet up, and Hale shakily climbed the ladder that would soon be kicked away for the drop. Next to the tree there was a freshly dug grave awaiting.

At the apex of the ladder, Hale was permitted the traditional last words. His were certainly not "I only regret that I have but one life to lose for my country"; that phrase, lifted from Joseph Addison's contemporary play *Cato*, was put into his mouth many years later by William Hull and other friends. Hull could not have known what Hale said in his final moments, though he did remember that Hale had been struck by *Cato* when at Yale, and that he and Hull and Tallmadge had talked excitedly of its brilliance. Perhaps he had specifically cited the "I regret" line as representative of his patriotic views, and Hull, loyal as ever, allowed his friend the posthumous privilege of uttering it.[69]

What Hale really said was caught by Captain Frederick MacKenzie, who wrote in his diary for September 22: "He behaved with great composure and resolution, saying he thought it the duty of every good officer, to obey any orders given him by his commander in chief; and desired the spectators to be at all times prepared to meet death in whatever shape it might appear."[70] Later that day, a Howe aide wrote a terse, routine entry in the orderly book: "A spy from the enemy (by his own full confession) apprehended last night, was this day executed at 11 oClock in front of the Artillery Park."

Lynching was a tricky business. If the knot was not properly placed at the *side* of a prisoner's neck (under his jaw, actually) rather than at the nape, his head would be ripped off if he dropped too great a distance, which left an unsightly mess for the guards to clean up. Conversely, if the drop was not sudden or long enough, the condemned man would be left jerking in the air as the rope strangled him. In those instances, a merciful hangman would pull on the victim's legs before the audience started booing him for being so clumsy. A perfect hanging would break the man's neck instantly by severing his spinal cord, while leaving his head attached. In Hale's case, his hangman was a former slave freed by the British who was unlikely to be familiar with the latest methods. As underestimating the appropriate drop was much more common than overestimating it, and being pushed off a ladder was far less sudden than falling through a gallows trapdoor, it probably took Hale several agonizing minutes to die.

Hale's body was left swinging for a few days, to set an example. One British officer had a letter published in the *Kentish Gazette* on November 9 (but dated September 26) remarking, "We hanged up a rebel spy the other day, and some soldiers got, out of a rebel gentleman's garden, a painted soldier on a board, and hung it along with the rebel; and wrote upon it, General Washington, and I saw it yesterday beyond headquarters by the roadside." His corpse was thrown into the waiting grave soon after.[71]

The first the Americans heard of Hale's death was on the evening of the twenty-second, when Captain John Montressor, of the Engineer Corps and an aide-de-camp to General Howe, approached an outpost in northern Manhattan under a flag of truce. His main business, however, did not concern Hale, but was to transport to Washington a letter from Howe offering an exchange of high-ranking prisoners.

Joseph Reed, Washington's adjutant general, accompanied by General Israel Putnam and Captain Alexander Hamilton, rode to meet him. After passing over the letter, he casually added that one Nathan Hale, a captain, had been executed that morning. The next day, without mentioning the Hale incident, Washington accepted the prisoner offer in a letter carried by Tench Tilghman, who was escorted by Colonel Samuel B. Webb and Captain William Hull, who had specifically requested permission to be part of the embassy after Hamilton had told him about Montressor's information.[72] Montressor again confirmed, at Hull's insistence, that Hale was dead.

And that was that. Hull was shaken, but few others wished to talk about the humiliating debacle, and no announcement was made to the army, for fear of undermining morale. In any case, there were hundreds of other war dead to handle. Certainly Washington never spoke of the affair, while Colonel Tilghman wrote to his father on September 25 about the meeting under a flag of truce but conspicuously failed to mention Hale. As part of the cover-up, his official listing in the Nineteenth Regiment's casualty list was simple and sparse: "Nathan Hale—Capt—killed—22d September."[73]

Privately, however, American commanders seethed, and wanted to exact revenge. On October 3, Tilghman told Egbert Benson not to be so soft on the British and any sympathizers who fell into their hands. "I am sorry that your convention do not think themselves legally authorized to make examples of those villains they have apprehended [for] the General [Washington] is determined, if he can bring some of them in his hands under the denomination of spies, to execute them. General Howe hanged a captain of ours belonging to Knowlton's Rangers, who went into New-York to make discoveries. I don't see why we should not make retaliation."[74]

No one made the effort to tell Hale's family what had happened. It wasn't until September 30 that his brother Enoch, now a preacher, wrote in his diary that he "hear[d] a rumor that Capt. Hale belonging to the east side Connecticut River, near Colchester, who was educated at college, was sentenced to hang in the enemy's lines at New York, being taken as a spy, or reconnoitering their camp. Hope it is without foundation. Something troubled at it. Sleep not very well." Two weeks later, on October 15, a maudlin Enoch continues: "Accounts from my brother captain are indeed melancholy! That about the second week of September, he went to Stamford, crossed to Long Island...and had finished his plans, but, before he could get off, was betrayed, taken, and hanged without ceremony.... Some entertain hope that all this is not true; but it is a gloomy, dejected hope. Time may determine. Conclude to go to camp next week." It wasn't until October 26, when Enoch rode to White Plains to talk directly to officers of the Nineteenth Regiment, that his brother's death was confirmed.[75]

By every measure, the Hale mission was a fiasco. While the sacrifice of the obscure captain made no difference to Washington's grand strategy, the bad decisions and poor planning that led to his death reflect Washington's own confusion as to what his spy's purpose was. Washington, however, would learn from his mistakes.

CHAPTER TWO

The Year of the Hangman

*1777, that year which the Tories said, had
three gallows in it, meaning the three sevens.*

JOHN ADAMS

As he trudged toward his doom on Sunday morning, Nathan Hale saw swirling plumes of smoke in the distance, to the south, where the city lay, still smoldering where a fierce fire had burned a mile-long swathe the day before. On that otherwise grim Sabbath, perhaps Hale allowed himself a wry smile upon overhearing his guards cursing the rebel arsonists who had, they presumed, set New York ablaze. Now, happily, the only thing the enemy would be occupying was the smoldering sump of a city.[1] If the Americans would be forced to camp outdoors during the coming winter, then for Hale it was satisfaction enough to know that Washington had deprived some redcoats of their nice warm billets as well.

He hadn't, though. Grumbling mightily that "had I been left to the dictates of my own judgment, New York should have been laid in ashes before I quitted it," Washington had obeyed Congress's instruction to leave the city intact when he evacuated.[2] From his headquarters on Harlem Heights, Washington had seen the red glare, and was glad: "Providence, or some good honest fellow, has done more for us than we were disposed to do for ourselves."[3]

The fire, which had begun near the docks at Whitehall Slip, rapidly devoured the surrounding houses and stores. At first there was panic. "The king's officers, uncertain in whom to confide," distrusted the city's volunteer firemen, thinking them to be "rebel[s] at heart," and "franticly hurried them from place to place." Several officers became so terrified at the holocaust surrounding them they started "beating [the firemen] with their swords," and even drove a few into the flames, screaming.[4]

Some kept their heads. Admiral Howe immediately ordered his navy to weigh anchor and sail downriver—sufficiently far away to avoid being set alight by stray sparks—while rowboats ferried officers and sailors back to the city to help fight the fire. In the meantime, General James Robertson drafted two full regiments of soldiers into makeshift fire brigades.[5] They soon discovered that New York had been left defenseless. Short of metal suitable for casting into cannons, Washington had stripped the city of its alarm bells; the British also found many of the water pumps and fire engines were out of order—testament to prewar civil authorities' sloppiness.[6]

Conquering blocks at a time, the fire marched inexorably to the foot of Broadway and turned—when the wind shifted at 2 a.m.—west. By merest chance, the "ship docks, warehouses, and the commercial part of the city" located on the eastern side were left unharmed.[7] Some ten hours after its outbreak, the wind having again changed, the fire was finally baffled at Barclay Street by pulling down the houses in its path.[8]

The physical and financial damage was enormous, with contemporaries agreeing that between a sixth and a quarter of the city—including five hundred houses—had been razed.[9] Thousands were wretchedly "reduced to beggary," while "many hundreds of families have lost their all" and were "destitute of shelter, food or cloathing."[10] The blow would have fallen still harder—as well as severely hampering British military preparations for at least a year—had General Robertson not diverted the fire engine dousing his flaming house to the nearby docks, thus saving £200,000 worth of army supplies at the cost of his own residence, worth £2,000.[11]

The fire was the fruit of a "preconcerted, deliberate scheme" of fifth columnists, covert operatives, and sleepers, suspected the British.[12] It certainly looked likely. "A few minutes after the fire was discovered," the authorities claimed, "it was observed to break out in five or six other places, at a considerable distance."[13] Mr. Chew, one of the army's assistant commissaries, said that he had seen the original building at Whitehall Slip on fire, and then another—two hundred yards away— "which had the appearance of having been purposely set on fire."

The conspiracy theory of the Great Fire was gravely weakened by General Howe's admission that the "night was extremely windy," which naturally conveyed sparks some distance. Further, if the fire were the product of a rebel plot, it's strange that no one thought to *start* the fire in the commercial and residential heart of New York.[14] Instead, the flames blasted a narrow path, originating in the southeast and driving northwest—that mirrored the wind's shifting direction through the night.

The truth about how the fire started has only recently come to light. On the night in question, "several of the soldiers' wives" had gathered together "in a large frame building near Whitehall-dock"—a storehouse adjacent to the Fighting Cocks, an old tavern frequented by British troops and sailors on the town. Hoping to cook some hot food in a fireplace, the women "procured from an adjacent yard a number of pine boards, the ends of which they placed in the chimney, [with] their opposite points rested upon the cedar floor of the apartment." The "careless gypsies," having finished their feast, "had withdrawn from the heated and smoky atmosphere within, to enjoy the fresh seabreeze without." In the meantime, the flames, of course, consumed the boards and "the cry of fire was heard soon after."[15]

Although innocent of igniting the fire, or of acting on Washington's orders, or of organizing a vast plot to burn the city, Continental servicemen (either stay-behinds, escaped prisoners, or deserters who'd had second thoughts) and rebel sympathizers *were* guilty of taking advantage of the chaos to help the fire along and frustrate efforts to save the city. Indeed, American officers in northern Manhattan took it for granted that "some of our own people" were responsible for spreading the fire. Washington's own aide-de-camp, Tench Tilghman, told his father that if any of these arsonists were executed it would admittedly be "upon good grounds" (though he assured him that they had acted "without the knowledge or approbation of any commanding officer in this army").[16]

One such freelance arsonist was Abraham Patten, who would be hanged as a spy in Brunswick, New Jersey, in early June 1777 after bribing a British grenadier to carry four letters to Washington; the soldier had pocketed the fifty guineas and delivered the messages to his superiors. On the scaffold, Patten, who had been living in the city at the time, "said he was a principal in setting fire to New York, but would not accuse any of his accomplices."[17] Another accessory after the fact was a New England captain "seized, with matches in his pocket," who confessed he was determined to set fire to King's College.[18] This unfortunate was one William Smith—son of a Massachusetts clergyman—who was "sacrificed on the spot to the fury of the soldiers."[19] The captain had been taken prisoner during a skirmish and took it upon himself to do his bit for Washington. Poor Smith wasn't the only one caught red-handed: Captured the week before, Lieutenant Richard Brown, of a Pennsylvania regiment, was discovered by soldiers "setting fire to some of the houses in New York" and likewise executed in the street.[20]

Being thrown into the flames was often the on-the-spot penalty for suspected arsonists (and sometimes looters), though lynchings and stabbings were not unheard of, and there were several instances when individuals were "hung up by the heels, and afterwards had their throats cut" or were bayoneted.[21] Women were not excluded from retribution: In fact, the "first incendiary who fell into the hands of the troops" was a female shoved "without ceremony" into the inferno. Soon afterwards, several men seen "destroying a chain of buckets, in order to prevent their being made use of in extinguishing the confla-gration" were thrown into the flames after her.[22]

Unlike the Great Fire of London in 1666, which cleansed its alleys of beplagued vermin, blasted a millennium's worth of microbes out of the gutters, and razed the medieval hovels, so giving Sir Christopher Wren the opportunity to construct a modern city atop its ruins, the fire which ravaged New York left large parts of it a macabre pyre. A bustling mercantile metropolis descended into a degenerate mare's nest, the leading red-light district in North America, the black-market capital of the Revolution. The area around Whitehall Slip, for in-stance, was never rebuilt, and instead became "Canvas-Town," a hell where paupers, felons, and prostitutes huddled in burnt-out houses. The glittering balls thrown in the ostentatious mansions of parvenu merchants and hard-faced war profiteers disguised, like a cheap rug, the rotted floorboards of a city torn and conflicted.

A narcotic, poisonous atmosphere pervaded New York, whose in-habitants were forced to compromise their principles to survive the war. Surrounded by naught but devastation, often forced to flee from their homes by greedy Patriots, and facing an uncertain future, almost every man and woman, no matter how deep his or her attachment to the Crown or to Congress, traded illegally with the enemy. Ambigu-ity reigned—New York was a city schizophrenically under occupation but one also under siege—and the only means of emerging unscathed was to play both ends against the middle. Citizens tailored their poli-tics, allegiances, and beliefs as circumstances dictated: On one particu-lar morning—June 25, 1775—crowds cheered George Washington as he passed through the city on his way to Boston; that very afternoon, they cheerfully greeted William Tryon, the royal governor, on his re-turn from England.

The immolation of New York was the one bright spot for Washington that dismal fall of 1776. He would spend the rest of it on the run. Leaving two large detachments at Forts Washington and Lee, the commander-in-chief of a severely demoralized army retreated north of Manhattan, languidly followed—"chased" would be the wrong word—by Howe. At the end of October, the two sides clashed at White Plains, and yet again Washington came off worse. Much to Washington's pleasant surprise, however, Howe refrained from the kill and turned back to finish off the forts to his rear. On November 7, General Nathanael Greene—the officer commanding Fort Lee—could see the enemy's camp fires burning across the river.[23] It could not be long before Howe, lethargic as he was, reduced Fort Washington and advanced on his own vulnerable outpost. Taking advantage of the respite, Washington withdrew the rump of his army further north to Peekskill, his plan being to circle around, rendezvous with his remaining commanders in New Jersey, and then, hopefully, evade Howe until winter brought campaigning to a halt.

Given the chaotic circumstances, American intelligence was nonexistent. Deserters, who could sometimes bring in useful material about their regiments, had become a rare thing indeed, for no one abandons the winning side. Washington, however, suffered terribly from these turncoats, though one, William Demont, may have single-handedly, if inadvertently, saved the American cause. An ensign in the Fort Washington garrison, he "sacrificed all [he] was worth in the world" and brought plans of its fortifications and artillery emplacements to the British. It was this intelligence which convinced Howe, then north of New York, that of the two fish he had to fry, Fort, not General, Washington was the bigger. By letting his foe escape, Howe lost the opportunity to extinguish the rebellion.[24]

Washington's primary problem, however, lay in not possessing a secure, fixed headquarters. Without one, there was no guarantee that spies' messages would ever find him. Washington was obliged to forget about acquiring strategic intelligence and instead rely on tactical reports gleaned by scouts riding as close as they dared to the enemy lines. More often than not, they would return with "lame" and "imperfect" accounts of British movements, a result General Charles Lee—one of Washington's most senior (and supremely talented, at least in his own opinion) officers—ascribed to them not "ventur[ing] far enough."

He was very "far from being satisfied" with the conduct of the scouts, though Washington had no choice but to use them, especially after mid-November, by which time Forts Washington and Lee had fallen, and Washington was being relentlessly pursued through New Jersey by Lord Cornwallis, Howe's chief lieutenant, who boasted that he would trap Washington "as a hunter bags a fox."[25]

And an exhausted fox at that. Since August, the strength of Washington's army had fallen from 20,000 to just 3,000 (about half of whose contracts were due to end in December), and he had lost four battles (plus one surrender without a fight—at Fort Lee, where the entering British discovered General Greene had vacated it so precipitately "the pots were left absolutely boiling on the fire, and the tables spread for dinner of some of the officers"; they also found twelve Patriots, "all dead drunk," who had resolutely stayed behind and liberated the fort's rum stores).[26] "The fact is," concluded Lord Rawdon, "their army is all broken to pieces, and the spirit of their leaders and their abettors is also broken." Surely, he ventured, "it is well nigh over with them."[27]

Still, this old fox remained a sly one. On December 12—with Cornwallis threatening to advance on Philadelphia, the seat of Congress itself—Washington ordered Colonel John Cadwalader to "keep a good lookout for spies" and "magnify your numbers as much as possible" should he spot an opportunity to sow some disinformation.[28] A little more than two weeks later, the efficient Cadwalader reported that he had sent an anonymous but "very intelligent young gentleman" to Princeton who had found some friendly British officers with whom to share a bottle. They got to talking, and the officers boasted they had 5,000 men at their command, whereupon the young gentleman cheekily declared that Washington had 16,000 in fine trim. The officers looked shocked, as they had not believed "we had more than 5 or 6000"— itself an exaggeration—that were deserting and in poor shape. His job done, the enterprising agent even brought back a map of the local British deployments.[29]

These successes aside, Cadwalader—like Washington and most officers at the time—relied primarily on soldiers sneaking across enemy lines, memorizing troop positions, and returning later that night. "I have sent several persons over for intelligence," noted Cadwalader on December 15, "& last night sent Capt. Shippen with 20 good men," and that wasn't to overlook the "very intelligent spirited officer in the Jersey Regulars" who also went over on a separate mission.[30] The British, too, had their sources, though they tended to rely more on the information brought in by such helpful loyalists as Bazilla Haines of Burlington County, who stayed a night in an American camp and subsequently informed his masters that "they had only two field pieces" and that "there were not above eight hundred, near one half boys and all of them militia."[31]

Despite such heroics, the enemy was taken by surprise by Washington's counterattacks at the Battles of Trenton and Princeton in late December and early January, allowing him a respite after the rigors of the past months.[32] With the British withdrawing to New York to reassess their strategy and recover from the shock of being beaten, Washington wintered in the hills around Morristown, where he was finally able to consider his intelligence apparatus, or rather, how to build one that would serve him well in the coming campaign seasons.

While military officers would continue to handle purely tactical matters and scouting, Washington wanted to recruit more civilians into the nascent service. Whereas soldiers disguised in civvies found it difficult to shed their drill-bred habits of saluting superiors and walking in perfect time, civilians could easily enter enemy-held cities without attracting suspicion, especially if they were locals or possessed the requisite passes. As Washington advised one of his generals at the time, he should gather intelligence "by engaging some of those people who have obtained protections, to go in under pretence of asking advice."[33]

To this end, he discreetly requested William Duer, a member of New York's Committee for Detecting and Defeating Conspiracies—the enforcement arm of the political revolutionaries—to recommend a suitable candidate. On January 28, Duer forwarded the name of Nathaniel Sackett, a middle-aged colleague of his on the committee.

Not only was Sackett "a man of honor, and of firm attachment to the American cause," he was, more importantly, "a person of intrigue, and secrecy well calculated to prosecute such measures as you shall think conducive to give Success to your generous exertions."[34] A week later, Washington informed Sackett that the "advantage of obtaining the earliest and best intelligence of the designs of the enemy" and "your capacity for an undertaking of this kind, have induced me to entrust the management of this business to your care." A monthly salary of fifty dollars was arranged, and Sackett was additionally allowed a secret fund of five hundred dollars "to pay those whom you may find necessary to Imploy in the transaction of this business."[35]

If Sackett succeeded in recruiting agents, he would certainly require a deputy empowered to detail army riders to run their messages to headquarters, as well as able to soothe the snippier colonels annoyed that a civilian was interfering in matters they regarded as their own prerogative. To that end, Washington quietly appointed a freshly made captain, Benjamin Tallmadge of the Second Continental Light Dragoons, as Sackett's military contact.[36]

Tallmadge, dark-eyed, pale, delicately featured, with a prominent nose, a somewhat bulbous forehead, and a disconcerting habit of cocking his head like a quizzical beagle, had enjoyed an interesting war so far. After bidding adieu to his dearest friend Nathan Hale, he had become a schoolmaster in Wethersfield, Connecticut. Most of his letters to Hale between 1773 and 1775 talked about girls (the females in his town were "very agreeable" and he was looking forward to having "a colleague (of the fair sex) settled under me, (or rather over me), for she will dwell in the 2nd loft"), but Tallmadge was slowly being drawn into revolutionary circles. His landlady, a widow of the town's Congregational minister, introduced Tallmadge to Wethersfield's first citizens, many of whom—such as Silas Deane and John Chester—would go on to play significant roles in the coming years. Tallmadge also met Jeremiah Wadsworth of New Haven, like him a minister's son. That contact would prove especially beneficial.[37] Still, Tallmadge was reluctant to sign up after the skirmishes at Lexington and Concord in April 1775, telling

Hale in May that while "a great, flourishing state may arise" in America, he questioned whether "we ought at present desire it."[38] A June jaunt to see the American lines at Boston, followed by a heartfelt talk with his friend John Chester, now captaining a company of Connecticut militia, removed some of Tallmadge's doubts and went some way toward persuading him that rebellion was a divine mission. As he told Hale, "Our holy religion, the honour of God, a glorious country, and a happy constitution is what we have to defend."[39] Even so, still beset by worry that expressing Whiggish sentiments was quite a different thing from taking up arms against an anointed king, he refrained from signing up for the colors for another year. By the spring of 1776, it had become almost impossible for a young man of Tallmadge's upbringing and milieu to avoid the fateful decision. By chance, Chester had just been promoted to colonel, and he offered Tallmadge a lieutenancy. Tallmadge took the commission. On June 20, he proudly donned his dashing new uniform for the first time and prepared to meet the blast of war.[40]

Chester's regiment marched for New York soon afterwards, where it was absorbed into General Jeremiah Wadsworth's brigade. For Tallmadge, perhaps thanks to his connections, promotion was rapid, and he became the regimental adjutant on July 22.[41] In late August, Chester's regiment was transferred from Manhattan to Brooklyn to await the inevitable British attack. When it came, Tallmadge saw action around Flatbush and found himself, along with the exhausted remnants of Washington's army, awaiting evacuation at Brooklyn Ferry on the evening of August 29. Tallmadge departed on one of the last boats off Long Island and followed Washington north to White Plains. His eldest brother, William, who had signed on as a sergeant in a Connecticut regiment as early as 1775, did not accompany him: He had been captured during the battle and soon after died of starvation and neglect, aged twenty-four, aboard one of the British prison ships in New York harbor. If Tallmadge still nursed any doubts about the cause he served, they immediately disappeared.

In early October, John Wyllys, then serving as Wadsworth's brigade major, was killed in a skirmish, and Tallmadge was raised to his place.[42]

In this post, Tallmadge first came to Washington's attention; brigade majors met at the general's headquarters at 11 a.m. each day to receive their orders, which they would in turn read out to the regimental adjutants. As Washington retreated through New Jersey, however, Tallmadge and many of the New England regiments were directed to stay in northern New York, on the east side of the Hudson, to fend off British pursuit. Rejoining the main body of the army in early December, Tallmadge was offered a captaincy in one of Congress's four brand-new cavalry regiments, the Second Dragoons, commanded by Colonel Elisha Sheldon. These mounted troopers, who could also fight on foot, were to be deployed by Washington on reconnaissance missions, where they would often skirmish with enemy cavalry undertaking the same task.[43] Forty-three men were under the young officer's command: a lieutenant, a cornet (a commissioned officer), a quartermaster, two sergeants, two corporals, a trumpeter, a farrier, and thirty-four privates.[44]

Uniformed in dark blue coats, lighter breeches, and knee-high black boots with silver spurs, the dragoons were crowned with metal helmets—designed to ward off saber blows—stylishly decorated with a white horsehair plume sprouting from their crested peaks. Each man carried a cavalry saber, a pistol or two, and a short musket, while officers, befitting the dashing character of the cavalryman, wore a crimson sash around their waists.[45] Immediately after being raised, the regiment trekked to Connecticut to buy horses, so missing the Battles of Trenton and Princeton. Tallmadge ensured that his own troop (one of six) "was composed entirely of *dapple gray horses* . . . with black straps and black bear-skin holster-covers" that, he added modestly, "looked superb."[46]

It was while based in Connecticut in these early months of 1777 that Tallmadge first experienced the secret world, its shadows and thrills. There, he served a dual role: His day job entailed being a dragoon captain assigned the chore of purchasing horses for the regiment, while his extracurricular employment consisted of acting as Sackett's point man for espionage operations across Long Island Sound. Even though Washington's correspondence with Tallmadge about horses is dull—"I would not wish to have even dark greys, if others equally good could be got; but if they cannot, you may purchase them, and when they change colour by age, we must put them to other Uses in the army"—the fact that the commander-in-chief was writing to a mere captain about such humdrum matters is testament to the trust he reposed in him.[47]

Tallmadge's first mission was to ensure that Major John Clark safely arrived on British-occupied Long Island from the Connecticut shore. Clark was a young, large-built Pennsylvanian lawyer, "fond of fun and frolick," who volunteered for duty as a lieutenant in 1775 and was noticed by senior officers for his gallantry at the Battle of New York.[48] Over the following months, Clark turned to specializing in reconnoitering. General Nathanael Greene, in particular, thought him remarkably talented and audacious, made him his aide-de-camp, and sent him out by himself to probe far ahead of the army and even to scout deep within enemy territory, where he whiled away the lonely hours in the forests and hills reading Beccaria's *Essay on Crimes and Punishments* (which contested the era's emphasis on harsh punishments) and Laurence Sterne's *Sentimental Journey Through France and Italy*, an account of the comic, and often amorous, adventures enjoyed by the author's alter ego, the Reverend Mr. Yorick.[49] For a covert expedition to Long Island, perhaps using it as Nathan Hale had as a back way into New York, Clark was just the man.

Little is known of what exactly Clark did there—Clark was so habitually secretive that in the autobiographical sketch he published forty-five years later he omitted any mention of what he was doing between January and September 1777—but he was certainly traveling all along the northern coastal road, from Setauket in the east to Huntington about midway and probably still more west than Oyster Bay.[50] On February 25, he paid a whaleboatman who frequently crossed the Sound to carry a message to Tallmadge. In it, he reported that "there were no troops at Satauket [*sic*], but part of two companies at Huntington." And that "there are but few who are not friendly to the Cause—That they had beat up for volunteers in the western part of the county but that only three had inlisted."[51]

Setauket at the time was a very small town, remarkable in this context only because it was Tallmadge's birthplace, and it was where his father still lived. Thus, Clark was assured of a friendly welcome, safe sleeping, and warm food—all the things Hale had lacked. The intrepid Clark spent several more months reconnoitering Long Island, all the while honing his skills at blending into a population and learning from the inside how the British army worked.[52] (On June 1, Washington's private accounts book records that $946 for "secret services" had lately been paid, some of it to Clark, to refund his expenses.)[53]

After receiving the message, Tallmadge summarized it for Sackett and passed the new version on to Captain John Davis, of the Second Company, Fourth Battalion, Fourth New York Regiment, for delivery.[54] Tallmadge had become acquainted with Davis through his younger brother, Samuel Tallmadge (born 1755), once bound for a mercantile career but currently a sergeant in the Fourth New York's First Company of the Fourth Battalion.[55] Samuel was also great friends with the former ensign—the lowest rank of officerdom—of Davis's company, Caleb Brewster, with whom he and Benjamin had grown up in Setauket. Brewster was a former whaleboatman by trade, and it may well have been he who carried Clark's messages across the Sound from Setauket to Connecticut.[56] Though Tallmadge's letter was addressed to Sackett, the latter seems to have been absent and Davis entrusted it to William Duer, who sent on a copy to Washington.[57]

Earlier in the year, chafing at the regiment's inaction, Brewster had transferred to the Second Continental Artillery, an outfit which allowed him plenty of free time to participate in "semi-official" covert operations across the Sound.[58] One such was an amphibious raid on August 14 in which Colonel Parsons led 150 armed men in a sloop and six whaleboats—one commanded by Brewster—on an attack on Setauket's Presbyterian church, recently taken over by a prominent Long Island Loyalist, Colonel Richard Hewlett, to use as a fort. His men had overturned many of the gravestones in the churchyard, destroyed the pulpit, and ransacked the interior. The desecrated church happened to be the one ministered by Tallmadge's father, and his son approved heartily of Brewster and his friends paying Hewlett a surprise visit (Tallmadge himself couldn't go, as his regiment had already been recalled to the main army). Parsons did not succeed in taking Hewlett and his men prisoner, but he did give them a good scare: Having beached their whaleboats outside the village, they silently marched to Setauket and sent a flag of truce to the surprised inhabitants of the "fort." Hewlett refused to surrender and a fierce firefight erupted. After Parsons was tipped off by a friendly local that British warships were on their way, he ordered a retreat to the boats and the raiders scarpered for home, not omitting to steal a few of Hewlett's horses.[59]

In the meantime, Tallmadge had found himself made a major on April 7, 1777, and in early July his regiment rode from Connecticut to New Jersey to join Washington.[60] The dragoons ranged widely, frequently encountering the advance parties of their British equivalents. As Tallmadge wrote to Wadsworth, "I have had here & there a horse and rider or two wounded, but have lost none from my troop as yet, though several horsemen have been killed in the same skirmishes with me, from other regiments."[61] So busy was Tallmadge with his regular military duties that his intelligence function fell by the wayside.

In any case, it mattered little, for Sackett had, during Tallmadge's absence in Connecticut, turned himself into an astute and imaginative spy chief. Unfortunately for his relations with Washington, he was successful more at inventing new forms of tradecraft than actually acquiring hard intelligence. Most of his agents may have performed poorly, but Sackett's system protected them, and their secrets, better than had any other until that time.

On the same day as Tallmadge's promotion, Sackett compiled a lengthy report for Washington on his progress. Having served on the Committee for Detecting Conspiracies, Sackett would have known a thing or two about double agents and impersonators, but his letter discusses so many advanced techniques—especially for the time—it should be regarded as one of the founding documents of American espionage.

Following his appointment, he had spent a fortnight "almost desp[airing] of success" until a gentleman pledged to "secure me a proper person to go into the City of New York . . . who he recommend[ed] to be well educated and a good surveyor and every way calculated for the business." On the night of March 7, Sackett got him through the British lines, his mission being to "hire a room in the city and get a licence to carry on a secret trade for poultry to enable him to convey me intelligence once or twice a week." The luckless agent never returned. This particular spy was either a charlatan or a dead man, but Sackett had stumbled onto an important insight: Instead of dispatching scouts or spies when the occasion demanded and having them return the same day with their intelligence, Sackett had been determined to send an agent into enemy territory, to keep him there, to invent a legend (in this case, poultry trader), and to arrange regular communication.

After that, Sackett found another gentleman who—in order "to enable him to go in under proper circumstances to get the best intelligence"—had "for some time associated with the first rate Tories in these parts and carried matters so far as to get a written invitation from William Bayard [a senior loyalist] now in the City." Bayard's son, John, was a colonel in the King's Orange Rangers and had offered to recommend Sackett's agent to Colonel Abraham Van Buskirk and Captain Robert Timpany, both of the New Jersey Volunteers. It is unknown what information this anonymous spy amassed, but Sackett's idea of infiltrating men masquerading as sympathizers and ingratiating them with senior British commanders was a brilliant one.

Then there was Sackett's recruitment of a Hessian, resident in America for nearly forty years, who said he would attach himself to members of Hessian regiments in New York and use "such arguments with them as will prevail with great numbers to desert," and then "make use of the deserters as pipes to convey intelligence."

Finally, by posing as a secret friend to King and Country, Sackett went so far as to recruit an unwitting female agent to ferret out intelligence. This woman was the "wife of a man gone over to the enemy" whose grain had been stolen by American troops. When she came to Sackett to complain, he gently counseled her to go see General Howe. "She was pleased with the advice and set off to his lordship to let him know how she was oppressed and to request the time that she might expect relief." On March 28, she left New York with nothing in hand, and told Sackett—who nodded sympathetically with pursed lips, no doubt—that no relief was in sight, for "there is a large number of flat-bottomed boats in the harbour of New York which are intended for an expedition against Philadelphia and that the British army is going to subdue that city and the poor Tory sufferers here will not be relieved until that expedition is over."[62]

It was a sweet coup, but not enough to save Sackett's job. He was paid off with five hundred dollars in secret service funds and ceased his involvement in intelligence matters following some kind of fiasco.[63] Washington forever remained silent about what happened, though in 1789, when Sackett was importuning the general for a federal appointment (unsuccessfully), he wrote a letter begging Washington to recall his services during the war. In doing so, he left behind a comically obtuse clue as to what precisely ended his career: "I had gone through all those dangers that awaited me in getting a regular plan laid, and was beginning to carry it on with every appearance of success, [but] the Jersey [man fell] in love with his horse, the doctor narrowly escaped with his life, and the whole scheme was frustrated."[64] The mind boggles.

Washington, too, imbibed some lessons from these first, halting steps toward constructing an effective espionage apparatus. To Sackett he declared that "the good effect of intelligence may be lost if it is not speedily transmitted—this should be strongly impressed upon the persons employed as it also should be to avoid false intelligence." Not only intuitively understanding that intelligence of the enemy's designs and movements is only useful if delivered promptly, and that spies often embroidered paltry facts to earn their pay, Washington also grasped the importance of cross-referencing one agent's reports with other, competing versions ("A comparison of circumstances should be had, and much pains taken to avoid erroneous accounts") to prevent exaggerations. This was especially crucial when it came to estimating troop strengths, a notoriously tricky science to get right; many a promising offensive had been cancelled when the local commander relied on a report telling him the enemy possessed double or even triple his actual number. One thing Washington did not get right, however: "It runs in my head that I was to correspond with you [Sackett] by a fictitious name—if so I have forgot the name & must be reminded of it again."[65]

There would be fewer of these comic moments in future. By the time Sackett left, the secret war was beginning to turn into an exceedingly nasty one. Over the course of the "year of the hangman," the Americans became increasingly wary of not only British spies but covert Tories living in the areas under congressional control. When caught, for them the noose inevitably awaited. Perhaps because there were fewer American spies, the British tended to be more lenient, though even they sometimes made graphic examples of those they suspected of passing on information. General Howe, for example, was usually quite lax about delivering such awful punishments, but that did not stop him from hanging "three women, (two of them by the feet, at the head of his army) whom he imagined were spies," as one observer informed Washington in June.[66]

By and large, however, the Americans were more ruthless at weeding out agents and those sympathizers abetting them. Even the "great appearance of guilt" in a man's "countenance"—"a faithful index to the heart," declared Alexander McDougal of Simon Mabee, soon after hanged—could be enough to kill him.[67] An unguarded word to the wrong person also risked a death sentence. John Williams was tried on April 13 for "holding a treacherous correspondence with the enemy and enlisting men into their service." The prosecution produced Nicholas Outhouse, Israel Outhouse, and Christian House to swear that Williams had said to them at various times that he wanted to enlist some men for the British and had talked of going to New York. Despite an energetic defense by Williams, who said the Outhouses were biased against him because of a personal quarrel, and adding that he was entirely innocent, while introducing six character witnesses with Patriot sympathies who testified "he has been frequently on guard with them & they always took him to be a friend to his country," the court found him "guilty of the charge & do therefore sentence him to be hanged by the neck till he is dead."[68]

Miscreants were tried before military courts-martial, not civil courts, and could accordingly expect little sympathy from a jury.[69] In the spring of 1777, partly owing to the absence of reinforcements from overseas, the British made a determined effort to raise men for Loyalist regiments. They directed Loyalists, sometimes sent from New York, to travel to the country and offer pay and benefits to potential recruits. These men often stayed hidden in the houses of known sympathizers; if detected, their protectors often went to the gallows with them. Mass trials became increasingly common as the authorities sought to crack down on the enemies within. At the end of April, to take just one instance, thirteen men went on trial for being "soldiers in the service of the King of Great Britain" while "owing allegiance to the State of New York"; ten of them were hanged.[70]

In May, Simon Newall volunteered to act as an agent provocateur to rouse a ring of covert Tories. To this end, he befriended John Likely and masqueraded as "one dissaffected to his country and on my way to join General Howe and engage in his service as many as possible." Over dinner one night, Likely "manifested a firm attachment" to the British cause; Newall saw the opening and said he wanted "to spy out a way in which we could bring down a number of men for General Howe," and asked "how and when I should find friends to my purpose." The unsuspecting Likely then told him the names of several "friends," one of whom, Anthony Umans, was a member of the local Committee of Safety, and had even served in the Continental army, which he said was only "to still people's talk and save himself from trouble." Umans put him in touch with Reuben Drake, the chairman of the same committee Umans sat on. Through Drake, Newall was given an introduction to one "Huson," a recruiter who was looking for men to take to New

York, with whom he became friends. Over (many) drinks, Lent Far— one of Huson's associates—proudly declared that their "business was to plunder the Whigs and they had as good will to kill them as a dog." As for himself, he said, "he would go and join Howe...and fight his way through the rebel guards to get there or die." That night, reported Newall, "we all dined heartily, drank King George's health and Howe's, confusion to Congress and Washington."[71]

At the subsequent trial, only Likely and Umans were charged. The rest had run for either New York or the hills. Likely claimed that he had sent Newall to Umans—his fellow committeeman—so that he might be arrested. Umans said he had directed him to Drake for the same purpose. The court, this time, was lenient: Each man was sentenced to receive one hundred lashes on his bare back and to be jailed until the end of hostilities. Likely and Umans were lucky in their timing. A short time before, both would have certainly swung, but the pace of executions had been so incessant, even the stoutest of local Patriots and court officers were debating "the propriety of our determining the fate of our fellow creatures." Civilians "unacquainted with the Articles of War" or martial law should not be tried by courts-martial, especially when, as president of the court Colonel Henry Livingston chided, "skilled persons have been sent among them to draw the substance of their stupidity and ignorance" and had then manipulated the accused into giving evidence against themselves. Here Livingston had in mind Newall, though Likely and Umans still had to be punished for their undoubted acts of subversion.[72]

In the purely military realm, however, spies could not expect such leniency. In mid-July, for instance, General Israel Putnam at Peekskill, New York, told Washington that he captured one Edmond Palmer, who had "been lurking around here plundering & driving off cattle to the enemy, [and] breaking up & robbing houses." He had entered a Mr. Willis's house, "presented his pistol to his wife's breast as she sat in bed, strip'd the rings from her fingers, then fell upon the father an old gentleman, abused, beat, & left him, to appearance dead." Palmer was also known to have "been about recruiting for the enemy & spying our army." Putnam believed that "the speedy execution of spies is agreeable to the laws of nature & nations & absolutely necessary to the preservation of the army & without such power in the army, it must be incompetent for its own safety."[73] Despite Palmer's wife (carrying an infant in her arms) pleading with Putnam for mercy and a request from Sir Henry Clinton, then commanding the British troops in New York, that since Palmer held a lieutenant's commission in a Loyalist regiment he was a prisoner-of-war, Putnam remained unmoveable and Palmer was hanged. He also brusquely informed Clinton that "Edmond Palmer, an officer in the enemy's service, was taken as a spy lurking within our lines, has been tried as a spy, condemned as a spy, and shall be executed as a spy." Soon afterwards, he added a helpful P.S.: "And has been accordingly executed."[74]

Another of Washington's generals, Lord Stirling, was equally merciless. In late July, one of his detachments brought in five Tories, one of whom—Daniel Curvin—proved upon interrogation to be a spy. He confessed that he had been sent "to view the situation & motions of our army, that he came and remained in the neighbourhood of the army till Sunday" but was caught in northern New Jersey. There were several corroborative pieces of evidence. "Therefore I ordered him to be instantly hanged."[75]

That summer, as well, the Americans were faced with the threat of General John Burgoyne's army driving south from Canada, the grand strategy being to rendezvous with Clinton near Albany and thereby split New England from the rest of the rebel states. British high command tended to assume that the majority of Americans were not rebels, but were pushed into insurrection by fiery New England radicals; once the Bostonians were dealt with, so the theory went, the colonies would return to their natural allegiance. Burgoyne's plan, while strategically correct and boldly executed, suffered fatally from its complexity.

The general had envisaged a triple-pronged offensive in which he would push south along the Lake Champlain–Lake George waterway and occupy Albany, Colonel Barry St. Leger's eight-hundred-man contingent would circle west to Lake Ontario and then drive east to Albany, and General Howe would advance from New York up the Hudson—all at the same time. The major problem with the plan was that it required seamless coordination between the three prongs, an impossibility given the distances that separated the armies. Howe's usual lack of energy should also have been taken into account, though in his defense it had been left unclear what exactly he should have been doing, and when it should have been done. After all, Burgoyne was his junior in rank, and Howe received his orders from Lord George Germain, the Secretary of State for America in London (whose considered view of the rebellion's chances was that "these country clowns cannot whip us"): Should he take his commands from a man who was the illegitimate son of Lord Bingley and rumored to fleece drunks at cards?

In mid-June, Burgoyne's expedition left St. Johns in a large fleet of pinnaces and transports to sail south toward Fort Ticonderoga, the key to Lake George and the Hudson. Within a week of Burgoyne's arrival on July 1, the fortress had fallen, but the victor made a grievous mistake in advancing to the Hudson overland (the original plan had called to proceed by water) in order to circumvent Fort George. Out there, there were no roads, just rough, thick wilderness with uneven terrain crammed with pine and hardwoods. By the end of the summer, Burgoyne's army was down and bloodied, just as the enemy was continually receiving fresh volunteers. Worse, Burgoyne had heard that Barry St. Leger had turned back, and that Howe was not about to save him, as he had sailed instead for the Delaware Bay, intent on capturing Philadelphia, the rebel capital and seat of Congress.

In September, while Howe was engaged in the Philadelphia campaign, he left New York in the charge of Sir Henry Clinton, who was keener to help the beleaguered Burgoyne. At the time, since Howe had denuded him of troops and left him just four thousand regulars and three thousand Loyalists, Clinton couldn't achieve more than a diversionary feint, but on September 24 he received reinforcements from Britain and began preparing to march north to relieve the pressure on Burgoyne.

Clinton's feelings on the matter of Howe's adventure were revealed in a letter he sent to Burgoyne in August:

> You will have heard, Dr Sir I doubt not long before this can have reached you that Sir W. Howe is gone from hence. The Rebels imagine that he is gone to the Eastward. By this time however he has filled Chesapeak bay with surprize and terror. Washington marched the greater part of the Rebels to Philadelphia in order to oppose Sir Wm's. army. I hear he is now returned upon finding none of our troops landed but am not sure of this, great part of his troops are returned for certain. I am sure this countermarching must be ruin to them. I am left to command here, half of my force may I am sure defend everything here with much safety. I shall therefore send Sir W. 4 or 5 Bat[talio]ns. I have too small a force to invade the New England provinces; they are too weak to make any effectual efforts against me and you do not want any diversion in your favour. I can, therefore very well spare him 1500 men. I shall try some thing certainly towards the close of the year, not till then at any rate. It may be of use to inform you that report says all yields to you. I own to you that I think the business will quickly be over now. Sr. W's move just at this time has been capital. Washingtons have been the worst he could take in every respect. sincerely give you much joy on your success....

By a different courier, Clinton sent a single piece of paper with an hourglass-shaped hole cut out, a device known as a "grille" or "mask." He was using a "Cardano System," named after Giralamo Cardano, a sixteenth-century Italian cryptologist. What Clinton had done was write his *genuine* message within the borders of the grille and then filled in the rest of the above letter with suitably innocuous observations and deliberate misinformation. In case of interception, Clinton sent two express messengers; the enemy needed the letter *and* the grille to decipher the message. Thus, while Clinton openly says "Sr. W's move just at this time has been capital. Washingtons have been the worst he could take in every respect," when read with the grille, the true meaning is revealed as "I own to you that I think Sr. W's move just at this time the worst he could take."[76]

Be that as it may, Clinton was still expected to do something, and he prepared his troops for an expedition. He aimed for Forts Clinton and Montgomery, then commanded by General George Clinton (the governor of New York). Sir Henry Clinton captured the forts in early October, and sent a small force up the Hudson to Fort Constitution, which quickly surrendered. In short order, Clinton had done what he had intended to do: create a diversion to the south, demolish the American barrier of forts on the river, and open the Hudson for navigation for forty miles north of the forts. Even so, Fort Constitution lay one hundred miles south of Burgoyne's position.

On October 8, Henry Clinton dispatched Captain Daniel Taylor to find Burgoyne and acquaint him with the situation.[77] Cognizant that Taylor's route would be a hazardous one through wilderness occupied by roving detachments of American soldiers under General Horatio Gates's command and unsympathetic locals, Clinton—no slouch when it came to finding innovative ways to get his messages through—had cast a small, swallowable silver ball, oval in shape and about the size of a bullet, which could be unscrewed into halves to reveal a tiny piece of silk containing the message: "Nothing now between us but Gates. I sincerely hope this little success of ours may facilitate your operations."[78]

Clinton was being deliberately ambiguous in hoping that the beleaguered Burgoyne's operations would be "facilitated": No one wanted to be blamed for Burgoyne's loss of an army, and Clinton consciously avoided advising Burgoyne to advance or retreat from his isolated position. By passing the buck right back to Burgoyne, Clinton had ensured that what his comrade did next would be his own decision, and his sole responsibility.

Clinton's craftiness, nevertheless, did Taylor no good. He was caught a day later by a patrol and, when searched, was revealed to be carrying seven personal letters written by British and Loyalist officers to their friends in Burgoyne's army that Taylor had foolishly agreed to deliver.[79] That correspondence, in itself, was enough to condemn him, but Taylor panicked and forgot to swallow the silver ball, which he had secreted in his pocket. Dragged before General George Clinton, Taylor recovered his composure and slipped the casing into his mouth. As his captors pried open his jaws to retrieve it, Taylor managed to swallow the message. Clinton, a patient man, wasn't angry, and asked Dr. James Thacher to administer "a very strong emetic, calculated to operate it either way." Unfortunately, while this "had the desired effect," Taylor, "though close watched," enterprisingly swallowed the casing again. This time, Clinton "demanded the ball on pain of being hung up instantly and cut open to search [for] it. This brought it forth."[80]

On October 14, Taylor was taken before a court-martial and charged with espionage. He pleaded not guilty on the distinctly weak grounds that when a Lieutenant Howe and his men had captured him, they had been wearing British uniforms. "He was thereby deceived" when he approached them for directions. In fact, Taylor was quite correct about the patrol wearing enemy garb, but that was because they had recently taken some of Burgoyne's men prisoner and had stolen their red coats—which were rather better tailored and more durable than the American ones. Taylor's end was an inevitable one: A few days later he was brought to a nearby apple tree and hanged from one of its limbs.[81] As he mounted the ladder, Taylor—who had risked, and was about to lose, his life to save Burgoyne—heard the clatter of a messenger arriving from General Gates. Burgoyne had surrendered, but it was too late for Taylor.

Burgoyne's lack of support from New York had doomed him, but from General Howe's point of view, the conquest of Philadelphia was of vaster importance than the sideshow up north. He was content to allow Henry Clinton to launch a diversionary thrust that would attract Washington's attention to the Hudson while he himself transported the main army to the Delaware River by sea. At the end of August, Washington received word that Howe, believing the river defenses too strong to proceed to Philadelphia with his fifteen thousand men, had actually landed at the Head of Elk on the Chesapeake. From there, he intended to march northeast to the city. Washington planted himself midway between Howe's landing place and Philadelphia, on Brandywine Creek. On September 11, in what was a repeat performance of the Battle of New York a year earlier, Howe feinted toward Washington's center while executing a flanking maneuver with his main force. Washington seems not to have learned his lesson from his defeat the previous time, and at Brandywine he was again defeated by Howe and forced to retreat, leaving a thousand of his men dead and wounded. Howe, for his part, had yet again been unwilling or unable to launch a knockout blow to the staggered American forces. Though Washington escaped, the road to Philadelphia now lay open. On September 26, Lord Cornwallis and his legions entered the city, recently abandoned by Congress, which had decamped to Lancaster.

Some time before, Major John Clark had returned from Long Island and was attached to General Greene's staff, but shortly before Brandywine was "severely wounded" in his right shoulder during a skirmish.[82] He had had little time to recuperate when he was called back into service as a spy. Washington ascribed the Brandywine defeat to what he called "uncertain and contradictory" intelligence, which had prevented him from deploying his forces more effectively.[83] Since Clark's observational and undercover skills were unsurpassed, he wanted Clark to act as his eyes and ears as close as possible to Philadelphia and the key forts, Mifflin and Mercer, that guarded the Delaware. Clark immediately set out on his lonely mission and was soon running a remarkable stable of spies. Just two days after yet another defeat for Washington at Germantown on October 4, Clark dispatched his first letter to the general at five in the morning.[84] (He used a former barber turned soldier, Martin Nicholls, aged eighteen and five feet two inches tall with a yellowish complexion and a face badly pitted with smallpox, as his messenger.)[85] His second was sent the same day at 10 p.m.[86] Over the next three months—despite suffering grievously from shoulder pain—he would send another thirty of them, each carefully describing British troop movements and numbers, naval maneuvers, infantry positions, checkpoints, artillery emplacements, and Philadelphia gossip, all gleaned from local inhabitants (some of whom were so suspicious of the stranger, they "watch me like a hawk would a chicken") or his roster of agents.[87] Driven solely by duty—"Please give me every instruction you may think necessary, and I will endeavor to observe them, and obey your orders with all the exactitude of a better officer," he once wrote—Clark changed his hiding places so frequently and roved so distant (up to forty miles a day) he wore out three nags.[88] At other times, camped out there all alone in the winter darkness and sleeping fitfully for fear of discovery by an enemy patrol, he confessed that "my hands are so cold I can scarcely write to you."[89]

Clark so stringently guarded his sources that their names are today undiscoverable. Several were Quakers, that is certain. One of them, at no little risk to himself, participated in one of Clark's mischievous efforts at planting fake intelligence on the enemy. In early November, purporting to be a pro-British Quaker, Clark penned a "few lines to Sir William, informing him that the rebels had plundered me, and that I was determined to risque my all in procuring him intelligence," signing it with the name of a Quaker "who I knew assisted" (i.e., collaborated with) Howe. His "friend," described as "an exceedingly intelligent fellow," brought it to Howe, who "smiled when he saw the pains taken with it," and told the agent that if he would "return and inform me of your movements and the state of your army," he would be generously rewarded. Before he left to report back to Clark, the agent took the opportunity to walk around Philadelphia, busily memorizing where the army's ammunition dumps were and eavesdropping on soldiers discussing an imminent attack by Howe.[90]

Washington was most pleased with Clark's initiative, telling him that he thought "you have fallen upon an exceeding good method of gaining intelligence and that too much secrecy cannot be used, both on account of the safety of your friend and the execution and continuance of your design, which may be of service to us." The general, in excellent spirits at the thought of deceiving Howe, composed a completely invented summary of the Continental army's strength—adding, as a nice touch, a memorandum detailing his intended movements—and sent it to Clark for subsequent delivery to Howe's headquarters.[91] Clark would feed disinformation to Howe via this agent several more times over the coming months.[92]

Clark's favorite cover story for his agents was that they were low-level smugglers sneaking food and basic supplies in and out of the city. As British stockpiles were running low, they were generally allowed to pass checkpoints unhindered (perhaps after bribing the guards), but to make life easier, Clark somehow acquired a sheaf of blank passes allowing the bearer the right to travel freely within British lines. Generously, he even sent one to Washington, though he kept several for his own spies.[93] These passes, which required the signature of a senior officer, must have been stolen from some unsuspecting colonel's desk by one of Clark's operatives. Indeed, the most irritating aspect of Clark's job was suspicious *American* patrols stopping his agents as they went about their secret business. On December 3, he complained to Washington about Colonel Warner, whose Pennsylvania militia "took up one of my friends going into Philadelphia, which has prevented my getting some very material intelligence, as I had formed a channel through which everything, in that way, would have come with secrecy."[94] He recovered quickly from the loss, however, and within a week he had managed to send "several spies into the city" to discover the enemy's plans to raid the surrounding countryside for fodder and supplies.[95]

Still, despite his ingenuity, some of Clark's people were caught by the British, and may have been hanged, but none revealed the whereabouts and name of their mysterious manager.[96] One had a very close call when, as he approached an enemy checkpoint, a farmer grabbed him by the coat and loudly called out that he had caught a "damn'd Rebel." As the guards came to investigate, the spy spurred his mare and left his accuser "lying in the road." By happenstance, American soldiers soon after took the farmer prisoner, much to Clark's satisfaction.

"His name is Edward Hughes, is a papist, and lives in Springfield," Clark remarked. "I hope an example will be made to deter others."[97]

Clark, in any case, was always looking out for potential recruits, and easily replaced his lost operatives. Just two days after one of his men was taken, Clark had invested "a young fellow of character" (recommended "by a gentleman of my acquaintance in whom I can entirely confide"—a euphemism for agent) as his newest spy and had dispatched him into Philadelphia with orders "to mingle with the British officers," a task he boasted would be "easily effected."[98]

By late December, as the two armies settled into their winter quarters—Howe, rather comfortably, in Philadelphia; Washington not so comfortably at Valley Forge—Clark knew that his stint as spymaster was ending. His shoulder wound had not healed, and he was exhausted from the strain of three months' unceasing work and danger. He, unshaven and long unbathed, visited Washington in person to beg his permission to visit his wife, whom he hadn't seen in more than a year.[99] The commander-in-chief unbegrudgingly released his faithful retainer from his burdens, and introduced him to Henry Laurens, the president of the Congress, as being an "active, sensible and enterprising" soldier who "has rendered me very great assistance since the army has been in Pennsylvania by procuring me constant and certain intelligence of the motions and intentions of the enemy."[100]

Washington had hinted that Clark might not continue "in the military line" owing to his health, and Laurens offered him a desk job as auditor of the army's expenses, which the former spy gladly accepted. Clark also informed General Greene that he was obliged to resign as his aide-de-camp, and thus retired from not only the army but the secret world, too, and willingly entered the realm of respectable obscurity craved by so many spies, then and now.[101]

As dusk settled on Major Clark's espionage career, that of Major Tallmadge was about to dawn. Tallmadge's regiment accompanied Washington throughout the Philadelphia campaign, and were assigned to General Sullivan's division at the Battle of Germantown, where they led the advance against the British, only to later withdraw amid the confusion caused by the late arrival of General Greene and a fog sweeping in. As the American army wintered at Valley Forge in late 1777, Tallmadge had a few adventures as he ranged far and wide with his troopers. "I had to scour the country from the Schuylkill to the Delaware River, about five or six miles, for the double purpose of watching the movements of the enemy and preventing the disaffected from carrying supplies or provisions to Philadelphia. My duties were very arduous...by reason of the British light horse, which continually patrolled this intermediate ground. Indeed it was unsafe to permit the dragoons to unsaddle their horses for an hour, and very rarely did I tarry in the same place through the night."[102]

Once, at 1 a.m. on December 14 near Germantown, when out with a patrol, Tallmadge heard enemy cavalry nearby, but it was too late to retreat, and they were jumped. "We exchanged a few shots, but finding it impossible with 10 or 12 men to oppose 90 [or] 100," they succeeded in outpacing them and circled back to the rest of his dragoons' quarters, only to find they had already heard the news and skedaddled—all except for three unfortunates who had been captured as they fled. As Tallmadge watched from afar, "after taking from [them] their arms, etc., the officers directed that they should be killed. Notwithstanding the entreaties and prayers of the prisoners for mercy, the soldiers fell upon them with their swords, and after hacking, cutting, and stabbing them till they supposed they were dead, they then left them there (one excepted whom they shot) setting fire to the barn to consume any who might be in it. They also coolly murdered an old man of the house, first cutting and most inhumanly mangling him with their swords and then shooting him."[103] Within a week or two, however, Tallmadge's men captured thirteen troopers, "the Devils that murdered those lads of my troop, wish to God I could take some of them to show that we dare and will retaliate such unprecedented barbarities."[104]

In January 1778, the dragoons were ordered to winter at Trenton, New Jersey. Trouble began almost immediately afterward. The five hundred sailors already billetted on the town made finding suitable accommodation difficult, and that was before the inevitable navy-army brawls in the taverns and streets. Colonel Sheldon and Major Blagden, the two chief officers, loathed each other so intensely, Tallmadge worried they might fight a duel, and Count Casimir Pulaski, an exiled Polish nobleman Washington had recently put in charge of the cavalry, resigned when subordinates refused to take orders from a haughty foreigner. A move to new quarters in Chatham, New Jersey, put an end to the brawling, but there remained a shortage of sabers, pay, boots, horses, and uniforms, and morale plummeted even as the tedium and stress of confinement to barracks rose. While the regiment had had ten troopers killed during the Philadelphia campaign, that winter fully fifty-one deserted or were discharged. To raise the men's and officers' spirits, the regiment's commanders relaxed discipline and allowed more furlough. In February, Tallmadge traveled back to Wethersfield for more than a month to see his old friends and on his return was put in temporary charge of the fifth and sixth troops, when their captains in turn went home on leave.[105]

Since almost the day he had signed up, Tallmadge had been one of Washington's most promising golden boys, but in April 1778 his career, which had hitherto streaked across the firmament like a meteor, suffered an abrupt deceleration. During Tallmadge's vacation in Connecticut, the dragoon officer Colonel Stephen Moylan—an Irishman recently unhorsed in a most unfraternal joust by one of Pulaski's aides—had reported to Washington on the state of the cavalry. He singled out the Second Regiment as the most deficient. Of the regiment's fifty-four horses, ten were scarcely fit for duty. They had been starved "and the blame thrown from the officers on Mr. Caldwell, who acted as a Commissary of Forage." But "the true reason of their being in such condition," according to Moylan, "was that few or none of the officers had been with the regiment."[106]

On April 14, Tallmadge was sent a harshly chiding letter from a commander-in-chief disheartened by his favorite son's dereliction of duty. "I scarce know which is the greatest, my astonishment or vexation, at hearing of the present low condition of your horse." He recalled that Tallmadge had been "exempted from the fatigues of a winter campaign, & permitted to retire to the best quarters the country afforded" but "for what purpose did I do this? Why to furnish the officers & men it seems with opportunities of galloping about the country and by neglect of the horses reducing them to a worse condition than those which have been kept upon constant & severe duty the whole Winter." He concluded on a particularly bitter note: "How can you reconcile this conduct to your feelings as an officer, and answer it to your Country I know not."[107]

Tallmadge, horrified at receiving a personal chastisement that impugned his honor, tried to defend himself, but even he must have realized how thin his excuses sounded. He claimed that a third of the officers had been off supervising other duties, that the regiment had received few supplies, and that Caldwell—as well as the saddlers, armorers, and quartermasters—were "indolent and inattentive to duty." He finished by offering to resign his commission.[108] On May 13, Tallmadge tore open the reply from Washington, only to find that the general was neither angry nor mollified, just cold. He had written a noncommittal answer but one which held firm that the officers were "reproachable."[109] And he left it at that. The two, once in fairly regular communication, would not correspond again until the summer. Tallmadge had been frozen out.

In late May, the regiment was ordered to ride to General Horatio Gates at Peekskill on the Hudson River. On June 3, the Second left Chatham to take up their position at an advanced post at Dobbs Ferry, about nine miles north of Manhattan.[110] Two weeks later, Henry Clinton—since May 20 the commander-in-chief of the British army in America following General Howe's resignation—embarked on the long retreat from Philadelphia to New York. The capital had been impossible to supply and was leaving the army exposed to attack. Clinton wanted to regroup in New York, where at least he could be sure of reinforcements and good forage. At least three thousand Philadelphian Loyalists traveled with him to their new home. Washington and his army, reinvigorated by strict drills and musketry practice imposed by General "Baron" von Steuben, shadowed and harassed Clinton from the day he left, finally striking on June 28 at Monmouth Court House. Though the battle was a draw, Clinton had been unpleasantly surprised by the newfound skills of the Continental army, and he quickened his pace to New York. Washington set up camp in a large semicircle, stretching from the New Jersey Highlands across the Hudson to Dobbs Ferry and then on to the Connecticut coast.

Clinton was in New York; Washington surrounded it. He needed another Major Clark to enter the den.

Chapter Three

Genesis of the Culper Ring

New York was, intelligence-wise, dark and silent. Not just maddeningly senseless to the enemy's strategy and intentions, Washington now lacked such vital, timely information as troop strength, morale, army gossip, supply levels, naval reinforcements, and even the names of senior commanders. And then along came the hulking shape and commanding countenance of Lieutenant Caleb Brewster, whose fearsome looks belied a quick wit and ribald sense of humor.[1]

On August 7, Washington received from him an unexpected letter, written from the port of Norwalk on the Connecticut side of Long Island Sound. That original document has been lost, but we do have Washington's reply of the next day, from which we can gather that the lieutenant offered to report on the enemy. Having been burnt before by overzealous amateurs, Washington was curtly specific about what he expected and wanted from this new and untried source.

First, "do not spare any reasonable expense to come at early and true information; always recollecting, and bearing in mind, that vague and uncertain accounts of things . . . is more disturbing and dangerous than receiving none at all." Bearing that admonition in mind, Brewster was instructed to keep an eye out for naval transports, "whether they are preparing for the reception of troops and know what number of men are upon Long Island. Whether they are moving or stationary. What is become of their draft horses. Whether they appear to be collecting them for a move. How they are supplied with provisions. What arrivals. Whether with men, or provisions. And whether any troops have been embarked or elsewhere within these few days."[2]

Brewster's approach had come just at the right moment. Washington was in the midst of coordinating the Franco-American attack—a benefit stemming from the new Treaty of Alliance between the two countries— on British-held Newport, Rhode Island. The French had gleefully learned of Americans embarrassing their ancient foes at Saratoga the year before and were now willing to deploy French troops in the hopes of doing it again. To this end, a fleet of twelve ships of the line and five frigates, together carrying 11,384 sailors and soldiers, and commanded by Admiral Charles-Hector, Comte d'Estaing—a man blessed with so many quarterings of nobility he could realistically claim descent from the last king of the Visigoths—sailed from the Mediterranean port of Toulon in mid-April and had arrived on July 8 at Delaware Bay after an exceedingly languid and comfortable voyage. (Had d'Estaing traveled just a little faster, mused Washington, he would have caught Clinton ferrying his soldiers from Philadelphia to New York across the Delaware. If that had happened, the British commander would have shared Burgoyne's fate; the loss of two armies within less than a year would have caused a collapse of confidence in London and perhaps have led to a military withdrawal to Canada.)[3] Having missed the British, d'Estaing headed for New York, there to seek combat with the inferior forces of Admiral Howe. Beat the British at sea, and their army would starve.

Howe may have been weak on paper—he had just six 64-gunners, three 50s, and six frigates, while d'Estaing brought the *Languedoc*, a 90-gun behemoth, one 80, six 74s, and a 50—but New York harbor was a formidable redoubt and Howe's expertise at tactical deployments unsurpassed. D'Estaing, who possessed a lion's bravery but a cat's caution, weighed discretion against valor and decided in the former's favor. A few hours after his arrival on July 22, as Howe's crews beat to quarters and braced for the first thunderous broadside, d'Estaing ordered his captains to sail south out to sea. He had already concerted with Washington to meet the American general John Sullivan several miles north of Newport, there to land some four thousand French soldiers and marine riflemen, for their joint attack on the port. He arrived on July 29 and began disembarking the troops on Conanicut Island, to the south just opposite Newport, where the British garrison of six thousand was commanded by General Robert Pigot. Sullivan's ten thousand men were to cross over from the mainland from the north; Pigot would be crushed between d'Estaing and Sullivan's advances.

The attack was scheduled to begin on August 10, but things began going badly the day before. Sullivan jumped the gun and began ferrying troops over to the island, and then Admiral Howe unexpectedly appeared, having mustered no fewer than thirteen ships of the line. D'Estaing immediately recalled his troops, thereby leaving Sullivan in the lurch, and put to sea. As the French fleet approached, Howe led his pursuer into the Atlantic. By the late afternoon of August 11, d'Estaing and Howe were formed into lines of battle, and as the French prepared to attack the British rear—now fortified by Howe's heaviest warship, the *Cornwall* of seventy-four guns—the admiral saw d'Estaing's fleet suddenly call off the chase as a freshening wind pushed rain-heavy clouds toward them both.

Over the next two days, the two fleets were ravaged by a violent thunderstorm, which scattered their formations. Hardly a vessel remained unharmed, especially after the storm had passed and individual ships began preying on damaged ones, not always successfully. The *Languedoc* may have lost her bowsprit and all her lower masts, and a broken tiller rendered her rudder unserviceable, but even so, d'Estaing's flagship remained a dangerous beast, as the *Renown* discovered to her cost when she attacked it. The fifty-gun *Isis* was pounced upon by the seventy-four-gun *César*, but she put up a spirited fight and the French captain lost his arm when a cannonball tore away the wheel. The *Apollo*—which had briefly served as Howe's flagship—was fortunate in only having her foremast fall overboard.

D'Estaing gathered together the remains of his fleet and returned to Newport, where Sullivan had anxiously been awaiting him, having abandoned his own attack during the storm. Now, at last, thought Sullivan, the operation could belatedly begin, but d'Estaing refused to risk his fleet until it could be refitted in Boston. Sullivan pleaded with the admiral to stay just one more day to help, but d'Estaing was adamant. He departed at midnight on August 21.

Sullivan was livid. He resented "the conduct of the Count" and his officers, who had left "us on an island without any certain means of retreat." Half his ten thousand men came to the same conclusion and departed quietly back to their homes, prompting General Pigot to sally forth from his fortifications in Newport and launch an attack on Sullivan's positions. He was eventually pushed away by well-aimed musket volleys, but Sullivan had already decided to quit the island to save his force from disaster. It was a sound decision. The next day, September 1, Clinton himself arrived with ten fresh infantry regiments and two artillery brigades ferried from New York by Admiral Howe, the sailor who, with a force inferior throughout his brilliant defensive campaign, had saved not only Rhode Island but the British fleet and New York as well.[4]

On August 27, a few days before Clinton arrived in Newport, Brewster had sent his first intelligence report. He had watched Admiral Howe's warships, including "the *Isis* of fifty guns, the *Renown* of sixty four, the *Apollo* thirty six," limp into New York harbor. The *Isis* and the *Renown*, in particular, were "much shattered," which Brewster attributed to them having attacked "two seventy fours" on the high seas. (He was slightly wrong about the *Renown*, which actually battled a ninety-gunner.) He also reported that about a thousand British troops were around Brookhaven, on the northeast side of Long Island, and they were preparing to move out, while in Huntington's harbor there were between twenty-six and thirty ships expected to sail for Rhode

Island. Meanwhile, "several regiments [had] crossed from New York to Brookline Ferry, and encamped."[5]

While some of Brewster's intelligence was somewhat old—the *Isis* and her sisters had come home a week before his report—it was news to Washington. Thanks to his new agent inside them, New York's blank, forbidding walls had been breached, and intelligence was slowly leaking out. To know where Howe's fleet was, even several days late, was better than having to guess. And to know that several regiments of British troops were preparing to board transports clearly bound for one place—Newport—as a relief force was priceless.

Brewster was impressive, no doubt about that, but he needed to be managed. Washington directed General Charles Scott, who had fought at the Battles of Trenton, Germantown, and Monmouth, to handle Brewster and find additional agents. Scott was then in charge of the light infantry—troops selected for their toughness and skilled in scouting and skirmishing—at the forward positions in Westchester and Fairfield counties. Brewster would find it easier to get his messages through Scott than trying to reach Washington directly.[6] To aid Scott, Washington chose Benjamin Tallmadge of the dragoons—a unit that worked closely with the light infantry.[7] It was the first time Washington had communicated with the errant major since the winter and the imbroglio over the horses. The commander had determined Tallmadge's term in exile over. He was forgiven.

Though Scott was nominally in charge of gathering intelligence, he had onerous field duties to attend to, and was not much interested in the job in any case. In late September, Washington was forced to "earnestly entreat" him to "endeavour to get some intelligent person into the City, and others of his own choice to be messengers between you and him." It was "of great consequence," Washington reminded him, "to the French admiral [d'Estaing] to be early, and regularly advised of the movements of the British ships of war, at New York; and he depends upon me to give this advice."[8]

Much of the work thus devolved upon Tallmadge, who at least displayed some enthusiasm and aptitude for the task—as well as enjoying some experience thanks to his time with Sackett and Clark. Obsessively observant, he was possibly the only officer in the army whose roster of recruits contained not just the usual, humdrum facts— names, date of enlistments, discharges, and so forth—but a detailed description of each man's physiognomy, including his eye color, height, build, and complexion.[9] He soon told Washington about one potential contact for Brewster—a Long Islander named Abraham Woodhull.

A few months before the Newport business, Woodhull had been passing through the Sound between Connecticut and Long Island when his boat was stopped by an armed American sloop and he was taken prisoner on the grounds that he had been involved in what was euphemistically dubbed the "London Trade." Owing to the Royal Navy's command of the sea, New Yorkers enjoyed a bounty of im- ported luxury goods: Spanish olives, French mushroom ketchup, jel- lies, Gloucester cheese, Scottish smoked salmon, German mustard, Russian tongues, walnuts, anchovies, Indian spices, and Italian confec- tionery were all available at reasonable prices. However, because Washington controlled the rural areas surrounding the city and Long Island, there were shortages of staples. Thus, delicate Chinese tea, grown on the other side of the world, was sold in New York shops, but milk and beef were rationed even as rebel-owned cows nonchalantly grazed across the Hudson in New Jersey.

A busy black market inevitably evolved, one that paid no heed to ad hoc borders or personal politics. A Hessian officer in New York once wrote that "almost open trade is carried from here with the rebels; at least both sides close an eye."[10] Suffering under the same petty an- noyances bred by army rule, the strictest of Patriots were as keen to trade illegally as the firmest of Loyalists if it meant surviving the war—or maybe just treating oneself to a little something. For years re- signed to wearing homespun, scratchy dresses and coats to aid the boycott of British goods, and tired of dunking sage in their brew to give it taste, which American did not desire a stash of Ceylon tea and a bolt of lustrous Cathay silk, especially if it only meant exchanging a few pounds of beef and some garden vegetables?[11]

Hence the bizarre spectacle of the London Trade, in which hogs, chickens, and beef were smuggled from Connecticut into New York, and gold buttons, cut-glass decanters, and casks of Madeira returned in the opposite direction.[12] The simplest way to enter the trade was for customers to sidle up to whaleboatmen docked at one of New York's wharves or Long Island's many inlets, grease them the going commission, and hitch a ride. Passengers would be smuggled across the Sound late at night to a quiet Connecticut bay and barter their goods for, say, fresh produce brought there by an enemy boat.[13]

The situation for Woodhull, who happened to be a farmer, was somewhat different in that as a rural Long Islander he had access to vegetables and livestock that could easily be bartered for luxuries in New York. Having little use for buckskin gloves and vinegar cruets, Woodhull would sail across the Sound and sell them for hard currency; that is, British pounds, not worthless, Congress-issued Continental dollars.[14] For New Yorkers of all classes, it was ready *money*—money for bribes, money to pay the rent, money to mitigate wartime privation— that was in the shortest supply.

Illegal trading understandably alarmed Congress, where, quite apart from the financial problems it created by draining cash from already cash-strapped states, many felt that Americans ought to be weaned from their pathetic dependence on imported fripperies. Some representatives also suspected that the sight of civilians enjoying contraband they had acquired from the enemy damaged ill-fed soldiers' morale; others feared that so many contacts with the British might cause nostalgic royalist allegiances to reappear.[15]

Military men, perhaps surprisingly, were often less critical of the practice, believing it too widespread in Connecticut and New Jersey to be worth devoting the resources, already scarce, needed to stamp it out, and arguing that it was vital to buttress civilian morale during wartime— even at the cost of ostensibly succoring the enemy. (Sometimes, though, officers participated in the trafficking, which really was going a bit far. One such was Colonel Sylvanus Seely of the New Jersey militia, who ran a lucrative network of smugglers in Elizabethtown.)[16]

Washington himself was unperturbed by illegal trading. In November 1777, Governor Livingston of New Jersey had pleaded with him to clamp down on the Staten Island–Elizabethtown route (in which Seely was likely involved), which "plentifully supplied [the British] with fresh provisions." Clandestine trading with the enemy was bad enough, but Livingston was particularly incensed by the revelation that *Americans* had begun opening *stores* solely devoted to fencing smuggled merchandise to the patriotic public. Washington did nothing. About a year later, when he was again begged to investigate a similar situation in Shrewsbury in northern New Jersey, Washington asked General Stirling to look into it and punish anyone he caught— but that was only after Congress expressly instructed him to take the matter in hand.[17]

As for the British, they were well aware of illegal trading's negative political and economic impact on Congress, and turned a blind eye—so long as traffickers didn't get too greedy and run guns across the Sound. Thomas Jones, a respectable New York judge, was all in favor of the trade, for, among other advantages, "the merchants had a large vent for their merchandise. . . . It assisted the royal army, and it distressed rebellion."[18]

Woodhull, unfortunately, had been caught red-handed during one of the periodic swoops urged by Congress. Hence his imprisonment in Connecticut. He was detained some time before Governor Jonathan Trumbull, with whom Tallmadge had put in a quiet word, issued a permit for him to return home. Before he left in late August, Tallmadge and Woodhull had a talk about the latter joining Washington's new secret service. Woodhull's extracurricular activity hadn't bothered Washington; in fact, he quite approved of the practice in this instance, for if you could smuggle goods, you could also smuggle information. Already, several American spies had masqueraded as traffickers during the war, bringing home minor intelligence picked up on their trips into enemy territory. Alas, smuggling's fat profit margins proved too tempting for some of them.[19] Washington accordingly complained that agents were "attend[ing] more to their own emolument than to the business with which they are charged," and wanted to "take proper measures to curb this extravagant passion for gain" among his spies.[20]

Woodhull, promised Tallmadge, was not cut of the same cloth. On August 25, an impressed Washington said that "you should be perfectly convinced of the integrity of W—— previous to his embarking in the business proposed. This being done I shall be happy in employing him, but there will be an impropriety in his coming with you to headquarters, as a knowledge of the circumstances in the enemy might blast the whole design. You will let me see you this afternoon—if you can come to dinner at three o'clock I shall be glad."[21]

At that dinner, Tallmadge assured his chief of Woodhull's "integrity" and trustworthiness. Actually, if anyone was a security risk, it was Washington, who had used the first letter of Woodhull's real name in his letter. Henceforth, with Scott's approval, Tallmadge adopted a set of aliases: Tallmadge became the anodyne "John Bolton," and Woodhull, "Samuel Culper." Washington, Scott, and Tallmadge collaborated to invent the latter code name. Samuel Culper's reversed initials are those of Charles Scott, while Washington lightheartedly amended the name of Culpeper County, Virginia—where, aged seventeen, he had worked as a surveyor back in 1749—to "Culper." As for the first name, Benjamin Tallmadge's younger brother was named Samuel—a friend of Caleb Brewster's who the year before had helped convey messages from Major John Clark during his sojourn on Long Island. At this precise time, Benjamin was agitating on his behalf with Governor George Clinton to promote him; he chose a name not only on his mind, but also a kind of in-joke between him and Brewster.[22] Brewster himself preferred to forgo an alias: Being a bluff and reckless fellow willing to take his chances, he always insisted on scrawling his real name, in very prominent letters, on all of his correspondence.

The course of relations between the more capable Tallmadge and his distinctly inferior superior, Scott, were not running smooth at this time. Scott was a notoriously difficult boss with a history of undermining his subordinates if he deemed them a threat to his position. In April, he had repeatedly reported one such, Colonel John Parke, for being absent without leave "and even when present inattentive to your duty." Washington had him arrested, but found no one willing to second the charges. At his hearing, Parke was found guilty of being occasionally absent without leave but cleared of being inattentive. It was a minor matter and Parke was restored to his command. When Parke wrote to Washington to explain his position, he hinted enigmatically that the stories of his dereliction of duty were due to "the misrepresentations of enemies." Washington knew full well whom he was talking about.[23]

Tallmadge had always maintained a chilly formality with Scott and vice versa, but soon Scott was going out of his way to squelch Tallmadge. At the end of October, the already brittle relationship between the two came close to snapping when Tallmadge told Washington that Brewster was delivering messages to him, but that Scott was ignoring them because, as Scott explained, the intelligence was not received "through the proper channel" and therefore "I did not give credit to it." There was no apology for calling his own deputy an "improper" channel, though Scott knew—and was no doubt irritated by the fact—that Tallmadge was one of Washington's favorites.[24]

Even apart from their personal clashes, Scott and Tallmadge could not keep working together for much longer without destroying whatever little existed of the American intelligence service. They each represented fundamentally incompatible approaches to spying. Tallmadge had learned from Nathaniel Sackett how to disguise agents as enemy sympathizers using realistic cover stories, and from John Parke that a spy could nestle within the breast of an unsuspecting foe for months, perhaps years, at a time—provided he enjoyed a secure chain of communication back to base. Tallmadge ambitiously envisaged combining these two approaches to create a network of agents-in-place permanently embedded in occupied New York and running to Long Island, then across the Sound to his headquarters in Connecticut, where the intel would be digested and passed upstairs to the commander-in-chief—with Tallmadge's summary and analysis attached.

Scott thought more traditionally and wanted to stick to the tried-and-true method of military reconnaissance. He wanted to send in single, disposable spies on quick, Nathan Hale–style missions to observe what they could of the enemy's deployments and (attempt to) sneak back across the lines.

The risk inherent in Tallmadge's "underground railroad" system was that if one member of the network was blown or flipped by the enemy's counterespionage service, it rendered the rest of the chain useless, whereas if the same happened to Scott's agents, the loss would be limited to just the unfortunates captured (as happened with Hale). Where Tallmadge held the advantage was that if he could set up such a network, the intelligence it communicated back would be of a far higher quality than that gleaned by any one-time operative. But Scott could counter that simultaneously running several small-scale missions assured more *accurate*—if lower-level—intelligence because the case officer could verify his agents' independent estimates of, say, troop strengths, by cross-referencing them against each other. As Washington once wrote, to the leading American cryptographer of the time, "It is by comparing a variety of information, we are frequently enabled to investigate facts, which were so intricate or hidden, that no single clue could have led to the knowledge of them."[25]

For the time being, Washington was not entirely convinced by the merits of Tallmadge's radical scheme, and instead continued to rely on the older system. On September 10, accordingly, Scott informed Washington that "Capt. Leavenworth is now on the Sound in pursuit of intelligence," and that Scott had sent in three officers separately—Butler, Parker, and Grayham—to sniff out British positions on Long Island.[26] A Captain John Rathburn also went in, to observe the enemy fleet.

Rathburn and Leavenworth soon returned safely, but Scott feared the worst for the other three. On September 12, Scott informed Washington that one of them had been "stopped at the out lines contrary to the usual custom. Leaves it no longer a doubt about the others being detained." The British had unexpectedly tightened their perimeter, netting the three unlucky spies.[27]

Two weeks later—September 25—Washington had belatedly concluded that the traditional system was failing. He needed something new, and discreetly suggested to Scott that Tallmadge's progressive ideas ought to be tried. He asked Scott to "endeavour to get some intelligent person into the City and others of his own choice to be messengers between you and him, for the purpose of conveying such information as he shall be able to obtain and give." He now wanted a *chain of agents* stationed permanently in enemy territory. His choice of chief agent was Tallmadge's recruit, "Mr. C———," because if he "could be engaged in a work of this sort, his discernment, and means of information, would enable him to give important advices."[28]

Invigorated by this unexpected support, Tallmadge intended to forge Woodhull and Brewster into the nucleus of a network—what would become known as the Culper Ring—as a showcase for his scheme, and to take effective control of his little band from Scott. As early as October 22, for instance, Tallmadge was in direct contact with Brewster and thence to Washington, thereby neatly excising Scott from the chain of command.[29]

He began prepping Abraham Woodhull for active duty. Since Woodhull's return from Connecticut in the summer, he had been regarded with slightly raised eyebrows by his pro-British neighbors. Tallmadge needed to put their minds at ease that Woodhull was one of them, and as loyal as they were to the Crown—despite his suspiciously early release from prison by the rebel authorities. By coincidence, earlier that month, just before its members returned to London, the Carlisle Commission—fruitlessly sent by Britain to negotiate an end to hostilities—had proclaimed that all those who swore an oath to their sovereign would be pardoned after Congress's defeat. The spy chief hit upon the crafty idea of having Woodhull "take the benefit of the same and serve as in his present capacity." Woodhull, now "considered as one of their friends," would have "a better opportunity of acquainting himself with their proceedings," Tallmadge boasted to Washington.[30]

Scott soon after bowed out, reporting to Washington on October 29 (in a swipe at Tallmadge) that for certain reasons he had been having trouble fulfilling his duties as a spy manager. His spies were also failing him. One promising recruit, for example, had just returned from a visit to New York, but "he knows nothing and will not tell me any thing at all, I suspect he is a rascal and shall treat him accordingly." Worse, family issues were weighing him down, so "my unhappy misfortunes make it indispensably necessary that I should leave the army in a few weeks."[31] Washington graciously accepted his mostly welcome resignation, and gave Tallmadge the chance to head his own intelligence network.

Unlike Brewster's missives to Scott, which had been written somewhat stiffly with a full formal flourish, his letters to Tallmadge were casually written and signed with his name. Not just comrades in the war, the two were old friends. And so, too, was Abraham Woodhull.

Tallmadge was from coastal Setauket, in Suffolk County, the small town in which Woodhull still lived and whence Brewster had left in the years before the war. The three of them had grown up together. Setauket, in every other respect, was an entirely unexceptional Long Island settlement. In 1655, six pioneers from Massachusetts purchased land from the Setalcott Indians; within a half-decade, the capable Richard Woodhull—born in England thirty-five years before and emigrating to Massachusetts in 1640—had taken charge, and the town, and those around it, expanded by underhandedly encouraging its new arrivals to "take some likers [liquors] with them" when they went to talk to the Indians about buying property.[32] Woodhull's great-great-grandson was Abraham Woodhull, who lived with his parents on the family farm, a modest tract on Strong's Neck facing the placid waters of Old Field Bay. The Tallmadge residence was a few minutes' walk to the south.[33]

As for Caleb Brewster's people, they emigrated from England in the early 1660s, and had found their way to Setauket by the end of the decade. One, the Reverend Nathaniel Brewster, graduated from Harvard, and served as Setauket's Presbyterian minister between 1665 and

1680.[34] Since then, the family, or at least Caleb's father, had turned to farming and left the ministering of the flock to the able divine, the Reverend Benjamin Tallmadge, a Yale-educated Whig of stout persuasion and one fearsomely learned in the weightiest of Greek and Roman political philosophy, who alternately denounced the idolators, the damned, and the Episcopalians from his Presbyterian pulpit between 1754 and 1785. (Given the robustness of Tallmadge's convictions, it was hardly surprising that Colonel Hewlett's vengeful force of damned, idolatrous Episcopalian militiamen desecrated the church, for which they were duly punished by Brewster, among others, during the August 1777 raid.) His son was our Benjamin, who loved his God and General Washington in equal measure (even if he were perpetually disappointed that Washington was never "explicit in his profession of *faith in* . . . the finished Atonemont of our glorious Redeemer").[35]

In such an insular and isolated place as eighteenth-century Setauket, *everyone* knew each other. This complex web of personal relationships, continuing down through generations and concentrated in one compact locality, was key to the Culper Ring's later success. Its members refused to work with anyone they didn't know, and insisted on using Tallmadge as their sole channel to Washington. They were one-man dogs.

They shared not only a common background, but politics, as well. Those who signed a local petition dated June 8, 1775—seven weeks or so after the first shots at Lexington and Concord, and the formation of New York's radical First Provincial Convention—were Whigs good and true who resolved "never to become slaves" to tyrants, and most could be counted on to support Congress in its struggle against the Crown. The list itself consists of some seventy names, and includes Woodhull, Brewster, and "John Talmadge" (Benjamin Tallmadge's younger brother).[36]

Those of Tallmadge himself and his father are missing from this "List of Associators." Tallmadge's absence is easily explicable: At the time he was away "superintend[ing] the High School in Weathersfield"; as for his father, Tallmadge recalled that despite his zealous Whiggery, he was "very reluctant to have me enter the army." Like many other Americans trapped in the tempest of the mid-1770s, Tallmadge Senior may have happily boycotted Anglophile tradesmen and berated the Tories, but was in the end unwilling to fight the Mother Country. Cheering the bravery of the tea party was one thing; indulging the madness of the war party quite another.

Befitting its Presbyterian heritage, therefore, Setauket was a nest of Patriot sentiment. Religion in the American Revolution was enormously important. Indeed, George III once joked that the Revolution was a "Presbyterian War"—and he was largely right. New England, the most thoroughly Patriot region, was two-thirds Congregationalist and Presbyterian. These were not naturally revolutionary, but their core belief that kings must exercise their power righteously or risk rebellion by God's Chosen compelled in them a natural sympathy for the American cause.

High Church Anglicans, Low Church Anglicans, the Dutch, the Quakers, Methodists, and Irish Catholics—all doctrinally and historically opposed to the Yankees—populated the Middle Colonies, though in Pennsylvania, Quaker-loathing Ulster Presbyterians emerged as a powerful force. As a result, Long Island was peculiarly divided. Its eastern half, including Setauket, had once been part of Connecticut, and fire-and-brimstone Presbyterianism accordingly dominated. Few Presbyterians lived in its pro-British western half, where Anglicans and their allies predominated. The Quakers there—mostly merchants, professionals, and prosperous farmers—gravitated toward either neutrality or a diluted loyalty toward the Anglican status quo, partly owing to their distaste for Presbyterians, who had developed something of an expertise in persecuting them.

Despite these social, political, and religious reasons for backing the rebellion, not every resident of Setauket volunteered to risk his life spying for Washington. The Culper spies also had very personal motives. Aside from the profane abuses perpetrated by Colonel Hewlett against his father's church, Tallmadge held a grudge against the British occupiers for the death of his eldest brother, who had been captured during the Battle of New York and starved in prison.[37]

Unlike Tallmadge, Caleb Brewster's family doesn't seem to have suffered loss, either of blood or of treasure, by British troops. Brewster was a man who simply relished action, more so if hand-to-hand fighting was involved. His adventuring started early. Born in September 1747, Brewster chafed as a farmhand on his father's land in Setauket.[38] Bored unto death, when he was nineteen he signed on to a Nantucket whaler that voyaged to Greenland, whose chilly, dark waters concealed a ferocious quarry: the sperm whale, whose head contained the clearest and sweetest oil of all the cetaceans. Whaling was a man's work. For months, crewmen ate nothing but salt pork, rice, beans, and cornmeal dipped in a little molasses, and they knew they would stay way out there in the blue until either the food ran out, the captain fell overboard in a storm, or they hauled in enough oil to make the trip a profitable one.

Once a whale was spotted, the whaleboats were lowered and the hunt was on. Muscles tore as the men pulled at the oars to bring the high-paid harpooner within range. Once launched, the spear stuck in the beast and pulled the suddenly fragile craft rapidly through the churn of its wake. Should a sailor be careless enough to be entwined in the snarls of a whirring line, he was yanked from the boat, never to be seen again. Then came the most dangerous time. A wounded, and angry, whale could assault the boat with its fluke, or still more terrifyingly, charge it head-on. "She came at our boat," recalled one oarsman, "& furiously ran over us and oversat us & made a miserable rack of our boat in a moment."[39]

After a few years, having had his fill of whaling and with a nice stash of cash, Brewster joined a merchantman bound for London. Owing to his seafaring experience, Brewster served as a mate, and imbibed a great deal of invaluable nautical knowledge—which would come in useful as he navigated the Sound—the "Devil's Belt"—in the dark of the wartime night.

He was back home by May 1775, when he signed a petition backing Selah Strong for the post of delegate to the Provincial Convention.[40] Strong (born 1737) was a kinsman of Abraham Woodhull's, as well as his neighbor. Demonstrating how intricately Setauket's families were enmeshed, Strong's sister would later marry Tallmadge's father as his second wife, and his wife Anna's relative, Mary, would marry Woodhull.[41]

In December, Brewster joined the Suffolk County militia as second lieutenant, but was promoted to a full lieutenantcy in the spring of 1776 when Strong—now a captain—took command of the Seventh Company. In the confused aftermath of the Battle of New York, the four companies of minutemen disbanded, but those still willing to fight—including Brewster—made their way to New Haven and Rhode Island.[42]

His thirst for adventure was temporarily sated when on October 28, 1776, Brewster and thirty-five other men took six whaleboats and three transports across the Sound to "bring off the effects of Colonel [William] Floyd." Brewster and company instead captured two sloops taking on wood in Setauket bay. They returned to Long Island twice more. On November 6, they engaged a detachment of freshly enlisted troops, killed five or six of them, took twenty-three prisoner, and hauled in seventy-five muskets for the loss of one man, and one wounded. Two days later, they returned for Floyd's belongings but were interrupted by an especially unlucky band of militiamen. Result: ten Loyalists lying dead and another twenty-three prisoners. The raiders suffered a sergeant killed in the firefight.[43]

Later that month, Brewster volunteered as an ensign in the Second Company, Fourth Battalion, of the Fourth New York Regiment.[44] He wasn't long there. Three months later, in early 1777, Brewster, again a lieutenant, had transferred to the Second Continental Artillery, stationed in Connecticut. And there—apart from the time he dealt with Colonel Hewlett in Setauket—he remained until August 1778, when, tired of the land and homesick for the sea, Caleb Brewster wrote his first letter to General Washington.[45]

Born in 1750, Abraham Woodhull, conversely, preferred farming the land and was more than happy not to go gallivanting around the world hunting sperm whales. Despite his appearance as a placid man of toil, Woodhull was inwardly a distinctly odd bird, whereas Brewster was a simpler soul. Both men were patriotic, but in no letter of his correspondence did Brewster ever evince much dislike of the British: One gets the feeling that he was partly in the game because it was fun. Woodhull, on the other hand, turned into a fierce, if outwardly circumspect, partisan, often writing how greatly he loathed his overlords. He derived pleasure from tricking and betraying them secretly.

Aside from a couple of months as a lieutenant in the Suffolk militia in the fall of 1775, where he saw no action but was trained how to shoulder his musket and wheel smartly on command, Woodhull lacked the martial spirit of Brewster and Tallmadge.[46] He never volunteered for further service.[47] On a practical level, his two older brothers had died in 1768 and 1774, and Abraham was obliged to stay on the farm to keep it running and look after his aged parents.[48] And in any case, at least until the Battle of New York, Woodhull was more politically moderate than Brewster or Tallmadge, more loath to join the colors that attracted so many young men. But something happened during that battle that radicalized him, and made his enmity toward the British more visceral than Brewster's.

It was his pang to avenge the callous and needless murder of his kinsman General Nathaniel Woodhull (born 1722) that propelled Abraham into Tallmadge's secret world. Tallmadge, too, had lost a brother (as well as a near brother, Nathan Hale) during that battle, but as a hard-bitten soldier he understood, and had seen, that terrible things happened in war, and could accordingly rationalize their deaths as inevitable sacrifices in a glorious war of liberation. Brewster, as well, had witnessed shipmates sucked into the watery depths and accepted it as the natural course of events. Woodhull was gentler and unaccustomed to brutality. To him, the loss of Nathaniel came as a far more bitter and unfair blow, more so because his older cousin was an exemplar of moderation, not of revolutionary fervor.

General Woodhull had fought bravely in the French and Indian War, but by 1776 he was better known as a politician with connections in both Tory and Whig camps.[49] Woodhull, despite being the president of the Provincial Convention, did not sign New York's endorsement of the Declaration of Independence, thinking it too radical and aggressive. He, like many others of moderate persuasion who acknowledged that the colonists did have a point, was reluctant to take such a momentous step as declaring war on Britain and sought to reconcile the two sides. That did not stop him being, as the local arch-Loyalist judge Thomas Jones disapprovingly opined, a "flaming republican," an unfortunate trait he attributed to his being a "rigid Presbyterian."[50]

The general's death was no ordinary one. In late August 1776, General Woodhull was ordered to burn grain and round up livestock that could be used by the British once they invaded Long Island. On the twenty-eighth, he wrote his last letter, to the Convention, from Jamaica, Long Island, saying that "my men and horses are worn out with fatigue." He decided to stay the night at Increase Carpenter's tavern, a place two miles east of the town. That evening the inn was surrounded by men of the Seventeenth Light Dragoons and the Seventy-first Foot; Woodhull, apparently while attempting to escape, was wounded in the head and arm and taken prisoner. That was the official story laid out in the British military record.

Different versions soon emerged. A newspaper account said that Woodhull had refused to give over his sidearms, and so was "wounded on the head with a cutlass, and had a bayonet thrust through his arm." Other sources claimed that Major Baird of the Seventy-first Foot had ordered him to say, "God save the King," to which Woodhull replied, "God save us all," whereupon he was assailed by Baird's broadsword. And still others omitted Baird, and instead blamed one "Lieut. Huzzy" for striking the general, who was saved only by the intervention of "Major [Oliver] De Lancey." James Fenimore Cooper, the *Last of the Mohicans* novelist who married into the De Lancey family, recalled in 1849 that Oliver had told him this was the case.

The Continental Congress continued to investigate this dreadful instance of prisoner abuse into early 1777. Lieutenant Robert Troup, a New York militiaman who had been taken in a separate engagement, testified that having seen the "shocking mangled" Woodhull on board a transport, he approached him and asked "the particulars of his capture." Woodhull *himself* said the dragoons—"under the command of Capt. Oliver de Lancey"—had asked whether he wished to surrender. When he replied in the affirmative, but only on condition he was treated as a gentleman, they accepted his sword but then De Lancey knavishly "struck him, and others of the same party imitating his example, did cruelly hack and cut him." Taken to the Church of New Utrecht, the stricken Woodhull was deprived of medical care and food and died in agony on September 20. Some time later, Dr. Silas Holmes, a prisoner and assistant surgeon who attended the dying Woodhull, confirmed in a letter that "the wounded prisoners . . . were wallowing in their own filth, and breathed an infected and putrid air" during Woodhull's time in the hospital. A few days later, Dr. Richard Bailey took over as superintendent and rapidly improved the conditions, though by then it was too late for Woodhull.

However, John Sloss Hobart, who had been detailed by the Provincial Convention in October 1776 to negotiate for Woodhull's release, made no specific mention of any ill treatment of the general. He said in his report that "the wound in his arm mortified" and the arm was amputated; Woodhull nevertheless continued to suffer gangrene, which carried him off a few days later. Indeed, "he was attended to in his dying moments by his lady, who was permitted to remove the corpse to his seat, where it was interred" about September 23. The Provincial Convention, summing up the case, also failed to cite mistreatment during his captivity causing his death.[51]

It's an intriguing mystery, to be sure, and we'll never know whether De Lancey was Woodhull's savior or his tormentor. Troup could easily have gotten his story mixed up, but then so too could have Cooper, seventy-five years after the event. As for the ill treatment of prisoners, this did happen disturbingly often, but then so too did dying after an amputation, especially one carried out in a dirty, jerry-rigged prison.

It's most probable that Woodhull—a general, after all, not a common soldier, though only of militia—received slightly better treatment than other prisoners (which isn't saying much), but no one bothered to exert himself on a rebel's behalf.

For Abraham Woodhull, however, Troup's account, the reports widely printed in the Patriot press, and the rumor mill all rang truer than the cover-up by the respectable Convention. He believed in the perfidy of De Lancey. And so Woodhull single-mindedly devoted himself to destroying the British, their allies, and all that they stood for by spying the daylights out of them. Thus, he leapt at the chance to serve Tallmadge.

On October 29, 1778, after having sworn his oath of loyalty to His Majesty, Woodhull dispatched his first "Samuel Culper" letter. Hitherto he had passed on intelligence verbally for fear of incriminating documents falling into the enemy's hands, so Tallmadge had assured him that none but he and Brewster knew his real name, and that, if captured, they would destroy the letters before surrendering. For safety's sake, Tallmadge *did* destroy Woodhull's original letter after copying it verbatim in his own handwriting and passing that version to headquarters. There was nothing left now to trace it back to Woodhull—though the experience of transcribing Woodhull's epistles must have bored the busy Tallmadge, and he soon resorted to just sending on the originals—without telling his trusting correspondent.

Whereas Washington, equipped with a staff of private secretaries, and Tallmadge, nursed on Cicero's cadences and blessed with a Yale education, composed splendidly styled, flowing sentences, Woodhull's provincialism made his punctuation idiosyncratic and spelling atrocious. He used such words as "doth" and "hath"—antiquated even by the standards of the time—but as time progressed, so too did Woodhull's abilities. Tallmadge, for instance, never complained about his correspondent's letters.[52]

Woodhull's first espionage effort was not a masterpiece, but it did contain some useful tidbits, mostly concerning embarkations onto transports by British troops, which Woodhull speculated were on their way to the West Indies. (In this case, he was wrong: British command-ers quite often liked to keep the rebels on their toes by marching on and off ships, and up and down hills, to pretend major movements were afoot or for training purposes.)[53] Two days later, Woodhull—having overcome his initial reservations—wrote his second letter. The first third of it is meandering, but Woodhull belatedly gets down to the work at hand, even if, as was typical of these early Woodhull letters, he found it difficult to write concisely.

Because Tallmadge lacked a permanent agent in the city, Woodhull performed double duty by acting as Brewster's liaison in Setauket and then traveling to New York every few weeks to pick up news. Woodhull hated making that trip: It was by far the riskiest aspect of his job, for not only did villains, Tory plunderers, and British patrols in-fest the fifty-five-mile road to New York, but worse, he had to leave his aged parents for several days at a time, stay in expensive (for him) inns on the way, and travel by himself in the cold and through the muck. Most irritatingly, each person who wanted to travel from Brooklyn to Manhattan aboard a ferry was required to show a passport to the guards at the gate, and to leave most had to obtain a two-shilling per-mit from the authorities, who were apt to be suspicious of unfamiliar Long Island farmers who rarely brought any produce.

On October 31, at one British checkpoint where he was routinely questioned, Woodhull "received their threats for coming there that make me almost tremble knowing…my business." After that little scare, Woodhull's innate caution prompted him to tell his chiefs to "destroy every letter instantly after reading for fear of some unfore-seen accident that may befall you and the letter get into the enemies hands and probably find me out and take me before I have any warn-ing." (Woodhull would have suffered an apoplexy had he ever discov-ered that Washington's staff, despite Tallmadge's assurances that his agent's wishes were being carried out, actually kept his letters for ad-ministrative reasons—so allowing us to read them today—though Woodhull's real name was never used at headquarters.)[54]

Woodhull followed up with an unhelpful observation that some regiments of Loyalist militia had refused to embark for a destination that was a "profound secret." He was luckier on other matters: A fleet had recently arrived with stores and provisions, and there was "forage and wood sufficient for their needs this winter." It was crucial to Washington to know the status of the British supply fleet, as well as the quantities of fuel and oats the army had available. An abundance of such things, or evidence of stockpiling, signaled a renewed campaign in the coming season.

For their part, locked even as they were into their island fortress, the British authorities were alarmed at how vulnerable they were. The city they occupied absolutely depended on the outside world. Before the war, while New York (like the rest of the colonies) imported far more than it exported, after 1776, the city exported virtually nothing and became, instead, a vast urban parasite quarantined from the rest of the continent and its traditional inland trade routes. The army had to import even its footwear. General Howe announced on January 26, 1777, for instance, that the fleet had brought "16,000 pairs of soles, 250 sets of shoemaker's tools, 14 dozen lbs. of shoemaker's thread, 40 lbs. of shoemaker's bristles, 200,000 shoemaker's pegs, and 450 lasts."[55]

Any provisions that could not be supplied from Long Island had to be imported by sea, by what was known as the "Cork Fleet," as it sailed from Ireland, the army's westernmost port, several times a year.[56] The overriding importance of this victualing fleet to the survival of the British empire in America was a constant source of worry for city and military officials. "What would become of us should a Cork fleet miscarrie—which sooner or later may be the case—the army wou'd eat up the market and the inhabitants wou'd starve," wrote an alarmed David Sproat, Commissary of Naval Prisoners, to Joseph Galloway in London.[57] William Eden, the undersecretary of state, solemnly warned Sir Henry Clinton that "if the Cork Fleet fails... there can be no doubt that our removal [from New York and America] must take place."[58]

The nightmare came close to realization in the summer of 1778, when food reserves had run so low there were just five weeks' worth left and British commanders even debated abandoning the city. But thanks to Woodhull's letter, Washington—much to his chagrin—learned that the fleet had arrived with enough supplies for six months. Only there wasn't. Graft and thievery, the twin banes of the British army, would whittle six months' supplies down to just three months'. Greed, as usual, played a role: An investigation found that barrels of what purported to be government-approved "fine flour" actually contained "sweepings of stores and bake houses, rags, papers, and old hats," while some military contractors mixed sand with flour or sent shortweighted barrels of beef, disguising their fraud by placing stones at the bottom.[59]

Despite the bad tidings he brought, Woodhull was hoping this would be his last trip. "Blessed be God," cheered Woodhull on his return, I've been "particularly successful in engaging a faithful friend and one of the first characters in the City to make it his business and keep his eyes upon every movement and assist me in all aspects and meet and consult weekly in or near the City. I have the most sanguine hopes of great advantages will accrue by his assistance."[60]

Woodhull's mysterious "faithful friend" was Amos Underhill (1740–1803), a former mill owner in Glen Cove whose property had been razed by the British during the Battle of New York.[61] Soon afterwards, he moved into the city, became a merchant of sorts, and bought a house. By 1778, with a baby on the way, he and his wife, Mary, were forced to take in occasional boarders. They, like so many others, had been hit hard by the steep increases in the cost of living caused by the war. So tight was the financial situation that even Woodhull—who was Underhill's brother-in-law through Mary (1745–1815), Abraham's older sister—had to be charged £3 per week to stay with them.[62]

In September 1775, the normal peacetime price for a family-size portion of flour was 20 shillings; by 1781, it would be more than 70 shillings. Over the same period, beef rocketed from 65 shillings a pound to £8, while the price of fresh vegetables soared 800 percent. And this was before factoring in rent increases of 400 percent, caused by a combination of a housing shortage after the Great Fire and New York's burgeoning wartime population.[63]

New York's inhabitants were compressed into a tiny area, an inverted triangle measuring half a square mile.[64] There were about 25,000 residents in 1776—including 3,137 free, freed, and enslaved blacks, as well as Scots, Irish, Germans, Jews (some 300), Spaniards, and Portuguese—but this figure did not account for soldiers. In May 1776, 8,767 American troops were deployed in and around the city; by August, there were no fewer than 20,375 American and 34,614 British servicemen in the area, all demanding food, fuel, and shelter.[65] Within the month, the vast majority of civilians had fled the fighting, leaving just 5,000 living in the spookily deserted city. (Among those who remained, whoever's soldiery was in town, were the 500 hopeful prostitutes plying their trade in what was known as "Holy Ground"—it was land owned by the Church of England—that occupied the area later occupied by the World Trade Center.)[66]

Over the coming years, tens of thousands of civilians dribbled back. Whenever the British retreated to New York, a ragged, hopeful procession of Loyalists accompanied them. Those from Connecticut and New Jersey arrived first—by early 1777, the city's population had swollen to 11,000—and another 3,000 streamed in after the British evacuated Philadelphia in 1778. In 1783, on the eve of the British evacuation, there were 33,000 inhabitants.[67]

There were also, of course, the king's troops, who were rotated in and out of action as the fortunes of war required. In January 1777, immediately prior to Washington's victory at Princeton, there were 3,300 soldiers in New York, rising to 5,000 in November after General Burgoyne's surrender at Saratoga, and rising again to 9,000 in July 1778 following Clinton's withdrawal from Philadelphia. Eighteen months later, owing to British success in the South, the number of redcoats had fallen to 4,000, but in August 1781, on the eve of Yorktown, it had more than doubled, to 9,700, before reaching 17,200 in December 1782, that imposing figure ironically heralding the collapse of Britain's

American empire.[68] Even then, these numbers were underestimates. For example, if one includes in the July 1778 figures (i.e., 9,000) the cohorts of new recruits, deserters, Royal Navy sailors, Marines, privateers, soldiers on sick leave, Loyalist militiamen, and freebooters working off the books, the number was actually about 20,000.[69]

Though these numbers made life most unpleasant, Woodhull could also take solace in the realization that, owing to the flood of strangers and outsiders, he might easily blend into the background and evade recognition by alert British sentries. Though that fact greatly reassured him, Woodhull was not yet comfortable sneaking around as a spy, and tended to exaggerate to buttress his confidence. Thus, Woodhull boosted Underhill's importance in order to impress Washington and Tallmadge. By no means could his kinsman, upstanding and respectable as he was, be described as "one of the first characters in the City."

Even so, his chiefs were pleased at Woodhull's acquisition of an asset in New York, but not so much about the vagueness of their man's intelligence: the destination of the army being a "profound secret," for instance. On November 18, Washington instructed Tallmadge to tell Woodhull to "ascertain the following facts with as much precision, and expedition, as possible." These included which corps were in Manhattan and which on Long Island, whether any forts and strongpoints were being built in Brooklyn opposite Manhattan, the names of the commanders on Long Island, where they were based, whether the troops were ready to move, and other humdrum basics. He didn't care, having been burnt before by spies plucking numbers from the sky, about Culper's estimates of troop strength, since "I can form a pretty accurate opinion of the numbers from" knowing simply which corps were present. If his spy complained about the workload, Washington airily opined that discovering the location of sundry units was "a piece of knowledge that a man of common abilities may come at with precision by taking a little pains."[70]

It was a moot point, replied Tallmadge, because "I have been hourly waiting for two days" for the latest Culper letter. Getting information was one thing, receiving it quite another. "I am confident the failure must be attributed to those employed in crossing the Sound for such dispatches, as [Woodhull's] punctuality heretofore in fulfilling all appointments . . . leaves no room to doubt." The problem lay not with Brewster, but with his crew—most of whom could only be used if their commanding officers allowed them time off from their military duties to work "freelance" under Brewster, who had been released from the artillery for secret service. Unfortunately, the rub was that if sailors were detailed to work on the Culper missions exclusively, someone would eventually shoot his mouth off in a tavern that something secret was afoot. Tallmadge said he was about to ride to Fairfield, where Brewster was based, to try to work something out.

In the meantime, it was crucial to keep Brewster as the sole liaison between Tallmadge and Woodhull, for the latter's "extreme cautiousness, and even timidity, in his present undertaking would not admit of having his business made known to any persons who are not at present his confidantes." So jumpy was Woodhull that if his role were "communicated to any other persons he would most probably leave his present employment immediately." The same principle applied to Woodhull's letters. Though Tallmadge didn't fear that Culper's spying will be "made public at camp," if people at headquarters were "made acquainted with his present situation [it] would make him extremely unhappy, and as he [said] when he embarked in the business, he should leave the Island immediately" and flee to American-held Connecticut.[71] To which Washington immediately confirmed: "You will be pleased to observe the strictest silence with respect to C——, as you are to be the only person intrusted with the knowledge or conveyance of his letters."[72]

Whereupon Woodhull filed a report on November 23 that exceeded Washington's expectations. Not only did he provide names, corps, and movements ("the second division under Brig. Genl. Cambell that have laid some time at Sandy Hook . . . are to sail this day" and "the cannon and field pieces are removed from the common [in New York] to Fort George") but, disobeying the general's instructions, Woodhull added precise numbers: "the whole of the Kings troops on York Island including outposts, doth not exceed three thousand five hundred men" but the "best of their troops are on Long Island." Thus, "there is about 300, most of them Hessians, at Brooklyn Ferry. 350 New Town, British; 1500 British, Jamaica; 800 Yeagers [Hessian Jägers], Flushing; 200 Jerico, most of them Dragoons; 400 foot, 70 Dragoons Oyster Bay; 150 Lloyd's Neck, [new] Leveys; 400 Hempstead, Dragoons." Unlike the inflated figures habitually produced by other spies, Woodhull's estimates rang so true, a skeptical Washington could not help but be impressed.[73] "His account has the appearance of a very distinct and good one and makes me desirous of a continuance of his correspondence," declared the general. But then he, as had Tallmadge, fingered the issue that would vex the Ring throughout the war: How to get the intelligence through, on time and securely. "At the same time, I am at a loss how it can be conveniently carried on as he is so scrupulous respecting the channel of conveyance." He left it up to Tallmadge to come up with a scheme "in which the purpose of procuring his intelligence with expedition can be answered."[74]

Tallmadge never quite succeeded in reconciling Washington to Woodhull's (understandable) obsession with anonymity and safety. Security and timeliness were incompatible virtues—there would always be a trade-off between them. Whereas Woodhull's primary concern lay in keeping his neck out of a tightening noose, the general, preoccupied with winning battles, was rather more concerned with receiving timely intelligence about the enemy than about the personal comfort level of his agents, especially one as pernickety as Woodhull was turning out to be. Washington, even so, was willing to go halfway: "If you think you can really depend on C——s fidelity, I should be glad to have an interview with him myself; in which I could put the mode of corresponding upon such a footing that even if his letters were to fall into the enemy's hands, he would have nothing to fear, on that account."[75] (The meeting did not happen, Woodhull being reluctant to raise suspicions by being away from Long Island for so long.)[76]

Aside from the tardiness of his correspondence, two tics, both of them irritating to Washington, characterized Woodhull's letters. First, he liked to add his personal views. So, for instance, in November he attends a meeting of Loyalists, and noting that "with much satisfaction [I] beheld their dejected countenances," he pompously declares that "I am firmly of opinion that a sudden attack of ten thousand men would take the City and put an end to the War." There was "not much to be feared from the inhabitants" of Manhattan, he casually appends, as "the whole City [is] seized with a panic and a general dissatisfaction."[77] By December, Woodhull had convinced himself that if Washington waited but four months, "I am confident they will go themselves, Yes I am firmly of opinion and it is become general belief that in half the time we shall have the news of Great Britain acknowledging American independence."[78] Washington soon learned to filter out Woodhull's grand strategic visions.

Still, Woodhull's ruminations, especially his more mordant ones, provide an insight into what normal Americans thought of the British and their own political leaders at the time. "I cannot bear the thoughts of the war continuing another year," wrote Woodhull, "as could wish to see an end of this great distress. Were I to undertake to give an account of the sad destruction that the enemy makes within these lines I should fail. They have no regard to age, sex, Whig or Tory. I lament to hear [of the] civil dissensions among you [the Congress] at Philadelphia. I think them very alarming. It sinks the spirits of our suffering friends here and pleases the enemy. Cannot the disturbers see that they are working their own ruin. Is there no remedy to apply. Better had they be cut off from the land of the living than to be suffered to go on."[79]

The second annoying thing was more serious. Money. Woodhull was fanatical about getting his expenses reimbursed. Amazingly, for someone so strident about every other aspect of his security, Woodhull kept a cash book notated with the costs incurred by his espionage: travel, lodging, and food, mostly.[80] Though no doubt he kept it safely hidden, maintaining an itemized ledger was, of course, a major breach of the regulations. In one respect, however, it was a necessity: Woodhull, as he often pointed out, was not wealthy, his expenses were considerable, and hard cash was difficult to come by.

But Woodhull (and his colleagues) were adamant about one thing: They did not serve for pay, and would not accept any reimbursement apart from money rightfully owed to them for expenses. Had they been offered cash, they would have haughtily rejected it. Indeed, they—Woodhull, in particular—were ashamed of being spies, and never termed themselves as such, instead referring to spying as "this business" and other euphemisms.

During the eighteenth century, there were three distinct types of agent. One kind was perfectly respectable, and weren't spies per se but military scouts on reconnaissance missions to probe fortifications or map terrain. These intelligence gatherers were heirs to a tradition dating from Homer and the Peloponnesian War. Officers and gentlemen—the two being one and the same at the time—were permitted to practice this kind of "espionage," one reason being that they were rarely out of uniform, or if they did assume a disguise, it was merely temporary—and physical (such as a wig or cloak). They did not stay behind enemy lines and masquerade as adherents to the enemy cause.

Washington had been one of these "intelligencers," as he once said in his journals. In 1753, then a young officer during the French and Indian War, he was ordered to enter the wilderness and discover whether the French were building forts on British soil. As "cover," he was given a letter from the lieutenant governor of Virginia requesting that the French vacate their positions. Two months later, a uniformed Washington visited Fort Lebouef and, while the French commander was reading the letter, was allowed to wander around freely taking notes and sketching the defenses. In the end, the French ignored the lieutenant governor's warning and sent Washington home, whereupon he was directed to return and build a fort of his own.

The second type of agent was more secretive, but just as respectable, for he operated solely within the closed and cramped environments of European palaces and chancelleries. Diplomats, princes, and generals discreetly passed each other scraps of intelligence that eventually reached the ears of the various capitals. It was all very civilized and often took place over dinner.

Alternatively, the foreign ministries of the European powers conducted their activities through "Black Chambers," a set of offices whose entrance was usually on a side street off the main building. Aside from the collecting of gossip, most intelligence was acquired by intercepting the diplomatic mails, sliding a hot wire beneath the wax seal or melting it, breaking the cipher, and making copies before resealing it.

The practice was so ubiquitous that the British ambassador in Vienna once complained to the Austrian chancellor that his censors had kept the originals and accidentally passed on the copies. The latter, Count Kaunitz, did not bother denying his interceptors' activities, lightheartedly remarking instead "how clumsy these people are." He could afford to be so humorous: The Habsburg *Geheime Kabinets-Kanzlei* was the best in the world. The sacks of diplomatic dispatches due to be delivered to the embassies in Vienna were dropped off at the Black Chamber at 7 a.m. each day; by 9.30 a.m., they were back at the Post Office ready to go. (Owing to the stress of the job, Viennese cryptanalysts worked shifts of one week on, one week off, but were paid lavish bonuses when they cracked a code: eighteen, once, in a single year.) Over the centuries, the espionage process evolved into a ritual as stiffly stylized as Kabuki, and was viewed as just part of the ancient game played by Great Powers.[81]

It was the *third* kind of spy that was beneath contempt. These were agents who worked for wages, and whose loyalty was always in doubt. They were regarded as lowborn blackguards who insinuated themselves into better society and betrayed their colleagues' trust by selling information. Permanently embedded in enemy territory and *psychologically* disguised as "friendlies," they were the sneaky, shifty toadies who informed on Jacobites, Jacobins, and radicals of various kinds. By their masters, cash was earmarked for bribes ("Without money," reads one particularly clear-eyed Bavarian instruction of 1773, "one does not get far"), some £67,000 annually in London's case.[82] It was to these characters that Napoleon, always a shrewd judge of character, alluded in his dictum: that the only true reward for a spy was gold. The playwright Ben Jonson also amusingly captured the prevailing image of these creatures:

> *Spies, you are lights in state, but of base stuffe,*
> *Who, when you have burnt your selves down to the snuffe,*
> *Stinke, and are throwne away. End faire enough.*

Woodhull, a former (if temporary) militia officer and an eminently respectable (if unmoneyed) gentleman related to a martyred general, would have been horrified had he been regarded as a mere, snuffable "light in state" by his heroes, Washington and Tallmadge. Hence he sought to cleanse himself of espionage's taint by refusing offers of pay, and also his insistence on serving solely out of loyalty to the Cause of Liberty, a theme he repeatedly harped on.[83] As for Tallmadge, he, too, remained enigmatically discreet about his spying activities. In his *Memoir*, written half a century after the Revolution, he had only this to say: "This year [1778] I opened a private correspondence with some persons in New York [for General Washington] which lasted through the war. How beneficial it was to the Commander-in-Chief is evidenced by his continuing the same to the close of the war. I kept one or more boats continually employed in crossing the Sound on this business." Apart from that sole paragraph, the balance of the sixty-eight-page book is devoted to his more respectable soldierly achievements.[84]

Lest Washington ever suspected him of padding his expenses—the sort of thing low-class spies did—Woodhull repeatedly took great pains to explain how thrifty and "as sparing as possible" he was. "I have drawn on you for fifty pounds," he humbly wrote, "which please accept."[85] Washington, because "all the specie in my possession is with my baggage from which I shall be for some days separated," could not send the money directly, but mentioned to Tallmadge that "there is a sum about equal to what is now wanted in the hands of Col. Henley, whom I have directed...to pay what he may have, to you."[86] This was money originally allotted to Charles Scott, lately resigned, to fund secret services.

Though he understood that spying could not be done on the cheap, Washington was always concerned with keeping expenses down. A peculiar difficulty was presented by Woodhull, who required British currency or bullion, not the Congress-printed paper that was both worthless (by 1780, a pound of tea cost five hundred dollars and people used the bills as wallpaper) and useless (how was Woodhull expected to circulate enemy currency in British-occupied territory?).[87] As Washington explained, "specie is so scarce an article and so difficult to be procured, that we must use great oeconomy with it. If Continental money can be made to answer the purpose in part, it will be a very desirable circumstance, as it will facilitate the necessary supplies."[88] Be that as it may, replied Woodhull on January 22, 1779, quite sensibly if a touch testily, "Continental money will not serve me; It is much lower here."[89] Washington's remark about using "great oeconomy," however, continued to rankle his spy, who reminded the commander-in-chief that "I have not an independent fortune," but that "I can assure you...I have had nothing else in view. And in one word a sufficiency for...support."[90] To which Washington, hoping to soothe a ruffled amour propre, clarified, it was "the difficulty of furnishing specie, not the mere matter of expense which I had in view when I recommended oeconomy."[91]

Mollified, and good and faithful servant that he was, Woodhull continued to do his master's bidding.

CHAPTER FOUR

711 and the Sympathetic Stain

Winter was traditionally a quiet time for armies, summer being the accepted and most civilized season to recommence killing the enemy. For Tallmadge, however, the winter of 1778–79 offered no respite and he was instead kept exceptionally busy by his spy ring. Washington had directed him to find a faster method of conveying Culper's letters to headquarters, and to this task he devoted himself.

There were two bottlenecks. Since Woodhull was now doing much of his spying work in the city at Amos Underhill's house, messages were delayed between there and Caleb Brewster's pick-up spot fifty-five miles away in one of the quieter bays just outside Setauket where the surrounding woods concealed these illicit goings-on from prying eyes. Assuming Brewster's crew were available, he could transport the letters across the Sound in just a few hours. The second bottleneck was on the Connecticut side, where it was proving onerous for Tallmadge both to rendezvous with Brewster and then ride to Washington's headquarters.

The latter was easily fixed. At Washington's suggestion, Tallmadge stationed a dragoon officer at Danbury who relayed the letters up the line to camp "without his knowing the person from whom they came," as the general put it.[1] By January 2, 1779, this single officer was replaced by a chain of "regular expresses established between Danbury and the headquarters of the army" who were given special permits to ride through American checkpoints.[2] Even so, there was the occasional delay: A Culper letter of mid-January was days late owing to a dragoon's lame horse and his need to "get some repairs to his accoutrements."[3]

The New York–Long Island stretch was trickier. Just before Christmas 1778, Tallmadge brought Jonas Hawkins into the Ring to courier the letters to Setauket. He didn't omit to assure Washington that Hawkins was sound.[4] Hawkins officially began work in mid-January. Little is known of him apart from his family's longtime presence in Setauket— a Zachariah Hawkins arrived in the town two years after its founding—that he owned a tavern and store, that (like Woodhull and Brewster) he signed the List of Associators in 1775, and that he served in the militia after the war for a short time. He was some years younger than Woodhull, Brewster, and Tallmadge, and had known them as the "older boys" since his childhood.[5] Like Amos Underhill, he was never, however, a full-time operative of the Ring, and soon began splitting his courier duties with Austin Roe, another signatory to the Associators' list. The latter, born in 1749, was also of an old Setauket family (related to Hawkins) and he owned a tavern—about fifty yards from the house where Caleb Brewster had grown up—on the short road between Setauket and Port Jefferson. Roe had bought it from the Woodhulls.[6] At this stage, the growing cell was recruiting solely from the ranks of men its members knew they could trust implicitly, men who shared their religion, blood, class, and creed.[7]

With Hawkins and Roe undertaking the hazardous trip between Woodhull in New York and Brewster waiting off Setauket, the new system quickly demonstrated its superiority. At the end of January 1779, the Ring managed to convey a letter from New York to Washington in a week, at least half the time it had previously taken.[8] Information could also travel in a more regular fashion, as Washington happily noticed when he received two Culper letters—one from Woodhull, the other, Brewster—in late February.

Brewster's was a short report on a visit he'd paid to Long Island, and was mostly concerned with naval matters, such as his observation that "they are repairing all their flat bottom boats in New York and building a number at the ship yards"—indicating that the enemy was gearing for a landing somewhere, probably Connecticut. There was also a tip that "the inhabitants [are] fitting a number of privateers out in the City," so allowing American commanders to warn merchantmen to be on the alert.[9]

Any intelligence of privateer-building activity was bound to be worrisome. New York's geographical position between Canada, Europe, and the Caribbean had long allowed privateering—the practice of allowing armed, private ships to attack those owned by the enemy and take their cargoes as prizes—to flourish on the side, but during the war, when it was impossible to obtain certain goods on the open market, it turned into a cross between an indispensable lifeline and a speculative thrill. (One such venture was the *Royal Charlotte*, a vessel owned by a consortium of New York high-society ladies patriotically intended "to assist in humbling the pride and perfidy of France, and in chastising the rebels of America" while also turning a sweet profit for its proprietors.)[10]

For Americans, over the course of the war their fleet of congressionally approved privateers—which varied between 73 (in 1777) and 449 (1781)—brought in 3,100 merchant vessels, of which 900 were eventually recaptured or ransomed to their owners. Though British global trade was mostly undisrupted by these losses (the premiums at Lloyd's of London, the maritime insurers, rose but not so much as to stifle commerce), the money generated by Continental privateering helped nourish the sinews of the war on land.[11]

On the British side, however, privateering was a much bigger business, employing up to six thousand New York seamen.[12] Blacks comprised a disproportionate number of these. Privateers were color-blind, and their captains could count on black crewmen—most former slaves freed by the British—not to surrender at the first whiff of American grapeshot. The consequences of capture, for them, were too dreadful not to put up a fight. In April 1782, for instance, when a Continental privateer captured the frigate *Alert*, it found that eleven out of its forty-six men were blacks, nine of whom were subsequently sold in a Trenton tavern.[13] For whites, so attractive were the business's rewards that the Royal Navy found its own ships undermanned because potential recruits were signing on to privateers. Notwithstanding the public complaints about the degenerate practice of sailing for profit instead of fighting for glory, even high-ranking officers, such as Admiral Howe, took cuts from commerce raiders, and navy captains themselves turned privateer if a juicy Continental plum crossed their path.[14] And with good reason: A good take could double, or even triple, a sailor's annual wages.[15]

A privateer who made a living mugging merchantmen often found itself a tempting target preyed on by larger craft: On September 30, 1776, the *Industry*, an American raider of twenty-six guns, was jumped by the *Emerald*, a frigate, and suffered thirteen killed and twenty-nine wounded.[16] Yet privateers on both sides still found the risk worthwhile. Three enterprising Continental captains, for instance, sailed their sloops into New York harbor and hijacked a fully laden merchantman right from under the nose of the *Russell*, a mammoth seventy-four-gunner, which failed to do anything to stop it, much to the fury of the New York merchants who could see their stolen property vanishing over the horizon.[17]

The British alone authorized some two hundred New York–based privateers to prowl the seas.[18] And they did. Roaming as far south as Virginia and the West Indies, and as far north as New England, between September 1776 and March 1779, these hunters brought into port no fewer than 165 prizes worth a staggering £600,000.[19] Small wonder that Washington found Brewster's information most useful, and not a little alarming.

The second letter in the February package, Woodhull's, was more substantive, and was the longest dispatch he ever wrote—a full seven dense pages. Now relieved of the burden of traveling back and forth from Setauket, he'd been assiduously touring the British positions. As Woodhull says, explaining his absence over the past weeks, "I have been for some time engaged to find out the true state of the enemy." Which was: "The 44, 57, 63 [regiments], Colls. Robinson's and Emmerick with three German regiments all commanded by Governor Tryon, are cantoned [at] King's Bridge....From these posts to and within the city are two battalions of Guards, 28 Regm. Welch Fusiliers, the Volunteers of Ireland...and four German Regm. Also in the city are Genls. Clinton, Jones, Mathews, De Lancey, Knyphausen." He computed "the whole force of the enemy to be thirty four battalions, equal to two hundred and fifty in a battalion." Rather sweetly, in the margin he calculated the sums for Washington, arriving at 8,500 men. He also independently confirmed Brewster's report of shipyard activity: "I frequently see General Clinton amongst the carpenters [at the shipyard], in particular viewing the boats."[20]

The importance of Brewster and Woodhull's early warnings that the British were building flat-bottomed transports and that there were significant numbers of soldiers at King's Bridge at the northern tip of Manhattan would soon become apparent. At the time, the "royal governor" of New York, William Tryon, had been urging Clinton to authorize the use of "desolation warfare" upon the enemy. For Tryon and other Loyalist hard-liners, Clinton's reluctance to countenance attacks on pro-Patriot civilians was evidence of namby-pambyism; only by punishing popular support for the rebel regime could Americans be wooed back into the monarchical fold. Though he and Tryon had once been close, Clinton dismissed his comrade's schemes as mad and immoral. In an attempt to quiet him, at the end of February he allowed Tryon to march from King's Bridge at the head of his regiments to West Greenwich (more often known as Horseneck), some thirty miles away, his objective being to destroy American *military* stockpiles.

Tryon's raid was a successful one (his men also managed to scuttle three docked vessels), even if he was harried on the way back by Connecticut militiamen.

Clinton had in the meantime begun musing on a plan that would use Tryon as bait. Come the summer, he would give Tryon command of a small fleet to transport 2,600 troops to the Connecticut coast. That armada was now secretly under construction, explaining Clinton's interest in visiting the shipyards to inspect progress. The task of Tryon's expeditionary force was to create a diversion that would lure Washington and the eight-thousand-man army southeast from his main camp near West Point on the upper Hudson. Once he had left his secure defensive redoubts to deal with Tryon's raiders, Clinton would march rapidly with the main army from New York, capture Washington's supply depots in New Jersey, and threaten his strongholds on the Hudson. Washington would be forced to rush back to save his rear, thereby allowing Clinton an opportunity to meet him on the field of battle and inflict a decisive defeat.[21]

The latest Culper intelligence—Clinton building transports in the midst of winter and Tryon instigating raids on Connecticut—bemused Tallmadge and Washington. Perhaps the two were linked, and Tryon's next attack would be waterborne; if that were the case, the Connecticut coastline would have to be the target. As Clinton would never stay put in New York during the crucial summer months, what would he do while Tryon was unleashed on Connecticut?

If Clinton *was* up to something, Washington wanted to know about it before it happened, and he urged Tallmadge to improve the timeliness of the Culper letters by finding a quicker route. Tallmadge, however, was equally, if not more, concerned with strengthening security. Written as they were openly in black ink, all it would take would be one overly curious trooper on patrol to find the incriminating documents and disaster would befall the Ring.

Making the telltale ink disappear would provide a hedge against discovery, which is precisely what Tallmadge set out to do. Quite by happy circumstance, a few months before, John Jay—about to become the new president of Congress—had enigmatically written to Washington about "a mode of correspondence, which may be of use, provided proper agents can be obtained. I have experienced its efficacy by a three years' trial."[22]

Jay, a future coauthor of the Federalist Papers with Alexander Hamilton and James Madison, was referring to an extraordinary ink concocted by his older brother, Sir James Jay (1732–1815), a physician who had been living in London before the war. Sir James, knighted in 1763 by George III and described as "haughty, proud, overbearing, supercilious, pedantic, vain, and ambitious" (as well as being a notorious overcharger; his medical practice "became entirely confined among his own relations"), also happened to be a keen amateur chemist.[23]

Many years after the Revolution, Sir James described to Thomas Jefferson that "when the affairs of America...threatened to issue in civil war [in 1775], it occurred to me that a fluid might possibly be discovered for invisible writing, which would elude the generally known means of detection, and yet could be rendered visible by a suitable counterpart. Sensible of the great advantages, both in a political and military line, which we might derive from such a mode of procuring and transmitting intelligence, I set about the work." After "innumerable experiments, I succeeded to my wish."

Jay continues: "From England I sent to my brother John in New York, considerable quantities of these preparations." Sir James himself turned spy when, using his ink, he "transmitted to America the first authentic account which Congress received, of the determination of the British Ministry to reduce the Colonies to unconditional submission."[24]

It took nearly six months for Washington to receive a small supply of what Sir James called a "sympathetic" ink, that is, "fluids by which if one writes on the whitest paper the letters immediately become invisible" but which are magically "rendered visible" by the application of a different chemical liquid. Technically speaking, the writing fluid is termed the agent, and the developer, the reagent (in Washington's words, the "counterpart" or "counter liquor").[25]

Agent and reagent were difficult to produce, given the scarcity of the materials and the need for secrecy. When he moved back to America, Sir James brought a limited amount of the chemicals from England, but was eventually obliged, with Washington's permission, to appropriate hospital supplies for his requirements.[26] Between the two men, the ink was code-named "medicine," and Jay would ship it to the general in a small doctor's box. Even with the ingredients in hand, the ink was tricky to produce, for it "require[d] some assistance from chemistry" and, Jay reported, "I have no place where a little apparatus may be erected for preparing it" because "our house is so small, and so well inhabited, that there is not a corner left where a little brick furnace, which a mason could build in two hours time, can be placed." However, "a log hut for the purpose might be soon run up, but it is also out of my power to effect this. Neither bricks, boards nor lime are to be purchased here, nor a carpenter nor mason to be had without great difficulty, if at all."[27] Jay soon got the help he needed, courtesy of Washington, for whom the ink was a priority. Colonel Udne Hay was commanded to supply "the assistance of a few artificers for a day or two to erect a small laboratory. As [Sir James] purposes making some experiments which may be of public utility and has already furnished me with some chymical preparations, from which I have derived considerable advantages I think it proper to gratify him." And, added Washington, "should a few boards or such matters be wanting to complete the building which is to be of logs, you will also procure them, if it be in your power."[28] It was.

For the most part, in the eighteenth century secret inks were rarely used. This was because they were generally based on organic liquids, such as the juice of leeks, oranges, limes, cabbage, and potatoes, as well as milk, vinegar, or urine (in a pinch). To develop them, the recipient applied heat, either by pressing the letter with an iron or holding a candle beneath it. The very simplicity of the revelatory process tended to outweigh the advantages bestowed by invisibility, which may have been one reason why the British—Clinton, in particular—preferred to write openly, so to speak, in cipher or by grille.

Jay's recipe, however, was revolutionary enough to amaze Washington. Performing his own experiments with the liquid, the general marveled that "fire which will bring lime juice, milk and other things of this kind to light, has no effect on it. A letter upon trivial matters of business, written in common ink, may be fitted with important intelligence which cannot be discovered without the counter part." He soon dubbed this marvelous fluid the "sympathetic stain."[29]

So what was the "sympathetic stain"? Conducting tests on the Culper letters in the Washington collection at the Library of Congress is impossible, and even if performed would be unlikely to yield much of use owing to the age and brittleness of the surviving correspondence written in the stain. We can take a few stabs at what it *could* have been, using the few clues available.

The Culpers tended to write on new paper, despite the added expense and the difficulty of acquiring it, in order to use the whitest available. Washington once advised, when he suggested that the Culpers could write in the blank leaves of books, that they should choose such volumes on the basis of "the goodness of the blank paper, as the ink is not easily legible, unless it is on paper of a good quality."[30] As a result—keeping in mind that the basis of sympathetic-ink alchemy is a change of color (if written in red, say, the developed message might appear in green) caused by the reaction between the agent and reagent—when Washington developed their letters, the Culpers' writing appeared in the hoped-for black. Only by "wetting the paper with a fine brush" dipped in the reagent, specified Washington, could one render the writing visible.[31] Another clue is that Jay conducted "innumerable experiments" (as he said in his letter to Jefferson) to get the compounds and sequence right, so the solution could not be an obvious one. Nor were the ingredients easy to come by, since Jay needed to get the key chemicals from a hospital or dispensary. And finally, as Washington found, the ink was impervious to heat.

There are some five hundred known sympathetic-ink formulas, and no doubt many hundreds more could be concocted. The vast majority of these can be discarded, as they fail at least one of the above criteria, and in any case, at that time there were but three types of sympathetic inks known. There is one that does fulfill every requirement. Mix and dissolve 60 grains of gallic acid with 10 grains of powdered acacia, more commonly known as gum arabic. (Gallic acid is a colorless or slightly yellowish crystalline acid derived from gallnuts, primarily Chinese in origin and so hard to find except in hospitals, where they were used by eighteenth-century doctors as an antidiarrheal medication.) After several attempts, you should have a solution the color of pale straw. For the reagent, acquire 30 grains of ferrous sulphate and dissolve them in 8 ounces of distilled water, thereby producing a colorless developer. The reason why Washington specified using a "fine brush" to reveal the message is that the reagent has a tendency to smear the text if too much is swabbed over it. Once the "counter liquor" is properly applied, the writing will gradually appear, tinted a pale greenish or bluish black, but will eventually, with exposure to air, turn coal-black. The document itself will, thanks to the oxidation of the ferrous salts, turn slightly brownish, as indeed the Culper letters often are.[32]

In mid-April 1779, Woodhull finally received "a vial for a purpose that gives me great satisfaction" and immediately began using it.[33] Even so, it took a year to procure sufficient supplies. The Culpers, as a result, often found themselves grievously short, and Washington himself tended to write openly to Tallmadge to preserve the precious drops. When, however, Woodhull finally had enough of the ink, he tended to hoard it for fear of another shortage, leading Washington to remark crossly to Tallmadge that "what I have sent for him at different times would have wrote fifty times what I have recd. from him."[34]

Armed now with his sympathetic stain, Washington soon began to cast round for a permanent New York agent so that Woodhull could hold the fort in Setauket. His eye settled on Lewis Pintard, a merchant who had been appointed (with General Howe's acquiescence) in early 1777 as commissary to American prisoners in New York, his job being to ensure they received proper care. In his letter asking for Howe's permission to keep an American representative in the city, Washington had pledged that Pintard was "under parole to transmit no intelligence." By the late spring of 1779, he had evidently decided that Pintard was too valuable an asset to let lie fallow.[35]

On May 3, 1779, Washington sounded out Elias Boudinot, his commissary-general of prisoners. "It is a matter of great importance to have early and good intelligence of the enemy's strength and motions, and as far as possible, designs, and to obtain them through different channels. Do you think it practicable to come at these by means of P———d? I shall not press it upon him; but you must be sensible that to obtain intelligence from a man of observation near the head quarters of an army from whence all orders flow and every thing originates must be a most desirable thing." If Pintard were willing, he would "entitle himself not only to thanks but reward, at a proper season." Understandably, Pintard would be concerned about exposure—the British no doubt steamed open his dispatches to headquarters—but Washington alluded to the possibility of using his new weapon, the ink, to evade their snares. The general asked Boudinot "to hint the matter to the person mentioned, for trial of his willingness to engage in a correspondence of this kind."[36]

Nothing came of the scheme: A miffed and insulted Pintard refused to send any reports to Washington. Some time later, he gave his reasons when he complained of the "disagreeable circumstances attending my particular situation" that had "exposed me to the most dangerous . . . consequences imaginable." Pintard was too discreet to mention Washington's approach, but word had somehow leaked out and he was "considered as a person of the most dangerous principles to the safety of the City, as a spy and common enemy of the British Government." As he was "extremely unhappy," Pintard asked Washington to appoint "some other person . . . to take charge of the American prisoners in New York" so he could "retire to my farm."[37] (He later became Washington's wine supplier.)[38]

Despite his faux pas, Washington wasn't yet willing to give up his quest for a New York agent-in-place. On June 27, 1779, Washington suggested to Tallmadge, then stationed in Connecticut, that he make contact with "a man on York Island [Manhattan], living on or near the North River, of the name of George Higday who I am told hath given signal proofs of his attachment to us, and at the same time stands well with the enemy." This Higday had, the previous month, helped three stranded American officers cross the Hudson into New Jersey and they had cited him as a potentially useful friendly.[39]

A week later—on July 2—Colonel Banastre Tarleton, leading a two-hundred-man force comprised of part of his British Legion, the crack Seventh Light Dragoons, the Queen's Rangers, and the Hussars, struck Tallmadge's camp at about five in the morning. Sabers fiercely clanged, and the raiders were eventually repulsed with the help of the local militia, but not before the dragoons had suffered ten casualties and eight men captured, along with twelve horses taken—including Tallmadge's charger, whose saddlebags had contained twenty guineas from Washington intended for Woodhull and, worse, his letter of June 27 mentioning George Higday's name and location.[40]

Tallmadge was mystified by the attack: How had the British known exactly where to find him, and why had they undertaken such a risky operation? What he did not know was that a June 13 letter—not written in the stain—from Washington to Tallmadge that mentioned "C——r" and a "liquid" he was using had been intercepted by the British, who decided to venture capturing Tallmadge himself.[41]

Washington was composed, but was certainly annoyed at what he regarded as Tallmadge's carelessness. "The loss of your papers was certainly a most unlucky accident and shows how dangerous it is to keep papers of any consequence at an advanced post. I beg you will take care to guard against the like in future. If you will send me a trusty person I will replace the guineas." However, "the person most endangered by the acquisition of your letter is one Higday, who lives not far from the Bowery, in the Island of New York. I wish you could endeavour to give him the speediest notice of what has happened. My anxiety on his account is great."[42]

His chiding was not altogether warranted. It had been Washington, after all, who had blundered badly in using Higday's real name, not

Tallmadge. Though the plot to nab Tallmadge had been thwarted, the British couldn't believe their luck in intercepting a *second* letter from the commander-in-chief, and it was read at the highest levels—by Clinton himself. To make matters worse, the June 27 letter had also mentioned "C——r"—so now the enemy had a double confirmation that not only was there an active agent by that alias, but that Tallmadge was head of the intelligence service and was probably operating a ring on Long Island, through Connecticut, and across the Sound.

They could deal with this C——r later. On July 13, troopers broke down Higday's door and arrested him. Terrified for his life, and either convinced already, or persuaded by his interrogators, that Washington had had the letter deliberately intercepted to destroy him, Higday wrote a semiliterate, pathetic confession from prison to Clinton. After he had helped the officers across the Hudson, they said "what a fine thing it might be for me to fetch information over for Washington" and "that he would make me rich in so doing." Granted an audience with Washington, Higday offered his services for pay, and the general agreed to give him some money. Higday's modest intention had been to buy a cow with his wages, but Washington's money turned out to be counterfeit and Higday refused to work anymore. He assumed Washington had put his name "in the black book" and betrayed him out of spite.[43]

It's unlikely Higday was executed, because Clinton, as he told his sisters, was a forgiving man, especially to such confused and harmless small fish as Higday. "From good policy and perhaps a little more feeling than is usual for those in my situation...I have never executed a spy." Why? Because "I have made good use of them by employing them double"—a sentiment belying his self-regarding virtuousness.[44] Indeed, Clinton may have tried to recruit Higday as a "double," but he was useless, for Washington knew he had been compromised. A victim of the spy game, poor Higday went back to his little place on the Bowery and endeavored to disappear.

The Higday gaffe did at least demonstrate to Washington and Tallmadge the urgent need to encipher their letters. Given the chronic shortage of invisible ink, Tallmadge vowed never to allow his agents again to be placed in such danger, and set himself the task of creating a code that would serve as an additional hedge against discovery.

Inventing a workable code from scratch is a tall order. Today's cryptographers (those who create codes, as opposed to cryptanalysts, who break them) are fortunate enough to work for intelligence agencies able to draw on many decades of institutional experience. Tallmadge had no such luck. He lacked instruction manuals, professional advice, and even knowledge of which words to include. The code he eventually conceived may have been simple but it was not a bad one. Though it certainly wasn't up to the cutting-edge standards used by European diplomatic codemakers, Tallmadge was not obliged to shield his men from European diplomatic codebreakers. So long as it frustrated a casual reader, it would suffice.

His code was a distant descendant of the *Ave Maria* cipher created by a priest, Johannes Trithemius, author of the first book printed on the subject, the *Polygraphiae* of 1518.[45] (Men of the cloth made superb cryptographers owing to their ability to translate Hebrew, Greek, and Latin back and forth.) Trithemius constructed a table pairing the twenty-four "plaintext" letters of the alphabet with a selection of nouns, verbs, adjectives, and adverbs. The sender would substitute one of these corresponding words for each letter of the plaintext message to form a coherent prayer—hence *Ave Maria*. I've reproduced a partial example below for the letters A through D:

A—Deus	A—Clemens	A— creans	A—celos
B—Creator	B—clementissimus	B—regens	B—celestia
C—Conditor	C—pius	C—conseruans	C—supercelestia
D—Opifex	D—piussimus	D—moderns	D—mundum

So, if we wanted to encipher "Abbas Trithemius," we would select "Deus" from the A row of the first column, then "clementissimus" from the B row of the second column, then "regens" from the next B row in the third column, and "celos" from the last column and so on.

The Latin prayer of "Abbas Trithemius" would emerge as (once some "nulls," which don't mean anything and can serve as red herrings, and "joiners" to make the sentences intelligible, which I've italicized, were added): "Deus clementissimus regens celos manifestet optantibus lucem seraphicam *cum omnibus* dilectis *suis in* perpetuum *amen* suauitas potentissimi motoris deuotis *semper vbique*."[46]

Trithemius's cipher was clever but laborious, as it used an entire word to replace a single letter. A simple sentence could translate into a page-long prayer—suspiciously lengthy even for the most theologically fervent. It never really took off. Europe's few cryptographers instead relied on a French code system, also dating from the Renaissance, known as a one-part nomenclator.

For this, a codemaker compiled two parallel lists, the first containing plaintext words and the second, numerals in ascending order. Thus, "apple" might be represented by the number 9, and "meeting" by 256, "thunder" by 407, and so on all the way through to "zoo" at 522. Instead of writing words, the cryptographer substitutes a number, so that eventually the message appears as a series of digits separated by periods.

A one-parter does contain a major flaw that only gradually emerged: All words alphabetically between "apple" and "meeting" must necessarily bear numbers between 9 and 256. Given that the science of determining how frequently certain words, bigrams, and letters occurred was in its infancy (in English, for instance, "the" occurs 420 times in every 10,000 words, the bigram "th" 168 times in every 1,000 words, and "e" 591 times in 1,000 words), an observant cryptanalyst would notice a "bunching" of numbers around particular points.[47] Once he had three or four messages in his possession, and having verified that the numerals petered out at about 520, our cryptanalyst could hypothesize that the flurry of code numbers hovering around the 400 mark—or four-fifths of the way through the series—was signaling a frequently used word, probably beginning with "t" and therefore almost definitely "the." Likewise, a bunching in the single digits pointed a finger at the word "a," and in the mid-100s, "from," and in the low 500s, "which." From there, it was a matter of attrition to crack the code; i.e., "of" must be somewhere between 256 and 407, and most likely around the early 300s, so he would start looking for the telltale bunching in that area. Once this basic structure had been established, the cryptanalyst would scour for common military and diplomatic terms: "ambassador," "king," "army," and so on. Sooner or later, the pieces would fall into place.

By the early seventeenth century, the French master cryptographer Antoine Rossignol had worked out how to confound his peers by using a *two*-part nomenclator. The basic principle—turning words into numbers and back again—remained the same, but Rossignol partly randomized the system so that "apple" might be represented by 389 and "zoo" by 25.[48] He did this by giving the encoder a book listing alphabetically all the words that would ever need to be masked, with a random number in the next column. The decoder received a book with the digits in numerical order and the words they represented next to them, rather like a bilingual dictionary. A two-parter made codebreaking more difficult, because if, say, "the" was given the number 262, it did not necessarily mean that numbers 1 through 261 belonged to words running from "a" to "that." Even so, it still suffered from the same fundamental defect as its more primitive ancestor: A cryptanalyst could detect 262 occurring suspiciously often, thereby indicating a lurking "the," and so on down the line of frequency.

One way of getting around the problem was relatively simple: Don't encode common words like "the." Instead, encipher only the more important, but rarer, ones, such as "muskets," "France," and "negotiations." Nevertheless, if the cryptanalyst possessed several encoded messages, he could try to guess the meaning of a number from its context in a sentence by cross-referencing it with the other messages in which the same number was used.

In any case, French superiority in the field had eroded by the early 1700s. Other countries learned to baffle codebreakers by increasing the number of nomenclators from the traditional several hundred to two thousand or three thousand elements—so that each word could have *several* random numbers assigned to it—and including scores of nulls to throw decipherers off the scent. The French responded by using half a dozen sets of nomenclators simultaneously, a decision that caused immense confusion among recipients of enciphered letters who may not have received the newest update.

Despite the complexity of this new breed of cipher, it was often broken thanks to a willingness to cheat. Europe's Black Chambers dug deep in the diplomatic bags to find the freshly issued two-part lists destined for outlying embassies. By the time the local ambassador was perusing his new decrypted mail over breakfast, the local Black Chamber had already read it.

Human error was another major factor. At great expense, England's Decyphering Branch in the early 1700s developed an impregnable four-digit code for diplomatic use only to discover years later that the Foreign Office, thinking it would save some money, had gone on to use the same code in embassies from Gibraltar to Stockholm for more than a decade. Changing the code numbers *at least* three or four times a year, and allotting each embassy a different version, should have been automatic. As it was, the code had been leaked or broken so long before, the Foreign Office might as well have sent its messages directly to the enemy in plaintext.[49] Then there were the diplomats who, after receiving a document written in plaintext from their home government, sent their reply in cipher, so providing enemy codebreakers with a crib sheet of the newest version when they steamed it open about an hour later and compared it with their copy of the original document.

By the eve of the Revolution, it was clear that for the most sensitive diplomatic communications, two-part nomenclators were insecure. To the Americans' rescue rode Charles William Frederic Dumas, a German in his fifties living in the Netherlands, who had turned into a zealous Patriot partly owing to his friendship with Benjamin Franklin. Employed by the Americans as their agent in Holland, and acquainted with the practices of the Black Chambers, Dumas devised a robust system combining an early version of what is known as a "stream cipher" (encrypter and decrypter share the same text for their correspondence) and a randomized key in which any of maybe a dozen numbers could represent the same letter.

The concept is easier to grasp by looking at the first couple of sentences from the patriotic, 682-character-long passage Dumas and Franklin used as their shared source-text for their correspondence: "Voulez-vous sentir la différence? Jettez les yeux sur le continent septentrional de l'Amérique." (Translation: "Do you want to feel the difference? Glance at the continent of North America.")

Then Dumas numbered each character consecutively, e.g.:

V	O	U	L	E	Z	–	V	O	U	S	S	E	N	T	I	R
1	2	3	4	5	6	7	8	9	10	11	12	13	14	15	16	17

L	A	D	I	F	F	E	R	E	N	C	E	?
18	19	20	21	22	23	24	25	26	27	28	29	30

Once the entire passage is numbered thus, the encoder could choose between no fewer than 128 different numbers for "e" (or 63 for "r," 60 for "s," or 50 for "a"). In the sentence above, for example, "e" was represented by 5, 13, 24, 26, and 29. When it came to "w," however, or "k," he was out of luck, for the original passage did not contain them: Franklin and Dumas substituted "uu" and "c" for them. There was also but one number each for "y," "?," and "&"—flaws that no veteran cryptanalyst scouring for such regularities would overlook. Nor would he overlook the Dumas Cipher's other failing—that the encoder must choose between the 128 numbers for "e" as randomly as he can; what Franklin had a lazy habit of doing was repeatedly choosing the first couple of numbers that appeared. In the case of "e"—see example above—he would use 5 or 13 far more often than, say, 29. Again, the frequency of "e" was the dead giveaway.

As far as it went, however, the Dumas Cipher was simple to use and provided fairly good security. The same could not be said of the polyalphabetic system invented by the leading American cryptographer of the time, James Lovell (born in 1737 and Harvard educated), whose cipher was brilliant, yet so confusing that no one could work out how to use it, least of all John Adams, whom Lovell persisted in subjecting to his cipher, much to the former's dismay. For years, he couldn't read the missives the cryptographer sent him.

A boiled-down version follows, using just the first two letters of the keyword CRANCH (the name of a friend of Lovell's and Adams's).

1	C	R
2	D	S
3	E	T
4	F	U
5	G	V
6	H	W
7	I	X
8	J	Y
9	K	Z
10	L	&
11	M	A
12	N	B
13	O	C
14	P	D
15	Q	E
16	R	F
17	S	G
18	T	H
19	U	I
20	V	J
21	W	K
22	X	L
23	Y	M
24	Z	N
25	&	O
26	A	P
27	B	Q

To encipher "bankrupt," find "b" in the first column and write the number to its left; for the second letter, "a," look for it in the second column and write down the number; then for the third letter, return to the first column and continue to alternate. Thus, "bankrupt" becomes "27.11.12.21.16.4.14.3." If one isn't paying attention—and Adams often wasn't—it was easy to miscount and use the wrong column to substitute, thereby garbling the rest of the message. Indeed, Lovell himself used to miscount occasionally, leaving poor Adams still more befuddled than before. And this is all before accounting for Lovell's arcane "rules," such as the one laying down that "29.38" was a signal to the reader to begin deciphering *in reverse*, let alone his fondness for three- and four-letter keys (rather than the above two-letter), which made decipherment even more prone to miscounting. As Abigail Adams told Lovell, her husband was not "adept in investigating ciphers and hates to be puzzled for a meaning." Consequently, Adams switched to the basic, tried-and-true alphanumeric system that was highly insecure but comprehensible, at least. Thus, to his friend Francis Dana, Adams wrote in 1782: "19 presses 18 to come to him, and he thinks of going in ten days"—18 stood for Adams, and 19, John Jay.[50]

Tallmadge couldn't afford the luxury of a top-class diplomatic code—two reasons being the difficulty of training each Culper member in encipherment and ensuring he had the latest key-book—and was obliged to find a simpler, Adams-style solution. He began researching and compiling one in earnest in July 1779. However, almost from the very beginning, the Culper Ring had occasionally employed a stripped-down code consisting of precisely one element: Thus, Woodhull dated his letter of March 17, 1779, "*10* March 17 1779 [italics added]."[51] Subsequently, in April, Woodhull clarified that:

"No. 10 represents N. York
    20   Setauket
    30 and 40   2 Post Riders."[52]

The "Post Riders" were Jonas Hawkins and Austin Roe, and until July, the Ring used just those four numbers. By the end of that month, the Ring had switched to a full-scale Code Dictionary.[53]

The "Dictionary" was the sourcebook of the Culper Cipher, a creaky one-part nomenclator developed by Tallmadge. From his copy of the 1777 London edition of *Entick's Spelling Dictionary,* Tallmadge chose 710 words he thought most useful for his agents—*county, Congress, advise, gun, intrigue, longitude, navy, Tory, war,* and so on—and wrote them alphabetically in the left-hand column; in the next, he numbered the words consecutively. Thus:

many	384
mercy	385
moment	386
murder	387
measure	388

He added 53 numbers, running from 711 to 763, to represent proper names. These included the names of his agents, leading actors, and places. The most important ones, for our purposes at the moment, were:

General Washington	711
General Clinton	712
Tallmadge ("John Bolton")	721
Samuel Culper	722
Austin Roe	724
Caleb Brewster	725
New York	727
Long Island	728
Setauket	729

For those words not listed in the Dictionary, and for digits, Tallmadge added a bare-bones, mixed-alphabet scheme, which was as follows:

Original: a b c d e f g h i j k l m n o p q r s t u v w x y z
Code: *e f g h i j a b c d o m n p q r k l u v w x y ʒ s t*
Original: 1 2 3 4 5 6 7 8 9 0
Code: *e f g i k m n o q u*

Thinking ahead, Tallmadge included a few rules to simplify de-cryption. Transposed digits were to have a double line drawn under-neath to distinguish them from enciphered words; and for words in the past and future tenses and for plurals, a small squiggle, or "flourish," was added above the code number.[54]

Tallmadge's one-part nomenclator is a clone of early French cryp-tographic practice. Even so, in the American theater, it was counted as cutting-edge: It would not be until the fall of 1781 that this type of nu-merical code came into more widespread use.[55] Tallmadge's inspira-tion probably came, indirectly, from the Marquis de Lafayette, who would certainly have been *au fait* with elementary cryptography after his time at court and in the army of a country once the world leader in ciphering.

Lafayette arrived in America for the first time on June 13, 1777, and met Washington on July 31, 1777. The two became firm friends. He stayed until the beginning of 1779, and then returned from France in the spring of 1780. The Culpers began using Tallmadge's Dictionary in mid-1779— during Lafayette's absence. It might have been Washington—never averse to making proposals to improve the Ring's effectiveness—who, re-membering a conversation with Lafayette, described for Tallmadge the rudiments of a one-part nomenclator and code dictionary.

After a few false starts, the Ring quickly got accustomed to this strange new language. On August 6, for instance, part of one of their letters read:

Sorry 626.280 cannot give 707 an exact account 431.625 situation 431.625.635—707.373. think 626.280.249 not taken sufficient pains 634.442.284. I assure 707.626.280.249.190.284 more 146 than 280 expected. It is 282 some measure owing 683[?].379.414 having got 287.1.573 line 431.216 intelligence. To depend 668.80 reports 683.[?].183—I 537.5. conversed 680 two qjjcgilw 431 different 76 from 730 from 419.431 which 280 could 442.2 account 431.625 situation 431.625. army 630. I was afraid 430 being too 526.

The translation, made by one of Washington's aides, is:

Sorry that I cannot give you an exact account of the situation of the troops. You may think that I have not taken sufficient pains to obtain it. I assure you that I have, and find it more difficult than I expected. It is in some measure owing to my not having got into a regular line of getting intelligence. To depend upon common reports would not do. I saw and conversed with two officers of different corps from Kings-bridge from neither of whom I could obtain an account of the situation of the army there. I was afraid of being too particular.[56]

Tallmadge's cipher would not have withstood a Black Chamber specialist for long: The words and numbers were not randomized (so that "artillery" was represented by 46, and "troops" by 635); there were but 760-odd elements, whereas the minimum a one-parter should have had to delay breaking was between 1,500 and 3,000 (including nulls and multiples); and it contained 22 of the 27 most frequently used words— "the," "an," "at," "I"—in the English language. Even a novice cryptologist knew better than to hand out such free clues. Note, also, that the writer of the above letter has transposed "of," "that," and "with" but left "intelligence" and "army" in plaintext. This bad habit soon ceased when it was realized that keeping common words as plaintext while enciphering the rarer, less easily guessable ones, made messages far more secure. Tallmadge, of course, could hardly have been expected to know all this, and one error of his stands out: the omission of an obviously pertinent word, "officers," from his Dictionary, which obliged the sender of the letter above to transpose "qjjcgilw" (Tallmadge's oversight is inexplicable, though he did include "office").

Despite the Culper Cipher's weaknesses, it did the job it was meant for: turning plaintext into code strong enough to baffle an ordinary reader while avoiding the fiendish complexity of Lovell's keyword system. It was never intended to do more than provide backup security, for no matter how innocuous its contents, an encrypted letter is always bound to raise suspicions that something murky is afoot.

Armed with their code and ink, the Culper Ring was already the most "professional" of all Washington's spies. By the summer, having found another candidate for investiture, it would be the most effective.

CHAPTER FIVE

The Man of Parts and Halves

Pleased as Washington was with the Ring's progress in cipher and ink, Abraham Woodhull's failure to place a man in New York nagged at him. Amos Underhill was fine, so far as he went, but his role was to shelter Woodhull at the "safe house" during his stays, not to serve as a bona fide agent digging up material. For the time being, Woodhull would have to do until he could find a suitable candidate for investiture in the Ring. Washington's counsel in the meantime was that "C—— had better reside at New York, mix with, and put on the airs of a Tory to cover his real character, and avoid suspicion." Indeed, as the "temper and expectation of the Tories and [Loyalist] Refugees is worthy of consideration," Woodhull might find it "political and advantageous" to form "an intimacy with some well informed Refugee."[1]

During the spring of 1779, Woodhull heeded his chief's advice and submitted a nice amount of useful intelligence. On March 17, Woodhull followed up his January warning that Clinton was building transports with the news that the general was touring eastern Long Island to hire crews of Loyalists in preparation for a strike to "plunder and distress" the Connecticut seaboard.[2] Washington pondered this. A week later, he informed General Joseph Reed that "the enemy have some enterprize in view." According to "one of my most intelligent correspondants," he should be on his guard everywhere, for "General Clinton (under pretence of visiting the troops) is now at the east end of Long Island," and will doubtless "attempt something that will give éclat to his arms."[3] Washington advised General Israel Putnam in Connecticut to reinforce the militia and have them man the fortifications along the coast.[4] On April 1, Washington instructed his soldiers to come off full alert, as the raid now looked less likely: "Sir Henry Clinton is returned to New York...and accounts from New York mention that troops have been relanded upon Long Island which are thought to be those which went eastward." Even so, "except there should be certain intelligence obtained from Long Island [i.e., from Woodhull] that the matter which has been in agitation is entirely over," commanders must not take their troops fully off guard.[5]

Apart from his success in passing on that intelligence, April was a cruel month for Woodhull. Never comfortable as a spy, the stress of his double life was stretching Woodhull's nerves, and he confessed to Tallmadge that the only reason he remained in the business was because he hoped "it may be of some service towards alleviating the misery of our distressed country, nothing but that could have induced me to undertake it, for you must readily think it is a life of anxiety to be within...the lines of a cruel and mistrustful enemy that I most ardently wish and impatiently wait for their departure."

He was glad his intelligence had been helpful, but Woodhull was beginning to doubt his own fortitude. His lack of education, poor hand, and provincial manners caused Woodhull embarrassment, particularly whenever he compared himself to Tallmadge, whose time at Yale and his membership in the elite officer corps had bestowed a gracefulness and social ease lacking in his less privileged friend. "Whenever I sit down I always feel and know my inability to write a good letter," wrote Woodhull at one particularly low moment. "As my calling in life never required it," he continued, feeling ever more forsaken, "and much less did I think it would ever fall to my lot to serve in such public and important business as this, and my letters perused by one of the worthiest men on earth."[6]

Realizing that his man was liable to crack up, on April 16 Tallmadge sailed with Brewster to Setauket to reassure Woodhull that Washington was properly appreciative of his efforts. Owing to "a violent storm and contrary winds," as well as the unexpected decision by a couple of British officers to billet themselves on Woodhull, Tallmadge was forced to hide in the woods near Woodhull's house for five days. Whenever Woodhull sneaked food to him, the two old friends talked of ways to relieve the pressure. Woodhull was grateful for the fifty guineas Tallmadge brought with him, so at least his monetary concerns were sated, but Woodhull was adamant that if Washington wished him "to discontinue his present correspondence he will most cheerfully quit." However, while Woodhull was as eager as Washington to find a faster route, he worried that safety would be sacrificed for speediness. After much discussion, Tallmadge succeeded in persuading Woodhull to accept the *possibility* of having a man, personally vouched for by him but accepted also by Woodhull, on Staten Island "who will receive his dispatches and forward them at all times." But Woodhull stipulated that the man must "go across with a boat to an appointed place [in Manhattan]" to receive his letters. Under no circumstances would Woodhull go to Staten Island.

From Woodhull's point of view, this was a perfectly reasonable demand. Already taking an enormous risk traveling and staying in New York, there was no reason why Woodhull should be asked to assume another one talking his way past the sentries at the ferries (what business did a Setauket farmer have on Staten Island that required his presence there every two weeks?), and entering the maw of one of the most heavily guarded strongholds in British America—just to meet a contact unknown to him. He wanted to at least have the chance to walk away if he noticed anything untoward about the Staten Island agent when he landed at Woodhull's chosen "appointed place," presumably at one of the quieter wharves. In Washington's eyes, however, Woodhull was asking the impossible. How was he to find an agent on Staten Island who would pass muster by Woodhull when he didn't even have a permanent one in New York?

The Staten Island proposal died soon after, much to Washington's annoyance, for no solution had yet been found to accelerate transmission of the letters to him.[7] As it was, Woodhull continued to insist that, as Tallmadge put it, "any instructions which your Excellency may wish to communicate to Cr. you will please to forward to me as usual, no other person being appointed in this quarter with whom he would be willing to correspond." Jonas Hawkins, to make matters worse, cut back on his duties around this time, halving the number of couriers available and placing the entire burden on Austin Roe's shoulders.

Hoping to moderate Washington's ill temper about his picky spy, Tallmadge did pass on an anecdote, culled during his involuntarily prolonged sojourn in Setauket, that illustrated just how jumpy Woodhull had become. It seems, having received a vial of the stain and being "much pleased" with it, Woodhull sat down to write a dispatch. No sooner had he finished it, but "suddenly two persons broke into the room (his private apartment). The consideration of having several [British] officers quartered in the next chamber, added to his constant fear of detection and its certain consequences made him rationally conclude that he was suspected, and that those steps were taken by said officers for discovery. Startled by so sudden and violent an obtrusion he sprang from his seat, snatched up the paper, overset his table and broke his vial. This step so totally discomposed him that he knew not who they were, or even to which sex they belonged—for in fact they were two ladies who, living in the house with him, entered his chamber in this way on purpose to surprise him. Such an excessive fright and so great a turbulence of passions so wrought on poor C. that he has hardly been in tolerable health since." The two young ladies were actually, it seems, his mischievous nieces.

A few days later, Woodhull's spirits were hardly improved when, on his way to New York, he was mugged near Huntington and was glad to escape with his life. Tallmadge suspected the villains ("I know the names of several") were local privateers who had taken to landing on Long Island "and plunder[ing] the inhabitants promiscuously."[8]

Worn to a frazzle, Woodhull went on almost complete hiatus throughout May, but early June proved almost as hazardous to his health as had April. Writing from Setauket, Woodhull related to Tallmadge on June 5 that John Wolsey, a Long Islander privateer based in Connecticut, had been captured by the British. In order to secure his parole, Wolsey told his captors that while in Connecticut he had overheard—perhaps while one of Brewster's men was blabbing in a tavern—that Woodhull was up to something dubious. On his return to Long Island, Wolsey "lodged information against me before Col. Simcoe of the Queens Rangers."

John Graves Simcoe, a jowly Old Etonian and Oxonian born in 1752, was a junior officer in the Thirty-fifth Regiment of Foot when he arrived in Boston in 1775, but had bought a captaincy within the year and was wounded three times during the New York and New Jersey campaigns of 1776–77. On October 15, 1777, he was promoted to colonel of the Queen's Rangers—Robert Rogers's old outfit—and began turning it into a first-class line regiment, a far cry from the old days.[9]

Simcoe, "thinking of finding me at Setauket came down," but "happily I [had] set out for N. York the day before his arrival, and to make some compensation for his voyage he fell upon my father and plundered him in the most shocking manner." On his return, Woodhull's life was saved only by pleading with "a friend of mine" who contacted a general's adjutant and stood guarantor for Woodhull's Loyalist credentials. Nevertheless, "I am very obnoxious to them and think I am in continual danger."[10]

Woodhull's anonymous but well-connected "friend" was Colonel Benjamin Floyd (1740-1820), a well-meaning, gullible Loyalist militia officer who preferred the solitude of Setauket to campaigning. He was the younger brother of Colonel Richard Floyd, a rebel-rousing Tory militant, and the two of them were cousins of William Floyd, the high Patriot who signed the Declaration of Independence. They were also distantly related to Woodhull through the late General Woodhull's wife, Ruth Floyd (William's sister).[11]

Owing to his ravages of Patriot property, Richard was a popular target of raiders from Connecticut—Caleb Brewster particularly disliked him—suffering them at least thrice, each time "his cattle, sheep, and several of his slaves" being kidnapped. (The British had a contradictory, politically calculated relationship with slavery: They freed slaves owned by rebels, but did not liberate those owned by Loyalists; they freed runaways who joined the army or served as auxiliaries, but not those unable or unwilling to; they stopped the slave trade, but continued to allow female slave auctions and sold blacks captured in enemy uniform. Thus, while it was British policy to promise, as Clinton did in 1779, "every negro who shall desert the rebel standard, full security to follow within these lines any occupation which he shall think proper," this decree did not apply to slaves already living in New York.[12] It was a distinction that caused much jealousy between the enslaved, upright maids serving in rich merchants' houses and the free, but unlettered, farmhands newly arrived from the southern plantations.)

As for Colonel Benjamin, he periodically suffered plundering by his *own* side. Judge Thomas Jones, the acerbic Tory, recalls that in September 1778, Governor Tryon and General De Lancey marched two thousand soldiers and several battalions of militia to eastern Long Island to expropriate cattle belonging to rebel sympathizers. On the way, they stopped at Setauket and dined with Floyd. During supper, their "soldiers robbed him of all his apples, his Indian corn, potatoes, turnips, cabbages, the greatest part of his poultry, and burnt up all his fences."

Very soon after, the hapless Floyd was again plundered—this time by "a party from New England" who "took away his furniture, and robbed him of £1,000 in cash"—and was "carried to Connecticut."[13] Immediately afterwards, Woodhull successfully implored Washington to release Floyd from imprisonment and allow him to return to Setauket. This secret intercession was not prompted by personal regard for Floyd, but because "I am very likely to stand in need of his services."[14] Woodhull had already recognized the utility of having a well-placed—if unwitting—protector.

Thanks to his foresight, Woodhull, for the moment, was safe, but

"I dare say you will be filled with wonder and surprise, that I have had the good fortune to escape confinement. And am sorry to inform you that it hath rendered me almost unserviceable to you." As "I am now a suspected person I cannot frequent their camp as heretofore," continued Woodhull, and therefore "I [propose] quitting 10 [New York] and residing at 20 [Setauket]." To cushion the blow, Woodhull added, "I shall endeavour to establish a confidential friend [in New York] to step into my place if agreeable." Once done, "most probable I shall come to you [in Connecticut]. And shall wish to join in the common defence."[15] In truth, Woodhull was not keen on leaving his parents and his farm to join the army, but if his cover were blown, he would end up dead if he remained on Long Island.

If it had to be, it had to be. "Should suspicions of him rise so high as to render it unsafe to continue in New York," agreed Washington, "I should wish him by all means to employ some person of whose attachment and abilities he entertains the best opinion, to act in his place." It was a pity about Woodhull, but Washington thought his replacement, if one could be found, might be more receptive to "a mode of conveying [his intelligence] quickly," a matter he still regarded as being "of the utmost importance."[16] What Washington didn't know was that Woodhull *already* had his eye on a New York connection. And that Woodhull, his natural patriotism prevailed upon by Tallmadge and against his instinct to flee to Connecticut, would stay in Setauket to act as the new agent's handler.

Three days after offering to resign, Woodhull traveled to New York—for the last time, he expected and hoped—to "settle the plan proposed." He soon reported that "my success hath exceeded my most sanguine expectations." While there, Woodhull had "communicated [his] business to an intimate friend and disclosed every secret and laid before him every instruction that hath been handed to me; it was with great difficulty I gained his compliance, checked by fear." This "intimate friend" was "a person that hath the interest of our country at heart and of good reputation, character and family as any of my acquaintance. I am under the most solemn obligation never to disclose his name to any but the Post

[Austin Roe, by this time] who unavoidably must know it." He "will expect an ample support, at the same time he will be frugal. As long as I am here shall be an assistant and do all that I can."[17] Washington was most pleased with the acquisition, and sent Woodhull ten guineas to cover the money he had lost being mugged.[18]

At last, Washington and Tallmadge had a man in New York. The chain of agents Tallmadge had envisaged in the summer of 1778 was complete. The New York man would gather intelligence, compose his letter in invisible ink and code, and pass it to the courier at a prearranged time and place. The courier (Austin Roe) rode from New York to Setauket, and transferred the letter to Woodhull—either giving it to him in person or, for safety's sake, dead-dropping it in a buried container in one of Woodhull's fields—who would add his own letter containing observations, as well as information given to him by Roe. Then he would signal or arrange with Brewster to land outside town for the pick-up. Brewster took the package across the Sound and gave it to Tallmadge, who usually developed the letters, added his own gloss and comments, and handed all the messages to a dragoon for conveyance to Washington's headquarters.

The new agent was Robert Townsend—soon unimaginatively aliased "Samuel Culper, Junior" and bestowed the code number "723." A secretive, reserved man who found it difficult to form permanent attachments, Townsend remained a lifelong bachelor. He kept his spying activities so much to himself that even the nineteenth-century Townsend family history, which might otherwise be expected to laud him to the skies, contains precisely one unremarkable sentence on the man called Culper, Jr.: "Robert, son of Samuel, died unmarried, March 7, 1838."[19]

His anguished mind writhed with contradictions. He was a man of parts and halves in a time of wholes and absolutes. Half Quaker, half Episcopalian, partly secular, partly devout, somewhat idealistic, somewhat mercenary, Townsend was neither wholly pacifist nor entirely militant. He was an American who refused to fire a musket for his country, a Loyalist who struggled against the British.

Woodhull knew Townsend, then in his late twenties and from Oyster Bay (in western Long Island), because, owing to the shortage of accommodation in New York, Townsend also happened to lodge at Amos Underhill's boardinghouse. Underhill was not only Woodhull's brother-in-law but was also descended from the founder of Oyster Bay, Captain John Underhill, whose Quaker family still lived there. Townsend was probably directed to Amos's house by one of Underhill's Oyster Bay relatives. One can imagine how Woodhull, over the years, slowly warmed to Townsend over the dinner table or at a local tavern as they repeatedly bumped into each other staying at the Underhills'.[20] Robert's father, Samuel Townsend, a local politician of Whiggish bent, was well known the length and breadth of Long Island, and Woodhull no doubt knew, or was made aware, that Robert was one of his boys. Robert, in turn, would certainly have mentioned to Woodhull that he had served for a time under the command of his kinsman the late General Nathaniel Woodhull.

Always cautious about approaching possible recruits to his Ring for fear of betrayal, Woodhull gently sounded out this man with a sterling Patriot background, but one so innocuous he had slipped under the British radar. To all intents and purposes, Townsend was a Loyalist, but he, too, found he could trust Woodhull, another secret Patriot. Eventually, in early June 1779, Woodhull asked whether Townsend was interested in serving his country. Townsend was in.

Unlike Woodhull, Brewster, and Tallmadge (as well as Roe and Hawkins), who were stout Presbyterians with broadly similar backgrounds and whose motives for spying ranged from the adventurous (Brewster) to the vengeful (Woodhull) to the purposeful (Tallmadge), Townsend was a solitary creature prone to bouts of depression, insomnia, and guilt. Despite his "excellent symptoms of health," Townsend, for instance, slept but "middling well," and would spend much of one year "sunk under a low depressed and dejected state of mind."[21]

From his surviving papers emerges a learned, troubled man. Possessing a large library of the standards every gentleman was expected to own—Locke's philosophical tracts, Boswell's *Life of Samuel*

Johnson, Montesquieu's works, the *opera omnia* of Chaucer—and having a weakness for Alexander Pope, trade magazines, and current-affairs journals from London, Townsend's habit was to jot down meaningful passages from them, sometimes adding his own comments and criticisms.[22] Two of these in particular bear witness to his peculiar temperament and tricky predicament. For him, it was evident that "a gloomy and melancholy disposition is...a vice or imperfection; but as it may be accompanied with [a] great sense of honour and great integrity, it may be found in very worthy characters; though it is sufficient alone to imbitter life, and render the person affected with it completely miserable." Townsend's decision to spy was motivated partly by his desire to lighten his "gloomy and melancholy disposition" with a labor requiring "great integrity."

Townsend, who maintained a number of dual identities—Loyalist and Patriot, Anglican and Quaker—that forced him to condemn what he felt was right, was keenly aware of the distinction between public display and private opinion. "The gravest persons," he wrote, "betray an inward esteem for a statesman, who has been the contriver of a very notable piece of political management, at the same time they are... obliged outwardly to censure the immorality of the action."[23] Individuals, in other words, must often say one thing while doing another, sometimes something wicked, and sometimes merely questionable—like spying.

Luckily, we have a single, fragile portrait of Robert Townsend. His nephew Peter took up sketching about Christmas 1812, with Robert being one of his very first sitters the following January. It is a small charcoal picture—amateurishly executed, with thick lines and a clumsy pose—glued into a sketchbook, of a formally dressed, bespectacled Townsend in a chair, reading a book. It is a great pity that Peter drew his beloved uncle so early, for in the years to come, thanks to practice and three months' worth of lessons with one Archibald Robertson of 79 Liberty Street, he developed into a fine artist. The good news is that several distinct family similarities—present but unevolved in the rudimentary Robert portrait—can be seen in Peter's excellent sketch of Robert's sixty-five-year-old sister, Sarah, done twelve years later, as well as in other pictures of the Townsend family. As does her brother, she wears small round glasses perched on a long, aquiline nose; she has high, prominent cheekbones, thin, downturned lips, a firm chin, and an oddly wide space between the upper lip and the nose. Like other Townsends in Peter's sketchbook, Robert has a towering forehead, a slim, even spindly, figure, and short, curly dark hair.[24]

The Townsends were among the first to cross the water from New England and settle on Long Island—when most of it was still Dutch territory—but were relatively recent arrivals in Oyster Bay. In 1645, John Townsend was one of the patentees of Flushing, and he moved to Jamaica in 1656. Both Flushing and Jamaica were towns in what would become Queens County (which would encompass what is today the Borough of Queens and adjacent Nassau County), and John's descendants never left its confines. Samuel Townsend—John's great-great-grandson and Robert's father—originally conducted business from Jericho, but in 1740, when he was twenty-three, he bought a six-acre property in nearby Oyster Bay. Over the next three years, carpenters built a white wooden mansion—dubbed Raynham Hall, after the Townsends' ancestral home of Raynham, Norfolk—designed to accommodate Samuel's growing family.[25] An eighteenth-century real-estate agent later described the Hall as "a commodious two-storey house, with four rooms on a floor, situate near the centre of the village on the main road to the Mill, and about 50 rods from the harbour, with a good barn and other outhouses, a well of good water at the door, an excellent spring 20 rods from the house, a good garden [and] a good bearing orchard."[26] In 1743, when the house was completed, Samuel moved to Oyster Bay, and established himself as one of its leading citizens. Within a decade, he had become Justice of the Peace, eventually becoming town clerk.

On November 25, 1753, Robert—the third of Samuel's eight children (five sons, then three daughters)—was born. His mother was Sarah, the daughter of William and Mary Stoddard, local Episcopalians. The Townsends were Quakers, but Samuel—though a member by "birthright"—may have disappointed them by marrying out. Thankfully, she preferred the Friends, and they piously attended Quaker meetings together, but Samuel himself preferred worldly things. He carried a gold-topped cane and his shoes sported heavy silver buckles. Quakers disapproved as vanity the flaunting of precious metals, so Samuel cautiously avoided trouble with his fellows by otherwise dressing plainly. His conventional, if expensively cut, suits were invariably gray or snuff-colored and his shirts white—all good, sound Quaker colors.[27] Still, the snappy cocked hat he wore bespeaks in Samuel a certain rakishness, a degree of independent-mindedness that sometimes put him at odds with the leadership in Pennsylvania, homeland and cockpit of Quakerism.

This Townsend, though not religiously observant, was culturally Quaker—in education, upbringing, language, and outlook. He resembled, in a way, a modern Jew who eats pork but strongly identifies with humanistic Judaism, or a secular Catholic who, much to his dismay, can't help but perceive the world in terms of sin, confession, and good works. Samuel—whose marriage conveniently made him socially acceptable among New York's Anglican elites—was sometimes torn between his desire to fit into conventional society and the heavy load of a Quaker inheritance he could never quite bear to shake off.

Thus, in 1758—when Samuel is a man of status and wealth, a member of the county gentry, and one accustomed to his inferiors doffing their hats as he passes in the street—we see him writing an intemperate letter to New York's General Assembly calling for better treatment of prisoners; never a popular move during any war, and especially not in the midst of a very nasty French and Indian one. According to a diary entry of March 27 by Oyster Bay's schoolmaster, Zachariah Weekes, "Last Monday was a report about town that Justice Townsend was sent for to meet the Assembly and they said to be brought forthwith dead or alive.... However he went without compulsion and stayed there until last Saturday night."

What had happened was that when a rather shaky Townsend arrived in New York he was arrested by the sergeant at arms and held in custody for a few days. The Assembly found him "guilty of a high misdemeanor and most daring insult on the honour, justice and authority of this House," and fined him heavily. He was released after pledging to behave better in the future. Weekes added: "He returned and since it has been as still as a mouse in a cheese."[28]

What could have brought about this strange display of orneriness? Townsend was simply following the example set by the Philadelphia Quakers. In 1755, they had faced a crisis when the French and their Indian allies invaded western Pennsylvania. For the first time, settlers were being scalped and their towns razed, some a mere seventy-five miles from Philadelphia. In the provincial Assembly of thirty-six members, of whom three-quarters were Friends, there was a taxation bill to raise money for border defenses and militias—measures that offended the Quakers' dedication to pacifism. Politically, the Quaker leadership was uncomfortably divided between those who assented to the taxes in order to preserve Quaker power in the Assembly, and those who stood firm on Quaker pacifist principles, come what may. For a time, the politically minded compromisers held sway and the Quaker bloc voted to supply £15,000 "for the King's use."

Their more spiritually zealous brethren angrily dismissed them as sellouts. If the Quakers bent on their most sacred testimony to appease their critics, they argued, then what next would be sacrificed to gain a temporal advantage? In order to keep the church whole and unified, most of the compromisers—"the Politicals"—resigned their positions in the Assembly in June 1756.[29] By defending the rights of prisoners—while not condemning the war itself—Samuel Townsend had found a median between fortitude and moderation, and sided with the Politicals.

Thankfully, when the clock rolls forward to 1765, Townsend was not faced with another crisis of conscience. Quaker businessmen from north to south strongly opposed the imposition by Parliament of the Stamp Act and the Townshend Duties. Only six days after the Stamp Act came into force, for example, the Philadelphia merchants organized a Non-Importation Agreement; over eighty Friends signed it.[30] They could square this stand with their pacifist principles because American resistance to the government in the 1760s was generally confined to petitions and declarations, and there was nothing in Quakerism barring *peaceful* opposition to iniquitous laws and tyrannical behavior.[31]

By the mid-1770s, Samuel Townsend was known throughout Queens County as a moderate, respectably old-fashioned Whig opposed to radical independence talk; even so, the great majority of its residents regarded him as a dangerous firebrand dead set on dragging them into a war with the Mother Country.

Queens, in short, was for the King. In 1775, of the 3,074 white adult males living there, Whigs amounted to 368 (12 percent), while the number of Tories was more than double that, at 824 (or 27 percent). The "Don't Knows" came to a minuscule 27 (barely 1 percent), but the so-called neutrals outnumbered them all together at 1,855 (60 percent). Neutrals were not genuinely neutral. They were men who generally steered clear of signing petitions or of announcing their political allegiance. International affairs and highbrow perorations on Our Ancient Anglo-Saxon Liberties were of little interest to them, local and personal issues being of far greater concern. Most were farmers or other rural folk, and while they may have grumbled in their cups at the local tavern about the corrupt ministers in London, by their own inaction and acceptance of the status quo they were passive Tories/Loyalists.

Focusing on Oyster Bay, in 1775 there were 660 adult males; of these, 23 percent, or 150, were Quakers. And of that 150, fully 89 percent—or 134—can be classed as neutral or Tory. Which leaves Samuel Townsend as just one of 16 outright Quaker Whigs living in Oyster Bay.[32]

The geography of Queens County also helped define its politics. In the 1680s, following the English conquest, Long Island was divided in three. Kings, the westernmost county, was the smallest but also the nearest to the city of New York; occupying the eastern two-thirds of the island was Suffolk. Between them was Queens, thirty miles long. At 410 square miles, Queens stretched the width of Long Island so that the Sound formed its northern coast and the Atlantic, its southern. Its total population in 1771 was 10,980. Blessed with fertile soil and a leavening of commercial wealth from the city, northern Queens County was richer than the south, where the residents tended to be subsistence farmers. There were also more Anglicans in the south, further predisposing that already inherently conservative half to Loyalism (or neutralism, at least).

In Queens County, enthusiasm for the Congress and its works was distinctly lackluster, much to the Whigs' disappointment. "A great deal of pains has been taken to persuade the counties to choose delegates for the Congress," Lieutenant Governor Colden cheerfully informed the Earl of Dartmouth on October 5, 1774, yet "several counties have refused. In Queens county, where I have a house, and reside in the summer season, six persons have not been got to meet for the purpose, and the inhabitants remain firm in their resolution not to join in the Congress."[33]

Between December 30, 1774, when Samuel Townsend, as town clerk, moderated a public meeting in Oyster Bay to "take into consideration the resolves of the [First] Continental Congress" (which had convened in Philadelphia in September), and the British invasion of Long Island in the summer of 1776, he played some very dirty politics as he tried to wrest power from the Tory Loyalists who ran the county.

Local Tories were furious, for instance, after learning that Townsend had (self-)appointed an Oyster Bay Committee of Observation, as per Congress's instructions. Townsend also stumbled rather clumsily when he agreed to hold the December 30 meeting at the house of George Weeks, a longtime Whig agitator: Tories instantly realized that Townsend and Weeks, the Whig ringleaders, were hoping to ram through an "Oyster Bay Supports Congress!" resolution right under their noses. According to a Tory newspaper report of the affair, about ninety of Oyster Bay's freeholders showed up and voted the "meeting illegal and void" so "that no business could...be done." During the well-orchestrated filibuster, Townsend was heckled and catcalled.[34]

On March 16, 1775, the Committee of Observation (a sixty-strong body of New York Whigs detailed to organize province-wide protests against Parliament) sent a letter to Queens County towns ordering them to hold elections on April 20 to elect delegates to a Provincial Convention. From this Convention, delegates to the Second Continental Congress, due to meet in Philadelphia on May 10, would be selected.[35]

Still annoyed by his embarrassing defeat at the hands of the Tories, and angered that he had failed to capture control of the town, Townsend pioneered a dubious tactic to elect a delegate—by hook or by crook. On April 12, ignoring the wishes of the overwhelming majority of Oyster Bayers, he held a secret rump meeting of the town's Whigs. Predictably, they voted unanimously for their man, Zebulon Williams, to "represent" the town at the Convention.[36]

Despite Townsend's best efforts at ballot-rigging, Whigs could look upon affairs in Queens County only with dismay. In April 1773, Whigs had held 46 percent of all major town offices in Queens County; by April 1775, when they should have been surfing a wave of Patriotic fervor, that figure had plummeted to 32 percent. By way of contrast, in the same period the Tory share rose from 31 percent to 48 percent.[37]

But within a short time of Townsend's secret meeting, Whig spirits revived. On April 23, 1775, news of the Battles of Lexington and Concord reached New York, causing a sensation.[38] The Sons of Liberty paraded through the streets en masse and there were several assaults on soldiers. Lexington and Concord instantly transformed politics and hardened political divisions. As the middle ground slipped from beneath the moderates' feet, they were forced to choose between Loyalism and Patriotism. Townsend chose Patriotism. Then, in early May, the Second Continental Congress convened in Philadelphia, and by the middle of June, Congress had assumed control over the Boston militia as the nucleus of a new national army under Washington's command.

On May 29 the Congress ordered the formation of committees in each town to supervise observance of the boycott of British goods. Rather unpleasantly, activists were requested to provide to Congress by July 15 the names of those found breaking the rules. Samuel Townsend was on the Oyster Bay committee, where he kept a sharp eye out for sneakily recalcitrant Tories.[39]

How many names Townsend turned over to the Provincial Convention cannot be known, but it probably wasn't very many. Throughout Queens County, antagonism to the new regime ran extraordinarily high. Local chairmen were terrified of Tory reprisals and few of them submitted complete lists to the bosses in New York.[40] Their job was not made any easier by Congress's order in September that all weapons not belonging to Whigs were to be confiscated. Cleverly, the Congress had hit upon a ploy that simultaneously disarmed potentially lethal Tories while acquiring free guns for the new American militias.

Unfortunately, while clever, the scheme proved unworkable, even after Congress offered a "certificate of appraisal"—a sort of IOU—for any guns relinquished. The Tories threatened open rebellion: Richard Hewlett of Hempstead, a veteran of the guerrilla tactics during the French and Indian War (and future desecrator of the Reverend Benjamin Tallmadge's Setauket church), went so far as to raise his own, private militia company that he claimed would "warm the sides" of any rebel force that tried to take Tory guns. Even so, William Williams, a Patriot company commander from Suffolk County, was sent to Queens to enforce the law. After a few days, he gave up and reported to the Provincial Congress: "The people [of Queens] conceal all their arms that are of any value; many declare that they know nothing about the Congress, nor do they care anything for the order of Congress, and say they would sooner lose their lives than give up their arms; and that they would blow any man's brains out that should attempt to take them." Cheekily, some "hardy and daring" Tories were even breaking into Whigs' houses and stealing *their* firearms, and on a few occasions they were reported to be "collecting together, and parading in sundry places, armed, and firing their muskets by way of bravado." He specified that he needed at least a battalion to do his job.[41]

What Williams didn't know was that Richard Hewlett—now Captain Hewlett—had been in contact with the British and had arranged for the warship *Asia* to make secret arms drops beginning November 30. Powder, flints, balls, muskets, pistols, even a cannon (plus a gunner) were transferred to Hewlett's militiamen under cover of night on the south shore of Queens County. The Tories were gearing up for a fight.

Williams's problems in Queens notwithstanding, the Patriots were in good shape politically, at least for the moment. On October 13, Governor William Tryon, the Crown's representative in New York, boarded the *Dutchess of Gordon* in New York harbor to await the British troops who would put the rebels back in their place. Buoyant, the Provincial Congress called an election for November 7 so that its delegates—now including Samuel Townsend—could take their seats.

The turnout was better than expected—more than a thousand men across the county cast their votes—but the result was a great deal worse than anyone suspected. Faced with a slate of Whigs (Loyalists were not allowed on the ballot) and a straight yes-or-no question, Tories derived immense pleasure from humiliating their enemies. Samuel Townsend and his colleagues were crushed, 788 to 221.[42]

For the moment, the uppity Tories who dared to reject the candidates selected for them by the Whigs had to be punished. In the eighteenth century, votes were openly cast to minimize the risk of ballot-stuffing, so Congress knew the names and addresses of its 788 foes. Excommunicated from the protection of the law, they were turned into outlaws and the papers published their names as a warning.

On January 3, 1776, Colonel Nathaniel Heard of New Jersey and several hundred Minutemen arrived in Queens County with orders to find, disarm, and arrest the guilty 788. Heard's aggressive policy of stop-and-search (and raid-and-threaten) brought mixed results. Tories voluntarily surrendered six hundred weapons, but on closer inspection these turned out to be rusty or useless—and certainly not the brand-new English muskets delivered by the *Asia*. On the plus side, within a few weeks 471 of the 788 had sworn an oath of loyalty to Whig rule. Nevertheless, dozens of others had scarpered and joined the Loyalist militias.

Heard's replacement was General Charles Lee, who was commanded to "secure the whole body of professed Tories in Long Island." Isaac Sears, a self-made businessman and ringleader of the

Sons of Liberty's radical wing, administered, forcefully, new oaths to recalcitrant Loyalists. These arrests were pretty indiscriminate and at one point Whigs from Oyster Bay and Hempstead complained that the rough tactics were turning even Patriots into diehard Tories. Lee and Sears were recalled, but Continental units were permitted to embark on daily "Tory Hunting parties" in the countryside to scoop up suspects and terrorize sympathizers.

The hardline strategy succeeded, to a point. In the April 1776 elections, the number of Tory officeholders fell from 1775's 48 percent to 30 percent. But Whigs, who increased their share from 32 percent to an unspectacular 37 percent, did not replace them. The real winners were men who ran as independents (jumping from 19 percent to 33 percent). Clearly, Long Islanders were hedging their bets: They didn't like the Whigs, but were too scared to vote openly for the Tories. There was nothing for it but to sit tight and wait until the British army arrived to rescue them.[43]

Robert Townsend, therefore, matured in this hothouse of Whig politicking, though he doesn't seem to have participated in his father's shenanigans. He was too busy learning how to make money in New York, following the traditional path trod by aspiring young merchants, especially those of the Quaker variety. When he was in his mid-teens, his father had arranged for him to enter the "large mercantile House of Templeton & Stewart," whose store "was in Greenwich Street a little above Morris Street with the river shore as its immediate rear."[44] (Greenwich Street, until landfill expanded Manhattan's shoreline, was on the water.) Templeton's was located on the island's west side, a couple of minutes' walk south from Trinity Church; Broadway was virtually next door.

If Townsend walked north up Broadway, he would soon see on his right-hand side the main army barracks, the workhouse, and the jail, all located on the Common, now City Hall Park. The barracks were Spartan affairs: Two or three stories high and square shaped, and divided into small fourteen-man rooms, each contained weapons racks, stoves, cooking pots, candlesticks, and beds (two men to each) with straw mattresses six and a half feet long and four and a half feet wide. The sheets were supposed to be cleaned every thirty days, and sometimes were.[45]

If he happened to walk by between 6 a.m. and 6 p.m., Townsend would have seen soldiers on fatigue duty—monotonous but not back-breaking chores like shoveling snow, cutting wood, unloading provisions, and, hated more than anything else, standing on guard, which every man was required to perform once every three or four days.[46] For hours each day, there was drill, a repetitive series of facings, wheelings, and stiff-legged marching in the synchronized patterns needed to execute the era's complex tactical maneuvers on the battlefield. Mastering the art and science of gunnery required incessant, rote practice. Loading and firing one of the army's standard .75-caliber "Brown Bess" muskets was a twenty-four-step process that had to be repeated until it became second nature. A decently trained infantryman could fire two rounds a minute, though the British army was unique in being able to shoot thrice in that time.[47]

Small wonder that in their free time soldiers fled their barracks, crossed the street, and entered Holy Ground—on Townsend's left—the biggest red-light district on the continent. The Americans had done exactly the same, of course: During his time in New York in early 1776, Lieutenant Isaac Bangs of Connecticut complained that his men were indulging in "intimate connexion[s]" with the "worse than brutal creatures" inhabiting the area; worse, they, and officers, too, had picked up the clap and "the Fatal Disorder," by which he meant syphilis. No fewer than forty men from this single regiment contracted the disease during Bangs's time in New York. Even the upright Bangs may have succumbed to the temptation of a bit of slap and tickle: After all, "the whole of my aim in visiting this place at first" was "out of curiosity," but as he tantalizingly reveals, he subsequently went "several times" more.[48]

Holy Ground was a violent, murky place where one might easily find, as Bangs wrote, two soldiers "inhumanly murdered & concealed, besides one who was castrated in a barbarous manner." (Their mates returned the next day to the brothels where the men were rolled and "leveled them to the ground.") Another time, "an old whore who had been so long dead that she was rotten was this day found concealed in an outhouse."[49]

Killing "cracks," the slang for *nymphs du pave,* was rarely punished by either army, partly because it was so difficult to catch the murderer. So it was that a naval officer thought he could get away with stabbing a madame after one of her employees cheated him, and how in the local taverns, "fireships"—prostitutes known to have venereal disease—were set alight as punishment.[50]

The rest of the Holy Ground slum was a nest of rotgut joints, pawnshops, and questionable taverns, with a sprinkling of molly-houses (gay brothels) and astrologers' stands, and populated by assorted swindlers, hoods, and tallymen—loan sharks who could harry you into prison (or an early grave) if you didn't pay on the nose. Abortionists, unsurprisingly given the number of prostitutes, set up shop there, as well. These were mainly midwives and nurses, often German, working for extra pin money, but some men, usually failed doctors, were known to provide "cures for ladies." Abortion rates were high at the time: One in four children was born either dead or prematurely, both euphemisms for the practice. If a woman hadn't the desire to abort, she could leave her child somewhere—a church usually—as a foundling and hope he was adopted, hand him over to the almshouse (effectively a death sentence, as few infants survived there a year), strangle him, or rent him out to beggars for use as a prop. And in the gloomier recesses of New York's underworld there were always the baby farmers, who bought attractive babies and discreetly sold them to barren couples. It was a cash business and babies that the farmer overstocked and weren't adopted were terminated to keep down expenses.[51]

The house of Templeton & Stewart, which had long dealt with the Townsends, was a "vendue" and retailing operation that catered to the respectable working-class residents of the Holy Ground. A vendue house, essentially, was a combination of a flea market and a discounter used by small merchants to clear slow-selling or damaged stock. The public loved them, because they could pick up goods at everyday low prices, but the large retail stores, with their fat overheads, thought the vendue houses unfairly undercut them.[52] For more upmarket clients, Templeton's also had a retail arm, which sold everything from Connecticut pork to Irish butter to Philadelphia soap.[53] Townsend dealt more with the retail side. In early 1773 he left the firm and on April 1 opened his own dry-goods business ("dry-goods" usually meant one didn't import rum, but during the war, this old colonial distinction softened).[54]

Being concerned solely with his business career, Robert Townsend remained resolutely unpolitical in these tumultuous years. The war, however, would soon change that happy state of affairs. By late June 1776, it was a dead certainty the British were coming to New York. That month, three warships carrying the first contingents of troops under General Howe arrived in lower New York harbor. On July 2— the very same day that the Continental Congress approved a resolution for independence (followed, two days later, by its Declaration to that effect)—Howe occupied Staten Island. By mid-July, ten ships of the line, twenty frigates, and nearly three hundred transports and supply ships clogged the bay. Residents of the city and Long Island could see nothing but a forest of masts across the water. Over the next two months, Howe deployed 32,000 soldiers, the largest expeditionary force Britain had ever amassed.

In order to deprive the British of meat for their hungry army, Samuel Townsend and General Nathaniel Woodhull were ordered to herd the estimated 7,000 cattle, 7,000 sheep, and 1,000 horses in Queens County away from the expected British invasion spot.[55] On August 22, Howe's transports began ferrying 15,000 troops over to Gravesend Bay on Long Island. Washington and his subordinates, in the meantime, had covered the passes surrounding their positions in Brooklyn Heights. But, laboring under the misapprehension that one, Jamaica Pass, was too far away to do Howe much good, had left there just five officers. At 3.15 a.m. on August 27, the unlucky quintet received a rude shock when Howe and 10,000 redcoats poured through the pass after a silent night march. Howe wheeled westward, encircling the 2,500 Patriots manning the other three passes. By 11 a.m., Howe was two miles from Brooklyn Heights. The defenders there were saved only by an adverse wind and the ebb tide that prevented the British grand fleet from sailing up the North River and blasting them to pieces from the rear. Washington himself had come over to the Heights from the city at 8 a.m. only to see his disastrous position collapse around him.

For the moment, however, Howe's men were disorganized and so he dug in six hundred yards from the Heights, intending to besiege the American remnants. Surely, the man would see sense and surrender? On August 29, Washington realized he must evacuate his position or die. He ordered every boat he could find to come across the river, and at 1 a.m. on August 30, the men began boarding. A dense fog rolled in, helpfully obscuring the Americans' activities and allowing Washington and the last of the men—including Tallmadge and Hale—to reach Manhattan safely several hours later.

Meanwhile, Samuel Townsend had been helping General Woodhull herd the livestock onto Hempstead Plain. The operation had not been a success: Woodhull had managed to move fewer than 2,000 head of cattle eastwards. He had, however, only 190 militiamen at his disposal, which made the task an impossible one from the start. Given the dire state of affairs in Brooklyn, and the increasing likelihood of a British victory, each night another dozen of his men would desert.

It is here that Robert Townsend officially shuffles into our history for the first time, albeit briefly. On August 24, the Convention appointed him commissary—the man in charge of ensuring supplies and provisions—to Woodhull, now camped at Jamaica, a short distance from the British lines. The general received notice of this appointment on August 27, most likely when Robert Townsend himself rode out to Jamaica and handed General Woodhull his letter of introduction.[56] Young Robert was not allowed much of a chance to shine. Later that day, when a thunderstorm rolled over Long Island, Woodhull fatally sought refuge at Increase Carpenter's roomy inn. As for Robert, he evaded British advance units as they fanned through Queens County, and by the first days of September, he was almost certainly at home in Oyster Bay, as was his father.

Long Island was soon after cleansed of American insurgents. In the days before the fall, Patriots sent their wives, children, and slaves, as well as their livestock, grain, and stores to Connecticut. One in six Long Islanders departed as refugees, leaving behind their farms, belongings, and homes. In some places, it looked like the *Marie Celeste*. Tory Loyalists emerged with red cockades in their hats or red ribbons on their coats to greet the King's troops as they entered liberated towns. Having been humiliated by the "Tory Hunting parties" and the blacklist of "non-Associators," Loyalists were in no mood to forgive the men they regarded as collaborators with the illegal Revolutionary government. Loyalists informed on leading Whigs, who were taken into custody by the redcoats. Which is how Samuel Townsend came to be arrested in the first week of September 1776.

The day it happened, the sun glared at the troopers of the Seventeenth Light Dragoons—eight of them there were—lusting for water. It was searingly hot and humid, even for September. Their splendid uniforms smelled. Weeks' worth of dried sweat clung to the fibers of the thick, woolen red cloth spattered with muck. Tucked into knee-high black cavalry boots, their yellowish buckskin breeches, designed to ease chafing, were as scuffed and muddy as the once-bright white facings and linings of their coats. Their helmets, cast of brass, padded with leather, and decorated with a crest of dyed red horsehair falling to the shoulder, were heat traps. Whenever a man took his off, a glistening circlet of perspiration crowned him. Even so, a black, burnished plate attached to the front of the helmet added a designedly sinister touch: It featured a death's-head—the symbol usually favored by pirates—with the motto "Or Glory" scrolling underneath.

This little detachment was following up a tip from some Loyalists. They wheeled in front of Raynham Hall and dismounted. The young subaltern in charge, haughty as a warlord, clanked over to the nervous fifty-nine-year-old man sitting on the verandah and demanded whether "Sam" Townsend was at home. "I am the man," he replied. Discourteous to a fault, the officer ordered him to get ready, for he was under arrest and bound for prison. Shaken, Townsend asked whether he could send a servant to fetch his horse, a request rudely yielded (and accompanied, for good measure, by a blasphemous curse).

As he waited, the subaltern (a certain Lieutenant Nettles) strutted about the house, sneering at its plainness, which he naturally associated with backwardness and poverty—the marks of colonials cut off from civilization. True, like every Quaker residence, the furniture was modest and simple, the colors muted, the rooms uncluttered. Spotting a small musket the servants used for hunting fowl, the martinet strode over and shattered it. No rebel had the right to own such a weapon, he declared. In the corner, Samuel's wife and children—Sarah, Phebe, and Robert were present—grew frantic with worry as to his fate.

By now, drawn by the commotion, a knot of people had gathered outside. Among them were the informers who had denounced Townsend to the authorities. Witnessing this dreadful scene, even they were moved to sorrow and pity, according to one Tory present. Allowed only a change of clothes, Townsend was hustled onto his horse and escorted out of town. The dragoons were heading for Jericho, about five miles south of Oyster Bay, where their colonel had his field headquarters.

Along the way, the party met an in-law, Thomas Buchanan, an affluent merchant well known as a Loyalist, who demanded that the lieutenant allow him to accompany Townsend to Jericho. When they arrived at headquarters, Buchanan pleaded to Colonel Samuel Birch that Townsend was harmless. To his credit, and impressed by Buchanan's credentials, the colonel agreed to free Townsend on bail for several thousand pounds and on condition that he be produced with six hours' notice. The two men, one utterly unnerved, arrived home late that night.[57]

Less than a week later, the New York authorities summoned Townsend. There was no heroic defiance; it wasn't cinematic. Instead, Samuel Townsend showed up as directed and Whitehead Hicks, a judge of the Supreme Court, duly certified that "he hath submitted to government and taken the oath of allegiance to his Majesty King George this 10th Sept. 1776 before me."[58]

In swearing his loyalty to the Crown, Townsend's political career was finished. Like so many others on Long Island, he made his peace with the new rulers. His arrest was the first and last time during the war that Samuel Townsend ran afoul of the British authorities. Henceforth, he kept his Whiggish views to himself. Still, Samuel was not quite so tame as he seemed, according to an 1850s recollection of Elizabeth Titus, who knew every member of the Townsend clan, and met Washington thrice to boot. Throughout the war, she wrote, Townsend would arrange to meet some of his old Whig confreres to discuss Washington's progress: "Whenever they used to hear of the escapes of their countrymen on the main[land] they contrived to gather in each other's houses, and find in their joy and mutual congratulations at such auspicious news some consolation for the hardships and the suspense they had to endure on account of their insulated position."[59]

As for Robert, he too bent his knee, for the new British administration was surprisingly lenient and stopped Loyalist harassment of their former tormentors. So long as they could produce someone to vouch for them, most Whigs were released on bail. By the end of 1776, in Queens County alone, 1,293 men had sworn allegiance to their sovereign.[60] All in all, about 3,000 Long Islanders were given certificates proving their loyalty, according to a letter from Tryon to Lord Germain that December. He, said Tryon, "had the satisfaction to observe among them a general return of confidence in govern[men]t."[61]

Accordingly, a note in Robert Townsend's handwriting declares that he was "willing to testify our loyalty to our King," and resolved "to oppose this unprovoked rebellion now carried on against His Majesty's Government." Some decades later, Townsend's nephew recalled that Robert "inclined at first to the Royal cause [and] stood he admitted on one occasion sentinel" in front of the British commander's headquarters "in Broadway near the Battery."[62]

During the British occupation of the city, Robert Townsend, now cleansed of the taint of rebellion, focused on catering to the military class, especially the officers who could afford to spend lavishly on the rum, spirits, sugar, and lemons that went into making a punch with some kick. A Captain Willington, aide to Governor Tryon, was a regular customer. Townsend was also known for being a good source of navy grog, and many a sailor aboard one of His Majesty's ships owed his cracking hangover to Robert Townsend.[63] He even purchased a share in James Rivington's coffeehouse, an officers' favorite, where he would have been well placed to overhear talk of troop movements and army gossip—soon transmitted to Tallmadge.[64]

Rivington was one of the city's more notorious characters. A former bookseller and English emigrant, he founded the *Royal Gazette* newspaper in 1777 and soon became New York's godfather of journalistic hackdom. Newspapers of the era carried almost no local news (readers were expected to already know it) and no editorials (readers were aware of each newspaper's political slant and discounted its coverage accordingly), but they did print official proclamations, shipping reports, price listings, stock quotes, theatrical notices, foreign news, Parliamentary minutes and proceedings, extracts from other papers, and lengthy letters from readers (which essentially served as op-eds). In order to offset their low subscription prices, almost half of a newspaper's pages consisted of advertisements, Lost and Founds, and Help Wanteds.[65]

Upon buying a copy of the *Royal Gazette* from a vendor, who shouted "Bloody news! Bloody news! Where are the rebels now?" the visitor would read of the inexorable brilliance and glory of British arms.[66] As Rivington had an eye for atrocity stories and punchy tavern-talk, his readers were stunned to discover that Benjamin Franklin had been wounded by an assassin and would likely die; that Congress was about to rescind the Declaration of Independence; that the Tsar was sending thirty-six thousand Cossacks to stamp out the rebels; that Washington had been made Lord Protector; and that Washington fathered illegitimate children (a favorite theme of Rivington's, this one), or had died.[67]

He was also adept at spinning the news in such a way as to buoy New Yorkers' spirits, so there was a stream of exaggerated "reports" of Patriot misdeeds intended to persuade citizens they had chosen right by sticking with King George. To this end, *Gazette* readers were informed that nothing was "exempt from the fangs of those devouring locusts," the Whig legislatures; that two men in Dutchess County had been "crucified" by rebels for trying to join the British army, and that another volunteer had been strapped to a tree by rebels, and shot multiple times.[68] Most terrifying of all was the revelation that Washington had allied with France. As part of this diabolical agenda to Romanize stout Anglicans, Washington had agreed to allow French vessels to bring 50,000 mass books, 200 racks and wheels, 3,000,000 consecrated wafers, 70,000 rosaries, and 5 chests of "paint for the ladies' faces." Rivington predicted that Louis XVI would soon be crowned King of America if Loyalist hearts faltered.[69] Not all was doom-and-gloom, however. The *Royal Gazette* printed comic pieces, some amusing still today, like this spoof advertisement, which appeared in the Lost and Found section after the terrible American defeat at Camden: "Strayed, deserted, or stolen, from the subscriber, on the 16th of August last, near Camden, in the State of South Carolina, a whole army, consisting of horse, foot, and dragoons, to the amount of near ten thousand." Anyone possessing any leads as to its whereabouts—"a certain Charles, Earl Cornwallis" was suspected to be the thief—was asked to send the information directly to "Charles Thompson, Esq.; Secretary to the Continental Congress."[70]

Precisely for this sort of thing, Rivington had his detractors. One such was Robert Biddulph, a military contractor's agent sent from London, who observed that "the origin of every report is at a place called Rivington's Corner—which is at the bottom of this [Wall] Street. Before the door of that most facetious printer you will always see a crowd of redcoats, who as naturally repair there after breakfast, as the ox to his crib before breakfast, to hear and assist in the circulation of any thing that may be stirring. Within is the Venerable Rivington himself, clothed in a long gown, & may very properly be called The Priest of the Temple of Falsehood."[71]

Rivington's rag appeared twice a week—on Wednesdays and

Saturdays so as not to compete with Hugh Gaine's *New York Mercury,* which came out Mondays—and had 3,600 subscribers paying three dollars for an annual subscription, with advertisers being charged one dollar per fifteen lines of text.[72] While it took only 600 subscribers to make a paper self-sufficient, Rivington's costs were enormous, employing as he did sixteen men. Like many other newspaper barons, he found his influence greater than his profits. So, in keeping with traditional Grub Street practice, Rivington opened a business on the side. In his case, two. There was, first, a general store selling gloves, stationery, "a few very elegant pictures of the King and Queen," canes, walking sticks, paper hangings, fishing tackle, tea, "gentlemans dress frocks, of scarlet cloth," and "French raspberry brandy."[73] Second, along with at least one other silent investor—Townsend—he maintained his very fancy private coffeehouse, whose customers were forgiven their bills if they passed on stories Rivington could print (unattributed, of course).[74]

The Rivington investment brought Townsend a small income. For his everyday business, he maintained his old connections to Templeton & Stewart, who supplied him with sugar, coffee, molasses, wine, butter, pork, cloth, pepper, tobacco, and tea.[75] Townsend also supplied difficult-to-procure provisions (ribbon and fustian) for his father's firm in Oyster Bay, which, in turn, was patronized by local British and Loyalist units, and he was occasionally fortunate enough to receive fresh produce from Oyster Bay—thanks to his family connections with the area's farmers.[76]

Even with his army contacts providing much-needed revenue, the first years of the war were hard on Townsend (as they were for many a merchant in New York). In late 1779—a few months after joining the Culper Ring—he took on a partner, Henry Oakham, an experienced merchant who had been recommended by Oliver Templeton. The pair opened a store at 18 Smith Street, just off Hanover Square between Queen and Water streets. The partnership was not a happy one, with Townsend accusing Oakham of importing goods on his private account and covertly reselling them to the firm at a vast markup. Oakham and Townsend parted ways in the early spring of 1781.[77]

By that time, however, Townsend was firmly enough established to fly solo once more (and to leave the Underhills' boardinghouse). He rented a store on Pecks Slip from Hannah Cockle for £125 a year, paying her in moderate weekly installments.[78] He had rather good digs. In addition to the store, there was a spare room adjoining it, a cellar, a shared kitchen, and a small bedroom upstairs. Townsend went to Barclay & Co. for his home-furnishing needs. He bought andirons, a bellows, a poker and rake for the fireplace, candlesticks, a guest bed, chairs, and much else. Townsend, a lifelong bachelor, must have had an enthusiastic cook, owning as he did a ladle, a tureen, pepper grinder and salt cellar, milk pot, canisters, teapot, wineglasses (for company), mustard pot, decanters, tumblers, a vinegar cruet, a sugar dish, and cupboards full of pots, pans, cutlery, and plates.[79]

Townsend did well out of the war. According to his Cash Book, between May 1781 and July 1783, he brought in £16,786, and expended £15,161, leaving him a profit of £1,625, or about £750 per year. This was at a time when his monthly "house expenses for sundrys" ran him (depending on inflation and scarcity) between £6 and £14—let's assume it averaged £10. Adding his rent of £125 and those "sundry" costs of £120 a year comes to £255, or 34 percent of his annual income—leaving him more than enough for a young man-about-town to get by on.[80]

Yet, despite the flashy connections and a hefty disposable income, two and a half years after pledging his allegiance to the Crown, Townsend turned his coat in mid-1779 and joined the Culper Ring. Why?

During the crisis of the mid-1750s in Pennsylvania, when the "Political" Quakers broke away from their "Religious" brethren, the latter faction accused them of bending their most sacred pacifist principles to appease their critics. In the end, the majority of Politicals resigned their seats in the provincial Assembly, spelling the end of Quaker secular influence and heralding the rise of more doctrinally fundamentalist leaders. As a result, Quakerism's expansive, universalist experiment in irradiating the masses with the "Inner Light" flickered and died, and was replaced by a reformist, purifying emphasis on spirituality, exclusivity, and withdrawal from the slights of the corrosive outside world.[81] To that effect, the Philadelphia Yearly Meeting decreed that all Quakers must "cease from those national contests productive of misery and bloodshed," for glory and power and treasure were "as dust of the balance."[82] Good Quakers, in other words, would tend their own gardens, not toil in the jungle outside.

In the two decades before the Revolution, meeting attendances rose markedly, the most zealous adherents being the young. Though Robert Townsend, born in 1753 amid the reformist wave, never went as far as some contemporaries—judging by his enthusiasm for commerce, and perhaps because he was half Episcopalian—he did not escape the second, more powerful, undertow created by Quakerism's renewal.[83]

As part of their campaign to withdraw from the world, reformers focused on strict pacifism and obedience. So that outsiders would leave them alone, they espoused a creed of nonviolence and pledged never to rise up, or conspire against, a legal and constituted government. By the 1770s, accordingly, the Quakers had emerged as the stoutest defenders of British rule in the colonies. A torrent of missives to this effect emanated from Philadelphia to meetings north and south. As early as 1770, the Yearly Meeting warned Friends against participating in any activities "asserting or maintaining their civil rights and liberties [against British rule], which are frequently productive of consequences inconsistent with . . . our peaceable testimony."

In January 1775, the Yearly Meeting issued its official position on the looming war. First and foremost, Friends must "discountenance and avoid every measure tending to excite disaffection to the king." The Declaration of Independence not only marked the final rupture between Britain and America, but also that between Quakers and Patriots. In September 1776, the Yearly Meeting barred Quakers from holding any type of public office that could even remotely be tied to the war effort.[84]

However, as evidenced by Samuel Townsend and later Robert Townsend, Quakers never formed a *wholly* unified body of resistance to the war. All in all, some two hundred Friends were purged from their meetings in the first few years of the war either for joining the Continental army or for holding offices under the Revolutionary regime.[85] In particular, what persuaded Robert Townsend to volunteer as a Patriot commissary—a decision that put him at odds with the Quaker leadership—that summer as Washington desperately sought to fend off General Howe on Long Island?

The answer is the Revolution's most electrifying pamphlet, *Common Sense*, by Tom Paine. Almost immediately following its publication on January 10, 1776, *Common Sense* became the century's biggest bestseller; within a year, between 100,000 and 150,000 copies had been purchased, with every edition selling out immediately. Roughly 10 percent of the entire American population owned *Common Sense*, and even that remarkable figure underestimates how many humble colonials it really converted into rebels. Many scores of thousands more may not have owned or read it, but they were familiar with Paine's basic arguments thanks to the extracts run in the local newspapers (which also printed exchanges of letters on the subject) and the counterblasts streaming from the Loyalist presses.

The more ferocious parts of *Common Sense* and its magnificent prose impress themselves on the memory. Less well remembered is the extent to which *Common Sense* is suffused with Quaker tenets, images, and messages. We should not be surprised: Like Robert Townsend's, Paine's father was a Quaker (his mother was an Anglican), and though Paine himself eventually threw off Quakerism for Whiggery (and Deism), he was suckled, raised, and taught in the Quaker tradition.

In tone, *Common Sense* echoes the authors of early religious Quaker tracts, who stressed the responsibility of individuals to participate in the struggle against worldly hubris, corruption, and narcissism so that they, too, might live in a paradisiacal, divine future. For his rousing plea to overthrow the effete despotism of Britain and "begin the world over again" by creating "an asylum for mankind," Paine merely secularized his forefathers' message for republican readers.[86]

Where Paine differs from his Quaker contemporaries is in advocating resistance as the means to create this new world. "Every quiet method for peace [has] been ineffectual," he said, which left only the option of *defensive* war to safeguard Americans' rights, since "the violence which is done and threatened to our persons; the destruction of our property by an armed force; the invasion of our country by fire and sword" justified the use of arms.[87]

Reading these incendiary, heretical words by one of their own—if a fallen, disgraced one of their own—the Quaker leadership was horrified. Ten days after the publication of *Common Sense*, they retorted by issuing *The Ancient Testimony and the Principles of the People Call'd Quakers*. The broadside alleged that a conspiracy was afoot among Whigs to drag America into war with Britain, and sternly warned Quakers to dissociate themselves immediately from all such intrigues. It ended in a declaration of unbending loyalty to the Crown, and called for Friends to "unite in the abhorrence of all such writings" designed "to break off the happy connection we have heretofore enjoy'd" with Britain.[88]

It was blazingly clear to all to just which "Writings" the Quakers were referring. Whereas the original version of *Common Sense* had dealt but fleetingly with Quakerism, in mid-February 1776 a nettled Paine added a short, devastating indictment of the Society and their *Ancient Testimony* to the pamphlet's new edition. In it, Paine accused the leadership of hypocrisy and of turning their religion into a political hobbyhorse by declaring their loyalty to George III instead of maintaining a truly neutralist silence. Paine particularly loathed those reformists who deployed pacifist religious principles to justify their political Loyalism while claiming to stand aside from worldly affairs.[89] For Paine, the "Quaker junto" was "cringing" and "venomous," and little better, he would charge, than "three-quarter" Tories.[90]

Most damagingly, in the addendum to *Common Sense*, Paine declared that his antagonists were not *too* Quakerish, but not Quaker *enough*; the pacifists-at-any-price were not authentic Quakers. *Real* Quakers, the hardy men and women of a century before who suffered such awful persecutions, would never have bowed so humbly to their oppressors. The reformist Quakers had, in short, "mistaken party for conscience" and politicized pacifism, which they exalted as falsely as the Mosaic Jews had worshipped the Golden Calf. Paine countered that following one's conscience, one's soul, one's Inner Light—the founding tenet of the Quaker creed—truly marked the genuine Friend from his ersatz reformist fellows.[91]

Paine's assaults on the reformists inspired a small following among Friends. Patriotically minded dissenters in their ranks had found at last a Quaker (well, partly, anyway) who encouraged them to challenge the conformism imposed by their meetings. For the first time, it was suddenly possible, if not strictly permissible, to be both a Quaker and a Patriot without feeling that one had betrayed the Lord.[92] Still, while they avidly read their Paine, and nodded in agreement as he turned his guns on the reformists, they shuddered at the implications. True, the Quaker leaders erred in aligning themselves so openly with the Loyalists, but was violence the answer? Surely there was some way, a *via media* of some kind, to keep aglow the In-Dwelling Light *and* avoid jettisoning the Quakers' commitment to pacific resistance?

Robert Townsend was one of those ensnared and enraptured by Paine's arguments. *Common Sense* subverted everything he had taken for granted. In his reformist meetings, he had followed the strictures to obey his British masters with an increasingly reluctant heart, and was torn between his desire to fulfill his peace testimony and submit to his Inner Light. No longer was he forced to accept the proposition that the irresistible might of meekness would awe oppressors into submission.

Paine proved that pious Quakers could rebel against injustice without damning themselves. In his eyes, to be an authentic, heroic Quaker, one must *struggle* for liberty and security, and not idly accept the world as it is, fallen as it was. And so, just a few months after the publication of *Common Sense*, we find Robert Townsend volunteering to act as commissary—a logistics post that did not require shedding blood—to General Nathaniel Woodhull of the Queens County militia.

Still, why did Townsend ultimately accept Abraham Woodhull's blandishments? Life was good for well-connected Loyalists in New York, and Townsend was, despite his covert patriotism, a willing British collaborator. Yet he still agreed to spy for Washington, and risk his neck in the process, so by 1779—three years after his brief service with General Woodhull—he must have been seriously disaffected from British rule.

The answer lies in Queens County. Back in 1776, despite his attempts to woo erring Patriots back into the fold, General Howe's primary focus remained the annihilation of Washington as a military threat. But when he failed to trap his rival in Manhattan, Howe's priorities suddenly shifted.

Long Island, once seen as a mere pit stop on the road to victory, turned into the British army's trailer park. One of Howe's officers reported that "in this fertile island the army could subsist without succour from England or Ireland. Forming their camp on the plain, 24 miles long, they could in five or six days invade and seduce any of the colonies at leisure."[93] If the war was going to continue for years, as now seemed probable, Howe needed a place to quarter and feed his troops.[94]

Long Island was that place. Instead of being treated as liberated territory, much of the island became a military camp, and the sovereign's loyal subjects placed under martial law. Corruption became rampant among military administrators, and abuses against persons and property, commonly perpetrated. Where placation and politeness would have worked wonders in guaranteeing a satisfactory food and fuel supply, British officers and their troops needlessly antagonized and inflamed a once hospitable civilian population. By 1779, Patrick Ferguson, a Loyalist militia officer, could worry "that the people in general are becoming indifferent, if not averse, to a government which in place of the liberty, prosperity, safety, and plenty, under promise of which it involved them in this war, has established a thorough despotism."[95] As the years ticked by with no relief in sight, far stouter Loyalists than Ferguson began to wonder, would the Patriot oppressors really have been worse governors than their British liberators?

Queens County was especially hard done by. Even during the Battle of New York, there were reports of plundering and looting by sailors and enlisted men who did not bother distinguishing between Patriot and Loyalist. "These poor unhappy wretches who remained in their habitation through necessity or loyalty were immediately judged . . . to be rebels," wrote Charles Stuart to his father, Lord Bute, a former prime minister. "Neither their clothing or property [were] spared, but in the most inhuman and barbarous manner torn from them."[96]

It was after the battle that the real troubles began. General James Robertson, soon to become military commandant of New York, noticed that "when I first landed I found in all the farms poultry and cows, and the farms stocked; when I passed sometime afterwards I found nothing alive."[97] Some British officers, obsessed by the conviction that "the old hatred for kings and the seeds of sedition are so thickly sown [among] them, that it must be thrash'd out of them [because] New England has poyson'd the whole," experienced some genuinely psychotic moments.[98] "We should (whenever we get further into the country) give free liberty to the soldiers to ravage it at will, that these infatuated wretches may feel what a calamity war is," declared Lord Rawdon, who sometimes seemed a little too excited at the delicious prospect of teaching the locals what a calamity war was.[99]

All might have been forgiven after the violent spurt of looting had the British established a fair or effective system of compensation for the fuel, horses, fodder, transport, and supplies the army needed to requisition. As it was, residents felt that the looting never really ended: Their property continued to be expropriated, only now it was by official edict.[100]

Army transport was one field of particularly lucrative pickings. Quartermasters profited immensely by invoicing London for the official cost of compensating Loyalists for the requisition of their horses and wagons for military use, but paid out an unofficial lower rate to Long Island Tories desperate for cash. One senior quartermaster, after having cleared £150,000 from his scams, departed for England in 1778, where he "lived in the style of a prince." In 1779, his successor also left a rich man, as did *his* successor in 1780 and, finally, another in 1781. How much did they steal? Between 1777 and 1782, the British government blew the stupendous sum of £642,192 on wagon and horse hire alone; much of it was skimmed. To put that figure in perspective, in

1765 the government anticipated that its windfall from the introduction of the hated Stamp Act would amount to £60,000.[101] It would have been cheaper to have let the colonists go untaxed. As it was, the disgraceful and mercenary behavior of many officers, soldiers, and placemen during the occupation toward Loyalist property and sensitivities alienated the very people who had once cheered them as liberators.[102]

Fuel was also subject to graft. Coal was too expensive to ship from Britain, so the forests and orchards blanketing Long Island were chopped down instead.[103] At first, only trees on rebel-owned land were chopped down, but as the war drew on, the British were forced to requisition Loyalist stocks, promising to reimburse owners at a set price for regulation cords of four feet, nine inches. Enterprising barrackmasters, however, would only compensate residents for four feet's worth of wood, the nine-inch difference miraculously disappearing into their pockets amid the paperwork. Like compound interest, those nine inches accumulated over time—to the tune of £55,000 each year (at a time when a cord of walnut was set at £5).[104]

These frauds and swindles were common knowledge, mostly because so many Queens County residents suffered from them. The British imported a vast bureaucracy whose maw was nourished by the constant ingestion of backhanders and kickbacks. Thomas Jones spoke bitterly of the "barrack-masters, land commissaries, water commissaries, forage-masters, cattle commissaries, cattle feeders, hay collectors, hay inspectors, hay weighers, wood inspectors, timber commissaries, board inspectors, refugee examiners, refugee provision providers, and refugee ration deliverers, commissaries of American, of French, of Dutch, and of Spanish, prisoners, naval commissaries, and military commissaries," and their "train of clerks [and] deputy clerks" alongside assorted "pensioners and placemen."[105] Spluttered Jones, "we had *five* Commissaries of Prisoners when one could have done all the business."[106]

For Loyalists, who had long defended their idealized vision of the Mother Country against Whiggish charges of her sons' corruption and hypocrisy, the experience of reality was an unpleasantly jarring one. For Patriots, though it provided cold comfort given their subordinate position, British rule bore out their worst fears and justified the Revolution. As the war progressed, once-steadfast Loyalists quietly switched sides, not out of some newfound ideological principle, but because they reasoned that no matter how oppressive and corrupt Patriot rule was, it couldn't be any worse than what they were experiencing, and might even be a little less so.

No matter their politics, however, everyone in Queens County lived in a militarized zone where civil institutions had been suspended. New Yorkers were not unaware of the irony of their situation. Loyalists had sided with the British, who they believed were defending their rights as free Englishmen against the tyrannical American revolutionaries, yet in the very epicenter of Loyalism, such customary Englishman's rights as trial by jury, privacy, sanctity of property, and elected representation did not exist.[107] So, cheated they may have been, but there was no recourse to the courts.

Taught to believe in the effortless superiority of the British ruling class, Loyalists in New York and Long Island were shocked to discover how brittle these plaster saints actually were. Respect toward their masters plummeted. The British failure to defeat the rebels began to be ascribed not to Washington's ability to keep his army together in the darkest of moments, but to the incompetence, greed, and stupidity of their own side's commanders and civilian leaders.[108]

In Queens County, in particular, the disturbing number of thugs among the well-bred ranks of the officer corps did their bit to alienate the people. Few were punished for their transgressions. When Major Richard Stockton bought flour from one Paul Amberman, a miller, and was humbly asked for payment, Stockton inexplicably regarded it as a personal slight to his honor and allowed a junior officer to horsewhip Amberman. Stockton joined in with a sword and killed him. After Stockton was found guilty of murder at his court-martial, Clinton asked Amberman's widow to forgive the officer so he could be pardoned. She refused, but Stockton was pardoned anyway.

Governor Tryon's aide-de-camp, Colonel Archibald Hamilton, bordered on the insane. In 1779, he assaulted a prominent Tory judge "with all the fury of a mad man." Pulled off the man before he could kill him, Hamilton "got down on one knee in the dung in the Cow Yard" and prayed. Then, again seized by the Furies, he horsewhipped another man, thwacked another thirty times with his sword, and punched a third. He was never punished, and in 1784 Tryon testified that Hamilton "had served with great credit and reputation during the war."[109]

And lastly, Colonel Simcoe of the Queen's Rangers was another one for wanton brutality. It was he who beat up Abraham Woodhull's father. In 1778, Simcoe fell out with the Reverend Ebenezer Prime of Huntington when he commandeered his house. To teach the old man a lesson in humility, Simcoe allowed his men to break the furniture and burn the library. For good measure, they also ransacked the church. The minister never returned to his home and died soon after.

On November 19, 1778, the Townsends experienced the delights of Simcoe at first hand. He had settled on Oyster Bay as the winter, maybe even permanent, quarters for his Rangers regiment. De Lancey's brigade of Loyalists, as well as a force of Hessians, also arrived. Oyster Bay was expected to provide for their wants.[110]

Simcoe built a square wooden fortress on the town's hill, siting artillery at each corner. Inside, like a bailey, a guardhouse stood, immune to musketfire. Surrounding Simcoe's redoubt was a trench surmounted by a barricade of sharpened stakes pointing outward to fend off infantry attacks. For his purposes, Simcoe stripped Oyster Bay bare of wood. Boards from the town's churches were pulled up and used for firewood, and Samuel Townsend's prized orchard was cut down. To add insult to injury, Simcoe then billeted himself, his staff officers, and any friends of his who happened by at the finest house in Oyster Bay, Raynham Hall—the Townsend residence.

Simcoe made his presence felt. The Quaker meetinghouse on South Street was sacrilegiously converted into a commissary store and arsenal, with guards posted at the door. The navy began using Oyster Bay as a base for its enormous forage fleet (a gigantic haystack could be seen from Townsend's north window). Residents were subjected to curfew, and night patrols saw to it they obeyed. John Weeks, for example, was tied to "a locust tree in front of Townsend's" and whipped for defying one of these patrols. It is said he couldn't understand "the language of the Hessian soldiers."[111]

When Robert Townsend first visited his home—now an armed camp under total military control and crammed with drunken soldiers—after November 1778 (perhaps at Christmastime), his reaction can only be imagined. He was bound to have been at first horrified, then enraged, at seeing his father kowtowing to the likes of Simcoe and his sister subjected to the colonel's amorous intentions (including an unspeakably mawkish love poem, apparently the first Valentine card ever sent in America). And that was *before* he heard the tales of woe from his childhood friends and family about the excesses committed by their new, unwelcome occupiers.

Simcoe exemplified the worst aspects of the British army, and the British army in Long Island represented everything the Patriots were struggling against. By 1783, even the most hardened Tories were repulsed by their "liberators." When the British surrendered to Washington and evacuated New York, just one in twenty of the already heavily diminished Loyalist band of diehards left with them.[112] An ashamed British officer recalled, "We planted an irrecoverable hatred wherever we went, which neither time nor measures will be able to eradicate."[113]

As for Robert Townsend, when Abraham Woodhull approached him some six months (June 1779) after his visit, he eagerly volunteered to spy for Washington. At least now he could strike a strong, silent blow against the British. Many disparate elements combined in the making of Robert Townsend; the obscenities in Oyster Bay combusted them.

CHAPTER SIX

The Adventures of the Culper Ring

After his investiture into the Ring, Robert Townsend wasted no time. On June 29, 1779—just nine days after Woodhull informed Washington that he had "communicated [his] business to an intimate friend" in New York—Townsend sent his first dispatch. It was written in a stilted, stiff style, as if it were a letter compiled by an observant Tory telling a friend what had been happening in the weeks gone by. As it would be another month before Tallmadge's Code Dictionary was sent, and because (as he later wrote) Townsend was "not at that time being sufficiently acquainted with the character of 30 [Jonas Hawkins, the messenger]," the new agent preserved his cover by making it as nonincriminating as possible in case the plaintext letter fell into the wrong hands.[1] Hence, "We are much alarmed with the prospect of a Spanish war—Should that be the case, I fear poor old England will not be able to oppose the whole but will be obliged to sue for a peace." Townsend's missive did contain one useful warning: He'd heard from a Rhode Islander, who had briefly traveled with the troops in question, that two British divisions "are to make excursions into Connecticut . . . and very soon."[2] Washington soon had confirmation from General Horatio Gates that "a number of vessels with troops had left Rhode Island and directed their course up the Sound." A couple of days later, they were dropped off in New York.[3] It was a strange maneuver. If Clinton wanted to harry Connecticut, as Townsend had said, why had he not landed the troops on the coast instead of taking them all the way to Manhattan?

Woodhull had been hearing rumors similar to those related by Townsend. On July 1, Woodhull accordingly warned Tallmadge that he "must keep a very good look out or your shores will be destroyed."[4] Uncharacteristically, Tallmadge paid no heed to it, but that was because the next day—as was previously described—his camp was raided by Colonel Banastre Tarleton, who stole one of Washington's letters (as well as some money for Woodhull).

Tallmadge was so worried that the safety of the Culper Ring had been compromised by the attack that he omitted to ask himself why Tarleton's troopers were ranging so deeply into Connecticut in the first place. The reason would become clearer three days later, on July 5, when William Tryon, the royal governor of New York, swooped with 2,600 men—organized into two divisions—on New Haven, having departed New York on July 4 in the transports Woodhull had reported were being built months before. His assault was intended as a diversion to lure Washington out of his Hudson fastness toward the shore. Sir Henry Clinton, with the bulk of the army, would catch him in the open on the way back and finally bring the enemy to battle. Tarleton's raiders were part of Clinton's advance screen, and had taken the opportunity to try to capture Tallmadge.

The first of Tryon's divisions (under General George Garth) quickly suppressed New Haven's few defenders, seized the port, and burnt privateers and some storehouses. Tryon and his men had, in the meantime, taken East Haven. The next day, Garth and Tryon's forces re-formed aboard the transports and sailed to Fairfield, which was almost immediately abandoned by the Americans after the British landed on July 8. Following the precepts of his theory of "desolation warfare" against civilian property and morale, Tryon unleashed his regulars on the town. They were permitted to loot anything they wanted and burn everything they didn't. By the end of the day, 83 houses, 2 churches, 54 barns, 47 storehouses, 2 schoolhouses, the courthouse, and the town jail had been set aflame, and the soldiers returned to the ships dripping with booty. Tryon sailed to Huntington, Long Island, for a few days' rest and recreation. On July 11, he again put to sea and stormed Norwalk, now at least held by several score of militiamen. They proved no match for the Royal Welch Fusiliers and the Guards light infantry, and Norwalk fell within the hour. The takings, yet again, were lavish. Some fifty thousand dollars' worth of property belonging to rebel sympathizers was taken, most of the village was demolished, and almost every whaleboat, privateer, ammunition stockpile, and storehouse was burnt. After returning to Huntington for refitting for a raid the next day, Tryon was disgusted to find that Clinton had ordered a halt to the campaign.[5]

The Culper Ring had warned Washington of the operation in good time—indeed, four days before it actually happened—but the general received the crucial July 1 letter only in the late afternoon of Wednesday, July 7. Since dawn of the day before, he had been away from headquarters touring the American lines. Immediately after reading it, he sent an express to Governor Jonathan Trumbull to apprise him of the imminent attack.[6] By the time Trumbull received it, however, Tryon had already landed, thus explaining why the militia in New Haven, Fairfield, and Norwalk were unprepared. Still, none of this could be blamed on Woodhull, Townsend, Roe, or Brewster: Their message had taken just five days to reach Washington's headquarters from New York. And even then, it had been delayed by at least a day by Tarleton's sweep.

Though Tryon's raids inspired dread and significantly impoverished the inhabitants of the coastline, they were a failure, strategically speaking. They had been intended only as subsidiary to Clinton's attempt to destroy the main body of the enemy, but that had come to nothing. Thanks to the Culper warnings over the previous months, Washington had long been aware that Clinton was up to something and hard-heartedly did not budge from his Hudson strongholds and what he called his "defensive plan" to focus on "one essential point"— despite desperate entreaties from Governor Jonathan Trumbull of Connecticut to send men and arms.[7] ("I can do little more than lament the depredations of the enemy from a distance," Washington replied.)[8] He was right not to split his forces, already severely weakened by the recent expiration of service contracts and the dispatch of troops out west to fight the Indians.[9]

As Washington explained, retaining control of the Hudson "is of so great importance, and the enemy have such a facility, by the assistance of water transportation of moving from one place to another, that we dare not draw any considerable part of our force from this post." It was "very probable in the present case, that one principal object of the operations on [the Connecticut] coast may be to draw us off from the River, to facilitate an attack upon it."[10] On Sunday, July 11— the day Tryon attacked Norwalk—Washington received word from his advance posts that Clinton had marched to Mamaroneck, north of New York, and he ordered General William Heath and two brigades to act as a screen and engage the enemy if necessary while he stayed at his headquarters in New Windsor and plotted a little surprise for Clinton.[11]

At the end of May, Clinton had enterprisingly seized the half-built fort at Stony Point on the west side of the Hudson. On the opposite bank was Verplanck's Point, and between the two of them they not only provided a tight bottleneck on the Hudson but a key connection between Washington's troops in New York and those in New England. Clinton had left seven hundred soldiers and several pieces of heavy artillery in the ramparted redoubt—nicknamed "Little Gibraltar" by its cocky garrison—which was situated on a 150-foot-high promontory surrounded by water on three sides while its fourth was marshland that flooded at high tide. By every rule in the military book, Stony Point was impregnable.

In a brilliant commando strike, just before midnight on July 15, General "Mad Anthony" Wayne led two columns of light infantry (forbidden to load their muskets for fear of an accidental discharge) almost silently up to the very walls of the fortress. They were to rely on their bayonets at close quarters, itself a risky endeavor owing to the fearsome British reputation for fighting steel-on-steel. In twenty minutes, Stony Point had fallen and Wayne had, for the loss of 15 men and 83 wounded, taken 553 rather surprised prisoners and killed more than 60 of their comrades. Clinton was livid at the loss. It had been at Tryon's urging that he had denuded Stony Point of troops in order to provide the governor with enough men to launch his raids. To make matters worse, Tryon's wanton marauding was causing a great deal of trouble with everyone apart from the most hard-line Loyalists. The destruction of Fairfield's churches had particularly aggravated the public, as had the punishment of innocent civilians. Clinton had directed Tryon to harass the coast—though, in his typically ambiguous style, when Tryon requested the authority to raze the towns, Clinton did not *specifically* forbid burning, but just said that he detested that "sort of war"—and now Clinton felt compelled to demand why Tryon had disobeyed his orders. Tryon, not previously a vicious brute and once known as a humane man, had become a hostage of his own, tragic conviction that the rebels' insolence would be tamed by terrifying them. In his apologia for the Connecticut barbarities, Tryon said that no harm had been done by "irritat[ing] a few in rebellion if a general terror and despondency can be awakened among a people already divided...and impressible." Clinton never again entrusted Tryon with a major military command.[12]

Despite their dark warnings, Woodhull's letters of that July otherwise waxed avuncular, and he seemed newly buoyant, perhaps because now he wasn't exclusively relied upon to gather intelligence. Discussing "Mr. Saml. Culper Junr.," Woodhull pointed out that "he hath wrote in the style of Loyalty, I think through fear like me at first unaccustomed to the business," but, he assured Tallmadge, "the longer one continues in the business if unsuspected of more real service can he be." To that end, Woodhull promised to "repeat again to him those instructions that I have received from time to time from you and use my utmost endeavour to acquaint him with the steps I used to take... that a person unaccustomed [to the business] would not readily conceive of."[13]

Woodhull's word was his bond. Soon after, he visited "Mr. Culper, Junr. and repeated again all my instructions ever received from you. I have kept no secret from him." Townsend was, Woodhull reported, "determined to pursue every step that he may judge for advantage and is determined [to] disengage himself from every other business which at present affords him a handsome living." He would, of course, be "frugal of all moneys he may receive, and hath undertaken [spying] solely for to be some advantage to our distressed country."[14]

The "determined" Townsend rapidly proved his usefulness, alerting his masters that "Christopher Duychenik, sailmaker at 10 [New York], formerly chairman of the Committee of Mechanics, is amongst you and is positively an agent for David Mathews, mayor of 10, under the direction of Tryon." Warned Woodhull, "Be very cautious how you handle [this information] for if it should get to the above mentioned persons ears C. Jr. tells me they would immediately suspect him."[15] Indeed, Townsend was adamant that "the particulars [about Duychenik] must be kept a profound secret, as few persons but myself know them, and it is known that I do."[16] This was high-grade intelligence: Townsend was either associating with senior administrators, who had told him about Duychenik, a Loyalist double, or knew people who did.

By August—just a few months after beginning work as a Culper—Townsend was proving himself a difficult agent to run, more difficult even than Woodhull, who, as cell leader, now had to deal with these "human resources" issues instead of Tallmadge. "I have had much discourse with Culper, Jur.," he complained to Tallmadge. "Contrary to his intimation and my expectation, he continues in business, that engrosseth some part of his time, and interfereth with the important business he hath undertaken." Though "I have again most earnestly endeavoured and begged him to disengage himself from all concerns that may interfere with the public business he hath undertaken," Townsend's "reply in substance was this, that he feared his inability." Townsend, while "willing to do all he could to serve his country," would "not leave himself entirely out of the line of business," his reason being that he would be left "destitute of a support thereafter [in] employment when his services may not be required." Further, unlike the altruistic Woodhull, Tallmadge, Brewster, and the others, Townsend wanted, like the good merchant he was, a reward commensurate with the risks he was running. "I do not conceive his views are altogether mercenary yet [he] thinks he should have some compensation," concluded Woodhull, "but his chief aim is to have such a recommendation at the close of this war as will entitle him to some employment" or commission to public office under the new, postwar American government.[17] In his defense, Townsend claimed that he *had* originally intended to quit his business, but now could not, "owing to my having a partner"—Henry Oakham.[18]

Washington, playing Solon and Solomon as master of the Culper Ring, pondered the matter. On September 24, 1779, judgment was handed down. First, Woodhull must tell Townsend that he "may rest assured of every proper attention being paid to his services" after the war. Second, "it is not my opinion that Culper Junr. should be advised to give up his present employment. I would imagine that with a little industry, he will be able to carry on his intelligence with greater security to himself and greater advantages to us, under cover of his usual business, than if he were to dedicate himself wholly to the giving of information. It may afford him opportunities of collecting intelligence, that he could not derive so well in any other manner. It prevents also those suspicions which would become natural should he throw himself out of the line of his present employment."[19] His answer satisfied all parties.

Over the next several months, the Culper Ring honed its expertise and its members grew accustomed to working with each other. There were also a few personnel changes. Jonas Hawkins, the Ring's original messenger, having been only tangentially involved for some time, retired in September 1779. Whereas in April 1779, for instance, Woodhull listed both Hawkins and Austin Roe as the Ring's messengers, by July, Tallmadge had not bothered giving Hawkins a code number (Roe got 724) in his Code Dictionary, and on August 15, Woodhull, in an encrypted dispatch, was obliged to spell out his name: "*Dqpeu Beyocpu* [italics added] agreeable to 28 met 723 not far from 727 & received a 356." ("Jonas Hawkins agreeable to appointment met Culper Junior not far from New York & received a letter.")[20] His final mission in September was botched when Hawkins claimed it was too risky to come into New York. Forcing the annoyed merchant to expose himself by meeting him "at a place quite out of danger on Long-Island," Townsend testily told Tallmadge he believed Hawkins's fears were "merely imaginary" and accused him of "timidity."[21] It seemed clear that the once-courageous messenger was too burnt out, too jittery, to continue in the business. Hawkins was out, most likely voluntarily, but also because Townsend refused to work with him: in his very first letter, Townsend had said he was unsure about the content of Hawkins's character. In his place, Austin Roe became the Ring's sole, permanent messenger—except when Woodhull himself traveled to New York.

Townsend was being far too harsh on poor Hawkins. A month earlier, as Woodhull recorded, Hawkins had been forced to destroy one of the letters when he faced capture by enemy troops, and these days, he continued, "every house is opened at the entrance of New York and every man is searched." It was simply too dangerous to convey letters not written in the sympathetic stain because—owing to the recent raid on Tallmadge's camp—"they have some knowledge of the rout our letters take. I judge it was mentioned in the letter taken or they would not be so vigilant."[22] Indeed, in October, Woodhull judged that "it is too great a risk to write with [plain] ink in this country of robbers. I this day just saved my life. Soon after I left Hempstead Plains and got into the woods I was attacked by four armed men, one of them I had frequently seen in N.York. They searched every pocket and lining of my clothes, shoes, and also my saddle, which the enclosed [one of Townsend's letters] was in, but thank kind Providence they did not find it. I had but one dollar in money about me. It was so little they did not take it, and so came off clear." Woodhull finished by begging Tallmadge not to "mention this" to any of the others, "for I keep it a secret for fear it should intimidate all concerned here."[23] Hawkins's caution, it seems, had been warranted.

But thankfully, Woodhull continued, "I do not think [the vigilance] will continue long so I intend to visit New York . . . and think by the assistance of a 355 of my acquaintance, shall be able to outwit them all."[24] This mysterious "355"—decoded as "lady" in the Dictionary— is mentioned just once in the Culper correspondence. She was Anna Strong, Woodhull's neighbor and wife of Selah Strong, an active Whig and delegate to the provincial Congress before the war who was currently jailed aboard one of the British prison ships as a suspected insurrectionist. Selah's mother was Hannah Woodhull, the eldest sister of General Nathaniel Woodhull, making Abraham and him family.[25] (Incidentally, Selah's sister, Susannah, married Benjamin Tallmadge's father as his second wife.)[26]

The British, it seems, were not stopping and searching "every man," as Woodhull put it, but every *solitary* man, the sort that fit the profile of known spies. But sheer civility might dissuade troopers from stopping, let alone searching, respectable married men traveling to see in-laws with their equally respectable wives—even if that "wife," namely Anna, happened to be someone else's masquerading as your own (and was somewhat older than one might expect since she was born a decade before Woodhull). It was a risk, granted, but Woodhull appears to have been let alone, so he did, thanks to his brave accomplice, "outwit them all."[27]

That September, Woodhull's uncle, Captain Nathan Woodhull, then in his mid-fifties and of Whiggish inclination, was also brought into the Ring; like Anna Strong and Amos Underhill, the captain played a subsidiary role, serving only as needed, or when he could. Thus, on September 19, Woodhull records that "Pevbep Yqqhbwmm"

(Nathan Woodhull) recently returned from New York and had told him "there's a council of war holding of all the general officers... [and] that a large number of troops were embarking" aboard transports.[28] Two months later, Culper sent a "person" to check out troop positions "betwixt this and Huntington" who consequently submitted a lengthy, specialized report. As Captain Woodhull was a serving officer with the local Loyalist militia, and so took a professional interest in such matters, he was most certainly the unnamed "person" employed for the task.[29]

Gaining a mole within the enemy's ranks was a sweet scoop for the Ring, and that fall, there were moves afoot to recruit a still more senior officer in the same militia outfit—Colonel Benjamin Floyd. The idea originated with Tallmadge, who told Washington about Floyd—the hapless Loyalist kidnapped, imprisoned, paroled (on Woodhull's recommendation), and repeatedly plundered (by his own side, and sometimes by the Americans). Tallmadge thought him ripe for flipping: Rather like Robert Townsend, a former Loyalist disgusted by the abuses perpetrated by the British occupation, Floyd, Tallmadge speculated, might well be disaffected from his masters. "From a long and intimate acquaintance with this gentleman," Tallmadge reported to Washington, "I believe him to be of more service in the Whig interest in Setauket then every other man in it, tho' from his family connections I believe he has been in favour of Royal Government."[30]

That letter was written on November 1. Two days later—and certainly not by coincidence—Washington directed Governor George Clinton of New York to ensure that Floyd would not be robbed again by Patriot marauders. He never laid out his reasons for demanding that "proper measures" needed to be taken "to bring [the perpetrators] to justice, and prevent such acts of violence in future" by these minor miscreants, but if Tallmadge had hopes of enticing Floyd into the business it would not do to alienate him.[31]

Tallmadge accordingly requested Woodhull to put out feelers and "take all the pains possible to secure Col. Floyd"—only to be refused. Woodhull argued that Floyd had not, despite appearances, permanently changed sides. And, in any case, he had "no love for Col. Floyd, not for no *Tory* [italics added] under Heaven, but in my present situation am obliged to cultivate his friendship." For that reason, Woodhull "dare[d] not mention to him what you proposed. I do not doubt that he would be glad to hear it and perhaps keep it entirely secret for his own interests, but yet he would view me with an Evil Eye."[32] Floyd was more useful not knowing Woodhull's real business and to keep blithely believing that his distant kinsman was an unassuming Loyalist. Cover had to be maintained. It also didn't help that, as Townsend did Hawkins, Woodhull heartily disliked him. Given Floyd's connections with senior British commanders, his acquisition would have been a genuine intelligence coup, but Woodhull was right to suspect that he might betray the Ring and be turned into a double agent against them.

The fall of 1779 also witnessed a flurry of instructions from Washington, who remained intent on quickening the speed of communication and improving the expanded Ring's efficiency in the face of the increased British surveillance.[33] Townsend, he suggested, "should occasionally write his information on the blank leaves of a pamphlet; on the first second &c. pages of a common pocket book; on the blank leaves...of registers, almanacs, or any new publication or book of small value. He should be determined in the choice of these books principally by the goodness of the blank paper, as the [invisible] ink is not easily legible, unless it is on paper of a good quality. Having settled a plan of this kind with his friend, he may forward them without risk of search or the scrutiny of the enemy as this is chiefly directed against paper made up in the form of letters." Alternatively, "he may write a familiar letter, on domestic affairs, or on some little matters of business to his friend at Satauket or elsewhere, interlining with the stain, his secret intelligence or writing it on the opposite blank side of the letter. But that his friend may know how to distinguish these from letters addressed solely to himself, he may always leave such as contain secret information without date or place; (dating it with the stain) or fold them up in a particular manner, which may be concerted between the parties. This last appears to be the best mark of the two, and may be the signal of their being designed for me. The first mentioned mode, however, or that of the books, appears to me the one least liable to detection."[34]

This was sound counsel. But in fact Townsend had already hit upon a variation of the book idea. He would purchase a new quire of high-quality paper, write his message on a blank in the secret ink, and then insert the page at a predetermined place, say, the fifteenth sheet from the top.[35] Washington's idea was the better one, and less liable to crossed wires, as Tallmadge complained when he wasn't told of the prearranged position: He had to waste much of his precious stain swabbing several sheets to see which one contained Townsend's dispatch.[36] Washington's idea was cheaper as well, since "common pocket books," old pamphlets, and obsolete almanacs were less expensive in wartime New York than good paper imported from England, especially when Townsend was using an entire quire each time. Townsend agreed to change his method.[37]

Overall, Washington was most pleased with the Ring's progress and wanted to establish the Ring on a more "professional" basis. In early October, he summoned Tallmadge for a conference at the Robinson House at West Point.[38] Working together, the two composed a lengthy memorandum laying out Culper Senior's and Junior's responsibilities.

INSTRUCTIONS

C——r Junr, to remain in the City, to collect all the useful information he can—to do this he should mix as much as possible among the officers and refugees, visit the coffee houses, and all public places. He is to pay particular attention to the movements by land and water in and about the city especially. How their transports are secured against attempt to destroy them—whether by armed vessels upon the flanks, or by chains, booms, or any contrivances to keep off fire rafts.

The number of men destined for the defence of the City

and environs, endeavoring to designate the particular corps, and where each is posted.

To be particular in describing the place where the works cross the island in the rear of the City—and how many redoubts are upon the line from river to river, how many Cannon in each, and of what weight and whether the redoubts are closed or open next the city.

Whether there are any works upon the Island of New York between those near the City and the works at Fort Knyphausen or Washington, and if any, whereabouts and of what kind.

To be very particular to find out whether any works are thrown up on Harlem River, near Harlem Town, and whether Horn's Hook is fortifyed. If so, how many men are kept at each place, and what number and what sized cannon are in those works.

To enquire whether they have dug pits within and in front of the lines and works in general, three or four feet deep, in which sharp pointed stakes are pointed. These are intended to receive and wound men who attempt a surprise at night.

The state of the provisions, forage and fuel to be attended to, as also the health and spirits of the Army, Navy and City.

These are the principal matters to be observed within the Island and about the City of New York. Many more may occur to a person of C. Junr's penetration which he will note and communicate.

C—— Senior's station to be upon Long Island to receive and transmit the intelligence of C—— Junior . . .

There can be scarcely any need of recommending the greatest caution and secrecy in a business so critical and dangerous. The following seem to be the best general rules: To intrust none but the persons fixed upon to transmit the business. To deliver the dispatches to none upon our side but those who shall be pitched upon for the purpose of receiving them and to transmit them and any intelligence that may be obtained to no one but the Commander-in-Chief.[39]

That same month, recognizing the necessity of "establish[ing] a very regular communication with Long Island," he wrote no fewer than four letters requesting information on British movements and positions. The reason behind Washington's series of inquiries was that he had heard in late September several reports of the approach of a French fleet under Comte d'Estaing, who had wintered in the West Indies.[40] Any uptick in British activity at New York would signal that Clinton, too, knew of d'Estaing's movements. In the meantime, Washington ordered Generals Sullivan and Gates to ready their armies to march, and began calling up militiamen from Massachusetts (2,000), Connecticut (4,000), New York (2,500), New Jersey (2,000), and Pennsylvania (1,500) as a prelude to coordinating with the French a surprise assault on Clinton. Washington's ambitious hope was that d'Estaing would approve of "an attempt against New York."[41] As he explained, "New York is the first and capital object, upon which every other is dependant. The loss of the army and fleet there, would be one of the severest blows the English nation could experience."[42]

On October 9, a letter from Townsend arrived bearing the worst of news: Clinton's naval scouts *had* spotted d'Estaing. As a result, the New York garrison "was much alarmed," and "all the men of war and a number of armed transports were ordered down to [Sandy] Hook, with several old hulks to sink in the Channel in case d'Estaing should appear. They had also two or three fire ships preparing, and are building a very strong fort at the lighthouse." Clinton had also taken steps to prevent an amphibious assault from Connecticut by deploying the Seventeenth Dragoons and the Queens Rangers, as well as a "considerable number" of infantry at strategic points in western Long Island. Washington's dream of taking New York back was over.[43]

In any case, even had Clinton remained in total ignorance of d'Estaing's approach, the New York attack would never have

Benjamin Tallmadge as a young officer of dragoons. Pale, delicately featured, with a prominent nose and a somewhat bulbous forehead, Tallmadge had a disconcerting habit of cocking his head like a quizzical beagle.

New York in 1776. A ship approaches the southern tip of Manhattan. In late September, a fire would ravage the city and leave much of it a macabre pyre. A bustling mercantile metropolis descended into a degenerate mare's nest, the leading red-light district in North America, the black-market capital of the Revolution. Much of the area visible to the right was never rebuilt, and turned into "Canvas-Town," a hell where paupers, felons, and prostitutes huddled in the burnt-out houses.

(Photo Credit: New York Public Library)

[handwritten poem manuscript]

A fond, humorous poem written by the doomed Nathan Hale to his college friend Benjamin Tallmadge, ca. 1774. The two maintained a lively correspondence. Both of them were teachers at the time, and both would enter secret service. Captain Hale, said his army servant, "was too good-looking to go so. He could not deceive. Some scrubby fellows ought to have gone" instead on his mission.

(Photo Credit: Beinecke Rare Books and Manuscripts Library, Yale University)

The poem in part reads:

"Friend Tallmadge,

Although a first attempt prov'd vain,
I'm still resolv'd my end t'obtain.
My temper's such that I rare give out,
In what I 'tempt for one bad bout.
Were this the case, you'd never see
Lines, form'd to feet and rhyme from me.

But being sadly mortifiy'd
At thoughts of laying it aside;
Revived a little by your letter,
With hopes of speeding better,
At length I venture forth once more,
But fearing soon to run ashore."

Major Robert Rogers was described as "subtil & deep as Hell itself . . . a low cunning cheating back biting villain." Perhaps so, but he was an expert tracker, soldier . . . and spy-catcher.

(Photo Credit: Library of Congress)

Benjamin Tallmadge's first foray into the secret world. He acted as intermediary between Nathaniel Sackett—appointed spymaster by Washington in early 1777—and Major John Clark, who was to operate covertly on British-occupied Long Island. Tallmadge arranged for Clarke to cross the Sound at night using a whaleboat. This letter, dated February 25, 1777, is a summary of a message Tallmadge received from Clarke.

OPPOSITE: "Mr. Talmage writes that he received Intelligence from Long Island by one John Clarke that there were no Troops at Setauket, but part of two Companies at Huntington and one Company at Oyster Bay. That the said Clarke saw the said Companies at Huntington, that the Militia of Suffolk County was ordered to meet on the 16th Febr[uar]y in order to be drafted for the Ministerial Service but that they were Determined not to serve, however if their services were Insisted upon, they were determined to make their Escape in time.

That they are but few who are sufficiently to the Cause. That they had beat up for Volunteers in the Western part of the County but that only three had Inlisted.

I do hereby certify that the Intelligence I have Communicated to Mr. Sackett that came from Long Island I took from [a] Gent[lema]n whose Truth and Veracity I think be Depended on.

John Davis, Capt. 4th New York Regt."

(Photo Credit: Library of Congress)

The letter written from General Israel Putnam to British general Sir Henry Clinton on August 4, 1777—the Year of the Hangman. Putnam was merciless toward any British spies he caught; in this instance, he was succinctly replying to Clinton's plea for clemency for one of his agents.

"Edmond Palmer, an Officer in the Enemy's Service, Was taken as a Spy lurking within our lines, has been Tried as a Spy, Condemned as a Spy, and Shall be Executed as a Spy, and the Flag is ordered to depart immediately.

I. PUTNAM.
N.B. he has been accordingly Executed."
(Photo Credit: Library of Congress)

Two pages from Benjamin Tallmadge's Code Dictionary. On the first page, Tallmadge has written the most important code numbers.

Bolton John	721
Culper Saml.	722
Culper Junr.	723
Austin Roe	724
C. Brewster	725
New York	727
Long Island	728
Setauket	729

(Photo Credit: Library of Congress)

One of the first coded letters, this one written by the newest member of the Culper Ring, Robert Townsend. Unfamiliar with the system, he makes many elementary mistakes. A portion reads:

"Sorry 626.280 cannot give 707 an exact account 431.625 situation 431.625.635—707.373. think 626.280.249 not taken sufficient pains 634.442.284. I assure 707.626.280.249.190.284 more 146 than 280 expected. It is 282 some measure owing 683[?].379.414 having got 287.1.573 line 431.216 intelligence. To depend 668.80 reports 683.[?].183—I 537.5. conversed 680 two qjjcgilw 431 different 76 from 730 from 419.431 which 280 could 442.2 account 431.625 situation 431.625. army 630. I was afraid 430 being too 526."

The translation, made by one of Washington's aides, is:

"Sorry that I cannot give you an exact account of the situation of the troops. You may think that I have not taken sufficient pains to obtain it. I assure you that I have, and find it more difficult than I expected. It is in some measure owing to my not having got into a regular line of getting intelligence. To depend upon common reports would not do. I saw and conversed with two officers of different corps from Kings-bridge from neither of whom I could obtain an account of the situation of the army there. I was afraid of being too particular."

Townsend's most obvious error was to transpose such frequently used words as "of," "that," and "with" but leave key words ("intelligence" and "army") in plaintext. But that was more the fault of Tallmadge, who had compiled the Code Dictionary. Note also Tallmadge's omission of an obviously pertinent word in this context, "officers," from his Dictionary, which obliged Townsend to transpose "qjjcgilw."

(Photo Credit: Library of Congress)

An example of an early coded Culper letter, this one dated August 15, 1779, and written by Abraham Woodhull ("722") to Tallmadge. Woodhull is discussing the courier Jonas Hawkins's ("Dqpeu Beyocpu") destruction of a letter when he faced capture by a British patrol, and mentions that the enemy is stopping and searching civilians more often. However, he thinks that "by the assistance of a 355 of my acquaintance"—a female neighbor—he may "be able to out wit them all." The text reads:

"Sir. Dqpeu Beyocpu agreeable to 28 met 723 not far from 727 & received a 356, but on his return was under the necessity to destroy the same, or be detected, but have the satisfaction to inform you that there's nothing of 317 to 15 you of. There's been no augmentation by 592 of 680 or 347 forces, and everything is very quiet. Every 356 is opened at the entrance of 727 and every 371 is searched, that for the future every 356 must be 691 with the 286 received. They have some 345 of the route our 356 takes. I judge it was mentioned in the 356 taken or they would not be so 660. I do not think it will continue long so. I intend to visit 727 before long and think by the assistance of a 355 of my acquaintance, shall be able to outwit them all. The next 28 for 725 to be here is the 1 of 616 very long but it cannot be altered now. It is on account of their 660 that it is so prolonged. It may be better times before then. I hope there will be means found out for our deliverance. Nothing could induce me to be here but the earnest desire of 723. Friends are all well, and am your very humble servant, 722"

(Photo Credit: Library of Congress)

Robert Townsend expresses his willingness to come back to work for the Culper Ring. At the time, he was annoyed that Austin Roe, the Culpers' messenger, had been late for appointments several times. Townsend—"Samuel Culper, Jr."—sometimes wrote in the guise of a merchant replying to Colonel Floyd's wholly invented order for food and supplies. In reality, Roe picked up the letter from Townsend in New York and delivered it directly to Abraham Woodhull on Long Island for smuggling across the Sound to Washington's headquarters. The hapless Col. Floyd knew nothing of his name being used as cover. In this instance, Townsend could not resist a dig at Roe's tardiness.

"Sir,   New York August 6, 1780

I have recd. yours by Mr. Roe and note the contents. The articles you wanted could not be sent by him as the office was shut before he got down. They shall be sent by next conveyance.

I am, sir,
Your Humble servant,
Samuel Culper, Jun."

(Photo Credit: Library of Congress)

The one member of the Culper Ring who was never afraid to sign his real name was the whaleboatman Caleb Brewster. In this letter to Tallmadge, written at the height of the Whaleboat War in 1780, Brewster describes his encounter with the notorious Tory freebooters Captains Glover and Hoyt, who prowled the seas around Long Island. While Brewster was picking up a Culper letter at 2 a.m. on August 17, 1780, "I was attacked by Glover and Hoyght. I left one man taken and one wounded. We killed one on the spot." A few days later, Brewster went over with three boats "in search of Glover and Hoyght, but could hear nothing of them. They never stayed to bury their dead man. They carried another away with them mortally wounded." Still, the fact that the "cussed [Tory] refugees are so thick I can't go amiss of them" persuaded Brewster to try his luck once more with the wily Glover and Hoyt, but when he crossed again a week later, they had vanished. Soon after, Glover was in the pay of the British secret service. Brewster would have to bide his time to exact his revenge.

(Photo Credit: Library of Congress)

The spoiled poem "The Lady's Dress." During the Deausenberry fiasco, Townsend's cousin was frisked by the Americans and was found to be carrying nothing more than two folded sheets of paper, on which were written this poem. Townsend had followed Washington's directions and written his message invisibly between the lines, but had done so sloppily. When Washington later tried brushing the special chemical developer over the text he rendered it illegible. Judging by where the mess ends, he gave up about two-thirds of the way through. Luckily, or perhaps not, given their dire quality, one or two stanzas remain. The last three lines are, "You may take the dear charmer for life,/But never undress her—for, out of her stays/You'll find you have lost half your wife." Townsend was unmarried.

(Photo Credit: Library of Congress)

The most urgent note Abraham Woodhull ever penned. With the letter from Townsend he sent with it, the Culper Ring helped save Comte de Rochambeau and his newly arrived French troops from a surprise attack by the British at Rhode Island. It had been General Benedict Arnold, then working as a British agent, who had alerted his masters weeks before that "six French ships of the line, several frigates and a number of transports with six thousand troops are expected at Rhode Island."

"Sir,

The enclosed requires your immediate departure this day by all means let not an hour pass for this day must not be lost you have news of the greatest consequence perhaps that ever happened to your country. John Bolton must order your return when he thinks proper.

S.C."

John André, the charming British intelligence officer who managed the Benedict Arnold defection. Women—including Arnold's wife—thought him the handsomest man in America, but his own fiancée broke off the engagement because he lacked "the reasoning mind she required."

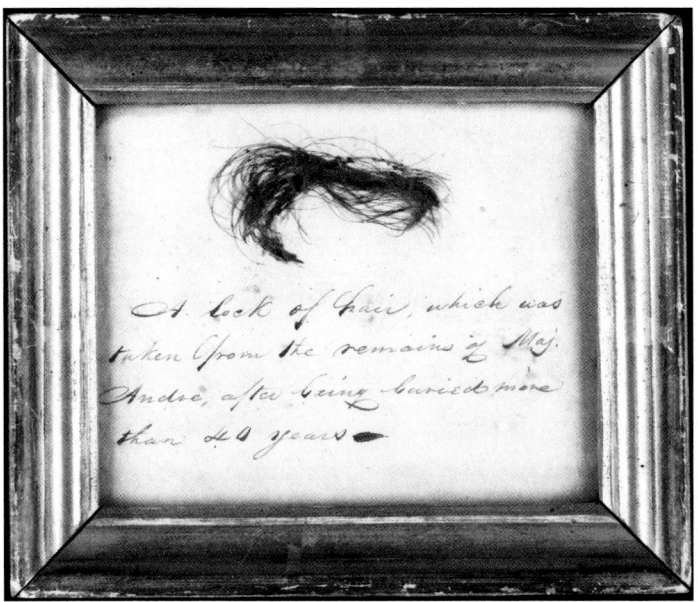

A lock of André's hair, snipped off by a rather gruesome collector forty years after his death.
(Photo Credit: Beinecke Rare Books and Manuscripts Library, Yale University)

Sergeant John Champe escapes his pursuers and embarks on his mission to kidnap Benedict Arnold.

(Photo Credit: New York Public Library)

The insolent letter Benedict Arnold sent Tallmadge proposing that he too defect to the British. "As I know you to be a man of sense, I am conscious you are by this time fully of opinion that the real interest and happiness of America consists in a reunion with Great Britain . . . I have taken a commission in the British Army, and invite you to join me with as many men as you can bring over with you. If you think proper to embrace my offer you shall have the same rank you now hold, in the cavalry I am about to raise." The letter so disgusted Tallmadge he wasted no time sending it directly to Washington, while noting that "I am equally a stranger to the channel through which it was conveyed . . . or the motives which induced the Traitor to address himself thus particularly to me."

(Photo Credit: Library of Congress)

A detailed map drawn for Comte de Rochambeau in 1781 of Lloyd's Neck and Fort Franklin—then commanded by Colonel Joshua Upham—based on information brought back by a Culper spy. Between 400 and 500 soldiers guarded the fort, and large numbers of Tory raiders used Lloyd's Neck as a base. Tallmadge's daring scheme envisaged simultaneously sweeping Long Island Sound with his flotillas of whaleboats to draw off the Royal Navy while up to 20 skilled pilots would land several hundred of his dragoons. Washington had advised Tallmadge to seek naval support from Rochambeau.

On the top left, one can see 1 "high cliffs," 2 "salt meadows," 3 "sand beach," and 4 "north creek" depicted. Also marked, on the beach, is 5 "an inlet where whale boats & barges may be secreted." To the lower left, there the 6 "Fort and Block House by ye enemy." Various houses—mostly belonging to the Lloyd family—are also pictured, as well as roads and ponds.

(Photo Credit: Library of Congress Geography and Map Division)

worked—the French admiral had decided to anchor his twenty-two warships and ten frigates off Georgia, instead, to take British-held Savannah in another show of Franco-American amity. His attack on October 9 was a disaster. Against a numerically inferior, but strongly entrenched, foe, d'Estaing and General Benjamin Lincoln suffered nearly 1,000 dead and wounded compared with British losses of 40 and 63, respectively.[44] D'Estaing, who had been hurt in the battle, sailed to the West Indies in high dudgeon.

Even before news of the British victory at Savannah had reached New York, Townsend was reporting that his officer friends were saying large detachments of Clinton's troops had embarked on transports. "It's generally believed that they are destined for Georgia"—an indication that Clinton was considering sending reinforcements to the South, now beginning to be regarded as Loyalist territory and Washington's weak point.[45] Townsend's intelligence was accurate, though in this case military scouts sent Washington more detailed information: A regular regiment and a force of light infantry and Grenadiers did sail.[46]

In the event, Clinton decided against the plan and recalled the reinforcements before they got too far. Instead, he adopted a defensive position in New York as winter drew in. Later in October, Townsend and Woodhull followed up. "The enemy have large magazines of wood and forage and are daily collecting more, particular hay. Some of the [commissaries] of provision say they have enough of all kinds to last 9 months. I believe they have plenty for six months."[47] From his end, Woodhull added that "they have collected nearly all the forage in Queens County and [are] carrying it to Brooklyn; in one word, every preparation is a making for their defence."[48]

Even if it seemed that the excitement was ending, Woodhull was getting jumpy, as he always did when soldiers were nearby. While naval activity was decreasing, the British were making threatening troop movements all over Long Island. On November 5, Captain Nathan Woodhull told him that the "Prince of Wales American Regt." was at Jamaica on their way to Huntington, and there was "much talk about their coming to this place soon, and we are greatly alarmed about it. Should they come here I [Abraham Woodhull] shall most certainly retreat to your side as I think it will be impossible for me to be safe."[49] A week later, Woodhull was beside himself with worry. On November 10, he had arranged to meet Townsend "at a house he appointed twelve miles west from here, and set out with all my letters to meet him, and just before I arrived at the appointed place I suddenly met a foraging party of 40 horse and 200 foot and about 100 wagons. Was much surprised but after answering a few questions passed them unmolested." However, "to my great mortification Culper Junior did not come that day. I waited all the next . . . I am much concerned."

The reason for Townsend's absence was probably due to either sickness or a reluctance to venture out to a secret rendezvous when British troops were on maneuvers. Woodhull, however, nervous at the best of times, was close to the end of his tether. "I am tired of this business, it gives me a deal of trouble, especially when disappointment happens." It required his every reserve of fortitude to stay in the game. As he confided to Tallmadge, he "could not consent to be any longer an assistant if I was not almost an enthusiast for our success. I [have suffered] a full year's anxiety, which no one can scarcely have an idea of, but those that experience. Not long since, there was not the breadth of your finger betwixt me and death. But so long as I reside here my faithful endeavours shall never be wanting."[50]

Just as Woodhull was faltering, Townsend hit gold and revived the Ring's spirits. If anything proved to Woodhull the necessity of his staying on, it was his colleague's news that the British "think America will not be able to keep an Army together another campaign. Truth reasons that [the Americans'] currency will be entirely depreciated, and that there will not be provision in the country to supply an Army [for] another campaign. That of the currency I am afraid will prove true, as they [the British] are indefatigable in increasing the quantity of it. Several reams of paper made for the last emission struck by Congress have been procured from Philadelphia."[51]

What Townsend had stumbled upon, most likely in his conversation with various officers and officials in Rivington's coffee-house, was the British campaign to undermine the American war effort by destroying the Continental currency. New York was the nexus of this counterfeiting trade. Though coin clipping and forging were hanging offenses, and counted in Britain as high treason, the orders to churn out hundreds of thousands of fake dollars came from as august a figure as Lord Germain, as the Americans discovered in January 1780, when one of their privateers boarded a Royal Navy vessel carrying a letter from Sir Henry Clinton confirming that "no experiments suggested by your Lordship; no assistance that could be drawn from the power of gold, or the arts of counterfeiting, have been left unattempted."[52]

Indeed, as early as four years before, Governor Tryon had supervised a counterfeiting operation aboard the *Dutchess of Gordon*, his maritime headquarters floating off New York. Later captured by Patriots, one Israel Young, who was up to his neck in the business, saved it by testifying to the Provincial Congress that an acquaintance of his, a hatter and felon named Thomas Vernon, had been aboard the *Dutchess* and had told him that "they had on board a number of Rivington's types and one of his printers" and that he had seen a chest full of fake—and professionally done—bills, though in Vernon's expert opinion the paper used was "rather thicker" than the original. Vernon had recruited Henry Dawkins, a noted forger already in jail for counterfeiting, for Tryon, who contracted to pay the latter "a hundred pounds for his trouble." Vernon had found, he told Young, "a plate to strike Pennsylvania money" in Dawkins's chest while rifling through it for things to steal—no honor even among forgers, it seems. (Dawkins was also jailed, but after being released some years later, he was engaged to engrave the seal of the State of New York.)[53]

In 1777, the British had shaken Patriots' confidence in their genuine dollars by telling them they were really fakes. Royalist papers like Hugh Gaine's *New York Gazette and Weekly Mercury* printed public "editorials" noting, by the by, that "there has lately been . . . a large distribution in the country of counterfeited Continental bills, so admirably executed, as not easily to be discerned from those issued by order of the Congress. This has contributed not a little to lower their value, and will be one effectual bar to their repayment or liquidation."[54] Gaine, of course, was fully aware—as were his British overseers—that this report would be digested and worried over in Patriot areas. A couple of months later, aiming to rile up the rebels against their own leaders, the *Gazette* cleverly spun the story that it was *Congress* perpetrating the fraud "in order...to increase the credit of the Continental currency." Warming to its theme, the paper added that "many reams have been brought over by merchants and others, and distributed for that purpose."[55]

The British still needed willing conduits to circulate the fake notes. One way of finding volunteers was to advertise all the free money available. One classified ad in the newspapers blatantly declared: "Persons going into the other Colonies may be supplied with any number of counterfeit Congress-Notes, for the price of the paper per ream. They are so neatly and exactly executed that there is no risk in getting them off, it being almost impossible to discover that they are not genuine. This has been proved by bills to a very large amount, which have already been successfully circulated. Enquire for Q.E.D. at the Coffee-House from 11 p.m. to 4 a.m. during the present month."[56] Such were the machinations of British intelligence that when Washington was sent a clipping of the ad, he stormed to Congress that it proved "that no artifices are left untried by the enemy to injure us."[57] By November 1777, Rivington's paper could observe that Continental bills had plummeted to seven to the silver dollar and that in Congress-controlled areas "the necessaries of life have risen to such exorbitant prices as makes them almost unattainable to those not concerned in the rebel army."[58]

A year later, the situation grew catastrophic as counterfeits flooded the rebel states and covert Loyalists paid their taxes with them, even as Washington insisted on death penalties to deter distributors.[59] John Blair and David Farnsworth, two New Hampshire Tories in the pay of British intelligence, were caught in Danbury, Connecticut, on October

7, 1778, carrying no less than $10,007 in American dollars printed in New York. Washington directed that it was "necessary to have them executed" and, quite profanely, ordered "a sensible clergyman to get as ample a confession from them as possible" for further intelligence on their masters.[60]

On December 16, 1778, belatedly grasping the efficacy of British dirty tricks, Congress recalled the bills of credit it had authorized at Philadelphia in May 1777 and at Yorktown in April 1778. "Counterfeits of those emissions," stated Congress, "have lately been issued by our enemies at New York, and are found to be spreading and increasing fast in various parts of these United States."[61] It did no good—despite a coup occasioned by the capture of the *Glencairn*, bound for New York, by the *Deane*, an American frigate. Before *Glencairn* was boarded, a sailor saw a crate being thrown overboard and fished it out. In it were discovered "materials for counterfeiting our currency, consisting of types, paper with silk and isinglass in it &c." intended, its original keeper confessed, for British forgers working for the government.[62]

By the summer of 1779, Continental bills became, literally, "not worth a Continental," having depreciated to 30 to a silver dollar, and a soldier's monthly pay being worth no more than two shillings in hard British currency. In New York itself, where a single guinea bought 200 dollars, you could use the stuff as wallpaper.[63] Matters were not helped by Congress's own free-and-easy recourse to the printing press to finance the war: In 1774, a man lucky enough to possess £100 could purchase 8,190 pounds of beef; seven years later, the same sum bought 25 pounds' worth.[64]

It was amid this drastic state of affairs that Townsend reported that the British had procured from Philadelphia "several reams of paper made for the last emission struck by Congress."[65] Now in possession of the actual blank paper, the enemy no longer would have to use a thicker substitute, and could accordingly print perfect copies of the Congressional notes. Upon receiving this missive, Washington composed a lengthy letter to Congress, warning them of the danger (while referring allusively to "a confidential correspondent in New

York").[66] On March 18, 1780, partly as a consequence of Townsend's intelligence, Congress was forced to retire and recall all its bills in circulation, effectively declaring bankruptcy to save itself. (Fourteen months later, a French subsidy and a Dutch loan helped rescue the country.)[67]

Washington's satisfaction with his "intelligencers," as he liked to call them, was short-lived. It all began with Washington's resurrected desire in December that the Culpers find a faster way of sending their reports. For the winter, he was to be based in Morristown, New Jersey, and was understandably worried that the letters' route through Connecticut was too circuitous. "It would be a very desirable thing [if] a channel of communication [could] be opened a cross the North river, or by way of Staten Island," he told Tallmadge. "If C—— can fall upon a line which he thinks he may safely trust I wish it to be adopted; but if this cannot be accomplished he will continue his communications in the old channel, and make them as constant as the season will admit."[68]

Still swollen with pride with Townsend's counterfeiting scoop, Woodhull had shrugged off his previous doubts and was unusually chipper in his reply, partly because the troops he had so feared had turned out to be inexperienced militiamen. "I have the pleasure to inform you my fears are much abated since the troops have been with us," he wrote to Washington, adding, "Their approach was like death to me. Did not know whether to stand or fall. Had they been the Queens Rangers or Legion should have been with you before now." He had been especially happy to learn that his nemesis, Colonel Simcoe, who had beaten up his father and made threats, had been captured and was being held in New Jersey. Indeed, "were I now in the State of New Jersey without fear of Law or Gospel, would certainly 344 Gqm. Ucngqi [kill Col. Simcoe], for his usage to me." Regarding a change in the route, Woodhull said he was intending to meet Townsend in New York on Christmas Day and would discuss it with him then.[69] Unfortunately, Woodhull forgot to mention it.

Washington wasn't amused. In early February 1780, annoyed that

Woodhull had dropped the ball, he instructed Tallmadge to "press him [Townsend] to open, if possible, a communication with me by a more direct rout than the present. His accts. are intelligent, clear, and satisfactory, consequently would be valuable but owing to the circuitous rout thro' which they are transmitted I can derive no immediate or important advantages from them." As "I rely upon his intelligence" and "am sensible of the delicacy of his situation, and the necessity of caution," he wanted to "name one or two men to him who will receive and convey to me (through others) such intelligence as he may think important." Woodhull, in other words, was becoming extraneous to Washington's needs, and the commander was willing to cut him out and deal directly with Townsend. Washington went so far as to suggest "a much better way" for Townsend to communicate with him so that even "if the agents should be unfaithful, or negligent, no discovery would be made to his prejudice." His advice? "Write a letter a little in the Tory style, with some mixture of family matters and between the lines and on the remaining part of the sheet communicate with the stain the intended intelligence."[70]

Owing to Washington's impatient decision to drop Woodhull, who hadn't sent him anything of interest in months, the Culper Ring came close to fissuring in the spring of 1780 as Townsend sought to explore this fabled passage through New Jersey. Townsend was too cautious to use any of the contacts Washington wanted to offer, and instead employed his teenaged cousin James Townsend (1763–1831) as the secret courier to go across the Hudson.[71] As that part of New Jersey was heavily Loyalist, James's cover story was that he was a Tory visiting his family in a rebel-controlled area and was seeking to recruit men for the British army. Unfortunately, James immersed himself a little too deeply in his false persona (and the bottle) and got carried away when he visited a house owned by the Deausenberrys, secret Patriots who astutely suspected him of being a spy but pretended to be Tories to catch him out. The mission was a disaster.

What we know of what happened is contained in a March 23, 1780, deposition by John Deausenberry, who said that

James Townsend came to his house . . . last evening and appeared to be something in liquor. The arrival, and appearance of said Townsend gave the family suspicion that he was an unusual person, and to know the truth the family retired, leaving only the two young women (daughters of the deponent's uncle) who undertook to [illegible] Townsend, pretending they were Friends to Britain &c. . . . [Deausenberry] heard the young women examine Townsend, and heard Townsend tell them that he (Townsend) was within two miles of New York City the day before yesterday, whither he went to carry a quantity of stockings to his uncle, and brother, that he went down with an intention to join the [British] army. But his uncle and brother advised him to return immediately and collect as many others as possible, to go [to] the enemy, when they came up the river, which they expected would be the latter part of the present week, or the beginning of next. . . . That he (Townsend) has persuaded many a good fellow, and sent them to join the enemy himself, and that he had very frequently in the course of last summer been backwards and forwards to and from the enemy, had piloted several companies to [British positions], and that he had carried in, and brought out, many valuable articles, that he had been taken once by the Damn'd Rebels, and left him confined and chained down flat upon his back, in the Provost three weeks . . . and finally made his escape by breaking out—this and no more the Deponent heard, for his spirits rose, he flew into the room upon Townsend, and took him prisoner.[72]

Dragged to the local Patriot headquarters by the jubilant Deausenberrys, Townsend was frisked, but was found to be carrying nothing more than two folded sheets of paper, on which were written a lengthy poem, "The Lady's Dress"—in Robert Townsend's handwriting, and perhaps composed by him. Townsend, of course, had followed Washington's directions and written his invisible message between the lines. He had done so sloppily, and when Washington later tried brushing the chemical reagent over the text, he rendered it illegible. He gave up about two-thirds of the way through. Luckily, or perhaps not, given their dire quality, one or two stanzas remain. The last three lines are, "You may take the dear charmer for life, / But never undress her—for, out of her stays / You'll find you have lost half your wife."[73]

Informed that a "British spy" by the name of Townsend had been arrested, Washington was livid, not at the Deausenberrys or at his own men, but at Culper Junior. It took the commander-in-chief's personal intervention, and a great deal of trouble, to secure the teenager's release. Townsend, for his part, was not only angry at the embarrassment he had brought upon himself, but scared: The debacle demonstrated just how simple it was to get caught, and his cousin had been fortunate indeed to fall into the hands of the Americans. James could quite easily have fluffed his lines among enemies, and Townsend, like anyone else, feared the sound of soldiers clumping up the stairs to arrest him after James was interrogated.

As for Woodhull, Tallmadge had filled him in about the Deausenberry venture before he went to New York to visit Townsend in early April. It wasn't a happy meeting. Townsend was petulant and curt, and Woodhull received "nothing but a short memorandum from C. Junr. on a scrap of paper which he said contained all worthy of notice." Woodhull, annoyed both at Townsend going behind his back and his foolhardiness in sending a green agent behind the lines, thought "him exceedingly to blame and guilty of neglect. And have given him my opinion in full upon the matter [and] hope that the like may never happen again."[74] Townsend responded by playing the diva, and told Tallmadge he would "continue no longer" in the business. On April 19, Woodhull again traveled to New York to dissuade Townsend from quitting, but "returned this day after making every effort possible with his utter denial."[75] At this point, Tallmadge stepped in and arranged a joint meeting for May 1 that he hoped would reconcile his warring spies, but it was canceled owing to Townsend's continued intransigence. A few days later, Woodhull, who disliked dissension, embarked on one last trip to the city to see Townsend. While the Quaker "declines serving any longer" as a correspondent, Woodhull was glad to report that Townsend *was* still willing to "give verbal information as he can collect" but would relate it only to him in person. It's clear that James's capture had seriously unmanned Townsend, and that he was now too afraid to compile written reports, which could be tracked back to him if intercepted. Still, the fact that he would pass on intelligence by mouth would do for the moment, even if poor Woodhull was obliged to assume the risk of going to the city for it.[76]

Washington, however, was rapidly losing his patience with Tallmadge's agents. His temper was not improved by Woodhull's incessant requests for money, such as this one: "I have recd 20 guineas sometime ago, which you sent me and with them have been paying off the expenses already accrued, and find a balance still due me. As soon as convenient could wish you to forward me an additional sum."[77] On May 19, Washington fired off a brusque letter to Tallmadge informing him that as Townsend had quit and Woodhull had seemingly lost his enthusiam, "I think the intercourse may be dropped, more especially as from our present position the intelligence is so long getting to hand that it is of no use by the time it reaches me." However, he kept his options open by asking Tallmadge to inform "the elder C. that we may have occasion for his services again in the course of the summer, and that I shall be glad to employ him if it should become necessary and he is willing."[78]

Woodhull was terribly shocked by his idol's coldness. He "intimates [that we] hath been of little service," Woodhull complained. "Sorry we have been at so much cost and trouble for little or no purpose. He also mentions of my backwardness to serve. He certainly hath been misinformed. You are sensible I have been indefatigable, and have done it from a principle of duty rather than from any mercenary end." Woodhull, now out quite a lot of money, had to add that he "perceive[d] there's no mention made of any money to discharge the remaining debts, which hath increased since I saw you."[79]

As quickly as Washington's anger had erupted, it passed. A little less than two months after he had shut down the Ring, he reactivated it upon hearing that a naval squadron under General Jean Baptiste Donatien de Vigneur, Comte de Rochambeau, was nearing Rhode Island. "As we may every moment expect the arrival of the French fleet a revival of the correspondence with the Culpers will be of very great importance," and he asked Tallmadge to see if he could engage "the younger" and "prevail upon the elder to give you information of the movements and position of the enemy upon Long Island."[80] Rochambeau, Washington hoped, would be less feckless than d'Estaing, and he might be willing to participate in a New York venture.

Tallmadge arrived in Fairfield on the morning of July 15—after gently reminding Washington that they were "something in arrears to [Woodhull], and in order to enable him to prosecute the business, it may be necessary to afford him a small supply of money."[81] Brewster, luckily, was hanging around the harbor, and agreed to sail to Setauket that night, but when he landed, Woodhull was too sick to leave his bed. Austin Roe, however, was available, and the next day he rode for New York to ask Townsend, first, whether he was interested in employment, and second, if he knew whether the British were aware of the French fleet's imminent arrival.[82]

What Roe brought back was explosive. So imperative was the intelligence that Townsend deigned to break his own rule and compiled a letter written in stain, hidden between the lines of an order for merchandise purportedly sent by the long-suffering Colonel Floyd—who unwittingly proved his usefulness once again. Cleverly, so as to provide Roe with a legitimate alibi in case he ran into a patrol, Townsend included a letter to Floyd saying, "Sir, I recd. your favor by Mr. Roe [which is crossed out but can be read] and note the contents. The articles you want cannot be procured, as soon as they can will send them. I am, Your humble Servant, SAMUEL CULPER."[83]

Unfortunately, the stain letter has been lost, but Woodhull, still ailing, paraphrased its contents in the package he gave to Brewster— along with the most urgent note he ever penned: "The enclosed [from Townsend] requires your immediate departure this day by all means let not an hour pass for this day must not be lost you have news of the greatest consequence perhaps that ever happened to your country."[84] Townsend, apparently, had warned that the British were aware that the French, carrying vital arms and troops, were close and were intending to ambush them. "Admiral Graves with six ships of the line," had just arrived, and had been "joined by three more out of New York [and] has sailed for Rhode Island," where the French had landed. "Also 8,000 troops are this day embarking at Whitestone for the before mentioned port."[85]

In fact, unsuspected by anyone, Clinton had known that Rochambeau's "six French ships of the line, several frigates, and a number of transports with six thousand troops are expected at Rhode Island in two or three weeks to act under General Washington" since June 12, which had given him plenty of time to plan a welcome party. His spy was General Benedict Arnold, who had been told all the details by Washington a few days before he betrayed them to his new British masters.[86] (Clinton also had an agent in Rhode Island who would send a map detailing the exact location and names of the French ships in the bay, as well as an estimate of their troop strength.)[87] As it usually took weeks to muster a force together, collect provisions, and gather the necessary transports—so making it obvious that some movement was afoot—Clinton's foreknowledge had allowed him this time to make his preparations on the quiet. If all went well, Rochambeau's soldiers—tired after their long voyage, unfamiliar with the terrain, and camped out in the open—would be surprised by Clinton's redcoated veterans and put to flight while the Royal Navy pounded the French squadron. Such a bloody blow after d'Estaing's embarrassing performances would surely cool Paris's ardor for her American allies. Washington would again be left to face the lion alone—and it was doubtful this time whether he would be able to pull off another Trenton or Princeton.

Woodhull's package, courtesy of Brewster, arrived in Connecticut on the morning of July 21, a Friday, but Tallmadge could not be found. Brewster roused a dragoon and ordered him to rush the letters to

Washington's headquarters. Washington, too, was away, and the dragoon left the package with Alexander Hamilton, who deciphered the dispatches and grew alarmed at their contents. At 4 p.m., with Washington still touring the lines, he made the decision to pen a letter for Rochambeau, the French commander, stating that he had "just received advice...that the enemy are making an embarkation with which they menace the French fleet and army. Fifty transports are said to have gone up the Sound to take in troops and proceed directly to Rhode Island." He sent express riders to catch up with the Marquis de Lafayette, who, unsuspecting that the British had caught wind of the landing, had left headquarters on the seventeenth and was leisurely wending his way to Newport to rendezvous with Rochambeau to help coordinate Franco-American operations.[88]

When Washington returned to camp that evening, Hamilton filled him in. The next evening at 9 p.m., Tallmadge, now having returned, was told by Brewster of what had happened; after forwarding the intelligence to Washington (who already had it, of course), Tallmadge urgently requested Generals Robert Howe and William Heath to steel themselves for a possible British attack.[89]

Washington, however, had shrewdly seen an opportunity to launch an attack of his own on the British. Knowing that Clinton would have to denude New York of troops for his expeditionary force, so leaving it vulnerable, Washington commissioned several senior officers to appraise the possibility of taking the city. Opinions were mixed, but tended to be negative; even emptied of troops, New York remained a formidable stronghold. Colonel Jean Gouvion of the Engineers thought that a siege could work but that it would take "forty or fifty days" to break through the fortifications, even if they were, as he judged, weak and poorly constructed. Washington would need, he continued, at least forty cannons, large amounts of ammunition for troops, a thousand shells for the artillery, plus another hundred for the mortars. It couldn't be done, in other words, before Clinton had returned from his hunting trip to Rhode Island.[90] Generals Greene and Knox were similarly pessimistic about the logistics of the operations, with Greene saying that the only way success could be achieved would be if Washington forcibly requisitioned supplies from the public—a politically difficult decision. In sum, "the time is by far too short to make the necessary preparations for such an important expedition."[91]

It was a moot point, in any case. "Though I seriously intended to attack New York if Clinton had gone to Rhode Island," Washington later told Lafayette, ultimately Clinton did not vacate New York.[92] "In the hope that I might yet be in time to undertake something offensive against the enemy," the British general explained to London in August, "I determined as speedily as possible to put a body of troops afloat in the Sound, ready for operation to the eastward, if further information should warrant it, and not too distant to return rapidly, and act against the rebel army, should they, in my absence, form an enterprise against these posts." Adverse headwinds at Hell Gate, it seems, "conspired to retard the arrival of transports at Frog's-neck," and he was only able to embark most of his troops on the twenty-seventh, during which time "all hope of success from a *coup de main* were of course wafted away." Like Washington with his New York plan, Clinton lacked the artillery and ammunition needed for a protracted siege of Rhode Island, and he chose to stay at home. Like Washington, too, Clinton enjoyed a secret service, and knew that his foe, "by a rapid movement, had, with an army increased to 12,000 men, passed the North-river, and was moving towards King's-bridge, when he must have learned that my armament had not proceeded to Rhode-Island. He (I apprehend in consequence of this) re-crossed the river, and is now near Orange Town."[93]

Robert Townsend, despite his critical assistance during the Rochambeau affair, was still proving reluctant "to continue the correspondence," though Washington belatedly authorized Tallmadge to give Woodhull whatever was owed to him as a reward for his good work.[94] On August 1, however, Tallmadge brought encouraging news. He had conceived a way of shortening the line by transporting the Culper letters "over at Cow Neck, to the westward of Oyster Bay. If this can be effected, dispatches may be brought from N.Y. to the White

Plains [headquarters] in twelve hours [in] emergencies, as the whole land course on [Long Island] would not exceed 22 miles, and the Sound not more than ten miles over." Townsend had been impressed by, if somewhat guarded about, the idea as he had "near relations living [near] Cow Neck whom if I can also engage, I am sure of Cr. Junr.'s services." A bonus for Townsend would be that "a change of men through whom letters may pass" in the future might be arranged: Austin Roe, it seems, had been tardy for several meetings with Townsend in the past and the courier's carelessness had contributed to Townsend's reluctance to pen letters. In short, Townsend "has consented to give intelligence but does not say how long."[95]

Woodhull by this time was also having trouble with Roe, whom he had begun mentioning in a slightly disparaging tone: "Being still in a feeble state (but mending) was obliged again to have recourse to Austin Roe," is one example.[96] It was also clear that keeping Roe on was proving expensive, according to an invoice sent by Woodhull. He had reimbursed Roe £34, more than double the £15 or so given to Townsend and thrice Woodhull's own expenditure of £11-odd. (Of the total of £60.18.8, Woodhull had received only £18.18.8, leaving him down £42—a great deal of money.)[97] Tallmadge, however, was reluctant to dispense with Roe just yet and reminded Washington, before he made a cost-cutting decision that might prove rash, that the messenger was "obliged always to ride to New York from the place where the boat lands and wait Culper's answer; his expenses on the road and in the city for himself and horse must be very considerable."[98] Washington agreed to wait.

Still, the Culper Ring was almost always most effective when Woodhull and Townsend communicated face-to-face rather than using an intermediary. Woodhull received a conciliatory note from his old comrade. Using his clever stratagem of writing to poor Colonel Floyd in the guise of a merchant, Townsend confided that the "articles you wanted" had not been sent because "the office was shut" before "Mr. Roe" finally showed up—a catty little comment—but signaled that he was again open for business, so to speak, by saying "they shall be sent by

next conveyance."[99] Woodhull, greatly heartened by Townsend's thaw-
ing, immediately prepared to depart for New York "for the benefit of
our 115 [correspondence]."[100] Ten days later, Woodhull returned from
the city, and was exceedingly "happy to inform you that Culper Junior
hath engaged to serve as heretofore."[101]

Washington was "very much pleased that the correspondence with
C—— is again opened. I have the greatest dependence in his good intentions and I am persuaded when he pleases to exert himself he can
give the most useful intelligence."[102] Tallmadge assured his chief that
"respecting the man, he is a gentleman of business, of education and
honor," and was willing to "shorten the route on certain conditions."[103]
A commercial animal, Townsend simply wanted to reconfirm that his
postwar needs would be taken care of before signing on. "Should
[Townsend] continue serviceable and faithful," replied Washington,
"and should the issue of our affairs prove as favorable as we hope, I
shall be ready to recommend him to the public, if public employ shall
be his aim, and if not that I shall think myself bound to represent his
conduct in the light it deserves and procure him a compensation of another kind."[104] The Culper Ring was back, but for how long?

CHAPTER SEVEN

On His Majesty's Secret Service

Bt the same time as the Culper Ring was resurrecting itself in the late summer of 1780, Sir Henry Clinton was poised to spring a trap. Clinton's goal in this round against Washington was the capture of West Point, a key American stronghold on the Hudson River that allowed Washington to move men, supplies, and arms between Massachusetts and Connecticut to New Jersey, Pennsylvania, Delaware, and Maryland.[1] His agent was General Benedict Arnold, who had persuaded Washington to appoint him West Point's commander.

Arnold's military laurels were undoubted by all. He had fought valiantly at Ticonderoga and had played a decisive role in the Saratoga campaign, at one point daringly, and almost single-handedly, preventing Burgoyne from escaping at the Battle of Bemis Heights. But he was resentful that he was continually passed over for promotion and not given the honors he felt were due him for his brave service. After Arnold was wounded badly in the leg, Washington put him in charge of Philadelphia during his recuperation, and it was while there he grew increasingly discomfited with the French alliance and more comfortable with Tory views, not least because of his engagement to Peggy Shippen, the vivacious daughter of a local Loyalist. Sensing blood in the water, his enemies arranged for a court-martial for two minor misdemeanors, which earned him a mild rebuke from Washington, who was aware of the ludicrousness of the proceedings and tried to salve Arnold's amour propre with the promise of high command. By then, however, Arnold had mulled too long on the injustices he had suffered and his thoughts had turned to treachery. And it was then that he asked for, and received, West Point.

Arnold's enemies had their reasons. Tallmadge, for one, greatly disliked him. He had become "acquainted" with Arnold, he told a friend, "while I was a member of Yale College & he residing at New Haven, & I well remember that I was impressed with the belief that he was not a man of integrity. The revolutionary war was coming on soon after I left college, & Arnold engaging in it with so much zeal, and behaving so gallantly in the capture of [General] Burgoyne, we all seemed, as if by common consent, to forget his knavish tricks."[2]

Arnold, a heroic and valiant soldier, was a low, sly Iago among traitors, but this defector was also the most senior mole in espionage history and a first-class intelligence asset. His betrayal poleaxed Washington. Even his peers, who thought him arrogant and snotty, had respected his undoubted martial talents, and none suspected him capable of treachery of the blackest dye. The British secret service, approached by Arnold in May 1779, ran him until September 1780, when the plot, by merest chance, was uncovered at the very last moment.

Until Arnold's recruitment, British intelligence operations had lagged behind Washington's, whose Culper Ring surpassed anything Clinton, let alone General Howe, had constructed. Washington, too, appreciated the craft of intelligence far more than did Clinton (or other senior commanders), and naturally grasped the need to acquire reports from myriad, often contradictory sources behind the lines, to cross-reference their information to distinguish between fact and fiction, and to analyze and evaluate their timeliness and utility before acting.

Washington understood that authentic intelligence gathering consists, not of flashy derring-do and glamorous escapades, but of piecing together an intricate, yet most tedious, jigsaw where every "fact" could be interpreted in several different ways. To Lord Stirling (William Alexander), Washington summarized that "as we are often obliged to reason on the designs of the enemy, from the appearances which come under our observation and the information of our spies, we cannot be too attentive to those things which may afford us new light. Every minutiae should have a place in our collection, for things of a seemingly trifling nature when conjoined with others of a more serious case may lead to very valuable conclusions."[3] Washington was always careful to keep a stern lookout for bloviating and unwarranted speculation in his agents' reports—an inevitable hazard in a game so often played by fantasists and adventurers. He told Matthias Ogden, an intelligence officer, in 1782: "It is my earnest wish that you impress upon the persons in whom you seem to place confidence, urging them to be pointed, regular and accurate in all their communications.... An account of the nature and progress of their [the enemy's] public works is of infinite more consequence than all the chit-chat of the streets and the idle conjecture of the inhabitants."[4] One reason why Washington valued the Culpers' dispatches so highly was owed to their proven veracity and absence of hyperbole.

The British, conversely, still preferred to use military scouts to reconnoiter enemy positions and to obtain tactical information as frequently as possible. Whereas Washington had appointed Tallmadge as his chief of intelligence and personal liaison with the Culper Ring, Clinton, until late in the day, acted as his *own* intelligence head and lacked any specialist staff to help him. Small wonder that he put little store in it, while Washington enjoyed the luxury of avoiding such humdrum chores as negotiating terms of service, dealing with uppity agents, and arranging the reimbursement of expenses incurred.

New York, of course, being the nexus of the imperial war effort, was the navel of all British intelligence operations. Two Loyalists, General Cortland Skinner and Colonel Beverley Robinson, set up their own private networks in their old stamping grounds (New Jersey, in Skinner's case, and the Hudson River, in Robinson's), and periodically sent Clinton packages of information and rumor gleaned from refugees, scouts, prisoners, and deserters, but these proved of little use and timeliness as they were jumbled and often contradictory. Consequently, Clinton complained of "too many ill-founded reports" finding their way to his desk.[5]

These problems were not entirely Clinton's fault. He was a product of the conventional military establishment, where spies were regarded with distaste, and in any case, there was little need for them in the European battlefields. The American theater, however, confronted British commanders with unique intelligence problems. The post service, for instance, was almost nonexistent, especially across enemy lines, and its lack of centralization foiled the kind of Black Chamber mail-intercepting operations common in Europe. Though bribes and baubles could still work their magic on the more mercenary of colonists (Benedict Arnold sold West Point for today's equivalent of half a million dollars and the promise of a knighthood), the leading ideologues remained barbarically immune to such blandishment.

Further complicating intelligence gathering, an ornery, diffuse population of constantly shifting degrees of loyalty lay spread over an area comprising one million square miles. In America, soldiers and militiamen foraging for food and supplies as they traversed the countryside was a time-honored necessity. In Europe, by contrast, tradition dictated that the military forgo foraging on the march, which forced generals to stick to roads and navigable rivers so that their supply lines could keep up with them. Any commander who took his army more than five days' march from a depot risked being cut off.

During wartime, then, collecting intelligence about the enemy's movements was not of prime concern since there were only certain, defined routes along which an army could travel, and topographers could thus accurately predict how long a formation would take to reach its destination. "The best way to discover the enemy's intent before the opening of a campaign," counseled Frederick the Great, who knew his onions, "is to discover where he has established his provision depot. If the Austrians, for example, made their magazines at Olmütz you could be sure that they planned to attack Upper Silesia, and if they established a magazine at Königgrätz, the Schweidnitz area would be threatened."

In Europe, the mark of a great captain was not his talent for deception or for divining intentions, but his ability to outmaneuver opponents on known ground and defeating them in the field as they marched and wheeled in lines and columns. In America's vast geographical spaces, however, armies (and guerrillas) could hide, live off the land, travel cross-country, appear out of nowhere, strike, and vanish. Possessing advance or intimate knowledge of what the enemy was doing, or was planning to do—the *raison d'être* of espionage—became of vital importance.

For both sides in the Revolutionary War, however, the pursuit of intelligence was initially hampered by the fact that no one was quite sure how to do it. There were no textbooks available on the principles and methods of agent (and double agent) recruitment, flipping sources, penetrating networks, verifying walk-ins, establishing dead drops, hiring cutouts, arranging secure data transmission, managing "black" budgets, finding safe houses, and inventing cover stories, let alone collecting, analyzing, and evaluating information.

Military writers had, of course, historically paid homage to the virtues of espionage. Frederick, Marshal de Saxe, and Julius Caesar had all stressed the need for spies, and everyone was familiar with the biblical story of Joshua sending agents to "spy out the land," but none had bothered to dictate practical instructions to their successors. Even as late as 1832, when *On War* appeared, the Prussian military genius Carl von Clausewitz cursorily cited the importance of intelligence while pointing out that "many intelligence reports in war are contradictory; even more are false, and most are uncertain," and left it at that. He managed only to advise commanders to "trust their judgment." Lacking instruction manuals, therefore, commanders in America were obliged to fashion a system of trial and error to evolve their secret services.[6] In hindsight, it's easy to illuminate the obvious mistakes made by both sides, but, to give Clinton and Washington their due, they were generally willing to learn from them.

Clinton, for example, improved his system as he gained control of particular areas, allowing him the time to establish spy networks in place. In May 1779, Clinton appointed Captain John André, his aide, as his specialist intelligence officer—the British equivalent of a Tallmadge. It was a radical step taken not because the general had experienced a brain wave, but for the more prosaic reason that Clinton, as supreme commander, was overwhelmed with work and needed to delegate some of it to a trusted subordinate. André may have been a dilettante but at least he was an *efficient* dilettante. He immediately put affairs on a sounder footing by extracting intelligence reports from the mass of general correspondence that daily arrived and filing it in chronological order in a hardbound book. Belatedly, one could at last distinguish intelligence (albeit of varying quality) from ordinary military orders, lists of promotions, transcripts of courts-martial, and other ephemera. André, unfortunately, went no further with his reorganization, and reports continued to go unevaluated. The "Intelligence Book" was dropped for lack of interest in August 1779, and only resumed the following July, when André began to concentrate heavily on news from the West Point area provided by his ace, Benedict Arnold, who became André's sole focus in the months leading up to his defection.[7]

Born in 1750, André was the son of a cold Swiss merchant and an exuberant Parisian mother. He grew up in Geneva but, after training in languages, music, dancing, and mathematics, left for London to work in his father's firm. Thankfully, when he was nineteen, André's father died, and he inherited a nice little fortune, thereby relieving him of the burden of labor. He got engaged to an Anna Seward, but she broke it off, believing he lacked "the reasoning mind she required." Bored, and newly single, André bought a second lieutenant's commission in a smart regiment, the Royal Welch Fusiliers, but transferred as a full lieutenant to the Seventh Foot, which was headed for Quebec in late 1775. Taken as a prisoner during the siege of Fort St. Johns shortly after, André charmed his captors and was exchanged after the Battle of New York in 1776. He soon became a staff officer at General Howe's headquarters, serving as a translator for the Hessian troops. When his benefactor left for England, he joined Sir Henry Clinton's staff in 1777–78. Clinton took a shine to him and André became the British commander's first friend and confidant. In three years, he had advanced from being a mere subaltern in the Fusiliers to Clinton's adjutant general, the eighteenth-century equivalent of chief of staff.[8]

In many respects Captain John André resembled Captain Nathan Hale: Both were gentle and graceful, and artistic and talented; both, too, were unsuited to espionage (André once admitted he, like Hale, was "too little accustomed to duplicity" to succeed in the game).[9] The André-Arnold correspondence even mirrors that which passed between the Culper Ring and *its* manager, with its manifold examples of crossed wires, elementary mistakes, and petty irritations.

Both teams used an alphanumeric substitution code, Tallmadge's being based on his own Code Dictionary, and André's on William Blackstone's legal *Commentaries*, a copy of which he and Arnold possessed.[10] Soon after making contact, they began using it as their common sourcebook (with Joseph Stansbury, a London-born Loyalist in Philadelphia, as their intermediary, and the Reverend Jonathan Odell in New York, who decrypted the messages).[11] "Three numbers make a word," instructed André, "the 1st is the page the 2nd the line the third the word."[12] So "general," which could be found in Blackstone on page 35, at the twelfth line, eight words from the left, became 35.12.8.

There were two fairly obvious drawbacks to the scheme—quite aside from the risk of someone discovering what the sourcebook was— as André and Arnold soon found. First, Blackstone had to have actually used the term. Otherwise, they were laboriously obliged to spell out the word, each time scratching through the last digit to indicate that this number referred not to a whole word but to the placement of a particular letter on the line. Since Blackstone never alluded to, say, "Poughkeepsie," the correspondents were often confronted with daunting strings of numbers for a single word (sixty, in Poughkeepsie's case). Second, even if Blackstone did use the word, it might require enormous stamina to find it. Arnold, rather enterprisingly, managed to dig up "militia," but only after he'd ploughed through 337 pages of legalese. Arnold and André tried it once and gave up, turning instead to the 21st edition of Nathan Bailey's *Universal Etymological English Dictionary*, which not only contained every common word, but also listed them, of course, alphabetically.[13]

Unlike Tallmadge, who insisted on using anodyne aliases ("John Bolton," "Samuel Culper") and simple code numbers, André preferred to assign colorful biblical names to people and places: Carlisle, Pennsylvania, for instance, became "Rome," the Susquehanna River "Jordan," Indians "Pharisees." Occasionally, his waspish sense of humor emerged, such as calling Congress "Synagogue" and Fort Wyoming, of all places, "Sodom." For himself, Arnold selected "Gustavus" or "Monk" for his aliases (after the seventeenth-century Scottish general who had restored monarchical rule to England, for which signal service he received a knighthood, a barony, an earldom, and a dukedom from an exceedingly grateful Charles II), while André broke from his own practice and, quite foolishly, used "John Anderson," or sometimes "James Anderson"—both names bearing too close a resemblance to his own. For a time, André used a cipher almost identical to Tallmadge's, in which, starting from the number 50, words were converted into digits; he even made the same mistake as Tallmadge by listing the words alphabetically, not randomly, so rendering the cipher relatively easy to crack.[14]

In some of their correspondence, as Townsend did with his letter to "Colonel Floyd," André and Arnold disguised the real meaning of their words within harmless contexts: a business deal between two crooked merchants, for instance, or "the complexion of affairs [of] an old woman's health."[15] André, like Tallmadge with Woodhull, cajoled and chided his secret servant, though, unlike his American counterpart, he did not quite trust him and it took several months of Arnold's importuning to persuade him that he had stumbled onto a bona fide, highly placed, and voluntary mole. The primary difference between Arnold and the Culper Ring, of course, is that the general was a mercenary entrepreneur, continually demanding more money for his treachery while his masters tried to gauge how fertile their man's supply of intelligence was likely to be.[16] André was perfectly blunt about what he desired: "Dispatches to & from foreign Courts, original papers, intimation of channels thro' which intelligence passes" plus "taking possession of a considerable seaport and defeating the troops assigned to the defense of the province." (At one point, he asked, "Could you obtain the command in Carolina?" though in that case Arnold one-upped him by offering possession of West Point.)[17] In reply to Arnold's pleas for more money, André remained businesslike, telling his spy that "services done are the terms on which we promise rewards; in these you see we are profuse; We conceive them proportioned to the risk."[18]

It was only in late August 1778 that Arnold's thirty shekels—twenty thousand pounds for West Point and its garrison, with a guaranteed minimum of ten thousand pounds should the plot fail but he came over anyway—was agreed, and André (now a major) and Beverley Robinson (who had been running agents on the Hudson and knew the area) arranged to meet their contact on the Hudson River to finalize the terms on September 11.[19] That plan was aborted when a British patrol boat fired on Arnold's barge as it neared Dobb's Ferry. For a week, they waited, and Arnold enticed his manager with the intelligence that Washington was in the vicinity and likely to visit him.[20] If all went well, not only would this key fortress fall into British hands, but so too would its three-thousand-strong garrison, plus, best of all, Washington himself.

On September 20, a second attempt was made. André and Robinson sailed upstream aboard H.M.S. *Vulture*, but could not make contact that night. The next evening, Arnold's intermediary, Joshua Smith, collected André, who was inexplicably posing as a merchant while dressed in regimental uniform, and brought him ashore to a grove at Haverstraw, on the west bank of the Hudson.[21] Upon meeting "Mr Anderson," recalled

Smith of André's "youthful appearance [and] the softness of his manners," he "did not seem to be qualified for the business of such moment. His nature seemed fraught with the milk of human kindness."[22]

At about two in the morning, André—still outfitted in his regimentals—discussed the topography and defenses of West Point with Arnold, who was waiting nervously a little north of Haverstraw. By the end of their long conversation, by which time daybreak was imminent, Arnold accompanied André and Smith to the latter's house to continue their talks, the plan being for him to leave the major in Smith's care until the following night, when he could be rowed back the six miles to the awaiting *Vulture*. It was only during the ride to the safe house that André realized, having seen in the dawn's early light a sentry post, that he was within American lines—dressed in the kit of an enemy officer. In the meantime, Arnold gave him a pass to travel unhindered through American territory, sketches of the fort, and maps of its artillery positions, all of which André hid in his stockings.

After Arnold's departure later that day, September 22, an American officer, having noticed the *Vulture*, decided to shell it with a howitzer, forcing the sloop to sail twelve miles downstream.[23] Rowing eighteen miles in a blazing red uniform, even at night, was far too risky an enterprise, and André, "vexed" (Smith's words), was persuaded to change into civilian dress, and don a round hat and blue cloak, and cross the river at Verplanck's Point with Smith and his black servant, so he could ride overland to the British lines at White Plains. Eight miles later, an American sentry stopped them and helpfully pointed out that Tory partisans were operating to the south, which was a no-man's-land terrorized by marauding gangs of Tory "Cowboys" and Patriot "Skinners."[24] Knowing that to continue would invite suspicion, André and Smith kipped near the outpost for the night, and after a breakfast of mush and milk early the following morning (September 23), Smith bade him farewell and handed him forty dollars to get home. André was confident he could make the fifteen-mile journey to White Plains by nightfall. That was the last time Smith saw him.[25]

All went well until 9.30 a.m., when, as André consulted a map,

John Paulding appeared in the road and pointed a musket at him. In the bushes to either side hid Isaac Van Wart and David Williams, also armed. Paulding demanded André's name and affiliation. A more hardened case officer would have precomposed the aptest response to a challenge from men equally likely to be rebel Skinners or loyal Cowboys: If the former, his pass from General Benedict Arnold of the Continental army would awe even them and he would be allowed to go; if the latter, the pass would guarantee they took him prisoner and conveyed him under guard to White Plains, where he could prove his credentials and be released. In the event, not unreasonably given the sentry's warning about Tory activity and that one of the party was wearing an ancient British redcoat, André misjudged the situation, and cheerily declared: "My lads, I hope you belong to our party." Paulding asked which party that might be. "The lower," said André, referring to the British side.

At that, they announced themselves to be Patriots. Startled, André stammered that he was "an officer in the British service on particular business in the country," and, mustering himself to look impressive, directed that they let him go. They didn't, instead ordering him to dismount. It was only then that André had the presence of mind to show his permit, but it was too late. Van Wart merely exclaimed, "Damn the pass!" and demanded money. The other two then mugged him— André's fine, white-topped, London-made boots being of particular interest to David Williams. As they unshod him, they found Arnold's incriminating plans of West Point hidden within his stockings. Paulding, the only literate one, stumbled through them and cried, "This is a spy!" Still, the highwaymen told André they would let him free if he gave them one hundred guineas, his horse, and his watch, an offer to which he readily agreed. Just as André thought he was home free, one of them suggested that there was nothing to lose by taking him in anyway.[26]

The trio trundled him—all the time debating André's desperate offers of a lucrative reward if they brought him south to New York instead—to the nearest commanding officer, Colonel Jameson at North Castle, who allowed them to keep André's belongings.[27] The twenty-eight-year-old colonel was befuddled, mostly because he had recently received a letter from Arnold informing him that an important friend to the American cause named Anderson might be crossing into Patriot territory *from* British lines, and here he had an Anderson who had claimed to be a royal officer heading *for* British lines carrying letters in Arnold's handwriting.

Tallmadge, who was out on patrol, was less puzzled than suspicious. In the secret world, as he knew, there was no such thing as a coincidence. He, too, had received a letter from Arnold a week earlier noting that a "Mr. James Anderson"—"a person I expect from New York"—might arrive; if he did, Tallmadge was to "give him an escort of two horse to bring him on his way to this place, and send an express to me that I may meet him." Ominously, Arnold had added, "if your business will permit I wish you to come with him," implying that the turncoat believed he might have a bonus for the British to scoop up: the American chief of intelligence.[28] Tallmadge, unfortunately for Arnold's scheme, did not open the letter until September 21—he had been "absent on command by special directions of His Excellency Genl. Washington"—which allowed him to avoid the trap set for him.[29] Unluckily for the captured spy, however, the letter's contents were fresh in Tallmadge's mind when he heard of this mysterious fellow in custody at Jameson's headquarters.

Even so, Arnold had enjoyed a lucky break. In Tallmadge's reply of September 21, after apologizing for the delay he said that he had received "private accounts from New York" noting the movements of Admiral Rodney with "10 sail of the line" and other warships leaving port to intercept the American fleet returning from the West Indies. Also, that several regiments, which he named, are "to embark in a few days," perhaps for the South or an attack on the French at Rhode Island. Tallmadge, of course, was extracting intelligence gleaned from a Townsend-Woodhull letter and passing it on, suitably disguised, to a superior officer whom he had no reason to suspect of treason. But what happened is that Arnold, just before his flight to the other side, was now certain that Tallmadge was running a man inside New York itself. When they read this letter soon afterward, Arnold's British masters started connecting the dots: They already knew that Tallmadge was based in southern Connecticut, they knew that whaleboatmen often smuggled information across the Sound, they knew that fifteen months before that Colonel Simcoe, a close friend of André's, had been notified there was a spy operating in coastal Setauket, and now they knew that a New York agent was somehow passing intelligence to Tallmadge, almost certainly using a courier. It was pretty good odds that all these individual facts were not random, but linked. To blow the network, they needed to find either Tallmadge, who was unlikely to talk, or, more promisingly, the Setauket connection, the courier, the whaleboatman, or the New Yorker. Any one would do.

In the meantime, Jameson called his officers (Tallmadge was still out) together to discuss the dilemma of what to do with this Anderson.[30] Jameson was particularly worried that no matter how suspicious the situation seemed, he could not avoid informing his superior officer Arnold about it for fear of being charged with insubordination. Instead, he decided to cover his bases by sending André, with his hands tied, to Arnold's headquarters near West Point with a note stating that papers of "a very dangerous tendency" were being conveyed to Washington, while giving a junior officer, Lieutenant Solomon Allen, the actual papers to bring to the commander-in-chief.[31]

In the late evening of September 23, Tallmadge arrived at Jameson's headquarters, where he heard the story of the capture. He was "surprised," according to his *Memoir*, to find Jameson had sent Arnold the letter and the prisoner, and the correspondence to Washington. "I did not fail to state the glaring inconsistency of this conduct to Lieut.-Col. Jameson, in a private and friendly manner. He appeared greatly agitated when I suggested to him a measure which I wished to adopt, offering to take the whole responsibility upon myself, and which he deemed too perilous to permit." This oblique reference to a "measure" amounted to a proposal to take a unit of dragoons and arrest Arnold, a suggestion Jameson, worried what should happen if Tallmadge's hunch proved wrong, quickly torpedoed. However, says Tallmadge, after much badgering "I finally obtained his reluctant consent to have the prisoner brought back to our headquarters," though Jameson, "strange as it may seem," insisted on "letting his letter go on to Gen. Arnold."[32]

On his return, André was handed over to Lieutenant Joshua King at South Salem for safekeeping. As André had at least three days' growth of beard, he asked for a man to shave him; King, quite perceptively, noticed that the prisoner had much powder in his hair, leading him to believe "I had no ordinary person in charge."[33] Indeed, "as soon as I saw Anderson" the next morning, recalled Tallmadge, "and especially after I saw him walk (as he did almost constantly) across the floor, I became impressed with the belief that he had been *bred to arms*." He asked Jameson to watch him, too, "to notice his gait, especially when he turned on his heel to retrace his course across the room."[34] After Tallmadge and Jameson had left, his jailer told André about the papers being sent to Washington. The jig was up. It was but a matter of time before exposure. At about 3 p.m. André requested that he be allowed to send a letter to Washington, a wish readily granted by Tallmadge.[35] When Tallmadge read André's letter—"he handed it to me as soon as he had written it"—and saw his confession that Anderson in fact was "Major John André, Adjutant-General to the British Army," his "agitation was extreme, and my emotions wholly indescribable." Tallmadge wanted to go arrest Arnold immediately, come what may, but there was little point: Jameson's letter would have reached Arnold "before I could possibly get to West Point."[36]

In the meantime, Jameson's messenger had arrived at Arnold's headquarters, where he found the general preparing to receive Washington, who was scheduled to breakfast with him before touring the defenses of West Point. Arnold's reaction, a picture of forced calm as his terrified eyes focused on Jameson's handwriting, can only be imagined. He immediately rushed upstairs as fast as his wounded leg would take him to converse with his wife, Peggy, before calling for his horse. Downstairs again, he told his subordinates that sudden business had arisen at West Point and that he would be back soon. He wasn't. Instead, Arnold galloped to the nearest British outpost and made his escape. While Washington was being given the tour by John Lamb, Arnold's deputy, Alexander Hamilton received the package from Jameson, as well as André's confession. Shaken, Hamilton handed the documents to his commander, who was shocked but recovered quickly enough to order Arnold's arrest and call out the garrison to man the defenses for a possible British attack.

Tallmadge volunteered to escort André to Tappan, well away from the threat of any British rescue operations and where the main army was waiting. The two spymasters got along well during their ride together. Tallmadge lamented to a friend that he "never saw a man whose fate I foresaw, whom I so sincerely pitied. He is a young fellow of the greatest accomplishments. . . . He has unbosomed his heart to me, and indeed, let me know almost every motive of his actions so fully since he came out on his late mission that he has endeared himself to me exceedingly. Unfortunate man!"[37]

In 1834, when he was eighty, Tallmadge wrote a letter to Jared Sparks, the eminent historian, narrating what transpired during André's last ride:

> Major Andre was very inquisitive to know my opinion as to the result of his capture. . . . I endeavored to evade the question, unwilling to give him a true answer. When I could no longer evade this importunity, I said to him that I had a much loved class mate in Yale College by the name of Nathan Hale, who entered the Army with me in the year 1776. After the British troops had entered N. York, Genl. Washington wanted information respecting the strength, position & probable movements of the enemy.

Then Tallmadge said:

> Do you remember the sequel of this story; "Yes," said Andre; "he was hanged as a spy; but you surely do not consider his case & mine alike." I replied, "precisely similar, and similar

will be your fate!" He endeavored to answer my remarks, but it was manifest he was more troubled than I had ever seen him before.[38]

Tallmadge's aged memory was playing him tricks. André, being a prisoner in Pennsylvania when Hale was hanged, was hardly likely to have "remembered" the details of an obscure spy in New York in General Howe's time. Rather more probable is that Tallmadge recounted the story, at which point André remarked that "surely [you] do not consider his case & mine alike." Unfortunately, Tallmadge did, and told him so.[39]

Like Nathan Hale, André had been caught red-handed in the act of espionage, and could not escape his fate. Hale, however, was not the adjutant general of the British army, and there were political implications. André could not simply be executed and be done with. Washington, for instance, was willing to entertain the notion of exchanging André for Arnold, a much bigger fish.[40] Sir Henry Clinton, though he adored André and made a touching intercession for his life, could never surrender such a high-ranking defector, not if he wanted any more to come over. Whereas Clinton—who privately seethed that Washington wanted to commit "premeditated murder [and] must answer for the dreadful consequences"—remained outwardly "calm, and deliberate in my resentment" over André's likely death, and addressed his pleas to his counterpart in stiff, but civil, language, Arnold wrote hotly to Washington, who was, at best, disinclined to listen to a disgraced traitor, to threaten a "torrent of blood" against American prisoners in retaliation if he killed André.[41] (Clinton later assured Washington that they "need be under no fears for their safety," despite Arnold's threats.)[42]

Even had Washington been willing to spare the spy's life, he had his army to think about. As it was, thanks to Arnold the men were becoming reluctant to trust their officers, and the officers were losing faith in their commanders. Public opinion also had to be appeased. Somebody had to be punished, and punishment had to be seen to be done to restore order. With Arnold safe behind enemy lines, André was the only possible victim apart from Joshua Smith, the intermediary, who had been arrested soon after Arnold's flight.

Smith, however, was a member of a prominent Whig family in New York, and requested an audience with Washington to prove he was innocent of *knowingly* abetting Arnold's defection. As Smith stood shackled in irons, Washington walked over to the terrified man, looked him sternly in the eye, and said that if he were guilty, he would hang him from the same tree he was about to use for André. Smith's defense was that Arnold had told him to expect an officer carrying a message from Clinton; that message Arnold said he would pass to Washington. Arnold made Smith promise to keep silent, telling him that the message might bring the war to an end. Smith claimed at his trial that his actions were motivated by the highest thoughts of patriotism—and he had presumed the same of Arnold. There were quite a few inconsistencies in Smith's story, but, though not numerous or gaping enough to hang him, they were sufficient to convict him. The court sentenced him to prison, and he spent much of the next two years being shuffled from guardhouse to guardhouse until he escaped on May 22, 1782, and made his way to the New York house of his brother—who happened to be Clinton's neighbor. It helped Smith nought. The British and their allies accused him of abandoning André on the road fifteen miles before White Plains and safety; had Smith accompanied André the whole way, as they believed he had promised Arnold, the solitary spy would never have been stopped, West Point would have fallen, and Washington would be a prisoner. (There is a postscript to this unfortunate tale. When the British evacuated New York in late 1783, Smith left for London, where some time later he was unexpectedly visited by Arnold. "The reception he received from me shortened the interview," is all Smith would say about the matter.)[43]

Unlike Smith, André had no chance of creating doubt in the minds of his judges. At his trial a Board of General Officers quickly found him guilty of espionage and recommended that he "suffer death."[44]

The method of André's death was a slightly tricky subject. André, having resigned himself to his doom, requested an honorable soldier's execution: by firing squad. Washington was initially inclined to grant this favor but, pressured to make an example of André, soon changed his mind and ordered the punishment traditionally meted out to common spies: hanging.[45] André, however, was deliberately left ignorant of the alteration.

When he was told of the verdict, wrote Tallmadge, "he showed no signs of perturbed emotion," but when he saw a gallows rather than a firing squad awaiting him, he was "startled, and enquired with some emotion whether he was not to be shot." Told no by Tallmadge, he said, "How hard is my fate!" adding, "It will soon be over."[46]

On October 2, at 12 p.m., said Tallmadge, "he met death with a smile, cheerfully marching to the place of execution, & bidding his friends, those who had been with him, farewell. He called me to him a few minutes before he swung off, and expressed his gratitude to me for civilities in such a way, and so cheerfully bid me adieu, that I was obliged to leave the parade in a flood of tears. I cannot say enough of his fortitude—unfortunate youth; I wish Arnold had been in his place."[47] André's last words? "Only this, gentlemen, that you all bear me witness that I meet my fate like a brave man."[48]

It had to be done. Washington, writing to Rochambeau on October 10, declared that "the circumstances [André] was taken in justified it and policy required a sacrifice; but as he was more unfortunate than criminal in the affair, and as there was much in his character to interest, while we yielded to the necessity of rigor, we could not but lament it."[49] Tallmadge concurred: "Enough of poor André, who tho' he dies lamented, falls justly."[50]

CHAPTER EIGHT

Spyhunters and Whaleboatmen

Benedict Arnold may not have brought an army with him, as he had so rashly promised Sir Henry Clinton, but he did carry in his head a list of American spies operating within British lines, as well as the knowledge that Tallmadge was running at least one agent in New York itself. Since the summer of 1780, Arnold had been assiduously collecting their names from his unsuspecting colleagues, who often organized local spies to pass on information to them about nearby enemy movements. On at least one occasion, he was unsuccessful, such as the time Arnold—who had heard that Washington, thanks to his spies (the Culpers, as it turned out), had warned Rochambeau of British preparations to pounce at Rhode Island—"innocently" asked the Marquis de Lafayette about these informants. Arnold's ostensible reason was that now that he was in charge of West Point, he, too, needed a few good men to serve as his eyes and ears. Lafayette refused to give their names, saying he had pledged secrecy, but also because *Tallmadge* had been careful not to divulge them even to him—precisely to prevent such accidental leakages.[1]

Arnold enjoyed a little more luck with his predecessor as West Point commander, General Robert Howe, to whom he wrote on August 5 explaining that "as the safety of this post and garrison... depends on having good intelligence of the movements and designs of the enemy...I must request (with their permission) to be informed who they are, as I wish to employ them for the same purpose. I will engage upon honour to make no discovery of them to any person breathing."[2]

Howe, a North Carolinian, kindly replied that he had two agents in South Carolina, but they would not permit him to reveal their names. Having said that, "I have a tolerable agent who acts by way of Long Island, and has been very faithful, intelligent and useful to me....He says that he will give you information of every circumstance which relates to your post or to any part under your command, that he will task himself to give every information of the enemy's intentions, and will faithfully report to you every movement which relates to you; he will correspond with you under the name of John Williams, and has made me pledge my honor that you will not endeavour by any means to learn his real name and if by accident you find it out that you never disclose it."[3]

"John Williams" was Captain Elijah Hunter, who had worked with Howe since December 1776, when he officially "retired" from the army. These days he posed as a Tory and served in the Second New York Militia while working as an assistant commissary of forage who occasionally came into the city to pick up information. He seems to have been acquainted with Clinton and Governor Tryon, but he reported rarely and did not supply the quality and quantity of material that the Culpers did. The only thing that saved his life after Arnold's defection was his insistence on his Williams alias, but even he went underground for a long while.[4]

Arnold's arrival in New York threw the Culper Ring into near panic when he appointed himself spyhunter-general and, with Clinton's authorization, rounded up a score of New York and Long Island residents who he strongly suspected had carried on "a treasonable correspondence with the rebels for many years [and] had acted as spies within the British lines." All of them had previously sworn oaths of loyalty to the king.[5] To General Heath, Tallmadge observed that "he has flung into the provost many of our friends whom he will have punished if possible. I fear it will injure the chains of our intelligence, at least for a little time [un]til the present tumult is over. I am happy that he does not know even a single link in my chain."[6]

Even so, Tallmadge was worried that his September 21 letter to Arnold about his receiving "private accounts from New York" had given away too much. "When he turned traitor and went off," he remembered, discreet as always, "I felt for a time extremely anxious for some trusty friends in New York." Tallmadge, however, consoled himself with the thought that "as I never gave their names to him, he was not able to discover them, although I believe he tried hard to find them out."[7]

His fears were not finally put to rest until early October when he heard from Woodhull saying he was still alive and well, and who mentioned that Townsend, too, remained free. "The present commotion that has arisen on account of the infamous Arnold together with little or no intelligence at this time was the reason he did not write," his cell leader reported. Woodhull had also arranged to meet Townsend in the coming weeks to discuss their future plans given the heightened state of alert in the city.[8]

The meeting did not go well. Townsend was antsy. Woodhull, too. Thanks to Arnold, reported Tallmadge to Washington, his agents were "at present too apprehensive of danger to give their immediate usual intelligence. I hope as the tumult subsides matters will go on in their old channels." Though Woodhull agreed to keep on working if anything pertinent arose, Townsend—despite Tallmadge's assurance that "his name or character are not even known by any officer but myself in the army"—decided to lie low until the heat dissipated.[9] "Happy to think that Arnold does not know my name," Townsend did not, however, go so far as to resign from the Ring, but he did call a halt for the time being to Tallmadge's plan to shorten the route by using Townsend's relatives in Cow Neck. Townsend opted, for safety's sake, to go solely through Woodhull, and thence Brewster to Tallmadge.[10]

During their meeting, Townsend and Woodhull had discussed André. Being in the same business themselves, they were less ready to damn him than their neighbors and fellow Patriots, but they were equally unwilling to view André, as Loyalists did, as an innocent martyr murdered by Washington. "I am sorry for the death of Major André but better so than to lose the post," observed Woodhull to Tallmadge. "He was seeking your ruin."[11] Townsend, it turns out, had been acquainted with André, a frequent visitor to his father's Oyster Bay house, Raynham Hall, whenever his pal Colonel Simcoe billeted himself there. "I never felt more sensibly for the death of a person whom I knew only by sight, and had heard converse, than I did for Major André," Townsend told Tallmadge. "He was a most amiable character. General Clinton was inconsolable for some days; and the army in general and inhabitants were much exasperated, and think that General Washington must have been destitute of feeling, or he would have saved him. I believe that General Washington felt sincerely for him, and would have saved him if it could have been done with propriety."[12]

Perhaps so, but Washington was more concerned with bringing Arnold to justice. That the Judas had gotten away with his crime rankled intensely. On October 13, he invited Major Henry "Light-Horse Harry" Lee—the father of future Confederate general Robert E.——to his headquarters to discuss "a particular piece of business." At their meeting the next day, Washington broached the possibility of kidnapping Arnold. Could he, Lee, find a man willing to embark on such a mission?[13]

It took Lee a week to find two volunteers "to undertake the accomplishment of your Excellency's wishes." He omitted to mention to them that they were acting on Washington's orders since, if they failed, the commander-in-chief's name could not be linked to such an unorthodox mission. The first man was a sergeant in Lee's regiment, John Champe, a tall Virginian in his early twenties whose taciturnity and total absence of cheerfulness masked a "remarkable intelligence."[14] His task would be to enter New York, somehow capture Arnold, and bundle him down to a waiting boat for removal to New Jersey. Modestly desirous of an officer's commission, all Champe asked for in reward for his services was a promotion.[15] The other volunteer, whose name was never revealed, would be the contact man in Newark, New Jersey, and Lee promised him "one hundred guineas, five hundred acres of land, and three negroes."[16]

Washington was most pleased at Champe's public-spiritedness. He had been reluctant to cast around for officers to undertake the business, which even he regarded as being a shade dishonorable.[17] After inquiring into Champe's details, his length of service, and his character, on October 20, in the strictest of confidences, he authorized the operation and approved the rewards Lee had arranged with "the conductors of this interesting business." He made one stipulation: Arnold was to be brought in alive. If he were killed during the mission, the British would put it about that "ruffians had been hired to assassinate him," whereas Washington's aim was "to make a public example of him."[18]

Late that night, Lee summoned Sergeant Champe to his quarters and ordered him to desert to the enemy immediately. For fear of raising British suspicions, Lee added that no help could be given to Champe during his flight. He would have to find his way to the British lines as if he were a real turncoat. The most Lee could offer was to delay pursuit for as long as he could if Champe's absence was noted before the next morning. And with that, Champe collected his belongings (including the regiment's orderly book, for added authenticity) and rode his horse out of camp at about 11 o'clock. He was given three guineas to cover his immediate expenses (Washington refused him any more, saying it would ring too many alarm bells) and the names of two known friendlies in New York. To prevent betrayal, Champe was told not to let one know the existence of the other. Who these two men were remains unknown; it is most unlikely one was Townsend, as Washington preferred not to run overlapping operations.

No one stopped him leaving, but just half a mile later, at a crossroads, a mounted patrol returning from duty issued a challenge. Champe kept silent, pulled up his hood, plunged his spurs into his steed's flanks, and galloped past them. The patrolmen gave chase but their horses were tired and they soon quit. Unfortunately, the patrol belonged to Lee's regiment, and half an hour later Captain Carnes reluctantly woke up Lee to tell him of the incident. Lee grasped instantly what had happened and played dumb, forcing the captain to repeat his entire story, questioning tiny details, dismissing Carnes's belief that the mysterious rider, judging by his riding style, was a cavalryman and suggesting instead he was "a countryman" in a hurry. Lee could see Carnes wasn't convinced and directed him to muster every man and horse and see if any were missing. That would waste at least an hour, he thought.

Sooner than he expected, Carnes returned and declared that Champe was gone, but Lee offhandedly said he must have gone out for a midnight ride of some sort. Still, it had come to the point when not to do anything would invite suspicion, and Lee called out the regiment. A pursuit party was selected and Lee included a young cornet named Middleton, whom he knew lacked Carnes's experience and, moreover, was of a gentle enough disposition that he would not kill Champe outright if he captured him. In his quarters with Middleton, Lee managed to waste ten minutes going over in tedious detail exactly which route he should take, which equipment he might need, and how many men he should bring. Finally, after waiting for a time for Lee to sign his orders and reiterate how Champe should be treated humanely, an impatient Middleton was allowed to go. Champe, thanks to Lee's intervention, had gained an hour's head start—enough to get to New York ahead of the law, barring some unforeseen event. At that point, it unexpectedly began to rain: not hard enough to prevent pursuit, but sufficient to leave tracks on the muddy roads. Lee's men were dragoons, and none in the army knew better than they how to follow footprints.

Worse, the regiment had one farrier, who used a single, peculiar pattern of horseshoe, which made it difficult ever to lose the trail.

Unlike his pursuers, Champe could not afford to gallop through the countryside. Quite aside from the risk of laming his horse, the place swarmed with militiamen and was studded with checkpoints whose guards would set off a hue and cry at the sight of a lone, becloaked horseman running at full pelt so late at night. At dawn, therefore, Champe was still several miles north of Bergen on a wide and open plain where he could be easily spotted. In the distance, he could hear the faint clatter of hooves, and knew his pursuers were closing. Looking behind him, Champe was horrified to see several horsemen pausing at the crest of a hill half a mile away and signaling to their comrades that the quarry was near. Champe gave spur to his horse and he made for the bridge traversing the Hackensack River. Most of the hunters, including Middleton, were local men and knew the terrain better than did Champe. The cornet was familiar with a narrow path through the nearby woods that acted as a shortcut to the bridge, and he sent his sergeant and a few dragoons down that route while he took the rest of the squadron and chased Champe. Caught between the two forces, Champe would be forced to surrender.

Middleton made two miscalculations. First, Champe, too, knew of the path, having ridden along it a dozen times on patrol, and was aware that the sergeant's detachment would beat him to the bridge; and second, assuming that Champe's destination was Paulus Hook, the British fortress on the Jersey shore that guarded the western entrance to New York harbor. That had been Champe's original intention, it is true, but seeing that there was no hope of outpacing Middleton and his men, Champe charged straight into Bergen itself and rode down one paved street after another before taking the road leading to the Hudson River, not the one heading to Paulus Hook. The sergeant's detachment, in the meantime, had reached the bridge and were concealed beside the road, waiting for Champe. Bemused why he had not yet approached, they asked passing villagers if they had seen a speeding dragoon. They pointed out that he had gone the other way. With a curse, the sergeant and his men clambered atop their horses and set off through Bergen in hot pursuit. Soon after, Middleton heard the same news and gave chase.

Champe could see two British ships anchored a mile ahead of him. Behind him, also a mile away, were the knot of cavalrymen. There was nothing for it but to lighten the horse's load and make a break for it. After shrugging off his cloak and tossing away his scabbard and belongings, Champe reached the shore in quick time but lost valuable minutes trying to attract the crews' attention by dismounting and waving his arms. Middleton had closed the distance and was just two hundred yards away. Fortunately, a sentry noticed Champe, who splashed through the marsh on the bank and plunged into the chilly river to swim toward the vessels. As Middleton pulled up and cried out for Champe to surrender, marksmen aboard the ships opened fire, driving the dragoons away.

Friendly hands reached down and hauled an exhausted Champe from the water. He was taken into New York and brought before Clinton, who had heard of the sergeant's adventure. The general was interested in Champe: He was only the second man ever to have deserted from Lee's legion, a unit famed for its fidelity. Champe played along admirably, telling Clinton that Arnold's defection would only be the first of many among the dispirited Americans. Clinton chatted to him for an hour, and he was particularly interested in knowing how fondly Washington was regarded by the troops, whether other senior officers seemed disaffected, and which measures might prompt large-scale desertions.

Once finished with his inquiries, Clinton recommended that Champe see Arnold, who was then busy raising a regiment of deserters and Tories. It was an unexpected offer, but one Champe could not refuse. Arnold took an instant shine to the young man, and made him a recruiting sergeant a day after he enlisted. For several weeks, Champe paid close attention to his chief's movements. Arnold's house was situated on one of the city's principal streets, which made it impossible to take him through the front door, but Champe noticed that Arnold had a habit of taking a midnight stroll in his garden before going to bed. This garden bordered an obscure alley, a wooden fence separating the two. One night, Champe sneaked along the alley and loosened several palings to allow enough space for a man to pass through. At that point, he contacted one of the two incognitos provided by Lee and asked him to get a message across the Hudson to the Newark contact, whose task it was to tell Lee to have a boat and several dragoons waiting on a particular night on the Jersey shore. At a prearranged time, they were to row to a darkened, deserted Manhattan wharf and pick up the "package." His other New York contact would accompany Champe to the alley, and they would hide themselves in Arnold's garden. On the day Champe had chosen for the deed, he prepared his kit: a gag and a cosh to bludgeon the general. The plan was to tackle Arnold, hit and silence him, push him through the fence, pull his hat down over his face, and hold him up with his arms sagging around their shoulders. To passersby, it would look like two friends taking their drunken friend home after a hard night. Once at the wharf, Arnold would be tied up and bundled into the boat, and Champe would leave with the dragoons. The first face a groggy Arnold would have seen the next day would have been Washington's rockily peering into his.

Just as pure luck had saved Arnold's hide before, when Colonel Jameson had sent him news that André was under arrest, it would do so again. The very evening that Champe was to kidnap the general, he discovered that Arnold had transferred to new quarters to oversee the embarkation of his "American Legion" aboard naval transports: Clinton that day had issued emergency orders directing the legion to proceed to Virginia. Champe and the rest of the regiment, accordingly, were immediately confined to barracks and then marched to the docks—the only person being kidnapped, it seems, was Champe himself. The depth of his disappointment can only be imagined. Lee, meanwhile, had been impatiently waiting with his dragoons on the banks of the Hudson all night, and it was only a few days later that he realized that Champe would never be coming.

Months went by. Then, without any warning, a bedraggled, bearded

Sergeant Champe appeared in Lee's camp. Soon after landing in the South and being obliged to fight against his compatriots, he had deserted—for real, this time—and lived rough in the country, traveling only at night through Virginia and North Carolina to evade Loyalist sympathizers and British pursuers. Lee immediately called the regiment to muster and proceeded to narrate Champe's story and affirm that he had been acting under the commander-in-chief's orders. Then he took Champe to Washington, who in place of the promised lieutenancy offered him a lavish bounty and a discharge from military service. When Champe objected and said he would like to rejoin his regiment, Washington wisely counseled against any such notion. If Champe were to be taken prisoner, he would inevitably be recognized and his life would end on a gibbet.[19]

Champe, his day done, bid farewell to his commanders and mounted the horse given to him by Washington. He went back to Loudoun County, Virginia, riding right out of the picture. The last time anyone saw the mysterious Sergeant John Champe was sometime in the 1780s, when Angus Cameron, a Scottish captain in Arnold's regiment who had married a Virginia lass of sound republican principles, happened to get lost while traveling deep in the Loudoun County woods one summer night. A terrible storm rolled over him, and he spotted a cottage—the first he had seen in many miles—by the flash of the lightning. A man ushered him inside, a man strangely familiar to Cameron. And there he was—"Sergeant Champe stood before me." Cameron's shock at seeing him was not altogether pleasant. Champe was, after all, a two-time deserter; Cameron was an unarmed outsider hours away from help, and his host might not relish this blast from the past turning up unexpectedly....

His misgivings were, thankfully, misplaced. "Welcome, welcome, Captain Cameron!" exclaimed Champe, "a thousand times welcome to my roof." After joining Arnold's legion, Champe had been placed in Cameron's company, and he was, as the former sergeant said, "the only British officer of whose good opinion I am covetous" owing to his kindly behavior toward him during the Virginia expedition. And so it was to Cameron that Champe told the entire story. The next day, Cameron bid adieu to Champe and went on his way.[20] A few years later, having married and had six children, Champe moved to Hampshire County, Virginia (now in West Virginia). In 1798, while negotiating to buy land in Morgantown, on the banks of the Monongahela River, he died. His widow moved to Madison, Ohio.[21]

Even as Sergeant Champe was in New York vainly plotting Arnold's downfall, "the person in whom [Washington had] the greatest confidence is afraid to take any measures for communicating with me just at this time, as he is apprehensive that Arnold may possibly have some knowledge of the connection, and may have him watched."[22] Washington was referring to Robert Townsend, who had gone completely quiet since Arnold's arrival in the city.

Washington subsequently reminded his intelligence chief that "I should be exceedingly glad to hear from C. Junior, because all my accounts from other quarters are very defective as to the number of troops to be embarked, or, indeed, whether an embarkation is seriously in contemplation." Tallmadge had suggested that he cross the Sound to buck up the faltering Townsend, but this idea was sensibly vetoed by Washington, who pointed out that "the enemy would act with more than common vigor just now should an officer be taken under circumstances the least suspicious."[23]

And then came a bitter blow. Washington's insistence on shortening the route, which Tallmadge repeatedly mentioned to Woodhull, combined with his alarm over Arnold's defection, was placing too much pressure on Townsend. At their recent meeting in New York, Townsend looked haggard, and Woodhull was "sorry to inform you that the present commotions and watchfulness of the enemy at New York hath resolved C. Jur. for the present to quit writing and retire into the country" until the tumult subsided. "The enemy are very severe," Woodhull continued, "and the spirits of our friends very low. I did not think myself safe there for a moment, and as nothing is like to be done about New York, perhaps it may not be much disadvantage to drop [the correspondence]" temporarily. However, "if need requires C. Junr. will undertake again," possibly in the spring.

What had finally broken Townsend's fortitude was Arnold's arrest of one Hercules Mulligan. According to Woodhull, the imprisonment of "one that hath been ever serviceable to this correspondence" had "so dejected the spirits of C. Junr. that he resolved to leave New York for a time."[24]

Mulligan was born in 1740 in Ireland, the second of Hugh and Sarah Mulligan's three sons (Hugh was the elder, Cooke the younger); he had a little sister, too, named after their mother. The family emigrated to New York about 1746. All three Mulligan boys became merchants. In the 1760s, Hugh Junior joined the upmarket import-export firm of Kortwright & Company, whose seven ships plied the West Indian–New York trade. Importantly, Townsend's father, Samuel, had been using Kortwright as his West Indian agents in St. Croix since at least 1757, and therefore was well acquainted with Hugh, and certainly Hercules as well.[25] An assiduous type, Hugh soon made junior partner—and in 1773 took over the company by buying out his colleagues.[26] That year, Hugh met the impecunious Alexander Hamilton, recently off the boat from St. Croix; he had worked for Kortwright's bureau (Kortwright & Cruger) in the West Indies, and the firm's representatives out there, impressed by the boy's talents, had persuaded the partners to sponsor his voyage to New York.[27] Hugh introduced Hamilton to Hercules, who took the orphan under his wing. When Hamilton attended King's (Columbia) College, he boarded with Hercules, and they collaborated in hauling off a cannon from the Battery in the summer of 1775. A year later, "about the 10 or 12 July 1776," Hercules helped Hamilton obtain his commission in the army when they recruited twenty-five men in a single afternoon.[28]

When Hamilton arrived, Hercules Mulligan was living on Water Street—between Burling's Slip and the Fly Market—but in 1774 he moved to 23 Queen Street, an altogether tonier area.[29] There, he opened a clothing emporium that outfitted New York's assorted gentlemen, fops, bucks, and dandies. His newspaper ads provide a flavor of the fashionable boulevardier's tastes. He specialized in "superfine cloths of the most fashionable colours," "gold and silver lace," "gold and silver spangled buttons and loops," "a large assortment of gold and silver fringe ornaments with bullion knots and epaulets," and gold "epaulets for gentlemen of the army and militia."[30]

Mulligan may have started in the rag trade, but by the time he moved to Queen Street he was the owner of an enterprise that employed several tailors. He himself was on hand to welcome customers, and may have taken their measurements while letting his employees do the basic cutting and sewing. At this time, as well, thanks to his conversion to Anglicanism, Mulligan was able to marry Elizabeth Sanders, the niece of Admiral Sanders of the Royal Navy. Given his success, his well-connected wife, and his brother's status, Mulligan was able to associate with a certain class of officers and gentlemen on a nearly equal level, which made them comfortable enough to chat with him about military strategy and troop movements.[31]

Outwardly, Mulligan was a paragon of bourgeois respectability; underneath, he nursed a roiling rebelliousness. In 1765 or so, he helped produce *The Constitutional Courant*, an anti–Stamp Act paper so incendiary the British banned it. Undaunted, Mulligan smuggled *samizdat* copies from New Jersey into the city for discreet distribution to interested readers. Five years later, Hercules was a secret member of the militant arm of the Sons of Liberty. He and his comrades dismissed boycotts and petitions as a limp-wristed exercise in futility and demanded a more muscular approach guaranteed to get results—fast.

Understandably, considering his notoriety in Loyalist circles, Mulligan felt that vacating New York after Washington's Long Island defeat might be the most sensible option, and he and his family joined the exodus of Patriot sympathizers. He didn't get far. Within a few days, a party of Tory militiamen roaming the countryside captured him and dragged him back to the city with a blanket over his head the whole way.[32]

Released, and adapting to the new reality, Mulligan made do as best he could by compromising his republican ideals. He stayed in New York and made a decent income from catering to British officers and the businessmen who profited from every defeat Washington's army suffered. With a young family to support, his duty was to survive the war living in an enemy-occupied city; talk of regretting that one had but a single life to give for the cause of liberty was for bachelors and romanticists. Like many other New Yorkers, Mulligan was obliged by circumstances to collaborate, but he refused to betray.

Later in the war, Mulligan becalmed his conscience by becoming, like Amos Underhill, a subagent of the Culper Ring, probably in the summer of 1779. It was then that Woodhull first mentioned that "an acquaintance of Hamilton's" had passed on information that "4 or 5 regiments were embarking, generally said for Quebec [and] had taken altogether thick clothing, yet nevertheless he thought most likely for Georgia, and believed they all had but a short time to stay here."[33]

This "acquaintance" started work a mere six weeks after Robert Townsend, his recruiter, sent his first Culper letter. Through his father, Townsend had known the older man since he had been a child, and knew he could trust him unhesitatingly. Washington, for his part, would have been reassured by Alexander Hamilton, his aide, that Mulligan was sound.[34] Mulligan, however, wrote no letters of his own. According to the recollection of his son John Mulligan, Hercules used to rendezvous on Long Island with an unnamed American agent, who transferred the information he gave to Washington's headquarters.[35] It's possible this hazy memory confused the actuality that Mulligan passed on information verbally to Townsend (who was *from* Long Island)—whose store was just around the corner from Mulligan's— who integrated it into his own reports to Woodhull and Tallmadge.

Arnold did not hold Mulligan for long. As a known former agitator, he had been arrested only on suspicion of having questionable contacts with the enemy, not on hard evidence of espionage. Still, the Irishman's imprisonment did succeed in scaring Townsend enough to drop the correspondence for fear of exposure. He needn't have worried: There wasn't a chance that Mulligan would talk, but Townsend was more alarmed that if Arnold started nosing around people's pasts, his own might come to light and he, too, would face an uncomfortable few weeks in prison.

Until Tallmadge could persuade Townsend to come back, he turned his mind to reorienting the Culper Ring away from conducting undercover operations in New York and toward providing timely intelligence on the ground for Tallmadge's dragoons to launch rapid strikes across the Sound to hit British soldiers and sabotage the Loyalist privateers commerce-raiding and harassing coastal towns. These same privateers were heavily to blame for the delays in conveying the Culper letters—the source of Tallmadge's problems in the first place. Tallmadge also predicted that occasional raids of fifty or sixty dragoons would provide him with "a good opportunity of opening a correspondence on the other side without being suspected by friends and foes"; in other words, he could shorten the line of communications by "attacking" Setauket as a diversion and meeting Woodhull to pick up letters.[36]

The "swarm of [Tory] refugee boats which cruise along the shore of Long Island" had annoyed Tallmadge—and the Culpers, and Long Islanders, and Connecticuters, for that matter—for a long time.[37] Brewster, for instance, complained of "a constant communication kept up for trade and intelligence by the enemy boats, bringing over goods and taking provisions in return, and in such force that renders it impossible and many times makes it dangerous to transact my business with my present command."[38]

Likewise, the Loyalists and the British had been harassed by flotillas of Patriot vessels ever since Washington had abandoned New York in 1776. For the course of the Revolution, a low-intensity guerrilla conflict raged in the Sound that was colloquially known as the "Whaleboat War," named after the swift, thirty-foot-long boats rowed by freebooters on either side. The whaling companies once based on Long Island and Connecticut had owned these whaleboats, originally carried aboard whalers and lowered into the water when hunting their prey on the high seas. With the outbreak of fighting, these companies wound themselves up, leaving their well-trained, hardy crews unemployed.[39] The boats were designed to be easily maneuverable and light enough to be borne on the shoulders of their crew, which numbered anywhere from twelve to twenty-four, one man to each eighteen-foot oar.[40] The whaleboatmen could lift the vessels onto their shoulders and hide them in the bushes when on a raid, shelter under them if a storm broke while on land, or even transport them miles across country and relaunch them on the other side of Long Island to spring a surprise attack.[41] Some were modified with collapsible masts and a swivel gun or two for close-quarters fighting.[42] Amid the roiling waves, in the dark, and with their sails down, the boats' low silhouette camouflaged them from even short distances, and the first a victim knew about an attack was when he saw boarders armed with pikes, cutlasses, and pistols clambering over the stern.

The Whaleboat War began as a legitimate enterprise. The governors of New York and Connecticut had originally handed out privateering commissions to Patriots—Caleb Brewster possessed one dating from October/November 1776—that legally entitled them to find forage and supplies for the needy American army, destroy provisions before the British could get to them, and capture any enemy vessel they found.[43] Thus, in May 1777, General Samuel Parsons ordered Colonel Meigs—a well-born, if rakish, Connecticut man who had been sentenced to death for passing counterfeit money in New York before the war—to destroy the British stockpiles at Sag Harbor. Meigs took 234 men in thirteen whaleboats, along with two sloops for protection, and managed to scuttle no fewer than twelve brigs and sloops, and destroy 120 tons of hay, corn, and oats, as well as a huge quantity of rum, while also killing six and taking ninety militiamen prisoner.[44]

Tories, too, received authority from Sir Henry Clinton to plunder whatever they wanted from the enemy, provided there were "no excesses, barbarities or irregularities."[45] This form of privateering, which was in accordance with the laws of war as they stood at the time, quickly degenerated into piracy on both sides.[46] Whereas once Tories and Patriots had confined themselves to capturing units of soldiers, they soon graduated to kidnapping individuals—usually eminent or rich (or both), but some not so much, such as the luckless carpenter Jonathan Darrow of Southport who was carried off in July 1779 and died on a prison ship a year later. It was a practice that resulted in a series of tit-for-tat raids across the Sound. A typical report in, say, the *New York Gazette* issue of July 17, 1780, ran as follows: "We hear from Setauket, that last Friday a party of rebels surrounded the dwelling house of Doctor Punderson, took him prisoner, and carried him off to Connecticut; and on that night the same party took Mr. William Jayne, Jun. The rebels told Mrs. Punderson that they had taken the doctor to exchange for John Smith, and Mr. Jayne for William Phillips, who were taken at Smithtown, at the widow Blydenburgh's, on a trading party [i.e., illegal smuggling mission]."[47]

Though both sides indulged in hostage taking, the Tories had begun it in May 1779 when Captain Bonnell and his deputy, Newtown-born carpenter Captain Glover, gained Clinton's imprimatur to kidnap the commander of Connecticut's coastal defenses, General Gold Selleck Silliman, who lived two miles outside of Fairfield. Taking seven men with them, Glover and his second-in-command, Lieutenant Hubbell, began beating at the general's door at 1 a.m. on Sunday only to hear the sound of smashing glass as the doughty old warrior thrust a musket through a pane and tried to fire. The powder flashed in the pan, allowing the Tories time to break in. Taking Silliman and his son prisoner, "these ruffians said it was fortunate for him that his gun missed fire [*sic*], for had he killed a man they would have burned the house & murdered all who were in it." As it was, the prisoners were roughly bundled onto the awaiting boats and spirited to Long Island. "On arriving at [Lloyd's Neck] they were hailed by Col. Simcoe," who asked, "'Have you got him?' 'Yes.' 'Have you lost any men?' 'No.' 'That's well,' says Simcoe, 'Your Sillimans and your Washingtons are not worth a man.'"[48] Soon afterwards, the detested Simcoe himself was the target of, as he recalled in his memoirs, "a party of twenty men" from Connecticut who lay "concealed" on Long Island for three weeks, but they failed to nab him.[49]

A month after the Silliman raid, a party of rebels under Major Jesse Brush landed at Treadwell's Farm and kidnapped Justice Hewlett and a Captain Youngs. Brush, a small man with red hair and a sandy complexion, had been a Long Islander before the war, but was forced to flee to Connecticut and his property was expropriated by a Tory. In August 1780, addressing the interloper, he took out an ad in, of all places, Rivington's *Gazette,* warning that "I have repeatedly ordered you ... to leave my farm. This is the last invitation. If you do not, your next landfall will be in a *warmer* climate than any you ever lived in yet. 20 days you have to make your escape." Warning his foe of his intentions may not have been the smartest move, as Brush and his gang were ambushed by the waiting British when they landed in late September to make good the threat; two were killed by musket fire, and the rest, including Brush, were dragged to the clink.[50] Soon after the Brush raid of June 1779, Tories raided Greenwich and took thirteen prisoners, including "a Presbyterian parson, named Burrit, an egregious Rebel, who has frequently taken arms, and is of great repute in that Colony" (according to Rivington's *Gazette* of June 23), plus forty-eight head of cattle and four horses.[51]

In early November 1779, aiming to shanghai a senior Tory to avenge General Silliman, Captain David Hawley and twenty-five men landed near Smithtown, fifty-two miles away from the house of the ultra-Tory Thomas Jones, a justice of the Supreme Court of New York. Hiding their boats in the undergrowth, they trekked for two nights (sleeping during the day in the woods) until they reached Oyster Bay at 9 p.m. on Saturday. They rapped at the door, but Jones was holding a party and no one answered it. Hawley burst through the door and "laid hold of the judge, whom he found in the entry," as well as his nephew. Later, as they marched back to the boats, Jones saw British sentries and "hemmed"; Hawley told him to shut up, whereupon Jones "hemmed" again, only to hear Hawley snarl that "he would run him through" if he did it again. He didn't, and the guards continued on their way none the wiser. Billeted, fittingly, on Mrs. Silliman, who grew quite fond of him, Jones and his nephew were exchanged six months later for Silliman and his son.[52] (The judge and the general maintained an active correspondence after the war.)

It was money that severed the political bonds of the privateers on either side. Loyalists not only soon discovered the profits inherent in smuggling—the so-called London Trade—goods out of New York to the Connecticut shore, but also the delight gained by mugging suspected Whigs (or anyone, for that matter) living on Long Island. In June 1781, for instance, Woodhull mentioned to Tallmadge that "a number of men commanded by one Stephen Smith a deserter from Col. Ludlow's [Loyalist] regiment, much abused and plundered several houses at a place called Drowned Meadow [now Port Jefferson]; broke their windows, fired into their houses, whipped and threatened both old and young."[53]

Patriots, for their part, conveniently interpreted their official marques to imply that they could plunder at will behind enemy lines, stealing everything from furniture to coins to horses. What happened, inevitably, is that since Long Island was controlled by the enemy, *anyone* who lived there was a potential target, be he Tory or Whig. The Culpers had long complained of the predations of their own side: "It is the nature of the people here, they will do any thing to get money," lamented Woodhull in June 1779.[54] Brewster once wrote to Governor Clinton about the atrocities that had occurred in the first two weeks alone of August 1781. Two boatloads of men banged on the doors of the houses of Captain Ebenezer Miller and Andrew Miller. The captain's young son was shot dead, and then Mr. Miller was hit "with the breech of a gun" which "broke the bone over his eye, tore his eye all to pieces [and] broke his cheek bone." The gang left him for dead. Another time, Gilbert Flint was hanged from his own rafters "till he was so near dead, that they had to apply the doctor to fetch him to." And then there was Major Richard Thorn, whose Patriotic credentials were impeccable, who received a visit at his house in Great Neck. They "hung him up to make him tell where his money was till they thought him dead, then cut him down and after awhile finding life yet in him, one of the party took his knife and cut him under his jaw from one ear to the other" before heading for Mr. Coulne's place, where they "hung him up in the same manner to get his hard cash and plundered his house." "There's not a night but they are over; if boats can cross people can't ride the roads but what they are robbed," concluded Brewster.[55]

A month later, relates another petition to Clinton, there was a crime spree between Friday, September 14, and Sunday the sixteenth. On the first night, two Connecticut crews stole sheep from Joseph Havens of Southampton; the second, they ransacked the houses of Nicoll Havens, Captain James Havens, and Mrs. Payne, a widow, all on Shelter Island; the third, this time at Southold, they burgled David Gardiner, assaulted Joseph Peck, beat up Mr. L'Hommedieu and his wife (described as "aged persons"), and tried to raze the house of Mrs. Moore (another widow).[56]

Like Brewster, Tallmadge also nursed a particular dislike of these men who declaimed their Revolutionary principles while acting like *banditi*. The "crime of plundering the destroyed inhabitants of Long Island" is having a terrible effect on morale, he reported to Washington in 1779, because "the marauders from our shore make no distinction between Whig and Tory." Moreover, "the boat [used] for dispatches from C—— has been chased quite across the Sound by these plunderers... while our crew has supposed them the enemy." Worse, owing to their menaces, "C—— will not risk, nor 725 [Brewster] go over for dispatches."[57]

Indeed, about six weeks before, one of Townsend's last letters had been lost when Woodhull, awaiting Austin Roe at Stony Brook for a drop-off, was disturbed by the sound of the militia being mustered "to pursue and lay wait for Ebenezar [*sic*] Dayton and his companions, that last night plundered two houses." "Dayton's excursion," he complained, "was the sole cause of the loss" of Townsend's letter as "the refugees and some troops were filling the road that the express was to pass." Brewster had had to return to Connecticut empty-handed. "These things you will readily conceive lay me open, and I desire you to take such measures to prevent the like again," pleaded Woodhull.[58]

This Ebenezer Dayton was a notorious freebooter who caused

havoc up and down the Long Island shore throughout the war. Before it, Dayton had been a peddler who sold goods on credit and was for a time a minuteman, but the British invasion obliged him to move his wife, Phebe, and their three children to New Haven, Connecticut, while he sailed back and forth across the Sound to recover money owed to him by former customers. Within a year, Dayton, having noticed that plundering was easier than debt collection, had drifted into "privateering." By 1778, he was cruising the Sound in his own schooner, the *Suffolk*, escorted by no fewer than four heavily armed whaleboats, each with fourteen men. On June 5, Dayton and Company jumped four British merchant vessels (*Dispatch, Polly, Jane,* and *Lively*) and captured them all. The next year, as Woodhull's letter attested, Dayton found it compatible with his patriotic conscience to launch inland raids on Long Island and to make no distinction between friend and foe. (In 1786, it was reported that Dayton, charged for his privateering activities, had drowned in the Housatonic River. In 1853, his son, the Reverend Smith Dayton, revealed that Ebenezer had faked his death and had actually died in New Orleans in 1802 of yellow fever, aged fifty-eight.)[59]

Washington agreed with Tallmadge and his agents that "the piracies upon the inhabitants of Long-Island . . . are in their very nature injurious to our cause, and altogether unjustifiable," and promised to take up the matter with Governors Clinton (of New York) and Trumbull (of Connecticut).[60] Little came of Washington's intervention. While Clinton proved willing to revoke their privateering commissions, saying they meant well but in fact were hurting more than they helped the cause, Trumbull reiterated that the whaleboatmen had paid two-thousand-pound bonds for the right to attack enemy assets and that any Whigs who were allegedly robbed by them enjoyed recourse to the law.[61] (It was only in August 1781 that a congressional committee finally ordered Trumbull to cancel their privileges.)[62]

Brewster, characteristically, had little time for such legalities and tackled the problem directly. His particular bugbears were Captains Glover (who had helped kidnap General Silliman) and Hoyt, his accomplice, who prowled the seas around Setauket. While Brewster was picking up a Culper letter at 2 a.m. on August 17, 1780, "I was attacked by Glover and Hoyght [*sic*]. I left one man taken and one wounded. We killed one on the spot. The man that was taken went after water. I shall want two men before I come across again. I have got two boats in fine order. I wish you send me seven men and I engage to take some of their boats."[63] A few days later, without waiting to hear back from Tallmadge, Brewster went over with three boats "in search of Glover and Hoyght, but could hear nothing of them. They never stayed to bury their dead man. They carried another away with them mortally wounded." Still, the fact that the "cussed [Tory] refugees are so thick I can't go amiss of them" persuaded Brewster to try his luck once more with the wily duo, but when he crossed again a week later, they had disappeared.[64] He would have to bide his time.

His efforts did not entirely go unrewarded. The British troops on the Island had become distinctly lackadaisical, and Brewster thought it "a fine time to take some of the officers. They are out with their hounds every day." Indeed, as Brewster holed up in Selah and Anna Strong's back garden in Setauket waiting for Woodhull, "there came a lieutenant of 17th Regiment within gunshot of us" who was out hunting. Brewster and his men pulled the officer down from his horse and were hauling him back to Connecticut, "but he begged so hard I thought it not best to take him as it was so near [Strong's] house." Pity was not among Brewster's virtues, but he correctly perceived that if the lieutenant were kidnapped, the British would strengthen their guard in the area, not only casting suspicion on Mrs. Strong—Woodhull's occasional accomplice—as a harborer of rebels but making it still more difficult to pick up Culper letters. As it was, the freed lieutenant would assume his assailants were thieves who chanced upon him rather than whaleboatmen on a more sensitive mission.[65]

Brewster would be luckier—though Glover and Hoyt continued to evade him—the following February, when he was cruising off Long Island with three whaleboats. As they prepared to leave, he spotted a "boat rowing from eastward. I lay concealed till she came opposite to me when I detached one of my boats in pursuit." It turned out that she was a Tory privateer with an eight-man crew. Back in Connecticut, he sent the prisoners (Captain Joseph Trowbridge, Henry Gibbs, Benjamin Prescott—who had already been jailed for illicit trading, but had escaped—James Smith, a captain in the King's Militia Volunteers, Thomas Davis, Thomas Wilson, Christopher Young, and Job Mosier) under the care of a corporal and six men to General Parsons's headquarters for safekeeping.[66] Unfortunately, two of them escaped along the way, presumably to plunder again.[67]

Brewster's adventures notwithstanding, taking on the privateers one by one would not deter their future attacks. The Americans needed to hit their center of operations, to sever the head from the limbs, so to speak. In this respect, the Loyalists were vulnerable. While the Patriot whaleboatmen dispersed their forces by using the Connecticut seaports of Stratford, Fairfield, Norwalk, Stamford, and Greenwich as their bases, Tory privateers—who now conglomerated under the official-sounding moniker of the "Board of Associated Loyalists"—camped just outside Fort Franklin at Lloyd's Neck, Long Island, an elevated promontory between Oyster Bay and Huntington. Sir Henry Clinton maintained a garrison—at one point numbering five hundred—there for the purpose of protecting these guerrillas.[68] When they weren't at sea, Woodhull complained, "parties of them" hid in the woods "laying wait for the unwary and ignorant" and then deceived them by "putting on the character of people from your shore." They had recently "carried off 10 or 12 men and stripped their houses lately from about 20. The roads from here to [New York] is infested by them, and likewise the shores."[69]

Eliminating this nest of piracy became, for obvious reasons, of key importance to the Americans. In 1779, General Parsons planned an attack, but at the time he had only the frigate *Confederacy* and the ship of war *Oliver Cromwell* available—vessels too valuable to risk in a raid, quite aside from their bulk barring any hope of surprise—so he gave it up.[70] "Having a great desire to break up this band of freebooters," Tallmadge revived it in early September of that year, when he daringly took 130 of his dismounted dragoons across the Sound in a small, sleek armada of sloops and whaleboats commanded by Brewster, landed near the Tories' camp at 10 p.m., and took them completely by surprise. He destroyed their boats and burned their huts, netted several prisoners, and returned to Connecticut without the loss of a single man.[71] This would be but the first of Tallmadge's great amphibious raids.

The camp may have gone but Fort Franklin, however, still stood. In August 1780, prompted by General Parsons, who had sent in a spy, Tallmadge began pondering with Caleb Brewster and Woodhull a scheme to attack it. To this end, the latter provided a rough diagram of the fort on August 6, but Washington did "not think it advisable under present circumstances. Although the enemy appear to be small, dispersed parties, yet the risk in an attempt more than counterbalances the advantage which might be obtained."[72] Tallmadge, however, was already nursing doubts about "the character" of the agent Parsons had sent in, and it was greatly to his relief that Washington again refused to approve it. Afterwards, Tallmadge learned, "that on the night we had appointed to cross, a large body of the garrison were stationed at the place appointed for our landing, which probably would have annoyed us greatly."[73] The agent had betrayed them. If nothing else, Tallmadge learned from this experience to trust only his own spies and no one else's, especially Parsons's, who recruited men of shadowy, shifting loyalties, by-products of the Sound's guerrilla raids and whaleboat wars. It would soon emerge as one of the most valuable lessons of all—when the spy code-named "Hiram," the most adept triple agent of the war, began operating.

Arnold's defection had also prompted Tallmadge to plot a suitable revenge to lift the deflated spirits of the Patriots. For some months, Woodhull had been describing the state and readiness of the local troops in uncomplimentary terms. One time, for instance, Woodhull noticed that "there [are] about 50 refugees at and about Tredles farm near Smiths Town [who] possess a small fort, two field pieces, but are under no command [since] each man thinks himself [his own] captain... and are disagreeing continually. Good judges say they can be taken at any time with ease and is thought they will leave that quarter soon, if they should not be attacked."[74] On September 4, 1780, to give another example, thirty-four Queen's Rangers had recently left Setauket. "For God's sake attack them," pleaded Woodhull, "you'll certainly be successful, if you are secret about it. Trust not to small boats at this season, you have three strong vessels on your shore that will be sufficient to bring five hundred men. Setauket is exceedingly distressed."[75] Nothing came of it, but in late October Woodhull noticed a nearby foraging force of 150 wagons accompanied "with a very small guard of militia troops," about seventeen. "Yourself [Tallmadge] with fifty men might do as you would with them. They are much off their guard. I think if you undertake and call on me you will do something handsome."[76] The foragers left before Tallmadge could organize a quick hit-and-run, but by that time the colonel was cooking up a raid that would truly shock the enemy.

It had been Woodhull who, some time before, had first mentioned that at Coram—seven or eight miles inland from Setauket—the British were stockpiling hay, forage essential for running their war machine.[77] In the first few days of November 1780, Tallmadge asked Brewster to call on Woodhull for more details. On November 6, Brewster returned with news, gleaned from Woodhull (who had ridden there for a look), that *three hundred* tons of hay had already been gathered for transport to New York. And there was more. Tories from Rhode Island had confiscated General John Smith's house at Smith's Point, at Mastic, on the south shore of Long Island, about eight miles further on from Coram, and had built a formidable triangular stockade they had christened, patriotically, Fort St. George. At two corners were stronghouses, the third consisting of Smith's house fortified with a deep ditch and encircled by sharpened stakes protruding at a 45-degree angle. The stockade itself was "quite high" and every post was "fastened to each other by a transverse rail strongly bolted to each." Once work was completed, Fort St. George would likely prove a nettlesome irritant. As it was, the British were already using it as a safe storehouse for wood, "stores, dry goods, groceries, and arms" due to be exported into

New York, and it was not far-fetched to predict that oceangoing privateers would soon seek protection in its bay. Tallmadge immediately urged Washington to let him mount a raid "with about 40 or 50 dismounted dragoons" to destroy the stockpile *and* the fortress in one ambitious (and highly risky) swoop.[78]

Washington, too, sensed a strategic opportunity to denude the British of their supplies just as winter was settling in: Without fuel, the despicable Arnold would have to endure a most unpleasant few months as the temperature dropped. Thus, he told Tallmadge in a letter written on November 11, the hay at Coram "is of so much consequence that I should advise the attempt to be made. I have written to Col. Sheldon to furnish a detachment of [100] dismounted dragoons, and will commit the execution to you." Brewster was to accompany him. Regarding Fort St. George, however, if it can be done "without frustrating the other [aim] or running too great a hazard...I have no objection—what you must remember [is] this is only a secondary object."[79] Not for Tallmadge it wasn't, who quietly determined to attack the fort after he heard from Brewster (and Woodhull, indirectly) that "their remains about forty Ruffigeus yet at Mastick on Mr. Smith's place. They have no connon, nothing but muskets."[80] For the time being, Fort St. George was an easy mark.

On November 21, at four in the afternoon, Tallmadge met his hundred chosen dragoons at Fairfield and took them across to a place called the Old Man's, a few miles east of Setauket. At 10 p.m., after they had silently marched five miles inland, a fierce wind began to blow, driving rain hard into their faces. There was nothing for it but to return to the beach, where the whaleboats had been concealed in the bushes, and shelter under them for the night. The next night, the rain having abated, they set off again and were within two miles of Fort St. George by 4 a.m. Tallmadge divided his company into three, he commanding the major part, and two subalterns "of high spirit" (one was Lieutenant Thomas Tredwell Jackson, who left a bloodthirsty memoir of the event) taking the balance. They were to circle around the fortress and conceal themselves until they heard the enemy "fire upon my column." By dawn, all were ready. Tallmadge's "pioneers"—commandos skilled at breaking through stockades—surged forward first and got to within forty yards of the wall before a formerly drowsy sentry rather foolishly left the stockade, "halted his march, looked attentively at our column, and demanded 'Who comes there?' and fired." But "before the smoke from his gun had cleared his vision, my sergeant, who marched by my side, reached him with his bayonet, and prostrated him" (as Tallmadge delicately put it).

The sentry's shot was the signal to charge. The two other detachments "all seemed to vie with each other to enter the fort," Tallmadge later wrote. Lieutenant Jackson recalled in greater detail that he scrambled out of the ditch surrounding the southeastern stronghouse only to meet Brewster with his blood up barging through the main gate. All this had been achieved without loss and without an American musket fired. Brewster, and Jackson's unit of fifteen men, stormed the stronghouse: "The poor dogs had not time to rub their eyes, or gasp before they were obliged to cry quarters." Soon after, the remaining stronghouse and Smith's house were taken, at which point "the watchword, 'Washington and glory,' was repeated from three points of the fort at the same time." It was too soon for celebration. "While we were standing, elated with victory, in the centre of the fort, a volley of musketry was discharged from the windows of one of the large houses, which induced me," said Tallmadge, "to order my whole detachment to load and return the fire." Even so, the diehards barricaded themselves in, obliging Tallmadge to send his pioneers to break the doors down with axes. "As soon as the troops could enter, the confusion and conflict were great." Those who had fired after the fort was taken, and its colors struck, "were thrown headlong from the windows of the second story to the ground." "Having forfeited their lives by the usages of war," judged Tallmadge, "all would have been killed had I not ordered the slaughter to cease." After that, the victors destroyed "an immense quantity of stores" and demolished "the enemy's works." Tallmadge is guilty of omitting a few unpleasant facts in his sunny report, though Jackson alluded to them when he wrote to a friend that there "was a scene ... of war my eyes never beheld nor description cannot equal. The cries of the wounded in the agonies of death. The screeching of the women and children while the parent and friend were entreating pity and compassion, called forth every tender feeling." Tallmadge never mentions these "women and children," but the Loyalist journalist James Rivington, in his story in the *Royal Gazette* of December 2, did. Rivington reminded his readers that "a body of respectable loyal Refugees ... who were establishing a post in order to get a present subsistence for themselves and their distressed families" manned Fort St. George. Taking into account Rivington's politics, and his habitual spinning of the news, it cannot be true that these "respectable loyal Refugees" were quite as angelic as he said. Fort St. George was, after all, a legitimate military target whose garrison continued to fight after the colors were struck; even so, Tallmadge seems to have lost control of some of his men temporarily. One woman, for instance, was "barbarously wounded through both breasts, of which wound she now lingers a specimen of rebel savageness and degeneracy." As for the sentry who had fired the first shot and was "prostrated" by the sergeant's bayonet, he was Isaac Hart, formerly of Newport and once an eminent merchant, who, after falling to the ground, was "wounded in fifteen different parts of his body, and beat with their muskets in the most shocking manner in the very act of imploring quarter, and died of his wounds in a few hours after."[81]

What to do with the haul of prisoners, some fifty, including a colonel, a captain, a lieutenant, and a surgeon? They were pinioned two-by-two and forced to carry heavy bundles of "dry goods." At 8 a.m., Tallmadge's company left whatever was left of Fort St. George and marched away. The colonel selected about a dozen men and together they took horses from the fort while the rest, with the prisoners, were ordered to rendezvous with them at a spot "at the middle of the island." Tallmadge and his now-mounted dragoons (including Brewster) rode to Coram, "made a vigorous charge upon the guard placed to protect" the stores of hay, "set it all on fire," and left to meet the rest. By four o'clock that afternoon, the company reached the shore and pulled their boats from their hiding places, and nine hours later they were all safely back in Fairfield. Not a man had been lost, and just one was badly wounded. The enemy, however, suffered seven killed and wounded, most mortally.[82]

For this mission, Tallmadge received the thanks of Congress. More personally, Washington congratulated him on the success, particularly the destruction of the hay "which must...be severely felt by the enemy at this time." Tallmadge must accept his commander's "thanks for your judicious planning and spirited execution of this business" and asked that "you will offer them to the officers and men who shared the honor of the enterprise with you." (As a reward, Washington allowed his "gallant party" to split "the little booty" they had acquired.)[83] Just as heartfelt, and as deeply appreciated, was Woodhull's excited letter of November 28: "I congratulate you on your success within the bounds of 729 [Long Island]. The burning the forage is agreeable to me and must hurt the enemy much."[84] Still better news followed: In January 1781, Woodhull went to New York for the first time in months and saw Townsend. The latter, he said, "intends to undertake the business again in the spring."[85]

With that knowledge, not even a letter of mind-boggling impudence Tallmadge received from Benedict Arnold could dampen his mood. The missive, originally written on October 25, but not delivered until late January, was an invitation to come over the water. "As I know you to be a man of sense, I am conscious you are by this time fully of opinion that the real interest and happiness of America consists in a reunion with Great Britain.... I have taken a commission in the British Army, and invite you to join me with as many men as you can bring over with you. If you think proper to embrace my offer you shall have the same rank you now hold, in the cavalry I am about to raise."

Arnold's letter so disgusted Tallmadge he wasted no time sending it directly to Washington, while noting that "I am equally a stranger to the channel through which it was conveyed, the reason why it was so long on its way, or the motives which induced the Traitor to address himself thus particularly to me."[86]

CHAPTER NINE

The Wilderness of Mirrors

André's death prompted a reformation of the British counterintelligence system under his successor, Major Oliver De Lancey of the Seventeenth Light Dragoons, and his aides, Captain George Beckwith and Colonel Beverley Robinson. De Lancey—he who had knavishly struck General Nathaniel Woodhull in 1776—was described in 1775 as "a lusty, fat, ruddy young fellow, between twenty and thirty years of age."[1] Immediately after taking over, he directed that more attention be paid to acquiring political and tactical intelligence. Unlike the American setup, in which case-officers like Tallmadge looked after their own small networks and conceived their own ciphers and procedures, De Lancey ensured that his aides shared sources, dealt with agents on a rota, and used the same standard codes. This meant that none of them was indispensable; if one manager was captured, his agents and codes wouldn't disappear with him. The American system's disadvantage was that if Tallmadge was taken out of the picture, the Culper Ring would have instantly gone dark and silent. On the other hand, because he dealt with his assets personally, Tallmadge knew his men's characters, fears, and desires far better, and could coddle and chastise them more effectively than his British counterparts. The Culpers, too, trusted Tallmadge implicitly, and he them, unlike the British managers and their agents, who maintained more of a cold business relationship. Another systemic difference is that while Washington insisted on cross-referencing overlapping, and often tedious, intelligence reports to sift out exaggerations, De Lancey preferred to file reports in chronological order in an Intelligence Book—an idea inherited from André.[2]

Whereas the more experienced Washington was aware of the perils of intelligence provided by sometimes flawed agents, De Lancey's mind was not attuned to the tricks agents play in a business where the ability to lie, dissemble, manipulate, and impersonate was a virtue. Which is why he fell so hard for the Hiram Hoax: "Hiram" being the triple agent William Heron—he worked for the Americans, for the British, but above all, for himself—a Freemason whose code name was a personal in-joke: The character of Hiram plays a central role in Freemasonry as the master of the construction of Solomon's Temple who refused to divulge to outsiders the secrets of the craft. Heron covered his tracks so expertly his own dark secret would not emerge for another century.

Heron entered the secret world accidentally. In late August 1780, he had business to attend to in New York, and he applied for a flag—essentially, a pass recognized by both sides—from General Samuel Holden Parsons, a "plain, mean-looking old man" with long hair who wore "shoes that I fancy were made by himself" (a catty allusion to his former trade as a cobbler).[3] As New York was out of his purvey, Parsons sent him to General Arnold—whose defection was just a few weeks away—for the necessaries along with a letter of recommendation stating that Heron "is a neighbour of mine, for whose integrity and firm attachment to the cause of the country I will hold myself answerable."[4]

Heron was hoping to obtain a license to ship goods to Ireland, and for one of those, he needed the approval of the British authorities. To that end, while he was in the city, he paid a visit to William Smith, the chief justice, and told him that "the majority of the Continent have long been for a reunion with Great Britain." Pleased to find an American expressing such stout Loyalist sentiments, Smith wrote Heron a letter of introduction to General Robertson, then the commandant of New York, who subsequently reported to London that Heron "ever was an enemy to the Declaration of Independency, but he thought it prudent to be silent, except to a few of the most trusty Loyalists." Most interesting to Robertson was Heron's claim that he was "intimate" with General Parsons, who commanded the Connecticut lines, and that Parsons was "greatly dejected under the prevailing disinclination of the people to continue the war."[5] This tidbit—one didn't often hear of possibly disaffected generals—was duly filed. Soon after, Heron received his license to ship goods.

It's difficult to unsnarl the truth from the coils of Heron's obfuscations. Was he "ever . . . an enemy to the Declaration"? Had Parsons merely expressed, in the way grizzled old soldiers do, a few annoyed remarks about the incompetence of his superiors and lamented the public's reluctance to send him more troops? These were questions the British unfortunately never asked themselves. They might have been forgiven, at least partly, for their lack of curiosity. Traditionally, the British had believed that most Americans were loyal at heart but had been seduced by the revolutionaries. So Heron's intimations would have rung true with them.[6] It was also known that Washington was faced with mutinous units, that Congress was essentially bankrupt, and that the Revolutionary effort was faltering. And they additionally knew, though Heron didn't, that Arnold was intending to betray West Point: Could it be that *more* generals were willing to come over?

Heron's motives, in other words, were *so* credible, the British felt they could trust the man while overlooking his more questionable aspects. Among these was the absence of anything in Heron's past to indicate a secret hankering for royal rule. Quite the opposite, in fact. Born an Irishman in 1742, Heron emigrated from Cork to Connecticut several years before the Revolution, and established himself at Redding, where he and Parsons found themselves living next door to each other. Originally a merchant, Heron sought a political career and by April 1777 sat on several local Patriot committees, including one charged with hiring soldiers for the Continental army. Beginning in May 1778, he represented the town in Connecticut's General Assembly.[7]

And second, Heron's principles were easily compromised by the lure of lucre. A grinding snob, Heron's favorite phrase was "We must keep the underbrush down," a sentiment that put him at odds with the uppity underbrush of his adopted state. He had a talent for embellishing his social and financial credentials, and claimed to be a graduate of Trinity College, Dublin, yet never attended that institution. He enjoyed the delights of cash, and spent a great deal on gold-headed canes, laced waistcoats, and velvet breeches—not items easy to come by in the midst of Revolutionary Connecticut.[8] It wasn't entirely beyond the realm of possibility that, despite his airy proclamations of allegiance, Heron's primary aim was profit.

On the other hand, Parsons, like Robertson and Smith, regarded him highly. As Parsons wrote to Washington, Heron was "a man of very large knowledge, and a great share of natural sagacity, united with a sound judgment," and mentioned that he was of "as unmeaning a countenance as any person in my acquaintance."[9] Heron's "unmeaning countenance" always reflected whatever people wanted, or expected, to see.

Parsons's faith was further strengthened on Heron's return to Connecticut, when he told the general about the British fortifications he had seen in New York. But what had originated as a dubious business deal turned into a major confidence scam once news of Arnold's defection emerged. Heron suddenly appreciated how much money the British were willing to pay for high-ranking turncoats. So he invented one: General Parsons. And thus began William Heron's remarkable career in secret service. In the winter of 1780–81, he volunteered his talents to Oliver De Lancey, who keenly accepted them.

Hiram's first letter was written on February 4, 1781. It contained one vital piece of intelligence—culled from his chats with the unwitting

Parsons, who was well acquainted with the whaleboatmen operating out of Connecticut. "Private dispatches are frequently sent from your city to the Chieftain [Washington] here by some traitors. They come by the way of Setalket [*sic*], where a certain Brewster receives them at, or near, a certain woman's." Hiram had provided yet another lead in the dossier the British were keeping on this mysterious Setauket leak they had been hearing about for years. The main problem was that Brewster remained at large, and the "certain woman"—Anna Strong—was untraceable without him. [10]

Cultivating his newfound taste for intrigue, Heron also began working for *Parsons* as a spy. In late February, Washington had written to Parsons requesting him to unearth a "plot among the tories of Stratford and Fairfield" he had heard about. He suggested finding a local man to go undercover as a Tory, and pledged to ensure the agent received "generous compensation."[11] Since money was involved, Heron was happy to help out, though, suspiciously, he was never able to provide "a sufficient degree of precision to make any attempt to secure the persons concerned," Parsons reported. After all, to have exerted himself too greatly in that respect would at once have ended that stream of "generous pay for his time and services" and ended his utility to Parsons. So he ran out the clock for as long as he could.[12]

For Heron, acting as a Tory—on Washington-approved "official" business—bore rich fruit. In order to further the deception, he was allowed to travel to New York and around Connecticut freely, and he could even trade illegally with the British as part of his cover. During one of his trips to New York, Heron had another interview with De Lancey. During it, he raised the possibility that it was in the British "power to tamper with" Parsons, since from his "mercenary disposition, there is little doubt of success."[13] He further embellished the story by telling De Lancey that Parsons was "a person possessed of a low Jesuitical cunning, but far from being a great character [he] is in needy circumstances, consequently avaricious, which was most ironic coming from the likes of Heron."[14]

In short order, Heron had begun working two parts and was

profiting both ways. His theatrical role as William Heron, Esq., covert Patriot and American spy, brought him closer to Parsons, who innocently provided the intelligence Heron then sold to De Lancey in his alternate guise as Hiram, covert Loyalist and British spy. Likewise, whenever he returned from New York, Heron passed on to Parsons nuggets of intelligence he'd picked up either from De Lancey or on the way home to Connecticut.[15]

On April 24, Hiram again reported to De Lancey. After returning to Connecticut, he wrote, "In order to break the ice (as says the vulgar adage)" with Parsons about "the business" (i.e., his proposed defection), Heron told Parsons that he had a conversation with "a gentleman" in New York. This suspiciously anonymous acquaintance said a soldier such as Parsons could do much good by "lending his aid in terminating this unhappy war in an amicable re-union with the parent state." Should he undertake the burden of making peace, the "Government will amply reward him, both in a lucrative and honorary way and manner." Parsons, according to Heron, "listened with uncommon attention" and said he was "disposed to a reconciliation," though stipulating that "he must have a reasonable...compensation."[16] At this point, Heron mentioned the matter of his own compensation to De Lancey, and asked for two hundred pounds to cover his expenses.[17] De Lancey authorized the payment.

Heron's conversation with Parsons was entirely fraudulent. At the time, Parsons was on maneuvers deep in Connecticut, after which he contracted a near-fatal fever that laid him up at camp.[18] Heron was not able to see him, and even if he had, the stricken general was unlikely to have discussed treason—for he well knew what the code word "reconciliation" meant after Arnold's flight—on what he thought was his deathbed.

It hooked De Lancey, even so. On the day following Heron's faked report, De Lancey excitedly drew up a list of items Heron had promised to get from his counterfeit traitor. These included: "the exact state of West Point," "who commands," "what troops," and "what P——s wish is, how we can serve him." As usual, Heron was telling De

Lancey what he wanted to hear, and what should have remained a hypothesis about the *possibility* of Parsons being disaffected transubstantiated into the established fact that he did intend to defect.[19]

On June 17, Hiram apologized for not sending on all the information De Lancey had requested, and promised to do so as soon as he could. In reality, as a civilian Heron had no way of discovering the "exact state" of the West Point defenses, but he continued the fiction of Parsons's imminent defection. He had discussed the matter again with the general and found "him disposed to go some lengths (as the phrase is) to serve you, and even going thus far is gaining a great deal" but "he will not at present explicitly say that he will go such lengths as I could wish." Parsons, apparently, was struggling with his "scruples"—those of "education, family connections and military ideas of honor." However, Heron thought that an appeal to "interest...rather than principle" might overcome these. Heron here was discreetly hinting at cash payments, though again, this conversation could not have occurred. Parsons, at the time, was one hundred miles away from Redding on the march with his troops.[20]

De Lancey, for whom the phrase "hook, line, and sinker" could have been invented, was so thrilled by Heron's progress he compiled a twelve-point list of further intelligence he wanted Hiram to acquire. He even made a concrete offer: three guineas for Parsons for every man he "puts in our possession" (by way of comparison, Arnold was promised just two), plus an unspecified sum, when he defected. Even better for Heron, he promised that "gratitude will prompt us to keep pace in our recompense to you, with the rewards given to our friend."

Heron again masterfully evaded handing over any hard intelligence. Parsons, he said, "does not wish to take an open and avowed part at present," though he was willing to "communicate any material intelligence" through his self-appointed intermediary. However, Heron suggested that it might prove persuasive if "something generous" were provided immediately for Parsons, and to that end, Heron selflessly volunteered to convey the money to the general, money which Heron pocketed.

By late June, and having paid over the required retainer, De Lancey at last began insisting on getting some results out of Heron. The spy was now in a bit of a fix. He had to show proof that Parsons was viable. After brooding on the matter for a few weeks, Heron decided to bluff it out. The "ascendancy I have over him, the confidence he has already reposed in me, the alluring prospect of pecuniary, as well as honorary rewards, together with the plaudits of a grateful nation," he grandly declared to De Lancey, made him think that Parsons himself would answer De Lancey's questions in a letter "and entrust me with the care of communicating" it.[21]

In mid-July, Heron duly provided a letter from Parsons fulfilling De Lancey's laundry list of questions. According to Heron, Parsons had written "as to a confidential friend, anxious to know those matters and occurrences, which may in anywise affect the cause of the country." For once, Heron was telling the truth—sort of. Parsons's letter *was* written in such a style, and did contain many details, such as where his camp was, how many men he had under his command, who was commanding the other regiments, and how little ammunition he had. But that was because in order to get De Lancey off his back, Heron had specifically asked Parsons about these matters and was merely sending on Parsons's polite reply, which revealed no sensitive plans. Heron, to recap, was a long-standing and respectable member of the Connecticut Assembly, and it would not have perturbed Parsons to mention such things to a respectable politician of pronounced Whig views. So, Parsons's letter to Heron *was* exactly what the latter declared it to be: a letter reassuring an "anxious" correspondent that all was well with the war. As Parsons wrote, while he running low on ammunition and provisions, "your fears for them are groundless," as the stockpiles "are principally at West Point, Fishkill, Wapping's Creek & Newburgh, which puts them out of the enemy's power." It was all junk, yet so pleased was De Lancey with Heron's "coup" that he authorized the payment of four hundred pounds for Parsons (or Heron, rather).[22]

Although Heron continued to scheme in fits and starts until March 1782, De Lancey eventually realized that Parsons was never going to come over and lost interest. In any case, Heron couldn't have kept up the pantomime much longer, for Parsons resigned from the army in May 1782 for reasons of "extreme ill health," and De Lancey himself was replaced by Beckwith as head of the secret service in July (probably as a result of Clinton's annoyance over the Parsons goose chase).[23]

Even if it would prove a mixed year for British intelligence, for the Culpers, 1781 opened brightly enough. Woodhull's letter of January 14 stating that Townsend "intends to undertake the business again in the spring" was soon followed by his observation that "it appears to me that we need not doubt of success, and that it is not far distant."[24] In early February, nonetheless, a note of annoyance did creep into Woodhull's missives, the subject being money—and how much he was owed. "It is now a full year that I have supported this correspondence and have forwarded frequent dispatches—and the expenses incurred amounts to one hundred and seven pounds eighteen shillings, and all I have received is 29 guineas. The balance is due me and in want thereof, wish it could be forwarded soon."[25]

Woodhull would soon have a lot more than money to worry about. Townsend, after a promising start ("C. Jur. is again in 727 [New York] and entering into business as heretofore and you may soon I hope receive his dispatches," reported Woodhull in mid-March), quickly faltered and seems to have gone on strike.[26] Sometime in late April, said the cell leader, "I had a 657 [visit] from C. Junr and am sorry to inform you that he will not 691 [work] any more on any account whatever." That wasn't entirely accurate: Townsend *was* willing to work, if just to provide "verbal accounts," but only if his expenses were taken care of. Like those of Woodhull, Washington had let them slide.[27]

Tallmadge rode, or rather sailed, to the rescue. He went to Long Island to see Woodhull, where "the matter of a future correspondence" was "fully discussed." It turned out Woodhull (and Townsend) had *two* concerns, not one. First was the payment of a "sufficient sum of money to defray the contingent expenses," said Tallmadge. "C. Senior observes that he is already considerably in advance for the business" but he recognized that "if in the present state of our public affairs it should be found difficult to furnish money for the purpose, he will advance 100 guineas or more if needed, receiving your Excellency's assurance that it shall be refunded by the public, with reasonable interest, after the War."

The second, more difficult to resolve than the first, was security. Jonas Hawkins had left their service some years before, and Austin Roe—who Townsend disliked, in any case—appears to have become more reluctant to undertake the dangerous and uncomfortable rides to and from New York. Neither Townsend nor Woodhull was willing to leave their posts, and Woodhull had stipulated, with Townsend's agreement, "that some confidential person must of course be employed to carry dispatches as it would cause suspicions which might lead to detection if either of the Culpers should be frequently passing from New York to Setauket, &c. they being men of some considerable note."[28]

The Culpers, Senior and Junior, were not exaggerating. In recent months, as part of their beefed-up intelligence apparatus, the British had established new checkpoints, were sending out more frequent patrols, and had recruited dozens of informers. Mostly owing to Hiram's tips, they were already aware that an intelligence network was operating in New York, passing through Setauket, and from there it wasn't difficult to guess that Tallmadge—who the British knew, thanks to Arnold, was its manager—was arranging transport across the Sound. The British secret service wanted to roll it up.

Tallmadge himself had noticed the reinvigorated efforts of the enemy: In early April, he reported, British intelligence had adopted a "regular system" to "open a more effectual communication with the disaffected in this state [Connecticut]. Chains of intelligence, which are daily growing more dangerous, and the more injurious traffic [across the Sound], which is constantly increasing, are but the too fatal consequences, which this system is calculated to promote."[29]

One of the men responsible for these "chains of intelligence" was Colonel Joshua Upham. A former Massachusetts Loyalist turned colonel of dragoons and aide-de-camp to Sir Henry Clinton, he had recently been placed in charge of the Lloyd's Neck whaleboatmen, who had rebuilt the camp outside Fort Franklin that Tallmadge had destroyed in September 1779 and were busy disrupting communications across the Sound as part of the British plan to unsettle the Culpers. Being well acquainted with De Lancey, Upham was also involved in a bit of spying. In June he sent "two refugees of fair character" to Connecticut to see "several friends to Government [i.e., British] who reside in that country"; they brought back news of four French divisions having left Rhode Island, the first proceeding to Danbury, and the second and third to Hartford (the destination of the fourth was unknown). "Their object," he wrote, "is universally believed by the rebels, and friends of government to be New York." Upham's intelligence, which was accordingly filed in De Lancey's Intelligence Book, was substantially accurate: Rochambeau was moving his troops in order to participate in Washington's scheme to surround a Loyalist corps at Kingsbridge in combination with an attack on Fort Washington from the New Jersey side of the Hudson.[30] Indeed, two weeks after writing that letter, Upham reported that about 450 French troops had landed about two miles away from Lloyd's Neck, and had marched, rather foolishly, to within four hundred yards of his twelve-pounders. Upham stoutly put the enemy to a "disgraceful retreat" by firing grapeshot at them, leaving the "grass besmeared with blood." His men were, said Upham gloatingly, "in the best spirits imaginable."[31]

Given its importance to British whaleboating, morale, and intelligence operations, Tallmadge determined to wipe this nest out—again. It would not be such an easy touch this time around. Now there were alert soldiers guarding the promontory, and the navy had provided a sixteen-gunner, two small frigates, and a galley as a defensive screen for the docked whaleboats. About eight miles away, there were another 140 armed men, so ruling out a flanking assault. Tallmadge's daring scheme envisaged simultaneously sweeping the Sound with his flotillas of whaleboats to draw off the navy while up to twenty skilled pilots would land several hundred of his dragoons and artillery pieces on Lloyd's Neck in a proto-D-Day.[32] Washington backed the plan, but stipulated that it "must depend, on the absence of the [main] British Fleet, the secrecy of the attempt, and a knowledge of the exact situation of the enemy."[33]

The last, at least, was quickly resolved. Woodhull sent a "faithful person" (i.e., Captain Woodhull) who, he was careful to say, "knows not the smallest link in the [Culper] chain" but was knowledgeable about "armies and fortifications," to survey the positions, and he confirmed that "the number of men at Lloyd's Neck is certainly not more than 500 nor less than 400 fighting men."[34] Fortunately for Colonel Upham, wrote a disgruntled Tallmadge, "the British fleet have returned to New York" from an oceangoing cruise, and he was obliged to postpone the assault.[35] Washington suggested he talk to Rochambeau about providing French warships to attack the fleet in the harbor, but owing to their naval commitments elsewhere, Tallmadge eventually concluded that it was "impossible to put the plan proposed in evolution at this time."[36] So that was that. In the end, Colonel Upham, along with General Arnold, launched a major raid on New London, Connecticut, that coming September. Upham, who always relished a good skirmish with the rebels so long as the odds were heavily in his favor, said that "everything required was cheerfully undertaken and spiritedly effected by the party I had the honor to command."[37]

In the meantime, Tallmadge attempted to restore the Culper Ring on a stronger footing, financially speaking. Washington, too, had noticed that their irregular reports had been very "vague and uncertain" in recent months, and told Tallmadge that he was "fully impressed with the idea of the utility of early, regular, and accurate communications" from them once again. To this end, Washington belatedly authorized "in behalf of the United States" a "liberal reward for the services of the C———s, (of whose fidelity and ability I entertain a high opinion)," but stipulated that in return "their exertions should be proportionably great."[38] This was easier said than done, given improved British security. As Woodhull told Tallmadge on May 8 after a trip to New York, "I can only obtain verbal accounts for you and that but seldom, as the enemy have lately been made to believe that a line of intelligence is supported here. They are jealous of every person that they may see from this part."[39] Worse, Townsend was still adamant that he would not set pen to paper for fear of interception, and though Wood-hull and he "racked our invention to point out a proper person" to copy down Townsend's nuggets and compose the intelligence letters, "no person will write." By May 19, Woodhull himself had become too antsy to continue for much longer, since the "enemy have got some hint of me for when passing at Brooklyn Ferry was strictly examined and told some villain supported a correspondence from this place. I do assure you am greatly alarmed—and wished to be relieved from my present anxiety. I shall not think it safe for me to go to New York very soon—and can only supply you with verbal accounts as hath been the case for some time." The only positive note was struck by Woodhull's mentioning that Austin Roe was willing to work occasionally as a courier, but Tallmadge realized that in itself wouldn't be enough to save the Ring.[40]

Instead, Tallmadge began mooting the possibility of using tempo-rary spies, or agents who were willing to pass information on occa-sionally and lived for short periods on Long Island. So long as they reported just once or twice before returning to Connecticut, their chances of being caught, he believed, were less than that of permanent agents-in-place. The downside, of course, was that they could not be trusted as implicitly as the Culpers, nor would they be willing to work just for expenses. Most of these temps, it turned out, were acquain-tances of Brewster's. In mid-May, Tallmadge noted to Washington that if Townsend couldn't be tempted back into the game, he would "send a person from this side (a native of Long Island) to engage an-other person, entirely independent of C.[ulper] and who lives much [closer] to New York."[41] The "native of Long Island" was Brewster, and his contact was the pseudonymous "John Cork," who was paid six guineas to go into New York on several occasions and see what he could find. Nothing more is known of him, not even his real name.[42]

An agent known as "S.G." was also recruited by Tallmadge, again through Brewster, in the same month. He was, Tallmadge told

Washington, "a person heretofore unknown in my private correspondence, but from whom I should expect important services if he could be engaged in this way."[43] "S.G."—probably one George Smith—seems to have acted as a replacement for Brewster whenever the latter was away on his Tory-hunting missions, and was in service as late as August 1782, when Tallmadge mentioned that he had "repaired to Fairfield, and effected an interview with S.G. [and] forwarded, by him, similar instructions to S.C. Senior and Junr."[44] Given the Culpers' unwillingness to deal with contacts unfamiliar to them, he was likely one of Brewster's longtime deputies aboard the whaleboats.

Another was Nathaniel Ruggles, a schoolmaster and physician born in 1713 and educated at Yale, who had helped arrange accommodation and subsistence in Connecticut for Whig refugees from Long Island at the beginning of the war.[45] Brewster and Tallmadge evidently persuaded him to do some secret service work on the side, and he was placed temporarily at Old Man's, an isolated spot a few miles east of Setauket, in the spring of 1781. From there he visited New York several times. His cover was blown within months, thanks to the testimony of Ebenezer Hathaway, a Loyalist captain of the privateer *Adventure*.

On April 7, while cruising off Huntington, Hathaway's boat had been surprised by a flotilla of seven whaleboats and his crew taken prisoner. They were transported to the Simsbury Mines, a former copper mine converted into a nightmarish subterranean prison in Connecticut—the American equivalent of the British prison ships. The captives were led through a series of trapdoors with iron bars progressively deeper underground. At the last one, they climbed down a six-foot ladder, which led to another grate covering a three-foot-wide hole sunk into solid rock that the guards told them led to a "bottomless pit." The men "bid adieu to the world" and descended down more ladders another eighty feet or so where they discovered "the inhabitants of this woeful mansion." Down there, the other prisoners were using pots of charcoal to dispel the foul air, aided by a narrow ventilation shaft bored from the surface. Hathaway and his friends stayed there for twenty days, and plotted to break out. On May 18, when twenty-eight of the prisoners were brought upstairs to what passed for a kitchen to cook, they cracked the lock to the grate connecting the kitchen with the ladder leading to the guardroom. At 10 p.m., the grate above was unlocked by the sentries, who were allowing in one of the prisoners' wives, and Hathaway and his accomplice, Thomas Smith, seized the opportunity to barge their way into the guardroom, where they scuffled with the two soldiers on duty. Hathaway was wounded in three places before the rest of the prisoners could rush through. After that, they surprised the remaining twenty-four guards, who were sleeping, and took them captive before pushing them into the black hole below. Seizing their arms and ammunition, they dispersed and made their way as best they could back to Long Island or Westchester.

When Hathaway reached New York, he contacted Major De Lancey with information that one of the prisoners, "Clarke"—no first name was ever mentioned—had told him when they were both locked up. Clarke was a whaleboatman of no fixed allegiance who had plundered both sides but had "frequently come over with Brewster" to Long Island. He doesn't seem to have been a member of Brewster's regular crew for conveying the Culper dispatches, but was probably used as a stand-in during the opening months of 1781. According to the record of Hathaway's June debriefing in the British intelligence archives, he said "that one Nathaniel Ruggles who lives at Setalket [*sic*] sends over intelligence once every fortnight by Brewster who comes from Connecticut and lands at the Old Man's. Ruggles comes to New York frequently." After his escape, Hathaway, moreover, had originally landed on the northeastern shore of Long Island, where, on his way to New York, he met "Major Talmadge," who was "purchas[ing] clothing for the rebel army."[46]

William Heron had first mentioned Brewster and the Setauket connection back in February, and the British now had a name and an address (though not Woodhull's)—as well as confirmation that Tallmadge was still operating. Ruggles, however, doesn't appear to have been arrested, most likely because he had scarpered back to Connecticut. Ruggles was unaware that his near-neighbor, Abraham Woodhull, was an agent—

Tallmadge was too canny to let that slip—but had the British captured him, they might have mounted an ambush for Brewster and Tallmadge next time they arranged a rendezvous with Ruggles. At that point, all it would have taken to scoop up Woodhull was someone recalling the gossip from June 1779 about the unassuming Setauket farmer being involved with dubious activities on the Sound, or someone remarking that Austin Roe was in New York an awful lot for a tavern-keeper. It wouldn't have taken long to link Woodhull to Roe to Townsend.[47]

It was the greatest of luck, then, that at that moment Woodhull— as a result of the increased British activity and perhaps also due to Tallmadge's warning him that he had seen Hathaway, who was *supposed* to be in prison—quit. I "live in daily fear of death and destruction. This added to my usual anxiety hath almost unmanned me," he wrote on June 4. "I dare not visit New York myself and those that have been employed will serve no longer, through fear." He was "fully persuaded by various circumstances and observation" that if he continued the correspondence "regular without any interval" his "ruin" would be assured, "and it appears clear to me that it would be presumption to take one step further at present." No longer, he felt, could he "expect that protection from Heaven that have hitherto enjoyed. You must acknowledge and readily conclude that have done all that I could, and stood by you when others have failed, and have not left you in the darkest hour but when our affairs appear as clear as the Sun in the Heavens, and promiseth a speedy and I hope a happy conclusion."[48]

Woodhull was soon tempted back into the Ring on an ad hoc basis by that old faithful, Tallmadge.[49] But he never again played a central role in Washington's deliberations, and the same can be said for the rest of the gang. The Culper Ring had done its job well and had served with great valor, but they were amateurs overtaken by the rapid evolution of espionage: From 1781 onwards, a new breed of spy had emerged, men like William Heron whose allegiances and motives were distinctly murky. They were agents who lacked the simple patriotic virtue of Benjamin Tallmadge, Abraham Woodhull, Anna Strong, and Captain Nathan Woodhull, the bravery of Robert Townsend and

Hercules Mulligan, the doggedness of Caleb Brewster and the two couriers Austin Roe and Jonas Hawkins. The Culper Ring's day was almost over, and that of the professional, the cynic, and the mercenary was dawning.

Thus, in the preparations for the showdown with Lord Cornwallis at Yorktown, and the subsequent winding down of the war, the Culper Ring are virtually invisible. Beginning in the summer of 1781, Woodhull's letters became steadily more infrequent, while Tallmadge occupied himself with more purely military matters (he was seconded to Rochambeau for a time) and Washington was focused on calming an army restless for payment after the great struggle and the peace negotiations in Paris.[50] Between June 1781 and April 1782, for instance, Woodhull wrote not a single letter, even though Townsend continued to submit the occasional verbal report. The former's reticence was prompted by his betrothal to a local lass, Mary Smith, on November 24, 1781: No longer a single man, had he come to grief, Mary, as the wife of a traitor and a spy, would have lost everything.[51] When Woodhull did finally write, it was to convey a happy event. He reported directly to Washington on May 5, 1782, that "a cessation of arms is ordered, to take place within these lines both by land and sea—and terms of peace are given to Congress, but the conditions is here unknown, but generally supposed independence is offered." He also warned that "the enemy still continue to fortify, nevertheless, both on York and on Long Island. I have nothing further to inform you of but hope soon to have peace in our land."[52] By any lights, Woodhull's intelligence was a scoop: Official news of British acceptance of independence reached New York only in August. "The inhabitants of York & loyal refugees are very much hurt at this sudden change of affairs, saying that their loyalty to their King and Mother Country, has sold them, & made them worse than slaves," wrote Captain William Feilding, a British officer in New York, to the Earl of Denbigh.[53]

In the spring of 1782, perturbed by British activity in New York under the new "Commander-in-Chief of His Majesty's Forces between Nova Scotia and the Floridas"—Sir Guy Carleton—when they were expected to be preparing to evacuate, Washington temporarily reactivated the Ring, whose members proved willing now that imminent victory had greatly reduced the risks of being executed if caught.[54] Having dispatched Austin Roe to reconnoiter British positions, and after receiving a report from Townsend, Woodhull soon wrote that

> At York Island they are encamped from the City to the bridge, and fortifying on the banks of the rivers near the City and it is expected they will contract their lines and only attempt to defend a part of York Island near the town if they should be attacked. They have a number of ships ready to sink in the river if an enemy should appear. There's only two ships of any consequence in the harbor, the *Lion* and *Centurion*. Their design appears only to act on the defensive and be as little expense to the Crown as possible. God grants their time may be short for we have much reason to fear within these lines that Carleton's finger will be heavier than Clinton's. . . . He is called a tyrant at N. York by the inhabitants in general and makes them do soldier's duty in the City without distinction.[55]

While Carleton informed him on August 2 that the new Whig administration in London had accepted the principle of American independence, given Woodhull's account of British activity, Washington was not quite ready to drop his guard. "From the former infatuation, duplicity and perverse system of British policy, I confess I am induced to doubt every thing, to suspect every thing," he cautiously confided to General Greene.[56]

On August 10, Washington instructed Tallmadge that he found "it very important, from a variety of considerations, to have the most definite and regular information of the state of the enemy at New York, which can possibly be obtained; particularly with regard to the naval force which now is in that harbour, or shall be there in the course of the summer or autumn." Since he had gone "to the southward last campaign," the general desired Tallmadge to utilize "the channel of intelligence through the C——s . . . to keep me continually and precisely advised of every thing of consequence that passes within the enemy's lines." He understood that "the only great difficulty has been in the circuitous route of communication," but urged yet again "the greatest diligence and dispatch."[57]

Little came of it. Washington lost interest in the affairs in New York when it became clear Carleton would not mount a last-ditch defense of the city. For some time, especially in the New Year of 1783, when Washington was notified of the conclusion of the peace treaty in Paris, Woodhull continued to go through the motions of sending letters, but they are only a poor shadow of his previous efforts, being one-page affairs, messily and hurriedly written. No one in Washington's headquarters cared anymore about his reports of troop movements on Long Island. They were dutifully read—with a sigh of boredom—and filed away. Woodhull's last "Culper" intelligence report is dated February 21, 1783.[58]

The one Culper Washington continued to take an interest in was the indomitable Caleb Brewster, who had been long intent on settling accounts with his old foes, Captains Glover and Hoyt. The whereabouts of Glover were a mystery, though it was known he was in the pay of the British secret service. In March 1781, for instance, he was acting as the conveyor of intelligence reports from Connecticut-based agents *to* Long Island; in traveling the opposite way across the Sound from Brewster, and essentially doing the same job, Glover was his Loyalist equivalent in the Clinton-Washington spy game.[59] Then in June of that year he was collaborating with Captain Nehemiah Marks, another Loyalist whaleboater based at Lloyd's Neck, keeping an eye on French naval movements for Major De Lancey.[60] After that, nothing. Brewster, unfortunately, never caught up with the slippery Glover. As many of the Loyalist whaleboatmen departed for Nova Scotia and New Brunswick at the war's close (as Marks did), it's likely Glover, too, sought refuge well away from the likes of Brewster and his Long Island countrymen.

Brewster would enjoy better luck with Captain Hoyt, who in July 1781 was commanding the obsequiously named *Sir Henry Clinton* and working with Colonel Upham at the Lloyd's Neck stronghold. Hoyt, said Upham, was "very serviceable to us."[61] Before Brewster's show-down, however, Tallmadge had a run-in with him. In the winter of 1781, the latter recalled, Hoyt's new ship, the *Shuldham*, was preying heavily on American *and British* commerce in the Sound. It seems that since July Hoyt had, or so he said, switched patrons, and was now op-erating under rebel auspices from Norwalk, Connecticut. Unfortu-nately, he was playing both sides—and in more ways than one, since a "Mr. Hoyt" was also working for British intelligence—and was in-volved in smuggling goods out of Connecticut to Long Island, and back again.[62] Intending to warn Hoyt off the practice, Tallmadge clam-bered aboard the *Shuldham* at Norwalk. After saluting the captain, Tallmadge took him below to discuss the matter, whereupon "he flew into a great passion, and first threatened to throw me overboard." Tallmadge calmly ordered him to obey his commands, but Hoyt "im-mediately ordered the anchor to be weighed and the sails hoisted, and stood out to sea." Tallmadge ordered him to return to Norwalk, to which Hoyt snarled that he would throw him overboard before it came to that. "I assured him if he made any such attempt I would certainly take him along with me." Tallmadge could see that Hoyt was heading for Lloyd's Neck. Asking him what he intended to do, Hoyt replied, "with an oath," that he was kidnapping Tallmadge, who informed him, with remarkable cool, "that for such an offense, by our martial law, he exposed himself to the punishment of death." Hoyt was un-moved, and "professed to care nothing for the consequences," though Tallmadge sensed his fortitude beginning to waver. Again, Tallmadge said that "I would have him hanged as high as Haman hung, if I ever returned, as I did not doubt I should." In the distance—they were now more than halfway across the Sound—Tallmadge saw the waiting whaleboat fleet at Lloyd's Neck. "The time now became critical," and "I again demanded that he should put his ship about." Only now did Hoyt hesitate, soon ordering his crew to steer back to Connecticut. As soon as they were back, "the captain went ashore in his boat, and I never saw him again." Tallmadge determined this Hoyt to be a "man devoid of principle."[63]

Finding himself now persona non grata among the Americans, Hoyt reappeared in British service a short time later. In November 1782—about a year after his initial encounter—Tallmadge was planning a raid on Huntington, where the Seventeenth Light Dragoons were camped. The attack was set for December 5. As the whaleboat crews and their complements of dragoons were waiting at Stamford, hail and rain began to pelt, delaying their departure. It wasn't for another two days that the weather abated sufficiently to allow them to leave, and it was as his dragoons were boarding that Tallmadge noticed three Loyalist whaleboats sniffing around off the coast. He ordered Brewster to pursue them before they returned to Lloyd's Neck to sound the alert. The interlopers immediately started running for home, but Brewster's three boats raised their sails and used their oars to catch up in the middle of the Sound. As he closed with them, Brewster recognized their admiral—the slippery Captain Hoyt.

Battle was joined. Hoyt's boat had a small cannon that was fired into the side of Brewster's, though it was too far away to do much damage. Brewster, racing toward Hoyt, held his fire until he came within 120 feet, then launched one broadside, and then another at 60. The two crashed together, throwing everyone off their feet, but Brewster recovered first and led his men over the side into a melee with Hoyt's. One of Hoyt's crew, a bulky Irishman, swung his broadsword to and fro, injuring some of the Americans, until Hamilton, a Massachusetts man, snatched the weapon from him and slashed his throat from ear to ear with it. Brewster, meanwhile, had been shot in the shoulder, and was further struck several times by Hoyt in the back with one of the heavy steel rammers used to load the cannon. Thankfully, one of Brewster's doughty Connecticuters came to the rescue and slew his assailant. The boat was theirs. Only one man aboard Hoyt's whaler escaped death or injury, while Brewster's had four wounded, one mortally (Judson Sturges, aged thirty-five, who died five days later). Meanwhile, the second of Hoyt's boats was blasted by a swivel gun mounted on one of Brewster's fleet, killing two men instantly and prompting its surrender immediately after. The third escaped unharmed back to its base. Having lost the element of surprise, Tallmadge aborted his raid.[64]

Two weeks later, as reward for "the signal gallantry of Captain Caleb Brewster of the 2nd Regiment of Artillery, and the officers and men under his command, in capturing on the Sound two armed boats then in service of the King of Great Britain," Washington ordered that the proceeds of selling the boats be shared among them.[65] Hoyt's death and Brewster's little victory earned him Washington's plaudits—while his wound earned him a pension of seventeen dollars a month for life. Washington also effusively congratulated Tallmadge on his efforts throughout the war, and though this particular operation had not been executed, "I cannot but think your whole conduct in the affair was such as ought to entitle you still more to my confidence and esteem." Indeed, waxed Washington, "for however it may be the practice of the world...to consider that only as meritorious which is attended with success, I have accustomed myself to judge of human actions very differently, and to appreciate them, by the manner in which they are conducted."[66]

As for the rest of the Culpers, there remained only a toting up of accounts. In July 1783, Woodhull submitted his bill for services rendered. Over the course of the war, Woodhull had spent a total of £500.15.8, of which £375.9.4 had been repaid at various times. The balance he was owed was £125.6.4. Considering that this number had covered the expenses of several individuals over roughly four years, the figure compares favorably with William Heron's demands for at least £500 during the Hiram Hoax. Still, it couldn't be called an insignificant sum. Over the course of the war, Washington spent about £1,982 on gaining secret intelligence; that fully a quarter of his budget was devoted to the Culper Ring testifies to its importance.[67] Still, Washington's expenditure paled next to the £1,000 per month Major Beckwith—De Lancey's newly promoted replacement—was having to pay his sources.[68]

Woodhull's invoice sheds some interesting light on how the Culper Ring worked, and who worked for it. Woodhull himself had incurred nearly a third of the total (£154.15.10) on travel and boarding in New York, which included keeping, on Tallmadge's instructions, "a horse at N. York which in about 9 months or a little more cost me £25." The horse, presumably, provided readily available transport for Woodhull and his couriers. "J.H."—Jonas Hawkins—came second with £145.2.6, and after him, "A.R." (or Austin Roe), with £116.16. Townsend racked up £51.9.4, mostly for buying paper, and there is an entry for a mysterious "J.D.," who cost £18. J.D.'s identity is troublesome: On the 1775 List of Associators in Setauket and its locale, two men—Joseph Davis and Jonas Davis—bear these initials, but there is also a Joshua Davis who served as a whaleboat captain on the Sound. He acted as Brewster's deputy whenever he was away on other business. An individual known only as "G.S." spent £4. This stood for George Smith (dubbed "S.G." by Tallmadge), who helped convey the Culpers' dispatches for a short time near the end of the war. An "S.S." is also listed as having expended £4: This was Selah Strong, or more properly, Anna Strong. Lastly, Brewster had spent £6.12.6 on supplies "when here in distress by bad weather."[69] Woodhull, ever respectable, was always concerned with appearances, and explained to Tallmadge that he could not "particularise dates for I only kept the most simple accounts that I possibly could for fear it should betray me," but was confident that his invoice was "a just one." He wanted to "assure you I have been as frugal as I possibly could. I desire you would explain to the Genl. the circumstances that attended this lengthy correspondence that he may be satisfied that we have not been extravagant."[70]

Tallmadge in turn forwarded the invoice to Washington, remarking that it was for "monies due S. Culper and others for Secret Services." He himself had seen "some of the principals in this business," had verified Woodhull's receipts, and was "convinced that he has been as attentive to the public interest as his circumstances and peculiar situation would admit."[71]

Washington's reply contained a note exemplifying the ingratitude that spies, then as now, often experience from their masters once their usefulness has been exhausted. While he did not doubt, "because I suppose S.C. to be an honest man," that "the monies charged in his account have been expended, and therefore should be paid," Washington felt that "the services which were rendered by him (however well meant) was by no means adequate to these expenditures." Absent the requests of Tallmadge and Rochambeau, "I should have discontinued the services of S.C. long before a cessation of hostilities took place, because his communications were never frequent, and always tedious in getting to hand."[72]

Taken as read, this was an unworthy remark—especially considering the praise Washington had heaped upon the Culpers' heads in years past, and his repeated pleas for them to come back to work—but can be explained by recalling that after 1781, the Culper Ring had declined precipitously in importance. Nearly all of the expenses still owing dated from that time onwards, so Washington was referring to that two-year period, not the Culpers' service as a whole.

Tallmadge, of course, never told Woodhull of Washington's hurtful remarks. His prime concern was "to insure the safety" of his agents, who were, of course, considered by their neighbors "to be of the Tory character," the better to further their designs. He obtained special permission from Washington to enter New York soon after the signing of the Treaty of Paris on September 3, 1783 (which ended the Revolutionary War) but before the last British troops finally quit the city (which they did on November 25).

As he rode down Broadway for the first time in seven years, in American uniform and escorted by a few of his dragoons, Tallmadge was alarmed to see he was surrounded by "British troops, tories, cowboys, and traitors," though he was treated "with great respect and attention" by army and navy officers, and especially well when he dined with General Carleton one convivial evening. "While at New York," he said, "I saw and secured all who had been friendly to us through the war, and especially our emissaries, so that not one instance occurred of any abuse, after we took possession of the city, where protection was given or engaged."[73]

That may have been true of his "emissaries"—Tallmadge was too polite to use the insulting term "spies"—but not of regular Loyalists, many of whom were dispossessed, abused, and beaten by their angry neighbors and those newly returned exiles who had fled the British invasion in 1776. The more farseeing of New York's Tories had begun leaving for Britain as early as the summer of 1782, but London wasn't keen on a sudden influx of penniless refugees and soon proposed a resettlement scheme in Canada. Heads of families were offered five hundred acres of land (bachelors, three hundred), given an allowance of three weeks' rations, a year's worth of supplies, clothing, medicine, and arms. Still, relatively few—convinced that Britain had not yet truly begun to fight—took up the offer to start again in the chilly realm of Nova Scotia. It was only after the cessation of hostilities in mid-February 1783 that there was a rush for the door as despairing and desperate Loyalists realized the Mother Country was not going to save them. Expensive china and imported furniture were dumped at whatever prices could be got for them at auction, some Tories going so far as to dismantle their houses to sell the bricks and wood. There were many reported instances of ruined Tories hanging, drowning, and shooting themselves, and waves of Loyalist refugees cleansed by Patriot militiamen from their homes in areas once under British control threatened to cause outbreaks of disease in the city. To his credit, Carleton realized that if he evacuated New York too quickly with his troops, American reprisals against any Loyalists not yet evacuated might well turn into a massacre.

A particularly tricky problem was posed by the situation of the many thousands of blacks freed by the British during the war whose former, and unforgiving, American masters were intent on reenslaving them. Carleton, writing that "I had no right to deprive them of that liberty I found them possessed of," decided to allow them to embark upon the Canada-bound ships but compiled a registry in case their former owners sued the British government for compensation. The preliminary articles of the peace agreement, however, forbade the conveyance of "American property," which of course included slaves, from American shores. To this end, Washington, at the behest of Congress, complained mightily to Carleton about this theft of valuable people, but the latter casually referred him to his registry and said that should his policy later be found to violate the peace treaty, the Crown would compensate their ex-masters. (Even so, old, sick, or "troublesome" blacks would have been exceptionally fortunate to land a berth aboard one of the transports.) By mid-November 1783, thanks to Carleton's go-slow policy, the transition had been more or less peaceable: Some twenty-nine thousand Loyalists had been shipped out, their vacated houses and stores gradually filled by incoming Patriots. On November 25, there remained only a core force of British troops, who began marching down the Bowery to the East River wharves at eight in the morning.

As the British boarded the transports for the Atlantic crossing, American soldiers paraded down Queen Street before turning west on Wall Street to Broadway. At the foot of the street, they could see the royal ensign fluttering from the flagpole at Fort George. An infantry and artillery detachment were sent to haul it down and replace it with the stars and stripes. Unfortunately, in one last parting prank, some redcoats had mischievously greased the pole, cut away the halyards, and removed the cleats. It took a sailor four attempts, aided by the tallest ladder available, to clamber up high enough to nail sufficient cleats to reach the top and tear down the offending flag.[74]

A little later, Tallmadge went home to Setauket to see his father, Woodhull, Roe, Hawkins, the Strongs, and Brewster. Much of the town congregated on the public green to celebrate their emancipation "from their severe bondage" by roasting an entire ox. Tallmadge was invited to serve as master of ceremonies, and "after a blessing from the God of Battles had been invoked by my honored father," he "began to carve, dissect, and distribute" the "noble animal" to "the multitude around me."[75]

With the war over, the British had packed their bags, but not all of them left town. Closet Tories everywhere abounded, many of them willing to pass on snippets, and many former agents went underground, poised for reactivation. The secret service itself relocated, along with thousands of Loyalist refugees, to Canada, where it kept a beady eye on American developments. There might still be a use for the spies.

For the cabinet in London, the war had finished, but not yet the struggle. Washington's government was weak and suffered an economic and diplomatic embargo. In the west, Indian confederations attacked settlers, while separatist movements arose on the Vermont, Maine, Kentucky, and Tennessee frontiers. In the years to come, predicted thoughtful observers, the newfangled United States might collapse, necessitating British intervention. Perhaps the rebellious colonists—as some in London persisted in regarding them—might even call upon British arms to save them from themselves—or the French or the Spanish. If that happened, an efficient spy service could quickly be resurrected.

From 1786, Lord Dorchester (the former Sir Guy Carleton, now elevated to the peerage) ran intelligence operations from his perch in Quebec. Carleton retained the services of another old America hand, George Beckwith, aged thirty-four. New York, however, had declined in importance, at least in terms of espionage, though Beckwith did report on anti-congressional sentiment among the merchants and their desire to create an American monarchy with Washington as their sovereign. For the most part, Beckwith focused on finding assets in such potentially troublesome areas as Vermont, the Florida border, Kentucky, Tennessee, and the new western Appalachian territories. For the next few years, Beckwith fomented problems wherever he could, but by the early 1790s, British troublemaking was the least of Washington's worries. (Beckwith himself went on to glittering things, becoming governor of Bermuda in 1797, a knight in 1808, and a general in 1814.)

In fact, it was French and Spanish espionage that was of greater concern. In an address after the war, Washington—no doubt remembering his financial difficulties during it, especially when he needed to slip cash to his agents—stressed the need to establish a "competent fund" to pay for espionage services. Such a fund would "enable me to fulfill my duty in that respect, in the manner which circumstances may render most conducive to the public good, and to this end [allow] the compensations to be made to the persons who may be employed." Accordingly, in 1790, Congress created a "Contingent Fund for Foreign Intercourse," earmarking toward it forty thousand dollars. Within three years, this figure had ballooned to one million dollars, or nearly one-eighth of the national budget.

What had caused this fiscal explosion? The revolution in France, followed by her declaration of war on Britain in February 1793, was mostly to blame. Despite France's invaluable aid during the war, Paris—no matter whether under the *ancien régime* or the newer radical one—was not an entirely natural ally of the United States. Her intervention had been prompted more by a desire to do ill to Britain than good for the Americans. Indeed, having read of the horrors in France, many of her most ardent American admirers were rethinking their Anglophobia. Washington, famously, maintained a position of strict neutrality.

Statesmanlike his decision was, but neutrality invited trouble from the spooks. Like neutral Spain and Switzerland in the Second World War, America became infested with spies from every land fighting their countries' battles on someone else's turf. France, for instance, immediately began plotting against Spain, Britain's ally, and sought to tip the Americans into Paris's camp. France's chief diplomat in America, Edmond Genêt, coordinated covert attacks on Spanish territories in Louisiana and the Floridas, while his successor, Joseph Fauchet, opened a secret channel with Edmund Randolph, the American secretary of state. Documents captured by a British vessel, *Cerberus*, in an attack on the *Jean Bart*, a French corvette, and helpfully passed to Washington, seemed to indicate that Randolph, a Francophile, had been soliciting a bribe as he attempted to torpedo the signing of the Jay Treaty with Britain. Though Randolph denied doing any such thing or acting improperly, the French government certainly regarded him as a volunteer agent of influence within the Cabinet, if not a paid partisan. Heightening American suspicions of France's motives was the arrival of some twenty-five thousand Jacobin refugees after Robespierre's execution. It was not beyond the realm of possibility that some of these might be sleepers and agents-in-place deserving of closer surveillance. However, instead of creating a domestic counterintelligence agency dedicated to unearthing, uprooting, or penetrating the enemy networks, the government instead decided to pass the Alien and Sedition Acts of 1798 that allowed the legal prosecution of suspects on a broad, and not terribly well-defined, range of charges.

As for Spain, her principal objective from 1786 was to separate the western territories from the United States and attach them to her possessions in Louisiana. To this end, James Wilkinson, a former brigadier general in the Continental army, was hired at an annual salary of two thousand dollars. Wilkinson, an accomplished cheat, blackguard, and traitor, settled in Kentucky (formerly part of Virginia) and sought to persuade his fellows to secede from the United States and become part of the Spanish empire. Upon the recognition of Kentucky's statehood, Wilkinson's intrigues fizzled out, and while he continued taking Spanish gold (at a reduced level), he was forced to regain a commission in the U.S. Army to pay the bills. In 1796, Wilkinson was appointed commander-in-chief of the army, which means that a former Spanish agent was running the United States military for a time, even if Spain and America had signed a treaty the year before Wilkinson's elevation.[76]

It was a new and dangerous secret world that awaited this young nation.

"Lord, Now Lettest Thou Thy Servants Depart in Peace"

None of the Culpers ever told a soul what they had done. Almost as if the war had never happened, they resumed their normal lives. Two were betrothed within the year. Brewster married Anne Lewis, daughter of Jonathan Lewis of Fairfield (who partly owned a wharf there, much used by Brewster during his whaleboating days), and Tallmadge settled down with Mary Floyd, the eldest daughter of William Floyd, signer of the Declaration of Independence and kinsman of the long-suffering Colonel Benjamin Floyd.[1]

In 1791, the hated Colonel Simcoe became the first Lieutenant-Governor of Canada, where he abolished slavery and has a lake named after him. The later career of Nathaniel Sackett, the great innovator of American espionage, was one of perennial disappointment. In 1785, his plan to establish a new state in the west bordering the Ohio, Scioto, and Muskingum rivers and Lake Erie was ignored by Congress. Four years later, evidently suffering from grave mental illness, he wrote a disjointed, incoherent letter to Washington begging him to remember the services he had rendered. It, too, was ignored.[2] The intrepid John Clark fared better. After peace was declared, he went on to practice law in Pennsylvania. His wife inherited land, so he was never obliged to exert himself greatly, but he was always on call to liven up a dull evening with his wit and sarcasm. Rousing himself for battle one last time, he volunteered for service in the War of 1812, unsuccessfully ran for Congress in March 1819, and died on December 27 that same year.[3]

After returning to Long Island, Robert Rogers, captor of Nathan Hale, continued to annoy British regular officers with his recruitment of "Negroes, Indians, Mulattos, Sailors and Rebel prisoners," according to Alexander Innes, who in January 1777 was appointed Inspector-General of the Provincial Forces. Innes found that the Rangers had declined to one-fifth of its original size through desertion, and reports of their voracious pillaging were becoming embarrassing. General Howe asked for Rogers's resignation, to which he, uncharacteristically, assented, because he was getting too old and was also disheartened by his imminent divorce from his beloved Elizabeth. He never saw her again, nor his son.[4] In the fall of 1778 he was in Quebec recruiting soldiers. Then he was seen in London, but was back in New York in April 1779, all the time in desperate debt and drinking heavily—a habit acquired in debtors' prison. He was finally captured by the Americans while aboard a schooner bound for New York from Quebec, and jailed in 1781. A broken man, he left for England with the rest of the army after the British defeat. For the rest of his life, he lived penuriously in London, boozing, and boring listeners—who thought this grizzled, muttering Yankee mad—with his interminable war stories. He contracted a wasting cough which made him spit up blood-clotted phlegm and prone to frenzies. The wretched end came on May 18, 1795, when, following a fall that "hurt his mind," Rogers died.

From the day his treachery was uncovered to the day he died, Benedict Arnold never escaped his past. After the War, in London, Arnold did not find the adulation he craved; the Whigs loathed him and the Tories distrusted him. His enemies knew Arnold could never return to the United States for fear of hanging, but then again, opined one newspaper, "as to hanging, he ought not so much to mind it. He thought the risk of it was but a trifle for his friend Major André to undergo."

André was Arnold's personal albatross. André was everywhere feted as the handsome, doomed, Romantic hero: There was a marble monument dedicated to André, erected in Westminster Abbey—the ancient burial chamber of sovereigns and warlords—and the bestowal of a knighthood on his brother, just for being related. Worse was to come. Every one of Arnold's financial and military schemes in Britain, the West Indies, and Canada came to nought, and he rapidly gained the reputation of being an embarrassing nuisance. By the late 1790s, Arnold was broken in spirit and in body.

Owing to an asthmatic cough, he got two hours' sleep a night. On June 8, 1801, his throat grew so hellishly inflamed he could barely draw breath. Two days later, he became delirious: It is said that he dressed in his old Continental uniform and fearfully begged God to forgive him for ever donning another. On June 14, "after great suffering, he expired . . . without a groan." The papers barely noticed his death.

After the war, William Heron—blessed with a resoundingly positive recommendation written by Parsons to Washington—retired to Redding and led a blameless life as a public official in the new republic.[5] He was elected to the Connecticut assembly several more times between 1784 and 1796, and died on January 8, 1819, his knavery undetected to the last. On his tombstone in Christ Church Yard is piously inscribed, "I know that my Redeemer liveth, and that he shall stand at the latter day upon the earth."[6] Parsons drowned in the Big Beaver River in November 1789. Oliver De Lancey continued in the army after the war, was appointed barrack-master general in 1794, and was elevated to the rank of full general in 1812. He died a decade later, never the wiser that Heron had played him for a fool all along. Indeed, no one suspected Heron's extracurricular activities until *1882*, when a collection of Sir Henry Clinton's intelligence records containing the complete De Lancey—Hiram correspondence was put up for sale at a London auction house.[7]

As for Robert Townsend—the tortured, flawed Oskar Schindler to Woodhull's selfless Raoul Wallenberg—he forever remained a bachelor, to the last an enigma. Of all the Culpers, only Townsend became embittered by what he perceived as his ill treatment: Washington never fulfilled his wartime pledges to provide a reward or public office for him. In the same year his comrades married, 1784, Townsend may have fathered an illegitimate son, also named Robert, by his housekeeper (Mary Banvard), to whom he would leave five hundred dollars in his will. Townsend, at the time of the child's birth, was living with his brother and cousin, and many decades later Solomon Townsend (a nephew) suspected that the real father of Robert Junior, whom he intensely disliked, was the *brother*, and that Robert Senior had taken it upon himself to provide for the boy's schooling, set him up as a grocer, and pay for French lessons. After all, Junior, with his "large head, broad face, large prominent blue eyes & large solemn features" (in the words of Peter, another nephew) bore no resemblance to his alleged father. There was perhaps something to this hunch: The brother in question, William, "a dissipate young man" who drowned a few years after the Revolution while cutting a vessel from the ice, was known by Oyster Bay's young women as the "Flower of the Family." He may have occupied himself in the occasional deflowering as well, such as that of Mary Banvard, while Robert took over the boy's care after William's death. On the other hand, Junior does seem to have suffered from the same depression that afflicted Robert Townsend. Thus, he often felt, he said, that there was "no bright prospect of any kind in the future" and he often "became hopeless—dispirited."

Robert Junior later became a figure in the Tammany movement, and succumbed, in the words of his horrified conservative cousin, Peter, to "radical visionary politics." For this reason, he claimed in a speech, recalled by one attendee, that he was a "working man" whose mother, "a confiding girl," had "been deceived by a gentleman of high standing," and that as a young boy—"the son of nobody, an outcast"—he had been "exposed to reproach and suffering." Given Robert's kindness toward him, there may have been an element of class-based, politically motivated hyperbole about this story since he was then hoping to run for the lieutenant governorship of New York State. He died in 1862.[8]

Townsend went into business with another brother, Solomon, at the end of the war, but their relationship soured (Solomon said his brother "conducted himself without temperance or moderation") and Robert left New York, with much money owing to him, and went to live permanently in Oyster Bay with his sisters, Sarah and Phebe. He died, quietly and forgotten, on March 7, 1838, aged eighty-four. Townsend left behind, among other things, twenty shares of Manhattan Bank stock (worth $1,200), sixteen shares of the Mercantile Insurance Company ($400), three shares of the Life and Fire Insurance Company (worthless), five shares of Merchants Exchange Company stock ($350), and $4,043 in cash "in the hands of S. Townsend of New York"—he was referring to his nephew, not his estranged brother, who had died in 1811. There wasn't much else, apart from his large and wide-ranging library, some clothes, a few trunks, two gold sleeve buttons, and one "Silver Watch not worth repair."[9]

Austin Roe, who alone had married before joining the Culper Ring, ran a tavern after the war. On April 22, 1790, during Washington's tour of Long Island, he stayed at Roe's inn for a night, which he found "tolerably decent with obliging people in it." It is said that Roe was so excited to meet the great warlord he fell off his horse and broke his leg. He served in a Suffolk County militia regiment after the war, and was appointed lieutenant of the First Company in 1786, with Captain Jonas Hawkins—his fellow courier—being his immediate superior, and Major Nicoll Floyd—son of William, Tallmadge's new brother-in-law—commanding both of them. The next year, Floyd departed, Hawkins took his place, and Roe was promoted to the vacated captaincy.[10] Roe died in 1830 in Patchogue, Suffolk County, aged eighty-one, the father of eight children. Jonas Hawkins seems to have opened a twenty-room tavern and store down the road in Stony Brook, but nothing more is known of him.[11] Selah and Anna Strong died in 1815 and 1812, respectively, having lived quietly in Setauket their entire lives.[12]

Brewster, after moving to Fairfield with his wife, became a black-smith before joining the forerunner of the Coast Guard in 1793 by taking command of the revenue cutter *Active,* whose job it was to stop his former colleagues' smuggling. He held that post until 1816 (barring three years, during the Adams administration, when he left the service in protest of the president's politics), when he retired to his farm in Black Rock, dying there on February 13, 1827, aged eighty.[13] He is buried in Fairfield's cemetery. The elements have erased the lettering on his tombstone, but, like Roe, he left behind no fewer than eight children and his wife, who herself died eight years later.

Little is known of the great Abraham Woodhull, who uncontroversially served as "First Judge of Suffolk County" between 1799 and 1810.[14] His wife, Mary Smith—whom he had wed in November 1781—bore him three children (Elizabeth, Jesse, and Mary), and she died in 1806. Elizabeth and Jesse both married Brewsters. In 1824, Woodhull, now quite old and probably lonely, married again, this time to Lydia Terry, and they had no offspring. Woodhull died, mum to the last about his wartime secret service, on January 23, 1826.

Benjamin Tallmadge, who settled in Litchfield, Connecticut, became a wealthy man thanks to his investments in the Ohio Company and was in 1801 voted to Congress on the Federalist ticket, from which perch he attacked Jefferson and Madison on several occasions. Described as a "Puritan humanitarian" by his biographer, Tallmadge believed the continued acceptance of slavery will "ere long . . . call down the vengeance of Heaven on our heads," cofounded the Litchfield Auxiliary Society for Ameliorating the Condition of the Jews, and donated large amounts to local churches.[15] He retired in 1817, and devoted himself to establishing a training school for Native American and Asian missionaries. In 1824, he met once more the Marquis de Lafayette, who was traveling through New Haven. Aged eighty-one, he died on March 7, 1835—like his Culper colleagues, Tallmadge proved exceptionally long-lived for the time—his last letter (to his son) noting that "I have had a swollen face which gave me much pain, and for several days was very uncomfortable."[16]

Like the rest of the Ring, Tallmadge cast off the cloak of the secret world for the raiment of a brave new one, but just once, he felt compelled to break his self-imposed silence in order to honor the memory of the sacrifices made by his friends. It was in 1817, on the eve of Tallmadge's departure from Congress, that John Paulding, one of the trio who had captured André in no-man's-land, applied for an increase in the war pension he (and the others) had been awarded by Congress by way of thanks for their services.[17] Most Americans, recalling his virtuous acts of nearly forty years before against the supreme traitor, Arnold, were inclined to grant him his petition, and Paulding enjoyed vociferous support in Congress, where Tallmadge was one of the few surviving members who had fought in the war.

"A debate of no little interest arose on this question," the *Annals of Congress* diplomatically records of what happened next. The aged Tallmadge rose to his feet and furiously denounced the three men as nothing less than murderous scoundrels who would have happily released André had he happened to have more cash on him. When they removed André's boots, "it was to search for plunder, and not to detect treason." The three, he continued, "were of that class of people who passed between both armies, as often in one camp as the other." Indeed, declared Tallmadge, if he and his dragoons had come across Paulding, Isaac Van Wart, and David Williams that night, he would have arrested them himself, "as he had always made it a rule to do with these suspicious persons."[18]

Tallmadge recalled his long and bitter experiences with the rapacious Skinners and their Tory counterparts, the Cowboys, the terrestrial equivalents of the whaleboatmen who had preyed on Whig and Tory civilians alike. To him, and to the last remaining soldiers of the Revolution, the Skinners and whaleboatmen were charlatans who sanctimoniously disguised their violent avarice with protestations of patriotic idealism, and they were disgraces to the republican virtues exemplified by Washington and his Continental army. It was these same sorts who had harassed Caleb Brewster on his covert missions across the Sound, who had menaced poor Abraham Woodhull on several occasions, and who had forced Austin Roe and Jonas Hawkins to take more circuitous routes than they otherwise would have taken, thereby endangering the Revolution by delaying the Culpers' messages. Had Robert Townsend, or any of the others, fallen into their hands, they, too, would have been sold to the British as booty. That Paulding and his friends had hijacked the Patriot cause for their own ends was simply too bitter a pill to keep swallowing. In the end, Paulding's petition came to nought, as the House Committee on Pensions, which examined his case, was concerned that if it was granted, a flood of similar applications for increases would arrive from other old soldiers. Still, Tallmadge, driven out of his habitual discretion, had finally had his say.

Tallmadge had another reason to come to André's posthumous rescue. For all his faults, André had been involved in the same business as Tallmadge, and among spies a certain solidarity, a peculiar sense of honor, existed. His execution had been a necessary murder to repay the British for killing Hale. That was just business. But that did not erase the fact that the circumstances of his capture had been dishonorable.

Like Tallmadge, André had worked out of nothing but a sense of duty to his country—wrongheaded as that may have been in Tallmadge's eyes. So, too, had the Culper Ring, whose brave participants had had the decency, modesty, and honor not to keep demanding pensions, medals, and recognition for their services. By defending André's memory and attacking Paulding and Company, in short, Tallmadge was fighting to protect his old friends Woodhull, Townsend, Brewster, Hawkins, Roe, and their assistants. He could not abide to see villains profiting while good and faithful men languished unheeded, untrumpeted, and unknown.

ACKNOWLEDGMENTS

It remains a necessary pleasure in life to repay the debts one incurs when writing a book. To that end, I must thank the late William Pencak of Pennsylvania State University for some much-needed advice before I started, as well as Richard Brookhiser, Edwin Burrows, Harry Macy (of the New York Genealogical and Biographical Society), John Hammond (the town historian of Oyster Bay), John Catanzariti (the archivist of the Underhill Society of America), Thomas M. Savini (director of the Chancellor Robert R. Livingston Masonic Library of Grand Lodge in New York), Dennis Barrow of the Fairfield Historical Society, David Smith of the New York Public Library, Mark Lilla, and Kirk Davis Swinehart, Mark Lee, Mark Lamster, and Joseph Kanon—may the Light of Bestsellerdom shine upon thee—for helping out along the way. A special thanks must go to Sarah Abruzzi and Lisa Cuomo at the Raynham Hall Museum for providing not only access to the Townsend Papers but also an invaluable thesis detailing the family's financial affairs in the eighteenth century.

I would also like to thank the staffs of the New-York Historical Society, the Manuscripts Division of the Department of Rare Books and Special Collections at Princeton University Library, and the Beinecke Rare Books and Manuscripts Library at Yale University, for providing permission to use and cite material held in their collections. The Manuscript Division of the Library of Congress—with the support of Reuters America, Inc., and the Reuters Foundation—has digitized the papers of George Washington, an extraordinary resource available freely to all at its website.

The Allen Room at the New York Public Library is a haven for every writer, and I've been fortunate enough to have long enjoyed its sanctuary owing to Jay Barksdale, who keeps the place ticking along smoothly. I'm also, of course, immensely thankful for the unparalleled resources of the grand old NYPL, which time and time again reminds me that we all should be grateful to the antiquaries, archivists, librarians, and scholars without whose dedication and diligence our knowledge of the past would be paltry indeed. It is owing solely to them that books like this can be written.

No book would be complete without thanking those who midwifed, nurtured, and raised it. Emma Parry and Christy Fletcher took my initial emailed query to the proposal stage and thence a sale to John Flicker at Bantam Dell. Ryan Doherty, Maggie Oberrender, Lindsey Kennedy, Anne Speyer, and Jonathan Jao at Random House; Eric Lupfer at William Morris Endeavor, and Theresa Beyer, Sarah Carragher, and Kate Mann at AMC have all helped immeasurably in bringing this edition to press at short notice.

I think it would be difficult to overstate my gratitude to, and admiration for, those overseeing the transition of this story to the screen. Barry Josephson and Craig Silverstein have performed genuine miracles in re-creating the lost world of Revolutionary America and bringing the adventures of the Culper Ring to fruition. Without them, their unstinting energy, and their unfailing good humor (and patience for this neophyte), there would be no *Washington's Spies*—quite literally. I must extend enormous thanks, too, to Lauren Whitney at WME for seeing potential in the book, as well as to Charlie Collier, Joel Stillerman, Susie Fitzgerald, Benjamin Davis, Brian Bockrath, and everyone else at AMC who took a gamble on the show and saw it through. Rupert Wyatt and the cast—Jamie Bell, Seth Numrich, Heather Lind, Burn Gorman, Daniel Henshall, Samuel Roukin, JJ Feild, Angus Macfadyen, and Kevin McNally— have all done marvelous jobs of breathing life and suffusing soul into characters once found only on the page. Everyone in the *Washington's Spies* writers' room—Mitchell Akselrad, Andrew Colville, Ada Croal, Elizabeth Friz, and Michael Taylor, in particular—has been wonderfully imaginative in placing those characters in some unenviable predicaments throughout a succession of fantastic scripts. It's been a pleasure working with them.

My parents and siblings—Olivia, Zoë, Ari—as well as Stephen and Craig, have all stood by through thick and the thinnest of thins, for which I'm truly grateful. Thanks and accolades, too, must be bestowed upon Erna Olafson, David and Carolyn Hellerstein, Chad and Elizabeth, and Ben and Jamie. Neither may I forget Sabrina and Romy, Kyla and Iliana.

And finally, the real secret agents behind all that *Washington's Spies* is and will be are my beloved wife, Rebecca, and fine son, Edmund. To them I owe everything.

NOTES

Chapter One: "As Subtil & Deep as Hell Itself": Nathan Hale and the Spying Game

1. "The Testimony of Asher Wright," in George Dudley Seymour, *Documentary life of Nathan Hale, comprising all available official and private documents bearing on the life of the patriot, together with an appendix, showing the background of his life* (New Haven, privately printed, 1941), pp. 315–18. Throughout this book, I have tended to modernize and standardize the original spelling, punctuation, and capitalization of writers. I have strived, however, not to alter grammar unless the meaning is unclear.

2. William Hull, who had begged his friend not to go spying a day or two before, had died in 1825. Stephen Hempstead, Hale's faithful sergeant and his escort to the ship that would transport him from Connecticut across Long Island Sound, had died in faraway St. Louis, Missouri, four years earlier. And Captain Charles Pond, who had commanded the sloop that had taken Hale over the water into British-held territory, had followed Hempstead to the grave seven months later.

3. "Testimony of Asher Wright," in Seymour, *Documentary life of Nathan Hale*, pp. 315–18.

4. On Hale's family, early life, and the Yale years, see H. P. Johnston, *Nathan Hale, 1776: Biography and memorials* (New Haven, 1914), pp. 3–24.

5. B. Tallmadge, *Memoir of Col. Benjamin Tallmadge* (New York, 1858), p. 6.

6. C. S. Hall, *Benjamin Tallmadge: Revolutionary soldier and American statesman* (New York, 1943; rep. 1966), pp. 7–8.

7. On Hillhouse, see B. J. Lossing, *The two spies: Nathan Hale and John André* (New York, 1886), p. 7.

8. Johnston, *Hale: Biography and memorials,* pp. 34–35, 31–32.

9. Johnston, *Hale: Biography and memorials,* Appendix, pp. 211–13.

10. Johnston, *Hale: Biography and memorials,* p. 36.

11. See T. Jones (ed. E. F. De Lancey), *History of New York during the Revolutionary war, and of the leading events in the other colonies at that period* (New York, 2 vols., 1879), I, p. 3; and letter, Thomas Gage to William Johnson, September 20, 1765, in L.G. Bishop (ed.), *Historical register of Yale university, 1701–1937* (New Haven, 1939), p. 14.

12. Johnston, *Hale: biography and memorials,* pp. 40–45, 49–55.

13. Alice would go on to live until she was eighty-eight, and would marry William Lawrence, the son of the former treasurer of Connecticut. A friend of hers recalled in 1901 that "many and many a time I talked with her about Nathan Hale. She, with tears in her eyes, told of his noble character and fine talents and personal appearance. . . . Happy as she was in her second marriage, she never forgot Nathan Hale." (Johnston, *Hale: Biography and memorials,* pp. 57–60.) Alice owned the only known portrait of Hale, a miniature he gave her, which she kept after her betrothal to Lawrence. Soon afterwards it disappeared. "Mrs. Lawrence in her latter days once said that she always suspected that her husband destroyed it," presumably in anger or out of jealousy, reported the *American Antiquarian* in 1889. But a descendant of Alice's corrected the magazine, a touch starchily, by asserting that "Mrs. Lawrence did not *suspect* her second husband of making away with it; it disappeared in some way, but allusions to her husband's complicity were always made with a laugh." (Johnston, *Hale: Biography and memorials,* p. 151.) Though we might wish Alice had taken better care of the portrait, for now we have no accurate likeness—the statues of him that exist are "artists' impressions"—we do owe Alice for her physical description of Nathan (as remembered by her granddaughter): Just over six feet tall, "he had a full and beautifully-featured face and a firm and sympathetic almost benign expression; his complexion was rosy; his hair was soft and brown; and his eyes light blue; his form was erect, slender, powerful, and remarkable for grace; he was an athlete in his college days, and could with ease leap out of one hogshead into another placed beside it; his chest was broad for his height and he was a great runner." (Johnston, *Hale: Biography and memorials,* p. 152.) In 1914, George Seymour, a researcher, discovered in the files of the pension bureau in Washington another description of Hale, this time written by Lieutenant Elisha Bostwick, a friend of his in the Nineteenth Regiment. It backs up Alice's granddaughter's recollection to a remarkable degree. He was "a little above the common stature in height, his shoulders of a moderate breadth, his limbs straight

& very plump: regular features—very fair skin—blue eyes—flaxen or very light hair which was always kept short—his eyebrows a shade darker than his hair & his voice rather sharp or piercing—his bodily agility was remarkable. I have seen him follow a football & kick it over the tops of the trees in the Bowery at New York, (an exercise which he was fond of)—his mental powers seemed to be above the common sort—his mind of a sedate and sober cast, & he was undoubtedly Pious; for it was remarked that when any of the Soldiers of his company were sick he always visited them & usually Prayed for & with them in their sickness." (See I. N. P. Stokes, *The iconography of Manhattan Island, 1498–1909: Compiled from original sources and illustrated by photointaglio reproductions of important maps, plans, views, and documents in public and private collections* [New York, 6 vols., 1915–28], V, p. 1025.) A Dr. Munson, whose father Hale used to visit during his Yale days, remembered in 1848 that "all the girls in New Haven fell in love with him and wept tears of real sorrow when they heard of his sad fate." Benson Lossing visited Munson in that year and interviewed him. Munson's description of Hale closely tallies with the others: "He was almost six feet in height, perfectly proportioned, and in figure and deportment he was the most manly man I have ever met. His chest was broad; his muscles were firm; his face wore a most benign expression; his complexion was roseate; his eyes were light blue and beamed with intelligence; his hair was soft and light brown in color, and his speech was rather low, sweet, and musical. His personal beauty and grace of manner were most charming." (Lossing, *The two spies*, p. 5.)

14. For these figures, see J. F. Roche, *The Colonial colleges in the war for American independence* (Millwood, 1986), p. 90.

15. Johnston, *Hale: Biography and memorials*, p. 216. See also Tallmadge, *Memoir*, pp. 6–7.

16. For the rest of his vivid narrative of the battle, see P. Oliver (ed. D. Adair and J. A. Schutz), *Peter Oliver's origin and progress of the American rebellion: A Tory view* (Stanford, Calif., 1967), pp. 118–24.

17. H. S. Commager and R. B. Morris (eds.), *The spirit of 'seventy-six: The story of the American Revolution as told by participants* (New York, 3rd ed., 1978; rep. 1995), p. 152.

18. On Hale's movements, see D. W. Bridgwater (preface), *Nathan Hale to Enoch Hale: Autographed letter, signed 3 June 1776* (New Haven, 1954), which contains a facsimile of the original letter, in Hale's handwriting.

19. W. Heath, *Memoirs of Major-General William Heath, containing anecdotes, details of skirmishes, battles, etc., during the American War* (Boston, 1798; rep. New York, 1901), diary entry for July 9, 1776, p. 41.

20. Johnston, *Hale: Biography and memorials*, pp. 70–93.

21. On the New Englander–New Yorker debate over the fate of the city, see W. H. Shelton, "What was the mission of Nathan Hale?" *Journal of American History*, IX (1915), 2, pp. 271–74.

22. Letter, Greene to Washington, September 5, 1776. All letters, unless otherwise noted, may be found in the George Washington Papers at the Library of Congress, Manuscript Division, Washington, D.C. This immense collection of letters, commonplace books, diaries, journals, financial accounts, military records, reports, and notes has, thanks to a generous grant by Reuters America, Inc., and the Reuters Foundation, been put online.

23. Letter, New York Legislature to Washington, August 22, 1776.

24. Letter, Washington to New York Convention, August 23, 1776.

25. Letter, Washington to Continental Congress, September 2, 1776.

26. Letter, Washington to Continental Congress, September 11, 1776.

27. Letter, Mercer to Washington, July 14, 1776; P. Force (ed.), *American archives: Consisting of a collection of authentick records, state papers, debates, and letters and other notices of publick affairs, the whole forming a documentary history of the origin and progress of the North American colonies; of the causes and accomplishment of the American Revolution; and of the Constitution of government for the United States, to the final ratification thereof* (Washington, 9 vols., 1837–53), 5th ser., I, p. 369; letters, Mercer to Washington, July 16, 1776; Livingston to Washington, August 21, 1776.

28. See annotation to Washington's Revolutionary War Expense Account, January–May, 1777, for January 1, 1777. This informant was either a captain of New Jersey militia, John Mersereau, or his brother Joshua, who lived in a remote house on Staten Island, who both spied for Washington in 1780, but only from time to time before that. Their material was specifically military in nature—they were particularly good on numbers and regiments—but it was intermittent and sparse. For instance, Washington's letter of June 2, 1779: "Sir: If you could fall upon some method to obtain knowledge of the strength and situation of the enemy on Staten Island and this in as short a time as possible, I shall thank you. After putting this business in a proper train for execution, I should be glad to see you at this place, if it could be tomorrow morning it would suit me best. I will pay the persons you employ, but wish the undertaking to appear as proceeding wholly from your own curiosity; for a surmise of its coming from me may defeat all I have in view. The particular regiments that are on the Island, their exact quarters, whether at their forts, and if not at what distance from them, are matters I wish to be solved in; also whether any troops have been sent off or brought on the Island lately. Whether any vessels lies in or just out of the narrows, and whether any fleet has arrived lately? where from and the contents of it. I am, &c." See also, letter, Washington to Continental Congress, November 14, 1776. Regarding the brother, see Force (ed.), *American archives*, 5th ser., I, p. 369; letter, Mercer to Washington, July 16, 1776.

29. Letter, Washington to Continental Congress, August 22, 1776.

30. Quoted in Johnston, *Hale: Biography and memorials,* pp. 100–1.

31. H. Hastings and J. A. Holden (eds.), *Public papers of George Clinton, first governor of New York, 1777–1795, 1801–1804* (New York, 10 vols., 1899–1914), I, no. 173, letter, Clinton to Washington, September 10, 1776, pp. 343–45.

32. Hastings and Holden (eds.), *Public papers of George Clinton,* I, "General Clinton sends two spies to the State Convention" (reprinted from the Proceedings of the New York Provincial Congress), p. 346; and no. 175, "Rather wild statements by Messrs. Treadwell and Ludlum," September 15, 1776.

33. G. Rothenburg, "Military intelligence gathering in the second half of the eighteenth century, 1740–1792," pp. 99–113, in K. Neilson and B. J. C. McKerchen (eds.), *Go spy the land: Military intelligence in history* (Westport, Conn., 1992), provides a useful guide.

34. Quoted in B. Schecter, *The battle for New York: The city at the heart of the American Revolution* (New York, 2002), p. 197.

35. Force (ed.), *American archives,* 5th ser., I, p. 369; letter, Mercer to Washington, July 16, 1776.

36. According to William Hull's memoirs, quoted in Johnston, *Hale: Biography and memorials,* pp. 106–7. Hull likely jazzed up Hale's brave speech on his "peculiar service" for the post-Revolutionary generation's moral edification. Nobody, even in the eighteenth century, spoke like that, especially to a friend.

37. Johnston, *Hale: Biography and memorials,* p. 108.

38. General Orders, June 16, 1776.

39. Since the nineteenth century, the essential history of the mission has often run, however, as follows: Hale was captured in *New York* after being betrayed (or recognized) by his Tory cousin, the assumption being that Manhattan was his destination and that he was making his way through the British lines to the Americans in Harlem. It follows, naturally, that Nathan had *completed* his observations and was caught on the cusp of safety: Hale was the ace of spies, in other words, whose death was caused not by ineptitude but darkest treachery. There are some wrinkles to this theory. For instance, that instead of a Tory cousin turning him in, one legend has it that Hale was captured by a passing ship after he had accomplished his mission *in* Manhattan; another, that he was arrested in Huntington, Long Island, following his return *from* Manhattan. However, the "Manhattan thesis" is inherently flawed. In the first place, it is difficult to believe that Hale would have been sent to reconnoiter the British positions in Manhattan this early in September, the reason being that there *were* no British positions in Manhattan until September 15, when Howe landed at Kip's Bay and sent the American troops fleeing. Until then, the British were stationed in Brooklyn or on Staten Island. Why would Hale be sent to sketch fortifications in a city that Washington himself had fortified, and

indeed, still controlled? And in any case, why would Hale undertake a hazardous and circuitous journey to New York City from Harlem through Connecticut, across the Sound, along Long Island, and into Brooklyn? Surely it would have been far easier, and much faster, to amble down the road from Harlem—past American sentries guarding American-held territory—that led directly to Broadway? The only possible reason is that Hale was only to go to Long Island to see where the hammer was planning to strike the anvil. The confusion that has arisen during the last two centuries was caused by Hale's tragicomic talent of being in the right place at the wrong time. Just as Knowlton's Rangers got into a firefight at Harlem a few days after he'd departed—one that proved fatal to Knowlton—so, too, did Hale land on Long Island at the precise moment when the British were leaving it. His entire mission, then, was a waste: Washington did not need intelligence on enemy positions in Brooklyn when the enemy was directly in front of him, shooting, but by then Hale was out of contact.

40. Hempstead had a sharp memory for detail: Regarding that "plain suit of citizen's brown clothes," Nathan had written to Enoch on June 3 that "Sister Rose talked of making me some Linen cloth similar to Brown Holland for Summer ware. If she has made it, desire her to keep it for me." Quoted in Johnston, *Hale: Biography and memorials*, pp. 155–56 and n. 2. After the war, in which he served heroically, Hempstead lived in New London, where his wounds prevented him from undertaking too much hard labor. He kept the county jail, and acted as overseer of the town's poor. In 1811, he and his family (including ten children) moved to St. Louis. In his declining years, Hempstead lived on a farm six miles from the city, where he regularly attended the First Presbyterian Church. His son Edward was Missouri's first delegate to Congress. Hempstead died in October 1831, and was buried in Bellfontaine Cemetery, on land that used to belong to his farm. On Hempstead's subsequent life, see I. Stuart, *Life of Captain Nathan Hale, the martyr-spy of the American Revolution* (Hartford/New York, 1856), Appendix H, pp. 251–56.

41. Pond served aboard the *Schuyler* until December 1777, when the vessel was captured off Huntington as it transported Colonel S. B. Webb's men for a raid on Long Island. Three years later, having been released, Pond was recaptured after a fierce running battle. He died aged eighty-eight, on May 18, 1832, and was buried in Milford. On privateering, see H. S. Commager and R. B. Morris (eds.), *The spirit of 'seventy-six: The story of the American Revolution as told by participants* (New York, 3rd ed., 1978; rep. 1995), pp. 964–81.

42. See, for instance, letter, New York Safety Committee to George Washington, August 29, 1776.

43. Cited in Johnston, *Hale: Biography and memorials*, p. 111.

44. The Rogers biographical material is based on J.R. Cuneo, *Robert Rogers of the Rangers* (Oxford University Press, 1959), and B.G. Loescher, *Rogers Rangers: The first*

Green Berets: the Corps and the revivals, April 6, 1758–December 24, 1783 (San Mateo, Calif., 1969).

45. Cuneo, *Robert Rogers,* pp. 47–56.

46. Force (ed.), *American archives,* 4th ser., III, p. 865.

47. Force (ed.), *American archives,* 4th ser., III, p. 866.

48. Letter, Howe to Dartmouth, November 26, 1775. Force (ed.), *American archives,* 4th ser., III, p. 1674. And see also the positive letter in reply, Germain to Howe, January 5, 1776. *American archives,* 4th ser., IV, p. 575.

49. Letter, Rogers to Washington, December 14, 1775.

50. Letter, Wheelock to Washington, December 2, 1775.

51. Letter, Washington to Schuyler, January 16, 1776.

52. Loescher, *Rogers Rangers,* p. 169.

53. Indeed, Clinton proved his own nemesis by devoting more of his time to ensuring his own preservation than to hunting Washington. Convinced from the beginning that he would somehow lose this war, and thinking ahead to the inevitable official enquiry he would have to endure back in London, Clinton preserved every scrap of paper—from high-level military correspondence to dinner receipts—he received or sent in his personal archive.

54. Quoted in Cuneo, *Robert Rogers,* p. 261.

55. Letter, Continental Congress to George Washington, July 6, 1776, with Resolutions.

56. Cuneo, *Robert Rogers,* p. 265.

57. See captured copy of Rogers's "Authorization for British Recruiting," December 30, 1776, in the Washington Papers.

58. Quoted in Cuneo, *Robert Rogers,* p. 268. I have corrected their names, some of which were misspelled by the original reporter.

59. Cuneo, *Robert Rogers,* p. 268.

60. Loescher, *Rogers Rangers,* Appendix II, No. 124A, p. 229.

61. Letter, New York Safety Committee to George Washington, August 30, 1776.

62. Letter, George Washington to Continental Congress, October 4, 1776. See also, especially, letters, Washington to Continental Congress, September 24, 1776; and Washington to Congress, September 2, 1776.

63. Loescher, *Rogers Rangers,* Appendix IV, "Uniforms of Rogers Rangers, 1758–1783," p. 249.

64. Cuneo, *Robert Rogers,* p. 270; Loescher, *Rogers Rangers,* p. 171.

65. Letter, Jonathan Trumbull to Washington, October 13, 1776.

66. Quoted in J. G. Rogers (a distant kinsman of Rogers, incidentally), "Where and by whom was Hale captured: An inquiry," in Seymour, *Documentary life of Nathan Hale,* p. 444.

67. Only in 2000, when C. Bradford Tiffany donated a manuscript that had been in his family for generations to the Library of Congress (which published portions three years later), did the true story of Hale's capture and Rogers's part in it belatedly emerge after more than two hundred years of speculation. The manuscript is a history of the Revolutionary War, written at the time by a Connecticut shopkeeper of Tory bent named Consider Tiffany. Why should we trust Tiffany's word? He knew Connecticut Tories who had fled to Long Island, where stories of what happened between Rogers and Hale had circulated, especially since Connecticut Loyalists had been central to identifying the suspicious Connecticut rebel. It was a good local story, in other words, related (either in person or by letter) to him by friends who were there. Furthermore, as his account was written during the war, at a time when the name Nathan Hale meant nothing and the British looked likely to smash Washington any day, there was no reason for Tiffany to embellish or embroider his tale. The relevant parts are printed in J. Hutson, "Nathan Hale revisited: A Tory's account of the arrest of the first American spy," *Library of Congress Information Bulletin*, LXII (2003), nos. 7–8, pp. 168–72. Tiffany's account of Rogers's involvement is lent additional veracity by a diary entry written by the otherwise unremarkable Captain William Bamford, an Irish soldier in the Fortieth Regiment of Foot. At the time of Hale's hanging, he was camped about a mile away, at what is now between Eighty-second and Ninetieth streets in Manhattan, and so heard of the American's death almost as soon as it happened. Within an hour of Hale's death, Bamford saw his corpse swinging at the end of the rope, and may even have watched his burial: "22 Su. bright hot M^g. Nathan Hales, a Capt in ye Rebel Army & a spy was taken by Maj^r Rogers & this m^g hang'd he had several Papers w^t acc^{ts} of our Force &ca he confess'd . . . [H]e was a spy." See "The diary of Captain William Bamford, September 22, 1776," printed in Seymour, *Documentary life of Nathan Hale*, p. 446.

68. Enoch Hale records in his diary that Wyllys told him the story of the Yale diploma. Quoted in Seymour, *Documentary life of Nathan Hale*, pp. 56–57. Regarding Cunningham's appearance and his confession, see Lossing, *The two spies*, p. 24 n.

69. From the moment he died, Hale was virtually forgotten, and remembered only by his friends, like Benjamin Tallmadge and William Hull. The first mention of the Hale affair seems to have run in the *Essex Journal* of Newburyport, Massachusetts, of February 13, 1777, which alleged that the spy had cried, at the scaffold, that "if he had ten thousand lives, he would lay them all down, if called to it, in defence of his injured, bleeding country." The tone and thrust of this line make it sound suspiciously like invented propaganda, and it was no doubt placed by one of Hale's comrades, probably Hull. Only four years later do we find a second mention: in the Boston *Independent Chronicle* on May 17, 1781. This article was certainly written or informed by Hull, and it was only then that a concentrated effort was made to sanctify Hale as

the martyr-spy. Thus, "just before he expired, [he] said, aloud: "I am so satisfied with the cause in which I have engaged, that my only regret is, that I have not more lives than one to offer in its service." Over the coming years, Hull streamlined this clumsy sentence into the memorable version we have today. Even so, Hale was hardly a household name, with just two articles to his credit during the entire course of the war. It was only in 1799, when Hannah Adams published her *Summary History of New England*, which included a section on Nathan Hale, that the story began receiving some attention. It was at Adams's request that Hull contributed the section in question, and we can see the pieces of the grand mythic melodrama already slipping into place. "He passed in disguise to Long Island, examined every part of the British army, and obtained the best possible information respecting their situation and future operations," said Hull, adding that William Cunningham, the provost marshal who guarded Hale in the greenhouse, cruelly destroyed his prisoner's last letters so "that the rebels should not know that they had a man in their army who could die with so much firmness." Hull clearly invented this: How could he have known what happened? And then he concluded, "His dying observation, 'that he only lamented, that he had but one life to lose for his country.'" Hull admitted, though, that "Hale has remained unnoticed, and it is scarcely known such a character ever existed." And so he stayed: Mercy Warren's famous *Rise, Progress, and Termination of the American Revolution* (1805), Paul Allen's *History of the Revolution* (1822), and James Thatcher's *History of the Revolution* (1823) do not mention Hale. It was only in 1824, when the Revolutionary generation—rather like the Second World War generation—was disappearing, that Nathan Hale was rediscovered as an exemplar of selfless virtue and heroism. Thus, in 1824, Jedediah Morse's *Annals of the American Revolution* highlighted the episode, in the process unleashing a Krakatoa of histories, biographies, novels, and magazine articles devoted to the Hale cult. Hale's old acquaintances, like Stephen Hempstead and Asher Wright, suddenly found themselves roused from obscurity and their memories and letters (a Missouri paper in 1827 published a lengthy one from Hempstead detailing all he recalled of his captain and the mission) in huge demand. In 1829, Samuel L. Knapp produced his well-known *Lectures on American Literature*, where he declared that "it is time we should be familiar with [Hale's] reputation. This staking one's life and reputation together—and staking them for love of country . . . is the highest of all mortal resolves." Seven years later, at almost the same time as Congress announced that it intended to build a monument at Coventry, Hale's birthplace, the *American Historical Magazine* placed Nathan Hale "in the Pantheon" as an "early and distinguished victim in the cause of his country." Congress failed to come through, but the citizens themselves did it in 1846. Later, his schoolhouses at East Haddam and New London were preserved, and two bronze statues erected in Hartford, as well as others in New York and Yale, beside the Justice Department in

Washington, and outside the CIA headquarters (where the former director William Casey thought it did seem a little incongruous to be celebrating a failed spy). In 1848, Hull's own memoirs appeared, though they were actually written by his daughter, as he had died in 1825. In crucial respects, the Hale story differed from Hull's original account in Hannah Adams's book half a century before. Now, Hull (or rather, his daughter) said that Captain Montressor had told him directly "that Captain Hale had passed through their army, *both on Long Island and York Island* [italics added]." Originally, Hull said that Hale had "passed in disguise" only on Long Island. Clearly, as Hale had become more famous, his exploits assumed a grander hue, and so he walked upon "York Island" (i.e., Manhattan) as well. The role of William Cunningham experienced a transformation, as well: From being merely a brute who tore up Hale's two final letters, he became a man "hardened to human suffering and every softening sentiment of the heart" who refused Hale a clergyman and a Bible. (Oddly, in the 1848 version, it seems that Montressor took Hale away from Cunningham, and permitted him to write the two last letters, "one to his mother and one to a brother officer." Hale's mother had died years before his execution, which renders this version more dubious still.) And, lastly, there was a subtle alteration of Hale's last words. In the 1799 version, Hale speaks indirectly ("he only lamented, 'that he had but one life to lose for his country'"), but in 1848, this construction has been rendered, more pithily, as, "He said 'I only regret that I have but one life to lose for my country.'" In and of themselves, these changes are perhaps not hugely significant, but together they helped set into stone the version we still know. Ultimately, in 1856, came the final act: the publication of I. W. Stuart's full-scale biography, which mythologized its subject as much as the great Parson Weems did his. The last word on Nathan Hale should be left to Stuart's breathless reviewer in *Putnam's Magazine*: "His death *proved* what his life had only indicated. It showed in him a true heroic greatness, which could, in calm dignity, endure to die wronged and unasserted. The common pathway to glory is trodden with comparative ease; but to go down to the grave high-spirited but insulted, technically infamous, unfriended in the last great agony, with an all-absorbing patriotism, baffled and anxious, and burning for assurance of his country's final triumph—thus to have done and borne in unfaltering dignity, was the ultimate criterion and evidence of a genuine nobility of nature. Had this sharp ordeal been spared, the man's strong, true spirit might have remained ever unrecognized."

70. MacKenzie was the well-educated son of a Dublin merchant. He came to America in 1774 as a lieutenant, and was promoted to captain in the fall of 1775. He served during the siege of Boston, as well as in New York and Rhode Island. He died in England in 1824. For his diary entry, see J. Rhodehamel (ed.), *The American Revolution: Writings from the War of Independence* (New York, 2001), p. 229.

71. Stokes, *Iconography of Manhattan Island*, V, p. 1025.

72. Letter, Washington to Howe, September 23, 1776.

73. Force (ed.), *American archives*, 5th ser., III, p. 725.

74. Force (ed.), *American archives*, 5th ser., II, p. 854.

75. Johnston, *Hale: Biography and memorials*, pp. 131–32. Note the confusion, already seeping in, about factual details; i.e., "Stamford," caused by the slowly spreading rumor.

Chapter Two: The Year of the Hangman

1. Letter, General Howe to Lord Germain, September 23, 1776, in P. Force (ed.), *American archives: Consisting of a collection of authentick records, state papers, debates, and letters and other notices of publick affairs, the whole forming a documentary history of the origin and progress of the North American colonies; of the causes and accomplishment of the American Revolution; and of the Constitution of government for the United States, to the final ratification thereof* (Washington, D.C., 4th and 5th ser., 1848–53), 5th ser., II, col. 380.

2. See his letter to Lund Washington, quoted in B. Schecter, *The battle for New York: The city at the heart of the American Revolution* (New York, 2002), pp. 207–8. On Congress's refusal, see letter, Hancock to Washington, September 3, 1776, in Force (ed.), *American archives*, 5th ser., II, col. 135.

3. Quoted in E. G. Burrows and M. Wallace, *Gotham: A history of New York City to 1898* (New York, 1999), p. 242.

4. Undated article, "Reminiscences of the American Revolution," no page number, in H. Onderdonk, *New York City in olden times, consisting of newspaper cuttings arranged by Henry Onderdonk, Jr.* (Jamaica, Long Island, unpub. personal scrapbook, 1863).

5. *St. James's Chronicle*, November 7–9, 1776; *New York Mercury*, September 30, 1776; letter, General Howe to Germain, September 23, 1776, in Force (ed.), *American archives*, 5th ser., II, cols. 462–63; "Extract from a letter from New-York to a gentleman in London," September 23, 1776, in ibid., col. 463. Diplomatically, Robertson avoided mentioning that the sailors "did the best part of it, taking care to pay themselves well by plundering other houses near by that were not on fire," as General Major Baurmeister ironically noticed. See C. Baurmeister, "Narrative of the capture of New York, September 1776," in *Magazine of American History*, I (1877), p. 38; letter, from an American officer in Harlem, September 25, 1776, printed in Force (ed.), *American archives*, 5th ser., II, col. 524.

6. *New York Mercury*, September 30, 1776; letter, Tryon to Germain, September 24, 1776, in Force (ed.), *American archives*, 5th ser., II, cols. 493–94.

7. Letter, Governor Tryon to Lord George Germain, September 24, 1776; in E. B. O'Callaghan (ed.), *Documents relative to the colonial history of the state of New York; procured in Holland, England and France* (Albany, 15 vols., 1856–87), VIII, p. 686.

8. See letter, Tryon to Germain, September 24, 1776; in Force (ed.), *American archives*, 5th ser., II, cols. 493–94; also, O'Callaghan (ed.), *Documents relative to the colonial history of the state of New York*, VIII, p. 686.

9. *New York Mercury*, September 30, 1776, which also notes that "nearly a fourth of the whole City" was destroyed, though its edition of two days earlier judged that it was a "6th part." On the number of houses destroyed, see D. Grim, "Account of the Fire of 1776 [by] David Grim," *Collections of the New-York Historical Society*, III (New York, 1870), p. 276.

10. *New York Mercury*, September 28, 1776; *New York Mercury*, September 30, 1776.

11. O'Callaghan (ed.), *Documents relative to the colonial history of the state of New York*, VIII, pp. 798–99.

12. *New York Mercury*, September 30, 1776.

13. Ibid.

14. Letter, Howe to Germain, September 23, 1776, in Force (ed.), *American archives*, 5th ser., II, cols. 462–63. See also, letter, Tryon to Germain, September 24, 1776, in O'Callaghan (ed.), *Documents relative to the colonial history of the state of New York*, VIII, p. 686.

15. Undated article, "Reminiscences of the American Revolution," no page number, in Onderdonk, *New York City in olden times*. In the New York Public Library, by chance I found this ragged scrapbook of newspaper clippings cut out and glued in by Henry Onderdonk, a mid-nineteenth-century local historian of Long Island. This particular article, "Reminiscences of the American Revolution," was written sometime in the first decades of that century by an anonymous "soldier of seventy-six," and tells the fullest story of how the fire started, though his version has, as far as can be told, escaped historians' notice. (It's possible the memoirist was a Hessian, or maybe even a Briton, who settled in America after the war.)

16. Letter, Colonel Silliman to his wife, September 25, 1776, quoted in I. N. P. Stokes, *The iconography of Manhattan Island, 1498–1909: Compiled from original sources and illustrated by photo-intaglio reproductions of important maps, plans, views, and documents in public and private collections* (New York, 6 vols., 1915–28), V, p. 1023; S. A. Harrison, *Memoir of Lieut. Col. Tench Tilghman, secretary and aid to Washington, together with an appendix containing Revolutionary journals and letters, hitherto unpublished* (Albany, 1876), letter, Tilghman to his father, September 25, 1776, pp. 139–40.

17. Cutting, June 9, 1777, reproduced in F. Moore (ed.), *Diary of the American Revolution from newspapers and original documents* (New York, privately printed, 2 vols., 1865), I, p. 446. Washington himself took notice of the case, and recommended that Congress consider a "private donation"—given Patten's sensitive undercover work, he thought a "public act of generosity" would attract too much attention—to his family, as the agent had "conducted himself with great fidelity to our cause rendering services and has fallen a sacrifice in promoting her interest." Letter, Washington to John Hancock, June 13, 1777.

18. *St. James's Chronicle*, November 7–9, 1776.

19. W. H. Shelton, "What was the mission of Nathan Hale?" *Journal of American History*, IX (1915), 2, pp. 269–89, far-fetchedly claims this captain was Nathan Hale. For the real identity of the New Englander, see the report in the *St. James's Chronicle*, November 9–12, 1776. For his background, see letter, Samuel Curwen (who knew Smith's family) to George Russell, December 20, 1776, in G. A. Ward (ed.), *The journal and letters of Samuel Curwen, an American in England, from 1775 to 1783* (Boston, 4th ed., 1864).

20. *London Packet*, December 2–4, 1776, quoted in Stokes, *Iconography*, V, p. 1024.

21. Letter, Washington to Governor Jonathan Trumbull, September 23, 1776. "The gentleman who brought the letter from General Howe [i.e., regarding Nathan Hale] last night . . . informed Col. Reed, that several of our countrymen had been punished with various deaths on account of it [the fire], some by hanging, others by burning, &c.; alleging that they were apprehended when committing the fact." On the incidents of being hung up by the heels, see letter from John Sloss Hobart, in Force (ed.), *American archives*, 5th ser., II, col. 503; regarding bayoneting, see *St. James's Chronicle*, November 16–19, 1776.

22. *St. James's Chronicle*, November 9–12, 1776. Edmund Burke, the political philosopher, later extolled this woman's patriotism in the House of Commons. See *Parliamentary Register*, VI, p. 60, November 6, 1776, quoted in Stokes, *Iconography*, V, p. 1023.

23. On Greene, see T. Golway, *Washington's general: Nathanael Greene and the triumph of the American Revolution* (New York, 2005).

24. Demont appears to have sought refuge in London after the war. See letter, Demont to the Reverend Dr. Peters, January 16, 1792, which contains his version, and Captain Frederick Mackenzie's diary entry for November 3, 1776 (where he is called "Diamond"), both printed in H. S. Commager and R. B. Morris (eds.), *The spirit of 'seventy-six: The story of the American Revolution as told by participants* (New York, 3rd ed., 1978; rep. 1995), pp. 491–92.

25. Letter, Lee to Washington, November 12, 1776.

26. Letter, Robert Auchmuty to the Earl of Huntington, January 8, 1777, in F. Bickley (ed.), *Report on the manuscripts of the late Reginald Rawdon Hastings, Esq., of the Manor House, Ashby de la Zouch* (London, Historical Manuscripts Commission, 4 vols., 1928–47), III, pp. 189–92. Auchmuty copied the contents of the November 25 report from Francis, Lord Rawdon (see below).

27. Letter, Rawdon to Robert Auchmuty, November 25, 1776, printed in Commager and Morris (eds.), *Spirit of 'seventy-six*, pp. 496–97.

28. Orders to Colonel John Cadwalader, December 12, 1776.

29. Letter, Cadwalader to Washington, December 31, 1776.

30. Letter, Cadwalader to Washington, December 15, 1776. William Shippen, a Philadelphia merchant, was killed a couple of weeks later at the Battle of Princeton. See also, letter, Cadwalader to Washington, December 27, 1776.

31. Quoted in Commager and Morris (eds.), *Spirit of 'seventy-six*, p. 509.

32. The essential text in this regard is D. H. Fischer, *Washington's crossing* (New York, 2004).

33. Orders, Washington to Lord Stirling, February 4, 1777.

34. Letter, Duer to Washington, January 28, 1777.

35. Letter, Washington to Sackett, February 4, 1777.

36. Tallmadge had been promoted to his captaincy on December 12, 1776. See F. B. Reitman, *Historical register of officers of the Continental Army during the War of the Revolution, April 1775 to December 1783* (Baltimore, 1967 ed., orig. pub. 1914), pp. 531–32. The most detailed narrative of the Second Continentals is contained in B.G. Loescher, *Washington's eyes: the Continental Light Dragoons* (Fort Collins, Colo., 1977), pp. 23–62.

37. C. S. Hall, *Benjamin Tallmadge: Revolutionary soldier and American businessman* (New York, 1943), pp. 12–13.

38. Letter, Tallmadge to Hale, May 9, 1775, quoted in Hall, *Tallmadge*, p. 12.

39. Letter, Tallmadge to Hale, July 4, 1775, quoted in Hall, *Tallmadge*, p. 13.

40. Reitman, *Historical register of officers*, pp. 531–32.

41. Hall, *Tallmadge*, p. 15.

42. Washington's orders, October 11, 1776; Reitman, *Historical register of officers*, pp. 531–32.

43. C. S. Hall, *Benjamin Tallmadge: Revolutionary soldier and American statesman* (New York, 1943), p. 27.

44. Letter, Washington to Sheldon, December 16, 1776.

45. B. Tallmadge, *Memoir of Col. Benjamin Tallmadge* (New York, 1858; rep. 1968), p. 19; Loescher, *Washington's eyes*, pp. 29–30.

46. Tallmadge, *Memoir*, p. 19.

47. See, for example, letters, Washington to Tallmadge, March 1, 1777; Tallmadge to Washington, March 16, 1777.

48. For a brief description of Clark, see I. H. McCauley's contribution at the end of E. W. Spangler, "Memoir of Major John Clark, of York Co., Pennsylvania," *Pennsylvania Magazine of History and Biography*, XX (1986), pp. 85–86.

49. See R. K. Showman and others (eds.), *The papers of General Nathanael Greene* (Chapel Hill, N.C., 12 vols. to date, 1976–), I, p. 343 n. On Clark's reading matter and espionage, see letter, Clark to Greene, November 8, 1776, in *Papers of Nathanael Greene*, I, pp. 340–42.

50. Spangler, "Memoir of Major John Clark," *Pennsylvania Magazine of History and Biography*, XX (1986), pp. 77–79.

51. "Abstract of a letter from Mr. Talmage to Mr. Sackett dated 25th February 1777," enclosed with letter, William Duer to Washington, March 2, 1777.

52. In a letter to Washington of February 20, 1777, Clark's mentor Nathanael Greene—based in Basking Ridge, New Jersey—said that Clark had given him an account of the enemy's strength and "the places they are posted at." Mysteriously, there is no mention of Clark again until July 17, when Greene told his wife that his aide was still "absent." See correspondence in Showman (ed.), *Papers of General Nathanael Greene*, II, pp. 24 (for the February letter), 121 (for the July letter).

53. See Revolutionary War Expense Account, May–August 1777, and especially the annotation for June 1, the Washington Papers at the Library of Congress.

54. Davis had joined the colors as a lieutenant on June 28, 1775, made captain on November 21, 1776, and would be wounded at Stillwater on September 19, 1777. Three years later, he was promoted to major and retired from the army on January 1, 1780. Reitman, *Historical register of officers*, p. 188.

55. On Samuel, see A.W. Lauber (ed.), *Orderly books of the Fourth New York regiment, 1778–1780 and the Second New York regiment, 1780–1783 by Samuel Tallmadge and others with diaries of Samuel Tallmadge, 1780–1782 and John Barr, 1779–1782* (Albany, 1932), pp. 7–8.

56. See "List of the officers of four battalions to be raised in the State of New York," November 21, 1776, in *Calendar of historical manuscripts relating to the War of the Revolution, in the office of the secretary of state* (Albany, 2 vols., 1868), II, pp. 35, 49, 164.

57. "Abstract of a letter from Mr. Talmage to Mr. Sackett dated 25th February 1777," enclosed with letter, Duer to Washington, March 2, 1777.

58. B. F. Thompson (ed. C. J. Werner), *History of Long Island, from its earliest settlement to the present time* (New York, 3 vols., 3rd ed., 1918; orig. 1839), III, p. 475.

59. "Historical discourse prepared and delivered at Setauket, L.I. N.Y.—July 2nd and 16th, 1876 by Rev. William Littell, 9th pastor of the First Presbyterian Church of Brookhaven," available at http://www.setauket.presbychurch.org/littell-history.htm; Thompson, *History of Long Island*, III, p. 475.

60. Reitman, *Historical register of officers*, pp. 531–32.

61. Letter, Tallmadge to Wadsworth, July 9, 1777, quoted in Hall, *Tallmadge*, p. 25.

62. Letter, Sackett to Washington, April 7, 1777, published in full in P.D. Chase, F.E. Grizzard, Jr., D.R. Hoth, E.G. Lengel et al. (eds.), *The papers of George Washington: Revolutionary War series* (Charlottesville, Va., 14 vols. to date, 1985–), IX, pp. 79–82. The original is kept at the Washington Headquarters and Museum in Newburgh, New York. I have corrected much of Sackett's erratic spelling and grammar.

63. Note to letter, Washington to Sackett, April 8, 1777, printed in Chase et al. (eds.), *Papers of George Washington*, IX, p. 95.

64. Note quoting letter, Sackett to Washington, May 23, 1789, printed in Chase et al. (eds.), *Papers of George Washington*, IX, p. 81. I have amended some of Sackett's spelling and grammar.

65. Letter, Washington to Sackett, April 8, 1777, printed in Chase et al. (eds.), *Papers of George Washington*, IX, p. 95.

66. Anonymous report to Washington, quoted in Chase et al. (eds.), *Papers of George Washington*, X, pp. 71–72.

67. See letter from McDougal to the Convention, April 14, 1777, printed in *Calendar of historical manuscripts relating to the War of the Revolution, in the office of the secretary of state* (Albany, 2 vols., 1868), II, pp. 84–85.

68. "Proceedings of a general court martial on John Williams and others," April 13, 1777, in *Calendar of historical manuscripts*, II, pp. 85–86.

69. Washington sometimes expressed alarm at the prevalence of courts-martial, saying that he was "not fully satisfied of the legality of trying an inhabitant of any State by military law, when the Civil Authority of that State has made provision for the punishment of persons taking Arms with the Enemy." See letter, Washington to William Livingston, April 15, 1778.

70. "Proceedings of a court martial," April 30, 1777, in *Calendar of historical manuscripts*, II, pp. 120–25.

71. "Affidavit of Simon Newall," May 20, 1777, in *Calendar of historical manuscripts*, II, pp. 165–68. I have amended Newall's idiosyncratic spelling and grammar.

72. "Trial of John Likely and Anthony Umans," in *Calendar of historical manuscripts*, II, pp. 179–82.

73. Letter, Putnam to Washington, July 18, 1777.

74. Letter, Putnam to Clinton, August 4, 1777.

75. Letter, Stirling to Washington, July 24, 1777.

76. The letter (and grille) can be seen at http://www.si.umich.edu/spies/letter-1777august10-1.html. The originals are kept at the William L. Clements Library, University of Michigan. On Cardano, see D. Kahn, *The codebreakers: The story of secret writing* (New York, 1967), pp. 144–45.

77. "Confession of Daniel Taylor at New Windsor, October 9, 1777," in H. Hastings and J. A. Holden (eds.), *Public papers of George Clinton, first Governor of New York, 1777–1795, 1801–1804* (Albany, 10 vols., 1899–1914), II, no. 825, pp. 398–99.

78. Letter, George Clinton to the Council of Safety, October 11, 1777, in Hastings and Holden (eds.), *Public papers of George Clinton,* II, no. 836, pp. 412–14.

79. "Daniel Taylor the spy sentenced to death," October 14, 1777, in Hastings and Holden (eds.), *Public papers of George Clinton,* II, no. 858, p. 443; and, for the soldiers' letters, "Confession," no. 825, pp. 399–401.

80. Letter, Clinton to Council of Safety, October 11, 1777, in Hastings and Holden (eds.), *Public papers of George Clinton,* II, no. 836, p. 413. See also Dr. Hames Thacher's diary entry for October 14, 1777, printed in Commager and Morris (eds.), *Spirit of 'seventy-six,* pp. 587–88.

81. "Daniel Taylor the spy sentenced to death," October 14, 1777, in Hastings and Holden (eds.), *Public papers of George Clinton,* II, no. 858, pp. 443–44 and note.

82. Spangler, "Memoir of Major John Clark," *Pennsylvania Magazine of History and Biography,* p. 78.

83. Letter, Washington to Continental Congress, September 11, 1777.

84. Letter, Clark to Washington, October 6, 1777.

85. On the Nicholls description—issued by Clark when his messenger deserted some months later to visit his family in Philadelphia—see J. F. Reed (ed.), "Spy chief to army chief," *Valley Forge Journal,* V (1991), 3, p. 190.

86. Letter, Clark to Washington, October 6, 1777 (second of same day).

87. Letter, Clark to Washington, October 27, 1777.

88. See, for example, letters, Clark to Washington, November 3, 1777; November 18, 1777; and November 25, 1777.

89. Letter, Clark to Washington, November 18, 1777.

90. Letter, Clark to Washington, November 3, 1777.

91. Letter, Washington to Clark, November 4, 1777.

92. See letter, Clark to Washington, November 22, 1777: "This will inform you one of my spies has this moment come to me from Philadelphia; he delivered the despatches to Sir William."

93. See P.S. in letter, Clark to Washington, November 22, 1777, at 6 p.m.

94. Letter, Clark to Washington, December 3, 1777.

95. Letter, Clark to Washington, December 10, 1777.

96. See, for example, letter, Clark to Washington, November 16, 1777.

97. Letter, Clark to Washington, December 10, 1777. He also suggested that "if a troop of horse was stationed in this quarter, and patrol[led] the roads, 'twould be of infinite service."

98. Letter, Clark to Washington, November 18, 1777.

99. Letter, Clark to Washington, December 30, 1777.

100. Letter, Washington to Laurens, January 2, 1778.

101. Letters, Clark to Washington, January 13, 1778; Washington to Clark, January 24, 1778.

102. Tallmadge, *Memoir*, p. 26.

103. Letter, Tallmadge to Jeremiah Wadsworth, December 16, 1777, quoted in Hall, *Tallmadge*, pp. 30–31. For a near-identical version, see Tallmadge to Washington, December 16–17, 1777.

104. Letter, Tallmadge to Wadsworth, December 30, 1777, quoted in Hall, *Tallmadge*, p. 30.

105. Hall, *Tallmadge*, pp. 31–33.

106. Moylan's complaint was paraphrased in a letter, Washington to Tallmadge, May 13, 1778.

107. Letter, Washington to Tallmadge, April 14, 1778.

108. Letter, Tallmadge to Washington, May 4, 1778.

109. Letter, Washington to Tallmadge, May 13, 1778.

110. Hall, *Tallmadge*, p. 36.

Chapter Three: Genesis of the Culper Ring

1. B. F. Thompson (ed. C. J. Werner), *History of Long Island, from its earliest settlement to the present time* (New York, 3 vols., 3rd ed., 1918; orig. 1839), III, p. 478. Thompson was the son of Samuel Thompson, who was Brewster's neighbor when the latter was a boy.

2. Letter, Washington to Brewster, August 8, 1778.

3. Letter, Washington to Thomas Nelson, August 20, 1778.

4. This section based on A. T. Mahan, *The major operations of the navies in the war of American independence* (London, 1913), pp. 59–80; H. S. Commager and R. B. Morris (eds.), *The spirit of 'seventy-six: The story of the American Revolution as told by participants* (New York, 3rd ed., 1978; rep. 1995), pp. 715–21.

5. Letter, Brewster to Washington, August 27, 1778.

6. J. W. Wright, "The Corps of light infantry in the Continental Army," *American Historical Review*, XXXI (1926), pp. 454–61.

7. The most detailed narrative of the Second Continentals is contained in B. G. Loescher, *Washington's eyes: The Continental Light Dragoons* (Fort Collins, Colo., 1977), pp. 23–62.

8. Letter, Washington to Scott, September 25, 1778.

9. Loescher, *Washington's eyes*, pp. 27–28.

10. Letter of December 19, 1781, printed in R. W. Pattengill (trans.), *Letters from America, 1776–1779: Being letters of Brunswick, Hessian and Waldeck officers with the British armies during the Revolution* (New York, 1924), pp. 232–33.

11. As Potter, a character in Crèvecoeur's *Sketches* speaking for "we poor folks, who have nothing to do with the affairs of the county," says, "Deal with the enemy? Aye, aye, that's to be sure; and so we do." H. St. J. de Crèvecoeur (ed. A. E. Stone), *Letters from an American farmer and sketches of eighteenth-century America* (New York, 1981 ed.), pp. 445, 443.

12. On "the London Trade," see F. G. Mather, *The refugees of 1776 from Long Island to Connecticut* (Albany, 1913), pp. 209–14; O. T. Barck, Jr., *New York City during the War for Independence, with special reference to the period of British occupation* (New York, 1931; rep. Port Washington, N.Y., 1966), p. 133; J. L. Van Buskirk, *Generous enemies: Patriots and Loyalists in Revolutionary New York* (Philadelphia, 2002), p. 127.

13. See Mather, *Refugees of 1776*, pp. 210, 212; T. Jones (ed. E. F. De Lancey), *History of New York during the Revolutionary War, and of the leading events in the other colonies at that period* (New York, 2 vols., 1879), II, pp. 12–13; B. Tallmadge, *Memoir of Col. Benjamin Tallmadge* (New York, 1858; rep. 1968), p. 33; *New York Mercury*, April 15, 1782.

14. Individuals like Woodhull could dispose of their foreign goods to the New Englanders "at an amazing profit," said Jones (ed. De Lancey), *History of New York*, II, p. 13.

15. W. A. Polf, *Garrison town: The British occupation of New York City, 1776–1783* (Albany, 1976), p. 14.

16. Van Buskirk, *Generous enemies*, pp. 120–21.

17. Letter, William Livingston to Washington, November 22, 1777; letter, Washington to Lord Stirling, October 21, 1778. See also, Livingston's letter to General John Sullivan, this time about "Doctor Barnet, a captain of horse," who along with many others is trafficking with the enemy, August 19, 1779, in Commager and Morris (eds.), *The spirit of 'seventy-six*, pp. 809–10.

18. Jones (ed. De Lancey), *History of New York*, II, p. 14.

19. See letter, William Livingston to Washington, November 22, 1777.

20. Letter, Washington to Samuel Parsons, December 18, 1779; letter, Washington to Stirling, November 19, 1778.

21. Letter, Washington to Tallmadge, August 25, 1778, in Mather (ed.), *The refugees of 1776*, p. 1074.

22. On Samuel, see the previous chapter, and regarding Tallmadge's suit on his behalf, A. W. Lauber (ed.), *Orderly books of the Fourth New York regiment, 1778–1780 and the Second New York regiment, 1780–1783 by Samuel Tallmadge and others with diaries of Samuel Tallmadge, 1780–1782 and John Barr, 1779–1782* (Albany, 1932), p. 8.

23. Letters, Washington to Parke, April 11, 1778; Parke to Washington, April 10, 1778.

24. See letters, Tallmadge to Scott, October 29, 1778; Scott to Washington, October 30, 1778.

25. Letter, Washington to James Lovell, April 1, 1782.

26. Letter, Scott to Washington, September 10, 1778.

27. Letter, Scott to Washington, September 12, 1778; for Rathburn and Leavenworth, see their letters to Washington and Scott, respectively, of September 12, 1778.

28. Letter, Washington to Scott, September 25, 1778.

29. Letter, Brewster to Tallmadge, October 22, 1778.

30. Letter, Tallmadge to Washington, December 11, 1778, Folio 7, in the Benjamin Tallmadge Papers held at the Manuscripts Division, Department of Rare Books and Special Collections, Princeton University Library.

31. Letter, Scott to Washington, October 29, 1778.

32. Quoted from the chapter on the township of Brookhaven in P. Ross, *The history of Long Island, from its earliest settlement to the present time* (New York, 3 vols., 1902), reproduced in full at http://freepages.genealogy.rootsweb.com/~jdevlin/newyork/brookhaven_hist.htm. See also Thompson (ed. Werner), *History of Long Island*, III, pp. 384–85.

33. Woodhull genealogy in M. Pennypacker, *General Washington's spies on Long Island and in New York* (New York, 2 vols., 1939, 1948), II.

34. D. L. Jacobus, "The family of Nathaniel Brewster," *The American Genealogist* (1936–37), reproduced in full at http://longislandgenealogy.com/brewster/surnames.htm.

35. Quoted in C. S. Hall, *Benjamin Tallmadge: Revolutionary soldier and American statesman* (New York, 1943), p. 167.

36. The list may be found in Mather (ed.), *Refugees of 1776*, Appendix H, p. 1058, dated June 8, 1775. The full text of the Form of Association is reproduced in Mather, pp. 141, 1050.

37. Tallmadge, *Memoir*, p. 9.

38. For a general biographical summary of Brewster, see the address given by William Brewster Minuse, president of the Three Village Historical Society, at Caleb Brewster's grave in Fairfield, Connecticut, on August 9, 1976, in MS no. 33, Folder I:H, in the Brewster Papers, kept at the Fairfield Historical Society.

39. On whaling, see D. Vickers, "Nantucket whalemen in the deep-sea fishery: The changing anatomy of an early American labor force," *Journal of American History*, LXXII (1985), 2, pp. 277–96; R. C Kugler, "The whale oil trade, 1750–1775," *Publications of the Colonial Society of Massachusetts*, LII (1980), esp. pp. 155–56.

40. Petition dated May 19, 1775, in *Calendar of historical manuscripts relating to the War of the Revolution, in the office of the secretary of state* (Albany, 2 vols., 1868), I, p. 44. See also H. Onderdonk (ed.), *Revolutionary incidents of Suffolk and Kings counties, with an account of the battle of Long Island, and the British prisons and prison-ships* (New York, 1849), no. 541, p. 17.

41. I have compiled this information from a variety of specialist genealogical sources on the Web, which are themselves compiled from genealogical journals, family histories, and historical sources. Selah was the nephew of Selah Strong, Sr. (born 1712), the husband of Hannah Woodhull (born 1718), the sister of Abraham's first cousin once removed, General Nathaniel Woodhull. For Selah and Anna Strong, see http://homepages.rootsweb.com/~drmott/Mott/g0000112.html#I3325; for Selah's parents, see http://homepages.rootsweb.com/~drmott/Mott/g0000119.html#I3324; for Hannah Woodhull's parentage, see http://homepages.roots web.com/~dr mott/Mott/g0000130.html#I1205; and for Hannah's relationship to General Woodhull, see http://homepages.rootsweb.com/~drmott/Mott/g0000 133.html. On Woodhull's marriage to Mary Smith, see "Marriage Licenses Issued by the State of New York," November 24, 1781, at http://homepages.rootsweb.com/~rbillard/ny_marriage_licenses.htm. The table in Pennypacker, *George Washington's spies*, II, contains some useful information but is incomplete. Some of these URLs may change in the future.

42. Minuse, "Address," p. 2, Brewster Papers.

43. Onderdonk (ed.), *Revolutionary incidents of Suffolk and Kings counties*, no. 621, p. 62.

44. Minuse, "Address," p. 2; "List of the officers of four battalions to be raised in the State of New York," November 21, 1776, in *Calendar of historical manuscripts*, II, p. 35.

45. Thompson, *History of Long Island*, III, p. 475.

46. Mather (ed.), *The refugees of 1776*, Appendix G, p. 990.

47. This was a not uncommon reluctance. Governor Tryon wrote to Lord George Germain on December 24, 1776, observing that "three companies, I learned,

had been raised out of Suffolk county for the rebel army, most of whom, I was made to understand, would quit the service if they could get home." Quoted in Thompson, *History of Long Island*, I, p. 303.

48. For his brothers' deaths, see Thompson, *History of Long Island*, III, p. 387.

49. On Woodhull's connections, see his entry in *American National Biography*, written by Wendell Tripp, pp. 798–99.

50. Jones (ed. De Lancey), *History of New York*, II, pp. 331–32.

51. This section is based on note XLIX, "The capture and subsequent death of General Woodhull—the documents relating thereto—the different versions of the story," printed in Jones (ed. De Lancey), *History of New York*, II, pp. 593–612. It's worth remembering that Jones's editor, and the author of the note, was Edward De Lancey, a relative of Oliver, who consequently exonerated his ancestor of Troup's calumny. On Troup, in particular, see Thompson, *History of Long Island*, III, p. 403, which also contains a chapter on Nathaniel Woodhull. The letter from Dr. Silas Holmes, which contains the information on Dr. Richard Bailey, is printed in Onderdonk, *Revolutionary incidents of Suffolk and Kings counties*, p. 40.

52. For one such, virtually illegible, letter—a consequence of Woodhull's habit of using cheap quills that produced thick, smudgy lines—see Woodhull to Tallmadge, December 12, 1778.

53. Letter, Tallmadge to Scott, October 29, 1778.

54. Letter, Woodhull to Scott, October 31, 1778. Scott had resigned a few days before, not that Woodhull was to know that (owing to the slowness of communications), but in any case Woodhull addressed his communications to Scott only as a formality—they were always handled by Tallmadge, and he dealt with him exclusively. On the requirements to get in and out of the city, see Thompson, *History of Long Island*, I, pp. 343–44.

55. "Gen. Sir William Howe's orders," January 26, 1777, in S. Kemble, *Kemble's journals, 1773–1789*, in *Collections of the New-York Historical Society* (New York, 2 vols., 1883–84), XVI, p. 440.

56. E. E. Curtis, *The organization of the British army in the American Revolution* (New Haven, 1926; rep. 1969), pp. 81–84.

57. I. N. P. Stokes, *The iconography of Manhattan Island, 1498–1909: compiled from original sources and illustrated by photo-intaglio reproductions of important maps, plans, views, and documents in public and private collections* (New York, 6 vols., 1915–1928), V, p. 1081.

58. Letter, Eden to Clinton, July 1776, in Stevens (ed.), *Facsimiles*, IV, no. 512.

59. Barck, *New York City during the War for Independence*, pp. 107, 110; Curtis, *The British army in the American Revolution*, pp. 98–99. In the early fall of 1779, another fleet arrived carrying enough "provisions for 60,000 men . . . for six months."

other fleet arrived carrying enough "provisions for 60,000 men . . . for six months."
See V. Biddulph (ed.), "Letters of Robert Biddulph, 1779–1783," *American Historical
Review*, XXIX (1923), letter of October 9, 1779, p. 91. Another arrived in the subsequent October, see ibid., letter of October 16, 1780, p. 96. Despite the many problems
with food supply, the logistics of the Cork Fleet are astounding. Between 1776 and
1778 alone, 229 transports sailed fully laden into New York with nearly six million
pounds of beef, more than twenty million pounds of pork, forty million pounds of
flour and bread, five million pounds of oatmeal and rice, and two million pounds of
butter. Notwithstanding these tens of millions of pounds of food in the ships' holds,
civilian New Yorkers suffered from a chronic lack of staples (hence their reliance on
the London Trade): Nearly all of it was earmarked for army use, some of it rotted
during the month-long, unrefrigerated voyage, and a portion fell off the back of a
wagon and ended up in the hands of black marketeers. Still, enough food did get
through to enable army commissaries to establish a daily ration for enlisted men of
one and a half pounds of bread or flour, one pound of beef or half a pound of pork, an
ounce of butter and one of rice, and a quarter-pint of peas. There was often another
half a pound of a strange new Hessian monstrosity, sauerkraut, plus the most important foodstuff of all—booze, between a quarter and half a pint of rum per man each
day. See Curtis, *The British army in the American Revolution*, Chart, pp. 90, 172; S. R.
Frey, *The British soldier in America: A social history of military life in the Revolutionary
period* (Austin, Tex., 1981), p. 30.

60. Letter, Woodhull to Scott, October 31, 1778.

61. A. P. Underhill, "William Underhill, his ancestors and his descendants," *New
York genealogical and biographical record*, LVIII (1927), p. 356. For much of the following information, I am indebted to John Catanzariti, archivist of the Underhill Society
of America, who sent me an e-mail (January 18, 2005) describing the contents of relevant materials drawn from the *Underhill genealogy*, vols. II (1932) and VII (2002).
Underhill was later described as "a Goodman of considerable property (near Oyster
Bay) and has the greatest respect of his fellow burghers." Beyond that, hardly anything is known.

62. On the Underhills' March 1774 marriage, see Thompson, *History of Long
Island*, III, p. 387; also, Pennypacker, *George Washington's spies*, p. 8. On rent, letter,
Woodhull to Tallmadge, February 26, 1779.

63. E. G. Schaukirk, *Occupation of New York City by the British* (originally
published in *Pennsylvania Magazine of History and Biography*, January 1887; New
York, rep. 1969), diary entry for February 1, 1782, p. 23; Barck, *New York City during
the War for Independence*, p. 103; Stokes, *Iconography*, V, p. 1042.

64. B. M. Wilkenfeld, "Revolutionary New York, 1776," in M. Klein (ed.), *New

York: The centennial years, 1676–1976 (Port Washington, N.Y., 1976), p. 45; C. Abbott, "The neighborhoods of New York, 1760–1775," *New York History*, XV (1974), p. 51.

65. Polf, *Garrison town*, p. 4; S. R. Zabin, "Places of exchange: New York City, 1700–1763" (unpub. Ph.D. thesis, Rutgers University, 2000), p. 7; Wilkenfeld, "Revolutionary New York," in Klein (ed.), *New York: The centennial years*, p. 44; E. J. McManus, *A history of Negro slavery in New York* (Syracuse, N.Y., 1966), pp. 197–99; J. G. Lydon, "New York and the slave trade, 1700 to 1774," *William and Mary Quarterly*, 3rd ser., XXXV (1978), 2, p. 388, Table VIII; N. A. Rothschild, *New York City neighborhoods: The 18th century* (San Diego, 1990), pp. 8–9. There is some dispute over the exact numbers of troops. I have used George Washington's tallies (plus official numbers for the British figure), reproduced in Jones (ed. De Lancey), *History of New York*, I, note XXXVI, pp. 599–603.

66. P. M'Robert (ed. by C. Bridenbaugh), *A tour through part of the north provinces of America* (New York, 1935; rep. 1968), p. 5.

67. On New York's population figures, see Barck, *New York City during the War for Independence*, pp. 74–78; Stokes, *Iconography*, V, p. 1129 (quoting *Lloyds Evening Post*, April 27, 1781).

68. These numbers are collated from various sources: A useful summary may be found in Barck, *New York City during the War for Independence*, p. 75. Also, *Kemble's Journals, 1773–1789*, in *Collections of the New-York Historical Society*, XVI, p. 156.

69. On July 17, 1778, Kemble stated there were nine thousand troops, but on July 29, he amended this to twenty thousand. See Kemble, *Journals*, XVI, pp. 156–58; for a slightly higher number, letter, Clinton to Lord George Germain, July 27, 1778, in Stevens (ed.), *Facsimiles*, XI, no. 1123. Kemble, an aide, may have taken his figure from Clinton.

70. Letter, Washington to Tallmadge, November 18, 1778. Thus, see Washington's letter to General Putnam of August 11, 1777: "Deserters and people of that class always speak of numbers from report, indeed scarce any person can form a judgment, except they see the troops paraded and can count their divisions. But if you can by any means obtain a list of the regiments left upon the island, we can compute the number of men within a few hundreds, over or under."

71. Letter, Tallmadge to Washington, November 19, 1778.

72. Letter, Washington to Tallmadge, November 20, 1778.

73. Letter, Woodhull to Tallmadge, November 23, 1778.

74. Letter, Washington to Tallmadge, November 29, 1778.

75. Letter, Washington to Tallmadge, November 29, 1778.

76. Letter, Washington to Tallmadge, December 17, 1778: "I did not know his

present situation. I now see the danger that so long an absence would incur and I must leave it entirely to you to manage the correspondence in such a manner as will most probably ensure safety to him and [achieve] the desired end."

77. Letter, Woodhull to Tallmadge, November 23, 1778.

78. Letter, Woodhull to Tallmadge, December 12, 1778.

79. Letter, Woodhull to Tallmadge, February 26, 1779.

80. Pennypacker, *George Washington's spies,* p. 8.

81. The best discussion of this subject is in D. Kahn, *The codebreakers: The story of secret writing* (New York, 1967), pp. 163–65.

82. G. Rothenburg, "Military intelligence gathering in the second half of the eighteenth century, 1740–1792," pp. 99–113, in K. Neilson and B. J. C. McKerchen (eds.), *Go spy the land: Military intelligence in history* (Westport, Conn., 1992), p. 100.

83. The spy's unwholesome image changed over the course of the nineteenth century. James Fenimore Cooper—a very distant kinsman of Woodhull through his wife, interestingly enough—tackled the subject in *The spy: A tale of the neutral ground* (1821), one of the first instances of espionage fiction. Cooper wrote *The Spy* to commemorate the lessons of the Revolutionary War he believed were being forgotten as the last of the greatest generation died off. Thus, his daughter recounted that in 1821 "the writer was walking in Broadway, when he saw a gentleman, well known to him, cross the street, and advance to meet him; it was a prominent merchant, a man of money, very well known in Wall street. He came on a friendly errand, to congratulate his acquaintance on the new book and its success. Lavish in his praise, the merchant told of sitting up through the night to finish the story. 'My friend Harvey [Birch, the spy-hero of the novel] is much obliged to you,' was Cooper's response. Then the merchant hesitated: 'I have one criticism to make, however . . . the character of Harvey is excellent in most regards—but there lies the difficulty . . . you have given the man no motive! . . . Just look at the facts. Here is a man getting in all kinds of scrapes, running his neck into the noose, of his accord, and where, pray, is his motive? I thought he would be well paid for his services—but just as I expected to see it all made clear as day, he refuses to take the gold General Washington offers him. That was your great mistake—you should have given Harvey some motive!'" The merchant had woefully misunderstood Cooper's book. That this little incident on Broadway occurred just forty years after the war underscored Cooper's desire to write it in the first place. Harvey Birch's sole motive is pure patriotism. He was an honest, common man (in fact, a rather earthy peddler with a 'baccy-spitting habit) living in a time of treachery and trimming, a time when loyalties were ambiguous and the country ravaged by hordes of freebooters, traitors, pirates, renegades, and mercenaries. He becomes, much to his own disgust, not just a spy—itself a low occupation—but a double agent, a still lower one. In the book, in the course of which he is suspected to be in British pay and faces execu-

tion, Birch's quietly heroic role as Washington's man is only revealed on the very last page—set thirty years later. Birch is never proud of what he did, but he did it because he needed to—for the good of the country. But he remains a darkly ambivalent figure who is needfully sacrificed in the War of 1812 to symbolize the triumph of the common weal. The invention of a new type of fiction—the mass-produced, dime-a-time spy novel—simplified matters. To their penny-a-word authors and panting audiences, the subtleties of Cooper's *The Spy* needlessly complicated a good read, so novelists created the Good Spy and the Bad Spy. The former were heroes who spy for their country using whatever means are available (though in espionage fiction, they tended to fight clean), and the latter, those who betray their country for cash (or for more nefarious reasons). Today, this fairly legitimate distinction still stands. Historically speaking, it is the reason why Nathan Hale is cheered as a truly towering figure while his British/Loyalist counterparts are condemned to ignominy.

84. Tallmadge, *Memoir*, p. 29.

85. Letter, Woodhull to Tallmadge, November 20, 1778.

86. Letter, Washington to Tallmadge, November 29, 1778. See also his letter to Colonel Henley of the same date: "I do not exactly recollect what sum of hard money General Scott left in your hands, but whatever you may now have be pleased to pay to Major Tallmadge, who has occasion for it for a special purpose, and let me know the amount."

87. On this subject, see the chapter, "Of bills of credit, and colonial and Continental money," in Thompson, *History of Long Island*, I, pp. 420–33.

88. Letter, Washington to Tallmadge, November 29, 1778. See also, Washington to Tallmadge, March 21, 1779: "With this letter you will receive fifty guineas [in gold] for S—— C——r, which you will cause to be delivered as soon as possible, with an earnest exhortation to use them with all possible oeconomy, as I find it very difficult to obtain hard money."

89. Letter, Woodhull to Washington, January 22, 1779.

90. Letter, Woodhull to Tallmadge, April 12, 1779.

91. Letter, Washington to Tallmadge, April 30, 1779.

Chapter Four: 711 and the Sympathetic Stain

1. Letter, Washington to Tallmadge, November 29, 1778.

2. Letter, Washington to Tallmadge, January 2, 1779.

3. Letter, Washington to Tallmadge, January 18, 1779.

4. Letter, Tallmadge to Washington, December 23, 1778.

5. See the listing of the town's earliest inhabitants in Ross, *History of Long Island*, at http://freepages.genealogy.rootsweb.com/~jdevlin/newyork/brookhaven_hist.htm;

F. G. Mather (ed.), *The refugees of 1776 from Long Island to Connecticut* (Albany, 1913), Appendix H, p. 1058, dated June 8, 1775.

6. See http://www.3villagecsd.k12.ny.us/Elementary/minnesauke/3village hist/RoeTavern.htm. It is today a private house. Regarding the kinship of Hawkins and Roe, the latter's ancestor Timothy Roe had married Mary Hawkins, from whom Jonas Hawkins was descended. Regarding the List of Associators, it may be found in Mather (ed.), *Refugees of 1776*, Appendix H, p. 1058, dated June 8, 1775. There is, however, an error in Mather's list: Austin Roe is not included. In an official version of the list in the *Calendar of historical manuscripts relating to the War of the Revolution, in the office of the secretary of state* (Albany, 2 vols., 1868), I, p. 53, Roe does appear. The reason for the discrepancy is that Mather's concentration slipped and he forgot to include Roe when he was copying it from this, the original source.

7. Compared to today's smaller and geographically widespread families, men of that time defined as "close" kin we often think of as distant: obscure in-laws, second cousins once removed, and the like. I deal with this subject in greater detail, for those of you who are interested in its medieval manifestation, in my *Kings in the North: The house of Percy in British history* (London, paperback ed., 2002), pp. 55–56.

8. See, for instance, letter, Tallmadge to Washington, January 28, 1779, enclosing Woodhull's January 22 letter to Tallmadge.

9. Letter, Brewster to Tallmadge, February 26, 1779.

10. *Royal Gazette*, January 6, 1779, and March 3, 1779. Patriots, too, were liable to conflate the right to make a return with the fight for liberty; as Alexander McDougall crowed to Samuel Adams in 1774, "Stocks have risen in favor of Liberty." P. Maier, *The old revolutionaries: Political lives in the age of Samuel Adams* (New York, 1980), p. 99. See also, in the same book, the chapter "Isaac Sears and the business of revolution," pp. 51–100.

11. See B. W. Labaree, W. M. Fowler, Jr., E. W. Sloan, J. B. Hattendorf, J. J. Safford, and A. W. German, *America and the sea: A maritime history* (Mystic, Conn., 1998), pp. 136–41.

12. O. T. Barck, Jr., *New York City during the War for Independence, with special reference to the period of British occupation* (New York, 1931; rep. Port Washington, N.Y., 1966), pp. 129–31.

13. J. L. Van Buskirk, *Generous enemies: Patriots and Loyalists in Revolutionary New York* (Philadelphia, 2002), p. 136; B. Quarles, *The negro in the American Revolution* (Chapel Hill, N.C., 1961; rep. 1996), pp. 152–56.

14. See letter, William Whipple to Dr. Josiah Bartlett, July 12, 1778, printed in H. S. Commager and R. B. Morris (eds.), *The spirit of 'seventy-six: The story of the American Revolution as told by participants* (New York, 3rd ed., 1978; rep. 1995), pp. 967–68.

15. T. J. Wertenbaker, *Father Knickerbocker rebels: New York City during the Revolution* (New York, 1948), p. 210.

16. I. N. P. Stokes, *The iconography of Manhattan Island, 1498–1909: Compiled from original sources and illustrated by photo-intaglio reproductions of important maps, plans, views, and documents in public and private collections* (New York, 6 vols., 1915–1928), V, p. 1027.

17. William Smith (ed. W. H. W. Sabine), *Historical memoirs from 16 March 1763 to 12 November 1783 of William Smith, historian of the province of New York; member of the governor's council, and last chief justice of that province under the Crown; chief justice of Quebec* (New York, 3 vols., in 2, rep. 1969–71), entry for May 10, 1780, III, p. 261.

18. For slightly varying figures, see Stokes, *Iconography*, V, p. 1047; Wertenbaker, *Father Knickerbocker rebels*, p. 208; Barck, *New York City during the War for Independence*, pp. 129–31.

19. Barck, *New York City during the War for Independence*, pp. 129–31; Stokes, *Iconography*, V, pp. 1075, 1086.

20. Letter, Woodhull to Tallmadge, February 26, 1779.

21. P. D. Nelson, *William Tryon and the course of empire: A life in British imperial service* (Chapel Hill, N.C./London, 2005), pp. 167–69.

22. Letter, Jay to Washington, November 19, 1778.

23. This was the determined opinion of Thomas Jones, in his *History of New York during the Revolutionary War, and of the leading events in the other colonies at that period* (New York, 2 vols., 1879), II, pp. 223–25. In 1782, Jay was captured by the British, to whom he confided his fear of growing French influence. After expressing a desire for reconciliation between the Mother Country and America, he was released and allowed to leave for Britain, giving rise to suspicions as to the robustness of his Patriotism. (For individuals to switch sides during the Revolution was common, but at that stage of the war, it was often to the Cause of Liberty, which also happened to be the one winning.) John Jay, hearing the news of his brother's apparent defection, wrote to a friend that "if after making so much bustle in and for America, he has . . . improperly made his peace with Britain, I shall endeavour to forget that my father has such a son." The two brothers corresponded rarely after the war. See Appendix XXXIX, in Jones, *History*, II, p. 540.

24. Letter, James Jay to Jefferson, April 14, 1806, Thomas Jefferson Papers, Manuscript Division, Library of Congress. "My method of communication was this: To prevent the suspicion which might arise were I to write to my brother John only, who was a member of Congress, I writ with black ink a short letter to him, and likewise to 1 or 2 other persons of the family, none exceeding 3 or 4 lines in black ink. The

residue of the blank paper I filled up, invisibly, with such intelligence and matters as I thought would be useful to the American Cause. All these letters were left open, and sent in that condition to the Director or Secretary of the General Post Office, with a letter insinuating that I thought it could not be the intentions of Government, in their restraining laws, to put a stop to family intercourse; and therefore requesting the party to read over the letters, and if nothing improper appeared in them, that he would permit them to pass in the mail to New York. They passed accordingly, and on their arrival in New York were sent into the American Lines. In this invisible writing I sent to Franklin and Deane, by the mail from London to Paris, a plan of the intended Expedition under Burgoyne from Canada." James Jay adds that he and his brother often corresponded using the ink, but once came close to discovery because John Jay had kept the letters and sent them to what he thought was a place of safety in New Jersey. When General Howe landed at Staten Island in the summer of 1776 in preparation for the assault on New York, his troops advanced within seven miles of the letters' hiding place. John Jay burned them shortly afterwards. For more on John Jay and Deane, see V. H. Paltsits, "The use of invisible ink for secret writing during the American Revolution," *Bulletin of the New York Public Library*, XXXIX (1935), no. 5, pp. 361–4.

25. Letter, Washington to Elias Boudinot, May 3, 1779.

26. Letters, Washington to Jay, April 9, 1780; Jay to Washington, April 13, 1780.

27. Letter, Jay to Washington, April 13, 1780.

28. Letters, Washington to Jay, May 12, 1780; Washington to Hay, May 13, 1780.

29. Letter, Washington to Boudinot, May 3, 1779.

30. Letter, Washington to Tallmadge, September 24, 1779.

31. Letter, Washington to Tallmadge, July 25, 1779.

32. S. Rubin's exhaustive *The secret science of covert inks* (Port Townsend, Wa., 1987) has a chapter on sympathetic inks; the one here may be found on p. 15. Sympathetic inks were not altogether unheard of at the time, though very few, excepting some specialists and antiquarians, knew about them. For his correspondence with the British, the extraordinary Tory spy Benjamin Thompson—soldier, charlatan, brilliant physicist—distilled gallotannic acid from gallnuts that could be developed with ferrous sulphate, an idea gleaned from Giovanni Battista Porta's sixteenth-century tome *Natural Magick*. (Thompson would go on to become Count Rumford of the Holy Roman Empire—it was quite a career.) Despite Jay's claims of uniqueness, this solution bears a distinct resemblance to his. Even so, the solution was such a rarity, the chances of discovery by the British are too remote to consider. On Thompson's concoction, see S. C. Brown and E. W. Stein, "Benjamin Thompson and the first secret ink letter of the American Revolution," *Journal of Criminal Law, Criminology and Police Science*, XL (1950), 5, pp. 627–36.

33. Letters, Woodhull to Tallmadge, April 12, 1779; Woodhull to Washington, April 29, 1779.

34. Letter, Washington to Tallmadge, February 5, 1780, copy in the Benjamin Tallmadge Papers held at the Department of Rare Books and Special Collections at Princeton University Library. This version contains a P.S. containing the words quoted here that does not appear in the Library of Congress copy.

35. Letter, Washington to Howe, January 20, 1777.

36. Letter, Washington to Boudinot, May 3, 1779. In the version of the letter actually sent, Washington cautiously wrote "——" in place of "P——," but used the latter in his draft. For a follow-up, see letter, Washington to Boudinot, May 17, 1779.

37. Letter, Pintard to Washington, March 25, 1780.

38. Letters, Pintard to Washington, May 14, 1783; Washington to Pintard, May 21, 1783.

39. Letter, Washington to Tallmadge, June 27, 1779.

40. On this encounter, see B. G. Loescher, *Washington's eyes: The Continental Light Dragoons* (Fort Collins, Colo., 1977), p. 41; B. Tallmadge, *Memoir of Col. Benjamin Tallmadge* (New York, 1858; rep. 1968), p. 32. Tallmadge seems to misremember in saying that Lord Rawdon led the attack. Rawdon was an infantry commander, of the Volunteers of Ireland, and his biographer does not mention the incident. See P. D. Nelson, *Francis Rawdon-Hastings, marquess of Hastings: Soldier, peer of the realm, governor-general of India* (Madison, Wis./Teaneck, N.J., 2005).

41. The letter, Washington to Tallmadge, June 13, 1779, is kept in draft in the Washington Papers, but the original may be found in Sir Henry Clinton's papers at the William L. Clements Library, University of Michigan.

42. Letter, Washington to Tallmadge, July 5, 1779.

43. Quoted in C. Van Doren, *Secret history of the American Revolution* (New York, 1941), p. 238.

44. Letter, Clinton to his sisters, October 4 and 8, 1780, printed in Van Doren, *Secret history,* Appendix, no. 67, pp. 477–80.

45. Though there are fuzzy distinctions between a code and a cipher that D. Kahn, *The codebreakers: The story of secret writing* (New York, 1967), pp. xiv–xv, discusses, I have tended to use the terms interchangeably, not only to save the reader confusion but because Kahn says that between 1400 and 1850 the nomenclator system commonly used was half-code, half-cipher, which makes it difficult to draw hard and fast lines.

46. G. F. Strasser, "Diplomatic cryptology and universal languages in the sixteenth and seventeenth centuries," pp. 73–97, in K. Neilson and B. J. C. McKerchen (eds.), *Go spy the land: Military intelligence in history* (Westport, Conn., 1992), pp. 75–76.

47. On frequencies, see F. Pratt, *Secret and urgent: The story of codes and ciphers* (London, 1939), Tables I, VIII, and IX, pp. 252, 260–61.

48. On Rossignol, see Kahn, *Codebreakers,* pp. 157–62.

49. Kahn, *Codebreakers,* pp. 173–74.

50. I have relied, for the section on the Dumas and Lovell ciphers, on two sources primarily: R. E. Weber, *United States diplomatic codes and ciphers, 1775–1938* (Chicago, 1979), esp. pp. 22–46; and the same author's *Masked dispatches: Cryptograms and cryptology in American history, 1775–1900* (2nd ed., 2002), published by the National Security Agency's Center for Cryptologic History. On p.16, Weber reproduces a three-letter key (B.R.A.) for the Lovell Cipher, but provides a transcription using the two-letter key (C.R.), so I have reconstructed the latter for those readers who are interested in this sort of thing.

51. Letter, Woodhull to Tallmadge, March 17, 1779.

52. Letter, Woodhull to Tallmadge, April 10, 1779.

53. Letter, Townsend to Tallmadge, July 29, 1779.

54. An original copy of the July 1779 Code Dictionary is kept in the Washington Papers, though Weber, *Masked dispatches,* pp. 44–51, reprints it. Robert Townsend became "723."

55. E. C. Burnett, "Ciphers of the Revolutionary period," *American Historical Review,* XXII (1917), 2, p. 332.

56. Letter, Townsend to Tallmadge, August 6, 1779.

Chapter Five: The Man of Parts and Halves

1. Letter, Washington to Tallmadge, March 21, 1779.

2. Letter, Woodhull to Tallmadge, March 17, 1779.

3. Letter, Washington to Reed, March 28, 1779.

4. Letter, Washington to Putnam, March 27, 1779.

5. Letter, Washington to Putnam, April 1, 1779.

6. Letter, Woodhull to Tallmadge, April 10, 1779.

7. Regarding the end of the Staten Island plan, see letter, Washington to Tallmadge, April 30, 1779.

8. Letter, Tallmadge to Washington, April 21, 1779.

9. The regiment, now the Queen's York Rangers, still exists as a Canadian armored reconnaissance unit.

10. Letter, Woodhull to Tallmadge, June 5, 1779.

11. See B. F. Thompson (ed. C. J. Werner), *History of Long Island, from its earliest settlement to the present time* (New York, 3 vols., 3rd ed., 1918; orig. 1839), III, p. 363.

12. *Royal Gazette*, July 3, 1779.

13. T. Jones (ed. E. F. De Lancey), *History of New York during the Revolutionary War, and of the leading events in the other colonies at that period* (New York, 2 vols., 1879), I, pp. 268–69, 287–88. Floyd is buried in the graveyard of Setauket's Presbyterian church. Jones, ignorant of Woodhull's letter, of course, did not speculate why Floyd was released so quickly.

14. Letter, Woodhull to Tallmadge, February 26, 1779. J. G. Staudt, "Suffolk County," in J. S. Tiedemann and E. R. Fingerhut (eds.), *The other New York: The American Revolution beyond New York City, 1763–1787* (Albany, 2005), p. 65, says that Benjamin Floyd was a major.

15. Letter, Woodhull to Tallmadge, June 5, 1779 (second of the same date).

16. Letter, Washington to Tallmadge, June 13, 1779.

17. Letter, Woodhull to Tallmadge, June 20, 1779. This letter was not sent for at least a week after its composition—an indication of the sudden slowness of communications caused by Hawkins's departure.

18. Letter, Washington to Tallmadge, June 27, 1779.

19. J. C. and C. A. Townsend, *A memorial of John, Henry, and Richard Townsend, and their descendants* (New York, 1865; rep. and new ed., 1976), p. 101.

20. Woodhull said he had been acquainted with Townsend for "several years." Letter, Woodhull to Tallmadge, July 9, 1779.

21. Letter, Captain Farley to Townsend, February 27, 1797, in the Townsend Family Papers, Raynham Hall Museum.

22. The list of his books is as follows (taken from an inventory of Robert Townsend's "Goods, Chattels and Credits," May 26, 1838, Townsend Family Papers, Raynham Hall Museum, FX 88.30.22.2): *Dictionary, Book of Plays, Elements of the English Language, Rasselas,* Denham's *Poems,* Shaftesbury's *Works,* Burke's *Works,* Godwin's *Justice,* Mair's *Bookkeeping,* Chaucer's *Poems,* Ovid's *Epistles,* Shenstone's *Poems,* Hooker's *Works, Covent Garden Magazine,* Walker's *Geography, Human Species, Turkish Spy in Paris* (8 vols.), *Latin Vocabulary,* Meignon's *Charter, History of Pennsylvania,* Montesquieu's *Works,* Leland's *Demosthenes, Free Thinker,* Churchill's *Poems, Spectator,* Chesterfield's *Letters, British Theatre,* Moore's *Journals, Principles of Government,* Johnson's *Arithmetic, Mariners Compass,* Hume's *History,* Raynal's *History,* Butler's *Analogy,* Woolstonecraft's *History of the French Revolution,* Smith's *Essays, Complete Merchant,* Carver's *Travels,* Love's *Survey,* Beattie's *Essays,* Johnson's *Dictionary,* Smith's *Moral Sentiments,* Anderson on *Industry,* Pope's *Iliad, Life of Pope, Tatler, Reverie, World, French Revolution,* Moore's *Journal,* Boswell's *Johnson, The Court of Cupid,* Barlow's *Writings, La Vie Prince,* Bellamy's *Life, Life of John Elvers, Letters of Junius,* Butler's *Sermons,* Mackenzie on *Health,* Prior's *Poems,* Condorcet's *Philosophical Dictionary,* Necker, Waller's *Poems, Freeholder,*

Murphey's *Tacitus*, Macpherson's *History*, Webster's *Political Essays*, Blair's *Lectures*, *Books of Fairs*, Seamen's *Vade Mecum*, Ferguson's *Philosophy*, Ash on *Education*, Fasquahar's *Works*, Pope's *Works*, Gregory's *View*, Whitehead's *Poems*, Hutchinson's *Enquiry*, *Picture of the Times*, Plowden's *British History*, Sidney on *Government*, Sheriden's *Revolution of Sweden*, *London Magazine*, Gillies' *Frederick II*, *Annals of Queen Anne's Reign*, *Present State of Great Britain*, Atkinson's *Navigator*, Bruce's *Memoirs*, Locke on the *Understanding*, Reid's *Essays*, Bertrand's *Mathematics*, Jones's *Bookkeeping*, *Duty of the Justices of the Peace*, Leyden's *Papers*, and four pamphlets on the *Laws of England*.

23. Personal notes by Robert Townsend, in the Townsend Family Papers, Raynham Hall Museum.

24. Peter Townsend sketchbook, F89.11.9, in the Townsend Family Papers, Raynham Hall Museum.

25. Which made them exceedingly distant relatives of Viscount Townshend, he of the hated Townshend Duties.

26. On the house, see F. Irwin, *Oyster Bay in history, a sketch* (New York, n.d. but 1950–1975), p. 71.

27. Samuel's appearance and his wife's affection for the Quakers were described by his grandson, Dr. Peter Townsend, in his personal notebook. Quoted in Irwin, *Oyster Bay in history*, p. 98.

28. M. Pennypacker, *George Washington's spies on Long Island and in New York* (New York, 2 vols., 1939, 1948), p. 104; I have also used Weekes's diary, reproduced in Irwin, *Oyster Bay in history*, pp. 79–80.

29. R. L. Ketcham, "Conscience, war, and politics in Pennsylvania, 1755–1757," *William and Mary Quarterly*, XX (1963), 3, pp. 416–39; I. Sharpless, *A Quaker experiment in government*, vol. 1 of *History of Quaker government in Pennsylvania* (Philadelphia, 2 vols., 1898).

30. A. J. Mekeel, *The relation of the Quakers to the American Revolution* (Washington, D.C., 1979), p. 20; the complete list of signatories is given in J. T. Scharf and T. Westcott, *History of Philadelphia, 1609–1884* (3 vols., Philadelphia, 1884), I, pp. 412–13.

31. W. H. Conser, Jr., R. M. McCarthy, and D. J. Toscano, "The American independence movement, 1765–1775: A decade of nonviolent struggles," in Conser et al. (eds.), *Resistance, politics and the American struggle for independence, 1765–1775* (Boulder, Colo., 1986), p. 17.

32. I have drawn on numbers unearthed by J. S. Tiedemann from church records, court minutes, family papers, Bible records, conveyances, mortgages, military records, newspapers, tax lists, town records, voting returns, and wills, and printed in "Queens County, New York Quakers in the American Revolution: Loyal-

ists or neutrals?" *Historical Magazine of the Protestant Episcopal Church*, LII (1983), 3, pp. 215–27.

33. Note to the "Meeting at Jamaica and election of a committee," in H. Onderdonk (ed), *Documents and letters intended to illustrate the Revolutionary incidents of Queens County with connecting narratives, explanatory notes, and additions* (New York, 1846), no. 2, held December 6, 1774.

34. "Meeting at Oyster Bay," in Onderdonk (ed.), *Revolutionary incidents of Queens County*, no. 8, December 30, 1774.

35. "A Provincial Convention to be held," in Onderdonk (ed.), *Revolutionary incidents of Queens County*, no. 11, March 16, 1775; Jones (ed. De Lancey), *History of New York*, I, note XVI, pp. 477–89.

36. "Certificate of minority at Oyster Bay," in Onderdonk (ed.), *Revolutionary incidents of Queens County*, no. 17, April 12, 1775. This document contains the complete list of all Whigs in Oyster Bay.

37. J. S. Tiedemann, "A Revolution foiled: Queens County, New York, 1775–1776," *Journal of American History*, LXXV (1988), 2, p. 427.

38. Jones (ed. De Lancey), *History of New York*, I, note XVI, p. 487.

39. "List of committee men in Queens County," in Onderdonk (ed.), *Revolutionary incidents of Queens County*, no. 24, May 29, 1775.

40. M. H. Luke and R. W. Venables, *Long Island in the American Revolution* (Albany, 1976), p. 9.

41. "Arms impressed from non-Associators," in Onderdonk (ed.), *Revolutionary incidents of Queens County*, no. 31, September 1775.

42. "Vote of Queens County of deputies," in Onderdonk (ed.), *Revolutionary incidents of Queens County*, no. 34, November 7, 1775.

43. Tiedemann, "A Revolution foiled," *Journal of American History*, pp. 429–31. On the preceding subjects, see also Jones (ed. De Lancey), *History of New York*, I, note XXVIII, pp. 568–73.

44. According to a personal note in the Scrapbook of Solomon Townsend II (Robert's nephew), F89.11.8, in the Townsend Family Papers, Raynham Hall Museum.

45. S. R. Frey, *The British soldier in America: A social history of military life in the Revolutionary period* (Austin, Tex., 1981), pp. 38–39.

46. Frey, *The British soldier in America*, p. 95.

47. Frey, *The British soldier in America*, pp. 99–102. There's some debate over the exact measurements, caliber, and weight of the musket. I've used Frey's figures, but see also E. E. Curtis, *The organization of the British army in the American Revolution* (New Haven, 1926; rep. 1969), p. 16 and n. 38.

48. E. Bangs (ed.), *Journal of Lieutenant Isaac Bangs, April 1 to July 29, 1776* (Cambridge, 1890), p. 29.

49. Bangs (ed.), *Journal of Lieutenant Isaac Bangs*, pp. 30, 31.

50. C. Abbott, "The neighborhoods of New York, 1760–1775," *New York History*, XV (1974), p. 50.

51. L. Picard, *Dr. Johnson's London: Coffee-houses and climbing boys, medicine, toothpaste and gin, poverty and press gangs, freak shows and female education* (New York, 2002 ed.), p. 78; G. Ellington, *The women of New York; or, the underworld of the great city* (New York, 1869), p. 448.

52. T. H. Breen, *The marketplace of revolution: How consumer politics shaped American independence* (Oxford, 2004), pp. 140–42.

53. J. Baldwin and G. Rossano, *Clan and commerce: The Townsend family of Oyster Bay* (no date, thesis in possession of Raynham Hall Museum, Oyster Bay), p. 108. Regarding the Townsends' business affairs, throughout this book I have heavily relied on this invaluable dissertation, available only at the Raynham Hall Museum. I am indebted to Lisa Cuomo of the Museum for bringing it to my attention.

54. Baldwin and Rossano, *Clan and commerce*, p. 108.

55. "Report to the president of Congress on driving off stock," in Onderdonk (ed.), *Revolutionary incidents of Queens County*, no. 79, July 1776; and also, letter dated July 12, 1776, in Pennypacker, *George Washington's spies*, p. 107

56. On the appointment, see Pennypacker, *George Washington's spies*, pp. 108–9.

57. This section is based on the detailed contents of a family document describing the incident, reproduced in Pennypacker, *George Washington's spies*, pp. 105–6. For the names of the officers in question, see Onderdonk (ed.), *Revolutionary incidents of Queens County*, no. 505, which lists the officers of the Seventeenth Light Dragoons. On Thomas Buchanan's background, see V. D. Harrington, *The New York merchant on the eve of the Revolution* (New York, 1935; rep. Gloucester, Mass., 1964), pp. 51, 351. On Townsend's oath of allegiance, Pennypacker, p. 107. After the war, in common with many Loyalists, Buchanan sold up and left for Nova Scotia with his family.

58. Certificate, in Box 1, 1776 Folder, of the Townsend Family Papers at the New-York Historical Society.

59. Her letter, which survived two attempts to destroy it, is lodged in the Long Island Collection at East Hampton Public Library. It is reproduced as a footnote in Pennypacker, *George Washington's spies*, pp. 112–13.

60. "Petition and representation of Queens County," in Onderdonk (ed.), *Revolutionary incidents of Queens County*, no. 123, October 21, 1776.

61. Letter, Tryon to Germain, December 24, 1776, in E. B. O'Callaghan et al.

(eds.), *Documents relative to the Colonial history of the State of New-York* (Albany, 15 vols., 1856–87), VIII, p. 693.

62. Undated note in Box 1, 1776 Folder, in the Townsend Family Papers, New-York Historical Society. His nephew's recollection is written on the note.

63. Baldwin and Rossano, *Clan and commerce*, p. 137.

64. Pennypacker, *George Washington's spies*, p. 12.

65. Barck, *New York City during the War for Independence*, pp. 150–51; B. Fay, *Notes on the American press at the end of the eighteenth century* (New York, 1927) is also very useful.

66. O. T. Barck, Jr., *New York City during the War for Independence, with special reference to the period of British occupation* (New York, 1931; rep. Port Washington, N.Y., 1966), p. 153.

67. *Royal Gazette*, March 7, 1778; January 3, 1778; November 1, 1777; S. Curwen (ed. G. A. Ward), *The journal and letters of Samuel Curwen, an American in England, from 1775 to 1783* (Boston, 4th ed., 1864); letter, Curwen to the Reverend Isaac Smith, April 30, 1777, p. 125.

68. *Royal Gazette*, March 20, 1782.

69. J. L. Van Buskirk, *Generous enemies: Patriots and Loyalists in Revolutionary New York* (Philadelphia, 2002), pp. 41–42.

70. *Royal Gazette*, September 16, 1780. See also *Royal Gazette*, January 31, 1781, for Congress's "Last Will and Testament."

71. Quoted in the *Magazine of American History*, XX (1915), p. 124.

72. The reader is directed to L. Hewlett, "James Rivington, Loyalist printer, publisher and bookseller of the American Revolution, 1724–1802: A biographical bibliographical study" (unpub. Ph.D. thesis, University of Michigan, Ann Arbor, 1958); B. M. Wilkenfeld, "Revolutionary New York, 1776," pp. 43–72, in M. Klein (ed.), *New York: The centennial years, 1676–1976* (Port Washington, N.Y., 1976), p. 59; on Loosley, see I. N. P. Stokes, *The iconography of Manhattan Island, 1498–1909: Compiled from original sources and illustrated by photo-intaglio reproductions of important maps, plans, views, and documents in public and private collections* (New York, 6 vols., 1915–1928), V, p. 1055; on the lamps, *Royal Gazette*, November 22, 1782.

73. Stokes, *Iconography*, V, p. 1059. The store's opening was announced on December 20, 1777.

74. Henry Wansey's entertaining recollections of a postwar tour has this: "June 23rd [1794], I dined with James Rivington, the bookseller, formerly of St. Paul's Churchyard; he is still a cheerful old man. . . . During the time the British kept possession of New York, he printed a newspaper for them, and opened a kind of coffee-house for the officers; his house was a place of great resort; he made a great deal of money during that period, though many of the officers quitted it considerably in arrears to

him." H. Wansey, *The journal of an excursion to the United States of North America in the summer of 1794* (New York, orig. 1796; rep. 1969). On Townsend's involvement, see Pennypacker, *General Washington's spies*, p. 12.

75. On his dealings with Templeton & Stewart, see various entries in his Cash Book, 1781–1784, in the Townsend Family Papers, Box 4, New-York Historical Society.

76. Baldwin and Rossano, *Clan and commerce*, pp. 137–38.

77. Baldwin and Rossano, *Clan and commerce*, p. 139; and Pennypacker, *George Washington's spies*, p. 54 n. (Pennypacker calls him "Oakman.")

78. For his rent payments, see Townsend's Cash Book, 1781–1784, in Townsend Family Papers, Box 4, New-York Historical Society. In the Townsend Papers at Raynham Hall, there is a black-and-white photograph, marked Gold. 35&6, of a note written by Peter Townsend, the subject's nephew, recording that Robert "kept Bachelors Hall over his store on Peak Slip on the East Side near Pearl St."

79. This list is taken from Baldwin and Rossano, *Clan and commerce*, pp. 138–39.

80. See his Cash Book, 1781–1784, in the Townsend Family Papers, Box 4, New-York Historical Society.

81. The doctrine of the Inward, or Inner, Light is covered in H. H. Brinton, *The religious philosophy of Quakerism* (Wallingford, Pa., 1973), pp. 5–7; S. V. James, "The impact of the American Revolution on Quakers' ideas about their sect," *William and Mary Quarterly*, XIX (1962), 3, pp. 360–61; W. M. Goering, "'To obey, rebelling': The Quaker dilemma in *Moby-Dick*," *New England Quarterly*, LIV (1981), 4, pp. 520–22. For discussions of Quaker reformism, see S. V. James, *A people among peoples: Quaker benevolence in eighteenth-century America* (Cambridge, Mass., 1963), pp. 141–68; J. D. Marietta, "Conscience, the Quaker community and the French and Indian War," *Pennsylvania Magazine of History and Biography*, XCV (1971), pp. 3–27; D. J. Boorstin, *The Americans: The colonial experience* (New York, 1958), pp. 56–60.

82. See *An epistle from our general spring meeting of ministers and elders for Pennsylvania and New-Jersey, held at Philadelphia, from the 29th of the third month, to the 1st of the fourth month, inclusive* (1755), pp. 2–3, quoted in F. B. Tolles, *Meeting house and counting house: The Quaker merchants of Colonial Philadelphia, 1682–1763* (Chapel Hill, N.C., 1948; rep. New York, 1963), pp. 235–36; see also, Mekeel, *Relation of the Quakers*, p. 6, and P. P. Moulton, *The journal and essays of John Woolman* (New York, 1971), pp. 48–50.

83. Townsend owned a copy of the *History of Pennsylvania*, and so was well acquainted with Quaker affairs. See the inventory of Robert Townsend's "Goods, Chattels and Credits," May 26, 1838, in the Townsend Family Papers, Raynham Hall Museum, FX 88.30.22.2.

84. P. Brock, *The Quaker peace testimony, 1660–1914* (York, 1990), pp. 143–44.

85. I. Sharpless, *A Quaker experiment in government; history of Quaker government in Pennsylvania, 1682–1783* (1902 ed.), p. 234.

86. As pointed out by W. C. Kashatus III, "Thomas Paine: a Quaker revolutionary," *Quaker History*, LXXIV (1984), 2, pp. 57–60.

87. Paine, *Common Sense* (Mineola, N.Y., 1997 ed.), p. 51.

88. *The ancient testimony and the principles of the people call'd Quakers renewed with respect to the king and government, and touching the commotions now prevailing in these and other parts of America, addressed to the people in general,* cited in Mekeel, *Relation of the Quakers,* p. 138.

89. See Paine, *The American Crisis,* no. 3, April 19, 1777: "What more can we say of ye than that a religious Quaker is a valuable character, and a political Quaker a real Jesuit."

90. Paine, *American Crisis,* nos. 1 (13 January, 1777) and 3.

91. Paine, *Common Sense,* p. 55.

92. To the most famous dissident of all, General Nathanael "the Fighting Quaker" Greene, who took on Paine as his aide-de-camp in 1776, peace was certainly not the answer. Only by beating their plowshares into swords, and their pruning hooks into spears, and learning how to war, could Quakers stay true to the Inner Light. The way to guarantee Quakers' religious rights—including the right to preach pacifism—was not to cozy up to a tyrannical regime or retreat into Stoic asceticism. No, Quakers must forcefully carve themselves a place in the new United States by fighting for their liberties with bayonet and musket. So, when the Revolution came, Greene accepted the bitter cup while others passed it on. By 1781 there was even a small Paineite splinter group called the "Free Quakers"—Betsy Ross, she who allegedly sewed the first flag, was one—animated by the pang for freedom from oppression and from every sort of ecclesiastical tyranny (including their own). But Greene and the Free Quakers were extreme examples of Paineite enthusiasm, and never gained much traction outside their own circle. See Kashatus, "Thomas Paine," pp. 48–49; and T. Thayer, *Nathanael Greene, strategist of the American Revolution* (New York, 1960). Mekeel, *Relation of the Quakers,* has a short chapter on the Free Quakers, pp. 283–89; C. Wetherill, *History of the religious Society of Friends called by some the Free Quakers, in the city of Philadelphia* (Philadelphia, 1894), is also useful.

93. Quoted in Irwin, *Oyster Bay in history,* p. 96.

94. The essential text on this material is R. A. Bowler, *Logistics and the failure of the British army in America, 1775–1783* (Princeton, N.J., 1975).

95. J. S. Tiedemann, "Patriots by default: Queens County, New York, and the British army, 1776–1783," *William and Mary Quarterly,* XLIII (1986), 1, pp. 49–50.

96. Letter, Stuart to Bute, February 4, 1777, in E. Stuart-Wortley (ed.), *A prime minister and his son* (London, 1925), pp. 96–99.

97. *The detail and conduct of the American war under Generals Gage, Howe, Burgoyne, and Vice Admiral Lord Howe: With a very full and correct state of the whole of the evidence as given before a committee of the House of Commons* (London, 3rd ed., 1780), p. 119.

98. William Bamford, "Bamford's diary: The Revolutionary diary of a British officer," *Maryland Historical Magazine*, XXVIII (1933), p. 13.

99. Letter, Lord Rawdon to the Earl of Huntington, September 23, 1776, in F. Bickley (ed.), *Report on the manuscripts of the late Reginald Rawdon-Hastings, Esq., of the Manor House, Ashby de la Zouch* (London, Historical Manuscripts Commission, 1934), III, p. 185. On this topic, see Tiedemann, "Patriots by default," *William and Mary Quarterly*, pp. 38–39.

100. On this subject, see Jones (ed. De Lancey), *History of New York*, I, pp. 115–122; Barck, Jr., *New York City during the War for Independence*, pp. 100–1. Both books are vital resources for this subject.

101. Jones (ed. De Lancey), *History of New York*, I, pp. 334–36; Tiedemann, "Patriots by default," *William and Mary Quarterly*, pp. 42–44; Bowler, *Logistics and the failure of the British army*, pp. 24–25, 183–85, 190–99; on the Stamp Act revenue, see J. C. D. Clark, "British America: What if there had been no American Revolution?" in N. Ferguson (ed.), *Virtual history: Alternative and counterfactuals* (London, 1997), p. 153.

102. The situation was almost as bad on the American side. They, too, would roust pro-independence civilians from their house if an officer took a liking to it, and forcibly billeted soldiers on homeowners who could ill afford to feed them. (Still, they often put a brave face on it. Anna Zabriskie of Kingston, New York, whose Patriotic credentials were impeccable, complained of the rudeness of the American officers staying with her: "One must always bear with the insolence of the lower sort," she mused.) When Mary Hay Burn of Hackensack, whose husband was fighting for Washington, was ordered to relocate by an American official, she replied, vainly, "Why should I not have liberty whilst you strive for liberty?" Whereas the British were more overtly corrupt, whenever the Continental army liberated Loyalist territory around New York, there were score-settling vendettas and arrests as local Patriots informed on and harassed their Tory neighbors under the guise of instilling the requisite civic virtue. Hector St. John de Crèvecoeur, a Loyalist of French background living in New York State, described in his *Sketches* the kind of pompous cant adopted by a greedy Whig deacon and his wife, and the other "low, illiterate, little tyrants" bossing other people about, to justify the cruel imprisonment and plundering of a Tory squire: " 'Tis a bleeding cause, as

our minister says of it; therefore sufferings must come of it." (Van Buskirk, *Generous enemies*, pp. 37–39; H. St. J. de Crèvecoeur [ed. A. E. Stone], *Letters from an American farmer and sketches of eighteenth-century America* [New York, 1981], "Landscapes," pp. 428–39. For the remark about "little tyrants," see p. 450.) Then again, when Crèvecoeur fled to New York in 1778 to escape Patriot persecution, some anonymous snitch tipped off the British, who imprisoned him for being a suspicious Frenchman. As Eccleston, a Crèvecoeur character described as "an *American* gentleman [italics added]," presciently remarked of the predicament faced by his nonpolitical, moderate countrymen, "We are . . . suspended between poverty, neglect, and contempt if we go to New York, and fines, imprisonment, and exile if we stay!" His acquaintance Iwan, a gloomily philosophical Russian, advises him to "learn to bear the insolence of men. Societies, like individuals, have their periods of sickness. Bear this as you would a fever or a cold." (From Stone's introduction to Crèvecoeur, *Letters from an American farmer*, p. 12. See also W. Smith [ed. W. H. W. Sabine], *Historical memoirs from 16 March 1763 to 12 November 1783 of William Smith, historian of the province of New York; member of the governor's council, and last chief justice of that province under the Crown; chief justice of Quebec* [New York, 3 vols. in 2, rep. 1969–71], II, entries for February 10 and 15, 1779, pp. 74–75; July 8, 1779, p. 126; July 16, 1779, p. 133; August 1, 1779, p. 146; for Eccleston and Iwan, see p. 447.) It was left to a Hessian, Major Baurmeister, to express the shared feeling among Patriots, Loyalists, and neutrals alike that "no matter how this war may end, as long as this mess continues, the people suffer at the hands of both friend and foe. The Americans rob them of their earnings and cattle, and we burn their empty houses; and in moments of sensitiveness, it is difficult to decide which party is more cruel. These cruelties have begotten enough misery to last an entire generation." (B. A. Uhlendorf [trans.], *Revolution in America: Confidential letters and journals 1776–1784 of Adjutant General Major Baurmeister of the Hessian forces* [New Brunswick, N.J., 1957], p. 362.)

103. Barck, *New York City during the War for Independence*, p. 111.

104. Barck, *New York City during the War for Independence*, p. 112; Tiedemann, "Patriots by default," *William and Mary Quarterly*, pp. 42–44.

105. Jones (ed. De Lancey), *History of New York*, II, p. 227.

106. Jones (ed. De Lancey), *History of New York*, I, p. 352. Americans, too, complained of the new, heavy burden of wartime government they bore. A character in Crèvecoeur's *Sketches* observes that "we have so many more masters than we used to have. There is the high and mighty Congress, and there is our governor, and our senators, and our assemblymen, and there is our captain of light-horse . . . and there is . . . our worthy colonel; and there are the honourable committee. And there are, let me see, one, two, three, four, five commissaries who want nothing but our horses, grain, hay, etc., and from whom we can never get any recompense." Crèvecoeur, *Letters from an American farmer*, p. 461.

107. M. M. Klein, "Why did the British fail to win the hearts and minds of New Yorkers?" *New York History*, LXIV (1983), no. 4, p. 366; and Jones (ed. De Lancey), *History of New York*, II, p. 136.

108. See, for instance, Jones's attack on Clinton in his (ed. De Lancey), *History of New York*, I, p. 285; and also E. G. Schaukirk, *Occupation of New York City by the British* (originally published in *Pennsylvania Magazine of History and Biography*, January 1887; New York, rep. 1969), diary entry for December 16, 1780, p. 17: "The general language even of the common soldiers is, that the war might and would have been ended long before now, if it was not for the great men, who only want to fill their purses; and indeed it is too apparent that this has been and is the ruling principle in all departments, only to seek their own private interest . . . and when they have got enough to retreat or go home—let become of America what will!" There was more. Henry Clinton—"haughty, morose, churlish, stupid," in Thomas Jones's characteristically bitter words—was nicknamed "The Knight" owing to his fondness for fox-hunting when he should have been campaigning. Lord Cornwallis was dismissed as a "blockhead." General James Pattison, for a time the commandant of New York, was "warm, vain, and weak." Governor Tryon was widely regarded as "hot, rash, vain, and ignorant." Admiral James Gambier was a "money getting pompous fool." General James Robertson—now aged nearly eighty—not only "lavish[ed] away the City funds upon every well-dressed little female" but personally clipped and shaved gold coins to pay off his creditors (the counterfeits being known as "Robertsons" around town). (See Jones [ed. De Lancey], *History of New York*, I, pp. 318; Smith [ed. Sabine], *Historical memoirs*, III, entries for June 24, 1780, p. 288; December 26, 1779, p. 201; October 5, 1779, p. 173; February 10, 1779, p. 79; on Gambier, see S. Kemble, *Kemble's journals, 1773–1789*, in *Collections of the New-York Historical Society* [New York, 2 vols., 1883–84], XVI, p. 167; Jones, *History*, I, pp. 164, 162.) Indeed, commanders didn't even think much of each other, a sign of the dissension and infighting within the upper ranks that often paralyzed British decision-making. The German general Leopold Philip von Heister tangled with his British counterpart, William Howe, whom he thought "as valiant as my sword but no more of a general than my arse," while Admiral Arbuthnot condemned Clinton as "a vain jealous fool." Robertson was of similar mind about his boss: Clinton lacked "the understanding necessary for [even] a corporal." (L. F. S. Upton, *The loyal Whig: William Smith of New York and Quebec* [Toronto, 1969], p. 123; Smith [ed. Sabine], *Historical memoirs*, III, entry for June 21, 1780, pp. 284–5; for Arbuthnot and Clinton's antagonism, Jones [ed. De Lancey], *History of New York*, I, p. 361; for Robertson on Clinton, see Smith [ed. Sabine], *Historical memoirs*, II, entry for September 4, 1778, p. 9.)

109. Tiedemann, "Patriots by default," *William and Mary Quarterly*, pp. 47–49.

110. J. G. Simcoe, *Simcoe's military journal: A history of the operations of a partisan*

corps, called the Queen's Rangers, commanded by Lieut. Col. J.G. Simcoe, during the war of the American Revolution; now first published, with a memoir of the author and other additions (New York, 1844 ed.), pp. 93–94.

111. Luke and Venables, *Long Island in the American Revolution*, pp. 42–43; Irwin, *Oyster Bay in history*, pp. 100–2.

112. Tiedemann, "Patriots by default," *William and Mary Quarterly*, p. 62.

113. Letter, Charles Stuart to Lord Bute, September 16, 1778, in Stuart-Wortley (ed.), *A prime minister and his son*, p. 132.

Chapter Six: The Adventures of the Culper Ring

1. Letter, Townsend to Tallmadge, July 15, 1779.

2. Letter, Townsend to Tallmadge, June 29, 1779.

3. Letter, Washington to Congress, July 9, 1779.

4. Letter, Woodhull to Tallmadge, July 1, 1779.

5. P. D. Nelson, *William Tryon and the course of empire: A life in British imperial service* (Chapel Hill, N.C./London, 1990), pp. 169–70.

6. Letter, Washington to Congress, July 9, 1779. As Washington mentions receiving a report from Trumbull dated July 10, his own letter to Congress must have been sent either on July 10 or July 11.

7. See, for instance, Trumbull to Washington, July 10, 1779; and also, letter, Washington to Thaddeus Betts and Colonel Stephen St. John, July 11, 1779. On his "defensive plan," see letter, Washington to Congress, July 9, 1779 ; for the "one essential point," see letter, Washington to Trumbull, July 12, 1779.

8. Letter, Washington to Trumbull, July 12, 1779.

9. Letter, Washington to Congress, July 9, 1779.

10. Letter, Washington to Trumbull, July 12, 1779.

11. Letter, Washington to Trumbull, July 12, 1779.

12. Nelson, *William Tryon*, pp. 171–72.

13. Letter, Woodhull to Tallmadge, July 1, 1779.

14. Letter, Woodhull to Tallmadge, July 9, 1779.

15. Letter, Woodhull to Tallmadge, July 15, 1779.

16. Letter, Townsend to Tallmadge, July 15, 1779.

17. Letter, Woodhull to Tallmadge, August 12, 1779.

18. Letter, Townsend to Tallmadge, September 11, 1779.

19. Letter, Washington to Tallmadge, September 24, 1779.

20. Letter, Woodhull to Tallmadge, August 15, 1779.

21. Letter, Townsend to Tallmadge, September 11, 1779.

22. Letter, Woodhull to Tallmadge, August 15, 1779.

23. Letter, Woodhull to Tallmadge, October 10, 1779.

24. Letter, Woodhull to Tallmadge, August 15, 1779.

25. For Selah and Anna Strong, see http://homepages.rootsweb.com/~drmott/Mott/g0000112.html#I3325; for Selah's parents, see http://homepages.rootsweb.com/~drmott/Mott/g0000119.html#I3324; for Hannah Woodhull's parentage and siblings, see http://homepages.rootsweb.com/~drmott/Mott/g0000133.html#I1203; and for Hannah's relationship to General Woodhull, see http://homepages.rootsweb.com/~drmott/Mott/g0000133.html. These URLs may change in the future.

26. F. G. Mather (ed.), *The refugees of 1776 from Long Island to Connecticut* (Albany, 1913), pp. 582, 587; B. Tallmadge, *Memoir of Col. Benjamin Tallmadge* (New York, 1858; rep. 1968), p. 5. On Selah Strong, see B. J. Thompson (ed. C. J. Werner), *History of Long Island, from its earliest settlement to the present time* (New York, 3 vols., 3rd ed., 1918; orig. 1839), II, p. 306.

27. Pennypacker, in *General Washington's spies*, II, pp. 34–35, spins an utterly fantastical and fanciful tale out of this single, brief mention of the woman, whom others have dubbed "Agent 355." (See also C. Ford's fictionalized *A peculiar service: A narrative of espionage in and around New York during the American Revolution* [Boston, 1965], especially pp. 206–8, which adds to the romance.) The trouble begins when Pennypacker misreads the letter: Instead of accepting that Woodhull was referring, as he openly states in his dispatch, to "a 355"—*a lady*—he drops the "a" and argues that Woodhull was talking about a female agent code-named 355. Agent 355, the story goes, was Townsend's paramour, but she was captured by the British and detained aboard the prison ship *Jersey*, where she was interrogated (but kept stoutly mum) and died—but not before giving birth to Townsend's love child. A charming story, though it's nonsense, not least because females were not kept aboard the prison ships, there's no record whatsoever of a birth, and, I think most pertinently, the son who claimed Robert Townsend as his father was born some years *after* the war. His mother, rather prosaically, was Townsend's housekeeper, not the fictional "Agent 355"—and it's questionable whether Townsend was even the real father. Also, rather importantly, the actual letter is written by *Woodhull* (who accordingly signed it "722," his code number), not Townsend, as others have assumed.

28. Letter, Woodhull to Tallmadge, September 19, 1779. Captain Nathan Woodhull signed the List of Associators, printed in Mather (ed.), *Refugees of 1776*, Appendix H, p. 1058, dated June 8, 1775.

29. Letter, Woodhull to Tallmadge, November 13, 1779.

30. Letter, Tallmadge to Washington, November 1, 1779.

31. Letter, Washington to Clinton, November 3, 1779.

32. Letter, Woodhull to Tallmadge, November 13, 1779.

33. See, for instance, letter, Washington to Tallmadge, August 28, 1779, in which

he reiterates: "The period is now come (in the arrival of the enemy's reinforcement) when the intelligence of C——r Junr. may be interesting and important. To delay his communications till they are matters of public notoriety, is answering no valuable purpose; but to be early precise and well informed in the several accots. transmitted, is essential. To know as nearly as may be the amount of the enemy's reinforcements with Arbuthnot. how many and the names of the complete Corps which compose it; whether there is any bustle in preparing for a movement of troops by land or water, or both, and the destination of it, as far as can be discovered from appearances, information or surmise are much to be wished, and if you can with safety, request these matters of him I shall thank you."

34. Letter, Washington to Tallmadge, September 24, 1779.

35. Letter, Townsend to Tallmadge, September 29, 1779.

36. Letter, Tallmadge to Washington, November 1, 1779.

37. Letter, Townsend to Tallmadge, October 21, 1779.

38. C. S. Hall, *Benjamin Tallmadge: Revolutionary soldier and American statesman* (New York, 1943), p. 51.

39. Instructions, passed on by Tallmadge to Woodhull and Townsend, October 14, 1779.

40. Letter, Washington to Jonathan Trumbull, William Livingston, and George Clinton, September 27, 1779.

41. Letter, Washington to Congress, October 4, 1779.

42. Letter, Washington to d'Estaing, October 4, 1779.

43. Letter, Townsend to Tallmadge, October 9, 1779.

44. Samuel Davis, father of future Confederate president Jefferson Davis, and Major Pierce Charles L'Enfant, the future architect of Washington, D.C., fought at Savannah.

45. Letter, Townsend to Tallmadge, October 9, 1779.

46. Letter, Washington to d'Estaing, October 4, 1779.

47. Letter, Townsend to Tallmadge, October 21, 1779.

48. Letter, Woodhull to Tallmadge, October 26, 1779. See also, letter, Townsend to Tallmadge, October 29, 1779.

49. Letter, Woodhull to Tallmadge, November 5, 1779.

50. Letter, Woodhull to Tallmadge, November 12, 1779.

51. Letter, Townsend to Tallmadge, November 29, 1779.

52. Quoted in K. Scott, "Counterfeiting in New York during the Revolution," in *Narratives of the Revolution in New York: A collection of articles from the New-York Historical Society Quarterly* (New York, 1975), p. 140.

53. On this subject, see Scott, "Counterfeiting," pp. 145–51; John Broome, "The

counterfeiting adventures of Henry Dawkins," *American Notes and Queries,* VIII, (1950), pp. 179–84.

54. *New York Gazette and Weekly Mercury,* January 20, 1777.

55. *New York Gazette and Weekly Mercury,* March 31, 1777.

56. *New York Gazette and Weekly Mercury,* April 14, 1777.

57. Letter, Washington to Congress, April 18, 1777.

58. Quoted in Scott, "Counterfeiting," p. 155.

59. Woodhull alerted Washington that he had met a man who said "he had left 20 odd thousand pounds of counterfeit money of your late emissions in the hands of the Toreys—to pay their taxes with." Letter, Woodhull to Washington, September 1, 1780.

60. Letter, Washington to Horatio Gates, October 7, 1778. See also K. Scott, "New Hampshire Tory counterfeiters operating from New York City," *New-York Historical Society Quarterly,* XXXIV (1950), pp. 31–57.

61. Quoted in Scott, "Counterfeiting," p. 163.

62. *Virginia Gazette,* October 2, 1779, quoted in Scott, "Counterfeiting," p. 164.

63. Letter, Lieutenant Samuel Shaw to Francis and Sarah Shaw, June 28, 1779, printed in J. Rhodehamel (ed.), *The American Revolution: Writings from the War of Independence* (New York, 2001), p. 528; Scott, "Counterfeiting," pp. 163–64.

64. See Table C, in H. S. Commager and R. B. Morris (eds.), *The spirit of 'seventy-six: The story of the American Revolution as told by participants* (New York, 3rd ed., 1978; rep. 1995), p. 789.

65. Letter, Townsend to Tallmadge, November 29, 1779.

66. Letter, Washington to Congress, December 7, 1779. Washington errs slightly in dating Townsend's letter to November 27.

67. See Commager and Morris (eds.), *The spirit of 'seventy-six,* p. 793.

68. Letter, Washington to Tallmadge, December 6, 1779.

69. Letter, Woodhull to Tallmadge, December 12, 1779.

70. Letter, Washington to Tallmadge, February 5, 1780.

71. On James Townsend, who later became a successful merchant in New York, see J. C. and C. A. Townsend, *A memorial of John, Henry, and Richard Townsend, and their descendants* (New York, 1865; rep. and new ed., 1976), p. 118.

72. Deposition by John Deausenberry, March 23, 1780.

73. Poem, "The Lady's Dress," March 23, 1780.

74. Letter, Woodhull to Tallmadge, April 5, 1780.

75. Letter, Woodhull to Tallmadge, April 23, 1780.

76. Letter, Woodhull to Tallmadge, May 4, 1780.

77. Letter, Woodhull to Tallmadge, May 4, 1780.

78. Letter, Washington to Tallmadge, May 19, 1780.

79. Letter, Woodhull to Tallmadge, June 10, 1780.

80. Letter, Washington to Tallmadge, July 11, 1780.

81. Letter, Tallmadge to Washington, July 14, 1780.

82. Letter, Tallmadge to Washington, July 18, 1780.

83. Letter, "Samuel Culper" [Townsend] to Floyd, July 20, 1780.

84. Note, Woodhull to Brewster, July 20, 1780.

85. Letter, Woodhull to Tallmadge, July 20, 1780.

86. Letter, Arnold to John André, June 12, 1780, printed in C. Van Doren, *Secret history of the American Revolution* (New York, 1941), Appendix, no. 32.

87. See Plate II, in W. B. Willcox, "Rhode Island in British strategy, 1780–1781," *Journal of Modern History*, XVII (1945), 4, pp. 304–31.

88. Letter, Hamilton to Lafayette, July 21, 1780. About a week after the Culpers' report, Hamilton received a note from the mysterious agent "L.D.," who sounded as if he lived somewhere outside the city in what today would be Queens. Nothing more is known of him. It is officially dated July 21 in the Washington Papers, but it was written over the course of four days as the author updated it, the last entry being written on the twenty-fifth. The first section was written in the evening of July 21. It reports that the troops ordered to embark are "in motion." The second part, written on the afternoon of the twenty-second, says that the troops were moving up the North and East rivers, but the main fleet was staying the night between the "shipyards and Hellgate." L.D. had seen sailors engaged in painting a frigate a "muddy yellow so that she may not be known." His report was accurate, but late, too late to be of any use. See Intelligence Report, "L.D." to Washington, July 21, 1780.

89. Letter, Tallmadge to Washington, July 22, 1780.

90. Letter, Gouvion to Washington, July 22, 1780.

91. Letter, Greene to Washington, July 21, 1780.

92. Letter, Washington to Lafayette, August 5, 1780.

93. Letter, Clinton to Germain, August 1780, printed in Pennypacker, *George Washington's spies*, pp. 85–87. A similar letter, though much angrier in tone, was addressed to William Eden, August 18 and September 1, 1780, in B. F. Stevens, *Facsimiles of manuscripts in European archives relating to America, 1773–1783. With descriptions, editorial notes, collations, references and translations* (London, 25 vols., 1889–98), VII, no. 730. The best discussion of this subject is W. B. Willcox, "Rhode Island in British strategy, 1780–1781," *Journal of Modern History*, XVII (1945), 4, pp. 304–31.

94. Letter, Washington to Tallmadge, July 24, 1780.

95. Letter, Tallmadge to Washington, August 1, 1780.

96. Letter, Woodhull to Tallmadge, August 6, 1780.

97. Invoice, Woodhull to Tallmadge, September 18, 1780.

98. Letter, Tallmadge to Washington, September 19, 1780.

99. Letter, "Samuel Culper, Jr." [Townsend] to Floyd, August 6, 1780.

100. Letter, Woodhull to Tallmadge, August 6, 1780.

101. Letter, Woodhull to Tallmadge, August 16, 1780.

102. Letter, Washington to Tallmadge, August 11, 1780.

103. Letter, Tallmadge to Washington, September 13, 1780.

104. Letter, Washington to Tallmadge, September 16, 1780.

Chapter Seven: On His Majesty's Secret Service

1. On this subject, see G. C. Stowe and J. Weller, "Revolutionary West Point: 'The key to the continent,'" *Military Affairs*, XIX (1955), 2, pp. 81–98.

2. Letter, Tallmadge to Sparks, February 17, 1834, printed as a footnote in H. Hastings and J. A. Holden (eds.), *Public papers of George Clinton, first governor of New York, 1777–1795, 1801–1804* (Albany, 10 vols., 1899–1914), VI, p. 262.

3. Letter, Washington to Stirling, October 6, 1778.

4. Letter, Washington to Ogden, April 2, 1782.

5. R. Kaplan, "The hidden war: British intelligence operations during the American Revolution," *William and Mary Quarterly*, 3rd ser., XLVII (1990), 1, pp. 119–20.

6. This section is heavily based on Kaplan's excellent article "Hidden war," *William and Mary Quarterly*, pp. 115–38.

7. Kaplan, "Hidden war," *William and Mary Quarterly*, pp. 123–26. For an interesting angle—from a professional viewpoint—on André's management of Arnold, see R. Amory, Jr., "John André, case officer," *Studies in Intelligence* (1961), pp. A1–A15. I am indebted to the CIA's Public Affairs Division for providing a copy of this declassified article.

8. This biographical information is taken from B. A. Rosenberg, *The neutral ground: The André affair and the background of Cooper's* The spy (Westport, Conn., 1994), pp. 19–25.

9. See letter, André to Washington, September 24, 1780.

10. See letter, Joseph Stansbury to Jonathan Odell, May 1779, in C. Van Doren, *Secret history of the American Revolution* (New York, 1941), Appendix, no. 6, p. 442.

11. Van Doren, *Secret history*, pp. 196–200.

12. Letter, André to Joseph Stansbury, May 10, 1779, in Van Doren, *Secret history*, Appendix, no. 1, p. 440.

13. D. Kahn, *The codebreakers: The story of secret writing* (New York, 1967), pp. 176–77. On André's sourcebooks, see Van Doren, *Secret history*, pp. 200, 204, and letters, Stansbury to André, May 1779, in Van Doren, *Secret history*, Appendix, no. 4,

p. 441; and Arnold to André, no date but mid-1779, no. 5, pp. 441–42. It was strange that Arnold did not suggest using a dictionary from the start, as that idea had been discussed as early as 1776 within the secret Patriot committees, but it was André who chose the sourcebook and Arnold went along with it. On the dictionary, see Arthur Lee's letter to the committee of secret correspondence in P. Force (ed.), *American archives: Consisting of a collection of authentick records, state papers, debates, and letters and other notices of publick affairs, the whole forming a documentary history of the origin and progress of the North American colonies; of the causes and accomplishment of the American Revolution; and of the Constitution of government for the United States, to the final ratification thereof* (Washington, D.C., 4th and 5th ser., 1848–53), 4th ser., VI, p. 686.

14. On André's codes, see J. Bakeless, *Turncoats, traitors and heroes: Espionage in the American Revolution* (New York, 1959), pp. 269–70. On the use of "Gustavus," see letter, Stansbury to André, July 11, 1779, in Van Doren, *Secret history*, Appendix, no. 16, p. 449; on "Monk," see letter, André to Stansbury, May 10, 1779, in Van Doren, *Secret history*, Appendix, no. 1, p. 439.

15. See letters, Arnold to André, August 30, 1780, no. 52, p. 470; and André to Joseph Stansbury, May 10, 1779, no. 1, p. 440, both in Van Doren, *Secret history*, Appendix.

16. See, for instance, memorandum by General Knyphausen, May 1780, no. 29, p. 459; and letter, Arnold to André, July 11, 1780, no. 37, pp. 462–63, both in Van Doren, *Secret history*, Appendix.

17. Letter, André to Arnold, undated, in Van Doren, *Secret history*, Appendix, no. 13, pp. 446–47. In the event, this particular letter was never sent, but its contents were intimated to Arnold on several other occasions.

18. Letter, André to Arnold, July 24, 1780, Van Doren, *Secret history*, Appendix, no. 43, p. 466.

19. See, among others, letters, Arnold to André, July 15, 1780, no. 40, pp. 464–65; Odell to Stansbury, July 24, 1780, no. 42, pp. 465–66; André to Arnold, July 24, 1780, no. 43, p. 466, all in Van Doren, *Secret history*, Appendix. Also, Hatch, p. 231.

20. Letter, Arnold to André, September 15, in Van Doren, *Secret history*, Appendix, no. 58, p. 473.

21. Letter, Robinson to Clinton, September 24, 1780, in Van Doren, *Secret history*, Appendix, no. 61, pp. 474–75. See also, "Clinton's narrative," October 11, 1780, which was included in a package to Lord George Germain, printed in full in Van Doren, Appendix, p. 485.

22. Quoted in Amory, "John André, case officer," *Studies in Intelligence*, p. A8. See H. B. Dawson (ed.), *Record of the trial of Joshua Hett Smith, Esq., for alleged complicity in the treason of Benedict Arnold, 1780* (Morrisania, N.Y., 1866).

23. Letter, Robinson to Clinton, September 24, 1780, in Van Doren, *Secret history*, Appendix, no. 61, pp. 474–75.

24. Van Doren, *Secret history*, pp. 338–39. J. Judd, "Westchester County," in J. S. Tiedemann and E. R. Fingerhut (eds.), *The other New York: The American Revolution beyond New York City, 1763–1787* (Albany, 2005), p. 119; C. S. Crary, "Guerrilla activities of James DeLancey's Cowboys in Westchester County: Conventional warfare or self-interested freebooting?" pp. 14–24, in R. A. East and J. Judd (eds.), *The Loyalist Americans: A focus on greater New York* (Tarrytown, N.Y., 1975).

25. Rosenberg, *The neutral ground*, pp. 35–39; Amory, "John André, case officer," *Studies in Intelligence*, pp. A8–9.

26. Rosenberg, *The neutral ground*, pp. 41–44.

27. Van Doren, *Secret history*, p. 341.

28. Letter, Arnold to Tallmadge, September 13, 1780. Van Doren, *Secret history*, p. 311, cites a "Mr. John Anderson" in this letter, but in the original in the Washington Papers at the Library of Congress, it is rendered James Anderson.

29. Letter, Tallmadge to Arnold, September 21, 1780.

30. Accounts differ as to whether Tallmadge was present: Jameson says he was; Tallmadge says he arrived later and missed the conference. Thus, according to a letter, Jameson to Washington, September 27, 1780, he "mentioned my intention to Major Tallmadge and some others of the field officers, all of whom were clearly of opinion that it would be right, until I could hear from your Excellency" to write to Arnold about the capture of André. But Tallmadge's *Memoir of Col. Benjamin Tallmadge* (New York, 1858; rep. 1968), pp. 35–36, states that he arrived late in the evening to find that the letter had already been sent.

31. Letter, Jameson to Arnold, September 23, 1780, in "Clinton's narrative," no. 76, Van Doren, *Secret history*, Appendix, p. 486. On the name of the junior officer, see J. E. Walsh, *The execution of Major André* (New York, 2001), p. 116.

32. Tallmadge, *Memoir*, pp. 35–36.

33. Walsh, *Execution of Major André*, p. 123.

34. Tallmadge, *Memoir*, p. 36.

35. Letter, André to Washington, September 24, 1780.

36. Tallmadge, *Memoir*, p. 36.

37. Letter, Tallmadge to S. B. Webb, September 30, 1780, in W. C. Ford (ed.), *Correspondence and journals of Samuel Blachley Webb* (New York, 3 vols., 1839–94), II, pp. 293–97.

38. Letter, Tallmadge to Sparks, February 17, 1834, printed as a footnote in Hastings and Holden (eds.), *Public papers of George Clinton*, VI, pp. 263–64.

39. Tallmadge also makes no mention of this anecdote in his earlier *Memoir*, p. 37,

where he restricts himself to saying that he "escorted the prisoner to Head-Quarters." At the time of Tallmadge's letter to Sparks, the potency of the Nathan Hale legend had reached its zenith, which certainly affected Tallmadge's recollection of his conversation with André.

40. Letter, Hamilton to Clinton, September 30, 1780, in Van Doren, *Secret history*, Appendix, no. 63, p. 476.

41. Letters, Clinton to his sisters, October 4 and 9, 1780, no. 67, Van Doren, *Secret history*, Appendix, pp. 477–80; Arnold to Washington, October 1, 1780, no. 86, "Clinton's narrative," in Van Doren, Appendix, p. 491.

42. Letter, Clinton to Washington, October 9, 1780, no. 90, "Clinton's narrative," in Van Doren, *Secret history*, Appendix, pp. 494–95.

43. This section on Smith is based on W. B. McGroarty, "Sergeant John Champe and certain of his contemporaries," *William and Mary Quarterly*, XVII (1937), 2, pp. 172–74.

44. "Proceedings against John L. André as a spy, by Continental Army Board of General Officers," September 29, 1780, Washington Papers; Letter, Tallmadge to Sparks, November 16, 1833, printed as a footnote in Hastings and Holden (eds.), *Public papers of George Clinton*, VI, p. 259.

45. On the historicity of hanging for spies, see Rosenberg, *The neutral ground*, pp. 12–13. A 1643 text used by the British was the *Laws and Ordinances of Warre, established for the better conduct of the army*, which stated that "whosoever shall come from the enemy with a trumpet or drum [or a flag of truce], after the custom of war, within the quarters of the army or a garrison town, shall be hanged as a spy." Rosenberg points out that the "document says nothing about defining the status of a spy," and in André's case, there were several counterarguments the Board of General Officers took into consideration but ultimately rejected. These were, among others, that André had been caught out of uniform owing to extraordinary circumstances and wearing civilian clothing against his desire, that he had proceeded upriver under a flag aboard the *Vulture,* and that he had been captured *between* enemy lines—in "the neutral ground"—and not within American-held territory. Against these defenses was raised the objection that André was traveling in a "disguised habit" under a "feigned name" and carrying incriminating papers given to him by an infamous traitor. Had Washington been in a giving vein, or the circumstances less politically charged, there was probably sufficient gray area to commute the death sentence. For the official British view of the trial and hanging of André, see letters, Clinton to an unknown friend in England, October 1780, in no. 66, p. 477; and Clinton to his sisters, October 4 and 9, 1780, no. 67, pp. 477–80 (where he says that Washington "has committed premeditated murder [and] must answer for the dreadfull consequences," all in Van Doren, *Secret history*, Appendix). For Washington's considered view, see letter,

Washington to Clinton, September 30, 1780, in "Clinton's narrative," no. 81, Van Doren, Appendix, pp. 487–8.

46. Tallmadge, *Memoir*, p. 38.

47. Quoted in Hall, *Tallmadge*, p. 63.

48. Quoted in Walsh, *Execution of Major André*, p. 144.

49. Letter, Washington to Rochambeau, October 10, 1780.

50. Letter, Tallmadge to Webb, September 30, 1780, in Ford (ed.), *Correspondence and journals of Samuel Blachley Webb*, II, pp. 293–97.

Chapter Eight: Spyhunters and Whaleboatmen

1. See M.J.P.R.Y.G.M. Lafayette, *Memoirs, correspondence and manuscripts of General Lafayette* (London, 3 vols., 1837), I, p. 254; C. Van Doren, *Secret history of the American Revolution* (New York, 1941), pp. 287–88.

2. Letter, Arnold to Howe, August 5, 1780.

3. Letters, Howe to Arnold, August 14 and 16, 1780.

4. For background on Hunter, see J. Bakeless, *Turncoats, traitors, and heroes: Espionage in the American Revolution* (New York, 1959), pp. 241–43.

5. T. Jones, (ed. E. F. De Lancey), *History of New York during the Revolutionary War, and of the leading events in the other colonies at that period* (New York, 2 vols., 1879), I, p. 382.

6. Letter, Tallmadge to Heath, October 10, 1780, in "Letters and papers of General William Heath," *Collections of the Massachusetts Historical Society*, 7th ser., V, Part III, pp. 111–13.

7. Letter, Tallmadge to Sparks, February 17, 1834, printed as a footnote in H. Hastings and J. A. Holden (eds.), *Public papers of George Clinton, first governor of New York, 1777–1795, 1801–1804* (Albany, 10 vols., 1899–1914), VI, p. 262.

8. Letter, Woodhull to Tallmadge, October 2 and 3, 1780.

9. Letters, Tallmadge to Washington, October 11, 1780.

10. Letter, Townsend to Tallmadge, October 14, 1780.

11. Letter, Woodhull to Tallmadge, October 14, 1780.

12. Letter, Townsend to Tallmadge, October 14, 1780.

13. Letter, Washington to Lee, October 13, 1780, printed in H. Lee, *Memoirs of the war in the southern department of the United States* (New York, 1869 ed.), p. 407.

14. See a contemporary description of Champe in W. C. Hall, "Sergeant Champe's adventure," *William and Mary Quarterly*, XVIII (1938), 3, p. 327; W. B. McGroarty, "Sergeant John Champe and certain of his contemporaries," *William and Mary Quarterly*, XVII (1937), 2, p. 155.

15. Hall, "Sergeant Champe's adventure," *William and Mary Quarterly*, p. 334.

16. McGroarty, "Sergeant John Champe," *William and Mary Quarterly*, pp. 152–53.

17. Lee, *Memoirs*, p. 396.

18. Letter, Washington to Lee, October 20, 1780.

19. This section is based on the accounts in McGroarty, "Sergeant John Champe," *William and Mary Quarterly*, pp. 145–75; Hall, "Sergeant Champe's adventure," *William and Mary Quarterly*, pp. 322–42; Lee, *Memoirs of the war*, pp. 394–411.

20. Cameron's diary would first emerge in the *United Service Journal* of December 1834, where it was promptly forgotten. It turned up again in the *William and Mary Quarterly*, which published it in its entirety in July 1938 (Hall, "Sergeant Champe's adventure"). While Cameron's account of his meeting with Champe is sound, some caution is required when reading his suspiciously detailed version of Champe's story. As shown by McGroarty, "Captain Cameron and Sergeant Champe," *William and Mary Quarterly*, XIX (1939), 1, pp. 49–54, Cameron cribbed large portions from Lee's *Memoirs*. As a result, both Lee and Cameron make the identical error of saying that Champe departed for New York in late September—that is, before André's execution—whereas the idea of kidnapping Arnold first occurred to Washington in mid-October, roughly two weeks *after* André's death. Lee's motive for confusing the dates may be ascribed to either faulty memory or an attempt to present the Arnold kidnapping plot—which some might have seen as a dishonorable or illegal tactic on Washington's part—as an attempt to save André's life. Once Washington had Arnold, so the story goes, he would have virtuously returned André to Clinton. McGroarty, in "Sergeant John Champe and certain of his contemporaries," restores the correct chronology.

21. McGroarty, "Sergeant John Champe," *William and Mary Quarterly*, esp. p. 164.

22. Letter, Washington to Congress, October 15, 1780.

23. Letter, Washington to Tallmadge, October 17, 1780.

24. Letters, Woodhull to Tallmadge, October 26, 1780, and November 12, 1780.

25. J. Baldwin and G. Rossano, *Clan and commerce: The Townsend family of Oyster Bay* (available only at the Raynham Hall Museum), p. 79.

26. M. J. O'Brien, *Hercules Mulligan: Confidential correspondent of General Washington* (New York, 1937), pp. 41–42.

27. R. Chernow, *Alexander Hamilton* (New York, 2004), pp. 29–41, has a good account of Hamilton's time in the West Indies and his business experience there.

28. "In the evenings," recalled Mulligan fondly in his seventies, "Mr H" sat "with my family and my brother's family and write dogerel [sic] rhymes for their amusement he was all ways amiable and cheerful and extremely attentive to his books."

Some years later, "he evinced his gratitude for the attentions of my brother & myself by his attentions to us through life & by taking one of my sons to study Law without charging the least compensation." "Narrative of Hercules Mulligan," reprinted in O'Brien, *Hercules Mulligan*, Appendix III, pp. 181–84.

29. O'Brien, *Hercules Mulligan*, pp. 33–34.

30. O'Brien, *Hercules Mulligan*, p. 38.

31. Indeed, Washington, who could be starchy about observing the social hierarchy, hardly regarded Mulligan as unutterably gauche. Even so, one grinding snob of the late nineteenth century scribbled, on the back of one of Mulligan's bills to Andrew Eliot, the complaint that "he is made out to be a member of an important [West Indian] merchant but on this bill we see him the vulgar tradesman." Andrew Eliot Papers, Miscellaneous MSS E. folder, at the New-York Historical Society.

32. O'Brien, *Hercules Mulligan*, pp. 49, 87.

33. Letter, Woodhull to Tallmadge, August 12, 1779.

34. Townsend certainly knew Mulligan. Among the family's papers at the New-York Historical Society there is a receipt from Mulligan, dated February 24, 1783, acknowledging payment for "Making a coat" (£1.14.0), plus "pockets & sleve linings" and "1 dozen of buttons" for about 11 shillings. Receipt, in 1783 Folder, Townsend Family Papers, New-York Historical Society.

35. Cited in O'Brien, *Hercules Mulligan*, p. 95.

36. Letter, Tallmadge to Washington, August 1, 1780.

37. Letter, Tallmadge to Washington, October 11, 1780.

38. Letter, Brewster to Tallmadge, February 14, 1781.

39. C. B. Todd, "Whale-boat privateersmen of the Revolution," *Magazine of American History*, VIII (1882), p. 169.

40. J. F. Collins, "Whaleboat warfare on Long Island Sound," *New York History*, XXV (1944), no. 2, p. 197; E. N. Danenberg, *Naval history of the Fairfield County men in the Revolution* (Fairfield, Conn., 1977), p. 44. I am indebted to Dennis Barrow, librarian of the Fairfield Historical Society, for providing a copy of this invaluable book.

41. B. F. Thompson (ed. C. J. Werner), *History of Long Island, from its earliest settlement to the present time* (New York, 3 vols., 3rd ed., 1918; orig. 1839), I, p. 316.

42. Todd, "Whale-boat privateersmen," p. 180.

43. F. G. Mather (ed.), *The refugees of 1776 from Long Island to Connecticut* (Albany, 1913), p. 220.

44. On Meigs and the raid, see Thomas Jones, the Loyalist judge, in his (edited by E. F. De Lancey) *History of New York*, I, pp. 180–82. Collins, "Whaleboat warfare," pp. 197–98; and Thompson, *History of Long Island*, I, pp. 304–5, differ in a few minor

details from Jones's account of the raid. Meigs was later made Postmaster General under President Madison.

45. Collins, "Whaleboat warfare," p. 199.

46. C. E. Nelson, "Privateering by Long Islanders in the American Revolution," *Journal of Long Island History*, XI (1974), no. 1, pp. 27–28.

47. Quoted in Thompson, *History of Long Island*, I, p. 314.

48. As recounted in Jones (ed. De Lancey), *History of New York*, II, note XLII, pp. 565–67.

49. J. G. Simcoe, *Simcoe's military journal: A history of the operations of a partisan corps, called the Queen's Rangers, commanded by Lieut. Col. J.G. Simcoe, during the war of the American Revolution; now first published, with a memoir of the author and other additions* (New York, 1844 ed.), p. 100.

50. On this affair, see H. Onderdonk (ed.), *Revolutionary incidents of Suffolk and Kings counties, with an account of the battle of Long Island, and the British prisons and prison-ships* (New York, 1849), pp. 94–95.

51. Mather, *Refugees of 1776*, p. 206.

52. Jones (ed. De Lancey), *History of New York*, II, Note XLII, pp. 568–69; Todd, "Whale-boat privateersmen," pp. 173–74.

53. Letter, Woodhull to Tallmadge, June 4, 1781.

54. Letter, Woodhull to Tallmadge, June 20, 1779.

55. Letter, Brewster to George Clinton, August 20, 1781, in H. Hastings and J. A. Holden (eds.), *Public papers of George Clinton, first governor of New York, 1777–1795, 1801–1804* (Albany, 10 vols., 1899–1914), VII, pp. 233–34.

56. For the petition, see Mather, *Refugees of 1776*, p. 205.

57. Letter, Tallmadge to Washington, November 1, 1779.

58. Letter, Woodhull to Tallmadge, September 19, 1779.

59. On Dayton, see Nelson, "Privateering by Long Islanders," pp. 30–33; "Patriot peddler," an address by Hervey Garrett Smith to the Long Island Forum, April 1975, reproduced at http://www.longwood.k12.ny.us/history/bio/edayton.htm; and Pennypacker, *George Washington's spies*, p. 254n.

60. Letter, Washington to Tallmadge, November 2, 1779.

61. See, for instance, letter, Clinton to Trumbull, August 20, 1781, Hastings and Holden (eds.), *Public papers of George Clinton*, VII, no. 3918, pp. 234–35.

62. Mather, *Refugees of 1776*, p. 208. See also Hastings and Holden (eds.), *Public papers of George Clinton*, VI, pp. 778–79, 803–04.

63. Letter, Brewster to Tallmadge, August 18, 1780.

64. Letters, Brewster to Tallmadge, August 21 and 27, 1780.

65. Letter, Brewster to Tallmadge, August 27, 1780.

66. Letter, Brewster to Tallmadge, February 14, 1781.

67. Letter, Washington to Brewster, February 23, 1781.

68. B. G. Loescher, *Washington's eyes: The Continental Light Dragoons* (Fort Collins, Colo., 1977), pp. 43–44; Collins, "Whaleboat warfare," p. 196.

69. Letter, Woodhull to Tallmadge, July 9, 1779.

70. Mather, *Refugees of 1776*, p. 219.

71. B. Tallmadge, *Memoir of Col. Benjamin Tallmadge* (New York, 1858; rep. 1968), pp. 32–33; Loescher, *Washington's eyes*, pp. 43–44.

72. Letters, Woodhull to Tallmadge, August 6, 1780 (enclosing map); Washington to Tallmadge, August 11, 1780.

73. Tallmadge, *Memoir*, p. 34.

74. Letter, Woodhull to Tallmadge, November 28, 1780.

75. Letter, Woodhull to Tallmadge, September 5, 1780.

76. Letter, Woodhull to Tallmadge, October 26, 1780.

77. Letter, Woodhull to Tallmadge, November 28, 1780, in which Woodhull states that he spoke to Brewster about the hay "some time ago."

78. Letters, Brewster to Tallmadge, November 6, 1780; Tallmadge to Washington, November 7, 1780; Mather, *Refugees of 1776*, p. 233; Tallmadge, *Memoir*, pp. 39–40.

79. Letter, Washington to Tallmadge, November 11, 1780.

80. Letter, Brewster to Tallmadge, November 13, 1780. Brewster also noted that "I took a prize a coming across today. A fine large boat from New Haven, which had been to carry passengers over. We run up long side of them and made them believe we came from Lloyd's Neck [i.e., that they were Tories].... We got two thirds across the Sound before they found out their mistake and I got them safe under guard."

81. *Royal Gazette*, December 2, 1780, printed in C. S. Crary (ed.), *The price of loyalty: Tory writings from the Revolutionary era* (New York, 1973), p. 171.

82. The lengthiest description of the Fort St. George raid may be found in Tallmadge, *Memoir*, pp. 39–42. Thomas Tredwell Jackson's account is printed in Pennypacker, *George Washington's spies*, pp. 192–94. Tallmadge's letter to Washington narrating the story of November 25, 1780, differs in a few small details from his later account in the *Memoir*.

83. Letter, Washington to Tallmadge, November 28, 1780.

84. Letter, Woodhull to Tallmadge, November 28, 1780.

85. Letter, Woodhull to Tallmadge, January 14, 1781.

86. Letters, Arnold to Tallmadge, October 25, 1780; Tallmadge to Washington, January 28, 1781.

Chapter Nine: The Wilderness of Mirrors

1. Quoted in L. Sabine, *Biographical sketches of Loyalists of the American Revolution* (Boston, 2 vols., 2nd ed., 1864), I, p. 367.

2. On the British system, see R. Kaplan, "The hidden war: British intelligence operations during the American Revolution," *William and Mary Quarterly*, 3rd ser., XLVII (1990), p. 131; for the daily intelligence reports, see E. F. De Lancey (ed.), "Sir Henry Clinton's original secret record of private daily intelligence," printed serially in *Magazine of American History*, X–XII (October 1883–August 1884), and which contains every single piece of documentation between January and July 1781.

3. The observer, as one might expect, was Thomas Jones, the acerbic Loyalist judge, in (ed. E. F. De Lancey) *History of New York during the Revolutionary War, and of the leading events in the other colonies at that period* (New York, 2 vols., 1879), I, pp. 183–84.

4. Letter, Parsons to Arnold, August 28, 1780.

5. See memorandum, "Mr. Heron's information at a conversation in New York" (and Smith's note at the end), Robertson to Lord Germain, September 4, 1781, in B. F. Stevens, *Facsimiles of manuscripts in European archives relating to America, 1773–1783. With descriptions, editorial notes, collations, references and translations* (London, 25 vols., 1889–98), VII, no. 733; William Smith (ed. W. H. W. Sabine), *Historical memoirs from 16 March 1763 to 12 November 1783 of William Smith, historian of the province of New York; member of the governor's council, and last chief justice of that province under the Crown; chief justice of Quebec* (New York, 3 vols., in 2, rep. 1969–71), III, entry for September 4, 1780. A copy may also be found in E. B. O'Callaghan et al. (eds.), *Documents relative to the colonial history of the state of New York; procured in Holland, England and France* (Albany, 15 vols., 1856–87), VIII, pp. 804–8, which differs in parts from the original draft.

6. On this subject, see S. Conway, "To subdue America: British army officers and the conduct of the Revolutionary War," *William and Mary Quarterly*, XLIII (1986), 3, pp. 381–407; and his "British army officers and the American War for Independence," *William and Mary Quarterly*, XLI (1984), 2, pp. 265–76.

7. The most complete biographical sketch of Heron is in W. E. Grumman, *The Revolutionary soldiers of Redding, Connecticut, and the record of their services* (Hartford, 1904), esp. p. 189.

8. For his comment, see Grumman, *Revolutionary soldiers*, p. 193; for his dress, C. S. Hall, *Life and letters of Samuel Holden Parsons: Major-general in the Continental army and chief judge of the Northwestern Territory, 1737–1789* (Binghamton, N.Y., 1905), p. 421.

9. Letter, Parsons to Washington, April 6, 1782.

10. Letter, "Hiram" to British Intelligence, February 4, 1781, in De Lancey (ed.), "Private daily intelligence," *Magazine of American History*, X, pp. 410–17

11. Letter, Washington to Parsons, February 22, 1781. Parsons subsequently confirmed to Washington that he had given Heron "assurances of generous pay for his time and services, and if he finds out the plan [by the Tories], and is detected and has to fly, he is to have one hundred dollars a year for life." Letter, Parsons to Washington, March 14, 1781.

12. Letter, Parsons to Washington, March 14, 1781. See also letter, Washington to Parsons, March 23, 1781.

13. Memorandum of interview, March 11, in De Lancey (ed.), "Private daily intelligence," *Magazine of American History*, X, p. 503.

14. Letter, Heron to De Lancey, March 11, 1781, quoted in C. Van Doren, *Secret history of the American Revolution* (New York, 1941), p. 396.

15. Letter, Parsons to Washington, April 6, 1782.

16. Letter, Heron to British Intelligence, April 24, 1781, in De Lancey (ed.), "Private daily intelligence," *Magazine of American History*, XI, pp. 62–64.

17. Letter, Heron to De Lancey, April 26, 1781, quoted in Van Doren, *Secret history*, p. 387.

18. As pointed out by Hall, *Life and letters*, pp. 433–34.

19. Memorandum "of a conversation with Hiram," April 25, 1781, in De Lancey (ed.), "Private daily intelligence," *Magazine of American History*, XI, pp. 64–65.

20. Letter from Heron to De Lancey, June 17, 1781, in De Lancey (ed.), "Private daily intelligence," *Magazine of American History*, XI, pp. 254–57.

21. "Questions by Major De Lancey to Hiram with his answers," June 20, 1781, in De Lancey (ed.), "Private Daily Intelligence," *Magazine of American History*, XI, pp. 347–51.

22. For this section, see letter, Hiram to De Lancey, July 15, 1781 (enclosing the letter from Parsons to Heron, July 8, 1781), in De Lancey (ed.), "Private daily intelligence," *Magazine of American History*, XII, pp. 163–67; Hall, *Life and letters*, pp. 452–54, for a copy of Parsons's letter to Mumford; Van Doren, *Secret history*, p. 399.

23. G. B. Loring, *A vindication of General Samuel Holden Parsons against the charge of treasonable correspondence during the Revolutionary War* (Salem, 1888), p. 29; Van Doren, *Secret history*, p. 399.

24. Letters, Woodhull to Tallmadge, January 14, 1781; February 8, 1781.

25. Letter, Woodhull to Tallmadge, February 8, 1781.

26. Letter, Woodhull to Tallmadge, March 18, 1781.

27. Letter, Woodhull to Tallmadge, April 23, 1781.

28. Letter, Tallmadge to Washington, April 25, 1781.

29. Letter, Tallmadge to Washington, April 6, 1781.

30. On Colonel Upham, see L. Sabine, *Biographical sketches of Loyalists in the American Revolution* (Boston, 2 vols., 2nd ed., 1864), II, pp. 372–73. See also letter, Upham to General Riediesel, June 30, 1781, in De Lancey (ed.), "Private daily intelligence," *Magazine of American History*, XI, p. 439.

31. Letter, Upham to Governor Franklin, July 13, 1781, which can be found in full at the useful website, The On-Line Institute for Advanced Loyalist Studies, at http://www.royalprovincial.com/history/battles/aslrep4.shtml.

32. Letter, Tallmadge to Washington, April 6, 1781.

33. Letter, Washington to Tallmadge, April 8, 1781.

34. Letter, Woodhull to Tallmadge, April 23, 1781.

35. Letter, Tallmadge to Washington, April 20, 1781.

36. Letter, Tallmadge to Washington, April 24, 1780.

37. Letter, Colonel J. Upham to Governor Franklin, September 13, 1781, printed in the *New England Historical and Genealogical Register*, X (1856), p. 127. Upham's letter was printed in the *New York Gazette* of September 24, 1781.

38. Letter, Washington to Tallmadge, April 30, 1781.

39. Letter, Woodhull to Tallmadge, May 8, 1781.

40. Letter, Woodhull to Tallmadge, May 19, 1781.

41. Letter, Tallmadge to Woodhull, May 12, 1781.

42. J. Bakeless, *Turncoats, traitors, and heroes: Espionage in the American Revolution* (New York, 1959), pp. 181, 357.

43. Letter, Tallmadge to Washington, May 29, 1781.

44. Letter, Tallmadge to Washington, August 18, 1782. This George Smith—whose identity was tracked down in 1959 by Virginia Eckels Malone, a columnist at the *Smithtown News*—was based in Nissequogue, a village about four and a half miles west of Setauket. Corey Ford's novel, *A peculiar service: A narrative of espionage in and around New York during the American Revolution* (Boston, 1965), mentions this fact briefly on p. 322, but I have not been able to find the original article. Whoever Smith was, he played a very small role, for a short amount of time, in the Culper Ring, and was used by Tallmadge just a couple of times.

45. Little else is known of Ruggles. What there is may be found in Mather, *Refugees of 1776*, p. 1093.

46. Memorandum, June 8, 1781, printed in De Lancey (ed.), "Private daily intelligence," *Magazine of American History*, XI, pp. 247–50. Hathaway's description of Simsbury Mines and his escape is contained in the notes accompanying the document. On "Clarke," see Mather, *Refugees of 1776*, Appendix H, No. 35, p. 1067.

47. See letter, Woodhull to Tallmadge, June 5, 1779, previously quoted.

48. Letter, Woodhull to Tallmadge, June 4, 1781.

49. Letter, Woodhull to Tallmadge, June 27, 1781.

50. See letter, Rochambeau to Washington, June 20, 1781, which encloses a Woodhull letter to Tallmadge that the latter had passed on to him.

51. See "Marriage licenses issued by the state of New York," at http://home pages.rootsweb.com/~rbillard/ny_marriage_licenses.htm.

52. Letter, Woodhull to Washington, May 5, 1782.

53. Letter, William Feilding to the Earl of Denbigh, August 10, 1782, printed in J. Rhodehamel (ed.), *The American Revolution: Writings from the War of Independence* (New York, 2001), pp. 769–70.

54. Letter, Tallmadge to Washington, April 27, 1782.

55. Letter, Woodhull to Tallmadge, July 5, 1782.

56. Letter, Washington to Greene, August 6, 1782.

57. Letter, Washington to Tallmadge, August 10, 1782.

58. Letter, Woodhull to Tallmadge, February 21, 1783.

59. Letter by Colonel Beverley Robinson, March 1, 1781, in De Lancey (ed.), "Private daily intelligence," *Magazine of American History*, X, p. 502 and note.

60. Letter, Marks to Major De Lancey, June 29, 1781, in De Lancey (ed.), "Private daily intelligence," *Magazine of American History*, XI, p. 440.

61. Letter, Upham to Governor Franklin, July 13, 1781, which can be found in full at http://www.royalprovincial.com/history/battles/aslrep4.shtml.

62. Letter by Mr. Shoemaker, February 27, 1781, in De Lancey (ed.), "Private daily intelligence," *Magazine of American History*, X, p. 500.

63. B. Tallmadge, *Memoir of Col. Benjamin Tallmadge* (New York, 1858; rep. 1968), pp. 50–51.

64. See the accounts in E. N. Danenberg, *Naval history of the Fairfield County men in the Revolution* (Fairfield, Conn., 1977), p. 53; B. G. Loescher, *Washington's eyes: The Continental Light Dragoons* (Fort Collins, Colo., 1977), pp. 58–60.

65. Letter, Washington to Tallmadge, December 26, 1782.

66. Letter, Washington to Tallmadge, December 10, 1782. On the pension, see New-York Historical Society's Miscellaneous Manuscripts, under "Caleb Brewster," where there is a letter dated December 2, 1822, noting that he is entitled to a pension "on account of wounds and disabilities received or occurred in the services of the United States during the Revolutionary war."

67. On Washington's total, see the *Final report of the* [Senate] *select committee to study governmental operations with respect to the intelligence activities of the United States,* Book VI, April 1976, p. 12.

68. F. T. Reuter, "'Petty Spy' or effective diplomat: The role of George Beckwith," *Journal of the Early Republic,* X (1990), 4, p. 473.

69. Invoice, Woodhull to Tallmadge, July 5, 1783.

70. Letter, Woodhull to Tallmadge, July 5, 1783.

71. Letter, Tallmadge to Washington, August 16, 1783.

72. Letter, Washington to Tallmadge, September 11, 1783.

73. Tallmadge, *Memoir*, pp. 61–62.

74. This section is based on R. Ernst, "A Tory-eye view of the evacuation of New York," *New York History*, LXIV (1983), 4, pp. 377–94.

75. Tallmadge, *Memoir*, pp. 61–62, 65.

76. This section based on G. J. A. O'Toole, *Honorable treachery: A history of intelligence, espionage, and covert action from the American Revolution to the CIA* (New York, 1991), pp. 69–81; Reuter, "'Petty Spy' or effective diplomat," *Journal of the Early Republic*, pp. 471–92; *Final report of the* [Senate] *select committee to study governmental operations*, pp. 15–17.

Epilogue: "Lord, Now Lettest Thou Thy Servants Depart in Peace"

1. E. N. Danenberg, *Naval history of the Fairfield County men in the Revolution* (Fairfield, Conn., 1977), p. 54; C. S. Hall, *Benjamin Tallmadge: Revolutionary soldier and American statesman* (New York, 1943), p. 88; B. Tallmadge, *Memoir of Col. Benjamin Tallmadge* (New York, 1858; rep. 1968), p. 66.

2. Letter, Sackett to Washington, May 23, 1789, in D. Twohig (ed.), *The papers of George Washington: Presidential series* (Charlottesville, Va., 1987), II, pp. 376–77 and note.

3. See Spangler, "Memoir of Major John Clark," *Pennsylvania Magazine of History and Biography*, XX (1986), pp.77–86.

4. J. R. Cuneo, *Robert Rogers of the Rangers* (Oxford University Press, 1959), pp. 274–75.

5. Letter, Parsons to Washington, April 6, 1782.

6. Grumman, *The Revolutionary soldiers of Redding*, p. 193.

7. See E. F. De Lancey (ed.), "Sir Henry Clinton's original secret record of private daily intelligence," printed serially in *Magazine of American History*, X–XII (October 1883–August 1884).

8. See H. Macy, Jr.'s definitive investigative series, "Robert Townsend, Jr., of New York City," *The New York Genealogical and Biographical Record*, CXXVI (1995), pp. 25–34, 108–12, 192–98. I disagree slightly with Macy, to whom I'm indebted for bringing this research to my attention, in believing that it could quite easily have been William who was Robert Junior's father. See also a small collection of photographs in the Raynham Hall Museum of notes by Peter Townsend, which say that he first met Robert Junior in 1837–38, and was "discouraged at his conduct (he being dissipated in many ways)." Though Robert had seen little of his son (adopted or otherwise), it was

in anticipation of receiving five hundred dollars that Junior contacted Peter. At their meeting, Junior complained of Robert's "indifference to him (unjustly, I think, for my uncle had expended nearly one half his mind in trying in early life to make his *reputed* [italics added] son a person of respectability) and mentioning at the same time his own mother's coincidence in the female sentiments as to my Uncle William's attractions—her ability to judge arose from being house keeper for the 3 young men. I could not refrain from the remark that I believe my Uncle Robert thought that he might as well have owed his paternity to his brother William as to himself (and what he had just said of his mother's preference rather confirmed the suspicion). The subject was *never again* renewed between us." There seems to be some confusion whether the author of this note was Peter or Solomon (Macy says the latter). See also the scrapbook of Solomon Townsend, F89.11.8, at Raynham Hall Museum.

9. Inventory of Robert Townsend's "Goods, Chattels and Credits," May 26, 1838, FX 88.30.22.2, at Raynham Hall Museum. M. Pennypacker, *General Washington's spies on Long Island and in New York* (New York, 2 vols., 1939, 1948), II, pp. 4–5, reprints Townsend's will.

10. H. Hastings and H. H. Noble (eds.), *Military minutes of the Council of Appointment of the state of New York, 1783–1821* (Albany, 4 vols., 1901–02), I, pp. 84, 120.

11. See http://www.3villagecsd.k12.ny.us/Elementary/minnesauke/3village hist/RoeTavern.htm. It is today a private house; Pennypacker, *George Washington's spies*, pp. 60–61n. For Hawkins, see http://www.3villagecsd.k12.ny.us/Elementary/minnesauke/3villagehist/Hawkins-Mount%20House.htm.

12. Pennypacker, *George Washington's spies*, p. 16n.

13. Address given by William Brewster Minuse, president of the Three Village Historical Society, at Caleb Brewster's grave in Fairfield, Connecticut, on August 9, 1976, in MS no. 33, Folder I:H, in the Brewster Papers, kept at the Fairfield Historical Society, and see also Karen Seeskas's article in the *Black Rock News*. The clipping is in the Brewster Papers.

14. Pennypacker, *George Washington's spies*, p. 3.

15. See Hall, *Tallmadge*, Chapter XX, pp. 263–84.

16. Letter from Tallmadge, January 29, 1835, in the Benjamin Tallmadge Collection, Manuscripts Division, Department of Rare Books and Special Collections, Princeton University Library.

17. See Hall, *Tallmadge*, p. 231.

18. *Annals of Congress*, House of Representatives, 14th Congress, 2nd Session, January 13, 1817, cols. 474–75. This may be found online, thanks to the Library of Congress's amazing electronic resources, at http://memory.loc.gov.

${\mathscr B}$IBLIOGRAPHY

Original Sources

George Washington Papers. Library of Congress.
Thomas Jefferson Papers. Library of Congress.
Benjamin Tallmadge Papers. Princeton University Library.
Townsend Family Papers. New-York Historical Society.
Townsend Family Papers. Raynham Hall Museum.
Caleb Brewster Papers. Fairfield Historical Society.
Andrew Eliot Papers. New-York Historical Society.

Newspapers

St. James's Chronicle
New York Mercury
Pennsylvania Journal
Royal Gazette

Primary Sources

Adlum, J. (ed. by H. H. Peckham). *Memoirs of the life of John Adlum in the Revolutionary War.* Chicago, 1968.

Annals of Congress. House of Representatives, 14th Congress, 2nd Session, January 13, 1817, cols. 474–75.

Bamford, W. "Bamford's diary: The Revolutionary diary of a British officer." *Maryland Historical Magazine,* XXVIII (1933).

Bangs, E. (ed.). *Journal of Lieutenant Isaac Bangs, April 1 to July 29, 1776.* Cambridge, Mass., 1890.

Baurmeister, C. "Narrative of the capture of New York, September 1776." *Magazine of American History,* I (1887), pp. 33–39.

———. (trans. by B. A. Uhlendorf). *Revolution in America: Confidential letters and journals 1776–1784 of Adjutant General Major Baurmeister of the Hessian forces.* New Brunswick, N.J., 1957.

Bickley, F. (ed.). *Report on the manuscripts of the late Reginald Rawdon Hastings, Esq., of the Manor House, Ashby de la Zouch.* London, Historical Manuscripts Commission, 4 vols., 1928–47.

Biddulph, V. (ed.). "Letters of Robert Biddulph, 1779–1783." *American Historical Review,* XXIX (1923).

Bridenbaugh, C. (ed). *Gentleman's progress: The itinerarium of Dr. Alexander Hamilton.* Chapel Hill, N.C., 1948.

Bridgwater, D. W. (preface). *Nathan Hale to Enoch Hale: Autographed letter, signed 3 June 1776.* New Haven, 1954.

Bushnell, C. I. (ed.). *Narrative of Maj. Abraham Leggett.* New York, 1865.

Butterfield, L. et al. (eds.). *Adams: The diary and autobiography, 1771–1781.* Cambridge, 4 vols., 1961.

Calendar of historical manuscripts relating to the War of the Revolution, in the office of the secretary of state. Albany, 2 vols., 1868.

Chase, P. D., F. E. Grizzard, Jr., D. R. Hoth, E. G. Lengel, et al. (eds.). *The papers of George Washington: Revolutionary War series.* Charlottesville, Va., 14 vols. to date, 1985–.

Collins, J. (ed. J. M. Roberts). *A Revolutionary soldier.* New York, 1979.

Commager, H. S., and R. B. Morris (eds.). *The spirit of 'seventy-six: The story of the American Revolution as told by participants.* New York, 3rd ed., 1978; rep. 1995.

Crary, C. S. "The Tory and the spy: the double life of James Rivington." *William and Mary Quarterly,* 3rd ser., XVI (1959), no. 1, pp. 61–72.

——— (ed.). *The price of loyalty: Tory writings from the Revolutionary era.* New York, 1973.

Crèvecoeur, H. St. J. de (ed. A. E. Stone). *Letters from an American farmer and sketches of eighteenth-century America.* New York, 1981.

Curwen, S. (ed. G. A. Ward). *The journal and letters of Samuel Curwen, an American in England, from 1775 to 1783.* Boston, 4th ed., 1864.

Custis, G. W. P. (ed. B. J. Lossing). *Recollections and private memoirs of Washington, by his adopted son.* New York, 1860 ed.

Dawson, H. B. (ed.), *Record of the trial of Joshua Hett Smith, Esq., for alleged complicity in the treason of Benedict Arnold, 1780.* Morrisania, N.Y., 1866.

De Lancey, E. F. (ed.). "Sir Henry Clinton's original secret record of private daily intelligence." *Magazine of American History,* X–XII (October 1883–August 1884).

The detail and conduct of the American war under Generals Gage, Howe, Burgoyne, and Vice Admiral Lord Howe: With a very full and correct state of the whole of the evidence as given before a committee of the House of Commons. London, 3rd ed., 1780.

Dring, Capt. T. (ed. A. G. Greene). *Recollections of the* Jersey *prison-ship.* Providence, 1829.

Fitch, J. (ed. W. H. W. Sabine). *The New-York diary of Lieutenant Jabez Fitch of the 17th (Connecticut) Regiment from August 2, 1776 to December 15, 1777.* New York, 1954.

Force, P. (ed.). *American archives: Consisting of a collection of authentick records, state papers, debates, and letters and other notices of publick affairs, the whole forming a documentary history of the origin and progress of the North American colonies; of the causes and accomplishment of the American Revolution; and of the Constitution of government for the United States, to the final ratification thereof.* Washington, D.C., 4th and 5th ser., 1848–53.

Ford, W. C. (ed.). *Correspondence and journals of Samuel Blachley Webb.* New York, 3 vols., 1839–94.

Graydon, A. (ed. J. S. Littell). *Memoirs of his own time with reminiscences of the men and events of the revolution of Alexander Graydon.* Philadelphia, 1846.

Grim, D. "Account of the Fire of 1776 [by] David Grim." *Collections of the New-York Historical Society,* III. New York, 1870.

Harrison, S. A. (ed.). *Memoir of Lieutenant Colonel Tench Tilghman, secretary and aide to Washington, together with an appendix containing Revolutionary journals and letters, hitherto unpublished.* Albany, 1876.

Hastings, H., and J. A. Holden. (eds.). *Public papers of George Clinton, first governor of New York, 1777–1795, 1801–1804.* Albany, 10 vols., 1899–1914.

Hastings, H., and H. H. Noble (eds.). *Military minutes of the Council of Appointment of the state of New York, 1783–1821.* Albany, 4 vols., 1901–02.

Heath, W. *Memoirs of Major-General William Heath, containing anecdotes, details of skirmishes, battles, etc., during the American War.* Boston, 1798; rep. New York, 1901.

Henry, J. J. *An accurate and interesting account of the hardships and sufferings of that band of heroes who traversed the wildness in the campaign against Quebec in 1775.* Lancaster, Pa., 1812.

Historical Manuscripts Commission. *Report on American manuscripts in the Royal Institution of Great Britain.* London, 4 vols., 1904–09.

————. *Report on the manuscripts of Mrs. Stopford-Sackville, of Drayton House, Northamptonshire.* London, 1910.

Institut Français de Washington (ed.). *Correspondence of General Washington and Comte de Grasse, 1781 August 17–November 4; with supplementary documents from the Washington Papers in the Manuscripts Division of the Library of Congress.* Washington, D.C., 1931.

Jones, T. (ed. E. F. De Lancey). *History of New York during the Revolutionary War, and of the leading events in the other colonies at that period.* New York, 2 vols., 1879.

Kemble, S. *Kemble's Journals, 1773–1789,* in *Collections of the New-York Historical Society.* New York, 2 vols., 1883–84.

Krafft, J. von. "Journal of Lt. John Charles Philip von Krafft, of the Regiment von Bose, 1776–1784." *New-York Historical Society Collections.* New York, 1882.

Lafayette, M. J. P. R. Y. G. M. *Memoirs, correspondence, and manuscripts of General Lafayette.* London, 3 vols., 1837.

Lauber, A. W. (ed.). *Orderly books of the Fourth New York regiment, 1778–1780, the Second New York regiment, 1780–1783, by Samuel Tallmadge and others, with diaries of Samuel Tallmadge, 1780–1782 and John Barr, 1779–1782.* Albany, 1932.

Lee, H. *Memoirs of the war in the southern department of the United States.* New York, 1869 ed.

M'Robert, P. (ed. by C. Bridenbaugh). *A tour through part of the north provinces of America.* New York, 1935, rep. 1968.

Mather, F. G. (ed.). *The refugees of 1776 from Long Island to Connecticut.* Albany, 1913.

Moore, F. (ed.). *Diary of the American Revolution from newspapers and original documents.* New York, privately printed, 2 vols., 1865.

O'Callaghan, E. B. et al. (eds.). *Documents relative to the colonial history of the state of New York; procured in Holland, England and France.* Albany, 15 vols., 1856–1887.

Oliver, P. (ed. D. Adair and J. A. Schutz). *Peter Oliver's origin and progress of the American rebellion: A Tory view.* Stanford, Calif., 1967.

Onderdonk, H. (ed.). *Documents and letters intended to illustrate the Revolutionary incidents of Queens County with connecting narratives, explanatory notes, and additions.* New York, 1846.

———— (ed.). *Revolutionary incidents of Suffolk and Kings counties, with an ac-*

count of the battle of Long Island, and the British prisons and prison-ships. New York, 1849.

————. *New York City in olden times, consisting of newspaper cuttings arranged by Henry Onderdonk, Jr.* Jamaica (Long Island), unpub. personal scrapbook, 1863.

Padelford, P. (ed.). *Colonial panorama, 1775: Dr. Robert Honyman's journal for March and April.* San Marino, 1939.

Paine, T. *Common Sense.* Mineola, New York, 1997 ed.

Paltsits, V. H. (ed.). *Minutes of the Commissioners for Detecting and Defeating Conspiracies in the state of New York.* Albany, 3 vols., 1909–10.

Pattengill, R. W. (trans.). *Letters from America, 1776–1779: Being letters of Brunswick, Hessian and Waldeck officers with the British armies during the Revolution.* New York, 1924.

Reed, J. F. (ed.). "Spy chief to army chief." *Valley Forge Journal,* V (1991), 3, pp. 165–94.

Reitman, F. B. *Historical register of officers of the Continental army during the War of the Revolution, April 1775 to December 1783.* Baltimore, 1967 ed., orig. pub. 1914.

Rhodehamel, J. (ed.). *The American Revolution: Writings from the War of Independence.* New York, 2001.

Schaukirk, E. G. *Occupation of New York City by the British.* Originally published in *Pennsylvania Magazine of History and Biography,* January 1887; New York, rep. 1969.

Scott, K. (ed.). *Rivington's New York newspaper: Excerpts from the Loyalist press, 1773–1783.* New York, 1973.

Seymour, G. D. *Documentary life of Nathan Hale, comprising all available official and private documents bearing on the life of the patriot, together with an appendix, showing the background of his life.* New Haven, privately printed, 1941.

Shaw, S. (ed. by J. Quincy). *The journals of Major Samuel Shaw, the first American consul at Canton.* Boston, 1847.

Showman, R. K. et al. (eds.). *The papers of General Nathanael Greene.* Chapel Hill, N.C. 12 vols., 1976–.

Sibley J. L. "Col. J. Upham and the attack on Groton, Conn." *New England Historical and Genealogical Register,* X (1856), pp. 127–28.

Simcoe, J. G. *Simcoe's military journal: A history of the operations of a partisan corps, called the Queen's Rangers, commanded by Lieut. Col. J.G. Simcoe, during the war of the American Revolution; now first published, with a memoir of the author and other additions.* New York, 1844 ed.

Smith (ed. W. H. W. Sabine). *Historical memoirs from 16 March 1763 to 12 November 1783 of William Smith, historian of the province of New York; member of the governor's council, and last chief justice of that province under the Crown; chief justice of Quebec.* New York, 3 vols. in 2, rep. 1969–71.

Spangler, E. W. "Memoir of Major John Clark, of York Co., Pennsylvania." *Pennsylvania Magazine of History and Biography,* XX (1986), pp. 77–86.

Stevens, B. F. *Facsimiles of manuscripts in European archives relating to America, 1773–1783. With descriptions, editorial notes, collations, references and translations.* London, 25 vols., 1889–98.

Stokes, I. N. P. *The iconography of Manhattan Island, 1498–1909: Compiled from original sources and illustrated by photo-intaglio reproductions of important maps, plans, views, and documents in public and private collections.* New York, 6 vols., 1915–28.

Tallmadge, B. *Memoir of Col. Benjamin Tallmadge.* New York, 1858; rep. 1968.

Townsend, J. C., and C. A. Townsend. *A memorial of John, Henry, and Richard Townsend, and their descendants.* New York, 1865; rep. and new ed., 1976.

Townsend, M. *Townsend-Townshend, 1066–1909.* New York, 1909.

Wansey. *The journal of an excursion to the United States of North America in the summer of 1794.* New York, orig. 1796; rep. 1969.

Willcox, W. B. *The American Rebellion; Sir Henry Clinton's narrative of his campaigns, 1775–1782, with an appendix of original documents.* Yale, 1954.

Theses

Barber, A. R. "The Tallmadge-Culper intelligence ring: A study of American Revolutionary spies." Unpub. M.A. thesis, Columbia University (1963).

Hewlett, L. "James Rivington, Loyalist printer, publisher, and bookseller of the American Revolution, 1724–1802: A biographical bibliographical study." Unpub. Ph.D thesis, University of Michigan, Ann Arbor (1958).

Zabin, S. R. "Places of exchange: New York City, 1700–1763." Unpub. Ph.D. thesis, Rutgers University (2000).

Secondary Sources

Abbott, C. "The neighborhoods of New York, 1760–1775." *New York History,* XV (1974), pp. 35–54.

Abbott, W. C. *New York in the American Revolution.* New York, rep. 1975.

Amerman, R. H. "Treatment of American prisoners during the Revolution." *Proceedings of the New Jersey Historical Society,* LXXVIII (1960).

Amory, R., Jr. "John André, Çase Officer." *Studies in Intelligence,* Summer 1961, pp. A1–A15.

Anderson, O. "The treatment of prisoners of war in Britain during the American War of Independence." *Bulletin of the Institute of Historical Research*, XXVII (1955).

Anon. *Final report of the [Senate] select committee to study governmental operations with respect to the intelligence activities of the United States.* April 1976.

Bailyn, B. *The ideological origins of the American Revolution.* Cambridge, Mass., 1992 ed.

Bakeless, J. *Turncoats, traitors and heroes: Espionage in the American Revolution.* New York, 1959.

Baldwin, J., and G. Rossano. *Clan and commerce: The Townsend family of Oyster Bay.* No date, thesis in possession of Raynham Hall Museum, Oyster Bay.

Barck, O. T., Jr. *New York City during the War for Independence, with special reference to the period of British occupation.* New York, 1931; rep. Port Washington, N.Y., 1966.

Bass, S. "Nathan Hale's Mission." *Studies in intelligence*, Winter 1973.

Batten, A. C. "Long Island's Loyalists: The misunderstood Americans." *The Freeholder*, III (1999), 4.

Batterberry, M., and A. Batterberry. *On the town in New York: The landmark history of eating, drinking, and entertainments from the American Revolution to the Food Revolution.* New York/London, 1999.

Berlin, I. *Many thousands gone: The first two centuries in North America.* Cambridge/London, 1998.

Bishop, L. G. (ed.). *Historical register of Yale University, 1701–1937.* New Haven, 1939.

Blanco, R. L. "Military medicine in northern New York, 1776–1777." *New York History*, LXIII (1982), 1, pp. 39–58.

Boorstin, D. J. *The Americans: The colonial experience.* New York, 1958.

Bowler, R. A. *Logistics and the failure of the British army in America, 1775–1783.* Princeton, N. J., 1975.

Bowman, L. G. "Military parolees on Long Island, 1777–1782." *Journal of Long Island History*, XVIII (1982), 1, pp. 21–29.

Bradford, A. *Memoir of the life and writings of Rev. Jonathan Mayhew, D.D.* Boston, 1838.

Breen, T. H. *The marketplace of revolution: How consumer politics shaped American independence.* Oxford, 2004.

Brinton, A. "Quaker profiles." *Bulletin of the Friends Historical Association*, XXIX (1940).

Brinton, H. H. *Quaker journals: Varieties of religious experience among Friends.* Wallingford, Pa., 1972.

Brock, P. *The Quaker peace testimony, 1660–1914.* York, Pa., 1990.

Brookes, G. S. *Friend Anthony Benezet.* Philadelphia, 1937.

Broome, J. "The counterfeiting adventures of Henry Dawkins." *American Notes and Queries,* VIII (1950), pp. 179–84.

Brown, S. C., and E. W. Stein. "Benjamin Thompson and the first secret ink letter of the American Revolution" *Journal of Criminal Law, Criminology and Police Science,* XL (1950), 5, pp. 627–36.

Burnett, E. C. "Ciphers of the Revolutionary period." *American Historical Review,* XXII (1917), 2, pp. 329–34.

Burrows, E. G., and M. Wallace. *Gotham: A history of New York City to 1898.* New York, 1999.

Central Intelligence Agency. *Intelligence in the War of Independence.* Washington, D.C., CIA Office of Public Affairs, 1976.

Champagne, R. "The military association of the Sons of Liberty." In *Narratives of the revolution in New York : A collection of articles from the New-York Historical Society quarterly,* pp. 1–11. New York, 1975.

Chernow, R. *Alexander Hamilton.* New York, 2004.

Clark, J. C. D. "British America: What if there had been no American Revolution?" In N. Ferguson (ed.) *Virtual history: Alternative and counterfactuals.* London, 1997.

Coggins, J. *Ships and seamen of the American Revolution: Vessels, crews, weapons, gears, naval tactics, and actions of the War of Independence.* Harrisburg, Pa., 1969.

Collins, J. F. "Whaleboat warfare on Long Island Sound." *New York History,* XXV (1944), 2, pp. 195–201.

Conser, W. H, Jr., R. M. McCarthy, and D. J. Toscano. "The American independence movement, 1765–1775: A decade of nonviolent struggles," In Conser et al. (eds.), *Resistance, politics and the American struggle for independence, 1765–1775.* Boulder, Colo., 1986.

Conway, S. "British army officers and the American War for Independence." *William and Mary Quarterly,* XLI (1984), 2, pp. 265–76.

———."To subdue America: British army officers and the conduct of the Revolutionary War," *William and Mary Quarterly,* XLIII (1986), 3, pp. 381–407.

———."'The Great Mischief Complain'd of': Reflections on the misconduct of British soldiers in the Revolutionary War." *William and Mary Quarterly,* XLVII (1990), No. 3, pp. 370–90.

Crary, C. S., "The Tory and the spy: The double life of James Rivington." *William and Mary Quarterly,* XVI, 3rd ser., no. 1 (January 1959), pp. 61–72.

———(ed.). *The price of loyalty: Tory writings from the Revolutionary era.* New York, 1973.

————."Guerrilla activities of James DeLancey's Cowboys in Westchester County: Conventional warfare or self-interested freebooting?" In R. A. East and J. Judd (eds.), *The Loyalist Americans: A focus on greater New York*, pp. 14–24. Tarrytown, N.Y., 1975.

Cray, R. E., Jr. "Anglicans in the Puritan domain: Clergy and laity in eastern Long Island, 1693–1776." *Long Island Historical Journal*, II (1989), 2, pp. 189–200.

Cuneo, J. R. "The early days of the Queen's Rangers, August 1776–February 1777." *Military Affairs*, XXII (1958), 2, pp. 65–74.

————.*Robert Rogers of the Rangers*. Oxford University Press, 1959.

Curtis, E. E. *The organization of the British army in the American Revolution*. New Haven, 1926; rep. 1969.

Custis, G. W. P. (ed. B. J. Lossing). *Recollections and private memoirs of Washington, by his adopted son*. New York, 1860 ed.

Danenberg, E. N. *Naval history of the Fairfield County men in the Revolution*. Fairfield, Conn., 1977.

Davison, R. A. *Isaac Hicks: New York merchant and Quaker, 1767–1820*. Cambridge, Mass., 1964.

Dawson, H. B. *The Sons of Liberty in New York*. New York, privately printed, 1859.

Dexter, F. B. *Biographical sketches of the graduates of Yale College with annals of the college history, 1701–1815*. New York/New Haven, 6 vols., 1885–1912.

Donaldson Eberlein, H. *Manor houses and historic homes of Long Island and Staten Island*. Port Washington, N.Y., 1928; rep. 1966.

Drake, T. E. *Quakers and slavery in America*. New Haven, 1950.

Duer, W. *Reminiscences of an old New Yorker*. New York, 1867.

Ellington, G. *The women of New York; or, the underworld of the great city*. New York, 1869.

Ellis, J. J. *After the Revolution: Profiles of early American culture*. New York, 2002 ed.

Ellis, K. *The Post Office in the eighteenth century: A study in administrative history*. Oxford, 1958.

Endy, M. B. "The interpretation of Quakerism: Rufus Jones and his critics." *Quaker History*, LXX (1981), 1, pp. 3–21.

Ernst, R. "A Tory-eye view of the evacuation of New York." *New York History*, LXIV (1983), 4, pp. 377–94.

Falk, R. P. "Thomas Paine and the attitude of the Quakers to the American Revolution." *Pennsylvania Magazine of History and Biography*, LXIII (1939), pp. 302–10.

Fay, B. *Notes on the American press at the end of the eighteenth century*. New York, 1927.

Field, T. W. *The battle of Long Island*. New York, 2 vols., 1869.

Fischer, D. H. *Washington's crossing*. New York, 2004.

Fleming, T. "George Washington, spymaster." *American Heritage*, February–March 2000, pp. 45–51.

Flexner, J. T. *The traitor and the spy*. New York, 1953.

Ford, C. *A peculiar service: A narrative of espionage in and around New York during the American Revolution*. Boston, 1965.

Fox, G. *Journal of George Fox: Being an historical account of the life, travels, sufferings, Christian experiences, and labour of love, in the work of the ministry, of that eminent and faithful servant of Jesus Christ*. London, 8th ed., 2 vols., 1891.

French, A. *General Gage's informers: New material upon Lexington and Concord. Benjamin Thompson as Loyalist and the treachery of Benjamin Church, Jr*. Ann Arbor, Mich., 1932.

Frey, S. R. *The British soldier in America: A social history of military life in the Revolutionary period*. Austin, Tex., 1981.

Frost, J. W. *The Quaker family in Colonial America: A portrait of the Society of Friends*. New York, 1973.

Fryer, M. B., and C. Dracott. *John Graves Simcoe, 1752–1806: A biography*. Toronto, 1998.

Gilfoyle, T. J. *City of Eros: New York City, prostitution, and the commercialization of sex, 1790–1920*. New York, 1992.

Goering, W. M. "'To obey, rebelling': The Quaker dilemma in *Moby-Dick*." *New England Quarterly*, LIV (1981), 4, pp. 519–38.

Goddrich, C. "Invasion of New Haven by the British troops, July 5, 1779." *Papers of the New Haven Colony Historical Society*, II (1877), pp. 31–92.

Golway, T. *Washington's general: Nathanael Greene and the triumph of the American Revolution*. New York, 2005.

Greenberg, D. *Crime and law enforcement in the colony of New York, 1691–1776*. Ithaca, N.Y., 1974.

———. "The effectiveness of law enforcement in eighteenth-century New York." *American Journal of Legal History*, XIX (1975), 3, pp. 173–207.

Grumman, W. E. *The Revolutionary soldiers of Redding, Connecticut, and the record of their services*. Hartford, 1904.

Hall, C. S. *Life and letters of Samuel Holden Parsons: Major-general in the Continental army and chief judge of the Northwestern Territory, 1737–1789*. Binghamton, N.Y., 1905.

———. *Benjamin Tallmadge: Revolutionary soldier and American statesman*. New York, 1943.

Hall, W. C. "Sergeant Champe's adventure." *William and Mary Quarterly*, XVIII (1938), 3, pp. 322–42.

Harrington, V. D. *The New York merchant on the eve of the Revolution*. New York, 1935; rep. Gloucester, Mass., 1964

Higginbotham, D. "And the Curtain Fell on Yorktown." *Studies in Intelligence*, Summer 1981.

———. "The early American way of war: Reconnaissance and appraisal." *William and Mary Quarterly*, XLIV (1987), 2, pp. 230–73.

Hutson, J. "Nathan Hale revisited: A Tory's account of the arrest of the first American spy." *Library of Congress Information Bulletin*, LXII (2003), nos. 7–8, pp. 168–72.

Irwin, F. *Oyster Bay in history, a sketch*. New York, n.d. but 1950–1975.

James, S. V. "The impact of the American Revolution on Quakers' ideas about their sect." *William and Mary Quarterly*, XIX (1962), 3, pp. 360–82.

———. *A people among peoples: Quaker benevolence in eighteenth-century America*. Cambridge, Mass., 1963.

Johnston, H. P. *The campaign of 1776 around New York and Brooklyn. Including a new and circumstantial account of the battle of Long Island and the loss of New York, with a review of events to the close of the year*. New York, 2 parts, 1878.

———. "The Secret Service of the Revolution." *Magazine of American History*, VIII, 2, February 1882.

———. *Nathan Hale 1776: Biography and materials*. New Haven, 1914.

Jones, R. M., I. Sharpless, and A. M. Gummere. *The Quakers in the American colonies*. New York, 1911.

Judd, J. "Westchester County." In J. S. Tiedemann and E. R. Fingerhut (eds.). *The other New York: The American Revolution beyond New York City, 1763–1787*. Albany, 2005.

Kahn, D. *The codebreakers: The story of secret writing*. New York, 1967.

Kaplan, R. "The hidden war: British intelligence operations during the American Revolution." *William and Mary Quarterly*, 3rd ser., XLVII (1990), 1, pp. 115–38.

Kashatus, W. C., III. "Thomas Paine: a Quaker revolutionary." *Quaker History*, LXXIV (1984), 2, pp. 38–61.

———. *Conflict of conviction: A reappraisal of Quaker involvement in the American Revolution*. Lanham, Md., 1990.

Keane, J. *Tom Paine: A political life*. London, 1995.

Ketcham, R. L. "Conscience, war and politics in Pennsylvania, 1755–1757." *William and Mary Quarterly*, XX (1963), 3, pp. 416–39.

Kim, S. B. "The Continental army and the American people: A review essay." *New York History*, LXIII (1982), 4, pp. 460–69.

Klein, M. M. *The politics of diversity: Essays in the history of Colonial New York.* Port Washington, N.Y., 1974.

————. "An experiment that failed: General James Robertson and civil government in British New York, 1779–1783." *New York History,* LXI (1980).

————. "Why did the British fail to win the hearts and minds of New Yorkers?" *New York History,* LXIV (1983), 4, pp. 357–75.

Klein, M. M., and R. W. Howard (eds.). *The twilight of British rule in Revolutionary America: The New York letter book of General James Robertson, 1780–1783.* Cooperstown, N.Y., 1983.

Kornhiser, R. "Tory and Patriot: Love in the Revolution." *Journal of Long Island History,* XII (1976), 2, pp. 37–45.

Kugler, R. W. "The whale oil trade, 1750–1775." *Publications of the Colonial Society of Massachusetts,* LII (1980).

Labaree, B. W., W. M. Fowler, Jr., E. W. Sloan, J. B. Hattendorf, J. J. Safford, and A. W. German. *America and the sea: A maritime history.* Mystic, Conn., 1998.

Lantzer, J. S. "Washington as Cincinnatus: A model of leadership." In E. Fishman, W. D. Pederson, and M. J. Rozell (eds). *George Washington: Foundation of presidential leadership and character,* pp. 33–51. Westport, Conn., 2001.

Lawson, J. L. "The remarkable mystery of James Rivington, spy." *Journalism Quarterly,* XXXV (1958), 3, pp. 317–23, 394.

Lindsey, W. R. *Treatment of American prisoners of war during the Revolution.* Emporia State Research Studies, XXII. Emporia, Kan., 1973.

Loescher, B. G. *Rogers Rangers: The first Green Berets: The Corps and the revivals, April 6, 1758–December 24, 1783.* San Mateo, Calif., 1969.

————. *Washington's eyes: The Continental Light Dragoons.* Fort Collins, Colo., 1977.

Loring, G. B. *A vindication of General Samuel Holden Parsons against the charge of treasonable correspondence during the Revolutionary War.* Salem, Mass., 1888.

Lossing, B. J. *The Two Spies: Nathan Hale and John André.* New York, 1886.

Luke, M. H., and R. W. Venables. *Long Island in the American Revolution.* Albany, 1976.

Lydon, J. G. "New York and the slave trade, 1700 to 1774." *William and Mary Quarterly,* 3rd ser., XXXV (1978), 2, pp. 375–94.

Lysing, H. *Secret writing: An introduction to cryptograms, ciphers, and codes.* New York, 1936.

McGroarty, W. B. "Sergeant John Champe and certain of his contemporaries." *William and Mary Quarterly,* XVII (1937), 2, pp. 145–75.

———. "Captain Cameron and Sergeant Champe." *William and Mary Quarterly*, XIX (1939), 1, pp. 49–54.

McManus, E. J. *A history of Negro slavery in New York*. Syracuse, N.Y., 1966.

Macy, H., Jr. "Robert Townsend, Jr., of New York City." *New York Genealogical and Biographical Record*, CXXVI (1995), pp. 25–34, 108–12, 193–98.

Mahan, A. T. *The major operations of the navies in the war of American independence*. London, 1913.

Maier, P. *The old revolutionaries: Political lives in the age of Samuel Adams*. New York, 1980.

Marietta, J. D. "Conscience, the Quaker community, and the French and Indian War." *Pennsylvania Magazine of History and Biography*, XCV (1971), pp. 3–27.

———. *The reformation of American Quakerism, 1748–1783*. Philadelphia, 1984.

Matson, C. *Merchants and empire: Trading in Colonial New York*. Baltimore, 1998.

Mekeel, A. J. *The relation of the Quakers to the American Revolution*. Washington, D.C., 1979.

Monaghan, F. *John Jay*. New York, 1935.

Moulton, P. P. *The journal and essays of John Woolman*. New York, 1971.

Nelson, C. E. "Privateering by Long Islanders in the American Revolution." *Journal of Long Island History*, XI (1974), 1, pp. 25–34.

Nelson, P. D. *William Tryon and the course of empire: A life in British imperial service*. Chapel Hill N.C./London, 1990.

———. *Francis Rawdon-Hastings, marquess of Hastings: Soldier, peer of the realm, governor-general of India*. Madison, Wisc./Teaneck, N.J. 2005.

O'Brien, M. J. *Hercules Mulligan: Confidential correspondent of General Washington*. New York, 1937.

Odell, G. C. D. *Annals of the New York stage*. New York, 15 vols., 1927–49.

O'Toole, G. J. A. *Honorable treachery: A history of intelligence, espionage, and covert action from the American Revolution to the CIA*. New York, 1991.

Paltsits, V. H. "The use of invisible ink for secret writing during the American Revolution." *Bulletin of the New York Public Library*, XXXIX (1935), 5, pp. 361–64.

Patrick, L. S. "The Secret Service of the American Revolution." *Journal of American History*, I, 1907.

Pearl, N. "Long Island's secret agents of General Washington during the Revolutionary War." *Nassau County Historical Journal*, VIII (1945), 1, pp. 5–12.

Pennypacker, M. *The two spies, Nathan Hale and Robert Townsend*. New York, 1930.

———. *General Washington's spies on Long Island and in New York*. New York, 2 vols., 1939, 1948.

Picard, L. *Dr. Johnson's London: Coffee-houses and climbing boys, medicine, toothpaste and gin, poverty and press gangs, freak shows and female education.* New York, 2002 ed.

Polf, W. A. *Garrison town: The British occupation of New York City, 1776–1783.* Albany, 1976.

Pratt, F. *Secret and urgent: The story of codes and ciphers.* London, 1939.

Quarles, B. *The Negro in the American Revolution.* Chapel Hill, N.C., 1961; rep. 1996.

Ranlet, P. *The New York Loyalists.* Lanham, Md., 2nd ed., 2002.

Reiss, O. *Medicine and the American Revolution: How diseases and their treatments affected the Colonial army.* Jefferson, N.C., 1998.

Relyea, Harold C. "The evolution and organization of the federal intelligence function: A brief overview (1776–1975)." Book VI of *The final report of the Select Committee to Study Governmental Operations with Respect to Intelligence Activities.* Washington, D.C., 1976.

Reuter, F. T. "'Petty spy' or effective diplomat: The role of George Beckwith." *Journal of the Early Republic,* X (1990), 4, pp. 471–92.

Roche, J. F. *The Colonial colleges in the war for American independence.* Millwood, N.Y., 1986.

Rosenberg, B. A. *The neutral ground: The André affair and the background of Cooper's* The spy. Westport, Conn., 1994.

Ross, P. *The history of Long Island, from its earliest settlement to the present time.* New York, 3 vols., 1902.

Rothenburg, G. "Military intelligence gathering in the second half of the eighteenth century, 1740–1792." In K. Neilson and B. J. C. McKerchen (eds.). *Go spy the land: Military intelligence in history,* pp. 99–113. Westport, Conn., 1992.

Rothschild, N. A. *New York City neighborhoods: The 18th century.* San Diego, Calif., 1990.

Rubin, S. *The secret science of covert inks.* Port Townsend, Wa., 1987.

Sabine, L. *Biographical sketches of Loyalists of the American Revolution.* Boston, 2 vols., 2nd ed., 1864.

Sayle, Edward F. "George Washington, manager of intelligence." *Studies in Intelligence,* XXVII, 4 (Winter 1983), pp. 1–10.

Scharf, J. T., and T. Westcott. *History of Philadelphia, 1609–1884.* Philadelphia, 3 vols., 1884.

Schecter, B. *The battle for New York: The city at the heart of the American Revolution.* New York, 2002.

Schwartz, B. "The character of Washington: A study in republican culture." *American Quarterly,* XXXVIII (1986), pp. 202–22.

Scott, D. C. *John Graves Simcoe.* Toronto, 1905; Oxford/New York, new ed., 1926.

Scott, K. "New Hampshire Tory counterfeiters operating from New York City." *New-York Historical Society Quarterly,* XXXIV (1950), pp. 31–57.

————. "Counterfeiting in New York during the American Revolution." In *Narratives of the Revolution in New York: A collection of articles from the New York Historical Society Quarterly,* pp. 138–69. New York, 1975.

Sharpless, I. *History of Quaker government in Pennsylvania.* Philadelphia, 2 vols., 1898.

————. *A Quaker experiment in government; history of Quaker government in Pennsylvania, 1682–1783.* Philadelphia, 1902 ed.

Shelton, W. H. "What was the mission of Nathan Hale?" *Journal of American History,* IX (1915), 2, pp. 269–89.

————. *The Jumel mansion: Being a full history of the house on Harlem heights built by Roger Morris before the revolution.* New York, 1916.

Singleton, E. *Social New York under the Georges, 1714–1776.* New York, 1902.

Sparks, J. (ed.), *The life and treason of Benedict Arnold.* New York, 1835.

Staudt, J. G. "Suffolk County." In J. S. Tiedemann and E. R. Fingerhut (eds.). *The other New York: The American Revolution beyond New York City, 1763–1787.* Albany, 2005.

Stowe, G. C., and J. Weller. "Revolutionary West Point: 'The key to the continent.'" *Military Affairs,* XIX (1955), 2, pp. 81–98.

Strasser, G. F. "Diplomatic cryptology and universal languages in the sixteenth and seventeenth centuries." In K. Neilson and B. J. C. McKerchen (eds.). *Go spy the land: Military intelligence in history,* pp. 73–97. Westport, Conn., 1992.

Stuart, I. W. *Life of Captain Nathan Hale, the martyr-spy of the American Revolution.* Hartford/New York, 1856.

Stuart-Wortley, E. (ed.). *A prime minister and his son.* London, 1925.

Swanson, C. E. "American privateering and imperial warfare, 1739–1748." *William and Mary Quarterly,* 3rd ser., XLII (1985), pp. 357–82.

Thayer, T. *Nathanael Greene, strategist of the American Revolution.* New York, 1960.

Thompson, B. F. (ed. C. J. Werner). *History of Long Island, from its earliest settlement to the present time.* New York, 3 vols., 3rd ed., 1918; orig. 1839.

Thompson, E. R. *Secret New England: Spies of the American Revolution.* Portland, Me., 1991.

Thompson, J. W., and S. K. Padover. *Secret diplomacy: Espionage and cryptography, 1500–1815.* New York, 1963.

Tiedemann, J. S. "Queens County, New York Quakers in the American

Revolution: Loyalists or neutrals." *Historical Magazine of the Protestant Episcopal Church*, LII (1983), 3, pp. 215–27.

————. "Patriots by default: Queens County, New York, and the British army, 1776–1783." *William and Mary Quarterly*, XLIII (1986), 1, pp. 35–63.

————."A Revolution foiled: Queens County, New York, 1775–1776." *Journal of American History*, LXXV (1988), 2, pp. 417–44.

————. "Queens County." In J. S.Tiedemann and E. R. Fingerhut (eds.), *The other New York: The American Revolution beyond New York City, 1763–1787*. Albany, 2005.

Todd, C. B. "Whale-boat privateersmen of the Revolution." *Magazine of American History*, VIII (1882), pp. 168–81.

Tolles, F. B. " 'Of the best sort but plain': The Quaker esthetic." *American Quarterly*, XI (1959), 4, pp. 484–502.

Truxes, T. M. *Irish-American trade, 1660–1783*. Cambridge, U.K., 1988.

Underhill, A. P. "William Underhill, his ancestors and descendants." *New York Genealogical and Biographical Record*, LVIII (1927).

Upton, L. F. S. *The loyal Whig: William Smith of New York and Quebec*. Toronto, 1969.

Van Buskirk, J. L. *Generous enemies: Patriots and Loyalists in Revolutionary New York*. Philadelphia, 2002.

Van Doren, C. *Secret history of the American Revolution*. New York, 1941.

Vickers, D. "Nantucket whalemen in the deep-sea fishery: The changing anatomy of an early American labor force." *Journal of American History*, LXXII (1985), 2, pp. 277–96.

Vincitorio, G. L. "The Revolutionary War and its aftermath in Suffolk County, Long Island." *Long Island Historical Journal*, VII (1994), 1, pp. 68–85.

Volo, D. Denneen, and J. M. Volo. *Daily life during the American Revolution*. Westport, Conn., 2003.

Walsh, J. E. *The execution of Major André*. New York, 2001.

Weber, R. E. *United States diplomatic codes and ciphers, 1775–1938*. Chicago, 1979.

————. *Masked dispatches: Cryptograms and cryptology in American history, 1775–1900*. National Security Agency, Md., 1993.

Wertenbaker, T. J. *Father Knickerbocker rebels: New York City during the Revolution*. New York, 1948.

Wetherill, C. *History of the Religious Society of Friends called by some the Free Quakers, in the City of Philadelphia*. Philadelphia, 1894.

Wilbur, C. K. *Revolutionary medicine, 1700–1800*. Chester, Conn., 1980.

Wilkenfeld, B. M. "Revolutionary New York, 1776." In M. Klein (ed.). *New York: The centennial years, 1676–1976*, pp. 43–72. Port Washington, N.Y., 1976.

Willcox, W. B. "Rhode Island in British strategy, 1780–1781." *Journal of Modern History*, XVII (1945), 4, pp. 304–31.

————. *Portrait of a general: Sir Henry Clinton in the War of Independence*. New York, 1962.

Wright, J. W. "The Corps of light infantry in the Continental Army." *American Historical Review*, XXXI (1926), pp. 454–61.

I N D E X

The Princess Diaries

PRINCESS IN LOVE

BOOKS BY
MEG CABOT

THE PRINCESS DIARIES

The Princess Diaries, Volume II:
PRINCESS IN THE SPOTLIGHT

The Princess Diaries, Volume III:
PRINCESS IN LOVE

The Princess Diaries, Volume IV:
PRINCESS IN WAITING

VALENTINE PRINCESS:
A Princess Diaries Book (Volume
IV and a Quarter)

The Princess Diaries, Volume IV
and a Half:
PROJECT PRINCESS

The Princess Diaries, Volume V:
PRINCESS IN PINK

The Princess Diaries, Volume VI:
PRINCESS IN TRAINING

THE PRINCESS PRESENT:
A Princess Diaries Book (Volume
VI and a Half)

The Princess Diaries, Volume VII:
PARTY PRINCESS

SWEET SIXTEEN PRINCESS:
A Princess Diaries Book (Volume
VII and a Half)
Illustrated by Chesley McLaren

The Princess Diaries, Volume VIII:
PRINCESS ON THE BRINK

The Princess Diaries, Volume IX:
PRINCESS MIA

The Princess Diaries, Volume X:
FOREVER PRINCESS

The Princess Diaries, Volume XI:
ROYAL WEDDING

PRINCESS LESSONS:
A Princess Diaries Book

PERFECT PRINCESS:
A Princess Diaries Book

HOLIDAY PRINCESS:
A Princess Diaries Book

The Princess Diaries

PRINCESS IN LOVE

MEG CABOT

HARPER

An Imprint of HarperCollinsPublishers

Princess in Love

Copyright © 2002 by Meggin Cabot

Printed in the United States of America.

For information address HarperCollins Children's Books, a division of
HarperCollins Publishers, 195 Broadway, New York, NY 10007.

www.harpercollinschildrens.com

Library of Congress Cataloging-in-Publication Data

Cabot, Meg.

Princess in love / Meg Cabot.

p.   cm. — (The princess diaries ; v. 3)

Summary: In a series of humorous diary entries, a New York City
ninth grader agonizes over her love life, final exams, and future role
as the princess of Genovia.

ISBN: 978-0-06-299847-7

[1. Princesses—Fiction.   2. Identity—Fiction.   3. Schools—
Fiction.   4. Love—Fiction.   5. New York (NY)—Fiction.
6. Diaries—Fiction.   7. Humorous stories.]   I. Title.   II. Series.

PZ7.C11165 Ps 2002   2001039815
[Fic]—dc21   CIP
                                                                        AC

Typography by Jenna Stempel-Lobell

20 21 22 23 24   PC/BRR   10 9 8 7 6 5 4 3 2 1

❖

Revised paperback edition, 2020

For Benjamin, with love

"One of Sara's 'pretends' is that she is a princess," said Jessie. "She plays it all the time—even in school. She wants Ermengarde to be one, too, but Ermengarde says she is too fat."

"She *is* too fat," said Lavinia. "And Sara is too thin."

"Sara says it has nothing to do with what you look like, or what you have. It has only to do with what you *think* of, and what you *do*," Jessie explained.

A Little Princess
FRANCES HODGSON BURNETT

ENGLISH CLASS

Assignment (Due December 8): Here at Albert Einstein High School, we have a very diverse student population. Over one hundred and seventy different nations, religions, and ethnic groups are represented by our student body. In the space below, describe the manner in which your family celebrates the uniquely American holiday, Thanksgiving. Please utilize appropriate margins.

MY THANKSGIVING
by Mia Thermopolis

6:45 a.m. Roused by the sound of my mother vomiting. She is well into her third month of pregnancy now. According to her obstetrician, all the throwing up should stop in the next trimester. I can't wait. I have been marking the days off on my 'N Sync calendar. (I don't really like 'N Sync. At least, not that much. My best friend, Lilly, bought me the calendar as a joke. Except that one guy really is pretty cute.)

7:45 a.m. Mr. Gianini, my new stepfather, knocks on my door. Only now I am supposed to call him Frank. This is very difficult to remember due to the fact that at school, where he is my first-period Algebra teacher, I am supposed to call him Mr. Gianini. So I just don't call him anything (to his face).

It's time to get up, Mr. Gianini says. We are having Thanksgiving at his parents' house on Long Island. We have to leave now if we are going to beat the traffic.

8:45 a.m. There is no traffic this early on Thanksgiving Day. We arrive at Mr. G's parents' house in Sagaponic three hours early.

Mrs. Gianini (Mr. Gianini's mother, not my mother. My mother is still Helen Thermopolis because she is a fairly well-known modern painter under that name, and also because she does not believe in the cult of the patriarchy) is still in curlers. She looks very surprised. This might not only be because we arrived so early, but also because no sooner had my mother entered the house than she was forced to run for the bathroom with her hand pressed over her mouth, on account of the smell of the roasting turkey. I am hoping this means that my future half brother or sister is a vegetarian, since the smell of meat cooking used to make my mother hungry, not nauseated.

My mother had already informed me in the car on the way over from Manhattan that Mr. Gianini's parents are very old-fashioned and are used to enjoying a conventional Thanksgiving meal. She does not think they will appreciate hearing my traditional Thanksgiving speech about how the Pilgrims are guilty of committing mass genocide by giving their new Native American friends blankets filled with the smallpox virus, and that it is reprehensible that we as a country annually celebrate this rape and destruction of an entire culture.

Instead, my mother said, I should discuss more neutral topics, such as the weather.

I asked if it was all right if I discussed the astonishingly high rate of attendance at the Reykjavik opera house in Iceland (over 98 percent of the country's population has seen *Tosca* at least once).

My mother sighed and said, "If you must," which I take to be a sign that she is beginning to tire of hearing about Iceland.

Well, I am sorry, but I find Iceland extremely fascinating, and I will not rest until I have visited the ice hotel.

9:45 a.m.–11:45 a.m. I watch the Macy's Thanksgiving Day parade with Mr. Gianini Senior in what he calls the rec room.

They don't have rec rooms in Manhattan.

Just lobbies.

Remembering my mother's warning, I refrain from repeating another one of my traditional holiday rants, that the Macy's Thanksgiving Day parade is a gross example of American capitalism run amok.

At one point during the broadcast, I catch sight of Lilly standing in the crowd outside of Office Max on Broadway and Thirty-Seventh, her video camera clutched to her slightly squished-in face (so much like a pug) as a float carrying Miss America and William Shatner of *Star Trek* fame passes by. So I know Lilly is going to take care of denouncing Macy's on the next episode of her public access television show, *Lilly Tells It Like It Is* (every Friday night at nine, Manhattan cable channel 67).

12:00 p.m. Mr. Gianini Junior's sister arrives with her husband, their two kids, and the pumpkin pies. The kids, who are my age, are twins, a boy, Nathan, and a girl, Claire. I know right away Claire and I are not going to get along, because when we are introduced she looks me up and down the way the cheerleaders do in the hallway at school and goes, in a very snotty voice, "*You're* the one who's supposed to be a princess?"

And while I am perfectly aware that at five foot nine inches tall, with no visible breasts, feet the size of snowshoes, and hair that sits in a tuft on my head like the cotton on the end of a Q-tip, I am the biggest freak in the freshman class of Albert Einstein High School for Boys (made coeducational circa 1975), I do not appreciate being reminded of it by girls who do not even bother finding out that beneath this mutant facade beats the heart of a person who is only striving, just like everybody else in this world, to find self-actualization.

Not that I even care what Mr. Gianini's niece Claire thinks of me. I mean, she is wearing a pony-skin miniskirt. And it is not even imitation pony skin. She must know that a horse had to die just so she could have that skirt, but she obviously doesn't care.

Now Claire has pulled out her cell phone and gone out onto the deck, where the reception is best (even though it is thirty degrees outside, she apparently doesn't mind. She has that pony skin to keep her warm, after all). She keeps looking in at me through the sliding glass doors and laughing as she talks on her phone.

Nathan—who is dressed in baggy jeans and has a pager, in addition to a lot of gold jewelry—asks his grandfather if he can change the channel. So instead of traditional Thanksgiving viewing options, such as football or the Lifetime Channel's made-for-TV movie marathon, we are now forced to watch MTV2. Nathan knows all the songs and sings along with them. Most of them have dirty words that have been bleeped out, but Nathan sings them anyway.

1:00 p.m. The food is served. We begin eating.

1:15 p.m. We finish eating.

1:20 p.m. I help Mrs. Gianini clean up. She says not to be ridiculous, and that I should go "have a nice gossip" with Claire.

It is frightening, if you think about it, how clueless old people can be sometimes.

Instead of going to have a nice gossip with Claire, I stay where I am and tell Mrs. Gianini how much I am enjoying having her son live with us. Mr. G is very good about helping around the house, and has even taken over my old job of cleaning the toilets. Not to mention the thirty-six-inch TV, pinball machine, and foozball table he brought with him when he moved in.

Mrs. Gianini is immensely gratified to hear this, you can just tell. Old people like to hear nice stuff about their kids, even if their kid, like Mr. Gianini, is thirty-nine and a half years old.

3:00 p.m. We have to leave if we are going to beat the traffic home. I say good-bye. Claire does not say good-bye back to me, but Nathan does. He advises me to keep it real. Mrs. Gianini gives us a lot of leftover turkey. I thank her, even though I don't eat turkey, being a vegetarian.

6:30 p.m. We finally make it back into the city, after spending three and a half hours in bumper-to-bumper traffic along the Long Island Expressway. Though there is nothing very express about it, if you ask me.

I barely have time to change into my baby-blue floor-length Armani sheath dress and matching ballet flats before the limo honks downstairs, and Lars, my bodyguard, arrives to escort me to my second Thanksgiving dinner.

7:30 p.m. Arrive at the Plaza Hotel. I am greeted by the concierge, who announces me to the masses assembled in the Palm Court:

"Presenting Her Royal Highness Princess Amelia Mignonette Grimaldi Thermopolis Renaldo."

God forbid he should just say Mia.

My father, the prince of Genovia, and his mother, the dowager princess, have rented the Palm Court for the evening in order to throw a Thanksgiving banquet for all their friends. Despite my strenuous objections, Dad and Grandmère refuse to leave New York City until I have learned everything there is to know about being a princess . . . or until my formal introduction to the Genovian people the day before Christmas, whichever comes first. I have assured them that it isn't as if I am going to show up at the castle and start hurling olives at the ladies-in-waiting and scratching myself under the arms. I mean, I am fourteen years old: I do have some idea how to act, for crying out loud.

But Grandmère, at least, does not seem to believe this, and so she is still subjecting me to daily princess lessons. Lilly recently contacted the United Nations to see whether these lessons constitute a human rights violation. She believes it is unlawful to force a minor to sit for hours practicing tipping her soup bowl away from her—"Always, always, *away* from you, Amelia!"—in order to scrape up a few drops of lobster bisque. The UN has so far been unsympathetic to my plight.

It was Grandmère's idea to have what she calls an "old-fashioned" Thanksgiving dinner, featuring mussels in a white wine sauce, squab stuffed with foie gras, lobster tails, and Iranian caviar, which you could never get before because of the embargo. She has invited two hundred of her closest friends, plus the emperor of Japan and his wife, since they were in town anyway for a world trade summit.

That's why I have to wear ballet flats. Grandmère says it's rude to be taller than an emperor.

8:00 p.m.–11:00 p.m. I make polite conversation with the empress while we eat. Like me, she was just a normal person until one day she married the emperor and became royal. I, of course, was born royal. I just didn't know it until September, when my dad found out he couldn't have any more kids, due to his chemotherapy for testicular cancer having rendered him sterile. Then he had to admit he was actually a prince and all, and that though I am "illegitimate," since my dad and my mom were never married, I am still the sole heir to the Genovian throne.

And even though Genovia is a very small country (population 50,000) crammed into a hillside along the Mediterranean Sea between Italy and France, it is still this very big deal to be princess of it.

Not a big enough deal for anyone to raise my allowance higher than ten dollars a week, apparently. But a big enough deal that I have to have a bodyguard follow me around everywhere I go, just in case some Eurotrash terrorist in a ponytail and black leather pants takes it into his head to kidnap me.

The empress knows all about this—what a bummer it is, I mean, being just a normal person one day, and then having your face on the cover of *People* magazine the next. She even gave me some advice: She told me I should always make sure my kimono is securely fastened before I raise my arm to wave to the populace.

I thanked her, even though I don't actually own a kimono.

11:30 p.m. I am so tired on account of having gotten up so early to go to Long Island, I have yawned in the empress's face twice. I have tried to hide these yawns the way Grandmère taught me to, by clenching my jaw and refusing to open my mouth. But this only makes my eyes water, and the rest of my face stretch out like I am hurtling through a black hole. Grandmère gives me the evil eye over her salad with pears and walnuts, but it is no use. Even her malevolent stare cannot shake me from my state of extreme drowsiness.

Finally, my father notices, and grants me a royal reprieve from dessert. Lars drives me back to the apartment. Grandmère is clearly upset because I am leaving before the cheese course.

But it is either that, or pass out in the *fromage bleu*. I know that in the end, Grandmère will have retribution, undoubtedly in the form of forcing me to learn the names of every member of the Swedish royal family, or something equally as heinous.

Grandmère always gets her way.

12:00 a.m. After a long and exhausting day of giving thanks to the founders of our nation—those genocidal hypocrites known as the Pilgrims—I finally go to bed.

And that concludes Mia Thermopolis's Thanksgiving.

SATURDAY, DECEMBER 6

Over.

That is what my life is. O-V-E-R.

I know I have said that before, but this time I really mean it.

And why? Why THIS TIME? Surprisingly, it's not because:

Three months ago, I found out that I'm the heir to the throne of a small European nation, and that at the end of this month, I am going to have to go to said small European nation and be formally introduced for the first time to the people over whom I will one day reign, and who will undoubtedly hate me, because given that my favorite shoes are my combat boots and my favorite TV show is *Baywatch*, I am so not the royal-princess type.

Or because:

My mother, who is expecting to give birth to my Algebra teacher's child in approximately seven months, recently eloped with said Algebra teacher.

Or even because:

At school they've been loading us down with so much homework—and after school, Grandmère's been torturing me so endlessly with all the princess stuff I've got to learn by Christmas—that I haven't even been able to keep up with this journal, let alone anything else.

Oh, no. It's not because of any of that. Why is my life over?

Because I have a boyfriend.

At fourteen years of age, I suppose it's about time. I mean, all my friends have boyfriends. All of them, even Lilly, who blames the male gender for most, if not all, of society's ills.

And okay, Lilly's boyfriend is Boris Pelkowski, who may, at the age of fifteen, be one of the nation's leading violin virtuosos, but that doesn't mean he doesn't tuck his sweater into his pants, or that he doesn't have food in his braces more often than not. Not what I would call ideal boyfriend material, but Lilly seems to like him, which is all that matters.

I guess.

I have to admit, when Lilly—possibly the pickiest person on this planet (and I should know, having been best friends with her since kindergarten)—got a boyfriend, and I still didn't have one, I pretty much started to think there was something wrong with me. Besides my gigantism and what Lilly's parents, the Drs. Moscovitz, who are psychiatrists, call my inability to verbalize my inner rage.

And then, one day, out of the blue, I got one. A boyfriend, I mean.

Well, okay, not out of the blue. Kenny started sending me all these anonymous love letters. I didn't know it was him. I kind of thought (okay, hoped) someone else was sending them. But in the end, it turned out to be Kenny. And by then I was in too deep, really, to get out. So *voilà*! I had a boyfriend.

Problem solved, right?

Not. So not.

And it isn't that I don't like Kenny. I do. I really do. We have a lot in common. For instance, we both appreciate the preciousness of not just human, but *all* life forms, and refuse to dissect fetal pigs and frogs in Bio. Instead, we are writing term papers on the life cycles of various grubs and mealworms.

And we both like science fiction. Kenny knows a lot more about it than I do, but he has been very impressed so far by the extent of my familiarity with the works of Robert A. Heinlein and Isaac Asimov, both of whom we were forced to read in school (though he doesn't seem to remember this).

I haven't told Kenny that I actually find most science fiction boring, since there seem to be very few girls in it.

There are a lot of girl characters in Japanese anime, which Kenny also really likes, and which he has decided to devote his life to promoting (when he is not busy finding a cure for cancer). I have noticed that most of the girls in Japanese anime seem to have misplaced their bras.

Plus I really think it might be detrimental to a fighter pilot to have a lot of long hair floating around in the cockpit while she is gunning down the forces of evil.

But like I said, I haven't mentioned any of this to Kenny. And mostly, we get along great. We have a fun time together. And in some ways, it's very nice to have a boyfriend. Like I don't have to worry now about not being asked to the Albert Einstein High School Nondenominational Winter Dance (so called because its former title, the Albert Einstein High School Christmas Dance, offended many of our non-Christmas-celebrating students).

And why is it that I do not have to worry about not being asked to the biggest dance of the school year, with the exception of the prom?

Because I'm going with Kenny.

Well, okay, he hasn't exactly asked me yet, but he will. Because he is my boyfriend.

Isn't that great? Sometimes I think I must be the luckiest girl in the whole world. I mean, really. Think about it: I may not be pretty, but I am not grossly disfigured; I live in New York City, the coolest place on the planet; I'm a princess; I have a boyfriend. What more could a girl ask for?

Oh, God.

WHO AM I KIDDING?????

This boyfriend of mine? Here's the scoop:

I DON'T EVEN LIKE HIM.

Well, okay, it's not that I don't like him. But this boyfriend thing, I just don't know. Kenny's a nice enough guy and all—don't get me wrong. I mean, he is funny and not boring to be with, certainly. And he's pretty cute, you know, in a tall, skinny sort of way.

It's just that when I see Kenny walking down the hall, my heart so totally doesn't start beating faster, the way girls' hearts start beating faster in those teen romances my friend Tina Hakim Baba is always reading.

And when Kenny takes my hand, at the movies or whatever, it's not like my hand gets all tingly in his, the way girls' hands do in those books.

And when he kisses me? Those fireworks people always talk about? Forget about it. No fireworks. Nil. Nada.

It's funny, because before I got a boyfriend, I used to spend a lot of time trying to figure out how to get one, and once I got him, how I'd get him to kiss me.

But now that I actually have a boyfriend, mostly all I do is try to figure out how to get out of kissing him.

One way that I have found that works quite effectively is the head turn. If I notice his lips coming toward me, I just turn my head at the last minute, so all he gets is my cheek, and maybe some hair.

I guess the worst thing is, when Kenny gazes deeply into my eyes—which he does a lot—and asks me what I am thinking about, I am usually thinking about this one certain person.

And that person isn't Kenny. It isn't Kenny at all. It is Lilly's older brother, Michael Moscovitz, whom I have loved for, oh, I don't know, MY ENTIRE LIFE.

Wait, though. It gets worse.

Because now it's like everybody considers me and Kenny this big Item. You know? Now we're Kenny-and-Mia. Now, instead of Lilly and me hanging out together Saturday nights, it's Lilly-and-Boris and Kenny-and-Mia. Sometimes my friend Tina Hakim Baba and her boyfriend, Dave Farouq El-Abar, and my other friend Shameeka Taylor and her boyfriend, Daryl Gardner, join us, making it Lilly-and-Boris and Kenny-and-Mia and Tina-and-Dave and Shameeka-and-Daryl.

So if Kenny and I break up, who am I going to hang around with on Saturday nights? I mean, seriously. Lilly-and-Boris and Tina-and-Dave and Shameeka-and-Daryl won't want just plain Mia along. I'll be just like this seventh wheel.

Not to mention, if Kenny and I break up, who will I go to the Nondenominational Winter Dance with? I mean, if he ever gets around to asking me.

Oh, God, I have to go now. Lilly-and-Boris and Tina-and-Dave and Kenny-and-Mia are supposed to go ice-skating at Rockefeller Center.

All I can say is, be careful what you wish for. It just might come true.

SATURDAY, DECEMBER 6, 11 P.M.

I thought my life was over because I have a boyfriend now and I don't really like him in that way, and I have to break up with him without hurting his feelings, which is, I guess, probably impossible.

Yeah, well, I didn't know *how* over my life could actually be.

Not until tonight, anyway.

Tonight, Lilly-and-Boris and Tina-and-Dave and Mia-and-Kenny were joined by a new couple, Michael-and-Judith.

That's right: Lilly's brother, Michael, showed up at the ice-skating rink, and he brought with him the president of the Computer Club—of which he is treasurer—Judith Gershner.

Judith Gershner, like Lilly's brother, Michael, is a senior at Albert Einstein High School.

Judith Gershner, like Michael, is on the honor roll.

Judith Gershner, like Michael, will probably get into every college she applies to, because Judith Gershner, like Michael, is brilliant.

In fact, Judith Gershner, like Michael, won a prize last year at the Albert Einstein High School Annual Biomedical Technology Fair for her science project, in which she actually cloned a fruit fly.

She cloned a fruit fly. At home. In her *bedroom.*

Judith Gershner knows how to clone fruit flies in her bedroom. And me? I can't even multiply fractions.

Hmmm. Gee, I don't know. If you were Michael Moscovitz—you know, a straight-A student who got into Columbia early decision—who would you rather go out with? A girl who can clone fruit flies in her bedroom, or a girl who is getting a D in Freshman Algebra, in spite of the fact that *her mother is married to her Algebra teacher?*

Not that there's even a chance of Michael ever asking me out. I will admit, there were a couple of times when I thought he might. But that was clearly just wishful thinking on my part. I mean, why would a guy like Michael, who does really well in school and will probably excel at whatever career he ultimately chooses, ever ask out a girl like me, who would have flunked out of the ninth grade by now if it hadn't been for all those extra tutoring sessions with Mr. Gianini, and, ironically, Michael himself?

But Michael and Judith Gershner, on the other hand, are perfect for each other. Judith even looks like him, a little. I mean, they both have the same curly black hair and pale skin from being inside all the time, looking up stuff about genomes on the internet.

But if Michael and Judith Gershner are so suited for each other, how come when I first saw them walking toward us while we were lacing up our rental skates, I got this very bad feeling inside?

I have absolutely no right to be jealous of the fact that Michael Moscovitz asked Judith Gershner to go skating with him. Absolutely no right at all.

Except that when I first saw them together, I was shocked. I mean, Michael hardly ever leaves his room, on account of always being at his computer, maintaining his webzine, *Crackhead*. The last place I'd ever expected to see him is the ice-skating rink at Rockefeller Center during the height of the Christmas-tree-lighting hysteria. Michael generally avoids places he considers tourist traps, like pretty much everywhere north of Bleecker Street.

But there he was, and there was Judith Gershner, in her overalls and Rockports and ski parka, chatting away with him about something—probably something really smart, like DNA.

I nudged Lilly in the side—she was lacing up her skates—and said, in this voice that I hoped didn't show what I was feeling inside, "Look, there's your brother."

And Lilly wasn't even surprised to see him! She looked over and saw him and went, "Oh, yeah. He said he might show up."

Show up with a *date*? Did he mention *that*? And would it have been too much for you, Lilly, to have mentioned this to me beforehand, so I could have had time for a little mental preparation?

Only Lilly doesn't know how I feel about her brother, so I guess it never occurred to her to break it to me gently.

Here's the subtle way in which I handled the situation. It was really smooth (NOT).

As Michael and Judith were looking around for a place to put on their skates:

Me: (Casually, to Lilly) I didn't know your brother and Judith Gershner were going out.

Lilly: (Disgusted for some reason) Please. They're not. She was just over at our place, working with Michael on some project for the stupid Computer Club. They heard we were all going skating, and Judith said she wanted to come, too.

Me: Well, that sounds like they're going out to me.

Lilly: Whatever. Boris, must you constantly *breathe* on me?

Me: (To Michael and Judith as they walk up to us) Oh, hi, you guys. Michael, I didn't know you knew how to ice-skate.

Michael: (shrugging) I used to be on a hockey team.

Lilly: (snorting) Yeah, Pee Wee Hockey. That was before he decided that team sports were a waste of time because the success of the team was dictated by the performance of all the players as a whole, as opposed to sports determined by individual performance such as tennis and golf.

Michael: Lilly, don't you ever shut up?

Judith: I love ice-skating! Although I'm not very good at it.

And she certainly isn't. Judith is such a bad skater, she had to hold on to both of Michael's hands while he skated backward in front of her, just to keep from falling flat on her face. I don't know which astonished me more: that Michael can skate backward, or that he didn't seem to mind having to tow Judith all around the rink. Obviously I may not be able to clone a fruit fly, but at least I can remain upright unaided in a pair of ice skates.

Kenny, however, seemed to really think Michael and Judith's method of skating was way preferable to skating the old-fashioned way—you know, solo—so he kept coming up and trying to get me to let him tow me around the way Michael was towing Judith.

And even though I was all, "Duh, Kenny, I know how to skate," he said that that wasn't the point. Finally, after he'd bugged me for like half an hour, I gave in, and let him hold both my hands as he skated in front of me, backward.

Only the thing is, Kenny isn't very good at skating backward. I can skate forward, but I'm not good enough at it that if someone is wobbling around in front of me, I can keep from crashing into him if he falls down.

Which was exactly what happened. Kenny fell down, and I couldn't stop, so I crashed into him, and my chin hit his knee and I bit my tongue and all this blood filled up my mouth, and I didn't want to swallow it so I spat it out. Only unfortunately it went all over Kenny's jeans and onto the ice, which clearly impressed all the tourists standing along the railings around the rink, taking pictures of their loved ones in front of the enormous Rockefeller Center Christmas tree, since they all turned around and started taking pictures of the girl spitting up blood on the ice below, a truly New York moment.

And then Lars came *shoosh*ing over—he is a champion ice-skater, thanks to his Nordic upbringing; quite a contrast to his bodyguard training in the heart of the Gobi Desert—picked me up, looked at my tongue, gave me his handkerchief and told me to keep pressure on the wound, and then said, "That's enough skating for one night."

And that was it. Now I've got this bloody gouge in the tip of my tongue, and it hurts to talk, and I was totally humiliated in front of millions of tourists who'd come to look at the stupid tree at stupid Rockefeller Center, not to mention in front of my friends and, worst of all, Judith Gershner, who it turns out also got accepted early decision at Columbia (great, the same school Michael's going to in the fall), where she will be pre-med, and who advised me that I should go to the hospital, as it seemed likely to her that I might need stitches. In my *tongue*. I'm lucky, she said, I didn't bite the tip of it off.

Lucky!

Oh, yeah, I'll tell you how lucky I am: I'm so lucky that while I lie here in bed writing this, with no one but my twenty-five-pound cat, Fat Louie, to keep me company (and Fat Louie only likes me because I feed him), the boy I've been in love with since like forever is up at midtown right now with a girl who knows how to clone fruit flies and can tell if wounds need stitches or not.

One good thing about this tongue, though: If Kenny was thinking about moving on to Frenching, we totally can't until I heal. And that could, according to Dr. Fung—whom my mom called as soon as Lars brought me home—take anywhere from three to ten days.

Yes!

TEN THINGS I HATE ABOUT THE HOLIDAY SEASON IN
NEW YORK CITY

1. Tourists who come in from out of town in their giant sports utility vehicles and try to run you over at the crosswalks, thinking they are driving like aggressive New Yorkers. Actually, they are driving like morons. Plus there is enough pollution in this city. Why can't they just take public transit, like normal people?

2. Stupid Rockefeller Center tree. They asked me to be the person who throws the switch to light it this year, as I am considered "New York's own Royal" in the press, but when I told them how cutting down trees contributes to the destruction of the ozone layer, they rescinded their invitation and had the mayor do it instead.

3. Stupid Christmas carols blaring from outside all the stores.

4. Stupid ice-skating with stupid boys who think they can skate backward when they can't.

5. Pressure to buy stupid "meaningful" gifts for everyone you know.

6. Final exams.

7. Stupid lousy New York weather. No snow, just cold, wet rain, every single day. Whatever happened to a white Christmas? I'll tell you: global warming. You know why? Because everybody keeps driving SUVs and cutting down trees!

8. Stupid manipulative Christmas specials on TV.

9. Stupid manipulative Christmas commercials on TV.

10. Mistletoe. This stuff should be banned. In the hands of adolescent boys, it becomes a societally approved excuse to demand kisses. This is sexual harassment, if you ask me.

Plus, all the wrong boys have it.

SUNDAY, DECEMBER 7

Just got back from dinner at Grandmère's. All my efforts to get out of having to go—even my pointing out that I am currently suffering from a perforated tongue—were in vain.

And this one was even worse than usual. That's because Grandmère wanted to go over my itinerary for my trip to Genovia, which, by the way, looks like this:

SUNDAY, DECEMBER 21

3 P.M.

Arrive in Genovia

3:30 P.M.–5 P.M.

Meet and greet palace staff

5 P.M.–7 P.M.

Tour of palace

7 P.M.–8 P.M.

Change for dinner

8 P.M.–11 P.M.

Dinner with Genovian dignitaries

MONDAY, DECEMBER 22

8 A.M.–9:30 A.M.

Breakfast with Genovian public officials

10 A.M.–11:30 A.M.

Tour of Genovian public schools

12 P.M.–1 P.M.

Meet with Genovian schoolchildren

1:30 P.M.–3 P.M.

Lunch with members of Genovian Teachers Association

3:30 P.M.–4:30 P.M.

Tour of Port of Genovia and Genovian naval cruiser (the *Prince Phillipe*)

5 P.M.–6 P.M.

Tour of Genovian General Hospital

6 P.M.–7 P.M.

Visit with hospital patients

7 P.M.–8 P.M.

Change for dinner

8 P.M.–11 P.M.

Dinner with the dowager princess, prince, and Genovian
military advisors

TUESDAY, DECEMBER 23

8 A.M.–9 A.M.

Breakfast with members of Genovian Olive Growers
Association

10 A.M.–11 A.M.

Christmas Tree Lighting ceremony, Genovia Palace
Courtyard

11:30 A.M.–1 P.M.

Meet with Genovian Historical Society

1 P.M.–3 P.M.

Lunch with Genovian Board of Tourism

3:30 P.M.–5:30 P.M.

Tour of Genovian National Art Museum

6 P.M.–7 P.M.

Visit Genovian War Veterans Memorial,
place flowers on grave of Unknown Soldier

7:30 P.M.–8:30 P.M.

Change for dinner

8:30 P.M.–11:30 P.M.

Dinner with Royal Family of Monaco

And so on.

It all culminates in my appearance on my dad's annual nationally televised Christmas Eve address to the people of Genovia, during which he will introduce me to the populace. I am then supposed to make a speech about how thrilled I am to be Dad's heir, and how I promise to try to do as good a job as he has at leading Genovia into the twenty-first century.

Nervous? Me? About going on TV and promising fifty thousand people that I won't let their country down?

Nah. Not me.

I just want to throw up every time I think about it, that's all.

Whatever. Not that I thought my trip to Genovia was going to be like going to Disneyland, but still. You'd think they'd have scheduled in *some* fun time. I'm not even asking for Mr. Toad's Wild Ride. Just like some swimming or horseback riding.

But apparently, there is no time for fun in Genovia.

As if going over my itinerary wasn't bad enough, I also had to meet my cousin Sebastiano. Sebastiano Grimaldi is my dead grandfather's sister's daughter's kid. Which I guess actually makes him my cousin a couple times removed. But not removed enough that, if it weren't for me, he wouldn't be inheriting the throne to Genovia.

Seriously. If my dad had died without ever having had a kid, Sebastiano would be the next prince of Genovia.

Maybe that's why my dad, every time he looks at Sebastiano, heaves this big shudder.

Or maybe it's just because my dad feels about Sebastiano the way I feel about my cousin Hank: I like him in theory, but in actual practice, he kind of bugs me.

Sebastiano doesn't bug Grandmère, though. You can tell that Grandmère just loves him. Which is really weird, because I always supposed Grandmère was incapable of loving anyone. Well, with the exception of Rommel, her miniature poodle.

But you can tell she totally adores Sebastiano. When she introduced him to me, and he bowed with this big flourish and kissed the air above my hand, Grandmère was practically beaming beneath her pink silk turban. Really.

I have never seen Grandmère beam before. Glare, plenty of times. But never beam.

Which might be why my dad started chewing the ice in his whiskey and soda in a very irritated manner. Grandmère's smile disappeared right away when she heard all that crunching.

"If you want to chew ice, Phillipe," Grandmère said, coldly, "you can go and have your dinner at McDonald's with the rest of the proletariat."

My dad stopped chewing his ice.

It turns out Grandmère brought Sebastiano over from Genovia so that he could design my dress for my nationally televised introduction to my countrymen. Sebastiano is a very up-and-coming fashion designer—at least according to Grandmère. She says it is important that Genovia supports its artists and craftspeople, or they will all flee to New York, or even worse, Los Angeles.

Which is too bad for Sebastiano, since he looks like the type who might really enjoy living in LA. He is thirtyish, with long, dark hair tied back in a ponytail, and is all tall and flamboyant-looking. Like for instance, tonight, instead of a tie, Sebastiano was wearing a white silk ascot. And he had on a blue velvet jacket with leather pants.

I am fully prepared to forgive Sebastiano for the

leather pants if he designs me a dress that is nice enough. A dress that, should he happen to see me in it, will make Michael Moscovitz forget all about Judith Gershner and her fruit flies, and fill his head with nothing but thoughts of me, Mia Thermopolis.

Only of course the chances of Michael ever actually seeing me in this dress are very slim, as my introduction to the Genovian people is only going to be on Genovian television, not CNN or anything.

Still, Sebastiano seemed ready to rise to the challenge. After dinner, he even took out a pen and began sketching—right on the white tablecloth!—a design he thought might accentuate what he called my narrow waist and long legs.

Only, unlike my dad, who was born and raised in Genovia but speaks fluent English, Sebastiano doesn't have a real keen grasp of the language. He kept forgetting the second syllables of words. So *narrow* became "nar." Just like *coffee* became "coff," and when he described something as magical, it came out as "madge." Even the butter wasn't safe. When Sebastiano asked me to please pass him the "butt," I had to practically stuff my napkin in my mouth to keep from laughing out loud.

All my efforts to stifle myself didn't do any good, though, since Grandmère caught me and, raising one of her drawn-on eyebrows, went, "Amelia, kindly do not make light of other people's speech habits. Your own are not even remotely perfect."

Which is certainly true, considering the fact that, with my swollen tongue, I can't really say any word that starts with *s*.

Not only did Grandmère not mind Sebastiano saying the word *butt* at the dinner table, she didn't mind his drawing on the tablecloth, either. She looked down at his sketch and said, "Brilliant. Simply brilliant. As usual."

Sebastiano looked very pleased. "Do you real think so?" he asked.

Only I didn't think his sketch was so brilliant. It just looked like an ordinary dress to me. Certainly nothing to make anyone forget the fact that I'm about as likely to clone a fruit fly as I am to use animal-tested hair products.

"Um," I said. "Can't you make it a little more . . . I don't know . . . sexy?"

Grandmère and Sebastiano exchanged looks. "Sexy?" Grandmère echoed, with an evil laugh. "How? By making it lower cut? But you haven't got anything there to show!"

Now, seriously. I would expect to hear this kind of thing from the cheerleaders at school, who have made demeaning other people—especially me—a sort of new Olympic sport. But what kind of person says things like this to her only grandchild? I had meant, of course, a side slit, or maybe some fringe. I wasn't asking for anything Jennifer Lopez-ish.

But trust Grandmère to turn it into something like that. Why do I have to be cursed with a grandmother who shaves off her eyebrows and seems to enjoy making light of my inadequacies? Why can't I have a normal grandmother, who bakes me cookies and can't stop bragging to her friends in her bridge club about how wonderful I am?

It was while Grandmère and Sebastiano were cackling to themselves over this great witticism at my expense that my dad abruptly got up and left the table, saying he had to make a call. I suppose it's every man for himself where Grandmère is concerned, but you would think my own father would stick up for me once in a while.

I don't know, maybe I was feeling odd about the giant hole in my tongue (which doesn't even have a nice hypoallergenic stud in it so I can pretend to have done it on purpose to be controversial). I sat there listening to Grandmère and Sebastiano chatter away about how pathetic it was that I would never be able to wear anything strapless, unless some miracle of nature occurred one night that inflated me from a 32A to a 34C, and I couldn't help thinking that probably, given my luck, it will turn out that Sebastiano isn't in town just to design me a dress for my royal introduction, but to kill me so that he can assume the throne of Genovia himself.

Or, as Sebastiano would say, "ass" the throne.

Seriously. That kind of stuff happens on *Baywatch* all the time. You wouldn't believe the number of royal family members Mitch has had to save from assassination.

Like supposing I put on the dress that Sebastiano has designed for me to wear when I'm introduced to the people of Genovia, and it ends up squeezing me to death, just like that corset Snow White puts on in the original version of the story by the Brothers Grimm. You know, the part they left out of the Disney movie because it was too gruesome.

Anyway, what if the dress squeezes me to death, and then I'm lying in my coffin, looking all pale and queenly, and Michael comes to my funeral and ends up gazing down at me and doesn't realize until right then that he has always loved me?

Then he'll *have* to break up with Judith Gershner.

Hey. It could happen.

Okay, well, probably not, but thinking about that was better than listening to Grandmère and Sebastiano talk about me as if I weren't even there. Seriously. I was roused from my pleasant little fantasy about Michael pining for me for the rest of his life by Sebastiano saying suddenly, "She has bute bone struck," which, when I realized I was the *she* he was referring to, I took to be a compliment about my bone structure.

Only a second later it wasn't such a compliment when he went, "I put makeup on her that make her look like a mod."

Implying I don't look like a model without makeup (although of course I don't).

Grandmère certainly wasn't about to come to my defense, however. She was feeding bits of her leftover veal marsala to Rommel, who was sitting on her lap, shivering as usual, since all of his fur has fallen out due to canine allergies.

"I wouldn't count on her father letting you," she said to Sebastiano. "Phillipe is hopelessly old-fashioned."

Which is so the pot calling the kettle black! I mean, Grandmère still thinks that cats go around trying to suck the breath out of their owners while they are sleeping. Seriously. She is always trying to convince me to give Fat Louie away.

So while Grandmère was going on about how old-fashioned her son is, I got up and joined him on the balcony.

He was checking his messages on his cell phone. He's supposed to play racquetball tomorrow with the prime minister of France, who is in town for the same summit as the emperor of Japan.

"Mia," he said, when he saw me. "What are you doing out here? It's freezing. Go back inside."

"I will, in a minute," I said. I stood there next to him and looked out over the city. It really is kind of awe-inspiring, the view of Manhattan from the penthouse of the Plaza Hotel. I mean, you look at all those lights in all those windows, and you think, for each light there's probably at least one person, but maybe even more, maybe even like ten people, and that's, well, pretty mind-boggling.

I've lived in Manhattan my whole life. But it still impresses me.

Anyway, while I was standing there looking at all the lights, I suddenly realized that one of them probably belonged to Judith Gershner. Judith was probably sitting in her room right this moment cloning something new. A pigeon, or whatever. I got yet another flashback of her and Michael looking down at me after I'd split open my tongue. Hmmm, let me see: Girl who can clone things, or girl who bit her own tongue? I don't know, who would *you* choose?

My dad must have noticed something was wrong, since he went, "Look, I know Sebastiano is a bit much, but just put up with him for the next couple of weeks. For my sake."

"I wasn't thinking about Sebastiano," I said sadly.

My dad made this grunting noise, but he made no

move to go back inside, even though it was about forty degrees out there, and my dad, well, he's completely bald. I could see that the tips of his ears were getting red with cold, but still he didn't budge. He didn't even have a coat on, just another one of his charcoal-gray Armani suits.

I figured this was invitation enough to go on. You see, ordinarily my dad is not who I would go to first if I had a problem. Not that we're not close. It's just that, you know, he's a guy.

On the other hand, he's had a lot of experience in the romance department, so I figured he might just be able to offer some insight into this particular dilemma.

"Dad," I said. "What do you do if you like someone, but they don't, you know, know it?"

My dad went, "If Kenny doesn't know you like him by now, then I'm afraid he's never going to get the message. Haven't you been out with him every weekend since Halloween?"

This is the problem with having a bodyguard who is on your father's payroll: All your personal business totally gets discussed behind your back.

"I'm not talking about Kenny, Dad," I said. "It's someone else. Only like I said, he doesn't know I like him."

"What's wrong with Kenny?" my dad wanted to know. "I like Kenny."

Of course my dad likes Kenny. Because the chances

of me and Kenny ever getting past first base are like nil. What father doesn't want his teenage daughter to date a guy like that?

But if my dad has any serious hope of keeping the Genovian throne in the hands of the Renaldos, and not allowing it to slip into Sebastiano's control, he had better get over the whole Kenny thing, because I'm pretty sure that Kenny and I will not be doing any procreating. In this lifetime, anyway.

"Dad," I said. "Forget Kenny, okay? Kenny and I are just friends. I'm talking about someone else."

My dad was looking over the side of the balcony railing like he wanted to spit. Not that he ever would. I don't think. "Do I know him? This someone else, I mean?"

I hesitated. I've never really admitted to anyone out loud that I have a crush on Michael. Really. Not to anybody. I mean, who could I tell? Lilly would just make fun of me, or worse, tell Michael. And Mom, well, she's got her own problems.

"It's Lilly's brother," I said in a rush, to get it over with.

My dad looked alarmed. "Isn't he in college?"

"Not yet," I said. "He's going in the fall." When he still looked alarmed, I said, "Don't worry, Dad. I don't stand a chance. Michael is very smart. He'd never like someone like me."

Then my dad got all offended. It was like he couldn't

figure out which to be, worried about my liking a senior, or angry that that senior didn't like me back.

"What do you mean, he'd never like someone like you?" my father demanded. "What's wrong with you?"

"Duh, Dad," I said. "I practically flunked Algebra, remember? Michael is going to an Ivy League school in the fall, for crying out loud. What would he want with a girl like me?"

Now my dad was *really* annoyed: "You may take after your mother as far as your aptitude with numbers is concerned, but you take after me in every other respect."

This was surprising to hear. I stuck out my chin and tried to believe it. "Yeah," I said.

"And you and I, Mia, are not unintelligent," my dad went on. "If you want this Michael fellow, you must let him know it."

"You think I should just go up to him and be like, 'Hey, I like you'?"

My dad shook his head in disgust. "No, no, no," he said. "Of course you must be more subtle than that. Tell him by *showing* how you feel."

"Oh," I said. I may take after my father in every respect except my math aptitude, but I had no idea what he was talking about.

"We'd better get back in," my father said. "Or your grandmother will suspect us of plotting against her."

So what else is new? Grandmère is always suspecting somebody of plotting something against her. She thinks the launderers at the Plaza are plotting against her. She blames the soap they use on their linens for making all of Rommel's fur fall out.

Reminded of plots, I asked my dad, "Do you think Sebastiano's plotting to kill me so he can ascend the throne himself?"

My dad made a strangled noise, but he managed not to burst out laughing. I guess that wouldn't have seemed very princely.

"No, Mia," he said. "I do not."

But my dad, he really doesn't have much of an imagination. I have decided to stay on alert about Sebastiano, just in case.

My mom just poked her head into my room to say that Kenny is on the phone for me.

I suppose he wants to ask me to the Nondenominational Winter Dance. Really, it is about time.

SUNDAY, DECEMBER 7, 11 P.M.

Okay. I am in shock. Kenny so did NOT ask me to the Nondenominational Winter Dance. Instead, this is how our conversation went:

> *Me:* Hello?
> *Kenny:* Hi, Mia. It's Kenny.
> *Me:* Oh, hi, Kenny. What's the matter?

Kenny sounded funny, which is why I asked.

> *Kenny:* Well, I just wanted to see if you were okay. I mean, if your tongue was okay.
> *Me:* It's a little better, I guess.
> *Kenny:* Because I was really worried. You know. I really, really didn't mean to—
> *Me:* Kenny, I know. It was just an accident.

This is when I started realizing I'd asked my dad the wrong question. I should have asked him what's the best way to break up with somebody, not what's the best way to let someone know you like them.

Anyway, to get back to what Kenny said:

Kenny: Well, I just wanted to call and wish you a good night. And say that I hope you feel better. And also to let you know . . . well, Mia, that I love you.

Me: . . .

I didn't say anything right away, because I was completely FREAKED OUT!!!! It wasn't exactly as if it happened out of the blue, because we are sort of going out, after all.

But still, what kind of guy calls a girl on the phone and says I love you??? Except for weird psycho stalkers? And Kenny's not a weird psycho stalker. He's just Kenny. So what's he doing calling me on the phone and telling me he loves me????

And then, brilliant me, here's what I do. Because he was still on the phone, waiting for an answer, and all. So I go:

Me: Um, okay.

Um, okay.

A boy says he loves me, and this is how I respond: "Um, okay." Oh, yeah, good thing my future career lies in the diplomatic corps.

So then, poor Kenny, he's like waiting for some response other than "Um, okay," as anybody would.

But I am perfectly incapable of giving him one. Instead, I just go:

Me: Well, see you tomorrow.

AND I HUNG UP!!!!!

Oh, my God, I am the meanest, most ungrateful girl in the world. After Sebastiano kills me, I am going to burn in hell.

Seriously.

TO DO BEFORE LEAVING FOR GENOVIA

1. Detailed list for Mom and Mr. G: How to care for Fat Louie while I am away
2. Stock up on cat food, litter
3. Christmas/Hannukah presents! For:

   Mom—electric breast pump? Check on this.

   Mr. G—new drumsticks

   Dad—book on vegetarianism. He should eat better if he wants to keep his cancer in remission.

   Lilly—what she always wants, blank videotapes for her show

   Lars—see if Prada makes a shoulder holster that would fit his Glock

   Kenny—gloves? Something NON-romantic

   Fat Louie—catnip ball

   Grandmère—What do you get for the woman who has everything, including an eighty-nine-carat sapphire pendant given to her by the sultan of Brunei? Soap on a rope?
4. Break up with Kenny. . . . Only how can I? He LOVES me.

But not enough to ask me to the Nondenominational Winter Dance, I've noticed.

MONDAY, DECEMBER 8, HOMEROOM

Lilly doesn't believe me about Kenny calling and saying he loves me. I told her in the car on the way to school this morning (thank God Michael had a dentist appointment and wasn't there. I would sooner die than discuss my love life in front of him. It's bad enough having to discuss it in front of my bodyguard. If I had to discuss it in front of this person I've been worshiping for half my life, I think I'd probably go completely borderline personality disorder).

Anyway, so Lilly went, "I categorically refuse to believe Kenny would do something like that."

"Lilly," I said. I had to keep my voice down so the driver wouldn't hear. "I am dead serious. He told me he loves me. *I love you*. That is what he said. It was completely random and weird."

"He probably didn't say that. He probably said something else, and you misunderstood him."

"Oh, what? I *glove* you?"

"Well, of course not," Lilly said. "That doesn't even make any sense."

"Well, then what? What could Kenny have said that sounded like *I love you*, but wasn't *I love you*?"

Lilly got mad then. She went, "You know, you have been acting weird about Kenny for the past month. Since the two of you started going out, practically. I don't know what's wrong with you. All I ever heard before was 'Why don't I have a boyfriend? How come everybody I know has a boyfriend but me? When am I going to get a boyfriend?' And now you've got one and you aren't the least bit appreciative of him."

Even though what she was saying was true, I acted offended, because I have been trying really hard not to let the fact that I am not in love with Kenny show.

"That is so false," I said. "I completely appreciate Kenny."

"Oh, yeah? I think the truth of the matter is, you, Mia, simply aren't ready to have a boyfriend."

Boy did I see red after *that* remark.

"*Me?* Not ready to have a boyfriend? Are you kidding? I've been waiting my whole life to have a boyfriend!"

"Well, if that's true"—Lilly was looking very superior—"why won't you let him kiss you on the lips?"

"Where did you hear *that*?" I demanded.

"Kenny told Boris, of course, who told me."

"Oh, great," I said, trying to remain calm. "So now

our boyfriends are talking about us behind our backs. And you're condoning this?"

"Of course not," Lilly said. "But I do find it intriguing, from a psychological point of view."

This is the problem with being best friends with someone whose parents are psychiatrists. Everything you do is interesting to them from a psychological point of view.

"Where I let anybody kiss me," I exploded, "is *my* business! Not yours, and not Boris's, either."

"Well," Lilly said. "I'm just saying, if Kenny did say what you say he said—you know, the L word—then maybe he said it because he can't express the depth of his feelings any other way. You know. Other than *verbally*. Since you won't *let* him, physically."

So I suppose that technically I should be thankful that Kenny chose merely to say the words I love you, rather than enacting them physically, which, God knows, might have actually involved his tongue.

Oh, God, I don't even want to think about it anymore.

MONDAY, DECEMBER 8, HOMEROOM

They just passed out the final exam schedules. Here is mine:

FINAL EXAM SCHEDULE

DECEMBER 15
Reading Day

DECEMBER 16
Periods One and Two

For me, that means the Algebra and English finals will be on the same day. But that's okay. I'm doing pretty good in English. Well, except for that sentence diagramming thing. As if I'll ever need to do *that* in my future role as princess of the smallest nation in Europe.

Unfortunately, Algebra, I am told, I will probably need to know. DAMN!

DECEMBER 17

Periods Three and Four

World Civ: Easy. I mean, Grandmère has told me enough stories about post–World War II Europe for me to pass any test. I probably know more about it than the teacher. And PE? How can you give a final in PE? We already had the Presidential Fitness Test (I did okay on everything but the V-sit reach).

DECEMBER 18

Periods Five, Six, and Seven

Gifted and Talented? No exam there. They don't give finals in classes that are basically study hall. That will be a snap. I have French sixth period. I do okay in oral, not so great in written. Fortunately Tina's in the same class. Maybe we can study together.

But I have Bio seventh period. That won't be so easy. The only reason I'm not flunking Bio is because of Kenny. He slips me most of the answers.

And if I break up with him, that will be the end of that.

DECEMBER 19

Nondenominational Winter Carnival and Dance

The Winter Carnival should be fun. All the different school clubs and groups are going to have booths, with traditional winter fare, like hot cider. This will be followed in the evening by the dance I am supposed to go to with Kenny. If he ever asks me to it, I mean.

Unless, of course, I do the right thing and break up with him.

In which case, I won't be able to go at all, because you can't go without a date.

I wish Sebastiano would just hurry up and off me already.

MONDAY, DECEMBER 8, ALGEBRA

WHY???? WHY can't I ever remember my Algebra notebook?????

FIRST—Evaluate exponents
SECOND—Multiply and divide in order, left to right
THIRD—Perform addition and subtraction in order, left to right
EXAMPLE: $2 \times 3 - 15 \div 5 = 6 - 3 = 3$

Oh, God. Lana Weinberger just tossed me a note.

What now? This can't be good. Lana's had it out for me forever. Don't ask me why. I mean, I could kind of understand her resenting me for when Josh Richter asked me to the Cultural Diversity Dance instead of her. But he only asked me because of the princess thing—and they got back together right after. Besides, Lana hated me long before that.

So I open the note. Here's what it says:

I heard what happened to you at the skating rink this weekend. Guess the BF is going to have to wait a little longer if he wants to see any tongue action, huh?

Oh, my God. Does *everyone* in the entire school know that Kenny and I have not yet French-kissed?

It is all Kenny's fault, of course.

What next? The cover of the *Post*?

I'm telling you, if our parents knew what actually goes on every day in the typical American high school, they would totally opt for homeschooling.

MONDAY, DECEMBER 8, WORLD CIV

It's clear what I have to do.

I've always known it, of course, and if it hadn't been for, you know, the dance, I would have done it long before now.

But it is clear now that I cannot afford to wait until after the dance. I should have done it last night when he called, but you can't really do something like that over the phone. Well, a girl like Lana Weinberger probably could, but not me.

No, I don't think I can put it off another day: I have got to break up with Kenny. I simply cannot continue living this lie.

Fortunately, I do have the support of at least one person in this plan: Tina Hakim Baba.

I didn't want to tell her. I didn't plan on telling anybody. But it all sort of slipped out today in the girls' room between second and third periods while Tina was putting on her eye makeup. Her dad won't let her wear makeup, you see, so Tina has to wait until she gets to school to put it on. She has a deal with her bodyguard, Wahim. Tina won't tell her parents how much Wahim flirts with Mademoiselle Klein, our French teacher, if Wahim doesn't tell Mr. and Mrs. Hakim Baba about Tina's Maybelline addiction.

Anyway, all of a sudden I just couldn't take it anymore, and I ended up telling Tina what Kenny said last night on the phone—

And a lot more than that actually.

But first the part about Kenny's phone call:

Unlike Lilly, *Tina* believed me.

But Tina also had the totally wrong reaction. She thought it was great.

"Oh, my God, Mia, you are so lucky," she kept saying. "I wish Dave would tell me he loves me! I mean, I know he is fully committed to our relationship, but his idea of romance is paying to have my fries super-sized at Mickey D's."

This was so not the kind of support I was looking for.

"But, Tina," I said. I felt Tina, with her extensive reading of romances, would understand. "The thing is, I don't love him."

Tina widened her mascaraed eyes at me. "You don't?"

"No," I said, miserably. "I really like him, as a friend. But I'm not in love, or anything. Not with him."

"Oh, God," Tina said, reaching out and grabbing my wrist. "There's someone else, isn't there?"

We only had a few minutes before the bell rang. We both had to get to class.

And yet, for some reason, I chose this moment to make my big confession. I don't know why. Maybe since I'd already spilled it to my dad, it didn't seem too hard to tell someone else, especially Tina. Also, I can't stop thinking about what my dad said. You know, about showing the guy I like how I feel. Tina, I felt, was the only person I knew who would know how to help me do that.

So I went, "Yes."

Tina nearly spilled her cosmetics bag, she was so excited.

"I knew it!" she yelled. "I knew there was a reason you wouldn't let him kiss you!"

My jaw dropped. "*You* know about that, too?"

"Well." Tina shrugged. "Kenny told Dave, who told me."

Jeez! What's that Oprah always complaining about, about how men aren't in touch with their emotions, and don't share enough? It sounds to me like Kenny's been doing enough sharing recently to make up for several centuries' worth of masculine reticence.

"So who is he?" Tina asked, all eager as she packed up her eyelash curler and lipliner. "The guy you like?"

I went, "It doesn't matter. Besides, the whole thing is completely futile. He sort of has a girlfriend. I think."

Tina whipped her head around to look at me, making her thick, black braid smack her in her own face.

"It's Michael, isn't it?" she demanded, grabbing my arm again. She was holding on so tight it hurt.

My instinct, of course, was to deny it. In fact, I even opened my mouth, all set to have the word *No* come out of it.

But then I was like, Why? Why should I deny it to Tina? Tina wouldn't tell anyone. And Tina might be able to help me.

So instead of saying *No,* I took a deep breath, and said, "If you tell anyone, I'll kill you, understand? KILL YOU."

Tina did a strange thing then. She let go of my arm and started jumping up and down in a circle.

"I knew it, I knew it, I knew it," she said, as she jumped. Then she stopped jumping and grabbed my arm again. "Oh, Mia, I always thought you two would make the cutest couple. I mean, I like Kenny and all, but he's, you know." She wrinkled up her nose. "Not Michael."

If I had thought it felt strange last night telling my dad the truth about my feelings for Michael, that was nothing—NOTHING—compared to how it felt to be telling someone my own age. The fact that Tina hadn't burst out laughing or gone, "Yeah, right," in a sarcastic way meant more to me than I ever would have expected.

And the fact that she seemed to understand—even applaud—my feelings for Michael made me want to fling my arms around her and give her a great big hug.

Only there was no time for that, since the bell was about to ring.

Instead, I gushed, "Really? You really don't think it's stupid?"

"Duh," Tina said. "Michael is *hot*. *And* he's a senior." Then she looked troubled. "But what about Kenny? And Judith?"

"I know," I said, my shoulders slumping in a manner that would have caused Grandmère to rap me on the back of the head, if she'd seen them. "Tina, I don't know what to do."

Tina's dark eyebrows furrowed with concentration.

"I think I read a book where this happened once," she said. "*Listen to My Heart,* it was called, I think. If I could just remember how they resolved everything—"

But before she could remember, the bell rang. We were both totally late to class.

But if you ask me, it was worth it. Because now, at least, I don't have to worry alone. I have somebody else worrying with me.

MONDAY, DECEMBER 8, G & T

Lunch was a disaster.

Considering that everybody in the entire school seems to know, in the minutest detail, exactly what I've been doing—or not doing—with my tongue lately, I guess I shouldn't have been surprised. But it was even worse than I could have imagined.

That's because I ran into Michael at the salad bar. I was creating my usual chickpea-and-pinto-bean pyramid when I saw him headed for the burger grill (despite my best efforts, both Moscovitzes remain stubbornly carnivorous).

Seriously, all I did was say "Fine" when he asked how I was doing. You know, on account of how last time he saw me, I was bleeding out of the mouth (what a nice picture that must have been. I am so glad that I have been able to maintain an appearance of dignity and beauty at all times in front of the man I love).

Anyway, then I asked him, just to be polite, you know, how his dentist appointment went. What happened next was not my fault.

Which was that Michael started telling me about how he'd had to have this cavity filled, and that his lips were still numb from the novocaine. Seeing as how I have experienced a certain amount of sensation-deadening, what with my gouged tongue, I could relate to this, so I just sort of, you know, *looked* at Michael's lips while he was talking, which I have never really done before. I mean, I have looked at other parts of Michael's body (particularly when he comes into the kitchen in the morning with no shirt on, like he does every time I have a sleepover at Lilly's). But I've never really looked at his lips. You know. Up close.

Michael actually has very nice lips. Not thin lips, like mine. I don't know if you should say this about a boy's lips, but Michael's lips look like if you kissed them, they'd be very soft.

It was while I was noticing this about Michael's lips that the very bad thing happened: I was looking at them, you know, and wondering if they'd be soft to kiss, and as I looked, I sort of actually pictured us kissing, in my head. And right then I got this very warm feeling—the one they talk about in all of Tina's romance novels—and RIGHT THEN was when Kenny went by on his way to get his usual lunch: Coke and an ice-cream sandwich.

I know Kenny can't read my mind—if he could, he

totally would have broken up with me by now—but maybe he caught some hint as to what I was thinking, and that's why he didn't say *Hi* back, when Michael and I said *Hi* to him.

Well, that and the whole part where I said, "Um, okay," after he said he loved me.

Kenny must have known something was up, if my face was anywhere near as red-hot as it felt. Maybe *that's* why he didn't say *Hi* back. Because I was looking so guilty. I'd certainly *felt* guilty. I mean, there I was, looking at another guy's lips and wondering what it would be like to kiss them, and my boyfriend goes walking by.

I am so going to bad-girl hell when I die.

You know what I wish? I wish everyone *could* read my mind. Because then Kenny would never have asked me out. He'd have known I don't think of him that way. And Lilly wouldn't make fun of me for not letting Kenny kiss me. She would know the reason I don't is that I'm in love with someone else.

The bad part is, she'd know who that someone else is.

And that someone probably won't even speak to me again, because it's totally uncool for a senior to go out with a freshman. Especially one who can't go anywhere without a bodyguard.

Besides, I'm almost positive he's going out with Judith

Gershner, because after he came back from the grill, he went and sat down next to her.

So that settles that.

I wish I were leaving for Genovia tomorrow instead of in two weeks.

MONDAY, DECEMBER 8, FRENCH

In spite of that disastrous incident at lunch, I had a pretty good time in Gifted and Talented. In fact, it was almost like old times again. I mean, before we all started going out with each other and everyone became so obsessed with the inner workings of my mouth, and all that.

Mrs. Hill spent the whole class period in the teachers' lounge across the hall, yelling at American Express on the phone, leaving us free to do what we usually do during her class . . . whatever we wanted. For instance, those of us who, like Lilly's boyfriend, Boris, wanted to work on our individual projects (Boris is learning to play some new sonata on his violin), which is what Gifted and Talented class is supposedly for, did so.

Those of us, however, like Lilly and me, who did not want to work on our individual projects (mine is studying for Algebra; Lilly's is working on her cable access TV show) did not.

This was especially satisfying, because Lilly had completely forgotten about the whole kissing thing between

Kenny and me. The reason for this is that now she's mad at Mrs. Spears, her honors English teacher, who shot down her term paper proposal.

It really was unfair of Mrs. Spears to turn it down, because it was actually very well thought out, and quite creative. I made a copy of it:

HOW TO SURVIVE HIGH SCHOOL
by Lilly Moscovitz

Having spent the past two months locked in that institution of secondary education commonly referred to as high school, I feel that I am a qualified authority on the subject. From pep rallies to morning announcements, I have observed high school life and all its complexities. Sometime in the next four years, I will be granted my freedom from this festering hellhole, and then I will publish my carefully compiled *High School Survival Guide*.

Little did my peers and teachers know that as they went about their daily routines, I was recording their activities for study by future generations. With my handy guide, every ninth grader's sojourn in high school can be a little more fruitful. Students of the future will learn that the way to settle their differences with their peers is not through violence, but through the sale of a really scathing screenplay—featuring characters based on those very individuals who tormented them all those years—to a major Hollywood movie studio. That, not a Molotov cocktail, is the path to true glory.

Here, for your reading pleasure, are a few examples of the topics I will explore in *How to Survive High School*, by Lilly Moscovitz:

1. High School Romance, or How I Cannot Open My Locker Because Two Oversexed Adolescents Are Leaning Up Against It, Making Out
2. Cafeteria Food: Can Corn Dogs Legally Be Listed as a Meat Product?
3. How to Communicate with the Subhumans Who Populate the Hallways
4. Guidance Counselors: Who Do They Think They're Kidding?
5. Get Ahead by Forging: The Art of the Hall Pass

Does that sound good, or what? Now look what Mrs. Spears had to say about it:

> *Lilly—Sorry as I am to hear that your experience thus far at AEHS has not been a positive one, I am afraid I am going to have to make it worse by asking you to find another topic for your term paper. A for creativity, as usual, however.*
> *—Mrs. Spears*

Can you believe that? Talk about unfair! Lilly's been censored! By rights, her proposal ought to have brought the school's administration to its knees. Lilly says she is appalled by the fact that, considering how much our tuition costs, this is the kind of support we can expect from our teachers. Then I reminded her that that isn't true of Mr. Gianini, who really goes beyond the call of duty by staying after school every day to conduct help sessions for people like me, who aren't doing so well in Algebra.

Lilly says Mr. Gianini probably only started pulling that staying-after-school thing so that he could ingratiate himself to my mother, and now he can't stop, because then she'll realize it was all just a setup and divorce him.

I don't believe that, however. I think Mr. G would have stayed after school to help me whether he was dating my mom or not. He's that kind of guy.

Anyway, the upshot of it all is that now Lilly has launched another one of her famous campaigns. This is actually a good thing, as it will keep her mind off me and where I am putting (or not putting) my lips. Here's how it started:

Lilly: The real problem with this school isn't the teachers. It's the apathy of the student body. For instance, let's say we wanted to stage a walkout.

Me: A walkout?

Lilly: You know. We all get up and walk out of the school at the same time.

Me: Just because Mrs. Spears turned down your term paper proposal?

Lilly: No, Mia. Because she's trying to usurp our individuality by forcing us to bend to corporate feudalism. Again.

Me: Oh. And how is she doing that?

Lilly: By censoring us when we are at our most fertile, creatively speaking.

Boris: (leaning out of the supply closet, where Lilly made him go when he started practicing his latest sonata) Fertile? Did someone say *fertile*?

Lilly: Get back in the closet, Boris. Michael, can you send a mass email tonight to the entire student body, declaring a walkout tomorrow at eleven?

Michael: (working on the booth he and Judith Gershner and the rest of the Computer Club are going to have up at the Winter Carnival) I can, but I won't.

Lilly: WHY NOT?

Michael: Because it was your turn to empty the dishwasher last night, but you weren't home, so I had to do it.

Lilly: But I TOLD Mom I had to go down to the studio to edit the last few finishing touches on this week's show!

Lilly's TV program, *Lilly Tells It Like It Is*, is now one of the highest-ranked shows on Manhattan cable. Of course, it's public access, so it's not like she's making any money off it, but a bunch of the major networks picked up this interview she did of me one night when I was half asleep and played it. I thought it was stupid, but I guess a lot of other people thought it was good, because now Lilly gets tons of viewer mail, whereas before the only mail she got was from her stalker, Norman.

Michael: Look, if you're having time-management issues, don't take it out on me. Just don't expect me to meekly do your bidding, especially when you already owe me one.

Me: Lilly, no offense, but I don't think this week's a good time for a walkout, anyway. I mean, after all, it's almost finals.

Lilly: SO???

Me: So some of us really need to stay in class. I can't afford to miss any review sessions. My grades are bad enough as it is.

Michael: Really? I thought you were doing better in Algebra.

Me: If you call a D plus better.

Michael: Aw, come on. You have to be making better than a D plus. Your mom is married to your Algebra teacher!

Me: So? That doesn't mean anything. You know Mr. G doesn't play favorites.

Michael: I would think he'd cut his own stepdaughter a little slack, is all.

Lilly: WOULD YOU TWO PLEASE PAY ATTENTION TO THE SITUATION AT HAND, WHICH IS THE FACT THAT THIS SCHOOL IS IN VITAL NEED OF SERIOUS REFORM?

Fortunately at that moment the bell rang, so no walkout tomorrow as far as I know. Which is a good thing, because I really need the extra study time.

You know, it's funny about Mrs. Spears not liking Lilly's term paper proposal, because she was very enthusiastic about my proposal, *A Case Against Christmas Trees: Why We Must Curtail the Pagan Ritual of Chopping Down Pine Trees Every December If We Are Going to Repair the Ozone Layer.*

And my IQ isn't anywhere near as high as Lilly's.

MONDAY, DECEMBER 8, BIO

Kenny just passed me the following note:

> *Mia—I hope what I said to you last night didn't make you feel uncomfortable. I just wanted you to know how I feel.*
> *Sincerely,*
> *Kenny*

Oh, God. *Now* what am I supposed to do? He's sitting here next to me, waiting for an answer. In fact, that's what he thinks I'm writing right now. An answer.

What do I say?

Maybe this is my perfect opportunity to break up with him. *I'm sorry, Kenny, but I don't feel the same way— let's just be friends.* Is that what I should say?

It's just that I don't want to hurt his feelings, you know? And he is my Bio partner. I mean, whatever happens, I am going to have to sit next to him for the next two weeks. And I would much rather have a Bio partner who likes me than one who hates me.

And what about the dance? I mean, if I break up with him, who am I going to go to the Nondenominational Winter Dance with? I know it is horrible to think things like this, but this is the first dance in the history of my life to which I already have a date.

Well, I mean, if he'd ever get around to asking me.

And how about that final, huh? Our Bio final, I mean. No way am I going to be able to pass without Kenny's notes. NO WAY.

But what else can I do? I mean, considering what happened today at the salad bar.

This is it. Good-bye, date for the Nondenominational Winter Dance. Hello, Friday-night television.

Dear Kenny,
It isn't that I don't think of you as a very dear friend. It's just that—

MONDAY, DECEMBER 8, 3 P.M., MR. GIANINI'S ALGEBRA REVIEW

Okay, so the bell rang before I had time to finish my note.

That doesn't mean I'm not going to tell Kenny exactly how I feel. I totally am. Tonight, as a matter of fact. I don't care if it's cruel to do something like that over the phone. I just can't take it anymore.

HOMEWORK

ALGEBRA: REVIEW QUESTIONS AT THE END OF
    CHAPTERS 1–3
ENGLISH: TERM PAPER
WORLD CIV: REVIEW QUESTIONS AT THE END OF
    CHAPTERS 1–4
G & T: NONE
FRENCH: REVIEW QUESTIONS AT THE END OF CHAPTERS
    1–3
BIOLOGY: REVIEW QUESTIONS AT THE END OF
    CHAPTERS 1–5

TUESDAY, DECEMBER 9, HOMEROOM

All right. So I didn't break up with him.

I totally meant to.

And it wasn't even because I didn't have the heart to do it over the phone, either.

It was something *Grandmère*, of all people, said.

Not that I feel right about it. Not breaking up with him, I mean. It's just that after Algebra review, I had to go to the showroom where Sebastiano is flogging his latest creations, so that he could have his flunkies take my measurements for my dress. Grandmère was going on about how from now on, I should really only wear clothes by Genovian designers, to show my patriotism, or whatever. Which is going to be hard, because, uh, there's only one Genovian clothing designer that I know of, and that's Sebastiano. And let's just say he doesn't make very much out of denim.

But whatever. I so had more important things to worry about than my spring wardrobe.

Which I guess Grandmère must have caught on to,

because midway through Sebastiano's description of the beading he was going to have sewn onto my gown's bodice, Grandmère shouted, "Amelia, what is the matter with you?"

I must have jumped about a foot in the air. "What?"

"Sebastiano asked if you prefer a sweetheart or square-cut neckline."

I stared at her blankly. "Neckline for what?"

Grandmère gave me the evil eye. She does this quite frequently. That's why my father, even though he has the neighboring hotel suite, never stops by during my princess lessons.

"Sebastiano," my grandmother said. "You will please leave the princess and me for a moment."

And Sebastiano—who was wearing a new pair of leather pants, these in a tangerine color (the new gray, he told me; and white, you might be surprised to know, is the new black)—bowed and left the room, followed by the slinky ladies who'd been taking my measurements.

"Now," Grandmère said imperiously. "Something is clearly troubling you, Amelia. What is it?"

"It's nothing," I said, turning all red. I knew I was turning all red because: a) I could feel it, and b) I could see my reflection in the three full-length mirrors in front of me.

"It is not nothing." Grandmère took in a healthy drag from her Gitanes, even though I have asked her repeatedly not to smoke in my presence, as breathing secondhand smoke can cause just as much lung damage as actually smoking. "What is it? Trouble at home? Your mother and the math teacher fighting already, I suppose. Well, I never expected *that* marriage to last. Your mother is much too flighty."

I have to admit, I kind of snapped when she said that. Grandmère is always putting my mother down, even though Mom has raised me pretty much single-handedly and I certainly haven't gotten pregnant or shot anyone yet.

"For your information," I said, "my mom and Mr. Gianini are blissfully happy together. I wasn't thinking about them at all."

"What is it, then?" Grandmère asked in a bored voice.

"Nothing," I practically yelled. "I just—well, I was thinking about the fact that I have to break up with my boyfriend tonight, that's all. Not that it's any of your business."

Instead of taking offense at my tone, which any self-respecting grandparent would have found insolent, Grandmère only took a sip of her drink and suddenly looked way interested.

"Oh?" she said, in a totally different tone of voice—the

same tone of voice she uses when someone mentions a stock tip she thinks might be useful for her portfolio. "What boyfriend is this?"

God, what did I ever do to be cursed with such a grandmother? Seriously. Lilly and Michael's grandma remembers the names of all their friends, makes them rugelach all the time, and always worries that they're not getting enough to eat, even though their parents, the Drs. Moscovitz, are wholly reliable at bringing home groceries, or at least ordering out.

Me? I get the grandma with the hairless poodle and the nine-carat diamond rings whose greatest joy in life is to torture me.

And why is that, anyway? I mean, why does Grand-mère love to torture me so much? I've never done anything to her. Nothing except be her only grandchild, anyway. And it isn't exactly like I go around advertising how I feel about her. You know, I've never actually *told* her I think she's a mean old lady who contributes to the destruction of the environment by wearing fur coats and smoking fil-terless French cigarettes.

"Grandmère," I said, trying to remain calm. "I have only one boyfriend. His name is Kenny." I've only told you about fifty thousand times, I added, in my head.

"I thought this Kenny person was your Biology

partner," Grandmère said, after taking a sip of her Sidecar, her favorite drink.

"He is," I said, a little surprised that she'd managed to remember something like that. "He's also my boyfriend. Only last night he went completely psycho on me, and told me he loves me."

Grandmère patted Rommel, who was sitting in her lap looking miserable (his habitual expression), on the head.

"And what is so wrong," Grandmère wanted to know, "about a boy who says he loves you?"

"Nothing," I said. "Only I'm not in love with him, see? So it wouldn't be fair of me to, you know, lead him on."

Grandmère raised her painted-on eyebrows. "I don't see why not."

How had I ever gotten into this conversation? "Because, Grandmère. People just don't go around *doing* things like that. Not nowadays."

"Is that so? Well, my observations of people are to the contrary. Except, of course, if one happens to be in love with someone else. Then shedding an unwanted suitor might be considered wise, so that one can make oneself available to the man one truly desires." She eyed me. "Is there someone like that in your life, Amelia? Someone— ahem—special?"

"No." I lied, automatically.

Grandmère snorted. "You're lying."

"No, I'm not." I lied again.

"Indeed you are. I oughtn't tell you this, but I suppose as it is a bad habit for a future monarch, you ought to be made aware of it, so that in the future, you can try to prevent it: When you lie, Amelia, your nostrils flare."

I threw my hands up to my nose. "They do not!"

"Indeed," Grandmère said, clearly enjoying herself immensely. "If you do not believe me, look in the mirror."

I turned around to face the nearby full-length mirrors. Taking my hands from my face, I examined my nose. My nostrils weren't flaring. She was crazy.

"I'll ask you again, Amelia," Grandmère said, in a lazy voice, from her chair. "Are you in love with anyone right now?"

"No." I lied, automatically. . . .

And my nostrils flared right out!

Oh, my God! All these years I've been lying, and it turns out whenever I do, my nostrils totally give me away! All anyone has to do is look at my nose when I talk, and they'll know for sure whether or not I'm telling the truth.

How could no one have pointed this out to me before? And Grandmère—Grandmère, of all people—was the one who figured it out! Not my mother, with whom I've lived for fourteen years. Not my best friend, whose IQ is higher than Einstein's.

No. Grandmère.

If this got out, my life was over.

"Fine," I cried dramatically, spinning away from the mirror to face her. "All right, yes. Yes, I am in love with somebody else. Are you happy now?"

Grandmère raised her painted-on eyebrows.

"No need to shout, Amelia," she said, with what I might have taken for amusement in anyone other than her. "Who might this special someone be?"

"Oh, no," I said, holding out both my hands. If it wouldn't have been totally rude, I'd have made a little cross out of my index fingers and held it up toward her— that's how much she scares me. And if you think about it, with her tattooed eyeliner, she does look a little like Nosferatu. "You are not getting that information out of me."

Grandmère stamped out her cigarette in the crystal ashtray Sebastiano had provided, and went, "Very well. I take it, then, that the gentleman in question does not return your ardor?"

There was no point in lying to her. Not now. Not with my nostrils.

My shoulders sagged. "No. He likes this other girl. This really smart girl who knows how to clone fruit flies."

Grandmère snorted. "A useful talent. Well, never mind that now. I don't suppose, Amelia, that you are acquainted with the expression dirty dishwater is better than none?"

I guess she must have been able to tell from my perplexed expression that this was one I hadn't heard before, since she went on, "Do not throw away this Kenny until you have managed to secure someone better."

I stared at her, horrified. Really, my grandmother has said—and done—some pretty cold things in her time, but this one took the cake.

"Secure someone better?" I couldn't believe she actually meant what I thought she meant. "You mean I shouldn't break up with Kenny until I've got someone else?"

Grandmère lit another cigarette. "But of course."

"But, Grandmère." I swear to God, sometimes I can't figure out if she's human or some kind of alien life force sent down from some other planet to spy on us. "You can't do that. You can't just string a guy along like that, knowing that you don't feel the same way about him that he feels about you."

Grandmère exhaled a long plume of blue smoke. "Why not?"

"Because it's completely unethical!" I shook my head. "No. I'm breaking up with Kenny. Right away. Tonight, as a matter of fact."

Grandmère stroked Rommel under the chin. He looked more miserable than ever, as if instead of stroking him, she was peeling the skin away from his body. He really is the most heinous excuse for a dog I have ever seen.

"That," Grandmère said, "is your prerogative, of course. But allow me to point out to you that if you break off your relationship with this young man, your Biology grade will suffer."

I was shocked. But mostly because this was something I had already thought of myself. I was amazed Grandmère and I had actually shared something.

Which was really the only reason I exclaimed, "Grandmère!"

"Well," Grandmère said, flicking ash from her cigarette into the ashtray. "Isn't it true? You are only making what, a C, in this class? And that is only because that young man allows you to copy his answers to the homework."

"Grandmère!" I squealed again. Because, of course, she was right.

She looked at the ceiling. "Let me see," she said. "With your D in Algebra, if you get anything less than a C in Biology, your grade-point average will take quite a little dip this semester."

"Grandmère." I couldn't believe this. She knew all about my grades! And she was right. She was so right. But still. "I am not going to postpone breaking up with Kenny until after the final. That would be just plain wrong."

"Suit yourself," Grandmère said with a sigh. "But it certainly will be awkward having to sit beside him for the next—how long is it until the end of the semester?—Oh, yes, two weeks. Especially considering the fact that after you break things off with him, he probably won't even speak to you anymore."

God, so true. And not something I hadn't thought of myself. If Kenny got mad enough over me breaking up with him to not want to speak to me anymore, seventh period was going to be plenty unpleasant.

"And what about this dance?" Grandmère rattled the ice in her Sidecar. "This Christmas dance?"

"It's not a Christmas dance," I said. "It's a nondenominational—"

Grandmère waved a hand. This spiky charm bracelet she was wearing tinkled.

"Whatever," she said. "If you stop seeing this young man, who will you go to the dance with?"

"I won't go with anybody," I said, firmly, even though, of course, my heart was breaking at the thought. "I'll just stay home."

"While everyone else has a good time? Really, Amelia, you aren't being at all sensible. What about this other young man?"

"What other young man?"

"The one you claim to be so in love with. Won't he be at this dance with the housefly girl?"

"Fruit fly," I corrected her. "And I don't know. Maybe."

The thought that Michael might ask Judith Gershner to the Nondenominational Winter Dance had never occurred to me. But as soon as Grandmère mentioned it, I felt that same sickening sensation I'd felt at the ice-skating rink when I'd first seen them together: kind of like the time when Lilly and I were crossing Bleecker Street and this Chinese food delivery man crashed into us on his bicycle, and I had the wind completely knocked out of me.

Only this time, it wasn't just my chest that hurt, but my tongue. It had been feeling a lot better, but now it started to throb again.

"It seems to me," Grandmère said, "that one way to get this young man's attention might be to show up at this dance on the arm of this other young man, looking perfectly divine in an original creation by Genovian fashion designer Sebastiano Grimaldi."

I just stared at her. Because she was right. She was so right. Except . . .

"Grandmère," I said. "The guy I like? Yeah, he likes girls who can clone *insects*. Okay? I highly doubt he is going to be impressed by a *dress*."

I didn't mention that I had, of course, just the night before, been hoping that very thing. But almost as if she could read my mind, Grandmère just went, "Hmmm," in this knowing way.

"Suit yourself," she continued. "Still, it seems a bit cruel to me, your breaking things off with this young man at this time of year."

"Why?" I asked, confused. Had Grandmère inadvertently stumbled across some TV channel playing *It's a Wonderful Life*, or something? She had never shown one speck of holiday spirit before now. "Because it's *Christmas*?"

"No," Grandmère said, looking very disgusted with me, I guess over the suggestion that she might ever be moved by the anniversary of the birth of anyone's savior. "Because of your exams. If you truly wish to be kind, I think you might at least wait until after the final exams are over before breaking the poor little fellow's heart."

I had been all ready to argue with whatever excuse for me not breaking up with Kenny Grandmère came up with next—but this one, I had not expected. I stood there with my mouth hanging open. I know it was hanging open, because I could see it reflected in the three full-length mirrors.

"I cannot imagine," Grandmère went on, "why you do not simply allow him to believe that you return his ardor until your exams are over. Why compound the poor boy's stress? But you must, of course, do what you think is best. I suppose this—er—Kenny is the sort of boy who bounces back easily from rejection. He'll probably do quite well on his exams, in spite of his broken heart."

Oh, God! If she had stabbed a fork in my stomach and twisted my intestines around the tines like spaghetti, she couldn't have made me feel worse. . . .

And, I have to admit, a little relieved. Because of course I can't break up with Kenny now. Never mind my Bio grade and the dance: You can't break up with someone right before finals. It's like the meanest thing you can do.

Well, aside from the kind of stuff Lana and her friends pull. You know, girls' locker-room stuff, like going up to someone who is changing and asking her why she wears a bra when she obviously doesn't need one, or making fun of her just because she doesn't happen to like being kissed by her boyfriend. That kind of thing.

So here I am. I *want* to break up with Kenny, but I can't.

I *want* to tell Michael how I feel about him, but I can't do that, either.

I can't even quit biting my fingernails. I am going to gross out an entire European nation with my bloody cuticles.

I am a pathetic mess. No wonder in the car this morning—after I accidentally closed the door on Lars's foot—Lilly said that I should really look into getting some therapy, because if there's anybody who needs to find inner harmony between her conscious and her subconscious, it's me.

TO DO BEFORE LEAVING FOR GENOVIA

1. Get cat food, litter for Fat Louie
2. Stop biting fingernails
3. Achieve self-actualization
4. Find inner harmony between conscious and subconscious
5. Break up with Kenny—but not until after finals/ Nondenominational Winter Dance

TUESDAY, DECEMBER 9, ENGLISH

What was THAT just now in the hallway? Did Kenny Showalter just say what I think he said to you?

> *Yes. Oh, my God, Shameeka, what am I going to do? I'm shaking so hard I can barely write.*

What do you mean, what are you going to do? The boy is warm for your form, Mia. Go for it.

> *People can't just be allowed to go around saying things like that. Especially so loud. Everyone must have heard him. Do you think everyone heard him?*

Everybody heard him, all right. You should have seen Lilly's face. I thought she was going to suffer one of those synaptic breakdowns she's always talking about.

> *You think EVERYBODY heard him? I mean, like the people coming out of the Chemistry lab? Do you think they heard?*

How could they not? He yelled it pretty loud.

Were they laughing? The people coming out of Chemistry? They weren't laughing, were they?

Most of them were laughing.

Oh, God! Why was I ever born????

Except Michael. He wasn't laughing.

He WASN'T? REALLY? Are you pulling my leg?

No. Why would I do that? And what do you care what Michael Moscovitz thinks, anyway?

I don't. I don't care. What makes you think I care?

Um, for one thing because you won't shut up about it.

People shouldn't go around laughing at other people's misfortunes. That's all.

I don't see what the big misfortune is. So the guy loves you? A lot of girls would really like it if their boyfriend yelled that at them between first and second period.

Yeah, well, NOT ME!!!!

USE <u>TRANSITIVE VERBS</u> TO CREATE BRIEF, VIGOROUS SENTENCES.

<u>TRANSITIVE</u>: HE SOON REGRETTED HIS WORDS.
<u>INTRANSITIVE</u>: IT WAS NOT LONG BEFORE HE WAS VERY SORRY THAT HE HAD SAID WHAT HE SAID.

TUESDAY, DECEMBER 9, BIO

Gifted and Talented was so not fun today. Not that Bio is any better, on account of the fact that I am stuck here next to Kenny, who seems to have calmed down a little since this morning.

Still, I really think that people who are not actually enrolled in certain classes have no business showing up in them.

For instance, just because Judith Gershner has study hall for fifth period is no reason that she should be allowed to hang around the Gifted and Talented classroom for fifty minutes during that period. She should never have been let out of study hall in the first place. I don't think she even had a pass.

Not that I would turn her in, or anything. But this kind of flagrant rule-breaking really shouldn't be encouraged. If Lilly is going to go through with this walkout thing, which she is still trying to garner support for, she should really add to her list of complaints the fact that the teachers in this school play favorites. I mean, just because a girl knows how to clone things doesn't mean she should be allowed to roam the school freely any time she wants.

But there she was when I walked in, and there's no doubt about it: Judith Gershner has a total crush on Michael. I don't really know how he feels about her, but she was wearing tan-colored panty hose instead of the black cotton tights she normally wears, so you *know* something is up. No girl wears tan panty hose without a good reason.

And okay, so maybe they are working on their booth for the Winter Carnival, but that is no reason for Judith to drape her arm across the back of Michael's chair like that. Plus he used to help me with my Algebra homework during G and T, but now he can't, because Judith is monopolizing all his time. I would think he might resent the intrusion.

Plus Judith really has no business butting into my private conversations. She hardly even knows me.

But did that stop her from letting me know, when she overheard Lilly's formal apology for not having believed me about Kenny's weird phone call—any doubts about the veracity of which he managed to scatter today with his display of unbridled passion in the third-floor hallway—that she feels sorry for him? Oh, no.

"Poor kid," Judith said. "I heard what he said to you

in the hallway. I was in the chem lab. What was it again? 'I don't care if you don't feel the same way, Mia, I will always love you,' or something like that?"

I didn't say anything. That's because I was busy picturing how Judith would look with a pencil sticking out of the middle of her forehead.

"It's really sweet," Judith said. "If you think about it. I mean, the guy's clearly got it bad for you."

This is the problem, see. Everyone thinks what Kenny did was so cute and everything. Nobody seems to understand that it wasn't cute. It wasn't cute at all. It was completely humiliating. I don't think I've ever been so embarrassed in my whole life.

And believe me, I've lived through more than my fair share of embarrassing incidents, especially since this whole princess thing started.

But I'm apparently the only person in this entire school who thinks what Kenny did was the least bit wrong.

"He's obviously very in touch with his emotions." Even Lilly was taking Kenny's side in the whole thing. "Unlike *some* people."

I have to say, this makes me so mad when I think about it, because the truth is, ever since I started writing things down in journals, I have gotten very in touch with my emotions. I usually know almost exactly how I feel.

The problem is, I just can't tell anyone.

I don't know who was the most surprised when Michael suddenly came to my defense against his sister—Lilly, Judith Gershner, or me.

"Just because Mia doesn't go around shouting about how she feels in the third-floor hallway," Michael said, "doesn't mean she isn't in touch with her emotions."

How does he do that? How is it that he is able to magically put into words exactly what I feel, but seem to have so much trouble saying? This, you see, is why I love him. I mean, how could I not?

"Yeah," I said triumphantly.

"Well, you could have said something back to him." Lilly always gets disgruntled when Michael comes to my rescue—especially when he does it while she is attacking me about the lack of honesty in my emotional life. "Instead of just leaving him hanging there."

"And what," I demanded—injudiciously, I now realize—"should I have said to him?"

"How about," Lilly said, "that you love him back?"

WHY? That's all I want to know. WHY was I cursed with a best friend who doesn't understand that there are some things you just don't say in front of EVERYONE IN THE ENTIRE GIFTED AND TALENTED CLASS-ROOM, INCLUDING HER BROTHER????

The problem is, Lilly has never been embarrassed about anything in her life. She simply does not know the meaning of the word *embarrassment*.

"Look," I said, feeling my cheeks begin to burn. I couldn't lie, of course. How could I lie, considering what I now knew about my nostrils? And okay, Lilly hadn't figured it out yet, but it was only a matter of time. I mean, if *Grandmère* knew . . . "I really and truly value Kenny's companionship," I said, carefully. "But love. I mean, *love*. That is a very big thing. I'm not, I mean, I don't . . ."

I dribbled off pathetically, acutely aware that everyone in the room, most especially Michael, was listening.

"I see," Lilly said, narrowing her eyes. "Fear of commitment."

"I do not fear commitment," I insisted. "I just—"

But Lilly's dark eyes were already shining in eager anticipation. She was getting ready to psychoanalyze me, one of her favorite hobbies, unfortunately.

"Let's examine the situation, shall we?" she said. "I mean, here you've got this guy going around the hallways, screaming about how much he loves you, and you just stare at him like a rat caught in the path of the D train. What do you suppose that means?"

"Have you ever considered," I demanded, "that maybe the reason I didn't tell him I love him back is because I—"

I almost said it. Really. I did. I almost said that I don't love Kenny.

But I couldn't. Because if I'd said that, somehow it would have gotten back to Kenny, and that would be even worse than my breaking up with him. I couldn't do it.

So all I said instead was, "Lilly, you know perfectly well I do not fear commitment. I mean, there are lots of boys I—"

"Oh, yeah?" Lilly seemed to be enjoying herself way more than usual. It was almost as if she was playing to an audience. Which, of course, she was. The audience of her brother and his girlfriend. "Name one."

"One what?"

"Name a boy that you could see yourself committing to for all eternity."

"What do you want, a list?" I asked her.

"A list would be nice," Lilly said.

So I drew up the following list:

GUYS MIA THERMOPOLIS COULD SEE HERSELF COMMITTING TO FOR ALL ETERNITY

1. Wolverine of the *X-Men*
2. Han Solo from original 1977 *Star Wars* movie
3. Batman

4. Tarzan from the Disney cartoon

5. The Beast from *Beauty and the Beast*

6. That hot soldier guy from *Mulan*

7. The guy Brendan Fraser played in *The Mummy*

8. Angel from *Buffy the Vampire Slayer*

9. Tom on *Daria*

10. Justin Baxendale

But this list turned out to be no good, because Lilly totally took it and analyzed it, and it works out that half the guys on it are actually cartoon characters; one is a vampire; and one is a mutant who can make spikes shoot out of his knuckles.

In fact, except for Justin Baxendale—the good-looking senior who just transferred from Trinity and who a lot of girls at Albert Einstein High School are already in love with—all the guys I listed are fictional creations. Apparently, the fact that I could list no guy I had a hope of actually getting together with—or who even lives in the third dimension—is indicative of something.

Not, of course, indicative of the fact that the guy I like was actually in the room at the time, sitting next to his new girlfriend, and so I couldn't list him.

Oh, no. Nobody thought of *that*.

No, the lack of actual attainable men on my list was

apparently indicative of my unrealistic expectations where men are concerned, and further proof of my inability to commit.

Lilly says if I don't lower my expectations somewhat, I am destined for an unsatisfactory love life.

As if the way things have been going, I've ever expected anything else.

Kenny just tossed me this note:

Mia—I'm sorry about what happened today in the hallway. I understand now that I embarrassed you. Sometimes I forget that even though you are a princess, you are still quite introverted. I promise never to do anything like that again. Can I make it up to you by taking you to lunch at Big Wong on Thursday?
—Kenny

I said yes, of course. Not just because I really like Big Wong's steamed vegetable dumplings, or even because I don't want people thinking I fear commitment. I didn't even say yes because I suspect that, over dumplings and hot tea, Kenny is finally going to ask me to the Nondenominational Winter Dance.

I said yes because in spite of it all, I really do like Kenny, and I don't want to hurt his feelings.

And I'd feel the same way even if I weren't a princess, and always had to do the right thing.

HOMEWORK

ALGEBRA: REVIEW QUESTIONS AT THE END OF
CHAPTERS 4-7
ENGLISH: TERM PAPER
WORLD CIV: REVIEW QUESTIONS AT THE END OF
CHAPTERS 5-9
G & T: NONE
FRENCH: REVIEW QUESTIONS AT THE END OF CHAPTERS
4-6
BIOLOGY: REVIEW QUESTIONS AT THE END OF
CHAPTERS 6-8

TUESDAY, DECEMBER 9, 4 P.M., IN THE LIMO ON THE WAY TO THE PLAZA

The following conversation took place between Mr. Gianini and me today after Algebra review:

Mr. G: Mia, is everything all right?

Me: (Surprised) Yes. Why wouldn't it be?

Mr. G: Well, it's just that I thought you'd pretty much grasped the FOIL method, but on today's pop quiz, you got all five problems wrong.

Me: I guess I've sort of had a lot on my mind.

Mr. G: Your trip to Genovia?

Me: Yeah, that, and . . . other things.

Mr. G: Well, if you want to talk about the, um, other things, you know I'm always here for you. And your mother. I know we might seem preoccupied with the baby coming and everything, but you're always number one on our list of priorities. You know that, don't you?

Me: (Mortified) Yes. But there's nothing wrong. Really.

Thank God he doesn't know about my nostrils.

And really, what else *could* I have said? "Mr. G, my boyfriend is a nut case but I can't break up with him on account of finals, and I'm in love with my best friend's brother?"

I highly doubt he'd be able to offer any meaningful advice on any of the above.

TUESDAY, DECEMBER 9, 7 P.M.

I don't believe this. I'm home before *Baywatch Hawaii* starts for the first time in, like, months. Something must be wrong with Grandmère. Although she seemed pretty normal at our lesson today. I mean, for her. Except that she stopped me in the middle of my reciting the Genovian pledge of allegiance (which I have to memorize, of course, for when I am visiting schools in Genovia. I don't want to look like an idiot in front of a bunch of five-year-olds for not knowing it) to ask me what I'd decided to do about Kenny.

It's kind of funny about her taking an interest in my personal life, since she certainly never has before. Well, not very much, anyway.

And she kept on saying stuff about how ingenious it had been of Kenny, sending me those anonymous love letters last October, the ones I thought (well, okay, *hoped*, not really thought) Michael was writing.

I was all, "What was so ingenious about *that*?" to which Grandmère just replied, "Well, you're his girlfriend now, aren't you?"

Which I never really thought about, but I guess she's right.

Anyway, my mom was so surprised to see me home so early, she actually let me be in charge of choosing the takeout (pizza margherita for me. I let her get rigatoni bolognese, even though the sausage in the sauce is probably steeped in nitrates that could harm a developing fetus. Still, it was sort of a special occasion, what with me actually being home for dinner for a change. Even Mr. Gianini got a little wild and had something with porcini mushrooms in it).

I am psyched to be home early, because you wouldn't believe all the studying I have to do, plus I should probably start my term paper, then there's figuring out what I'm going to get people for Christmas and Hannukah, not to mention going over the thank-you speech I have to make to the people of Genovia in my nationally televised (in Genovia, anyway) introduction to the people I will one day rule.

I had really better buckle down and get to work!

TUESDAY, DECEMBER 9, 7:30 P.M.

Okay, so I was taking a study break, and I just realized something. You can learn *a lot* from watching *Baywatch*. Seriously.

I have compiled this list:

THINGS I HAVE LEARNED FROM WATCHING BAYWATCH

1. If you are paralyzed from the waist down, you just need to see a kid being attacked by a murderer, and you will be able to get up and save him.
2. If you have amnesia, it is probably because two men love you at the same time. Just tell the two of them you only want to be friends, and your amnesia will go away.
3. It is always easy to get a parking place near the beach.
4. Male lifeguards always put a shirt on when they leave the beach. Female lifeguards don't need to bother.
5. If you meet a beautiful but troubled girl, she is probably either a diamond smuggler or suffering from split personality disorder: Do not accept her invitation to dinner.

6. Dick van Patten, though a senior citizen, can be surprisingly hard to quell in a fistfight.

7. If people are mysteriously dying in the water, it is probably because a giant electric eel has escaped from a nearby aquarium.

8. A girl who is thinking about abandoning her baby should just leave it on the beach. Chances are, a nice lifeguard will take it home, adopt it, and raise it as his own.

9. It is very easy to outswim a shark.

10. Wild seals make adorable and easily trained pets.

TUESDAY, DECEMBER 9, 8:30 P.M.

I just got an email from Lilly. I'm not the only one who got it, either. Somehow she figured out how to do a mass email to every kid in school.

Well, I shouldn't be surprised, I guess. She *is* a genius. Still, she has clearly developed atrophy of the brain from too much studying, because look what she wrote:

ATTENTION ALL STUDENTS AT
ALBERT EINSTEIN HIGH SCHOOL

Stressed from too many exams, term papers, and final projects? Don't just passively accept the oppressive workload handed down to us by the tyrannical administration! A silent walkout has been scheduled for tomorrow. At 10 a.m. exactly, join your fellow students in showing our teachers how we feel about inflexible exam schedules, repressive censorship, and having only one reading day on which to prepare for our finals. Leave your pencils, leave your books, and gather on East 75th

Street between Madison and Park (use doors by main
administration offices, if possible) for a rally against
Principal Gupta and the trustees. Let your voice be heard!

I am so sure. I can't walk out tomorrow at 10 a.m.
That's right in the middle of Algebra. Mr. Gianini's feelings will be so hurt if we all just get up and leave.

But if I say I'm not going to take part in it, Lilly will
be furious.

But if I do take part in it, my dad will kill me. Not to
mention my mom. I mean, we could all get suspended, or
something. Or hit by a delivery truck. There are a lot of
them on 75th at that time of day.

Why? Why must I be saddled with a best friend who is
so clearly a sociopath?

TUESDAY, DECEMBER 9, 8:45 P.M.

I just got the following Instant Message from Michael:

CRACKING: Did you just get that whacked-out mass email from my sister?

I replied at once.

FTLOUIE: Yes.

CRACKING: You're not going along with her stupid walkout, are you?

FTLOUIE: Oh, right. She won't be too mad if I don't, or anything.

CRACKING: You don't have to do everything she says, you know, Mia. You've stood up to her before. Why not now?

Um, because I have enough to worry about right now—for instance, finals; my impending trip to Genovia; and, oh, yeah, the fact that I love you—without adding a fight with my best friend to the list.

But I didn't say that, of course.

FTLOUIE: I find that the path of least resistance is often the safest one when dealing with your sister.

CRACKING: Well, I'm not doing it.

FTLOUIE: It's different for you. You're her brother. She has to remain on speaking terms with you. You live together.

CRACKING: Not for much longer. Thank God.

Oh, right. He's going away to college soon.

Well, not too far away. But about a hundred blocks or so.

FTLOUIE: That's right. You got accepted to Columbia. Early decision, too. I never did congratulate you. So, congratulations.

CRACKING: Thanks.

FTLOUIE: You must be happy that you'll know at least one other person there. Judith Gershner, I mean.

CRACKING: Yeah, I guess so. Listen, you're still going to be in town for the Winter Carnival, right? You're not leaving for Genovia before the 19th are you?

All I could think was, *Why is he asking me this? I mean, he can't be going to ask me to the dance. He must know I'm going with Kenny. If Kenny ever gets around to asking me, that is. Besides, it isn't as if Michael is available. Isn't he going with Judith? Well? ISN'T HE?*

FTLOUIE: I'm leaving for Genovia on the 20th.

CRACKING: Oh, good. Because you should really stop by the Computer Club's booth at the Carnival, and check out this program I've been working on. I think you'll like it.

I should have known. Michael isn't going to ask me to any dance. Not in this lifetime, anyway. I should have known it was just his stupid computer program he wanted me to see. Who even cares? I suppose dumb army guys will pop out at me, and I'll have to shoot them, or whatever. Judith's idea, I'm sure.

I wanted to write to him, *Don't you have the slightest idea what I'm going through? That the only person with whom I can see myself committing to for all eternity is YOU? Don't you KNOW that by now????*

But instead I wrote:

FTLOUIE: Can't wait. Well, I have to go. Bye.

Sometimes I completely hate myself.

WEDNESDAY, DECEMBER 10, 3 A.M.

You're never going to believe this. Something *Grandmère* said is keeping me awake.

Seriously. I was dead asleep—well, as asleep as you can be with a twenty-five pound cat purring on your abdomen—when all of a sudden, I woke up with this totally random phrase going around in my head:

"Well, you're his girlfriend now, aren't you?"

That's what Grandmère said when I asked her what was so ingenious about Kenny's having sent me those anonymous love letters.

And do you know what?

SHE'S RIGHT.

It seems totally bizarre to admit that Grandmère might be right about something, but I think it's true. Kenny's anonymous love letters *did* work. I mean, I *am* his girlfriend now.

So what's to keep me from writing some anonymous love letters to the boy *I* like? I mean, really? Besides the fact that I already have a boyfriend, and the guy I like already has a girlfriend?

I think this is a plan that might have some merit. It needs more work, of course, but hey, desperate measures call for desperate times. Or something like that. Too sleepy to figure it out.

WEDNESDAY, DECEMBER 10, HOMEROOM

Okay, I was up all night thinking about it, and I'm pretty sure I've got it figured out. Even as I sit here, my plan is being put into action, thanks to Tina Hakim Baba and a stop at Ho's Deli before school started.

Actually, Ho's didn't really have what I wanted. I wanted a card that was blank inside, with a picture on the front that was sophisticated but not too sexy. But the only blank cards they had at Ho's (that weren't plastered with pictures of kittens) were ones with photos of fruit being dipped into chocolate sauce.

I tried to choose a non-phallic fruit, but even the strawberry I got is kind of sexier than I would have liked. I don't know what's sexy about fruit with chocolate sauce dripping off it, but Tina was like, "Whoa," when she saw it.

Still, she gamely agreed to print my poem on the inside of the card, so Michael won't recognize my handwriting. She even liked my poem, which I came up with at five this morning:

Roses are Red
Violets are Blue
You may not know it
But someone loves you.

Not my best work, I will admit, but it was really hard to come up with something better after only three hours of sleep.

I hesitated somewhat over the use of the L word. I thought maybe I should substitute *like* for *love*. I don't want him to think there's a creepy stalker after him, and all.

But Tina said *love* was absolutely right. Because, as she put it, "It's the truth, isn't it?"

And since it's anonymous, I guess it doesn't matter that I am laying open my soul.

Anyway, Tina goes by Michael's locker right before we have PE, so she's going to slip it to him then.

I can't believe that this is the low I have stooped to. But like Dad once told me, *Faint heart never won fair lady.*

WEDNESDAY, DECEMBER 10, HOMEROOM

Lars just pointed out that I'm not exactly risking anything, seeing as how I didn't sign the card and even went to the extreme of having someone else write out the poem for me (Lars knows all about this, on account of I had to explain to him why we had to go into Ho's at eight fifteen in the morning). He helped pick the card, but I would be happy if that was the extent of his contribution to this particular project. Because he's a man, I cannot imagine his input is at all valuable.

Besides, he's been married like four times, so I highly doubt he knows anything about romance.

Also, he should know by now we're not allowed to talk during Homeroom.

WEDNESDAY, DECEMBER 10, ALGEBRA, 9:30 A.M.

I just saw Lilly in the hallway. She whispered, "Don't forget! Ten o'clock! Don't let me down!"

Well, the truth is, I did forget. The walkout! The stupid walkout!

And poor Mr. Gianini, standing up there going over Chapter Five, not suspecting a thing. It's not his fault Mrs. Spears didn't like Lilly's term paper topic. Lilly can't just arbitrarily punish all the teachers in school for something one teacher did.

It's already nine thirty-five. What am I going to do?

WEDNESDAY, DECEMBER 10, ALGEBRA, 9:45 A.M.

Lana just leaned back and hissed, "You gonna walk out with your fat friend?"

I take real objection to this. Only in a culture as screwed up as ours, where girls like Christina Aguilera are held up as models of beauty when clearly they are in fact suffering from some sort of malnutrition (scurvy?), would one's size even matter or be something to be judged by.

I hate it here.

WEDNESDAY, DECEMBER 10, ALGEBRA, 9:50 A.M.

Ten minutes until the walkout. I can't take this. I'm getting out.

WEDNESDAY, DECEMBER 10, 9:55 A.M.

Okay. I'm standing in the hallway next to the fire alarm by the second-floor drinking fountain. I got a hall pass from Mr. G. I told him I had to go to the bathroom.

Lars is with me, of course. I wish he'd stop laughing. He does not seem to realize the seriousness of the situation. Plus Justin Baxendale just walked by with a hall pass of his own, and he gave us this really weird look.

And yeah, I probably do look a little strange, hanging out in the hallway with my bodyguard, who is currently experiencing a fit of the giggles, but still—I do not need to be looked at weirdly by Justin Baxendale.

His eyelashes are really long and dark and they make his eyes look sort of smoky. . . .

OH, MY GOD! I CAN'T BELIEVE I AM WRITING ABOUT JUSTIN BAXENDALE'S EYELASHES AT A TIME LIKE THIS!

I mean, I am in a real bind here:

If I do not walk out with Lilly, I'll lose my best friend.

But if I do walk out with everyone, I will be totally dissing my stepfather.

So I really only have one choice.

Lars just offered to do it for me. But I can't let him. I can't let him take the fall for me if we get caught. I am the princess. I have to do it myself.

I just told him to get ready to run. This is one time being so tall comes in handy. I have a pretty long stride.

Well, here goes.

WEDNESDAY, DECEMBER 10, 10 A.M., EAST 75TH STREET, BENEATH SOME SCAFFOLDING

I don't get why she's so mad. I mean, yeah, if everyone evacuates the building due to a fire alarm going off, it's not the same thing as everyone leaving in protest against the repressive teaching techniques of some of the teachers.

But we're still all standing in the middle of the street in the rain, and nobody has coats on because they wouldn't let us stop at our lockers for fear we'd all be consumed in a fiery conflagration, so we're probably going to get hypothermia from the cold and die.

That's what she wanted, right?

But no. She can't even be happy about that.

"Somebody ratted us out!" she keeps yelling. "Somebody told! Why else would they schedule a fire drill for exactly the same time as my walkout? I'm telling you, these bureaucrats will stop at nothing to keep us from speaking out against them. Nothing! They'll even make us stand out in freezing drizzle, hoping to weaken our immune systems so we'll no longer have the strength to fight them. Well, I for one refuse to catch cold! I refuse to succumb to their petty abuses!"

I suggested to Lilly that she write her term paper on the suffragettes, because they, like us, had to put up with numerous indignities in their battle for equal rights.

Lilly, however, told me not to be facile.

God, being best friends with a genius is hard.

WEDNESDAY, DECEMBER 10, G & T

I can't tell if Michael got the note or not!!!!

Worse, stupid Judith Gershner is here AGAIN. Why can't she stay in her own class? Why is she always hanging around ours? We were all getting along perfectly well until *she* came along.

My life is pathetic.

I thought about going across the hall to the teachers' lounge and asking Mrs. Hill a question about something— like why she had the custodians remove the door to the supply closet so we can't lock Boris in there anymore—so she'd maybe look over and NOTICE that there's a girl in our classroom who is *not* supposed to be there.

But I couldn't bring myself to do it, because of Michael. I mean, Michael obviously *wants* Judith here, or else he'd tell her to go away.

RIGHT?????

Anyway, with Michael so busy and all with Miss Gershner, I guess I am on my own with the whole Algebra review thing.

That's all right. I'm completely fine with that. I can study on my own just fine. Watch:

A, B, C = disjoint partition of universal set
Collection of non-empty subsets of U that are pairwise disjoint and whose union is equal to the set of U

I get that. I totally get what that means. Who needs Michael's help? Not me. I am totally cool with the collection of non-empty subsets.
TOTALLY COOL WITH IT.

Oh, Michael
You have made my heart
a disjoint partition.

Why can't you see
that we were meant to be
a universal set?

Instead, you have turned my soul
into a collection
of non-empty subsets.

I cannot believe
that our love was meant to be
pairwise disjoint.

But rather
a union—
equal to the set of
U and me.

WEDNESDAY, DECEMBER 10, FRENCH

You know what else I just realized? That if this thing works—you know, if I do manage to get Michael away from Judith Gershner, and I break up with Kenny, and I end up, you know, in a potentially romantic situation with Lilly's brother—I will not know what to do.

Seriously.

Take kissing, for instance. I have only ever kissed one person before, and that's Kenny. I cannot believe that what Kenny and I did really encompassed the whole of the kissing experience, because it certainly wasn't as fun as people always make it look on TV.

This is a very disturbing thought, and has led me to an equally disturbing conclusion: I know very little about kissing.

In fact, it seems to me that if I am going to be doing any kissing with anybody, I should get some advice beforehand. From a kissing expert, I mean.

Which is why I am consulting Tina Hakim Baba. She may not be allowed to wear makeup to school, but she has been kissing Dave Farouq El-Abar—who goes to Trinity—for close to three months now, *and* liking it, so I consider her an expert on the subject.

I am enclosing the results of this highly scientific document for future reference.

Tina—

I need to know about kissing. Can you please answer each of the following questions IN DETAIL????

And DO NOT show this to anyone!!!! DO NOT lose this paper!!!!   —Mia

1. Can a boy tell if the person he is with is inexperienced? How does an inexperienced kisser kiss (so I can avoid that)?

The guy may sense a feeling of nervousness coming from you, or that you are uneasy, but everyone is nervous when they are kissing someone new. It's natural! But kissing is easy to catch on to—believe me! An inexperienced kisser might break away too soon because he or she is scared or whatever. But that is normal. It's SUPPOSED to be weird. That's what makes it fun.

2. Is there such a thing as a great kisser? If so, what are the qualifications? (So I know what to practice.)

Yes, there is such a thing as a great kisser. A great kisser is always affectionate and gentle and patient and not demanding.

3. How much pressure do you exert on his lips? I mean, do you push, or like in a handshake, are you just supposed to be firm? Or are you just supposed to stand there and let him do all the work?

If you want a gentle kiss (a caring one) don't apply too much pressure (this is also true if he is wearing braces—you don't want to cause any lacerations). If you give a guy a "harsh" kiss (too much pressure), he might think you are desperate or that you want to go further than you probably do.

Of course you aren't supposed to just stand there and let him do all the work: Kiss him back! But always kiss him the way YOU want to be kissed. That is how guys learn. If we didn't show them how to do everything, we'd never get anywhere!

4. How do you know when it's time to stop?

Stop when he stops, or when you feel like you've had enough, or don't want to go any further. Just gently (so you don't freak him out) move your head back, or if the moment is right, you can change the kiss into a hug, then step back.

5. If you are in love with him, is it still gross?

Of course not! Kissing is never gross!

Well, okay, I guess I could see that maybe with Kenny, it might be. It is always better with someone you actually like.

Of course, even with someone you really like, sometimes kissing can be gross. Once Dave licked me on the chin, and I was all, Get away. But I think that was by accident (the licking).

6. If he is in love with you, does he even care if you are bad? (Define bad kisser. See above.)

If the guy likes/loves you, he won't care if you are a good kisser or not. In fact, even if you are a bad kisser, he will probably think you are a good one. And vice versa. He should like you for what you are—not how you kiss.

DEFINITION OF BAD KISSER: A bad kisser is someone who gets your face all wet, slobbers on you, sticks his tongue in when you're not ready, has bad breath, OR *sometimes there can be kissers whose tongues are all dry and prickly like a cactus, but I have never experienced one of those, just heard about them.*

7. When do you know if it's time to open your mouth (thus turning it into a French)?

You will probably feel his tongue touch your lips. If you want to pursue the idea, open your lips a little. If not, keep them closed.

Coming au demain–Chapter II: How to French!!!!

HOMEWORK

ALGEBRA: REVIEW QUESTIONS AT THE END OF CHAPTERS 8–10

ENGLISH: ENGLISH JOURNAL: BOOKS I HAVE READ

WORLD CIV: REVIEW QUESTIONS AT THE END OF CHAPTERS 10–12

G & T: NONE

FRENCH: REVIEW QUESTIONS AT THE END OF CHAPTERS 7–9

BIOLOGY: REVIEW QUESTIONS AT THE END OF CHAPTERS 9–12

WEDNESDAY, DECEMBER 10, 9 P.M., IN THE LIMO ON THE WAY HOME FROM GRANDMÈRE'S

I am so tired I can hardly write. Grandmère made me try on every single dress in Sebastiano's showroom. You wouldn't believe the number of dresses I've had on today. Short ones, long ones, straight-skirted ones, poufy-skirted ones, white ones, pink ones, blue ones, and even a lime-green one (which Sebastiano declared brought out the "col" in my cheeks).

The purpose of all this dress-trying-on business was to choose one to wear on Christmas Eve, during my first official televised speech to the Genovian people. I have to look regal, but not too regal. Beautiful, but not too beautiful. Sophisticated, but not too sophisticated.

I tell you, it was a nightmare of hollow-cheeked women in white (the new black) buttoning and zipping and snapping me in and out of dresses. Now I know how all those supermodels must feel.

Actually, it *was* kind of hard to choose my dress for my first big televised event, because surprisingly, Sebastiano turned out to be a pretty good designer. There were several dresses I actually wouldn't be embarrassed to be caught dead in.

Oops. Slip of the tongue. I wonder, though, if Sebastiano really does want to kill me. He seems to like being a fashion designer, which he couldn't do if he were prince of Genovia: He'd be too busy turning bills into laws and stuff like that.

Still, you can tell he'd totally enjoy wearing a crown. Not that, as ruler of Genovia, he'd ever get to do this. I've never seen my dad in a crown. Just suits. And shorts when he plays racquetball with other world leaders.

Ew, I wonder if I will have to learn to play racquetball.

But if Sebastiano became prince of Genovia, he would totally wear a crown all the time. He told me nothing brings out the sparkles in someone's eyes like pear-shaped diamonds. He prefers Tiffany's. Or as he calls it, Tiff's.

Since we were getting so chummy and all, I told Sebastiano about the Nondenominational Winter Dance, and how I have nothing to wear to it. Sebastiano seemed disappointed when he learned I would not be wearing a tiara to my school dance, but he got over it and started asking me all these questions about the event. Like "Who do you go with?" and "What he look like?" and stuff like that.

I don't know what it was, but I found myself actually telling Sebastiano all about my love life. It was so weird.

I totally didn't want to, but it all just started spilling out. Thank God Grandmère wasn't there. . . . She'd gone off in search of more cigarettes, and to have her Sidecar refreshed.

I told Sebastiano all about Kenny and how he loves me but I don't love him, and how I actually like someone else, but he doesn't know I'm alive.

Sebastiano is actually quite a good listener. I don't know how much, if anything, he understood of what I said, but he didn't take his eyes off my reflection as I talked, and when I was done, he looked me up and down in the mirror, and just said one thing: "This boy you like. How you know he no like you back?"

"Because," I said. "He likes this other girl."

Sebastiano made an impatient motion with this hands. The gesture was made more dramatic by the fact that he was wearing sleeves with these big frilly lace cuffs.

"No, no, no, no, no," he said. "He help you with your Al home. He like you, or he no do that. Why he do that, if he no like you?"

I took "He help you with your Al home" to mean "He helps you with your Algebra homework." I thought for a minute about why Michael had always been so willing to do that. Help me with my Algebra, I mean. I guess just because I am his sister's best friend, and he isn't the type of person who can sit around and watch his sister's best friend flunk out of high school without, you know, at least trying to do something about it.

While I was thinking about that, I couldn't help remembering how Michael's knees, beneath our desks, sometimes brush against mine as he's telling me about integers. Or how sometimes he leans so close to correct something I've written wrong that I can smell the nice, clean scent of his soap. Or how sometimes, like when I do my Lana Weinberger imitation or whatever, he throws back his head and laughs.

Michael's lips look extra nice when he is smiling.

"Tell Sebastiano," Sebastiano urged me. "Tell Sebastiano why this boy help you, if he no like you."

I sighed. "Because I'm his little sister's best friend," I said sadly. Really, could there *be* anything more humiliating? I mean, clearly Michael has never been impressed with my keen intellect or ravishing good looks, given my low grade-point average and of course my gigantism.

Sebastiano tugged on my sleeve and went, "You no worry. I make dress for dance, this boy, he no think of you as little sister's best friend."

Yeah. Sure. Whatever. Why must all my relatives be so weird?

Anyway, we picked out what I'm going to wear on

Genovian national TV during my introduction. It's this white taffeta job with a huge poufy skirt and this light blue sash (the royal colors are blue and white). But Sebastiano had one of his assistants take photos of me in all the dresses, so I can see how I looked in them and then decide. I thought this was fairly professional for a guy who calls breakfast "breck."

But all that isn't what I want to write about. I'm so tired, I hardly know what I'm doing. What I want to write about is what happened today after Algebra review.

Which was that Mr. Gianini, after everyone but me had left, went, "Mia, I heard a rumor that there was supposed to have been some kind of student walkout today. Had you heard that?"

Me: (freezing in my seat) Um, no.

Mr. Gianini: Oh. So you wouldn't know then if somebody—maybe in protest of the protest—threw the second-floor fire alarm? The one by the drinking fountain?

Me: (wishing Lars would stop coughing suggestively) Um, no.

Mr. Gianini: That's what I thought. Because you know the penalty for pulling one of the fire alarms—when there is, in fact, no sign of a fire—is expulsion.

Me: Oh, yes. I know that.

Mr. Gianini: I thought you might have seen who did

it, since I believe I gave you a hall pass shortly before the alarm went off.

Me: Oh, no. I didn't see anybody.

Except Justin Baxendale, and his smoky eyelashes. But I didn't say that.

Mr. Gianini: I didn't think so. Oh, well. If you ever hear who did it, maybe you could tell her from me never to do it again.

Me: Um. Okay.

Mr. Gianini: And tell her thanks from me, too. The last thing we need right now, with tensions running so high over finals, is a student walkout. (Mr. Gianini picked up his briefcase and jacket.) See you at home.

Then he winked at me. WINKED at me, like he knew I was the one who'd done it. But he couldn't know. I mean, he doesn't know about my nostrils (which were fully flaring the whole time; I could *feel* them!) Right? RIGHT????

THURSDAY, DECEMBER 11, HOMEROOM

Lilly is going to drive me crazy.

Seriously. Like it's not enough I have finals and my introduction to Genovia and my love life and everything to worry about. I have to listen to Lilly complain about how the administration of Albert Einstein High is out to get her. The whole way to school this morning she just droned on and on about how it's all a plot to silence her because she once complained about the Coke machine outside the gym. Apparently the Coke machine is indicative of the administration's efforts to turn us all into mindless soda-drinking, Gap-wearing clones, in Lilly's opinion.

If you ask me, this isn't really about Coke, or the attempts by the school's administration to turn us into mindless pod-people. It's really just because Lilly's still mad she can't use a chapter of the book she's writing on the high-school experience as her term paper.

I reminded Lilly if she doesn't submit a new topic, she's going to get an F as her nine-week grade. Factored in with her A for the last nine weeks, that's only like a C, which will significantly lower her grade-point average, and put her chances of getting into Berkeley, which is her first-choice school, at risk. She may be forced to fall back on her safety school, Brown, which I know would be quite a blow.

She didn't even listen to me. She says she's having an organizational meeting of this new group (of which she is president) Students Against the Corporatization of Albert Einstein High School (SACAEHS) on Saturday, and I have to come, because I am the group's secretary. Don't ask me how *that* happened. Lilly says I write everything down anyway, so it shouldn't be any trouble for me.

I wish Michael had been there to protect me from his sister, but like he has every day this week, he took the subway to school early so he could work on his project for the Winter Carnival.

I wouldn't doubt Judith Gershner has been showing up to school on the early side, too, this week.

Speaking of whom, I picked up another greeting card, this one from the Plaza gift shop on the way to Sebastiano's showroom last night. It's a lot better than that stupid one with the strawberry. This one has a picture of a lady holding a finger to her lips. Inside, it says, *Shhhh . . .*

Under that, I am having Tina write:

Roses are red
But cherries are redder
Maybe she can clone fruit flies
But I like you better.

What I meant was that I like him more than Judith Gershner does, but I'm not really sure that comes through in the poem. Tina says it does, but Tina thinks I should have used love instead of like, so who knows if her opinion is of any value? This is a poem clearly calling for a like and not a love.

I should know. I write enough of them.

Poems, I mean.

English Journal

This semester, we have read several novels, including *To Kill a Mockingbird*, *Huckleberry Finn*, and *The Scarlet Letter*. In your English journal, please record your feelings about the books we have read, and books in general. What have been your most meaningful experiences as a reader? Your favorite books? Your least favorite?

Please utilize <u>transitive</u> verbs.

Books I Have Read, and What They Meant
to Me *by Mia Thermopolis*

Books that were good:

1. *Jaws*—I bet you didn't know that in the book version of this, Richard Dreyfuss and Roy Scheider's wife have sex. But they do.

2. *The Catcher in the Rye*—This is totally good. It has lots of bad words and talks about how awful high school is.

3. *To Kill a Mockingbird*—This is an excellent book. They should do a movie version of this with Bruce Willis as Atticus, and he should blow Mr. Ewell away with a flamethrower at the end.

4. *A Wrinkle in Time*—Only we never find out the most important thing: whether or not Meg has breasts. I'm

thinking she probably did, considering the fact that she already had glasses and braces. I mean, all of that, and flat-chested, too? God wouldn't be so cruel.

5. *Emmanuelle*–In the eighth grade, my best friend and I found this book on top of a trash can on East 3rd Street. We took turns reading it out loud. It was very, very good. At least the parts I remember. Maya, my best friend's housekeeper, caught us reading it and took it away before we'd gotten a chance to finish it.

Books that sucked*

1. *The Scarlet Letter*–You know what would have been cool? If there had been a rift in the space-time continuum, and one of those Eurotrash terrorists Bruce Willis is always chasing in the Die Hard movies dropped a nuclear bomb on the town where Arthur Dimmesdale and all those losers lived, and blew it sky high. That's about the only thing I can think of that would have made this book even remotely interesting.

2. *Our Town*–Okay, this is a play and not a book, but they still made us read it, and all I have to say about it is that, basically, you find out when you die that nobody cared about you and we're all alone forever, the end. Okay! Thanks for that! I feel much better now!

3. *The Mill on the Floss*–I don't want to give anything

away here, but midway through the book, just when things were going good and there were all these hot romances (not as hot as in *Emmanuelle*, though, so don't get your hopes up) someone very crucial to the plot DIES, which if you ask me is just a cop-out so the author could make her deadline on time.

4. *Anne of Green Gables*—All that blah-blah-blah about imagination. I tried to imagine some car chases or explosions that would actually make this book good, but I must be like all of Anne's drippy unimaginative friends, because I couldn't.

5. *Little House on the Prairie*—Little yawn on the big snore. I have all ninety-seven thousand of these books, because people kept on giving them to me when I was little, and all I have to say is if Half Pint had lived in Manhattan, she'd have gotten her you-know-what-kicked from here to Avenue D.

* Mrs. Spears, I believe the word *sucked* is transitive in this instance.

THURSDAY, DECEMBER 11, FOURTH PERIOD

No PE today!

Instead there is an assembly.

And it's not because there's a sporting event they want us all to show our support for. No! This was no pep rally. There wasn't a cheerleader in sight. Well, okay, there were cheerleaders in sight, but they weren't in uniform or anything. They were sitting in the bleachers with the rest of us. Well, not really with the rest of us, since they were in the best seats, the ones in the middle, all jostling to see who could sit next to Justin Baxendale, who has apparently ousted Josh Richter as hottest guy in school, but whatever.

No. Instead, it appears that there has been a major disciplinary infraction at Albert Einstein High School. An act of random vandalism that has shaken the administration's faith in us. Which was why they called an assembly, so that they could better convey their feelings of—as Lilly just whispered in my ear—disillusionment and betrayal.

And what was this act that has Principal Gupta and the trustees so up in arms?

Why, someone pulled a fire alarm yesterday, that's what.

Oops.

I have to say, I have never done anything really bad before—well, I dropped an eggplant out a sixteenth-floor window a couple of months ago, but no one got hurt or anything—but there really is something sort of thrilling about it. I mean, I would never want to do anything *too* bad, like anything where someone might get hurt.

But I have to say, it is immensely gratifying to have all these people coming up to the microphone and decrying my behavior.

I probably wouldn't feel so good about it if I'd gotten caught, though.

I am being urged to come forward and turn myself in even as I write this. Apparently, the guilt for my action is going to hound me well past my teen years, possibly even into my twenties and beyond.

Okay, can I just tell you how much I'm NOT going to think about high school when I am in my twenties? I am going to be way too busy working with Greenpeace to save the whales to worry about some stupid fire alarm I pulled in the ninth grade.

The administration is offering a reward for information leading to the identity of the perpetrator of this heinous crime. A reward! You know what the reward is? A free movie pass to the Sony Imax theater. That's all I'm worth! A movie pass!

The only person who could possibly turn me in isn't even paying attention to the assembly. I can see Justin Baxendale has got a Game Boy out, and is playing it with the sound off while Lana and her fellow cheer cronies look over his broad shoulders, probably panting so hard they're fogging up the screen.

I guess Justin hasn't put two and two together yet. You know, about seeing me in the hallway just before that fire alarm went off. With any luck, he never will.

Mr. Gianini, though. That's another story. I see him over there, talking to Mrs. Hill. He has obviously not told anyone that he suspects me.

Maybe he doesn't suspect me. Maybe he thinks Lilly did it, and I know about it. That could be. I can tell Lilly really wishes she'd done it, because she keeps on muttering under her breath about how, when she finds out who did it, she's going to kill that person, etc.

She's just jealous, of course. That's because now it seems like some kind of political statement, instead of what it actually was: a way to prevent a political statement.

Principal Gupta is looking at us very sternly. She says that it is always natural to want to burn off a little steam right before finals, but that she hopes we will choose positive channels for this, such as the penny drive the Community Outreach Club is holding in order to benefit the victims of Tropical Storm Fred, which flooded several suburban New Jersey neighborhoods last November.

Ha! As if contributing to a stupid penny drive can ever give anybody the same kind of thrill as committing a completely random act of civil disobedience.

LILLY MOSCOVITZ'S LIST OF THE
TOP TEN BEST MOVIES OF ALL TIME

(with commentary by Mia Thermopolis)

Say Anything: Kickboxing iconoclast Lloyd Dobler, as played by John When-Is-He-Going-to-Run-for-President-So-We-Can-Have-Someone-Cute-in-the-Oval-Office Cusack, goes after the class brain (Ione Skye), who soon learns what we all know: Lloyd is every girl's dream date. He understands us. He longs to protect us from broken glass in the parking lot of the local 7-Eleven. Need we say more? *(This movie also contains classic song* Joe Lies.)

Reckless: Rebel from wrong side of tracks (Aidan Quinn) goes after straight-arrow cheerleader (Daryl Hannah). A classic example of teens struggling to break the yoke of parental expectation. *(Plus you get to see Aidan Quinn's you-know-what!)*

Desperately Seeking Susan: Bored suburban housewife finds man of her dreams in East Village. An eighties manifesto about female empowerment. Also starring Madonna and that lady who played Roseanne's sister, Jackie. *(Also starring Aidan Quinn as the East Village hottie, only you don't really get to see his you-know-what in this one. But you do get to see his butt!)*

Ladyhawke: Star-crossed lovers are caught in an evil spell that only Matthew Broderick can help them break. Rutger Hauer makes a powerful Navarre, a knight who lives only to exact vengeance upon the man who wronged his fair Isabeau, played by Michelle Pfeiffer. An elegant and moving love story. *(But what is with Matthew Broderick's hair?)*

Dirty Dancing: Spoiled teenage Baby learns a lot more than the cha-cha from long-haired summer resort dance instructor Johnny. A classic tale of coming-of-age in the Catskills, with important messages about the class system in America. *(Only you don't get to see anyone's butt.)*

Flashdance: A welder by day and an exotic dancer by night, Jennifer Beals's Alex is a feminist in a thong, the Elizabeth Cady Stanton of the lap dance, who longs to audition for the Pittsburgh ballet. *(But first she sleeps with her totally hot boss, Michael Nouri, and throws a big rock through his window!)*

The Cutting Edge: Former hockey stud D. B. Sweeney is paired with figure skater and prissy rich girl Moira Kelly in an unlikely quest for Olympic gold. Interesting for its strategic build-up of sexual tension through ice dancing. *(Toe-pick. Toooooooe-pick.)*

Some Kind of Wonderful: Victory of tomboy Mary Stuart Masterson over prissy Lea Thompson for the heart of Eric Stoltz.

As usual, keen insight by John Hughes into the teen psyche/ social structure. *(Last movie in which Eric Stoltz was actually cute.)*

Reality Bites: Who will indie filmmaker Winona Ryder choose, smart-aleck slacker Ethan Hawke, or clean-cut go-getter Ben Stiller? *(Isn't it obvious?)*

Footloose: Out-of-towner flouts small town's anti-dancing laws. Starring Kevin Bacon, who saves Lori Singer from her abusive hick boyfriend. Most notable for scene at the PTA meeting in which Kevin Bacon's character reveals he has actually done homework, as illustrated by his quoting from several biblical passages that support dancing. *(In the movies* Wild Thing *and* Hollow Man *you get to see Kevin Bacon's you-know-what.)*

THURSDAY, DECEMBER 11, G & T

Today was my lunch with Kenny at Big Wong.

I really don't have anything to say about it, except that he didn't ask me to the Nondenominational Winter Dance. Not only that, but it appears that Kenny's passion for me has ebbed significantly since it hit its zenith on Tuesday.

I of course was beginning to suspect this, since he's stopped calling me after school, and I haven't had one Instant Message from him since before the great Ice-Skating Debacle. He says it's because he's so busy studying for finals and all, but I suspect something else:

He knows. He knows about Michael.

I mean, come on. How can he not?

Well, okay, maybe he doesn't know about Michael *specifically*, but Kenny must know *generally* that he is not the one who lights my fire.

If I had a fire, that is.

No, Kenny is just being nice.

Which I appreciate, and all, but I just wish he'd come out and say it. All this kindness, this solicitousness, it's just making me feel worse. I mean, how could I? Really? How could I have ever agreed to be Kenny's girlfriend, knowing full well I liked someone else? By rights, Kenny should go to *Majesty* magazine and spill all. "Royal Betrayal," they could call it. I totally would understand it, if he did.

But he won't. Because he's too nice.

Instead, he ordered steamed vegetable dumplings for me, and pork buns for him (one encouraging sign that Kenny might not love me as much as he used to insist: he's eating meat again) and talked about Bio and what had happened at assembly (I didn't tell him it was me who pulled the alarm, and he didn't ask me, so there was no need to shield my nostrils). He mentioned again how sorry he was about my tongue, and asked how I was doing in Algebra, and offered to come over and tutor me if I wanted (Kenny tested out of freshman Algebra), even though of course I live with an Algebra teacher. Still, you could tell he meant to be nice.

Which just makes me feel worse. Because of what I'm going to have to do after finals and all.

But he didn't ask me to the dance.

I don't know if this means we aren't going, or if it means he considers the fact we are going a given.

I swear, I do not understand boys at all.

As if lunch wasn't bad enough, G and T isn't too great, either. No, Judith Gershner isn't here . . . but neither is Michael. The guy is AWOL. Nobody knows where he is. Lilly had to tell Mrs. Hill, when she took attendance, that her brother was in the bathroom.

I wonder where he really is. Lilly says that since he started writing this new program that the Computer Club will be unveiling at the Winter Carnival, she's hardly seen him.

Which is no real change, since Michael hardly comes out of his room anyway, but still. You'd think he'd come home once in a while to study.

But I guess, seeing as how he already got into his first-choice college, his grades don't really matter anymore.

Besides, like Lilly, Michael is a genius. What does he need to study for?

Unlike the rest of us.

I wish they'd put the door back on the supply closet. It is extremely hard to concentrate with Boris scraping away on his violin in there. Lilly says this is just another tactic by the trustees to weaken our resistance, so we will remain the mindless drones they are trying to make us, but I think it's just on account of that time we all forgot to let him out, and he was stuck in there until the night custodian heard his anguished pleas to be released.

Which is Lilly's fault, if you think about it. I mean, she's his girlfriend. She should really take better care of him.

HOMEWORK

ALGEBRA: PRACTICE TEST
ENGLISH: TERM PAPER
WORLD CIV: PRACTICE TEST
G & T: NONE
FRENCH: *L'EXAMEN PRATIQUE*
BIOLOGY: PRACTICE TEST

THURSDAY, DECEMBER 11, 9 P.M.

Grandmère is seriously out of control. Tonight she started quizzing me on the names and responsibilities of all my dad's cabinet ministers. Not only do I have to know exactly what they do, but also their marital status and the names and ages of their kids, if any. These are the kids I am supposedly going to have to hang out with while celebrating Christmas at the palace. I am figuring they will probably hate me as much, if not more, than Mr. Gianini's niece and nephew hated me at Thanksgiving.

All my holidays from now on are apparently going to be spent in the company of kids who hate me.

You know, I would just like to say that it is totally not my fault I am a princess. They have no right to hate me so much. I have done everything I could to maintain a normal life in spite of my royal status. I have totally turned down opportunities to be on the covers of *CosmoGirl*, *Teen People*, *Seventeen*, *YM*, and *Girls' Life*. I have refused invitations to go on *TRL* and introduce the number-one video in the country, and when the mayor asked if I wanted to be the one to press the button that drops the ball in Times Square on New Year's Eve, I said no (aside from the fact I am going to be in Genovia for New Year's, I oppose the mayor's mosquito spraying campaign, as runoff from the pesticides used to kill the mosquitos that may be carrying the West Nile virus has infected the local horseshoe crab population. A compound in the blood of horseshoe crabs, which nest all along the Eastern Seaboard, is used to test the purity of every drug and vaccine administered in the US. The crabs are routinely gathered, drained of a third of their blood, then re-released into the sea . . . a sea that is now killing them as well as many other arthropods, such as lobsters, thanks to the amount of pesticide in it).

Anyway, I am just saying, all the kids who hate me should just chill, because I have never once sought the spotlight I have been thrust into. I've never even called my own press conference.

But I digress.

So Sebastiano was there, drinking aperitifs and listening as I rattled off name after name (Grandmère has made flashcards out of the pictures of the cabinet ministers—kind of like those bubble gum cards you can get of the Backstreet Boys, only the cabinet ministers don't wear as much leather). I was kind of thinking maybe I was wrong about Sebastiano's commitment to fashion, and that maybe Sebastiano was there to try to pick up some pointers for after he's thrust me into the path of an oncoming limo or whatever.

But when Grandmère paused to take a phone call from her old friend General Pinochet, Sebastiano started asking me all these questions about clothes, in particular what clothes my friends and I like to wear. What were my feelings, he wanted to know, on velvet stretch pants? Spandex tube tops? Sequins?

I told him all of that sounded, you know, okay for Halloween or Jersey City, but that generally in my day-to-day life I prefer cotton. He looked saddened by this, so I told him that I really felt orange was going to be the next pink, and that perked him right up, and he wrote a bunch of stuff down in this notebook he carries around. Kind of like I do, now that I think about it.

When Grandmère got off the phone, I informed her— quite diplomatically, I might add—that, considering how much progress we'd made in the past three months, I felt more than prepared for my impending introduction to the people of Genovia, and that I did not feel it would be necessary to have lessons next week, as I have FIVE finals to prepare for.

But Grandmère got totally huffy about it! She was all, "Where did you get the idea that your academic education is more important than your royal training? Your father, I suppose. With him, it's always education, education, education. He doesn't realize that education is nowhere near as important as deportment."

"Grandmère," I said. "I need an education if I'm going to run Genovia properly." Especially if I'm going to convert the palace into a giant animal shelter—something I'm not going to be able to do until Grandmère is dead, so I see no point in mentioning it to her now . . . or ever, for that matter.

Grandmère said some swear words in French, which wasn't very dowager-princessy of her, if you ask me. Thankfully right then my dad walked in, looking for his Genovian Air Force medal, since he had a state dinner to go to over at the embassy. I told him about my finals and how I really needed time off from princess stuff to study, and he was all, "Yes, of course."

When Grandmère protested, he just went, "For God's sake, if she hasn't got it by now, she never will."

Grandmère pressed her lips together and didn't say anything more after that. Sebastiano used the opportunity to ask me about my feelings on rayon. I told him I didn't have any.

For once, I was telling the truth.

FRIDAY, DECEMBER 12, HOMEROOM

HERE'S WHAT I HAVE TO DO:

1. Stop thinking about Michael, especially when I should be studying.
2. Stop telling Grandmère anything about my personal life.
3. Start acting more:
   A. Mature
   B. Responsible
   C. Regal
4. Stop biting my fingernails.
5. Write down everything Mom and Mr. G need to know about how to take care of Fat Louie while I'm gone.
6. CHRISTMAS/HANNUKAH PRESENTS!
7. Stop watching *Baywatch* when I should be studying.
8. Stop playing Pod-Racer when I should be studying.
9. Stop listening to music when I should be studying.
10. Break up with Kenny.

FRIDAY, DECEMBER 12,
PRINCIPAL GUPTA'S OFFICE

Well, I guess it's official now:

I, Mia Thermopolis, am a juvenile delinquent.

Seriously. That fire alarm I pulled was only the beginning, it appears.

I really don't know what's come over me lately. It's like the closer I get to actually going to Genovia and performing my first official duties as its princess, the less like a princess I act.

I wonder if I'll be expelled.

If I am, it is totally unfair. Lana started it. I was sitting there in Algebra, listening to Mr. G go on about the Cartesian plane, when suddenly Lana turns around in her seat and slaps a copy of *USA Today* down in front of me. There is a headline screaming:

TODAY'S POLL

MOST POPULAR YOUNG ROYAL

Fifty-seven percent of readers say that **PRINCE WILLIAM OF ENGLAND** *is their favorite young royal,*

163

with *Will's little brother,* **HARRY,** *coming in at 28 percent. America's own royal,* **PRINCESS MIA RENALDO OF GENOVIA,** *comes in third, with 13 percent of the votes, and Prince Andrew and Sarah Ferguson's daughters,* **BEATRICE** *and* **EUGENIE,** *round out the votes with 1 percent each.*

The reasons given for Princess Mia's third-place finish? "Not outgoing" is the most common answer. Ironically, Princess Mia is perceived as being as shy as Princess Diana—the mother of William and Harry—when she first stepped into the harsh glare of the media spotlight.

Princess Mia, who only recently learned she was heir to the throne of Genovia, a small principality located on the Cote d'Azur, is expected to make her first official trip to that country next week. A representative for the princess describes her as looking forward to her visit with "eager anticipation." The princess will continue her education in America, and will reside in Genovia only during the summer months.

I read the stupid article and then passed the paper back to Lana.

"So?" I whispered to her.

"So," Lana whispered. "I wonder how popular you'd be—especially with the people of Genovia—if they found out their future ruler goes around pulling fire alarms when there isn't any fire."

She was only guessing, of course. She couldn't have seen me. Unless . . .

Unless maybe Justin Baxendale did figure it out! You know, seeing me in the hallway like that, just before the alarm went off—and he mentioned it to Lana. . . .

No. Not possible. I am so far out of the sphere of Justin Baxendale's consciousness as to be nonexistent to him. He didn't tell Lana anything. Lana, like Mr. G, obviously thinks it's a little coincidental that on that fateful Wednesday, the fire alarm went off about two minutes after I'd disappeared from class with the pass to the bathroom.

But even so. Even though she could only have been guessing, it seemed to me like she knew, like she was going to make sure I never heard the end of it.

I really don't know what came over me. I don't know if it was

A. The stress of finals

B. My impending trip to Genovia

C. This thing with Kenny

D. The fact that I'm in love with this guy who is going out with a human fruit fly

E. The fact that my mother is going to give birth to my Algebra teacher's baby

F. The fact that Lana has been persecuting me practically my whole life and pretty much getting away with it, or

G. All of the above.

Whatever the reason, I snapped. Just snapped. Suddenly, I found myself reaching for Lana's cell phone, which was lying on her desktop beside her calculator.

And then the next thing I knew, I had put the tiny little pink thing on the floor, and crushed it into a lot of pieces beneath the heel of my size-ten combat boot.

I guess I can't really blame Mr. G for sending me to the principal's office.

Still, you would expect a little sympathy from your own stepfather.

Uh-oh. Here comes Principal Gupta.

FRIDAY, DECEMBER 12, 5 P.M., THE LOFT

Well, that's it then. I'm suspended.

Suspended. I can't believe it. ME! Mia Thermopolis! What is happening to me? I used to be such a good kid!

And okay, it's just for one day, but still. It's going on my permanent record! What are the Genovian cabinet ministers going to say?

I am turning into Courtney Love.

And yeah, it's not like I'm not going to get into college because I was suspended for one day in the first semester of my freshman year, but how totally embarrassing! Principal Gupta treated me like I was some kind of criminal or something.

And you know what they say: Treat a person like a criminal, and pretty soon, she'll end up like one. At least I think that's what they say. The way things are going, I wouldn't be surprised if pretty soon I start wearing ripped-up fishnet stockings and dying my hair black. Maybe I'll even start smoking and get my ears double pierced or something. And then they'll make a TV movie

167

about me, and call it *Royal Scandal*. It will show me going up to Prince William and saying, "Who's the most popular young royal now, huh, punk?" and then headbutting him or something.

Except I practically fainted the first time I got my ears pierced, and smoking is really bad for you, and I always thought it must hurt to headbutt someone.

I guess I don't have the makings of a juvenile delinquent after all.

My dad doesn't think so, either. He's all ready to set the royal Genovian lawyers on Principal Gupta. The only problem, of course, is that I won't tell him—or anybody else, for that matter—what Lana said to make me assault her cell phone. It's kind of hard to prove the attack was provoked if the attacker won't say what the provocation was. My dad pleaded with me for a while when he came to pick me up from school, after having received The Call from Principal Gupta. But when I wouldn't tell him what he wanted, and Lars just looked carefully blank, my dad just went, "Fine," and his mouth got all scrunchy like it does when Grandmère has one too many Sidecars and starts calling him Papa Cueball.

But how can I tell him what Lana said? If I do that, then everyone will know I'm guilty of not just one crime, but two!

Anyway, now I'm home, watching the Lifetime channel with my mother. She hasn't been doing much painting at her studio since she got pregnant. This is on account of her being exhausted. It's quite hard to paint lying down, she's discovered. So instead she has been doing a lot of sketching from bed, mostly line drawings of Fat Louie, who seems to enjoy having someone home all day with him. He sits for hours on her bed, watching the pigeons on the fire escape outside her window.

But since I'm home today, Mom did some drawings of me. I think she is making my mouth too big, but I'm not saying anything, as Mr. Gianini and I have discovered it's better not to upset my mother in her current hormonal state. Even the slightest criticism—like asking her why she left the phone bill in the vegetable crisper—can lead to an hour-long crying jag.

While she sketched me, I watched a very excellent movie called *Mother, May I Sleep with Danger?* starring Tori Spelling, of *Beverly Hills 90210* fame, as a girl who has an abusive boyfriend. I really don't get why any girl would stay with a guy who hits her, but my mom says it's all about self-esteem and your relationship with your father. Except that my mom doesn't have that great a relationship with Papaw, and if any guy ever tried to slug her, you can bet she'd put him in the hospital, so go figure.

As my mom drew, she tried to get me to spill my guts to her, you know, about what Lana said that made me go on a cell-phone-stomping rampage. You could tell she was trying really hard to be all TV mom about it.

I guess it must have worked, because all of a sudden I found myself telling her all of it, every last thing: the stuff about Kenny and about my not liking to kiss him and about him telling everybody, and about how I plan to break up with him as soon as finals are over.

And along the way, I mentioned Michael and Judith Gershner and Tina and the greeting cards and the Winter Carnival and Lilly and her protest group and how I'm secretary of it, and just about everything else, except the part about pulling the fire alarm.

After a while my mom stopped drawing and just looked at me.

Finally, when I was done, she said, "You know what I think you need?"

And I said, "What?"

And she said, "A vacation."

So then we had a sort of vacation, right there on her bed. I mean, she wouldn't let me go study. Instead, she made me order a pizza, and together we watched the satisfying but completely unbelievable end of *Mother, May I Sleep with Danger?*, which was followed, much to our joy, by the dishiest made-for-TV movie ever, *Midwest Obsession*, in which Courtney Thorne-Smith plays the local Dairy Princess, who goes around in a pink Cadillac wearing cow earrings and kills people like Tracey Gold for messing with her boyfriend. And the best part was, it was all *based on a true story*.

For a while, there on my mom's bed, it was almost like old times. You know, before my mom met Mr. Gianini and I found out I was a princess.

Except, of course, not really, because she's pregnant, and I'm suspended.

But why quibble?

FRIDAY, DECEMBER 12, 8 P.M., THE LOFT

Oh, my God, I just checked my email. I am being inundated with supportive messages from my friends!

They all want to congratulate me on my decisive handling of Lana Weinberger. They sympathize with my suspension and encourage me to stay firm in my refusal to back down from my stand against the administration (what stand against the administration? All I did was destroy a cell phone. It has nothing to do with the administration). Lilly went so far as to compare me with Mary, Queen of Scots, who was imprisoned and then beheaded by Elizabeth I.

I wonder if Lilly would still think that if she knew that the reason I smashed Lana's cell phone was because she was threatening to spill the beans about my having pulled the fire alarm that ruined Lilly's walkout.

Lilly says it's all a matter of principle, that I was banished from the school for refusing to back down from my beliefs. But actually, I was banished from school for destroying someone else's private property—and I only did it to cover up for another crime that I committed.

No one knows that but me, though. Well, me and Lana. And even she doesn't know for sure why I did it. I mean, it could have been just one of those random acts of violence that are going around.

Everyone else, however, is seeing it as this great political act. Tomorrow, at the first meeting of the Students Against the Corporatization of Albert Einstein High School, my case is going to be held up as an example of one of the many unjust decisions of the Gupta Administration.

I think tomorrow I might develop a case of weekend strep throat.

Anyway, I wrote back to everyone, telling them how much I appreciate their support, and not to make a bigger deal out of this than it actually is. I mean, I'm not proud of what I did. I would much rather have NOT done it, and stayed in school.

One bright note: Michael is definitely getting the cards I've been sending him. Tina walked by his locker today after PE and saw him take the latest one out and put it in his backpack! Unfortunately, according to Tina, he did not wear an expression of dazed passion as he slipped the card into his bag, nor did he gaze at it tenderly. He did not even put it away very carefully: Tina regretted to inform me that he slipped his iMac laptop into his backpack next, undoubtedly squashing the card.

But he wouldn't, Tina hastened to assure me, have

done that if he'd known it was from you, Mia! Maybe if you'd signed it . . .

But if I signed it, he'd know I like him! More than that, he'd know I love him, since I do believe the L word was mentioned in at least one card. And what if he doesn't feel the same way about me? How embarrassing! Way worse than being suspended.

Oh, no! As I was writing this, I got Instant Messaged by, of all people, Michael himself! I freaked out so bad, I shrieked and scared Fat Louie, who was sleeping on my lap as I wrote. He sank all his claws into me, and now I have little puncture marks all over my thighs.

Michael wrote:

CRACKING: Hey, Thermopolis, what's this I hear about you getting suspended?

I wrote back:

FTLOUIE: Just for one day.

CRACKING: What'd you do?

FTLOUIE: Crushed a cheerleader's cellular phone.

CRACKING: Your parents must be so proud.

FTLOUIE: If so, they've done a pretty good job of disguising it so far.

CRACKING: So are you grounded?

FTLOUIE: Surprisingly, no. The attack on the cell phone was provoked.

CRACKING: So you'll still be going to the Carnival next week?

FTLOUIE: As secretary to the Students Against the Corporatization of Albert Einstein High School, I believe my attendance is required. Your sister is planning for us to have a booth.

CRACKING: That Lilly. She's always looking out for the good of mankind.

FTLOUIE: That's one way of putting it.

We probably would have talked longer, but right then my mom yelled at me to get off-line, since she's waiting to hear from Mr. Gianini, who, surprisingly, still wasn't home from school, even though it was past dinnertime. So I logged off.

This is the second time Michael's asked if I'm going to the Winter Carnival. What's up with that?

FRIDAY, DECEMBER 12, 9 P.M., THE LOFT

Now we know why Mr. G was so late getting home:

He stopped along the way to buy a Christmas tree.

Not just any Christmas tree, either, but a twelve-footer that must be at least six feet wide at the base.

I didn't say anything negative, of course, because my mom was so happy and excited about it, and immediately lugged out all her Dead Celebrity Christmas ornaments (my mom doesn't use pretty glass balls or tinsel on her Christmas tree, like normal people. Instead, she paints pieces of tin with the likenesses of celebrities who have died that year, and hangs those on the tree. Which is why we probably have the only tree in North America with ornaments commemorating Richard and Pat Nixon, Elvis, Audrey Hepburn, Kurt Cobain, Jim Henson, John Belushi, Rock Hudson, Alec Guinness, Divine, John Lennon, and many, many more).

And Mr. Gianini kept looking over at me, to see if I was happy, too. He got the tree, he said, because he knew what a bad day I'd had, and he didn't want it to be a total loss.

Mr. G, of course, has no idea what my English term paper topic is.

What was I supposed to say? I mean, he'd already gone out and bought it, and you know a tree that size had to have cost a lot of money. And he'd meant to do a nice thing. He really had.

Still, I wish the people around here would consult me about things before just going out and doing them. Like the whole pregnancy thing, and now this tree. If Mr. G had asked me, I would have been like, Let's go to the Big Kmart on Astor Place and get a nice fake tree so we don't contribute to the destruction of the polar bear's natural habitat, okay?

Only he didn't ask me.

And the truth is, even if he had, my mom would never have gone for it. Her favorite part of Christmas is lying on the floor with her head under the tree, gazing up through the branches and inhaling the sweet tangy smell of pine sap. She says it's the only memory of her Indiana childhood she actually likes.

It's hard to think about the polar bears when your mom says something like that.

SATURDAY, DECEMBER 13, 2 P.M., LILLY'S APARTMENT

Well, the first meeting of the Students Against the Corporatization of Albert Einstein High School is a complete bust.

That's because nobody showed up but me and Boris Pelkowski. I am a little miffed that Kenny didn't come. You would think that if he really loves me as much as he says he does, he would take any opportunity whatsoever to be near me, even a boring meeting of the Students Against the Corporatization of Albert Einstein High School.

But I guess even Kenny's love is not that great. As should be obvious to me by now, considering the fact that there are exactly six days until the Nondenominational Winter Dance, and Kenny STILL HASN'T ASKED ME IF I WANT TO GO WITH HIM.

Not that I'm worried, or anything. I mean, a girl who set off a fire alarm AND smashed Lana Weinberger's cell phone, worried about not having a date to a stupid dance?

All right. I'm worried.

But not worried enough to pull a Sadie Hawkins and ask *him* to the dance.

Lilly is pretty much inconsolable over the fact that no one but Boris and me showed up for her meeting. I tried to tell her that everybody is too busy studying for finals to worry about privatization at the moment, but she doesn't seem to care. Right now she is sitting on the couch, with Boris speaking to her in a soothing voice. Boris is pretty gross and all—with his sweaters that he always tucks into his pants, and that weird retainer his orthodontist makes him wear—but you can tell he genuinely loves Lilly. I mean, look at the tender way he is gazing at her as she sobs about how she is going to call her congressmember.

It makes my heart hurt, looking at Boris looking at Lilly.

I guess I must be jealous. I want a boy to look at *me* like that. And I don't mean Kenny, either. I mean a boy who I actually like back, as more than just a friend.

I can't take it anymore. I am going into the kitchen to see what Maya, the Moscovitzes' housekeeper, is doing. Even helping to wash things has to be better than this.

SATURDAY, DECEMBER 13, 2:30 P.M., LILLY'S APARTMENT

Maya wasn't in the kitchen. She was here, in Michael's room, putting away his school uniform, which she just finished ironing. Maya is going around picking up Michael's things and telling me about her son Manuel. Thanks to the help of the Drs. Moscovitz, Manuel was recently released from the prison in the Dominican Republic where he'd been wrongfully held for suspicion of having committed crimes against the state. Now Manuel is starting his own political party, and Maya is just as proud as can be, except she is worried he might end up back in prison if he doesn't tone down the anti-government stuff a little.

Manuel and Lilly have a lot in common, I guess.

Maya's stories about Manuel are always interesting, but it is much more interesting to be in Michael's room. I have been in it before, of course, but never while he was gone (he is at school, even though it is Saturday, working in the computer lab on his project for the Carnival; apparently the school's modem is faster than his. Also, I suppose, though I hate to admit it, he and Judith Gershner can freely practice their downloading there, without fear of parental interruption).

So I am lying on Michael's bed while Maya putters around, folding shirts and muttering about sugar, one of her native land's main exports and apparently a source of some consternation to her son's political platform, while Michael's dog, Pavlov, sits next to me, panting on my face. I can't help thinking, *This is what it's like to be Michael: This is what Michael sees when he looks up at his ceiling at night* (he has put glow-in-the-dark stars up there, in the form of the spiral galaxy Andromeda) and *This is how Michael's sheets smell* (springtime fresh, thanks to the detergent Maya uses) and *This is what the view of Michael's desk looks like from his bed.*

Except that looking over at his desk, I just noticed something. It's one of my cards! The one with the strawberry on it!

It isn't exactly on display, or anything. It's just sitting on his desk. But hey, that's a far cry from being crumpled at the bottom of his backpack. It shows that the cards mean something to him, that he hasn't buried them under all the other junk on his desk—the DOS manuals and anti-Microsoft literature—or worse, thrown them away.

This is somewhat heartening.

Uh-oh. I just heard the front door open. Michael???
Or the Drs. Moscovitz???? I better get out of here. Michael
doesn't have all those *Enter at Your Own Risk* signs on
the door for nothing.

SATURDAY, DECEMBER 13, 3 P.M., GRANDMÈRE'S

How, you might ask, did I go from the Moscovitzes' apartment to my grandmother's suite at the Plaza in the space of a mere half hour?

Well, I'll tell you.

Disaster has struck, in the form of Sebastiano.

I always suspected, of course, that Sebastiano was not the sweet-tempered innocent he pretended to be. But now it looks like the only murder Sebastiano needs to worry about is his own. Because if my dad ever gets his hands on him, Sebastiano is one dead fashion designer.

Looking at it objectively, I think I can safely say I'd prefer to have been murdered. I mean, I'd be dead and all, which would be sad—especially since I still haven't written down those instructions for caring for Fat Louie while I'm gone—but at least I wouldn't have to show up for school on Monday.

But now, not only do I have to show up for school on Monday, but I have to show up for school on Monday knowing that every single one of my fellow classmates is going to have seen the supplement that arrived in the *Sunday Times*: the supplement featuring about twenty photos of ME standing in front of a triple mirror in dresses by Sebastiano, with the words "Fashion Fit for a Princess" emblazoned all over the place.

Oh, yes. I'm not kidding. Fashion Fit for a Princess.

I can't really blame him, I guess. Sebastiano, I mean. I suppose the opportunity was too much for him to resist. He is, after all, a businessman, and having a princess model your clothes . . . well, you can't buy exposure like that.

Because you know all the other papers are going to pick up on the story. You know, Princess of Genovia Makes Modeling Debut. That kind of thing.

So with just one little photo spread, Sebastiano is going to get virtual worldwide coverage of his new clothing line.

A clothing line that it looks like I have endorsed.

Grandmère doesn't understand why my dad and I are so upset. Well, I think she gets why my dad is upset. You know the whole "My daughter is being used" thing. She just doesn't get why *I'm* so unhappy. "You look perfectly beautiful," she keeps saying.

Yeah. Like that helps.

Grandmère thinks I am overreacting. But hello, have I ever aspired to tread in Claudia Schiffer's footsteps? I don't think so. Fashion is so not what I'm about. What about the environment? What about the rights of animals? What about the HORSESHOE CRABS??????

People are not going to believe I didn't pose for those photos. People are going to think I am a sellout. People are going to think I am a stuck-up model snob.

I would so rather that they think I am a juvenile delinquent, I can't tell you.

Little did I know when I heard the front door to the Moscovitzes' apartment opening, and I hustled out of Michael's room, that I was about to be greeted by the disastrous news. It was only Lilly's parents, after all, coming home from the gym, where they'd met with their personal trainers. Afterward, they'd stopped to have a latte and read the *Sunday Times*, large sections of which arrive, for reasons no one understands, on Saturday, if you have a subscription.

What a surprise they had had, when they'd opened up the paper and saw the Princess of Genovia hawking this hot new fashion designer's spring collection.

What a surprise I had, when the Drs. Moscovitz congratulated me on my new modeling career, and I was all, "What are you talking about?"

So, while Lilly and Boris looked on with curiosity, Dr. Moscovitz opened her paper and showed me:

And there it was, in all its four-color-layout glory.

I'm not going to lie and say I looked bad. I looked okay. What they had done was, they had taken all the photos Sebastiano's assistant had snapped of me trying to decide which dress to wear to my introduction to the people of Genovia and laid them all out on this purple background. I'm not smiling in the pictures, or anything. I'm just looking at myself in the mirror, clearly going, in my head, *Ew, could I look more like a walking toothpick?*

But of course, if you didn't know me, and didn't know WHY I was trying on all these dresses, I'd seem like some freak who cares WAY too much about how she looks in a party dress.

Which is exactly the kind of person I've always wanted to be portrayed as.

NOT!!!!!!!

I have to admit, I am a little hurt. I'd thought, when he'd asked me all those questions about Michael, Sebastiano and I had kind of made a connection. But I guess not. Not if he could do something like this.

My dad has already called the *Times* and demanded that they remove the supplement from all the papers that haven't been delivered yet. He has called the concierge of the Plaza and insisted on Sebastiano being listed as persona non grata, which means the cousin to the prince of Genovia won't be allowed to set foot on hotel property.

I thought this was a little harsh, but not as harsh as what my dad *wanted* to do, which was call the NYPD and press charges against Sebastiano for using the likeness of a minor without the consent of her parents. Thank God Grandmère talked him out of that. She said there'd be enough publicity about this without the added humiliation of a royal arrest.

My dad is still so mad he can't sit still. He is pacing back and forth across the suite. Rommel is watching him very nervously from Grandmère's lap, his head moving back and forth, back and forth, his eyes following my dad as if he were watching the US Open or something.

I bet if Sebastiano *were* here, my dad would smash up a lot more than just his cell phone.

SATURDAY, DECEMBER 13, 5 P.M., THE LOFT

Well.

All I can say is, Grandmère's really done it this time.

I'm serious. I don't think my dad is ever going to speak to her again.

And I know *I* never will.

And okay, she's an old lady and she didn't know that what she was doing was wrong, and I should really be more understanding.

But for her to do *this*—for her not to even take into consideration my feelings—I frankly don't think I will ever be able to forgive her.

What happened was, Sebastiano called right before I was getting ready to leave the hotel. He was completely perplexed about why my dad is so mad at him. He tried to come upstairs to see us, he said, but Plaza security stopped him.

When my dad, who'd answered the phone, told Sebastiano that the reason Plaza security stopped him was because he'd been PNG'd, and then explained why,

Sebastiano was even more upset. He kept going, "But I had your permish! I had your permish, Phillipe!"

"My permission to use my daughter's image to promote your tawdry rags?" My father was disgusted. "You most certainly did not!"

But Sebastiano kept insisting he had.

And little by little, it came out that he *had* had permission, in a way. Only not from me. And not my dad, either. Guess who, it appears, gave it to him?

Grandmère went, all indignantly, "I only did it, Phillipe, because Amelia, as you know, suffers from a terrible self-image, and needed a boost."

But my dad was so enraged, he wouldn't even listen to her. He just thundered, "And so to repair her self-image, you went behind her back and gave permission for her photo to be used in an advertisement for *women's clothing*?"

Grandmère didn't have much to say after that. She just stood there, going, "Uhn . . . uhn . . . uhn . . . " like someone in a horror movie who'd been pinned to a wall with a machete but wasn't quite dead yet (I always close my eyes during parts like this, so I know exactly what it sounds like).

It became clear that even if Grandmère had had a reasonable excuse for her behavior, my father wasn't going to listen to it—or let me listen to it, either. He stalked over to me, grabbed my arm, and marched me right out of the suite.

I thought we were going to have a bonding moment, like fathers and daughters always do on TV, where he'd tell me that Grandmère was a very sick woman and that he was going to send her somewhere where she could take a nice, long rest, but instead all he said was, "Go home."

Then he handed me over to Lars—after slamming the door to Grandmère's suite VERY loudly behind him, before storming off in the direction of his own suite.

Jeez.

It just goes to show, even a royal family can be dysfunctional.

Couldn't you just see us on *Ricki Lake*?

Ricki: Clarisse, tell us: Why did you allow Sebastiano to put your granddaughter's photos in that *Times* advertising supplement?

Grandmère: That's Your Royal Highness to you, Ms. Lake. I did it to boost her self-esteem.

I just know that when I get to school on Monday, everybody is going to be all, "Oh, look, here comes Mia, that big FAKE, with her vegetarianism and her animal-rights activism and her looks-aren't-important-it's-what's-on-the-inside-that-matters-ism. But I guess it's all right to pose for *fashion photo shoots*, isn't it, Mia?"

As if it wasn't enough to be suspended. Now I am going to be sneered at by my peers, too.

I'm home now, trying to pretend none of it ever happened. This is difficult, of course, because when I walked back into the loft, I saw that my mom had already pulled the supplement out of our paper and drawn little devil horns coming out of my head in every picture, then stuck the whole thing onto the refrigerator.

While I appreciate this bit of whimsy, it does not make the fact that I will have to show my face—now plastered all over advertising supplements throughout the tristate area—in school on Monday any easier.

Surprisingly, there is one good thing that's come out of all of this: I know for sure I look best in the white taffeta number with the blue sash. My dad says over his dead body am I going to wear it, or any other Sebastiano creation, again. But there isn't another designer in Genovia who could do as good a job, let alone finish the dress in time. So it looks like the dress by Sebastiano, which got delivered to the loft this morning, is it.

Which is one thing off my mind, anyway.

I guess.

SATURDAY, DECEMBER 13, 8 P.M., THE LOFT

I've already gotten seventeen emails, six phone calls, and one visitor (Lilly) about the fashion thing. Lilly says it's not as bad as I think, and that most people throw the supplements away without even looking at them.

If that's true, I said, why are all these people calling and emailing me?

She tried to make out like it was all members of the Students Against the Corporatization of Albert Einstein High School, calling to show their solidarity with my suspension, but I think we both know better:

It's all people who want to know what I was thinking, selling out like that.

How am I ever going to explain that I had nothing to do with it, that I didn't even *know* about it? Nobody is going to believe that. I mean, the proof is right there: I'm *wearing* the proof. There's photographic evidence of it.

My reputation is going down the drain, even as I sit here. Tomorrow morning, millions of subscribers to the *New York Times* are going to open their papers and be like, "Oh, look, Princess Mia. Sold out already. Wonder how much she got paid? You wouldn't think she'd need the money, what with being royal, and all."

Finally I had to ask Lilly to please go home, because I'd developed a bad headache. She tried to cure it with some shiatsu, which her parents frequently employ on their patients, but it didn't work. All that ended up happening was that I think she burst a blood vessel or something between my thumb and index finger, since it really hurts.

Now I am determined to start studying, even though it's Saturday night, and everyone else my age is out having fun.

But haven't you heard? Princesses never get to have any fun.

HERE IS WHAT I HAVE TO DO

ALGEBRA: REVIEW CHAPTERS 1–10

ENGLISH: TERM PAPER, 10 PAGES, DOUBLE SPACED;
UTILIZE APPROPRIATE MARGINS; ALSO, REVIEW
CHAPTERS 1–7

WORLD CIV: REVIEW CHAPTERS 1–12

G & T: NONE

FRENCH: *REVUE CHAPITRES UN–NEUF*

BIOLOGY: REVIEW CHAPTERS 1–12

WRITE OUT INSTRUCTIONS ON HOW TO CARE FOR
FAT LOUIE

CHRISTMAS/HANNUKAH SHOPPING:
MOM–BON JOVI MATERNITY T
DAD–BOOK ON ANGER MANAGEMENT
MR. G–SWISS ARMY KNIFE
LILLY–BLANK VIDEOTAPES
TINA HAKIM BABA–COPY OF *EMMANUELLE*
KENNY–VINTAGE SLIDE RULE (I DON'T THINK THIS IS
TOO EXTRAVAGANT. AND NO, IT'S NOT GUILT, EITHER.
HE REALLY WANTS ONE.)
GRANDMÈRE–NOTHING!!!!!!

PAINT FINGERNAILS (MAYBE PRESENCE OF FOUL-
TASTING POLISH WILL PREVENT BITING THEM OFF)

BREAK UP WITH KENNY

ORGANIZE SOCK DRAWER

I am going to start with the sock drawer, because that is clearly the most important. You can't really concentrate on anything if your socks aren't right.

Then I will move on to Algebra because that is my worst subject, and also my first test. I am going to pass it if it's the last thing I do. NOTHING is going to distract me. Not this thing with Grandmère, not the fact that four of those seventeen emails are from Michael, not the fact that two are from Kenny, not the fact that I am leaving for Europe at the end of next week, not the fact that my mother and Mr. Gianini are in the next room watching *Die Hard*, my favorite Christmas movie, NOTHING.

I WILL PASS ALGEBRA THIS SEMESTER, and NOTHING IS GOING TO DISTRACT ME FROM STUDYING FOR THE FINAL!!!!!!!!!!!!

SATURDAY, DECEMBER 13, 9 P.M., THE LOFT

I just had to go out and see the part where Bruce Willis throws the explosives down the elevator shaft, but now I am back at work.

I was really curious about what Michael could possibly want, so I read his emails—just his. One was about the supplement (Lilly had told him, and he wanted to know if I was thinking of abdicating, ha ha) and the other three were jokes that I guess were supposed to make me feel better. They weren't very funny, but I laughed anyway.

I bet Judith Gershner doesn't laugh at Michael's jokes. She's too busy cloning things.

SATURDAY, DECEMBER 13, 10 P.M., THE LOFT

HOW TO CARE FOR FAT LOUIE WHILE I AM AWAY

A.M.:

In the morning, please fill Fat Louie's bowl with DRY FOOD.
Even if there is already food in the bowl, he likes to have some
fresh served on top so he can feel like he is having breakfast like
the rest of us.

In my bathroom is a BLUE PLASTIC CUP sitting by the bathtub.
Please fill that every morning with water from the bathroom sink.
You must use water from the bathroom sink, because water
from the kitchen sink isn't cold enough. And you have to put it
in the BLUE CUP because that is the cup Fat Louie is used to
drinking out of while I am brushing my teeth.

He has a bowl in the hallway outside my room. Rinse that
out and fill it with water from the WATER FILTER PITCHER
in the refrigerator. It must be water from the WATER FILTER
PITCHER because even though New York tap is said to be

contaminant-free, it is good for Louie to get at least some water that is definitely pure. Cats need to drink a lot of water to flush out their systems and prevent kidney and urinary tract infections, so always leave lots of water out, and not just by his food bowls, but other places as well.

Do not confuse the bowl in the hall with the BOWL BY THE CHRISTMAS TREE. That bowl is there to discourage Louie from drinking out of the tree holder. Too much tree resin could make him constipated.

In the morning, Fat Louie likes to sit on the windowsill in my room and look at the pigeons on the fire escape. NEVER OPEN THIS WINDOW, but be sure the curtains are open so he can see out.

Also, sometimes he likes to look out the windows by the TV. If he cries while he is doing this, it means you should pet him.

P.M.:
At dinnertime, give Fat Louie CANNED FOOD. Fat Louie only likes three flavors: CHICKEN AND TUNA FEAST (FLAKED), SHRIMP AND FISH FEAST (FLAKED), and OCEAN FISH FEAST (FLAKED). He won't eat anything with BEEF or PORK. He must have the contents of the can on a new, CLEAN saucer,

or he won't eat. Also, he won't eat if the contents don't retain their CANLIKE SHAPE on the plate, so don't chop up his food.

After eating his canned food, Fat Louie likes to stretch out on the carpet in front of the front door. This is a good time to give him his exercise. When he stretches out, just put your hand under his front legs and straighten them (he likes this) until he bends like a comma. Then dig your thumbs between his shoulder blades and give him a kitty massage. He will purr if you do it right. If you do it wrong you will know, because he will bite you.

Fat Louie gets bored very easily, and when he gets bored, he walks around crying, so here are some games he likes to play:

Take some pieces of CAT TREAT and line them up on top of the stereo for Fat Louie to knock off and chase.

Put Fat Louie in my COMPUTER CHAIR and then hide behind the bookshelf and throw one end of a shoelace over the back of the chair so he can't see where it is coming from.

Make a FORT out of pillows on my bed and put Fat Louie inside of it and then stick your hand into any openings between the pillows (I recommend wearing an oven mitt during this game).

Put some catnip in an OLD SOCK and throw it to Fat Louie. Then leave him alone for four to five hours, because catnip makes him a little free with his claws.

The Litter Box

Mr. Gianini, this one is for you. Mom must not clean out the litter box or touch anything that may have come in contact with it, or she might develop toxoplasmosis, and the baby might get sick. Always wash your hands in warm, soapy water after changing Fat Louie's litter box, even if you don't think you got anything on your hands.

Fat Louie's box needs to be scooped out EVERY DAY. Always use clumping litter, and then just scoop out the clumps into a Grand Union bag and dispose. Nothing could be simpler. He tends to do number 2 about two hours after his evening meal. You will be able to tell from the odor wafting from his box in my bathroom.

Most Important of All

Remember not to disturb Fat Louie's SPECIAL AREA BEHIND THE TOILET in my bathroom. That is where he keeps his collection of shiny objects. If he takes something of yours and you find it there, be sure not to take it out while he is looking, or for weeks he will try to bite you every time he sees you. I talked to the vet about it, but she said short of hiring an animal behaviorist at $70/hr there is nothing that can be done. We just have to put up with it.

ABOVE ALL, BE SURE TO PICK FAT LOUIE UP SEVERAL TIMES A DAY AND HUG AND SQUEEZE HIM!!!!! (HE LIKES THIS.)

SATURDAY, DECEMBER 13, MIDNIGHT, THE LOFT

I can't believe it's midnight already, and I am still only on Chapter One of *An Introduction to Algebra*!

This book is incomprehensible. I sincerely hope whoever wrote it did not make very much money off it.

I should just go and ask Mr. G what's going to be on the final.

No, that would be cheating.

Wouldn't it?

SUNDAY, DECEMBER 14, 10 A.M., THE LOFT

Only forty-eight hours until the Algebra final, and I am still on Chapter One.

SUNDAY, DECEMBER 14, 10:30 A.M., THE LOFT

Lilly just came over again. She wants to study for World Civ together. I told her I can't worry about World Civ when I am only on Chapter One in my Algebra review, but she said we could alternate: She would quiz me on Algebra for an hour, then I could quiz her on World Civ for an hour. I said okay, even though it really isn't fair: She is getting an A in Algebra, so her quizzing me isn't really helping her any, while my quizzing her in World Civ helps me study for it, too.

But that's what friends are for, I guess.

SUNDAY, DECEMBER 14, 11 A.M., THE LOFT

Tina just called. Her little brother and sisters are driving her crazy. She wanted to know if she could come down and study here. I said sure.

What else could I say? Besides, she promised to stop at H and H for bagels and vegetable cream cheese. And she said she thought the photos of me in the supplement were beautiful and that I shouldn't care if people call me a sellout, because I look so hot.

SUNDAY, DECEMBER 14, NOON, THE LOFT

Michael told Boris where Lilly is, so now Boris is here, too.

Lilly's right. Boris really does breathe too loudly. It's very distracting.

And I wish he wouldn't put his feet on my bed. The least he could do is take his shoes off first. But when I suggested it, Lilly said that would be a bad idea.

Ew. I don't know why Lilly puts up with a boyfriend who is not only a mouth breather but also has stinky feet.

Boris may be a musical genius, but he has a lot to learn about hygiene, if you ask me.

SUNDAY, DECEMBER 14, 12:30 P.M., THE LOFT

Now Kenny's here. I don't know how I am supposed to get any studying done with all these people around. Plus, Mr. Gianini has decided that now would be a good time to practice his drums.

SUNDAY, DECEMBER 14, 8 P.M., THE LOFT

I told Lilly, and she agreed, that once Boris and Kenny showed up, the whole studying thing kind of went down the drain. Plus, Mr. G's drumming didn't help. So we decided it would be best to take a study break and go to Chinatown for dim sum.

We had a good time at Great Shanghai eating vegetable dumplings and dried sauteed string beans with garlic sauce. I ended up sitting by Boris, and he really made me laugh, engineering it so that whenever the waiters brought something new, the only empty spot on the table was in front of him, so they had to put it there, and then Boris and I got first dibs on it.

Which made me realize that in spite of the sweaters and the mouth-breathing, Boris really is a funny and nice person. Lilly is so lucky. I mean, that the boy she loves actually loves her back. If only I could love Kenny the way Lilly loves Boris!

But I don't seem to have any control over who I fall in love with. Believe me, if I did, I would NOT love Michael.

I mean, for one thing, he is my best friend's older brother, and if Lilly ever found out I liked him, she would NOT understand. Also, of course, he is a senior and is graduating soon.

And oh, yeah, he already has a girlfriend.

But what am I supposed to do? I can't *make* myself fall in love with Kenny any more than I can *make* him stop liking me, you know, in that special way.

Although he still hasn't asked me to the dance. Or mentioned it, anyway. Lilly says I should just call him and be like, "So are we going, or not?" After all, she keeps pointing out, I had the guts to smash up Lana's cell phone. Why don't I have the guts to call my own boyfriend and ask him whether he is taking me to the school dance?

But I smashed up Lana's cell phone in the heat of passion. I cannot summon up anything like passion where Kenny is concerned. There is a part of me that doesn't want to go to the dance with him at all, and that part of me is relieved that he hasn't mentioned anything about it.

Okay, it is a very small part of me, but it's still *there*.

So actually, even though I was having fun sitting by Boris at the restaurant and all, it was also a little depressing, on account of the whole Kenny thing.

And then things got even more depressing. That's because some little Chinese American girls came up to me as I was opening my fortune cookie and wanted to know if they could have my autograph. Then they handed me pens and the advertising supplement that had appeared in that day's *Times* for me to sign.

I seriously thought about killing myself, only I couldn't think how I'd do it, except for maybe stabbing myself through the heart with a chopstick.

Instead I just signed the stupid thing for them and tried to smile. But inside, of course, I was FREAKING OUT, especially when I saw how happy the little girls were to have met me. And why? No, not because of my tireless work on behalf of the polar bears or the whales or starving kids. Which I haven't actually done yet, but I fully intend to do.

No, because I'd been in a magazine in a bunch of pretty dresses, and I'm tall and skinny like a model.

Which is no accomplishment at all!

After that, my headache came back, and I said I had to go home.

Nobody protested very much, I think because everybody realized all of a sudden how much time we'd wasted, and how much studying we all had left to do. So we left, and now I am home again, and my mom says that while I was gone, Sebastiano called four times, AND he had another dress delivered.

Not just any dress, either. It is a dress Sebastiano

designed just for me, to wear to the Nondenominational Winter Dance. It's not sexy. It isn't sexy at all. It's dark green velvet with long sleeves and a wide, square neckline.

But when I put it on and looked at my reflection in the mirror in my room, something funny happened:

I looked good. *Really* good.

There was a note attached to the dress that said,

> *Please forgive me.*
> *I promise this dress will not make him think of you as his little sister's best friend.*
> *S.*

Which is very sweet. Sad, but sweet. Sebastiano can't know, of course, that the Michael situation is completely hopeless, and that no *dress* is going to make any difference, no matter how nice I look in it.

But hey, at least Sebastiano *apologized*. That's a lot more, I've noticed, than Grandmère has done.

Of course I forgive Sebastiano. I mean, none of it is his fault, really.

And I guess someday I'll probably forgive Grandmère, since she's too old to know any better.

But the person I will never, ever forgive is myself, for getting into this situation in the first place. I totally should have known better. I should have told Sebastiano,

No photos, please. Only I was so carried away, looking at myself in all those beautiful dresses, that I forgot that being a princess is more than just wearing pretty dresses: It's being an example to a lot of people . . . people you don't even know and may not ever even meet.

Which is why if I don't pass this Algebra test, I am dead.

MONDAY, DECEMBER 15, HOMEROOM

Here are the number of students at Albert Einstein High School who (so far) have felt compelled to make comments to me about my smashing Lana Weinberger's cell phone last Friday: 37

Here are the number of students at Albert Einstein High School who (so far) have felt compelled to mention my suspension last Friday: 59

Here are the number of students at Albert Einstein High School who (so far) have felt compelled to make comments to me about my appearance in an advertising supplement to the *New York Times* over the weekend: 74

Total number of comments made to me so far today by students at Albert Einstein High School: 170

Oddly, after wading through all of this, when I got to my locker, I found something that seemed extremely out of place: a single yellow rose, sticking out of the door.

What can this mean? Can there be someone in this school who does not despise me?

Apparently so. But when I looked around, wondering who my one supporter could be, I saw only Justin

Baxendale, being stalked (as usual) by a horde of worshipful girls.

I suppose my anonymous rose-leaver must be Kenny, trying to cheer me up. He will not admit it, but who else could it be?

It is Reading Day today, which means we are supposed to spend the whole day—except for lunch—sitting in Homeroom, studying for our finals, which begin tomorrow. This is fine by me, since at least this way, there's no chance I'll run into Lana. Her homeroom is on a whole other floor.

The only problem is that Kenny's in this class. We have to sit alphabetically, so he's way up at the front of this row, but he keeps passing notes back to me. Notes that say things like, *Keep on smilin'!* and *Hang in there, Sunshine!*

He won't fess up to the rose thing, though.

By the way, want to know the total number of comments made to me so far today by Michael Moscovitz? 1

And it wasn't even really a comment. He told me in the hallway that my combat boot had come untied.

And it had.

My life is so over.

Four days until the Nondenominational Winter Dance, and still no date.

Distance formula: $d - 10xrt$
$r = 10$
$t = 2$
$d = 10 + (10)(2)$
$= 10 + 20 = 30$

Variables are placeholders for numbers (letters)
Distributive law
$5x + 5y - 5$
$5 (x + y - 1)$

$2a - 2b + 2c$
$2 (-1) - 2(-2) + 2 (5)$
$-2 + 4 + 10 = 12$

Four times a number is added to three. The result is five times the number.
Find the number.

$x = the\ number$

$$4x + 3 = 5x$$
$$-4x \qquad -4x$$
$$3 = x$$

Regardes les oiseaux stupides.

Cartesian coordinate system divides the plane into four parts called quadrants

Quadrant 1 (positive, positive)
Quadrant 2 (negative, positive)
Quadrant 3 (negative, negative)
Quadrant 4 (positive, negative)

Slope: slope of a line is line denoted m

Find slope
negative slopes
positive slopes
zero slope
Vertical line has no slope
Horizontal line has 0 slope
Collinear—points that lie on the same line
Parallel lines have the same slope

$$4x + 2y = 6$$
$$2y = -4x + 6$$
$$y = -2x + 3$$

Active voice indicates that the subject of the verb is acting

Passive voice indicates that the subject of the verb is being acted upon

TUESDAY, DECEMBER 16

Algebra and English finals completed.

Only three more, plus term paper, to go.

76 comments today, 53 of them negative:

"Sellout" = 29 times

I-Must-Think-I'm-All-That = 14 times

Here Comes Miss Thang = 6 times

Lilly says, "Who cares what people are saying? You know the truth, right? And that's all that matters."

That's easy for Lilly to say. Lilly's not the one who people are saying all those mean things about. *I* am.

Somebody left another yellow rose in my locker. What is up with that? I asked Kenny again if it was him, but he denied it. Strangely, he seemed to get very red in the face about it. But this might have been because Justin Baxendale, who was walking by at the time, stepped on Kenny's foot. Kenny has very large feet, larger even than mine.

Three more days until the Nondenominational Winter Dance, and nada on the date front.

WEDNESDAY, DECEMBER 17

World Civ exam *finis*.

Two more, plus term paper, to go.

62 comments, 34 negative:

Don't give up your day job = 12 times

Sellout = 5 times

"If I was flat-chested like you, Mia, I could be a model, too" = 6 times

One rose, yellow, still no indication who left it. Perhaps someone is mistaking my locker for Lana's. She is, after all, always hanging out in that area, waiting for Josh Richter, whose locker is next door to mine, so that the two of them can suck face. It's possible that someone thinks he is leaving roses for her.

God knows no one at Albert Einstein High School would want to leave flowers for me. Unless I were dead, maybe, and they could fling them onto my grave and say, "Good riddance, Miss Thang."

Two more days until the dance. Still nothing.

THURSDAY, DECEMBER 18, 1 A.M.

It just occurred to me:

Maybe Kenny is lying about the roses. Maybe they really *are* from him. Maybe he's leaving them as kind of teasers, leading up to asking me to the dance tomorrow night.

Which is kind of insulting, really. I mean, him waiting this long to finally ask. For all he knows, I could have said yes to somebody else by now.

As if somebody else might have asked.

HA!

THURSDAY, DECEMBER 18, 4 P.M., LIMO ON THE WAY TO THE PLAZA

THAT'S IT!!!!!

I'M DONE!!!!!!

DONE WITH FINALS!!!!!!!!!!!!

And guess what?

I'm pretty sure I passed all of them. Even Algebra. The grades aren't posted until tomorrow, during the Winter Carnival, but I bugged Mr. G so much he finally said, "Mia, you did fine. Now leave me alone, all right?"

Got that????? He said I did FINE!!!!!!!!!! You know what *fine* means, don't you?

IT MEANS I PASSED!!!!!!!!!!!!!!!!

Thank God all of that's over. Now I can concentrate on what's important:

My social life.

I am serious. It is in a state of total disrepair. Everyone at school—with the exception of my friends—thinks I am this total sellout. They're like, "You talk the talk, Mia, but you don't walk the walk."

Well, I'm going to show them. Right after the World Civ exam yesterday, it hit me like a ton of bricks. I knew *exactly* what to do. It's what Grandmère would do.

Well, okay, maybe not *quite* what Grandmère would do, but it will solve the whole problem. Granted, Sebastiano isn't going to like it very much. But then, he should have asked ME, not Grandmère, if it was all right to run those photos in an ad for his clothes. Right?

I have to say, this is the most princessy thing I've done so far. I am very, very nervous. Seriously. You wouldn't believe how much my palms are sweating.

But I cannot continue to lie back and meekly take this abuse. Something must be done about it, and I think I know what.

The best part is, I am doing it all by myself, with no help from anyone.

Well, all right, the concierge at the Plaza helped by getting me a room, and Lars helped by making all the calls on his cell phone.

And Lilly helped me write down what I was going to say, and Tina did my makeup and hair just now.

But other than that, it was all me.

Okay, we're here.

Here goes nothing.

THURSDAY, DECEMBER 18, 7 P.M.

I have now watched myself on all four major networks, plus New York 1, CNN, Headline News, MSNBC, and Fox News Channel. Apparently, they are also going to show it on *Entertainment Tonight*, *Access Hollywood*, and *E! Entertainment News*.

And I have to say, for a girl who supposedly has issues with her self-image, I think I did a fine job. I didn't mess up, not even once. If I maybe spoke a little too fast, well, you could still *understand* me. Unless, you know, you're a non-English-speaker or something.

I looked good, too. I probably should have worn something other than my school uniform, but you know, royal blue comes off pretty good on TV.

The phone has been ringing off the hook ever since the press conference was first aired. The first time it rang, my mom picked it up, and it was Sebastiano, screaming incomprehensibly about how I've ruined him.

Only he can't say ruined. It just came out "rued."

I felt really bad. I mean, I didn't mean to ruin him.

Especially after he was so nice about designing me that dress for the dance.

But what was I supposed to do? I tried to make him look on the bright side:

"Sebastiano," I said, when I got on the phone, "I haven't ruined you. Really. It's just the proceeds from the sales of the dresses I'm wearing in the ad that will go to Greenpeace."

But Sebastiano completely failed to look at the big picture. He kept screaming, "Rued! I'm rued!"

I pointed out that, far from ruining him, his donating all the proceeds from sales of the dresses I modeled to Greenpeace was going to be perceived in the industry as a brilliant stroke of marketing genius, and that I wouldn't be surprised if those dresses flew off the racks, since girls like me, who are really the people his fashions are geared for, care a great deal about the environment.

I must have picked up a thing or two during my princess lessons with Grandmère, since in the end, I totally won him over. By the time I hung up, I think Sebastiano almost believed the whole thing had been his idea in the first place.

The next time the phone rang, it was my dad. I may have to scratch the plan to get him a book on anger management, because he was laughing his head off. He wanted to know if it had been my mom's idea, and when I said, "No, it was all me," he went, "You really *have* got the princess thing down, you know."

So, in a weird way, I feel like I passed that final, too.

Except of course that I'm still not speaking to Grandmère. Not a single one of the calls I've gotten tonight—from Lilly and Tina and Mamaw and Papaw back in Indiana, who saw the broadcast on a local affiliate—have been from her.

Really, I think she should be the one to apologize, because what she did was totally underhanded.

Almost as underhanded, my mom pointed out to me over dinner from Number One Noodle Son, as what *I* did.

Which is sort of shocking. I mean, I never thought about it before, but it's true: What I did tonight—it was as sneaky as anything Grandmère's ever done.

But I guess that shouldn't be very surprising. We *are* related, after all.

Then again, so were Luke Skywalker and Darth Vader.

Must go. *Baywatch* is on. This is the first time in a while I've been home to watch it.

THURSDAY, DECEMBER 18, 9 P.M.

Tina just called. She didn't want to talk about the press conference. She wanted to know what I got from my Secret Snowflake. I was all, "Secret Snowflake? What are you talking about?"

"You know," Tina said. "Your Secret Snowflake. You remember, Mia. We signed up for it like a month ago. You put your name in the jar, and then someone draws it, and they have to be your Secret Snowflake for the last week of school before Winter Break. They're supposed to surprise you with little gifts and stuff. You know, as a stress breaker. Since it's finals week, and all."

I dimly remembered, one day before Thanksgiving Break, Tina dragging me over to a folding table where some nerdy-looking kids from the student government were sitting on one side of the cafeteria with a big jar filled with little pieces of paper. Tina had made me write my name on a slip of paper, then pick someone else's name out of the jar.

"Oh, my God!" I cried. With all the stress of finals and everything, I had forgotten all about it!

Worse, I had forgotten that I had drawn Tina's name. No real coincidence, since she'd stuffed her slip of paper into the jar right before I picked. Still, what kind of heinous friend am I, that I would forget something like this?

Then I realized something else. The yellow roses. They hadn't been put in my locker by mistake! And they really weren't from Kenny, either! They had to be from my Secret Snowflake.

Which was kind of upsetting in a way. I mean, it's really starting to look as if Kenny has no intention whatsoever of asking me to tomorrow night's dance.

"I can't believe you forgot about it," Tina said, sounding amused. "You *have* been getting stuff for your Secret Snowflake, haven't you, Mia?"

I felt a rush of guilt. I had totally blown it. Poor Tina!

"Uh, sure," I said, wondering where I was going to find a present for her by tomorrow morning, the last day of the Secret Snowflake thing. "Sure, I have."

Tina sighed. "I guess nobody picked me," she said. "Because I haven't gotten anything."

"Oh, don't worry," I said, hoping the guilt washing over me wasn't noticeable in my voice. "You will. Your Secret Snowflake is probably waiting, you know, until the last day because she's—or he's—gotten you something really good."

"Do you think so?" Tina asked, wistfully.

"Oh, yes," I gushed.

Reassured, Tina got businesslike.

"Now," she said, "that finals are over . . ."

"Um, yes?"

". . . when are you going to tell Michael that you're the one who sent him those cards?"

Shocked, I went, "How about never?"

To which Tina replied, tartly, "Mia, if you don't tell him, then what was the point of sending those cards?"

"To let him know that there are other girls out there who might like him, besides Judith Gershner."

Tina said, severely, "Mia, that's not enough. You've got to tell him it was you. How are you ever going to get him if he doesn't know how you feel?" Tina Hakim Baba, surprisingly, has a lot in common with my dad. "Remember Kenny? That's how Kenny got you. He sent the anonymous notes, but then he finally fessed up."

"Yeah," I said, sarcastically. "And look how great *that* turned out."

"It'll be different with you and Michael," Tina insisted. "Because you two are destined for each other. I can just *feel* it. You've got to tell him, and it's got to be tomorrow, because the next day, you are leaving for Genovia."

Oh, God. In my self-congratulations over having successfully maneuvered my first press conference, I'd forgotten about that, too. I am leaving for Genovia the day after tomorrow! With Grandmère! To whom I am not even speaking anymore!

I told Tina that I'd confess to Michael tomorrow. She hung up all happy.

But it was a good thing she hadn't been able to see my nostrils, because they were flaring like crazy, on account of the fact that I was totally lying to her.

Because there is no way I am ever telling Michael Moscovitz how I feel about him. No matter what my dad says. I *can't*.

Not to his face.

Not ever.

FRIDAY, DECEMBER 19, HOMEROOM

They are holding us hostage here in Homeroom until they've passed out our final semester grades. Then we are free to spend the rest of the day at the Winter Carnival in the gym, and then, later this evening, the dance.

Really. We don't have any more classes after this. We are just supposed to have fun.

As if. I am so never having fun again.

That is because—you know, aside from my many other problems, including the fact that I don't love my boyfriend, who also apparently does not love me anymore, at least not enough to ask me to the school dance, but I do love my best friend's brother, who is not even remotely aware of my feelings—that I think I know who my Secret Snowflake is.

Really, there is no other explanation. Why else would Justin Baxendale—who, even though he's so new, is still totally popular, not to mention way good-looking—be hanging around my locker so much? I mean, seriously. This is the third time I've spotted him lurking around there this week. Why else would he be hanging around there, except to leave those roses?

Unless he's planning on blackmailing me about the whole fire-alarm thing.

But Justin Baxendale doesn't exactly strike me as the blackmailer type. I mean, he looks to me like somebody who'd have something better to do than blackmail a princess.

Which leaves only one other explanation for why he could possibly be spending so much time around my locker: He is my Secret Snowflake.

And how totally embarrassing is it going to be when I go out there when the bell rings, and Justin comes up to me to confess—because that's the rule, it turns out: You have to reveal your identity to your Secret Snowflake today— and I have to look up into his smoky eyes with those long lashes and give a big fake smile and go, "Oh, gee, thanks, Justin. I had no idea it was you!"

Whatever. This is actually the least of my problems, right? I mean, considering that I am the only girl in this entire school who does not have a date to the dance tonight. And that tomorrow I have to leave for a country I am princess of, with my lunatic grandmother who isn't speaking to my father, and who, I know from past experience, is not above smoking in the airplane lavatory if the urge strikes her.

Really. Grandmère is a flight attendant's worst nightmare.

But that's not even half of it. I mean, what about my mom and Mr. Gianini? Sure, they're acting like they don't mind my spending the holidays in another country, and yes, we're going to have our own private little Christmas among ourselves before I leave, but really, I bet they mind. I bet they mind a lot.

And what about my grade in Algebra? Oh, Mr. Gianini says it's fine, but what is fine, exactly? A D? A D is not fine. Not considering the number of hours I've put into raising my grade from an F, it isn't. A D is *not* acceptable.

And what—oh God, *what*—am I going to do about Kenny?

At least I got Tina's present out of the way. I went online last night and signed her up for a teen romance book-of-the-month club. I printed out the certificate, saying she is an official member, and will give it to her when the bell rings.

When the bell rings, which is also when I have to go out there and face Justin Baxendale.

It wouldn't be so bad if it weren't for those eyes of his. Why does he have to be so good-looking? And why did a good-looking person have to pick me as his Secret Snowflake? Beautiful people, like Lana and Justin, can't help but be repulsed by ordinary-looking people, like me.

He probably didn't even pull my name from that jar at all. Probably, he picked Lana's name and has been putting those roses in my locker, thinking it's Lana's, seeing as how God knows she never hangs out in front of her own locker.

What's even worse is, Tina told me yellow roses mean love *everlasting*.

Which of course was why I figured maybe it was Kenny after all.

Oh, great. They are passing around the printouts with our grades on them. I am not looking. I don't even care. I DO NOT CARE ABOUT MY GRADES.

Thank God for the bell. I'm just going to slip out of here—not looking at my grades, totally not looking at my grades—and go about my business like nothing out of the ordinary is going on.

Except of course when I get to my locker, Justin is there, looking for someone. Lana is there, too, waiting for Josh.

You know, I really don't need this. Justin revealing that he is my Secret Snowflake right in front of Lana, I mean. God only knows what she's going to say, the girl who has been suggesting I wear Band-Aids instead of a bra every day since the two of us hit puberty. Plus, it isn't like she's been super happy with me since the whole cellphone thing. I'll bet she'll have something extra mean all prepared for the occasion. . . .

"Dude," Justin says.

Dude? I'm not a dude. Who is Justin talking to?

I turn around. Josh is standing there, behind Lana.

"Dude, I've been looking for you all week," Justin says, to Josh. "Do you have those Trig notes for me, or not? I've got to make up the final in one hour."

Josh says something, but I don't hear him. I don't hear him because there's a roaring sound in my ears. There's a roaring sound in my ears because standing behind Justin is Michael. *Michael Moscovitz.*

And in his hand is *a yellow rose.*

FRIDAY, DECEMBER 19, WINTER CARNIVAL

Oh, God.

I am in so much trouble.

Again.

And it isn't even my fault this time. I mean, I couldn't help myself. It just *happened*, you know? And it doesn't mean anything. It was just, you know, one of those things.

And besides, it's not what Kenny thinks. Not even. I mean, if you think about it, it is a complete and total letdown. For me, anyway.

Because of course the first thing Michael says, when he sees me standing there gaping at him while he is holding that flower, is, "Here. This just fell out of your locker."

I took it from him in a complete daze. I swear to God my heart was beating so hard, I thought I was going to pass out.

Because I thought they'd been from him. For a minute there, I really did think Michael Moscovitz had been leaving me roses.

But of course this time, there's a note attached to the rose. It says:

*Good luck on your trip to Genovia! See you
when you get back!
Your Secret Snowflake,
Boris Pelkowski*

Boris Pelkowski. Boris Pelkowski is the one who's been leaving those roses. Boris Pelkowski is my Secret Snowflake.

Of course Boris wouldn't know that a yellow rose represents love everlasting. Boris doesn't even know not to tuck his sweater into his pants. How would he know the secret language of flowers?

I don't know which was actually stronger, my feeling of relief that it wasn't Justin Baxendale leaving those roses after all . . .

. . . or my feeling of disappointment that it wasn't Michael.

Then Michael went, "Well? What's the verdict?"

To which I responded by staring at him blankly. I still hadn't quite gotten over it. You know, those brief few seconds when I'd thought—I'd actually thought, fool that I am—that he loved me.

"What did you get in Algebra?" he asked, slowly, as if I were dense.

Which, of course, I am. So dense that I never realized how much in love with Michael Moscovitz I was until Judith Gershner came along and swept him right out from under my nose.

Anyway, so I opened the computer printout containing my grades, and would you believe that I had raised my F in Algebra all the way up to a B minus?

Which just goes to show that if you spend nearly every waking moment in your life studying something, the likelihood is that you are going to retain at least a little of it.

Enough to get a B minus on the final, anyway.

I'm trying really hard not to gloat, but it's difficult. I mean, I'm so happy.

Well, except for the whole not-having-a-date-to-the-dance thing.

Still, it's hard to be unhappy. There is absolutely no way I got this grade because the teacher happens to be my stepfather. In Algebra, either you get the right answer, or you don't. There's nothing subjective about it, like in English. There's no interpretation of the facts. Either you're right, or you're not.

And I was right. Eighty percent of the time.

Of course it helped that I knew the answer to the final's extra-credit question: *What instrument did Ringo, in the Beatles, play?*

But that was only worth two points.

Anyway, here's the part where I got into trouble. Even though, of course, it isn't my fault.

I was so happy about my B minus, I completely forgot

for a minute how much I am in love with Michael. I even forgot, for a change, to be shy around him. Instead, I did something really unlike me.

I threw my arms around him.

Seriously. Threw my arms right around his neck and went, "Wheeeeeee!!!!!"

I couldn't help it. I was so happy. Okay, the whole rose thing had been a little bit of a bummer, but the B minus made up for it. Well, almost.

It was just an innocent hug. That's *all* it was. Michael had, after all, tutored me almost the whole semester. He had some stake in that B minus, too.

But I guess Kenny, who Tina now tells me came around the corner right as I was doing it—hugging Michael, I mean—doesn't see it that way. According to Tina, Kenny thinks there's something going on between Michael and me.

To which, of course, I can only say, I WISH!

But I can't say that. I have to go find Kenny now, and let him know, you know, it was just a friendly hug.

Tina's all, "Why? Why don't you tell him the truth—that you don't feel the same way about him that he feels about you? This is your big chance!"

But you can't break up with someone during the Winter Carnival. I mean, really. How mean.

Why must my life be so fraught with trauma?

FRIDAY, DECEMBER 19, STILL THE WINTER CARNIVAL

Well, I still haven't found Kenny, but I really have to hand it to the administrators: Grasping they might be, but they sure do know how to throw a party. Even Lilly is impressed.

Of course, signs of corporatization are everywhere: There are McDonald's orange drink dispensers on every floor, and it looks as if there was a run on Entenmann's, there are so many cake-and-cookie-laden tables scattered around.

Still, you can tell they are really trying to show us a good time. All the clubs are offering activities and booths. There's ballroom dancing in the gym, courtesy of the Dance Club; fencing lessons in the auditorium, thanks to the Drama Club; even cheerleading lessons in the first-floor hallway, brought to us by—you guessed it—the junior varsity cheerleaders.

I couldn't find Kenny anywhere, but I ran into Lilly at the Students for Amnesty International booth (Students Against the Corporatization of Albert Einstein High

School did not submit their application for a booth in time to get one, so Lilly is stuck running the Amnesty International booth instead). And guess what? Guess who got an F in something?

That's right.

Lilly. I couldn't believe it.

"Mrs. Spears gave you an F in English? *YOU* got an F?"

She didn't seem too bothered by it, though.

"I had to take a stand, Mia," she said. "And sometimes, when you believe in something, you have to make sacrifices."

"Sure," I said. "But an *F*? Your parents are going to kill you."

"No, they won't," Lilly said. "They'll just try to psychoanalyze me."

Which is true.

Oh, God. Here comes Tina.

I hope she doesn't remember—

She does.

We're going over to the Computer Club's booth right now.

I don't want to go to the Computer Club's booth. I already looked over there, and I know what's going on. Michael and Judith and the rest of the computer nerds are sitting there behind all these color monitors. When somebody comes up, they get to sit down in front of one of the monitors, and play a computer game the club designed where you walk through the school and all the teachers are in funny costumes. Like Principal Gupta is wearing a leather dominatrix's outfit, and holding a whip, and Mr. Gianini is in footie pajamas with a teddy bear that looks exactly like him.

They used a different program when the club applied to be part of the Carnival, of course, so none of the teachers or administrators know what everyone is sitting there looking at. You would think they'd wonder why all the kids are laughing so hard.

Whatever. I don't want to do it. I don't want to go anywhere near it.

But Tina says I have to.

"Now's the perfect time to tell him," she says. "I mean, Kenny's nowhere to be seen."

Oh, God. This is what comes from telling your friends anything.

EVEN LATER ON FRIDAY, DECEMBER 19, STILL THE WINTER CARNIVAL

Well, I'm in the girls' room again. And I think I can state with certainty that this time, I'm never coming out.

No, I think I'll just stay in here until everyone has gone home. Only then will it be safe. Thank God I am leaving the country tomorrow. Maybe by the time I get back, everyone involved in this little incident will have forgotten about it.

But I doubt it. Not with my luck, anyway.

Why do these kinds of things always happen to me? I mean, seriously? What did I ever do to turn the gods against me? Why don't these kinds of things ever happen to Lana Weinberger? Why me? Why always *me*?

All right, so here's what happened.

I had no intention whatsoever of actually telling Michael anything. I mean, let me get that out right away. I was only going along with Tina because, well, it would have looked weird if I had completely avoided the Computer Club's booth. Plus Michael had asked me so many times to make sure I stopped by. So there was no way I could avoid it.

But I never intended to say a word about

You-Know-What. I mean, Tina was just going to have to learn to live with the disappointment. You don't love somebody for, like, as long as I have loved Michael and then just go up to him at a school fair and be like, "Oh, by the way, yeah, I love you."

Okay? You don't *do* that.

But whatever. So I went up to the stupid booth with Tina. Everyone was all giggly and excited, because their program was so popular that there was this really long line to see it. But Michael saw us, and went, "Come on up!"

Like we were supposed to cut in front of all these other people. I mean, we did it, of course, but everyone behind us grumbled, and who can blame them? They'd been waiting a long time.

But I guess because of the thing the night before—you know, when I explained on national television that the only reason I'd done that clothing ad was because the designer was donating all the proceeds to Greenpeace—I have been noticeably more popular (positive comments so far: 243. Negative: 1. From Lana, of course). So the grumbling wasn't as bad as it could have been.

Anyway, Michael was all, "Here, Mia, sit at this one." And he pulled out a chair in front of this one computer monitor.

So I sat down and waited for the stupid thing to come on, and all around me other kids were laughing at what they were seeing on their screens. I just sat there thinking, for some reason, *Faint heart never won fair lady.*

Which was stupid, because, number one, I was NOT going to tell him I like him and number two, Michael is dark-haired, *not* fair. And he isn't a lady either, obviously.

Then I heard Judith go, "Wait, what are you doing?"

And then I heard Michael say, "No, that's okay. I have a special one for her."

Then the screen in front of my eyes flickered. I sighed. *Okay,* I thought. *Here goes the stupid teacher thing. Be sure to laugh so they think you like it.*

So I was sitting there, and I was actually kind of depressed, because I really didn't have anything to look forward to, if you think about it. I mean, everybody else was all excited, because later on they were going to the dance, but no one had asked me to the dance—not even my supposed boyfriend—so I didn't even have that to look forward to. And everyone else I knew was going skiing or to the Bahamas or wherever for Winter Break, but what did I get to do? Oh, hang out with a bunch of members of the Genovian Olive Growers Society. I'm sure they are all really nice people, but come on.

And before I even leave for my boring trip to Genovia, I have to break up with Kenny, something I totally don't want to do, because I really do like him, and I don't want to hurt his feelings, but I guess I sort of have to.

Although I have to say, the fact that he still hasn't so much as mentioned the dance is making the idea of breaking up with him seem a lot less heinous.

Then tomorrow, I thought, *I'll leave for Europe on a plane with Dad and Grandmère, who still aren't speaking to each other* (and since I'm not speaking to Grandmère, either, it should be a really fun flight), *and when I come back, knowing my luck, Michael and Judith will be engaged.*

That's what I was sitting there thinking in the split second the screen in front of me flickered. That, and, *You know, I'm not really in the mood to see any of my teachers in funny outfits.*

Only when the flickering stopped, that's not what I saw. What I saw instead was this castle.

Seriously. It was a castle, like out of the Knights of the Round Table, or *Beauty and the Beast*, or whatever. The picture zoomed in until we were over the castle walls and inside this courtyard, where there was a garden. And in the garden, all these big, fat, red roses were blooming. Some of the roses had lost their petals, and you could see them lying on the courtyard floor. It was really, really pretty, and I was like, *Hey, this is cooler than I thought it would be.*

And I sort of forgot I was sitting there in front of a computer monitor at the Winter Carnival, with like two dozen people all around me. I began to feel like I was actually in that garden.

Then this banner waved across the screen, in front of the roses, like it was blowing in the wind. The banner had some words written on it in gold leaf. When it stopped flapping, I could read what the words said:

Roses are red
Violets are blue
You may not know it
But I love you, too

I screamed and jumped up out of my chair, tipping it over behind me.

Everyone started laughing. I guess they thought I'd seen Principal Gupta in her leather catsuit.

Only Michael knew I hadn't.

And Michael wasn't laughing.

Only I couldn't look at Michael. I couldn't look anywhere, really, except at my own feet. Because I couldn't believe what had just happened. I mean, I couldn't process it. What did it *mean*? Did it mean Michael knew I was the one who'd been sending him those notes, and that he felt the same way?

Or did it mean he knew I was the one who'd been sending him those notes, and he was trying to get back at me, as a kind of joke?

I didn't know. All I knew was that if I didn't get out of there, I was going to start crying . . .

. . . and in front of everyone in the entire school.

I grabbed Tina by the arm and yanked her, *hard*, after me. I guess I was figuring I could tell her what I'd seen, and maybe *she'd* be able to figure out what it meant, since I sure couldn't.

Tina shrieked—I must have grabbed her harder than I thought—and I heard Michael call, "Mia!"

But I just kept going, lugging Tina behind me, and pushing through the crowd for the door, thinking only one thing:

Must get to the girls' room. Must get to the girls' room before I start bawling my head off.

Somebody, with about as much force as I'd grabbed Tina, grabbed me. I thought it was Michael. I knew if I so much as looked at him, I'd burst into big baby sobs. I said, "Get *off*," and jerked my arm away.

It was Kenny's voice that said, "But Mia, I *have* to talk to you!"

"Not *now*, Kenny," Tina said.

But Kenny was totally inflexible. He went, "Yes, *now*," and you could tell from his face he meant it.

Tina rolled her eyes and backed off. I stood there, my back to the Computer Club's booth, and prayed, *Please,*

please don't come over here, Michael. Please stay where you are. Please, please, please don't come over here.

"Mia," Kenny said. He looked more uncomfortable than I'd ever seen him, and I've seen Kenny look plenty uncomfortable. He's an awkward kind of guy. "I just want to . . . I mean, I just want you to know. Well. That I know."

I stared at him. I had no idea what he was talking about. Seriously. I'd forgotten all about that hug he'd seen in the hallway. The one I'd given Michael. All I could think was, *Please don't come over here, Michael. Please don't come over here, Michael. . . .*

"Look, Kenny," I said. I don't even know how I got my tongue to work, I swear. I felt like a robot somebody had switched into the Off position. "This really isn't a good time. Maybe we could talk later—"

"Mia," Kenny said. He had a funny look on his face. "I *know*. I saw him."

I blinked.

And then I remembered. Michael, and the B-minus hug.

"Oh, Kenny," I said. "Really. That was just . . . I mean, there's nothing—"

"You don't have to worry," Kenny said. And then I realized why his face looked so funny. It was because he was wearing an expression on it that I had never seen before. At least, not on Kenny. The expression was resignation. "I won't tell Lilly."

Lilly! Oh, God! The last person in the world I wanted to know how I felt about Michael!

Maybe it wasn't too late. Maybe there was still a chance I could . . .

But no. No, I couldn't lie to him. For once in my life, I could not summon up a lie.

"Kenny," I said. "I am so, so sorry."

I didn't realize until I said it that it was too late to run for the girls' room: I had already started crying. My voice broke, and when I put my hands to my face, they came away wet.

Great. I was crying, and in front of the entire student body of Albert Einstein High School.

"Kenny," I said, sniffling. "I honestly meant to tell you. And I really do like you. I just don't . . . love you."

Kenny's face was very white, but he didn't start crying—not like me. Thank God. In fact, he even managed to smile a little in that weird, resigned way as he said, shaking his head, "Wow. I can't believe it. I mean, when it first hit me, I was like *no way*. Not Mia. No way would she do that to her best friend. But . . . well, I guess it explains a lot. About, um, us."

I couldn't look him in the face any longer. I felt like a worm. Worse than a worm, because worms are very environmentally helpful. I felt like . . . like . . .

Like a fruit fly.

"I guess I've suspected for a long time that there was someone else," Kenny went on. "You never . . . well, you never exactly seemed to return my ardor when we . . . you know."

I knew. Kissed. Nice of him to bring it up though, here in the gym, in front of everyone.

"I knew you just weren't saying anything because you didn't want to hurt my feelings," Kenny said. "That's the kind of girl you are. And that's why I put off asking you to the dance," Kenny admitted. "Because I figured you'd just say no. On account of you, you know, liking someone else. I mean, I know you'd never lie to me, Mia. You're the most honest person I've ever met."

HA! Was he joking? *Me?* Honest? Obviously, he did not have the slightest clue about my nostrils.

"That's how I know how much this must be tearing you up inside. I just think you'd better tell Lilly soon," Kenny said somberly. "I started to suspect, you know, at the restaurant. And if I figured it out, other people will, too. And you wouldn't want her to hear it from somebody else."

I had reached up to try to wipe some of my tears away with my sleeve, but paused with my hand only halfway there, and stared at him. "Restaurant? What restaurant?"

"You know," Kenny said, looking uncomfortable.

"That day we all went to Chinatown. You and he sat next to each other. You kept laughing. . . . You looked pretty chummy."

Chinatown? But Michael hadn't gone with us that day to Chinatown. . . .

"And you know," Kenny said, "I'm not the only one who's noticed him leaving you those roses all week, either."

I blinked. I could barely see him through my tears. "Wh–what?"

"You know." He looked around, then dropped his voice to a whisper. "Boris. Leaving you all those roses. I mean, come on, Mia. If you two want to carry on behind Lilly's back, that's one thing, but—"

The roaring in my ears that had been there just after I'd read Michael's poem came back. BORIS. BORIS PEL-KOWSKI. My boyfriend just broke up with me because he thinks I am having an affair with BORIS PELKOWSKI.

BORIS PELKOWSKI, who always has food in his braces.

BORIS PELKOWSKI, who wears his sweaters tucked inside his pants.

BORIS PELKOWSKI, my best friend's boyfriend.

Oh, God. My life is so over.

I tried to tell him. That Boris isn't my secret love, but my Secret Snowflake.

But Tina darted forward, grabbed me by the arm, and went, "Sorry, Kenny, Mia has to go now." Then she dragged me into the girls' room.

"I have to tell him," I kept saying, over and over, like a crazy person, as I tried to break free of her grip. "I have to tell him. I have to tell him the truth."

"No, you do not," Tina said, pushing me past the toilet stalls. "You two are broken up. Who cares why? You're through, and that's all that matters."

I blinked at my tear-stained reflection in the mirror above the sinks. I looked awful. Never in your life have you seen anyone who looked less like a princess than I did just then. Just looking at myself made me break out into a fresh new wave of tears.

Of course Tina says she's sure Michael wasn't trying to make fun of me. Of course she says that he must have figured out that I was the one who was sending him those cards and was trying to let me know that he felt the same way about me.

Only of course I can't believe that. Because if that were true—*if that were true*—why did he let me go? Why didn't he try to stop me?

Tina has pointed out that he did try. But my shrieking when I read his poem, and then running in tears from the room, might not have seemed to him like a very encouraging sign. In fact, it might have actually looked to him like I was displeased by what I'd seen. Furthermore, Tina pointed out, even if Michael had tried to go after me, there'd been Kenny cornering me on my way out. It had certainly looked as if the two of us were Having A Moment—which we most certainly were—and didn't wish to be disturbed.

All of which could be true.

But it could also be true that Michael had just been joking. It was a very mean joke, under the circumstances, but Michael doesn't know that I adore him with every fiber of my being. Michael doesn't know that I've been in love with him all my life. Michael doesn't know that without him, I will never, ever achieve self-actualization. I mean, to Michael, I'm just his kid sister's best friend. He probably didn't mean to be cruel. He probably thought he was being funny.

It isn't his fault that my life is over, and that I am never, ever leaving this bathroom.

I'll just wait until everybody is gone, and then I'll sneak out, and no one will see me again until next semester starts, by which time, hopefully, all of this will have blown over.

Or, better yet, maybe I'll just stay in Genovia. . . .

Hey, yeah. Why not?

FRIDAY, DECEMBER 19, 5 P.M., THE LOFT

I don't know why people can't just leave me alone.

Seriously. I may be done with finals, but I still have a lot to do. I mean, I have to pack, don't I? Don't people know that when you are leaving for your royal introduction to the people over whom you will one day reign, you have to do a lot of packing?

But no. No, people keep on calling, and emailing, and coming over.

Well, I'm not talking to anybody. I think I have made that perfectly clear. I am not speaking to Lilly or Tina or my dad or Mr. Gianini or my mother and ESPECIALLY not Michael, even though at last count, he'd called four times.

I am *way* too busy to talk to anybody.

And with my headphones on, I can't even hear them pounding on the door. It's kind of nice, I have to say.

FRIDAY, DECEMBER 19, 5:30 P.M., THE FIRE ESCAPE

People have a right to their privacy. If I want to go into my room and lock the door and not come out or have to deal with anyone, I should have a right to. People should *not* be allowed to take the hinges off my door and *remove* it. That is completely unfair.

But I have found a way to foil them. I am out on the fire escape. It's about thirty degrees out here, and snowing, by the way, but guess what? So far no one has followed me.

Fortunately I bought one of those pens that's also a flashlight, so I can see to write. The sun went down a while ago, and I have to admit, my butt is freezing. But it's actually sort of nice out here. All you can hear is the hiss of the snow as it lands on the metal of the fire escape, and the occasional siren or car alarm. It is restful, in a way.

And you know what I'm finding out? I need a rest. Big time.

Really. I need to, like, go and lie on a beach somewhere, or something.

There's a nice beach in Genovia. Really. With white sand, palm trees, the whole bit.

Too bad while I'm there, I'm never going to have time to visit it, since I'm going to be too busy christening battleships, or whatever.

But if I *lived* in Genovia . . . you know, moved there, and lived there full-time . . .

Oh, I'll miss my mom, of course. I've already considered that. She's leaned out the window about twenty times already, begging me to come inside or at least put on a coat. My mom's a nice lady. I'll really miss her.

But she can come visit me in Genovia. At least up until her eighth month. Then air travel might be a little risky. But she can come after my baby brother or sister is born. That would be nice.

And Mr. G, he's okay, too. He just leaned out and asked if I wanted any of the four-alarm chili he just made. He left out the meat, he says, just for me.

That was nice of him. He can come visit me in Genovia, too.

It will be nice to live there. I can hang out with my dad all the time. He's not such a bad guy either once you get to know him. He wants me to come in off the fire escape, too. I guess my mom must have called him. He says he's really proud of me, on account of the press conference and my B minus in Algebra and all. He wants to take me out to dinner to celebrate. We can go to the

Zen Palate, he says. A totally vegetarian restaurant. Isn't that nice of him?

Too bad he let Lars take my door down, or I might have gone with him.

Ronnie, our next-door neighbor, just looked out her window and saw me. Now she wants to know what I'm doing, sitting out on the fire escape in December.

I told her I needed some privacy, and that this appears to be the only way I can get it.

Ronnie went, "Honey, don't I know how that is."

She said I was going to freeze without a coat, though, and offered me her mink. I politely declined, as I cannot wear the skins of dead animals.

So she loaned me her electric blanket, which she has plugged into the outlet beneath her air conditioner. I must say, this is an improvement.

Ronnie's getting ready to go out. It's nice to watch her put on her makeup. As she does it, she keeps up a running conversation with me through her open window. She asked me if I was having trouble at school, and if that was why I'm on the fire escape, and I said I was. She asked what kind, and I told her. I told her I am being persecuted: that I am in love with my best friend's brother, but that to him it is apparently all this really big joke. Oh, and also that everyone apparently thinks I am having an affair with a mouth-breathing violinist who happens to be my best friend's boyfriend.

Ronnie shook her head and said it was good to know things haven't changed since she was in high school.

I told Ronnie that it really doesn't matter, because I'm moving to Genovia. Ronnie said she was sorry to hear that. She'll miss me, as I have really improved conditions in the apartment building's incinerator room since I insisted on installing separate recycling bins for newspapers and cans and bottles.

Then Ronnie said she has to go because she's meeting her boyfriend for cocktails at the Carlyle. She said I could keep using the electric blanket, though, so long as I remember to return it when I'm done.

Uh-oh. I hear footsteps in my room. Who's coming now?

Well. You could knock me over with a feather.

Guess who just came out onto the fire escape and sat with me for half an hour?

Grandmère.

I'm not even kidding.

I was sitting here, feeling all depressed, when all of a sudden this big furry sleeve appeared out my window, and then a foot in a high-heeled shoe, and then a big blond head, and next thing I knew, Grandmère was sitting there, blinking at me from the depths of her full-length chinchilla.

"Amelia," she said, in her most no-nonsense tone. "What are you doing out here? It's snowing. Come back inside."

I was shocked. Shocked that Grandmère would even consider coming out onto the fire escape (it's an indelicate thing for a princess to mention, but there is actually a lot of bird poop out here), but also that she would dare to speak to me, after what she did.

But she addressed that issue right away.

"I understand that you are upset with me," she said.

"And you have a right to be. But I want you to know that what I did, I did for you."

"Oh, right!" Even though I swore I was never going to speak to her again, I couldn't help myself. "Grandmère, how can you possibly say that? You completely humiliated me!"

"I didn't mean to," Grandmère said. "I meant to show you that you are just as pretty as those girls in the magazines you are always wishing you look like. It's important that you know that you are not this hideous creature that you apparently think you are."

"Grandmère," I said. "That's nice of you and all—I guess—but you shouldn't have done it that way."

"What other way could I do it?" Grandmère demanded. "You will not pose for any of the magazines that have offered to send photographers. Not for *Vogue*, or *Harper's Bazaar*. Don't you understand that what Sebastiano said about your bone structure is really true? You really are quite beautiful, Amelia. If only you'd just have a little more confidence in yourself, show off once in a while. Think how quickly that boy you like would leave the housefly girl for you!"

"Fruit fly," I said. "And, Grandmère, I told you, Michael likes her because she's really smart. They have a lot of stuff in common, like computers. It has nothing to do with how she looks."

"Oh, Amelia," Grandmère said. "Don't be naïve."

Poor Grandmère. It really wasn't fair to blame her, because she comes from such a different world. In Grandmère's world, women are valued for being great beauties—or, if they aren't great beauties, they are revered for dressing impeccably. What they do, like for a living, isn't important, because most of them don't do anything. Oh, maybe they do some charity work, or whatever, but that's it.

Grandmère doesn't understand, of course, that today being a great beauty doesn't count for much. Oh, it matters in Hollywood, of course, and on the runways in Milan. But nowadays, people understand that perfect looks are the result of DNA, something the person has nothing to do with. It's not like it's any great accomplishment, being beautiful. That's just genetics.

No, what matters today is what you do with the brain *behind* those perfect blue eyes, or brown eyes, or green, or whatever. In Grandmère's day, a girl like Judith, who could clone fruit flies, would be viewed as a piteous freak, unless she managed to clone fruit flies *and* look stunning in Dior.

And even in this remarkably enlightened age, girls like Judith still don't get as much attention as girls like Lana— which isn't fair, since cloning fruit flies is probably way more important than having totally perfect hair.

The really pathetic people are the ones like me: I can't clone fruit flies, *and* I've got bad hair.

But that's okay. I'm used to it by now.

Grandmère's the one who still needs convincing that I am an absolutely hopeless case.

"Look," I said to Grandmère. "I told you. Michael is not the type of guy who is going to be impressed because I'm in a *Sunday Times* supplement in a strapless ballgown. *That's why I like him.* If he were the kind of guy who was impressed by stuff like that, I wouldn't want anything to do with him."

Grandmère didn't look very convinced.

"Well," she said. "Perhaps you and I must agree to disagree. In any case, Amelia, I came over to apologize. I never meant to distress you. I meant only to show you what you can do, if you'd only try." She spread her gloved hands apart. "And look how well I succeeded. Why, you planned and executed an entire press conference, all on your own!"

I couldn't help smiling a little at that one. "Yes," I said. "I did."

"And," Grandmère said, "I understand that you passed Algebra."

I grinned wider. "Yes. I did."

"Now," Grandmère said, "there is only one thing left for you to do."

I nodded. "I know. I've been thinking a lot about it, and I think it might be best if I extended my stay in Genovia. Like maybe I could just live there from now on. What do you think about that?"

Grandmère's expression, I could see in the light coming from my room, was one of disbelief.

"Live in . . . live in Genovia?" For once, I'd caught her off guard. "What are you talking about?"

"You know," I said. "They have schools there. I could just finish ninth grade there. And then maybe I could go to one of those Swiss boarding schools you're always going on about."

Grandmère just stared at me. "You'd hate it."

"No," I said. "It might be fun. No boys, right? That would be great. I mean, I'm kind of sick of boys right now."

Grandmère shook her head. "But your friends . . . your mother . . ."

"Well," I said, reasonably. "They could come visit."

Then Grandmère's face hardened. She peered at me from between the heavily mascaraed slits her eyes had become.

"Amelia Mignonette Grimaldi Renaldo," she said. "You are running away from something, aren't you?"

I shook my head innocently. "Oh, no, Grandmère," I said. "Really. I'd like to live in Genovia. It'd be neat."

"NEAT?" Grandmère stood up. Her high heels went through the slots between the metal bars of the fire escape, but she didn't notice. She pointed imperiously at my window.

"You get inside right now," she ordered, in a voice I had never heard her use before.

I have to admit, I was so startled, I did exactly what she said. I unplugged Ronnie's electric blanket and crawled right back into my room. Then I stood there while Grandmère crawled back in, too.

"You," she said, when she'd straightened out her skirt, "are a princess of the royal house of Renaldo. A princess," she said, going to my closet, and rifling through it, "does not shirk her responsibilities. Nor does she run at the first sign of adversity."

"Um, Grandmère," I said. "What happened today was hardly the first sign of adversity, okay? What happened today was the last straw. I can't take it anymore, Grandmère. I'm getting out."

Grandmère pulled from my closet the dress Sebastiano had designed for me to wear to the dance. You know, the one that was supposed to make Michael forget that I am his little sister's best friend.

"Nonsense," Grandmère said.

That was all.

Just nonsense. Then she stood there, tapping her toes, staring at me.

"Grandmère," I said. Maybe it was all that time I'd spent outside. Or maybe it was that I was pretty sure my mom and Mr. G and my dad were all in the next room, listening. How could they not be? There was no *door*, or anything, to separate my room from the living room.

"You don't understand," I said. "I can't go back there."

"All the more reason," Grandmère said, "for you to go."

"No," I said. "First of all, I don't even have a date for the dance, okay? And it's a rule that you're supposed to have one. . . ."

"Rules don't apply to you, Amelia," Grandmère said. "You are a princess. And princesses do not run away when things become difficult. They throw their shoulders back, and they face what disaster awaits them head-on. Bravely, and without complaint."

I said, "Hello, we are not talking about marauding visigoths, okay, Grandmère? We are talking about an entire high school that seems to think that I am in love with Boris Pelkowski."

"Which is precisely," Grandmère said, "why you must show them that it doesn't matter to you what they think."

"Why can't I show them that it doesn't matter by not going?"

"Because that," Grandmère said, "is the cowardly way. And you, Mia, as you have shown amply this past week, are not a coward. Now get dressed."

I don't know why I did what she said. Maybe it was because somewhere deep inside, I knew that for once, Grandmère was right.

Or maybe it was because secretly, I guess I was a little curious to see what would happen.

But I think the real reason was because, for the first time in my entire life, Grandmère didn't call me Amelia.

No. She called me Mia.

And because of my stupid sentimentalism, I am in a car right now, going back to stupid, crappy Albert Einstein High School, the dust from which I thought I'd managed to shake permanently from my feet not four hours ago.

But no. Oh, no. I'm going back, in the stupid velvet party dress Sebastiano designed for me. I'm going back, with no date. I'm going back, and I will probably be ridiculed for being the dateless biological freak that I am.

I am, however, a princess, and apparently that means I am expected to take whatever is dished out at me, no matter how cruel, unfair, or undeserved it might be.

And regardless of what happens, I can always comfort myself with the knowledge of one thing:

Tomorrow, I will be thousands of miles away from all of this.

Oh, God. We're here.

I think I'm going to be sick.

SATURDAY, DECEMBER 20, ROYAL GENOVIAN JET

When I was about to turn six years old, all I wanted for my birthday was a cat.

I didn't care what kind of cat. I just wanted one. I wanted a cat of my very own. We had been to visit my mom's parents at their farm in Indiana, and they had a lot of cats. One of them had had kittens, little fluffy orange and white ones, which purred loudly when I held them under my chin, and liked to curl up inside the bib of my overalls and take naps. More than anything in the world, I wanted to keep one of those kittens.

I should mention that at the time, I had a thumb-sucking problem. My mother had tried everything to get me to stop sucking my thumb, including buying me a Barbie, in spite of her fundamental stand against Barbie and all that she stands for, as a sort of bribe. Nothing worked.

So when I started whining to her about wanting a kitten, my mom came up with a plan. She told me she would get me a kitten for my birthday if I quit sucking my thumb.

Which I did, immediately. I wanted a cat of my own *that badly.*

Yet, as my birthday rolled around, I had my doubts my mother would live up to her end of the bargain. For one thing, even at the age of six, I knew my mom wasn't the most responsible person. Why else was our electricity always being turned off? And about half the time I would show up at school wearing a skirt AND pants, because my mother let *me* decide what to wear. So I wasn't sure she'd remember about the kitten—or that, if she did remember, she'd know where to get one.

So as you can imagine, when the morning of my sixth birthday rolled around, I wasn't holding out much hope.

But when my mother came into my bedroom holding this tiny ball of yellow-and-white fur, and plopped it into my chest, and I looked into Louie's (he didn't become Fat Louie until about twenty-something pounds later) great big blue eyes (this was before they turned green), I knew a joy such as I had never known before in my life, and never expected to feel again.

That is, until last night.

I am totally serious.

Last night was the best night of my ENTIRE life. After that whole fiasco with Sebastiano and the photos, I thought I would never, ever feel anything like gratitude to Grandmère EVER again.

But she was SO RIGHT to make me go to that dance. I am SO GLAD I went back to Albert Einstein, the best, the loveliest school in the whole country, if not the whole world!!!!!!!

Okay, here's what happened:

Lars and I pulled up in front of the school. There were twinkly white lights in all the windows, which I guess were supposed to represent icicles, or whatever.

I was sure I was going to throw up and I mentioned this to Lars. He said I couldn't possibly throw up because to his certain knowledge I hadn't eaten anything since the Entenmann's cake way before lunch, and that was probably all digested by now. With that piece of encouraging information, he escorted me up the steps and into the school.

There were masses of people teeming around the coat check in the front entrance. Lars checked our coats while I stood there waiting for someone to come up and ask me what I was doing there without a date. All that happened, however, was that Lilly-and-Boris and Tina-and-Dave descended upon me and started acting all nice and said how happy they were that I'd come (Tina told me later that she'd already explained to everyone that Kenny and I had broken up, although she hadn't told them why, THANK GOD).

So, fortified, by my friends, I went into the gym, which was decorated all wintry, with cut-out paper snowflakes, one of those disco balls, and fake snow everywhere, which

I must say looked a lot whiter and cleaner than the snow that was starting to pile up on the ground outside.

There were tons of people there. I saw Lana and Josh (ugh), Justin Baxendale with his usual flock of adoring fans, and Shameeka and Ling Su and a bunch of other people. Even Kenny was there, though when he saw me, he turned bright red and turned around and started talking to this girl from our Bio class. Oh well.

Everyone was there, except the one person I'd been most dreading. Or hoping to see. I didn't know which.

Then I saw Judith Gershner. She had changed out of her overalls and looked quite pretty in this red Laura Ashley-ish dress.

But she wasn't dancing with Michael. She was dancing with some boy I'd never seen before.

So I looked around for Lilly, and finally spotted her using one of the pay phones. I went up to her and was like, "Where's your brother?"

Lilly hung up the phone. "How should I know?" she demanded. "It's not my turn to babysit him."

Oddly comforted by her demeanor—which simply proved that no matter how much other things change, Lilly always stayed the same—I went, "Well, Judith Gershner is here, so I just figured—"

"For God's sake," Lilly said. "How many times do I have to tell you? *Michael and Judith are not going out.*"

I went, "Oh, right. Then why have they spent every waking moment together for the past two weeks?"

"Because they were working on that stupid computer program for the Carnival," she said. "Besides, Judith Gershner already has a boyfriend." Lilly grabbed me by the shoulders and turned me around so I could see Judith on the dance floor. "He goes to Trinity."

I looked at Judith Gershner as she slow-danced with a boy who looked a lot like Kenny, only older and not as uncoordinated.

"Oh," I said.

"*Oh* is right," Lilly said. "I don't know what is wrong with you today, but I can't deal with you when you're acting like such a freak. Sit down right here—" She pulled out a chair. "And don't you dare get up. I want to know where to find you when I need to."

I didn't even ask Lilly why she might need to find me. I just sat down. I felt like I couldn't stand up anymore. I was *that* tired.

It wasn't that I was disappointed. I mean, I didn't want to see Michael. At least, part of me didn't.

Another part of me *really* wanted to see him and ask him just what he'd meant by that poem.

But I was sort of afraid of the answer.

Because it might not be the one I was hoping it would be.

After a while, Lars and Wahim came and sat down

next to me. I felt like a complete tool. I mean, there I was, sitting at a dance with two bodyguards, who were deep in a discussion about the advantages versus the disadvantages of rubber bullets. Nobody was asking me to dance. Nobody would, either. I mean, I'm a huge, colossal loser. A huge, colossal loser without a date.

Who, by the way, is supposedly in love with Boris Pelkowski.

Why was I even staying? I had done what Grandmère said. I had shown up. I had proved to everyone that I wasn't a coward. Why couldn't I leave?

I stood up. I said to Lars, "Come on. We've been here long enough. I still have a lot of packing to do. Let's go."

Lars said okay, and started to get up. Then he stopped. I saw that he was looking at something behind me. I turned around.

And there was Michael.

He had obviously just gotten there. He was out of breath. His bow tie wasn't tied. And there was still snow in his hair.

"I didn't think you were coming," he said.

I knew my face had gone as red as Judith Gershner's dress. But there wasn't anything I could do about that. I said, "Well, I almost didn't."

He said, "I called you a bunch of times. Only you wouldn't come to the phone."

I said, "I know." I was wishing the floor of the gym would open up, like in *It's a Wonderful Life*, and that I'd fall into the pool underneath it and drown and not have to have this conversation.

"Mia," he said. "With that thing today. I didn't mean to make you cry."

Or the floor would open and I could just fall, and keep falling, forever and ever and ever. That would be okay, too. I stared at the floor, willing it to crack apart and swallow me up.

"It didn't." I lied. "I mean, it wasn't that. It was something Kenny said."

"Yeah," Michael said. "Well, I heard you two broke up."

Yeah. Probably by now the whole school had. Now, I knew, my face was even redder than Judith's dress.

"The thing is," Michael went on, "I knew it was you. Who was leaving those cards."

If he had reached inside my chest, pulled out my heart, flung it to the floor, and kicked it across the room, it could not possibly have hurt as much as hearing that. I could feel my eyes filling up with tears all over again.

"You did?" You know, it's one thing to have your heart broken. But to have it happen at a school dance, in front of everyone . . . well, that's harsh.

"Of course I did," he said. He sounded impatient. "Lilly told me."

For the first time, I looked up into his face.

"*Lilly* told you?" I cried. "How did *she* know?"

He waved his hand. "I don't know. Your friend Tina told her, I guess. But that's not important."

I looked around the gym and saw Lilly and Tina on the far side of it, both staring in my direction. When they saw me looking at them, they turned around really fast and pretended to be deeply absorbed in conversation with their dates.

"I'm going to kill them," I murmured.

Michael reached out and grabbed both my shoulders. "Mia," he said, giving me a little shake. "It doesn't *matter*. What matters is that I meant what I wrote. And I thought you did, too."

I didn't think I could have heard him right. I went, "Of course I meant it."

He shook his head. "Then why did you freak out like that today at the Carnival?"

I stammered, "Well, because . . . because . . . I thought . . . I thought you were making fun of me."

"Never," he said.

And that's when he did it.

No fuss. No asking my permission. No hesitation whatsoever. He just leaned down and kissed me, right on the lips.

And I found out, right then, that Tina was right:

It *isn't* gross if you're in love with the guy.

In fact, it's the nicest thing in the whole world.

And do you know what the best part is?

I mean, aside from Michael being in love with me, and having kept it a secret almost as long as I have, if not longer?

And Lilly knowing all along but not saying anything up until a few days ago because she found it an interesting social experiment to see how long it would take us to figure it out on our own (a long time, it turned out)?

And the fact that Michael's going to Columbia next year, which is only a few subway stops away, so I'll still be able to see him as much as I want?

Oh, and Lana walking by while we were kissing, and going, in this disgusted voice, "Oh, God, get a room, would you please?"

And slow dancing with him all night long, until Lilly finally came up and said, "Come on, you guys, it's snowing so hard, if we don't leave now, we'll never get home"?

And kissing good night outside the stoop to my loft, with the snow falling all around us (and grumpy Lars complaining he was getting cold)?

No, the best part is that we moved right into Frenching without any trouble at all. Tina was right—it just seemed perfectly natural.

And now the royal Genovian flight attendant says we

have to put away our tray tables for takeoff, so I'll have to quit writing in a minute.

Dad says if I don't stop talking about Michael, he's going to go sit up front with the pilot for the flight.

Grandmère says she can't get over the change in me. She says I seem taller. And you know, maybe I am. She thinks it's because I'm wearing another one of Sebastiano's original creations, designed just for me, just like the dress that was supposed to make Michael see me as more than just his little sister's best friend . . . except that it turned out he did anyway. But I know that's not it.

And it isn't love, either. Well, not entirely.

I'll tell you what it is: self-actualization.

Well, that and the fact that it turns out I'm really a princess, after all. I must be, because guess what?

I'm living happily ever after.

ACKNOWLEDGMENTS

Many thanks to Beth Ader, Jennifer Brown, Barbara Cabot, Sarah Davies, Laura Langlie, Abby McAden, and David Walton.

Discover

The *Princess* Diaries

series by bestselling author
MEG CABOT!

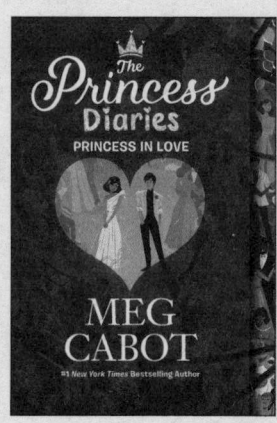

"Like reading a note from your best friend."
—ALA *Booklist*

HARPER
An Imprint of HarperCollinsPublishers

harpercollinschildrens.com